Definitive Guide to Excel VBA

Michael Kofler

Translated by David Kramer

Apress™

Definitive Guide to Excel VBA

ISBN (pbk): 1-893115-79-8

Printed and bound in the United States of America 2345678910

Editorial Directors: Dan Appleman, Gary Cornell, Karen Watterson
Translator and Editor: David Kramer
Project Editor: Carol A. Burbo
Page Composition and Production Services: Impressions Book and Journal Services, Inc.
Cover and CD Design: Karl Miyajima

Distributed to the book trade in the United States by Springer-Verlag New York, Inc.,175 Fifth Avenue, New York, NY, 10010
and outside the United States by Springer-Verlag GmbH & Co. KG, Tiergartenstr. 17, 69112 Heidelberg, Germany

In the United States, phone 1-800-SPRINGER; orders@springer-ny.com; http://www.springer-ny.com
Outside the United States, contact orders@springer.de; http://www.springer.de; fax +49 6221 345229

For information on this title, please contact Apress directly at 2560 Ninth Street, Suite 219, Berkeley, CA, 94710
Phone: 510-549-5930; Fax: 510-549-5939; info@apress.com; http://www.apress.com

Contents

Part II Foundation 59

Preface

Excel offers right out of the box an enormous variety of functions. So why does one need VBA macros? With VBA you can accomplish wonders:

- You can program your own worksheet functions that are easier to use than complicated formulas.
- You can configure Excel to suit your requirements and in this way achieve greater simplicity and efficiency.
- You can structure and simplify complex processes such as filling out forms by means of "smart" forms (templates).
- You can automate processes that are used frequently. This is particularly useful in dealing repeatedly with large data sets that must be processed, analyzed, and graphically displayed.
- You can create freestanding Excel programs that display their own menus, dialogs, and toolbars. This makes it possible to simplify an Excel application to the point where those unfamiliar with Excel can run the program corrcctly.

What's New in Excel 2000?

Changes in Excel's core functions have this time been kept within bounds. However, extensive changes in peripheral functions have occurred. For example, for the first time the **Scripting** library enables simple object-oriented access to files and folders. The ADO library now replaces the DAO library and simplifies access to external databases. Moreover, there are dozens of new properties, methods, and objects, which encompass a host of new functions (for example, HTML importation and exportation) and existing functions (such as pivot tables). Most of the changes apply to use of the Office Developer Edition. This version of Office is equipped with a large number of auxiliary tools, making it possible, for example, to develop COM add-ins (that is, ActiveX DLLs compiled to binary code).

Why This Book?

The real problem in VBA programming is not VBA itself. The formulation of a loop or test, the use of methods and properties, are easily understood as in any programming language and will cause you no trouble after a couple of days. The problem is to get a handle on the complex object libraries within Excel, with their more than a thousand keywords, and to use them efficiently. The focus of this book and the examples presented herein is to explain these object libraries. This book pulls no punches, however, and when there are problems and shortcomings in Excel, you will hear about them and get help in working around them. On the other hand, with the help of realistic examples you will be shown how far you can go with Excel programming: The possibilities are truly endless!

This Book Offers More!

If you open the file `Office2000/Office/Samples.xls`, you will be greeted with the following text:

Microsoft provides examples of Visual Basic for Applications procedures for illustration only, without warranty either expressed or implied, including, but not limited to the implied warranties of merchantability and/or fitness for a particular purpose. The Visual Basic procedures in this workbook are provided "as is" and Microsoft does not guarantee that they can be used in all situations. While Microsoft Technical Support Engineers can help explain the functionality of a particular macro, they will not modify these examples to provide added functionality, nor will they help you construct macros to meet your specific needs. If you have limited programming experience, you may want to consult one of the Microsoft Solution Providers.

Thus has Microsoft made it clear once again just what they mean by customer-friendliness. The express goal of this book is to offer more in every respect: clear language, accurate information, realistic examples, genuine assistance.

With this book you should be able to free yourself from Microsoft's *Technical Support Engineers* and *Solution Providers*. After a couple of weeks you will understand the Excel object model, and you may even find that programming in VBA is actually enjoyable. I wish you a pleasant journey and every success in your Excel programming!

Michael Kofler <excel@kofler.cc>, February 2000
http://www.kofler.cc

The Idea Behind This Book

Visual Basic for Applications is, to be sure, a modern object-oriented programming language that offers an incredible number of keywords, but at the same time it offers many difficulties. At the beginning one has no hope of gaining even an overview of VBA. And even after months of programming in VBA the on-line help will remain the most important source of advice on the details of a particular keyword. Therefore, this book attempts to compensate for the shortcomings in the original documentation and the on-line help by providing the following assistance:

- Genuine applications in the form of concrete, realistic examples
- Thematic syntax summaries (for example, all properties and methods for dealing with ranges of cells)
- Detailed information on the use of DLL functions, on ActiveX automation, on the creation of custom on-line help texts, on programming your own add-ins.
- Useful descriptions of all VBA objects and their arrangement in the object hierarchy
- Information on inconsistiencies and errors in VBA

However, there is one attribute that this book does not possess: completeness. There is no point, it seems to me, in filling hundreds of pages with a reference to all keywords when practically the same information can be found in the on-line help. Instead of seeking to give only the appearance of completeness, I have attempted to give preference to the most important topics and to deal with these in full detail.

Formalities

Keyboard shortcuts are given in the formCtrl+F2. Menu commands appear as follows: FILE|OPEN, CANCEL, or OK. The instruction EDIT|DELETE|SHIFT CELLS LEFT means that you first execute the menu command EDIT|DELETE and then in the dialog that appears select the button Shift cells left.

VBA keywords as well as variables and procedures are written in *italics,* for example, "*Application* object" or "*Visible* property." Worksheet functions are written in the same type style, but in all uppercase letters, as in *IF,* for example.

(In international versions of Excel it is necessary to distinguish worksheet functions from VBA keywords: VBA keywords are always in English, while worksheet functions must be given in the local language.) Keywords that appear in the text for the first time with an explanation or that are particularly important are printed in ***bold italics***.

Introduction

Here's a brief overview of the book:

Part I, "An Intuitive Approach," gets you started and tells you what is new in Excel 2000.

In Chapter 1, "Writing Your First Macro," we introduce some examples that while simple in execution are of great general value in showing how to create macros and how macros are used to configue Excel to your specifications, to manage a literature database, to create a "smart form," to define new worksheet functions, and so on.

Chapter 2, "What's New in Excel 2000," provides an overview of the most important new features of version 2000 (in comparison to versions 5, 7, and 97). This includes the new database library ADO, which facilitates access to external databases.

Part II, "Fundamentals," discusses basic information about Excel 2000, the development environment, VBA concepts, programming techniques, debugging, forms (the Microsoft Forms Library), and menus and toolbars.

Chapter 3, "The Development Environment," describes in detail the VBA development environment, which since Excel 97 has appeared in a separate window with its own menus and toolbars. The development environment facilitates the input of program code and the definition of new forms, helps with debugging, and contains such features as an object catalog with cross-references to the online help and an immediate window to test individual code segments and instructions.

In Chapter 4, "VBA Concepts," you will find useful explanations of variables, loops, branching, objects, methods, and properties. This chapter covers the formal aspects of the programming language VBA and describes the use and syntax of the elementary components of the language.

Chapter 5, "Techniques of Programming," provides answers to everyday questions that programmers ask: How do I access tables, ranges of cells, and individual cells? How do I carry out calculations with dates and times? How do I work with character strings? How are files managed? Where are Excel's configuration settings stored? Where can I obtain additional information?

In Chapter 6, "Debugging, Protection When Errors Arise," we will discuss the fact that not all computer programs are free of bugs (and will never be free of them). Software producers are continually coming out with new versions of their product that still contain errors. The theme of this chapter is how to find the bugs in your own programs and to protect your programs against disaster when errors occur.

In Chapter 7, "Forms (Microsoft Forms Library)," we will discuss dialogs and forms. These are usually small windows for the easy input of various data. Excel itself has countless forms such as those for file selection and for setting options. This chapter shows how you can create and manage your own forms with Excel's forms editor.

In Chapter 8, "Menus and Toolbars," you will learn how to customize the Excel user interface. Of particular importance is the creation of custom menus and toolbars (*CommandBar* object), which allow you to simplify the use of Excel and of your custom Excel applications.

Part III, "Application," covers the use of the application and its templates, smart forms, charts and drawing objects, data management in Excel, accessing external data, data analysis in Exel, and VBA programming for pros, Office Developer.

Chapter 9, "Templates, Smart Forms," covers an application that is as practical as it is simple. It is for the creation of so-called smart forms. The user of such a form is required simply to input particular numerical values, and the calculations on these values are then carried out automatically (which is why they are called "smart"). Finally, the complete form can be printed and its contents saved.

In Chapter 10, "Charts and Drawing Objects (*Shapes*)," you learn that charts play a central role in many Excel applications. This chapter describes how you can create and print charts via program code, and it also discusses the *Shape* object, which lets you decorate and label charts as well as normal Excel worksheets.

In Chapter 11, "Data Management in Excel," you learn that Excel is not itself a database program, but it facilitates the management of small data sets. This chapter describes how these functions can be employed in programs and discusses Excel's limits as a data management application.

Chapter 12, "Access to External Data," discusses how larger data sets are better handled by true database systems than in Excel. This chapter shows some of the possibilities for using Excel to access such data. At the center of this lies the new ADO library (ActiveX data objects).

In Chapter 13, "Data Analysis in Excel," you will learn that Excel's strengths lie less in the management of data than in the analysis of data. This chapter deals primarily with pivot tables, which are an incredibly powerful tool for grouping and subdividing tables according to various criteria.

Chapter 14, "VBA Programming for Pros, Office Developer," explains how to create add-ins, use DLL functions, and control external programs by means of ActiveX automation. In this respect the main focus is the numerous supplementary functions provided by the Office Developer Edition.

Part IV, "Reference," contains the Object Reference, information about the sample files for this book and references to other related works.

Chapter 15, the "Object Reference" describes in alphabetical order all Excel and ADO objects as well as the most important objects of other libraries.

Part I

An Intuitive Approach

CHAPTER 1

Writing Your First Macro

In this chapter you will learn about such concepts as "macro" and "Visual Basic for Applications." You will also record your very own macros, link macros with new tools (which you create) in the toolbar, change the menu structure, and put together a simple database application. This chapter offers—to the extent possible with simple examples—a brief glance at the material that will be covered in much greater detail in the remainder of this book. Welcome aboard!

Chapter Overview

Definition of Terms

Macro

This chapter is entitled "Writing Your First Macro." It thus seems appropriate at this point to explain the term "macro." *A macro is a sequence of instructions to the computer that the computer then carries out when ordered to do so.*

What is the purpose of macros? With macros it is possible to simplify and automate tasks that are frequently repeated. You can customize Excel to meet your particular needs and equip Excel with new menu commands and tools. Furthermore, you can simplify Excel for other users so that they can make use of particular Excel applications with almost no additional training. And finally, you can write full-blown "programs" that will be hardly recognizable as having originated from within Excel.

Since the computer unfortunately does not understand instructions such as "save this data" or "display the three selected cells in a larger font," macro instructions must be formulated in a special language. For reasons of compatibility, Excel offers two such languages from which to choose:

- The original macro programming language, called XLM, was created for early versions of Excel. Macros written in this language are referred to as XLM macros or Excel 4 macros, since the basic structure of this language has not been changed since version 4 of Excel.

- Beginning with version 5, the new language Visual Basic for Applications (VBA for short) was introduced. It offers more extensive and refined possibilities for the control of programs, though at first glance it may seem somewhat complex (especially for those who have written XLM macros).

> **NOTE** *In Excel version 5 several dialects of VBA in several languages were available, such as French, German, and Spanish. In version 7 these dialects were still supported, but they were no longer the default language. With version 97 they disappeared entirely.*
>
> *Foreign-language VBA code is now automatically converted to English when a file is loaded. This book describes English VBA exclusively.*

Here is an example in the two macro languages (first as an Excel 4 macro, then in VBA) that saves the current file:

```
=SAVE()                       'XLM macro (Excel 4)
ActiveWorkbook.Save           'VBA (Excel 5, 7, 97, 2000 etc.)
```

Our next example displays a group of selected cells in a larger font size (first as an Excel 4 macro, then in VBA):

```
=FONT.PROPERTIES(,,GET.CELL(19)+2)             'Excel 4
Selection.Font.Size = Selection.Font.Size + 2   'VBA
```

When the term "macro" is used in books or in on-line documentation it is not always made clear whether the XLM or VBA language is meant. In this book, however, the term "macro" will always mean a VBA macro.

> **NOTE** *The above examples are not usable in the form given. An Excel 4 macro must begin with the name of the macro and end with the command* =RETURN(). *VBA macros must be bracketed between* Sub Name() *and* End Sub. *The basic syntax of VBA should become clear from the examples presented in this chapter. A detailed description of VBA syntax will be presented in Chapter 4.*

Recording Macros

In general, there are two ways of creating macros: You can input the VBA commands from the keyboard, or you let Excel "record" the macro. By this is meant that (using the mouse and keyboard) you perform actions such as data entry, formatting of cells, and executing commands, and Excel follows your actions and writes the corresponding VBA instructions in a module. When later you execute the macro that has been created in this way, the exact same steps that you had previously executed by hand are executed.

In reality, macros are generally created by a combination of these two methods. You will certainly frequently let Excel record your actions, but it will also frequently be necessary to alter or supplement these macros by typing at the keyboard.

Executing Macros

The least satisfactory method of executing a macro is provided by the command TOOLS|MACRO, which produces a list of all the defined macros in all open workbooks. When you click on the name of a macro, the corresponding macro is executed.

However, there are quite a few more elegant methods available: You can link a macro to an arbitrary (new) tool in the toolbar, to a menu item, or to a keyboard shortcut Ctrl+ letter. The macro is executed when you choose the menu item, click on the tool, or type the keyboard shortcut. Macros implemented in this way can save a great deal of effort, as shown in the examples that appear in the following section.

There is even the possibility of having macros execute automatically when certain events occur. Excel knows about a large number of such events, such as a change in the active worksheet, the recalculation of a worksheet, and saving a workbook. Event procedures will be dealt with in detail in Chapter 4.

Programs

Many users of Excel, even those who have already created macros, are ready to tear out their hair when they hear the term "programming." One frequently hears the following opinion expressed: "Programming? *That* is something for computer professionals, for that you need an advanced degree." But relax! You are, in fact, already a programmer by virtue of having created your first macro, even if it is only three lines long. In principle, every macro is a program.

In this book the notion of a program will be construed for the most part somewhat more broadly. By a program we will mean a freestanding Excel application, distinguished in general by having its own menu commands, forms, and, usually, a large number of macros. This book will take you from the baby steps of your first macro (in this chapter) all the way to the giant steps of substantial programs.

What Is Visual Basic for Applications?

Visual Basic for Applications (VBA) is a macro programming language. With VBA you can automate Excel applications or simplify their use. The possibilities for using macros are so numerous and varied that you can create completely freestanding programs that can hardly be recognized as Excel applications. In this chapter you will find some introductory examples of simple macros.

Historical Note

Excel's XLM macro language arose originally from the desire to define new worksheet functions and to collect frequently occurring commands into a unit (into a macro, that is). Furthermore, to make Excel applications as easy as possible to use, XLM made it possible to alter menus and to define custom forms. The fact that Excel offers a large range of functions meant that by the time of Excel 4 a rather confusing macro language had developed.

To be sure, this macro language made possible almost unlimited programming of all Excel functions, though many programming problems could be solved only in a rather convoluted way. The programs that resulted were generally subject to error, and they often ran slowly. In large projects the limitations of this macro language became clear. Those who simultaneously used several Microsoft programs (Excel, Word, Access) were faced with the further problem that each program came equipped with its own macro language.

Because of all these shortcomings, Microsoft decided to develop a completely new macro language, designed first and foremost for Excel, but which by now has been integrated into all components of the Microsoft Office suite.

Special Features of VBA

- Unlike earlier macro languages, VBA is a complete programming language: VBA recognizes all variable types that are found in "real" programming languages, and it can handle such macho tasks as working with character strings, managing dynamic fields, and employing recursive functions.

- VBA is object oriented: Among the *objects* are to be found selected ranges of cells, worksheets, and charts. Typical characteristics of such objects—such as the orientation of cell contents, the background color of a chart—are set by means of manipulating their *properties*. Thus, properties are predefined keywords intended for the manipulation of objects. In addition to properties there are *methods*, which are used for executing complex operations, such as creating objects (new charts, pivot tables, for example) and deleting existing objects. Methods can be most nearly compared with XLM commands. The essential difference is that a method can be applied only to those objects that support that method.

- VBA is event oriented: Choosing a menu entry, clicking on a button or tool, results automatically in a call to the associated macro. As programmer you need not be concerned with the management of events, but only with creating macros, which then are called independently by Excel.

- VBA places professional assistance for debugging at your fingertips: Program segments can be run in step mode, while the contents of variables are examined. The execution of the program can be interrupted when particular conditions are met.

- VBA is extensible: In every VBA dialect one can make use of objects belonging to other applications. For example, it is possible in an Excel VBA program to use keywords (in computer jargon, the object library) from Access or Word. With add-ins you can create new Excel functions and objects. If you have access to Office Developer or the stand-alone programming language Visual Basic, you can even create ActiveX components, by means of which Excel is almost infinitely extensible.

- Integrated in VBA are form (dialog) and menu editors. The management of forms is handled in the same object- and event-oriented way as the management of Excel objects.

NOTE *Occasionally, there is a certain amount of confusion caused by the fact that Visual Basic is connected with a number of Microsoft products. The theme of this book is Excel, and how it can be controlled using the integrated language VBA. However, there is also the independent product "Visual Basic" (currently available in version 6): In this case we are dealing with a programming language that you can use to develop programs independent of the Office suite of applications; the execution of such programs does not presuppose that the user has installed Office. Visual Basic is also based on VBA. However, there are significant differences, such as in the available controls and libraries.*

Drawbacks

After describing the advantages of VBA you may have received the impression that with VBA you have landed in programmer's nirvana. That, however, would be an erroneous assessment of the situation. VBA has many advantages, but it has, alas, a number of drawbacks:

- The VBA language is quite large, and it is therefore difficult to obtain a broad overview of it. With well over one thousand keywords (without counting the predefined constants), VBA programming far exceeds the size that programmers previously had to deal with. In searching for a suitable method or property for a specific task you could end up missing both your dinner and next morning's breakfast.

- VBA programs are long-winded in their formulation. If you were to record the same macro once as an XLM macro and again as a VBA macro, you would find that the VBA code is on average at least fifty percent larger than the XLM code. (There is no dispute, however, that the VBA code is easier to read!)

Linking a Custom Style with a Tool

In our first example we shall begin by defining a style. (A style gathers together a collection of format information such as font, alignment, border, and color. Styles can be used for formatting cells.) Then we shall record a macro that assigns this style to selected cells. Then a new tool will be added to the toolbar, which will be linked to this macro. We will then be able to format previously selected cells with the style that we have defined by clicking on the new tool.

> **NOTE** *All the examples in this chapter can also be found in the example files at* `http://www.apress.com`: `Intro1.xls`, `Intro2.xls`, *etc.*

Before You Begin

We begin with two tips that will simplify your programming with Excel 2000:

- A new feature of Office 2000 that drives every user to despair is dealing with menus: In the default settings, only the most important menu items are shown, which, moreover, appear only after some time. To bring this nonsense to an end, execute VIEW|TOOLBARS|CUSTOMIZE, click on the OPTIONS tab, and there deactivate the option MENUS SHOW RECENTLY USED COMMANDS. From now on the full menus will be shown in all your Office applications.
- In the VBA development environment (which you may invoke by pressing Alt+F11) there are also some options whose preset values are a bit weird. You can reach the options form (dialog) by executing TOOLS|OPTIONS.
- When you get there, deactivate AUTO SYNTAX CHECK. (Syntax will still be checked; lines containing errors will be marked in red. But you will be spared the burdensome announcement of the error accompanied by a beep.)
- Then activate the option REQUIRE VARIABLE DECLARATION. (Extensive justification for this will be given in the first section of Chapter 4.)
- In the dialog page GENERAL deactivate COMPILE ON DEMAND (see Section 3.2).
- Finally, on the page DOCKING deactivate all of the options fields. (You will thereby obtain the result that in the development environment you will be able to place windows on top of each other. In the default setting the environment behaves as in Windows 1.0—and one would have thought that those times were long gone!)

Step 1: Definition of the Custom Style "Result"

We would like cells that contain an (intermediate) result of a calculation to look as follows:

Font: Arial, 14 point, bold
Border: double line below
Number format: two decimal places

If you wished, you could, of course, choose other formatting characteristics. The only point of the particular choice in this example is to define a new uniquely recognizable style.

To define a style, open a new workbook by executing FILE|NEW, type a number in an arbitrary cell, and format this cell according to the characteristics given above. Then execute the command FORMAT|STYLE. In the dialog that appears give the style the name "Result" and click first ADD and then OK.

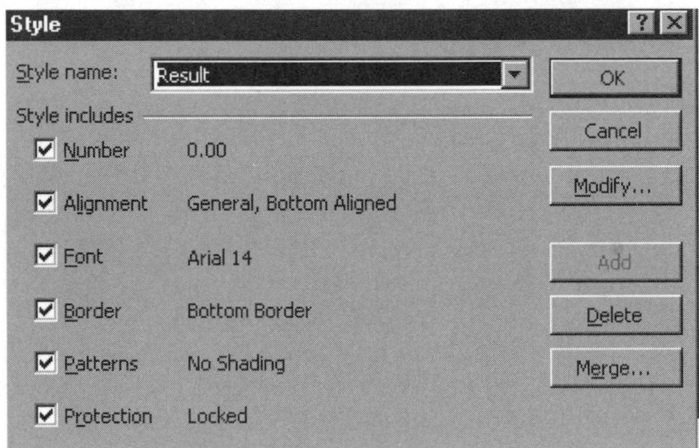

Figure 1.1. Defining a new style

Step 2: Recording a Macro

We would like the steps that we have just taken to format a test cell to be carried out in the future by a macro. Why should we have to do all the work? For this to happen we must first record these steps with the macro recorder. Move the pointer into a new cell and input a number (in order to verify the result). Terminate input by hitting Return, and move the pointer if necessary back into the cell that you have just altered. Now select the command TOOLS|MACRO|RECORD NEW MACRO, and give the macro the name "FormatAsResult"(see Figure 1.2).

As soon as you click on OK, Excel begins to record your new macro. Format the currently active cell with the style "Result"(just as you did at the end of Step 1 when you were testing the new style). Terminate the recording of the macro with TOOLS|MACRO|STOP RECORDING or by clicking on the small square that appeared on the little "Stop Recording" tool window that opened when you started recording.

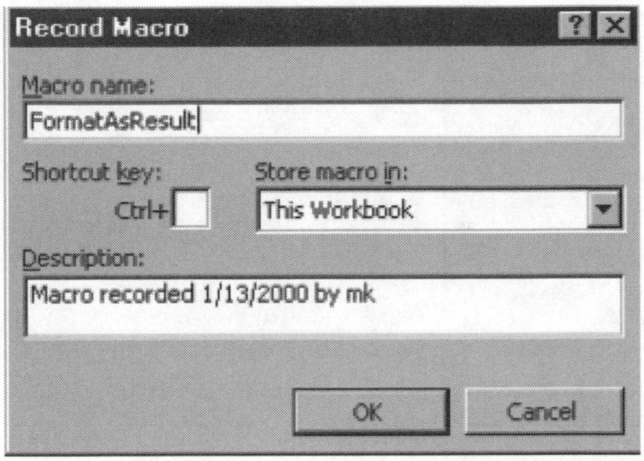

Figure 1.2. Form for recording macros

Now you can view the code of the completed macro by hitting Alt+F11 to switch into the development environment and there examining "Module1." (This module was created automatically during the recording of the macro. If "Module1" already exists, then Excel creates a new module with the name "Module2.") The new module will look something like the following:

```
Sub FormatAsResult()
' FormatAsResult macro
' Macro recorded 2/25/2000 by David Kramer
Selection.Style = "Result"
End Sub
```

We would now like to test the new macro. Return to your worksheet, input a number into an arbitrary cell, and terminate input by hitting Return. Execute Tools|Macro|Macros and select the macro "FormatAsResult." Excel executes your macro, and the cell should appear in the now familiar format.

Step 3: Defining a New Tool

In order to make the macro easier to summon when you need it, we would like to create a new toolbar. On this toolbar we will place a tool to invoke our macro. Executing View|Toolbars|Customize in Excel (not the VBA editor) brings up the form that we require. By pushing the button labeled New after clicking the Toolbars tab, you create a new empty toolbar, which for this example you can name "Intro1." Now click on the Commands tab in the Customize form. Select the category "Macros" and then with the mouse drag the command "Custom Button" into your new toolbar.

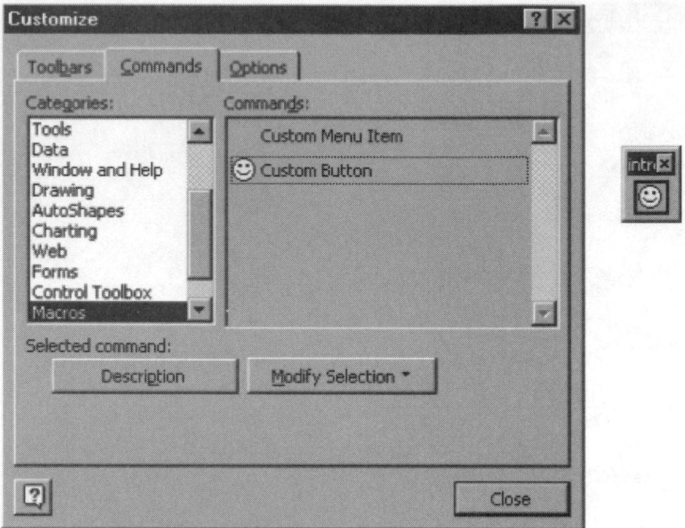

Figure 1.3. The form for changing menus and toolbars

Now the new tool must be modified and correctly labeled. Furthermore, it must be set to point to our macro *FormatAsResult.* These steps are accomplished by clicking on the tool with the right mouse button. (The CUSTOMIZE form will remain open during this operation.)

Figure 1.4. Modifying a tool

The label is changed in the field NAME. For example, you could give it the name "Style Result." (This text will appear in a yellow information field whenever the user pauses momentarily over the tool with the mouse.) Assigning the tool to a macro is accomplished by clicking on ASSIGN MACRO. This opens a form in which are shown all the macros available to you. Select "FormatAsResult" and click OK.

Step 4: Modify the Tool to Your Specifications

Since you will probably forget after a few days the precise meaning of the default smiley face tool, you should find a suitable graphical representation for the functionality of the tool. In the pop-up menu that you obtained by clicking on the new tool with the right mouse button you may select EDIT BUTTON IMAGE to enter a simple image editor. There we shall try to represent the formatting features of the style (boldface, double underline) on our button.

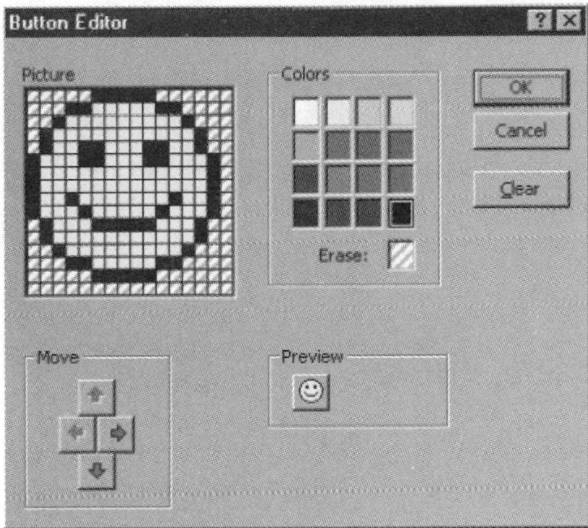

Figure 1.5. Button editor

Deleting the New Toolbar

When you have finished with this example, your new tool will probably be in your way. With VIEW|TOOLBARS|CUSTOMIZE you can select the new toolbar and delete it.

Remarks for Advanced Users

Although our example was quite simple, it raises some interesting problems. One cannot simply save all the information of this example (the definition of the style, the new tool, and the macro) in a workbook in such a way that another Excel user can use the new tool for formatting cells in his or her own spreadsheet. Even if they want to use the button only to format a cell in another workbook, they will get an error message. The reasons are these:

- Styles apply to a single workbook, and cannot be easily transferred to other workbooks. (The macro could, of course, be modified so that it first copies the style into the other workbook. But that would go beyond the bounds of a simple introductory example.)

- Tools are normally saved in their own file and belong to Excel's own configuration data. (Under Windows NT, `Windows\Profiles\username\Application Data\Microsoft\Excel\Excel.xlb` is used. Details as to the locations of the configuration files can be found in Chapter 5.)

- The newly defined tool is available only if you log in under your own name. Other users of the same computer can use the new tool only if you link the toolbar to the workbook: To do this you execute in Excel the command View|Toolbars|Customize|Attach for the toolbar in question.

The sample file `Intro1.xls` contains two procedures in the module "ThisWorkbook" that deal with automatically showing the toolbar when the file is opened and removing it when the file is closed. We will not go into more detail in this introductory example. Detailed information on event procedures and on dealing with custom menus and toolbars can be found in Chapters 4 and 8.

A New Tool for "Full Screen" Mode

Full screen mode exists for the purpose of allowing optimal use of the your monitor's valuable real estate. This is particularly useful when you are working with a small monitor or with a notebook computer. One minor irritation associated with this mode, though, is the fact that Excel can no longer be directly shrunk to an icon (for instance, to change to another program). Thus it is necessary first to deactivate full screen mode before the "Minimize" button on the Excel window again appears. It would be desirable to have a macro to accomplish this task, so let us create one.

Step 1: Record the Macro

Before recording the first draft of this macro, activate full screen mode (View|Full Screen). Open the "record" dialog by executing Tools|Macro|Record New Macro. This time store the macro in "Personal Macro Workbook." Give the macro the name *FullScreen_Icon*.

While the macro recorder is running, turn off full screen mode, minimize Excel to an icon in the Task toolbar, and then enlarge it again to its normal size by a mouse click. Finally, stop recording by executing TOOLS|MACRO|STOP RECORDING or click the square STOP button.

The resulting macro is located in the personal macro workbook, which belongs to the Excel configuration files. (Under Windows NT this file is saved as `Windows\Profiles\username\Application Data\Microsoft\Excel\Xlstart\Personal.xls`. Details on configuration files are discussed in Chapter 5.8.)

The code belonging to this workbook is shown in the development environment, but in Excel the file is invisible, since its window is hidden. (You can make the empty worksheet visible by executing WINDOW|UNHIDE, but this is seldom necessary.) The macro that you have just recorded looks something like the following:

```
' Sample file Intro2.xls
Sub FullScreen_Icon()
' FullScreen_Icon Macro
' Macro recorded 2/27/2000 by David Kramer
  Application.DisplayFullScreen = False
  Application.WindowState = xlMinimized
  ActiveWindow.WindowState = xlNormal
End Sub
```

The second-to-last line of this macro enlarges Excel to its normal window size. Since macro recording can be stopped only when Excel is visible, recording this line was unavoidable. However, it is not part of the intended purpose of the macro, which is to shrink Excel to an icon. Therefore, this line must be deleted manually.

Step 2: Defining a Tool

To make this macro easy to run, you will create a new tool (see also Steps 3 and 4 of the previous example). You can add the new tool to an already existing toolbar, or you can define a new toolbar. Finally, link the macro *FullScreen_Icon* that you have recorded to the tool, as in Figure 1.6.

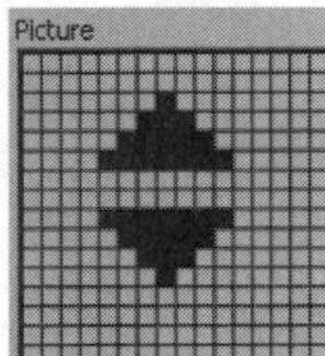

Figure 1.6. A tool for shrinking Excel to an icon

Test the new tool by first putting Excel in full screen mode and then clicking on the new tool. Excel should collapse into an icon.

Step 3: Improving the Macro

In its present form the macro can be used only to shrink the window to an icon. This is, to be sure, practical when Excel happens to be in full screen mode, but is otherwise unnecessary, since then the minimize button at the right end of the window's title bar is available. Therefore, it would make more sense to have the macro take over a second function, namely, switching into full screen mode. Adapt your macro according to the following model:

```
Sub FullScreen_Icon()
  If Application.DisplayFullScreen Then
    Application.DisplayFullScreen = False  'deactivate the mode
    Application.WindowState = xlMinimized  'shrink the window
  Else
    Application.DisplayFullScreen = True   'full screen mode
  End If
End Sub
```

Now the macro tests whether Excel is currently in full screen mode. If that is the case, then Excel shrinks to an icon (and thereby deactivates full screen mode). Otherwise, this mode is activated. In the macro this case differentiation is accomplished by means of an *If*-test: After the keyword *If* a condition is formulated. If the condition is met, then the program line appearing after *Then* is executed. Otherwise, the line after *Else* is executed. The end of the test is indicated by *End If*.

Saving the Personal Macro Workbook

When you exit Excel, you will be asked whether you wish to save the personal macro workbook (you should do this if you wish in the future to use the macro that you have recorded). The file `Personal.xls` will now be automatically opened every time the program is launched, and thus all macros defined there will be available for use.

Remark for Advanced Users

In the previous example program the keyword *Application* together with the period following could have been omitted. When an object is not specified in normal modules, Excel automatically assumes *Application* as the default object.

In order for you to be able to try out the example without difficulty, it has been saved in the file `Intro2.xls`. The toolbar "Intro2" is linked to this file, and it will be shown automatically when the file is loaded.

A Macro for Simplifying Input

In inputting data in tabular form it frequently happens that the number or text to be input into a cell is exactly the same as what was input into the cell immediately above it. Excel offers a variety of possibilities for copying into the cell below, but all of them require either using the mouse (which is a nuisance when you are using the keyboard for data entry) or engaging in elaborate movement of thc arrow cursors. It makes sense, then, to create a macro that can accomplish such copying with a simple keyboard combination (for example, Ctrl+K).

Preparatory Tasks

Excel can distinguish in macro recording between absolute and relative movement between cells:

- Absolute recording is the default mode. When you move the cell pointer during recording from B2 to D4, say, the resulting command is *Range("D4").Select.*

- In relative mode, however, the command would be *ActiveCell.Offset(2, 2).Range("A1").Select*: Here *ActiveCell.Offset(2,2)* denotes the cell two rows beneath and two columns to the right of the currently active cell, while *Range("A1")* refers to this new address.

The differences between these two variants become apparent when the macros are executed. In the first case cell D4 will always be involved, irrespective of where the cell pointer is located. In the second case the affected cell is to be chosen relative to the current cell.

Since Excel 97 there has been no menu command for switching between relative and absolute recording. Instead, one must click on the RELATIVE REFERENCE tool in the "stop recording" toolbar. This toolbar appears automatically when you begin recording a macro. If the tool appears as a pressed-in button, then relative recording is in effect, otherwise, absolute. The mode can be changed during the recording process. For the macro to be created in this section relative reference is necessary.

Figure 1.7. The button on the right toggles between absolute and relative recording

Recording the Macro

Before you begin recording the macro, prepare the table: Input some text into a cell, and then move the cell pointer into the cell immediately below.

Begin recording by executing TOOLS|MACRO|RECORD NEW MACRO, giving the macro the name *CopyFromCellAbove*. Then select as shortcut key Ctrl+K, and indicate that the macro is to be stored in the personal macro workbook. Finally, select relative recording mode if it has not already been selected. This mode is necessary for this macro because it should function for an arbitrary cell in the table (and always copy the cell above relative to the cell pointer).

While the recorder is running, execute the following keyboard entries and commands: Shift+↑ (this selects the current cell and the cell lying above it), EDIT|FILL|DOWN (this copies to the cell below), and finally, → (to move the cell pointer to the next cell to the right, where the next input can be made). End the recording with TOOLS|MACRO|STOP RECORDING.

The following Visual Basic macro can now be found in the personal macro workbook:

```
' Intro3.xls
Sub CopyFromCellAbove()
  ActiveCell.Offset(-1, 0).Range("A1:A2").Select
  ActiveCell.Activate
  Selection.FillDown
  ActiveCell.Offset(0, 1).Range("A1").Select
End Sub
```

If you now try out the macro, you will see that while in principle it runs, the cell pointer ends up one cell too high, to the right of the cell above rather than the cell below. There seems to be a slight contradiction between the recorded commands and the resulting code (that is, the automatic macro recorder has not functioned flawlessly). You can get around this shortcoming by changing the first *Offset* value in the last line of the macro as follows:

```
ActiveCell.Offset(1, 1).Range("A1").Select
```

> **NOTE** *If during recording you forgot to provide the keyboard shortcut* Ctrl+K, *you can always give an existing macro a keyboard shortcut. To do this execute in Excel (not in the development environment)* TOOLS|MACRO|MACROS, *select the macro, and insert the shortcut with* OPTIONS.

A Simple Literature Database

The following example is already a fairly concrete application (if perhaps still a bit elementary). It is located in the sample files under the filename `Intro4.xls`.

This workbook (or "program") makes possible the management of a collection of books, perhaps, for example, a small library. The list of books can be arbitrarily enlarged, sorted by title or by author, selected according to one or another of several criteria (for example, only books on the courting behavior of sea urchins), searched by subject, and so on. The use of the application is simplified by several buttons, so that to search for a book or to enlarge the database requires no Excel-specific knowledge.

Step 1: Preparing the Database, Arranging Windows

The construction of this application begins with the input of data on several books and constructing a table along the lines of Figure 1.8. This has nothing much to do with macro programming. It is merely a matter of constructing a normal Excel table. For now you should ignore the buttons and filter arrows.

(If you prefer, you could just as well create an address database, an index of students, or something else entirely. You do not need to adhere precisely to our presentation. The more creatively and independently you work, the more you will learn.)

Some suggestions for formatting the table: All cells of the table have been formatted with the text aligned vertically at the top of the cell (FORMAT|CELLS|ALIGNMENT). The cells in the title column have been given the attribute "wrap text" so that longer titles will automatically be displayed over several lines. The top two rows have had their height significantly enlarged. The entire second line has been formatted with a light gray background (FORMAT|CELLS|PATTERNS).

A comment is stored in cell C2 (content: Category). (Comments are input by executing INSERT|COMMENT. Beginning with Excel 7 comments are automatically displayed when the mouse is passed over a cell containing a comment.) The comment in cell C2 will be used to explain the category code: N=novels, C=computer books, etc. Cells in which a comment is stored are marked with a red triangle in the top right-hand corner. If this triangle is not shown, execute TOOLS|OPTIONS|VIEW, and activate the option "Comment indicator only."

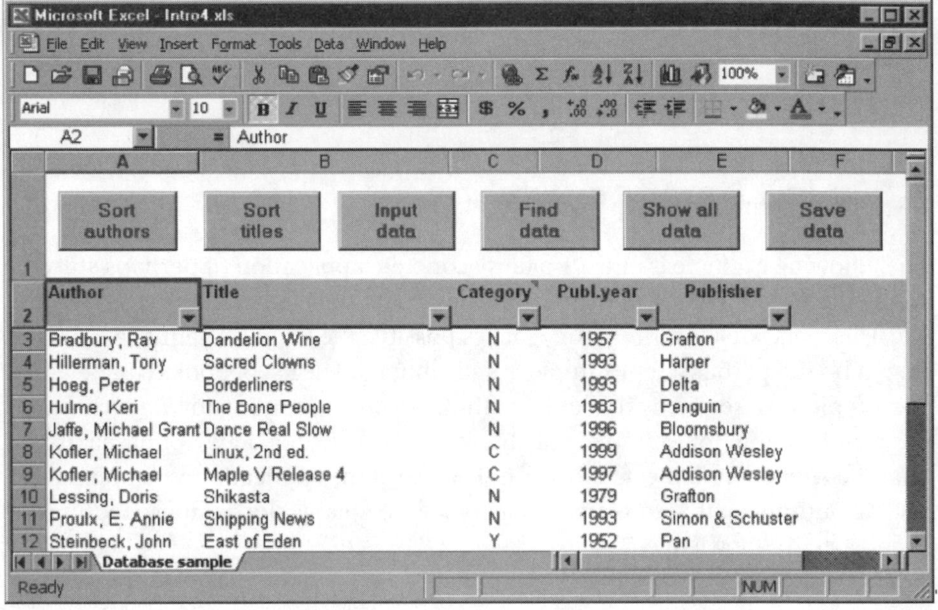

Figure 1.8. A simple database application

Some tips for arranging windows: The window was divided horizontally and arranged so that in the top region of the window the name of the database (two fairly high rows) is visible (WINDOW|SPLIT; arrange the dividing cross with the mouse, and fix it with WINDOW|FREEZE PANES). With TOOLS|OPTIONS|VIEW you can turn off the labeling of the row and column headers as well as the display of gridlines, the horizontal scroll bar, and the sheet tabs.

You do not need to inform Excel that it is dealing with a database. For Excel to recognize the database you have merely to move the cell pointer anywhere in the database. In Excel any connected range of cells is considered a database.

Therefore, you can immediately try out the database commands, such as sorting the table by a particular criterion (author, title, year of publication). Simply execute DATA|SORT. Another important database command is DATA: This opens a form for entry and editing of data.

Step 2: Equipping the Database with Filters

With the command DATA|FILTER|AUTOFILTER small filter arrows in the table's title cells are shown. When you click on these arrows with the mouse you can select filter criteria, such as a particular publisher or a publication year. The database will then display only those data that meet this criterion. To indicate that not all data are visible Excel turns the filter arrow blue. Several filtering criteria can be combined (such as all books of publisher *x* published in year *y*). You can even establish criteria such as showing all books that were published between 1980 and 1990 (a user-defined criterion).

Step 3: Buttons and Macros

As an experienced user of Excel you have presumably not had any problems using the database in its current configuration. Using the menu bar you can sort data according to chosen criteria, you can input and edit data, and so on. However, if you would like someone who is a total Excel novice to be able to use the database, then you need to make the interface a bit more user friendly. In the current example buttons have been added to the table that make it possible to execute the most important functions without a long search through the menu bar. (Of course, there are other possibilities for setting up the controls, such as a menu from which all but the truly important items have been deleted.)

To add buttons you activate the "control toolbox." (The control toolbox is part of the toolbars available for Excel. It can be shown using menu command VIEW|TOOLBAR.) Then click on the "Command Button" tool, and with the mouse click in the worksheet to insert the button. (This will automatically activate design mode, which enables further work on the button.)

Now comes the formatting of the button. In the pop-up menu obtained by clicking on the new button with the right mouse button choose COMMANDBUTTON OBJECT|EDIT. Ctrl+Return begins a new line, Esc terminates input.

All other properties of the button are entered via a properties window (Figure 1.9), which can be summoned either by using the button's pop-up menu or by clicking on the "properties" tool. There you should enter the following properties:

- *Name:* Give the control a meaningful name, such as btnSort for "sorting button."

- *Font:* Enlarge the font size to 10 points and choose the attribute "bold." You do this by clicking in the "font" field, which enables a button that if pressed opens a window in which font attributes can be edited.

- *ForeColor:* If you like buttons with a bit of pizzazz, here you can select a different text color.

- *TakeFocusOnClick:* Select the property *False,* so that the VBA code will be correct. (More on this in Chapter 7.)

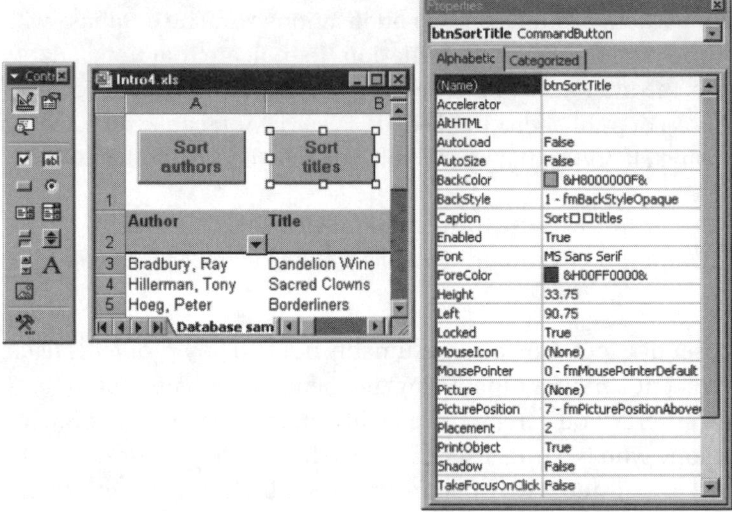

Figure 1.9. left: The control toolbox; middle: the table window; right: the properties window with settings for the selected button

> **NOTE** *You can save time by carrying out these formatting steps for the first button only. Then copy this button several times, which is accomplished by dragging the button with the mouse with the* Ctrl *key held down. If you hold down the* Shift *key as well, then the copied button has the same horizontal position as the original one, so that the buttons appear to belong together. Finally, you must define labels and names for each of the buttons.*

Now the buttons have to be linked to the program code. A double click on the button takes you to a template in the module "Sheet1" for an event procedure that will be automatically executed when the button is pressed. The name of the procedure is a combination of the control name (such as *btnSortAuthor*) and the event (usually *Click*).

```
' Intro4.xls, Module "Table1"
Private Sub btnSortAuthor_Click()
End Sub
```

The program code is recorded as in the previous examples. You then move the resulting instructions with Copy and Paste from the recorded module into the code template. If you have just been working on the example in the previous section, then "relative recording" mode is still active. You should be sure to deactivate it before recording.

Now onward to the content of the macro! For the two SORT macros first click cell A2, then execute DATA|SORT, and enter the desired sort criterion in the dialog (author or title). For data entry place the cell pointer once again in A2 and select DATA|FORM. Before you can record the macro DISPLAY ALL DATA, you must choose some filtering criterion (for example, show all books published before 1993). That is, the command DATA|FILTER|SHOW ALL is available only when at least one filtering criterion is active.

For the SAVE macro simply execute the command FILE|SAVE. The macro DATASEARCH must be input directly into the module via the keyboard (see below for the code). The macros should look something like this:

```
' Intro4.xls, "Table1"
' Sort by Author
Private Sub btnSortAuthor_Click()
  Range("A2").Select
  Selection.Sort Key1:=Range("A3"), Order1:= _
    xlAscending, Header:=xlGuess, OrderCustom:=1, _
    MatchCase:=False, Orientation:=xlTopToBottom
End Sub
' Sort by Title
Private Sub btnSortTitle_Click()
  Range("A2").Select
  Selection.Sort Key1:=Range("B3"), Order1:= _
    xlAscending, Header:=xlGuess, OrderCustom:=1, _
    MatchCase:=False, Orientation:=xlTopToBottom
End Sub
 'Show Database Form, Click on "New"-Button
Private Sub btnInput_Click()
  Range("A2").Select
  SendKeys "%w"
  ActiveSheet.ShowDataForm
End Sub
' Show Search Form
Private Sub btnFind_Click()
  SendKeys "^f"
End Sub
```

```
' Show All Data Records
Private Sub btnShowAll_Click()
  On Error Resume Next
  ActiveSheet.ShowAllData
End Sub
' Save
Private Sub btnSave_Click()
  ActiveWorkbook.Save
End Sub
```

NOTE *In order to try out the buttons you must exit design mode (the first tool in the "Control Toolbox" toolbar).*

Remarks for Advanced Users

Clicking cell A2 during the recording of a macro (it could be any cell in the range of the database) is necessary, because the database commands function only when the cell pointer is located within the range of the database. Since later the buttons will also be able to be pressed when the cell pointer is located elsewhere, at the beginning of the macro it must be placed explicitly in the range of the database.

In the macro *btnInput_Click* the *SendKeys* command must be inserted. It simulates the keyboard input Alt+W, by which in the dialog for the database form the button NEW is selected. This prevents the user from accidentally overwriting an existing entry. (Because of the not quite plausible operation of the database form this happens almost inevitably the first time.)

The order of the commands *SendKeys* and *ShowDataForm* seems illogical. It would appear as though first the form should be opened, and then the keyboard entry simulated. However, the command *SendKeys* merely has the function of placing the key combination Alt+W in a keyboard buffer, where (at some later time) it is made use of by Windows. If *SendKeys* appeared below *ShowDataForm* in the macro, then Excel would wait to execute *SendKeys* until the input in the database form was complete—and that, of course, would be too late.

The macro *btnFind_Click* also uses *SendKeys*, for invoking the SEARCH dialog. It would certainly be possible to show the dialog with *Dialogs(xlDialogFormulaFind).Show*, but it is not possible actually to find data. (The search is limited for unexplained reasons to the current cell.) This problem has been around since version 5!

Finally, an explanation of the macro *btnShowAll_Click* is necessary, in which the instruction *On Error Resume Next* may have caught your attention. This instruction has the effect of continuing the execution of the macro in the next row without an error message when an error occurs. In this macro an error can easily occur, namely, whenever the user clicks on the button DISPLAY ALL DATA when no filtering criterion is active.

A Form for Computing Interest in a Savings Account

Our next, and second to last, example of this chapter demonstrates that the design of a custom application is not inevitably associated with programming. In the table exhibited in Figure 1.10 there is a field with a yellow background in which four parameters can be entered: yearly interest rate, monthly deposits, day of first deposit, time during which the account is to run (saving time). The table is so constructed that the account can be set to run for at most six years.

From this input Excel calculates the date of the last deposit, the date the account terminates, the monthly interest, the crediting of interest, and the final total savings. Furthermore, Excel generates a table with monthly accrual of interest and balance, so that one can easily determine the balance at any time during the saving time.

The table can be used, for example, by a bank as the basis (and as promotional material) for convincing prospective customers of the value of opening a savings account. Creating a table tailored to the profile of a given customer can be accomplished in seconds. Finally, the table can be displayed in a suitable format.

> **NOTE** *This example can be managed without macro programming, instead of being based on rather complex* IF *expressions. If you have difficulties with* IF *expressions, then see the information in the first section of Chapter 9.*

The Model for the Table of Interest

The table is set up with a four-celled input region in which for simplicity of orientation input values have already been placed:

E5 (annual rate of interest): 6%
E6 (amount of each deposit): $100
E7 (first payment date): =*TODAY()*
E8 (time of savings): 1 year

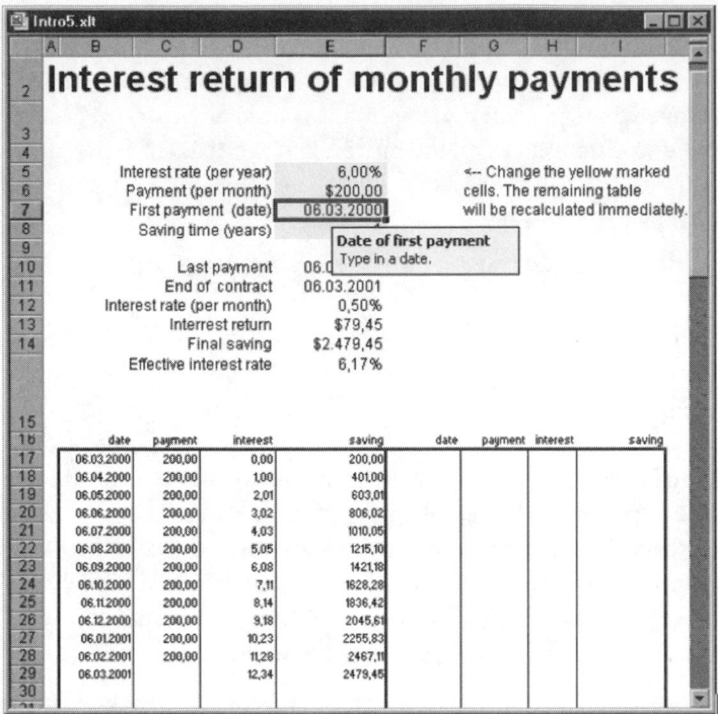
Intro5.xlt

Interest return of monthly payments

Interest rate (per year)	6,00%		<-- Change the yellow marked cells. The remaining table will be recalculated immediately.
Payment (per month)	$200,00		
First payment (date)	06.03.2000		
Saving time (years)		Date of first payment Type in a date.	
Last payment	06.0		
End of contract	06.03.2001		
Interest rate (per month)	0,50%		
Interrest return	$79,45		
Final saving	$2.479,45		
Effective interest rate	6,17%		

date	payment	interest	saving	date	payment	interest	saving
06.03.2000	200,00	0,00	200,00				
06.04.2000	200,00	1,00	401,00				
06.05.2000	200,00	2,01	603,01				
06.06.2000	200,00	3,02	806,02				
06.07.2000	200,00	4,03	1010,05				
06.08.2000	200,00	5,05	1215,10				
06.09.2000	200,00	6,08	1421,18				
06.10.2000	200,00	7,11	1628,28				
06.11.2000	200,00	8,14	1836,42				
06.12.2000	200,00	9,18	2045,61				
06.01.2001	200,00	10,23	2255,83				
06.02.2001	200,00	11,28	2467,11				
06.03.2001		12,34	2479,45				

Figure 1.10. Interest on monthly deposits

From these data three results will be computed: the date of the last deposit (*n* years minus 1 month after the first deposit), the end of the savings time (1 month thereafter), and the monthly rate of interest.

The determination of the date demonstrates the use of the *DATE* function, by which a valid date is created from the data *(year, month, day)*. The *DATE* function is quite flexible: *DATE(1997,13,1)* results 1/1/1998, *DATE(1998,2,31)* in 3/3/1998, *DATE(1998,-3,-3)* in 8/28/1997. It can be used almost without thinking; invalid month and day inputs are automatically translated into meaningful ones. The monthly rate of interest is simply one-twelfth of the annual rate (which yields an effective rate of –1 + (1 + 0.06/12)^12 = 0.06168, or 6.168%).

E10 (last deposit): =DATE(YEAR(E7)+E8, MONTH(E7)-1, DAY(E7))
E11 (end of account): =DATE(YEAR(E7)+E8, MONTH(E7), DAY(E7))
E12 (monthly interest rate): *=E5/12*
E15 (effective annual interest rate): *=(1+E12)^12-1*

The actual results of the table—the amount of interest credited to the account and the final balance—result from the monthly table in the bottom area of the form (B17:I53). The crediting of interest comes from the sum of all the monthly interest payments, while the final balance is derived from the largest entry to be found in the two balance columns. (Since the length of the table depends on the length of time the account runs, there is no predetermined cell in which the result lies).

E13 (total of interest payments): *=SUM(D17:D53, H17:H53)*
E14 (final balance): *=MAX(E17:E53, I17:I53)*

We proceed now to the monthly table, whose construction involves the greatest difficulties with formulas. For reasons of space the table is conceived as having two columns. Thus the whole table, up to a savings time of six years, can be printed on a single sheet of paper.

The first row of the table is trivial and refers simply to the corresponding cells of the input region. In the interest column the initial value is 0, since at the time of the first deposit no interest has been credited.

B17 (date): *=E7*
C17 (deposit): *=E6*
D17 (interest): 0
E17 (balance): *=C17*

With the second row the general formulas begin, which after once being entered by typing in or copying are distributed to the entire table. Of significance here is that while formulas appear in every cell of the table, they should be shown only in a certain number of cells determined by the length of time the account runs. In the remaining cells the formulas must know that the savings time has been exceeded, and therefore give as a result an empty character string "".

In the date column is tested whether the cell above contains a date (that is, is not empty) and whether this date is earlier than the date of account termination. If that is the case, then the new date is calculated by adding one month. In the deposit column is tested whether there is a date in the date column of the *previous month*. If that is the case, then the monthly deposit amount is shown, while otherwise the result is "". The previous month test is therefore necessary, because in the last row of the table (account termination) there are no further deposits, but a final crediting of interest.

The date test occurs in the interest column as well. The formula returns the previous month's balance multiplied by the monthly interest rate, or else "". In the balance column are added the previous month's interest and the deposit of the current month.

B18 (date): =IF(AND(B17<>"",B17<$E$11),
 DATE(YEAR(B17),MONTH(B17)+1,DAY(B17)),"")
C18 (deposit): *=IF(B19<>"",C17,"")*
D18 (interest): *=IF(B18<>"",E17*$E$12,"")*

E18 (balance): =IF(B18<>"",SUM(E17,C18:D18),"")

Note that during formula input some of the cell references ($E$11, $E$12) are absolute. Otherwise, there will be problems in copying or filling in cells.

The formulas given for one row can now be copied downwards by filling in. Select the four cells B18:E18 and drag the small fill handle (lower right corner of the cell region) down to cell E53.

Excel's fill-in function is not capable on its own of adapting the formulas in such a way that the table will be continued in the second column. However, you can give it a bit of help by filling in the formulas of the first column for two more cells (to E55) and then shifting the region B54:E5 to F17 (select the cells and drag on the selection boundary with the mouse). Finally, you can fill in the second column with formulas just as you did the first.

> **NOTE** *The formula for the date (B18) is in one respect not optimal: When 1/31/94 is given as start date, then the next date given is 3/3/94 (since there is no 2/31/94). Thereafter, all days of deposit are shifted by three days, the end date fails to agree with E11, and so on. This problem can be avoided if a new column is introduced containing a sequence of numbers for the deposits (1 for the first deposit, 2 for the second, etc.). Then the date of deposit can be calculated in the form*
> DATE(YEAR(E7); MONTH(E7)+counter-1; DAY(E7)).

Table Layout, Cell Protection, Printing Options

With the development of the formulas we have accomplished the most difficult task in our project. Now the table must be formatted in such a way that it presents a pleasing appearance (small, 8-point, type for the table of months, border lines, number and date formatting, alignment, background color for the input field, for example). With TOOLS|OPTIONS|VIEW you can deactivate the display of gridlines, row and column headers, horizontal scroll bar, and sheet tabs.

Now execute FILE|PRINT PREVIEW to see whether the table fits well on the page. If necessary you can adjust the height and width of individual rows and columns to obtain a better use of the space on the page. With the LAYOUT button (or the menu command FILE|PAGE SETUP) you can adjust the headers and footers (best is to select "none") and under the MARGINS tab select vertical and horizontal centering on the page.

Next you should protect your table against accidental changes made by the user. To do this, first select the input region and for these cells deactivate the option "Locked" (pop-up menu FORMAT CELLS|PROTECTION). Then protect the entire table (with the exception of the cells just formatted) using TOOLS|PROTECTION|PROTECT SHEET. In the dialog that appears do not give a password.

Validation Control

The four input cells have been protected against erroneous input. This was accomplished with DATA|VALIDATION, where the desired data format, validation rules, short information text, and a text for an error message (in the case of invalid input) were formulated. The possibility of formulating validation rules has existed since Excel 97.

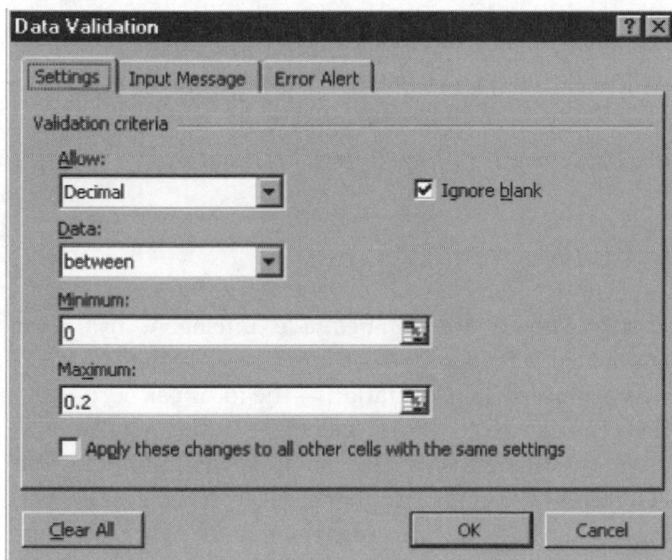

Figure 1.11. Formulation of validation rules for the interest table Templates

Templates

The table has now reached the stage where it can be used effortlessly: The user has merely to edit the four input areas and can then print out the result. To maintain the table in this condition and prevent it from being altered accidentally, save it with FILE|SAVE AS in Template format in the directory `Office2000\Office\Xlstart` (global) or `Windows\Profiles\username\Application Data\Microsoft\Templates` (user-specific) or `Windows\Application data\Microsoft\Templates.`

Templates are Excel files that serve as models for new tables. The user opens the template, changes certain information, and then saves the table under a new name. Excel makes sure automatically that the user gives a unique file name and does not overwrite the master template file with changes. In order for Excel to recognize templates, they must be saved in a particular format (filename `*.xlt`) and in a particular place (see above).

> **NOTE** *To test fully the special features of templates you should copy the sample file* Intro5.xlt *into one of the two above-mentioned locations. Furthermore, you must open it with the menu command* FILE|NEW, not FILE|OPEN*! (That would open the master file to allow you to make changes to it.)*

> **NOTE** *Further examples of templates and "smart sheets" can be found in Chapter 9, which is devoted entirely to the programming and application of such spreadsheets. For example, it is possible to write program code by means of which such tasks as automatically initializing the template on opening and providing buttons for printing are accomplished.*

User-Defined Functions

The previous example has shown how a table can be made "intelligent" by the inclusion of some fairly complicated formulas. The use of formulas as in the previous example soon runs up against certain limitations—the formulas become too long and unmanageable. You can avoid this problem by defining new functions yourself. However, your own functions can execute tasks that cannot be accomplished by formulas—such as changing a number into text (such as the number 12.34 into the character string "one two point three four," which is sometimes necessary, for example, in the preparation of checks in a payroll program.

The definition of one's own functions presupposes a fairly deep knowledge of VBA programming. The recording of macros is unfortunately unsuitable for this purpose, since here what is at issue is a calculation and not a sequence of commands. The following examples are actually quite simply constructed and should, in fact, be comprehensible without knowledge of programming.

Our first function will compute the area of a circle. Before you can use this new function in a table, you must input the code into a module sheet. Therefore, open a new workbook, and execute INSERT|MODULE.

```
' Example file Intro6.xls
Function CircleArea(radius)
  CircleArea = radius ^ 2 * Application.Pi
End Function
```

The keyword *Function* introduces a procedure, as did *Sub* in the earlier examples. The difference is that a *Function* procedure can return a value. For this reason the function name *CircleArea* in the second line is linked to the result of a calculation. The term *radius* is a parameter of the function. If you input the formula

=*CircleArea(5)* in a worksheet, then Excel executes the function and automatically substitutes for the parameter *radius* the value 5. With *Application.Pi* you access the number 3.1415927.

Now we proceed to our second function, which is somewhat more useful: It calculates the product of unit price and number of units, and if at least ten units are ordered, it computes an automatic discount of five percent. To deal with this special case an *If* statement is included.

```
Public Function Discount(unitprice, pieces)
  If pieces >= 10 Then
    Discount = pieces * unitprice * 0.95
  Else
    Discount = pieces * unitprice
  End If
End Function
```

NOTE *Normally, user-defined functions are provided for more demanding calculations. Details for programming user-defined functions are discussed in Chapter 5, in the section on user-defined worksheet functions.*

Analysis of Complex Tables

As an Excel user you are frequently confronted with complex worksheets that you yourself did not create, or if you did, it was so long ago that you do not remember how you constructed them. It is generally difficult to orient yourself in such worksheets. It is unclear which cells represent the results of which inputs, which cells are the results of formulas, and so on. The tools provided by the "Auditing" toolbar are, of course, helpful, but they are not quite suitable for our initial orientation. The macro that we will present here takes over this task: It analyzes all cells in the active worksheet. Character strings will be turned blue, formulas, red. (Of course, we could also investigate other aspects of the contents of the worksheet or produce other formatting, but we have enough on our plate as it is.)

This macro has the distinguishing feature, among others, that it cannot be created with the macro recorder—there are no comparable functions in Excel. The programming of a macro in this way thus requires a relatively extensive knowledge of Excel's object library and, in particular, knowledge of how to manipulate cells (see the first section of Chapter 5.1).

The program code begins with a test of whether the active page is a worksheet (it could be a chart). *TypeName* returns the name of the object type, for example, *Worksheet* or *Chart*. If a worksheet is present, then for the sake of speed, automatic recalculation and refreshing the screen are temporarily turned off. Finally, all used cells are analyzed in turn, as follows.

With *HasFormula* it can be simply determined whether the cell contains a formula. With *TypeName(c.Value)="String"* character strings are recognized. (With similar tests you can determine the presence of dates or currency values, e.g., $2.50.) For formatting purposes the *Color* property of the *Font* object of the cell being examined is altered.

```
' Intro7.xls
Sub AnalysisWorksheet()
  Dim c As Range   'cell
  If TypeName(ActiveSheet) <> "Worksheet" Then Exit Sub
  Application.Calculation = xlCalculationManual
  Application.ScreenUpdating = False
  For Each c In ActiveSheet.UsedRange
    If c.HasFormula Then
      c.Font.Color = RGB(192, 0, 0)
    ElseIf TypeName(c.Value) = "String" Then
      c.Font.Color = RGB(0, 0, 192)
    Else
      c.Font.Color = RGB(0, 0, 0)
    End If
  Next
  Application.Calculation = xlCalculationAutomatic
  Application.ScreenUpdating = True
End Sub
```

A Vocabulary Tutor

For the last example of the chapter we are going to have a bit of fun. This program will be an assistant for helping us to learn new vocabulary in a foreign language. The starting point is the table shown as in Figure 1.12 with vocabulary items in two languages. (Translator's note: In this edition they are English and German, as is appropriate for this translation from the German original. In the original, the languages were German and Swedish. Apologies to all you Swedes out there!) Columns C, D, E, and F indicate whether the word in one or the other direction (English → German or German → English) has already been correctly identified and how many times it has been looked up.

When you start the language tutor a dialog appears, as in Figure 1.13. A word is randomly selected from the vocabulary list, where preference is given for words that have not yet been tested and correctly identified. The vocabulary testing goes (also at random) in both directions. If you already know a word, you click on OK, otherwise, on ASK AGAIN LATER.

With CORRECT ENTRY and END TRAINER you exit the dialog. In the first case the input cursor is placed in the column of the vocabulary table from which the last test word was drawn. This makes it possible to make changes in the word list easily.

Vocabulary.xls

Start language trainer

	A	B	C	D	E	F
1			Language 1 --> Lang. 2 correct answers	tries	Lang. 2 --> Lang. 1 correct answers	tries
2	**English**	**German**				
3	evening	Abend	1	1	1	1
4	secret	Geheimnis	1	1		
5	thirst	Durst	1	1	1	1
6	ticket	Eintritts-/Fahrkarte	1	1	1	1
7	fire	Feuer		2		1

Words

Figure 1.12. Vocabulary list with lookup and correct answer information (columns C through F)

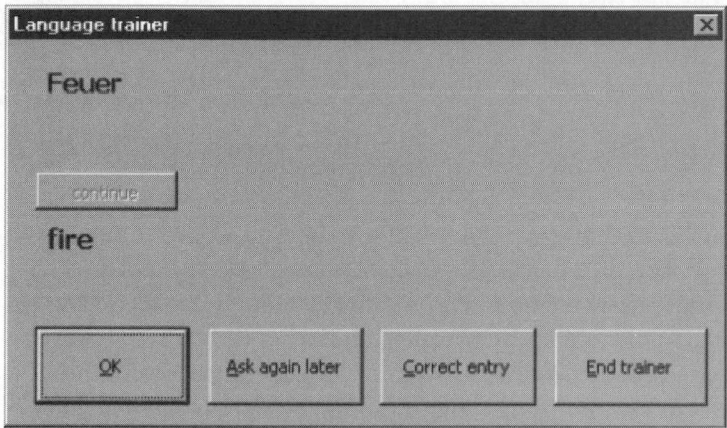

Figure 1.13. Form for the vocabulary tutor

Constructing the Form

NOTE *Almost all of the program code for this example is connected with the form (dialog) shown in Figure 1.13. The greatest hurdle to be jumped consists in constructing this form. If you have never worked with the form editor, you should perhaps take a peek at Chapter 7 in order to understand more fully the relatively brief discussion given here.*

Our work begins in the VBA development environment (type Alt+F11). There you produce a new form with INSERT|USERFORM. With VIEW|PROPERTIES you open the properties window, whose contents always relate to the object selected in the form. You set the internal name of the form as well as its label with the properties *Name* and *Caption*. In our example we will use *formQuery* as the object name and *Language trainer* as the title.

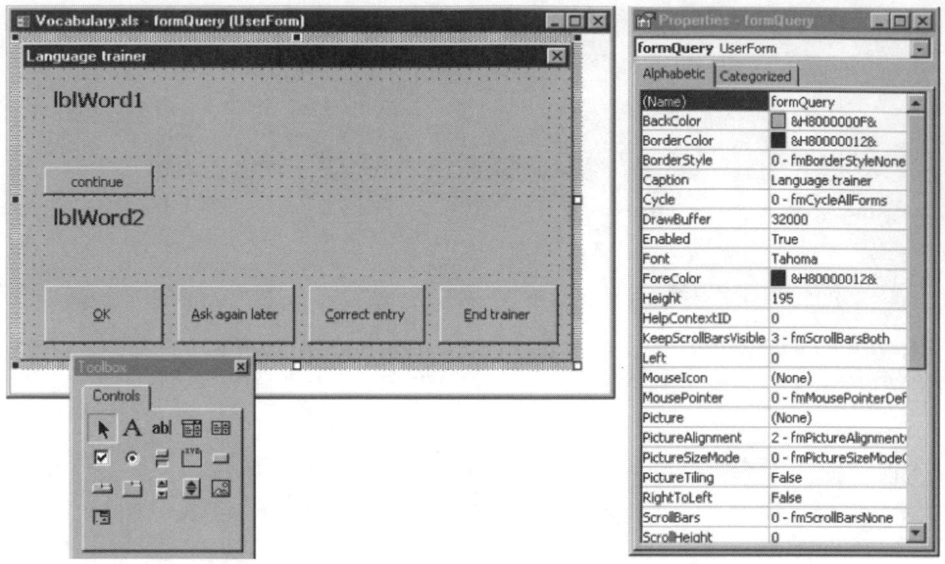

Figure 1.14. Constructing a Form

Insert into the form, as shown in Figure 1.14, two labels and five command buttons. To do this click on the appropriate control in the toolbox (VIEW|TOOLBOX) and then with the mouse draw the boundaries of the element in the form. The label field is indicated in the toolbox by a capital letter "A".

For each of the seven controls you must set, as you did previously for the form, the *Name* and *Caption* properties. In our example program we have made the following settings:

NAME	**CAPTION**	**PURPOSE**
lblWord1	lblWord1	Display the first word
lblWord2	lblWord2	Display the second word
btnNext	Continue	Second word is displayed
btnOK	OK	Word correct, proceed to next word
btnAgain	ASK AGAIN LATER	Word incorrect, continue
btnEdit	Correct ENTRY	Exit form, change word in table
btnEnd	END TRAINER	Exit form

Some of the other settings are not absolutely necessary for the proper functioning of the program, but they simplify its use: for the two labels you might set a larger font size with the attribute *Font*. For each of the buttons you can use the property *Accelerator* to allow the button to be selected later with Alt+letter. And finally, you can set the property *Cancel* to *True* for the END TRAINER button, so that this button can, as the cancel button, terminate the program and can be invoked with the Esc key as well as by a mouse click.

Program Code for the Form

> **NOTE** *Even the program code for this example is somewhat advanced. If you have no programming experience whatsoever, you should perhaps first look at Chapter 4, where elementary notions such as* variable *and* loop, *are discussed.*

We have now completed our preliminary work. Now we have to provide the form with procedures that will be executed when the form is invoked and the various buttons are pressed. To enable communication between these procedures, certain information must be stored in variables, which will be defined at the beginning of the code module for the form *queryForm.* (The ampersand ("&") serves to identify *Long* variables that store integer values.)

```
' Example file Vocabulary.xls
Option Explicit
Dim firstline&            'first line with words
Dim lastline&             'last line with words
Dim linenr&               'current line in word table
Dim querymode&            '  0: lang. 1 -> lang. 2,
                          '  1: lang. 2 -> lang. 1
Dim excelWindowstate&     'current window state of Excel
Dim startcell As Range    'current cell when trainer is started
Const maxTries = 20       'number of tries to find a yet untrained word
```

The procedure *UserForm_Initialize* is executed automatically when the form opens. As long as you are in the development environment, you can simply press the F5 key.

In this procedure the contents of the two label fields are cleared. Furthermore, the variables *startcell, firstline,* and *lastline* are initialized. The variable *startcell* denotes the first table cell of the vocabulary list and will be used in the rest of the program as the starting point for addressing further cells in the list. The variables *firstline* and *lastline* provide the first and last line numbers of the vocabulary range.

The calculation of *lastline* makes use of *CurrentRegion,* in order to determine the full range of the table (including the title). *Rows* decomposes this region into rows, while *Count* determines their number. (These properties will be described fully in the first section of Chapter 5.1.)

```
Private Sub UserForm_Initialize()
  lblWord1 = ""  'Erase the contents of the two label fields
  lblWord2 = ""
  Set startcell = Worksheets(1).Range("a3")
  firstline = startcell.Row
  lastline = startcell.CurrentRegion.Rows.Count
  Randomize        'initialize random number generator
  ShowNewWord      'display the first word
End Sub
```

The procedure *ShowNewWord* has the task of reading a word (one not yet learned, if possible) from the table and displaying it in the first label field. The search algorithm is rather trivial: With the random number function *Rnd*, which returns a number between 0 and 1, a row (*linenr*) and test direction (*querymode*) are generated. Then, with the method *Offset(row, column)* either column C or E—depending on *querymode*—of the vocabulary table is examined (see Figure 1.12). If the corresponding cell is empty or if it contains the value 0, then the word is considered not yet learned, and the loop is terminated.

If after *maxTries* attempts no unlearned word has been found, then a word that has already been learned is tested. For the running of the program this makes no difference—the word will be read via *Offset* and displayed in the first label field. The content of the second label field, which contains the word from the previous test, is erased. The following three instructions activate the button CONTINUE, and deactivate the buttons OK and ASK AGAIN LATER. Furthermore, the input focus is transferred to the CONTINUE button, so that this button can be operated with the **Return** key.

```
' randomly choose a word and display it
Sub ShowNewWord()
  Dim i&
  ' attempts to find an unlearned word
  For i = 1 To maxTries
    linenr = Int(Rnd * (lastline - firstline + 1))
    querymode = Int(Rnd * 2)
    If Val(startcell.Offset(linenr, 2 + querymode * 2)) = 0 Then
      Exit For
    End If
  Next
  lblWord1 = startcell.Offset(linenr, querymode)
  lblWord2 = ""
  btnNext.Enabled = True
  btnOK.Enabled = False
  btnAgain.Enabled = False
  btnNext.SetFocus
End Sub
```

The user now sees a form with a single word and attempts to guess the translation. Finally, he or she clicks on the CONTINUE button. In the procedure *btnNext_Click* the word is displayed in the target language in the second label field. The CONTINUE button is deactivated, and in exchange OK and AGAIN are activated.

```
' show the correct word in the target language
Private Sub btnNext_Click()
  lblWord2 = startcell.Offset(linenr, 1 - querymode)
  btnNext.Enabled = False
  btnOK.Enabled = True
  btnAgain.Enabled = True
  btnOK.SetFocus
End Sub
```

> **NOTE** *The procedure name* btnNext_Click *has its origin in the name of the object (here* btnNext*) and the name of the event (*Click*). To input the code simply execute a double click for the appropriate control in the form. This causes the lines* Private Sub name *and* End Sub *to be entered automatically in the program code.*

After typing in a response, if the user guessed correctly, he or she clicks OK, and the word will not be asked again. As a result, in *btnOK_Click* there is stored in column C or E (depending on *querymode*) how often the word has been translated correctly. Furthermore, in column D or F is stored how many times the word has been asked. Calling *ShowNewWord* triggers the display of the next word.

```
' word is identified
Private Sub btnOK_Click()
  ' Column C/E (correct answers)
  startcell.Offset(linenr, 2 + querymode * 2) = _
    Val(startcell.Offset(linenr, 2 + querymode * 2) + 1)
  ' Column D/F (tries)
  startcell.Offset(linenr, 3 + querymode * 2) = _
    Val(startcell.Offset(linenr, 3 + querymode * 2) + 1)
  ShowNewWord
End Sub
```

Here *btnAgain_Click* functions like *btnOK_Click*. The only difference is that column D/F is changed, but not column C/E.

```
' Word is not identified
Private Sub btnAgain_Click()
```

```
  startcell.Offset(linenr, 3 + querymode * 2) = _
    Val(startcell.Offset(linenr, 3 + querymode * 2) + 1)
  ShowNewWord
End Sub
```

Both procedures *btnEdit_Click* and *btnEnd_Click* terminate the form. For this the instruction *Unload Me* is used. In the first case the cell pointer is moved to the last displayed word, so that it can be corrected. In the second case a form is shown to ask whether the modified vocabulary list should be saved.

```
' vocabulary list should be corrected
Private Sub btnEdit_Click()
  Worksheets(1).Activate
  startcell.Offset(linenr).Activate
  Unload Me
End Sub
' Terminate form, save table
Private Sub btnEnd_Click()
  Dim result&
  Unload Me
  result = MsgBox("Should the vocabulary list be saved?", _
    vbYesNo)
  If result = vbYes Then ActiveWorkbook.Save
End Sub
```

Additional Code

In order to get the form started correctly, a button (*btnStartTrainer*) is inserted into the vocabulary table. In the event procedure the form is displayed with *Show*. This automatically causes *UserForm_Initialize* to be invoked, and the program proceeds as described above.

```
' Vocabulary.xls, Table 1
Private Sub btnStartTrainer_Click()
  formQuery.Show
End Sub
```

There Is Always Room for Improvement

Of course, there are countless ways in which this program could be improved: a convenient input dialog for new vocabulary, an options form for controlling the test mode (for example, testing only in one direction), a more refined algorithm for choosing the next word to test, extending the table with a column showing pronunciation.

Example Programs for You to Try

This section gives a brief description of the most interesting examples in this book. The figures should serve as invitations to you to go ahead and fire them up and try them out. At the same time, this section should give some indication as to just how extensive the possibilities of VBA programming are.

Install the example files in a directory on your hard drive as described in the Appendix.

> **NOTE** *If the programs correspond in some measure to ideas that you have for using Excel, then you can read the details in the indicated sections. A cross-reference as to which example files are described where in the book can be found in the Appendix.*

Calendar and Holidays

In many Excel applications the problem arises of dealing correctly with holidays. `Holidays.xls` shows how the occurrence of holidays is calculated. In addition, there is a small program for producing a calendar for any given year.

2000

January	February	March	April
New Year's Day	1	1	1
2	2	2	2
3	3	3	3
4	4	4	4
5	5	5	5
6	6	6	6
7	7	7	7
8	8	8	8
9	9	9	9
10	10	10	10
11	11	11	11
12	12	12	12
13	13	13	13
14	14	14	14
15	15	15	15
16	16	16	16
Martin Luther Kir	17	17	17
18	18	18	18
19	19	19	19
20	20	20	20
21	21	21	21
22	22	22	22
23	23	23	Easter Day

Figure 1.15. A calendar produced with Excel

A Macro for Using the Euro

Does your spreadsheet need to convert German marks into euros (or some other European currency)? This process cannot be completely automated, but in `Euro.xls` you will find some procedures to help you with the task.

Figure 1.16: Toolbar for the euro conversion tool

Design Your Own Forms

Excel offers the possibility to fashion forms, display them, and evaluate them with program code. A large number of such forms can be found in the file `Userform.xls`. The forms can be invoked with a mouse click.

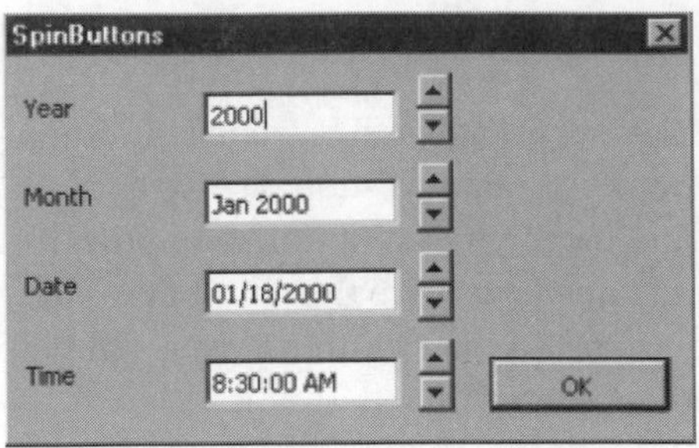

Figure 1.17. A user-designed form

"Intelligent" Billing Form for a Mail-Order Business

Creating invoices can be greatly simplified through the use of "intelligent" forms. The template `Speedy.xlt` provides a simple example. More refined variations on this theme are presented in the example files `DBCars.xls` and `Vertret.xls`.

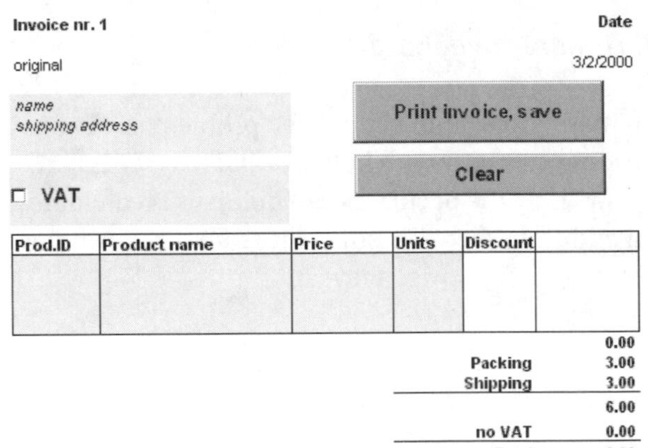

Figure 1.18. An intelligent form

Automated Data Presentation with Graphs

The extensive possibilities for creating graphs and charts in Excel are often used for presenting large quantities of data in graphic format. This process lends itself, of course, to automation. In `Chart.xls` is demonstrated how (using simulated test data) daily and monthly records of data can be created.

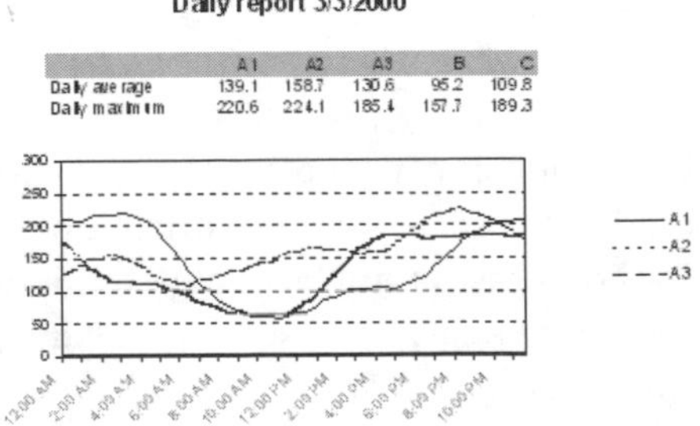

Figure 1.19: An automated chart

Balance Sheet for a Car-Sharing Club

As a member of a car-sharing club, you do not own your own automobile, but rather you borrow one from your club when you need it. The example `DB_Share.xls` shows how an "intelligent" form (namely, `Share.xlt`) can be extended to create a simple database application. With `DB_Share` you manage the fleet of cars, the names and addresses of members, and print out invoices for individual trips.

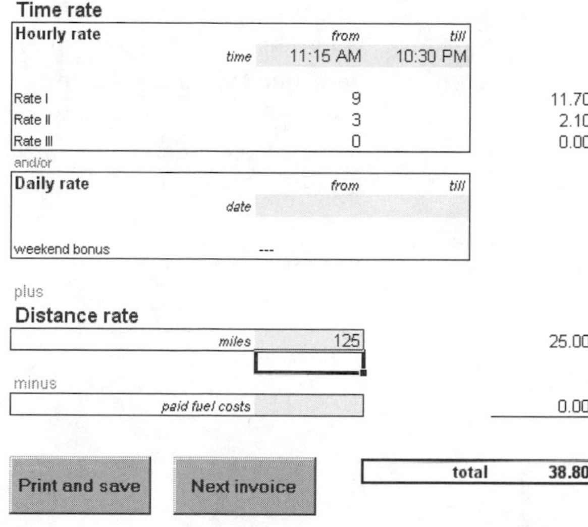

Figure 1.20. This form is linked to a small database application

Analysis of Survey Data

The evaluation of survey data is a labor-intensive occupation—so why not let Excel help out? In the directory survey you will find an example for an Excel-implemented survey form together with macros for automated analysis.

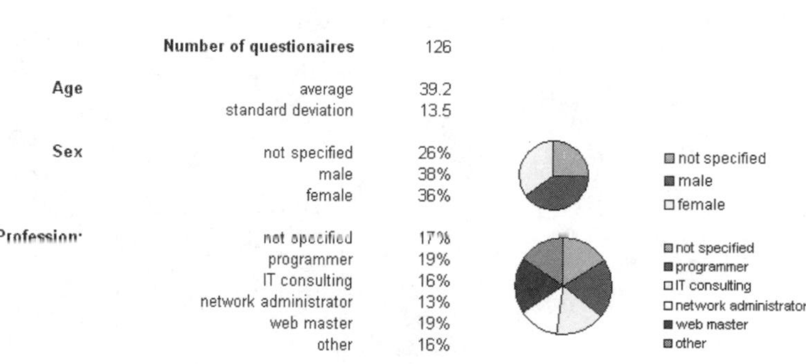

Figure 1.21. Analysis of survey data

Data Analysis with Excel (Pivot Tables)

Excel is an excellent tool for analyzing data, regardless of whether they reside in an Excel file or in an external database. The file `Pivot.xls` provides a host of examples of pivot tables and how to program them.

		qual.		
cat.	Data	I	II	Grand Total
a	Average of price	38.75	27.50	35.00
	Count of article	4	2	6
b	Average of price	83.75	60.00	75.83
	Count of article	4	2	6
c	Average of price	132.50	87.50	114.50
	Count of article	6	4	10
Total Average of price		91.79	65.63	82.27
Total Count of article		14	8	22

Figure 1.22. A simple pivot table

ActiveX Automation

The example ActiveX-Access.xls shows how Access—externally controlled via ActiveX automation—prints out a report on products in stock ordered by category from the *Northwind* database. It is, of course, assumed that you have access to Access!

Products by Category

07. Dez. 99

Category: Beverages

Product Name:	Units In Stock:
Chai	39
Chang	17
Chartreuse verte	69
Côte de Blaye	17
Ipoh Coffee	17
Lakkalikööri	57

Category: Condiments

Product Name:
Aniseed Syrup
Chef Anton's Cajun Seasoning
Genen Shouyu
Grandma's Boysenberry Spread
Gula Malacca
Louisiana Fiery Hot Pepper Sauce

Figure 1.23. Controlling external programs with Excel

Not only can Excel control external programs via ActiveX automation, the reverse direction is also possible. The Visual Basic program Vb6\Chart\ExcelChart.exe uses the chart functions of Excel to display its own data in an Excel chart.

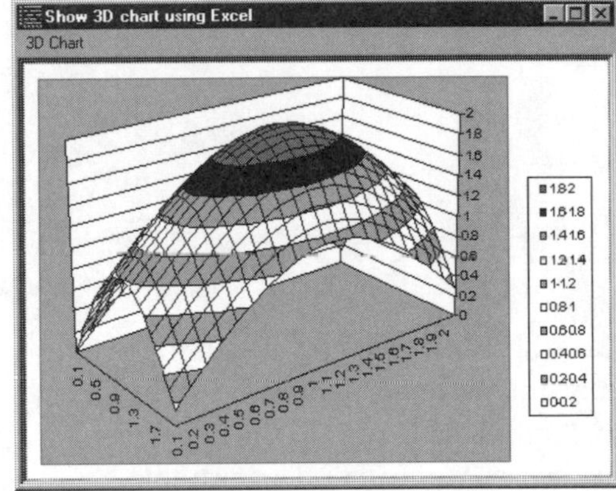

Figure 1.24. Controlling Excel via ActiveX automation

CHAPTER 2

What's New in Excel 2000

This chapter gives an overview of the most important innovations and changes in Excel 2000 in comparison to the earlier versions Excel 5, Excel 7 (alias Excel 95), and Excel 97.

We have no wish to dilly-dally, so let us come straight to the point: The differences between Excel 97 and Excel 2000 are limited in the standard version (fortunately!) to a manageable quantity, and in comparison to earlier updates from one version to the next there are relatively few compatibility problems. The most important new developments are the database library ADO, the FSO library for object-oriented access to files, and the new possibilities of internet import and export.

However, if you work with the Office 2000 Developer Edition, then you will have much more to learn. Microsoft has packed a host of useful new tools into this version of Office 2000.

Finally, if you are upgrading to Excel 2000 not from Excel 97 but from an earlier version, then prepare to be overwhelmed by numerous new libraries, objects, and compatibility problems.

Chapter Overview

Changes from Excel 97

> **NOTE** *The following overview of changes is not complete, but is limited to those details that in the author's view are most important for VBA programmers. Further information can be found in the on-line help system:*
>
> - *For general information, look in Microsoft Excel help via the Office Assistant for* What's New in Microsoft Excel 2000.
> - *For innovations for programmers, look in Microsoft Visual Basic help (call it from the development environment!) via the Office Assistant for* What's New for Microsoft Excel 2000 Developers.

Versions of Office

The version of Excel 2000 residing on your computer may have come from one of a number of sources. Either you acquired Excel as a stand-alone product, or you have installed one of the five (count them, five!) available Office suites: the Standard Edition, the Small Business Edition, the Professional Edition, the Premium Edition, the Developer Edition.

These editions differ primarily in how many and which components of the full Office suite they provide. In the context of programming in Excel, the numerous variants can be reduced to two:

- Perhaps you have the Office Developer Edition: In this case you have, in addition to all the components of the Premium Edition, a host of additional aids and functions, the most important of which will be described in Chapter 14.

- On the other hand, perhaps you are working with another version: In this case you still have access to all the possibilities of VBA programming, but not to the special functions of the Developer Edition.

The great majority of this book is valid for *all* versions of Excel. The special features of the Developer Edition will be mentioned, other than in Chapter 14, only in the form of cross-references or hints.

Language Features

VBA (Visual Basic for Applications) is the basis of all programming within Office. With Office 2000 is provided VBA version 6 (as opposed to VBA 5 in Office 97). Most of the changes are trivial:

- There are several new functions for working with and formatting character strings: *Join, InstrRev, Replace, Split, MonthName, WeekdayName, FormatCurrency, FormatDateTime, FormatPercent,* and *FormatNumber.*

- There are a few small improvements in object-oriented programming. You will still have to do without genuine inheritance (actually *the* determining feature of object-oriented programming languages), but at least now the keyword *Implements* makes possible the further—albeit halfhearted—use of existing classes.

- In any case, for the daily practice of programming in Excel it is more important to be able to define classes with their own properties (keywords *Event* and *RaiseEvent*).

New and Changed Objects, Properties, and Methods

Directories: The new property *UserLibraryPath* of the *Application* object provides the path to the local directory with add-in files. The effect of two *Application* properties has changed: *TemplatesPath* and *StartupPath* refer to the local `Templates`, respectively `Xlstart`, directories. (On the other hand, in Excel 97 the two properties give the path to the global `Templates` and `Xlstart` directories.) Unfortunately, there are no new properties to determine the global `Templates` or `Xlstart` directories.

Charts: The labeling of the coordinate axes can now be scaled. Thus instead of displaying numbers like 21,000,000 or 22,500,000, the scaling factor "millions" can be given, resulting in the numerical values 21 and 22.5. For VBA programming this feature is controlled by several new *DisplayUnitXxx* properties.

Also new are the so-called pivot charts: These are ordinary charts (*Chart* objects) whose contents, however, can be altered dynamically by certain pivot fields (as with pivot tables). The VBA control takes place via the new *PivotLayout* object, which is invoked by the property of the same name belonging to the *Chart* object.

Database Applications

Excel is, of course, a database program. However, it is very often used for the analysis of externally stored data (for example, in the form of charts or pivot tables). Therefore, access to external data has always been of great importance to Excel programmers.

Usually, the simplest way to extract data from a database is by means of the program MS Query, which is launched via DATA|GET EXTERNAL DATA|NEW DATABASE QUERY. The settings implemented in MS Query can be controlled with the *QueryTable* object. In Excel 2000 this object is equipped with a host of new properties.

The new ADO library (*ActiveX Data Objects*) offers considerably more flexibility and above all the possibility of making changes to databases. The DAO library, which was previously used for this purpose, can still be employed, but it will not be developed further by Microsoft. Therefore, new database applications especially should use the ADO library. (However, there is seldom any reason not to retain existing applications that make use of DAO.) An introduction to ADO programming can be found in Chapter 12.

A popular method of analyzing data within Excel—no matter whether the data come from traditional database systems or from a *Data Warehouse*—is by means of pivot tables. These tables have existed for a long time, but in Excel 2000 they come equipped with a variety of extensions (about thirty new properties and methods). Pivot tables are the main focus of Chapter 13.

If you have access to the Developer Edition, you will find in Chapter 14 further information about additional available ADO components and tools.

Internet

If you were to read what the marketing division of Microsoft has put out about Office 2000, you would get the impression that almost all changes in the new version are related to the internet. This impression, however, is totally misleading: To be sure, there are various improvements in Excel in this direction (especially in relation to simplified import and export of HTML files), but from the point of view of the VBA programmer there are comparatively few truly relevant innovations.

- **HTML Export/Import:** Excel offers new functions for exporting Excel objects (for example, a range of cells) in HTML format as well as for importation of data from HTML files. These functions can be run using program code with the objects *PublishObject* (Export) and *WebQuery* (Import).

- **Web Components:** These are controls suitable for the internet in which an Excel table (or diagram) can be represented. While not all Excel functions are available in the controls, many, in fact, are. The advantage is that the data can be manipulated dynamically in the HTML document. However, there are associated disadvantages, the most fundamental of which is that web components are supposed to be used only by those possessing an Office 2000 license. To this extent the web components are unsuitable for the internet, seeming to be rather designed for use in intranets (in large companies, for example).

- **E-Mail:** Thanks to the method *SendMail* it is now a simple matter to send the current workbook as e-mail. (Strictly speaking, *SendMail* is not an innovation of Excel 2000—the methods existed already in Excel 97. However, I neglected to describe the methods in the previous edition of this book, and that omission is remedied here.)

  What is truly new, on the other hand, is the *Workbook* property *EnvelopeVisible*: With this you can insert various text fields for the input of e-mail addresses and subject lines in the upper border of the table window. This makes it easier for the user to send the workbook interactively.

Miscellaneous

Dealing with Files (FSO Library): If you wish to access files or directories or need to read from or write to text files, then instead of the usual commands (*Open, Close, Print,* etc.) you can use the new FSO library (*File Scripting Objects*). The objects defined there offer not only greater elegance in accessing data, but also for the first time they offer unicode support. Unfortunately, the FSO methods are not suitable for working with binary data—for that you must still use the traditional functions.

Forms, or Dialogs (UserForm): Forms can now be opened independently (*Show vbModeless*). That is, Excel visible below the form, can be used without the form having to be closed. Just be sure not to use these new functions in combination with the *RefEdit* control for input of ranges of cells. Otherwise, Excel loses control over the keyboard focus and can be terminated only through brute force methods (task manager or Ctrl+Alt+Del)!

Importing Text: A frequent source of aggravation with previous versions of Excel was the attempt to automate the importation of ASCII files. Fortunately, there is progress to be reported. Finally, the decimal point and the thousands separator (for separating groups of three digits in the representation of numbers) can be controlled by additional parameters of the method *OpenText*. For importing text the revised *QueryTable* object can be used.

Configuration Files: The locations of configuration files have changed again—as has been the case with all previous versions. Everyone's favorite game is *Look for me!*

Help System: The entire help system has been completely revised and is now based internally on the so-called HTMLHelp System. As far as content goes, the information offered is, in fact, often correct, but the problem is in finding the information. The F1 key by no means always leads to the desired result, and the full text search that was available in the earlier help system has for some incomprehensible reason disappeared. In its place there is now the so-called Office Assistant, who (or which, depending on user preference), however, is not an adequate substitute. Its results are often quite good, but much more often are simply useless. (Don't we already have enough assistants, and even these are always in the way?)

If you wish to equip your own Excel applications with their own help files, you can now use HTMLHelp for that purpose. For developing your own help files you should make use of the HTMLHelp Workshop, which is provided only with the Office Developer Edition.

Euro Support: In older editions of Office the euro symbol could be used only after installation of special updates. In this respect Office 2000 has made a certain amount of progress, but there is much on the theme of the euro that seems not to have occurred to Microsoft. The function *EuroConvert,* which can be used as an Excel add-in function, is not documented, and one can seek in vain other aids for converting existing tables from a given European currency into euros. (The section on the euro in Chapter 5.9 attempts to redress this lack, to the extent that such redress is possible.)

Office Developer Edition

There has been a Developer Edition offered since Office 97, but it was of interest only to Access programmers and did not find wide application. With Office 2000 that might change. The Developer Edition now contains a large number of extensions and additional components that will be of interest to many VBA programmers.

The first section of Chapter 14 contains an overview of the most important features of Office Developer. Then throughout that chapter some of the new possibilities will be explicated in detail. (The remainder of the book is limited to functions that are available in all versions of Excel.)

> **NOTE** *The acronym division of Microsoft, whose sole responsibility consists in ceaselessly creating nice-sounding abbreviations, seems to have been unable to restrain its imagination. Thus for the Developer Edition there are two abbreviations: MOD (Microsoft Office Developer) and ODE (Office Developer Edition). Don't let yourself get confused!*

Changes from Previous Versions

Excel 7 → Excel 97

"Never give a programmer an even break" seems to have been Microsoft's motto at one point: What is new above all are the development environment and the idea of user-defined forms (dialogs) (MS forms library). Furthermore, about half of the approximately 120 Excel-7 objects have been replaced by new objects. Beyond that, countless new objects have been introduced.

Development Environment

The most obvious change in Excel 97 was the separation of the development environment from Excel. This separation takes some getting used to, but it has a number of advantages. The greatest advance is the extension of incomplete keywords by an automatically displayed list of choices or by Ctrl+spacebar.

Module Sheets: The division into application and programming components also has had effects on programming: The enumeration object *Modules* and the object class *Module* were no longer supported for module sheets and are currently available only for reasons of compatibility.

Protection of Module Sheets: Due to the separation of Excel into application and VBA components the protection functions for modules were also revised. That would not have been so bad if a minimum of compatibility had been retained. That is not, unfortunately, the case: Hidden and protected modules in Excel 7 are displayed in Excel 97 as though they were unprotected. After all, you always wanted your customers and users to know how you programmed all those functions, didn't you?

VBA Language Concepts

Events: The management of events was completely reworked in Excel 97. Whereas in Excel 5 and 7 a small number of predefined events were attached to *OnEvent* properties, now events are controlled in Visual Basic: For all possible events—such as activating a worksheet—the names of the event procedures are preset (such as *Worksheet_Activate*). When you fill this procedure with code, the code is then automatically executed when the event occurs. Even events associated to objects that in the development environment are not shown in their own modules can be received via the detour of a class module.

The down side of the new concept of an event is that Excel programmers were perhaps a bit too enthusiastic: Almost every object is equipped with countless events. In the process clarity has been lost. It remains to be seen whether there will really be applications for all these events.

Class Modules: Now in VBA as in Visual Basic new object classes with methods and properties can be defined (though without their own events and without *Enum* constants). However, the implementation gives the impression of being only half complete. Furthermore, there remains the question of whether there is a great need for programmer-defined class modules within Excel applications.

***Collection* Object:** The *Collection* object represents a convenient alternative to fields. The advantage over normal fields is that *Collections* do not have to be declared in advance in a particular size. Moreover, any text can be used as an index (instead of consecutive numbers).

User-Defined Functions: In Excel 5 and 7 one could associate user-defined worksheet functions of various categories, which were exhibited by the dialog INSERT|FUNCTION (the function assistant of the time). Since Excel 97 this possibility no longer exists officially, and all user-defined functions are associated with the data type *user-defined*. (This restriction can be gotten around; see Chapter 5.7.)

Changed and Extended Objects

A large number of Excel objects were introduced in version 97, or were changed or associated to other libraries (and thereby renamed). The most important changes—to the extent that they have not been made obsolete by Excel 2000—are discussed in the following pages. A complete listing can be found in the VB help in Excel 2000 (start in the development environment!), by searching in the office assistant for *Changes to the Microsoft Excel 97 Object Model*.

The most important additions to the *Workbook* object have to do with the shared use of an Excel file by several users (sharing functions). To make an Excel file available for shared use, you must save the file using *SaveAs* with *AccessMode:=xlShared* as a shared file. (Manually, the sharing of Excel files is accomplished not with SAVE AS, but with TOOLS|SHARE WORKBOOK.)

To terminate sharing, the method *ExclusiveAccess* is available. (With it the current workbook is saved under the current name.) The current state can be inferred from the property *MultiUserEditing*. There are a number of properties and methods for maintaining, managing, and synchronizing shared-use files: *AcceptAllChanges, AutoUpdateFrequency, AutoUpdateSaveChanges,*

HighlightChangesOnScreen, HighlightChangesOptions, KeepChangesHistory, ListChangesOnNewSheet, PersonalViewListSettings, PersonalViewPrintSettings, ProtectSharing, RejectAllChanges and *UnprotectSharing.*

With the *FormatCondition* object the formatting of a cell or range of cells (*Range* object) can be made dependent on the cell's contents. For example, you can arrange to have the color of a number change when the number exceeds a value contained in a comparison cell. There can be at most three conditions per cell. Manually, you can achieve this type of formatting with FORMAT|CONDITIONAL FORMATTING. (Similar effects could be achieved in earlier versions of Excel by conditional number formats. However, there were many fewer layout possibilities and no VBA interface.)

With the *Validation* object one can define validation controls for the input in cells. For example, input can be restricted to a particular format (e.g., date) or to within a range of values. Such rules can be formulated manually with DATA|VALIDATION.

With the *Hyperlink* object one can provide references to Excel worksheets as well as to other files (local or on the internet).

An entire family of objects (*Shape, ShapeRange, ShapeNode, GroupShapes,* etc.) replaces the drawing objects of Excel 5/7 (*Arc, Line,* etc.). Aside from the drawing objects, which are now called AutoShapes objects and offer much more in the way of layout possibilities, all the remaining objects in tables are controlled by *Shape* objects: controls, OLE objects, object groups, etc.

New Properties and Methods

By setting *AutoScaleFont=True* one can achieve for a variety of objects (*AxisTitle, LegendEntry,* etc.) that the size of the text is accommodated to the size of the object.

FormulaLabel=xlColumn/RowLabel the contents of a cell can be defined to be the name for the row or column the given cell heads. These names can then be used in formulas, thereby making formulas more readable. It is necessary that *AcceptLabelsInFormulas* be set to *True* (default setting). Manually, *FormulaLabel* can be changed with INSERT|NAME|LABEL.

In Figure 2.1 *FormulaLabel=xlColumnLabels* holds for the cells A1:C1. Thus in C2 the formula *=income-expenses* can be used. If a different text is input into A1 Text, then the formula is automatically changed!

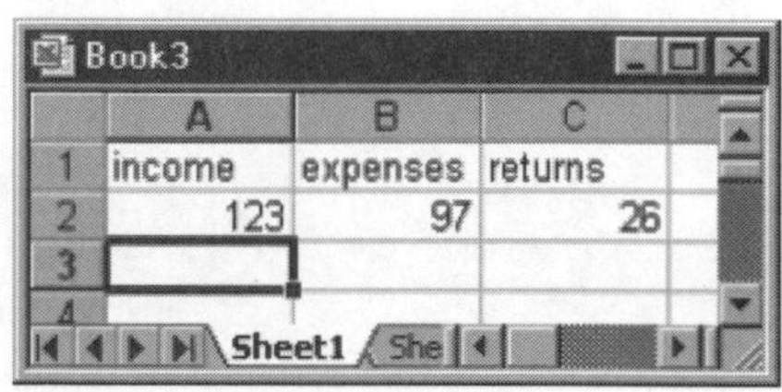

Figure 2.1: Example of FormulaLabel

> **WARNING** *The feature just described continues to exist in Excel 2000, but there it is deactivated by default! To use it in Excel 2000, you must first in* TOOLS|OPTIONS|CALCULATION *activate the option* ACCEPT LABELS IN FORMULAS.

A host of new formatting possibilities come from new properties of the *Range* object. *IndentLevel* sets how far the content of a cell is to be indented. (The permissible range is from 0 to 15.) With *Borders* it is now also possible to draw diagonal lines through a cell (previously, a cell could only be framed). With *Orientation* the text can be oriented between –90 and 90 degrees (previously, only multiples of 90 degrees were possible). The *Orientation* property can also be changed for many other objects, such as labels on charts.

Object Libraries

Menus/Toolbars (Office Library): You have no doubt noticed that the appearance of menus and toolbars has changed. The consequence for programmers is that the *Toolbar* and *Menu* objects have been replaced by a family of new *CommandBar* objects.

This results not only in serious changes for the management of custom menus and toolbars, but also in a number of incompatibilities. There is no longer a menu editor. Instead, in the creation of new menu bars one must allow oneself to be tormented by a number of incomprehensible pop-up menus (the starting point is VIEW|TOOLBARS|CUSTOMIZE). The only advantage in return for the time spent in adaptations and alterations is that the new menu bars and toolbars and the basic Office object library can be used together in all components of Office.

Forms (MS Forms Library): For setting up forms there is the new MS Forms Library. The forms created from it look just like the forms in Excel 5 and 7, but the forms editor is handled differently, and the management of the form by program code is considerably different. There are two fundamental advantages: You can now set up multipage forms (in the manner of the options forms) and use external controls (so-called ActiveX controls).

As opposed to the traditional menus and toolbars, Excel 5/7 forms are also supported in Excel 2000. That is, the forms editor is still provided. However, in the execution of VBA code for the management of forms one encounters frequent error messages. There are, then, considerable compatibility problems to some extent.

VBIDE Library: The development environment is programmable via its own library: Microsoft Visual Basic for Applications Extensibility, VBIDE in the object catalog, fundamental object *VBE*. The library is of benefit when you wish to improve the usefulness of the development environment or change the code of an Excel file by means of program code.

Excel 5 → Excel 7

Since version 7 the mechanism of ActiveX automation (which at the time was called object automation) has been used to incorporate various extensions into Excel. The extensions described in this section must be activated before use with TOOLS|REFERENCES. Furthermore, an entire library of new objects, methods, and properties is available, which can be used as Excel keywords in VBA code.

Office Library: To simplify and standardize the search for Office documents, when a document is saved, supplementary information is now saved with it. You can examine the possibilities available for searching for files from the dialog in FILE|OPEN and for the input of supplementary information in FILE|PROPERTIES. You can access the supplementary information in VBA code using the properties *BuiltinDocumentProperties* and *CustomDocumentProperties.*

Office Binder Library: A further innovation in the Office suite of applications is that a group of Office documents (text, worksheets, databases, etc.) can be assembled as if enclosed in a binder. The files thus assembled can then be more easily managed. Binders are controlled using program code by means of the new objects *Binder* and *Section.*

Old and New Errors; Compatibility Problems

NOTE *Every Excel developer cherishes the hope that the latest version of Excel will be better and more stable than the previous one. To some extent this hope is fulfilled, but nonetheless it always happens that in running or testing VBA code Excel crashes. (So save your files early and often!)*

Note that Excel doesn't always crash completely. Sometimes, of course, there is the obligatory announcement of a system error, but Excel remains in memory and allows the most recently opened files to be opened, though without the possibility of saving them. To be able to continue working properly, you must completely terminate Excel. Under Windows NT and Excel 2000 you use the Task Manager. Under Windows 9x hit Ctrl+Alt+Del. *A task list appears from which you can select Excel and forcibly terminate it.*

It brings me no pleasure to write about the on-line help. The new system is sadly immature. There is no central and complete index; the search possibilities are greatly reduced from the previous version (there is no longer a full-text search!). If you work with Office Developer, you must furthermore continually shuffle CD-ROMs, since the documentation of the MSDN library is distributed among three CDs.

If you have access to the MSDN library (for instance, it is included with Office Developer and is also available as a stand-alone product), you can search there for information about Excel with greater hope of success.

> **NOTE** *The greatest advantage of the MSDN library—the huge amount of information—is also a disadvantage: It is very difficult to restrict the search to information relevant to Excel. If you search for* Attributes *(a property of the* File *object in the* Scripting *library), you will find this word not only in the Visual Basic Scripting documentation, but also in another five hundred locations, including Java and API functions. Sometimes less is more!*

General Problems

- VBA is still, as always, unoptimized for evaluating conditionals. A test of the form *If x>=0 And Sqr(x)<3* leads in the case of negative *x* to an error. (This has been a problem with Visual Basic since its inception, so at this point I have given up all hope of any improvement on this score.)

- In program development there often arise strange "automation errors." Then every further attempt to execute VBA code leads to new errors. Even the attempt to exit Excel fails (or results in a crash). As a rule, Excel must be terminated via the Task Manager and then restarted.

- If individual worksheets in a workbook are deleted with *Worksheets(...).Delete,* it often happens that the resulting file is internally defective. It can be saved, but every subsequent attempt to load it leads to Excel crashing. It remains unclear under what circumstances this error occurs. (It has in itself nothing to do with the *Delete* method. The same problem can occur when the worksheet is deleted manually.)

- Just as in Excel 97, switching from the VBA development environment to Excel fails when the object catalog is the active window. You must first click in another window in the development environment. One would have thought that the three years that elapsed between Excel 97 and Excel 2000 would have sufficed for this trivial problem to be solved.

- Almost as troublesome is that toolbars from Excel always appear in the development environment, where they tend to be in the way. The moment they are clicked on, one experiences a (usually unwished for) switch back into Excel. Admittedly these are small points, but they do tend to get on one's nerves.

Problems with MS Forms Dialogs and Controls

Excel and most VBA commands are blocked as long as the input cursor is located in an MS Forms control in a worksheet. This can be prevented only in the case of buttons with *TakeFocusOnClick=False*. (The default setting, though, is *True*, and this is the reason that there are often problems with buttons in worksheets. The error messages that result are completely uninformative.)

If other controls are used in a worksheet, then the input cursor must be placed in a cell by means of program code (such as *Worksheets(n).[A1].Activate*) in order to make certain that it is not directed at a control.

Compatibility Problems with Respect to Excel 97

First, the good news: During the time that I was working on this book very few compatibility problems vis à vis Excel 97 arose. The VBA code in Excel 97 workbooks usually executed without any problem. In comparison to the change from Excel 5 to 7 and then to 97 the compatibility problems are minimal.

Needless to say, Excel 2000 is not fully compatible. The most frequent problems involve new locations of configuration files. New, for example, is that the "personal macro workbook" is for the first time actually personal. That is, this file is structured for each user and saved in its own location. Changes made to such a file are no longer effective globally for all Excel users. Fundamentally, this is an advantage, especially since there is always the possibility of defining global macros. Details on Excel configuration files can be found in Chapter 5, in the subsection on configuration files.

The *Application* properties *TemplatesPath* and *StartupPath* are also related to the configuration files. Their effects have changed with Excel 2000. They now refer to the personal `Templates` and `Xlstart` directories (instead of, as previously, the global directories). Further information on these properties can be found in Chapter 5, in the section on Excel-specific methods and properties.

Additionally, there was a series of sporadically occurring small problems whose cause has remained unclear. For example, Excel would crash until a previously undeclared variable was explicitly declared as *Variant*; there would occur an "automation error" until a *Select* was changed to an *Activate*; and so on.

Compatibility Problems with Respect to Excel 5/7

The following information is valid if you passed over Excel 97 and wish to upgrade directly from Excel 5 or Excel 7 directly to Excel 2000. In this case the situation is rather bleak.

> **NOTE** *Even Microsoft admits to upgrade problems and lists on its web site http://support.microsoft.com/support/kb/articles/q162/7/21.asp (this is the knowledge base article Q162721 in the MSDN library) no fewer than 75 separate problems.*

Needless to say, then, the following list is incomplete. It does, however, list the most important problems. Most of the problems mentioned here are, to be sure, niggling details. But it is often such "details" that cost a full day's work searching for errors.

- When a worksheet is accessed, many methods function only with *Worksheets(n)*, but not with *Sheets(n)* (even if in both cases the same worksheet is referenced).
- The formatting of charts via program code gives results different from those of Excel 7.
- VBA code that accesses *Selection* often gives difficulties. This is even more annoying in that as a rule the automatic recording of a macro is the source of the problematic code. Try the following remedy: Change the lines

  ```
  object.Select or object.Activate
  Selection.method
  ```

  to

  ```
  object.method
  ```

  This same course of action is also valid, of course, when *Selection* is used by means of *With* for several lines. (Give the actual object instead of *Selection* when using the *With* command.)
- Links to *OnEventXxx* properties have been stored in the Excel file since Excel 97, which was not the case with Excel 5/7. Most Excel 5/7 applications rely on the fact that when a file is loaded, all *OnEventXxx* properties are empty. This is no longer the case, which can result in serious problems.

There are, for the most part, problems with the attempt to replace *OnEventXxx* procedures by the event procedures newly introduced in Excel 97. Excel suddenly complains that it can no longer find the procedures stored in *OnEventXxx* properties.

The problem is exacerbated by the fact that there is no possibility to determine all initialized *OnEventXxx* properties. It is necessary, rather, to test whether the property is being used in the immediate window for every conceivable *OnEventXxx* property (for every worksheet!). If it is, then you must delete the property by defining an empty character string "". Enjoy!

- In Excel 7 the method *OpenText* provides *True* or *False* as a return value according to whether the importation of data was successful. Since Excel 97 this method can no longer be used as a function, and there is no longer a return value. Possible errors must be caught with an error-handling routine.

- The Syntax of the parameters *Destination* and *Connection* for specifying external sources of data using the method *PivotTableWizard* has changed. Excel 7 program code no longer runs in general.

Incompatibilities with Dialogs (Forms)

- MS Forms (new since Excel 97) can be decorated with drawing elements, text fields, or other Office objects. There are, however, many fewer visual formatting possibilities than there were for forms in Excel 5/7.

- In compatibility mode for the display and management of forms from Excel 5/7 a problem occurs when you attempt to link a range of cells to a listbox: Set listbox.List = Sheets("Table1").[a1:a4]

  The direct linking of ranges of cells to lists is apparently no longer supported. You must either execute a loop over all the cells and insert the entries individually with *AddItem* or use the MS Forms listbox of Excel 2000.

Incompatibilities with Menu Bars and Toolbars

Menu bars and toolbars, new since Office 97, are a chapter in themselves, and such a chapter would not be only about improvements.

- No new event procedures can be linked to existing menus that were created on the basis of the *Menu* objects of Excel 5/7. (Strictly speaking, the link functions, but it is not saved.) Thus you can continue to use existing menus, but you cannot change them. The transformation to new *CommandBar* menus is possible only manually and with considerable effort.

- There is no longer a menu editor. The manual production of new menus is accomplished through the form VIEW|TOOLBARS|CUSTOMIZE and is tied to hundreds of mouse clicks. Context menus can still be changed only with program code.

- Changes in predefined menus are no longer saved in the Excel file, but separately for each user in his or her own file. For this, additional code is necessary if changes in existing menus or toolbars are to be made in Excel applications. (New toolbars can be attached as in Excel 5/7.)

Part II

Fundamentals

CHAPTER 3

The Development Environment

This chapter describes in detail the operation of the VBA development environment, which since Excel 97 has appeared in its own window with its own menus, toolbars, etc. The development environment makes possible the input of program code and the definition of new forms, helps with debugging, and contains such delightful features as an object browser with cross-references to on-line help, and an "immediate window" for testing individual instructions.

Chapter Overview

The Components of a VBA Program

A VBA Program is always part of an Excel workbook. Thus it is impossible to save, edit, or execute an Excel program outside of a normal Excel file. In speaking about the components of a VBA program, we mean, then, the VBA components of an Excel file that are shown in the VBA development environment.

> **NOTE** *There are two special cases in saving VBA code: (1) You can export the code of a module or form as an ASCII file—you cannot, however, execute these files. (2) You can save an Excel file as an add-in. In this case the worksheets are invisible, and the code is saved in a compact format and cannot be changed. Although an Add-In has little in common visually with an Excel workbook and has quite a different purpose in life (see Chapter 14 on Excel add-ins), it is nonetheless nothing more than a special case of a normal Excel file.*

An Excel application can comprise the following VBA components:

- Normal program code (module): Program code with definitions of variables, subprograms, and functions is saved in so-called modules. A module is thus a group of specially programmed procedures (subprograms) that can be used in Excel. In the development environment a module is displayed in a text window for the code that it is to contain.

- Program code for defining new object classes (class modules): Purely visually, a class module looks like a normal module, that is, a text window with program code. The difference is that class modules serve to define new objects. An introduction to programming of class modules is given in Chapter 4.

- Program code with event procedures associated to Excel objects: Every Excel sheet (table, chart) as well as the entire Excel workbook understands events, such as changing from one sheet to another, or saving or printing a workbook. When such a predefined event occurs, a so-called event procedure can be automatically triggered. The program codes for these event procedures are located in their own modules, which, in turn, are associated to the corresponding Excel object. Detailed information about event procedures can be found in Chapter 4.

- Forms (*UserForm*): Since Excel 97 forms consist of two connected parts: the form itself with its controls, and the program code with the event procedures associated to the controls. (These event procedures are necessary for managing the form.) The creation and management of forms are the theme of Chapter 7.

- References: So long as you use only the standard Excel objects, you do not need to worry about references. However, as soon as you wish to use objects that are defined in external object libraries (such as in the ADO library for database programming), you must activate these with TOOLS|REFERENCES (in the development environment). The references to the object libraries used are saved in the Excel file.

The first four points in this list have the following in common: The VBA code is shown in code windows that always look the same. The tools for code input and for debugging are also the same in each case.

The Components of the Development Environment

The principal purpose of the development environment is to make possible the input of program code and the definition of "intelligent" forms. Since Excel 97 the VBA development environment is no longer integrated into Excel, but behaves almost like a freestanding application. The development environment is invoked by TOOLS|MACRO|VISUAL BASIC EDITOR or with the keyboard shortcut Alt+F11, and it then appears in an independent window.

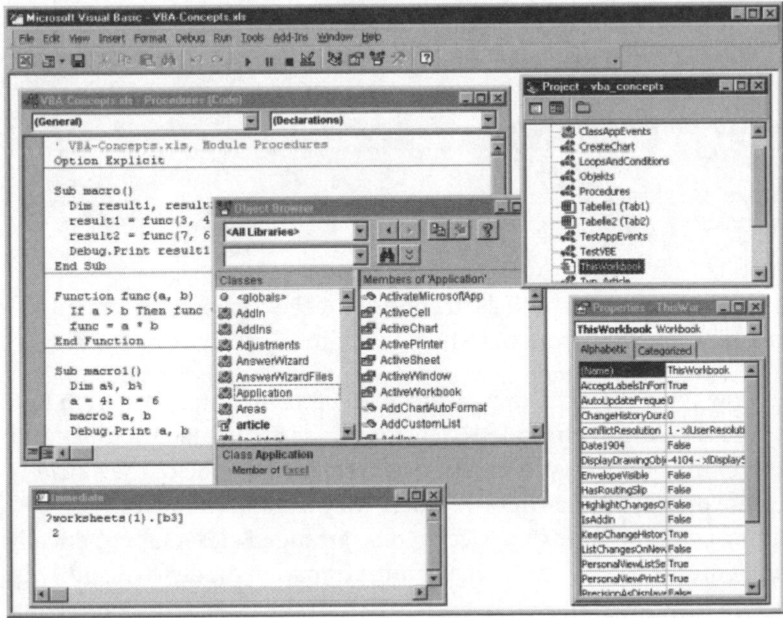

Figure 3.1. The VBA development environment

Instead of employing TOOLS|MACRO|VISUAL BASIC EDITOR or Alt+F11, the change from Excel to the development environment can be effected by means of a tool: In Excel (not in the development environment) execute VIEW|TOOLBARS|CUSTOMIZE|COMMANDS and with the mouse drag the button VISUAL BASIC EDITOR from the "tools" category into the standard toolbar. Now a simple mouse click suffices to move you into the window of the development environment.

For almost every component of the development environment there have been defined context (pop-up) menus, which can be invoked with the right mouse button. They enable the efficient invocation of the most important commands. Check them out!

NOTE *The changeover between Excel and the development environment functions only when no form is open in the currently active component. In Excel no cell or object can be in the process of manipulation. In the development environment the object catalog cannot be the active window. In all these cases the change will be denied (without an error message).*

POINTER *In fact, not every step in program development is carried out in the VBA development environment. For example, the recording of macros is controlled directly from within Excel. Likewise, the definition of new toolbars or menu items is done within Excel. For this reason, and in order that we may deal with related themes together, you will find further information on the development environment in other chapters:*

Background on the object catalog and library references: *Chapter 4*
Debugging aids: *Chapter 6*
Forms editor: *Chapter 7*
Definition of menus and toolbars: *Chapter 8*

Project Explorer

The project window (VIEW|PROJECT EXPLORER or Ctrl+R) provides an orientation to programming in Excel. With each loaded Excel file all the associated modules and forms are shown in the project explorer. By double clicking on one of the entries, its components are displayed in a window, where they can be worked on.

The individual components of a project can be arranged either alphabetically or, as shown in Figure 3.1 thematically. The change from one mode to the other is accomplished with the third tool icon in the project window (with the confusing name TOGGLE FOLDERS).

> **NOTE** *If you are working on several Excel files, you can close individual files ("projects") in the project explorer (click on the symbol + or –). All the windows of this project will then be hidden. This greatly simplifies orientation in the chaos of windows in the development environment.*
>
> *In the default setting the project explorer, as well as most other components, is not displayed as a freely movable window, but is fixed to the border area of the development environment. This is practical only if you are working with a large monitor. Otherwise, you will quickly use up all available real estate. To make the components of the development environment freely movable, execute* TOOLS|OPTIONS|DOCKING *and deactivate all the options on this tab of the dialog form.*

Properties Window

In the properties window VIEW|PROPERTIES WINDOW or F4) a number of characteristics of the current object can be set. As "objects" are considered modules and also forms and the controls contained within them. The most important role is played by the properties window in the creation of new forms: Every element of such a form has dozens of properties. In normal code modules, on the other hand, only the name of the module can be set. This name cannot contain a space character. With object modules the VBA name generally differs from the name of the Excel worksheet.

Just as in the project explorer, the entries in the properties window can be grouped (that is, first all the properties, then the methods, and finally the events, as in the tip below) or sorted alphabetically. The shift is accomplished here, however, with sheet tabs and makes sense only when objects support large numbers of properties.

If you embed controls directly in worksheets, you can also use the properties window in Excel. The invocation in Excel is, however, accomplished not with F4, but with the pop-up menu entry PROPERTIES or by clicking on the PROPERTIES tool in the "control toolbox."

Object Browser

Programming in Excel is based on a number of object libraries, of which the most important is the Excel library. Every library is equipped with a large number of objects, and the objects, in turn, with many properties, methods, and events. The only chance, then, to keep track of what is going on in this superfluity of keywords is provided by the object browser, which is displayed by executing VIEW|OBJECT BROWSER or hitting the F2 key. (If the cursor is located over a keyword in the code window, it will be automatically looked up in the object browser.) In many situations the object browser offers the shortest path into the on-line help.

In the object browser are shown the objects of all active libraries as well as (in boldface) all user-defined functions and subprograms. In the listbox in the upper left-hand corner you can limit the display to objects belonging to a specific library. This is especially useful when the search for a particular character string returns a large number of results. You carry out a search by giving a string as input in the second listbox and pressing Return.

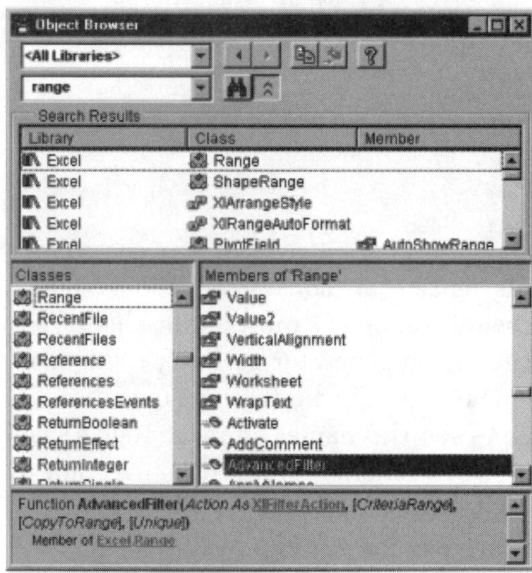

Figure 3.2. The Object Browser

Normally, in the browser are displayed only “officially” supported keywords. However, there are quite a few hidden keywords, which either are used internally or have been retained for reasons of compatibility with earlier versions. With the pop-up menu command SHOW HIDDEN MEMBERS you can also see these keywords, which appear grayed out.

> **TIP** *Under normal circumstances the keywords are listed alphabetically. By using the pop-up menu command* GROUP MEMBERS *you can have the entries ordered in groups, that is, first all the properties, then the methods, and finally the events. As a rule, in this form the list is easier to understand.*

Editor Options

With TOOLS|OPTIONS a four-sheeted form is displayed that allows you to control a variety of settings in the development environment. Most of the settings are more or less self explanatory. Here are a few notes for the others:

> AUTO SYNTAX CHECK (tab EDITOR): If this option is activated, an error message is displayed when a line containing an error is input. While you are still taking baby steps in VBA this is perhaps rather useful. However, after a couple of days these insistent error messages become burdensome. If you deactivate the option, lines with errors continued to be displayed in red, which is quite sufficient.
>
> REQUIRE VARIABLE DECLARATION: If this option is activated, in every new module the line *Option Explicit* is added. This means that you are allowed to use only those variables that you have declared with *Dim*. This option saves you from typos and supports the creation of correct code. Activate it by all means!
>
> AUTO LIST MEMBERS, AUTO QUICK INFO, AUTO DATA TIPS: These three options determine whether information about permitted methods and properties, the current content of variables, and, respectively, allowed parameters will be automatically inserted in the code window. Leave this option in the default setting, that is, activated. The information provided is extremely useful.
>
> DEFAULT TO FULL MODULE VIEW: This option has the effect of displaying in the code window not only an individual procedure, but all procedures belonging to the entire module.
>
> The tab EDITOR FORMAT: Here you can select the font of your choice and select a color for a variety of syntax elements.

General Options

> COLLAPSE PROJECT HIDES WINDOWS (tab GENERAL): If this option is activated, all windows of a project are closed as soon as the project is collapsed in the project explorer (click on the minus sign). When it is opened up, the windows appear again. This option serves the purpose of maintaining a certain degree of order in the development environment even when a number of projects are open.
>
> EDIT AND CONTINUE: With many changes in code—for example, in the declaration of new variables—all current contents of variables must be cleared.

When the option NOTIFY BEFORE STATE LOSS is activated, you will be warned before such changes are carried out.

BREAK ON ALL ERRORS: This option cancels the effect of error handling routines. In spite of *On-Error* instructions the program will be interrupted. This option is often very useful in debugging. (See also Chapter 6).

BREAK IN CLASS MODULE/BREAK ON UNHANDLED ERRORS: These two options yield differing results only when you develop class modules. If an error occurs in a class module, in the first case the program is interrupted in the class module, and in the second case it is interrupted where the method or property of the class that caused the error was called (see also Chapter 4, the section on programming your own classes).

COMPILE: VBA programs are automatically compiled into pseudocode, which can be executed more efficiently than the underlying ASCII code. (We are not talking about machine code, such as would be generated by a C compiler.) The two COMPILE options govern when compilation occurs. The default setting (both options activated) indicates that program execution begins at once, and procedures are compiled only as they are needed. The advantage of this is a rapid start. The disadvantage is that any obvious errors will be announced only later. With large projects it is usually a good idea to deactivate the options, since then you will be notified at once of any syntax errors in the code (and not sometime later, the first time the procedure is called).

Tab DOCKING: As mentioned in one of the "tips" above, in the default configuration most of the components in the development environment are so-called docked windows. These windows stick, as it were, to an end of the development environment. If you do not happen to be working with a 21-inch monitor, these docked windows take up too much space and represent a step backwards into the era of Windows 1 (when overlapping windows were not allowed). You can call a halt to this nonsense by unchecking most (or, even better, all) of the boxes on this page of the form. Now you can move the windows around and overlap them without any restrictions.

Project Properties

With TOOLS|VBAPROJECT PROPERTIES (PROJECT PROPERTIES) you open a dialog for setting properties of the current project. On the page with the tab GENERAL you give a short description of the project and file name of an associated help file (see Chapter 14). On the page PROTECTION you can hide the VBA part of an Excel file from view and protect it with a password.

> **CAUTION** *The status that Microsoft accords to password protection in Excel could be observed in the transition from Excel 7 to Excel 97. Modules that were hidden and password protected in Excel 7 were completely accessible to everyone with Excel 97! The password protection of Excel 2000 is, in fact, somewhat better, but it has already been broken. There are commercial tools available that allow anyone to recover a "forgotten" password or replace it with a known password (see* `http://soft4you.com/mso/vba.htm`*).*

Conditional Compilation

It often happens that along with a program you wish to manage a second version in parallel (say, a demo version with limited features or a debug version with additional tests). For this you can define a constant in PROJECT PROPERTIES|GENERAL in the text field CONDITIONAL COMPILATION ARGUMENTS such as *demo=1*. In the program code you can then make use of the value of the constant with *#If* instructions.

According to the result of the *#If* test one of two branches is executed. In contrast to normal *If* tests, here the result is determined during compilation. The compiled code contains only one variant and no *#If* tests, and therefore there is no loss of speed of execution. The following lines show some program code with *#If* instructions:

```
Sub Command1_Click()
  #If demo Then
MsgBox "In the demo version nothing can be saved"
  #Else
    ' ... program code for saving
  #End If
End Sub
```

Code Input in Modules

VBA code can be input into any code window. As mentioned above, there are numerous objects that can be fitted out with code: the Excel file as a whole (module *This Workbook* in the project explorer), every worksheet (*Sheet 1, Sheet 2,* etc.), forms, normal modules, and class modules.

While the objects *This Workbook* and *Sheet n* are provided by Excel, forms and modules must be created via INSERT|USERFORM, MODULE, or CLASS MODULE in the development environment. (When a macro is recorded a module is automatically created.)

Finally, you should give the form or module a meaningful name. To do this you use the properties window (F4). Blank characters and most special characters are prohibited.

While for a normal module the name is principally for orientation in negotiating large projects, the names of forms and class modules are also important for the execution of code. Subsequent changes then lead to additional expenditure of effort and should be avoided as much as possible.

First Experiments

For our first experiments with VBA open a new workbook, with via Alt+F11 into the development environment, and there execute INSERT|MODULE to create a new module. The shortest possible macro that you can create for test purposes should look something like this:

```
Sub example()
  Debug.Print "Wow, my very first program!"
End Sub
```

With the method *Print*, applied to the object *Debug*, this program will output the text "Wow, my very first program!" in the immediate window. You can launch this program simply by pressing F5 (with the input cursor placed within the procedure itself). The result will be displayed in the immediate window. Since this window is out of view under normal circumstances, it must be activated with VIEW|IMMEDIATE WINDOW or Ctrl+G.

When you input the program, you will observe that Excel emphasizes—by means of color—certain parts of the program, namely the keywords *Sub, Debug, Print, End,* and *Sub*. This not only improves clarity, it indicates that the program lines are syntactically correct.

If Excel detects an error in the input of a program line, it announces that an error has occurred. You may ignore such announcements temporarily. Then the entire line will be displayed in red. The macro cannot be executed until all syntax errors have been removed.

Automatic Completion of Keywords and Variable Names

Code input is simplified by the so-called *IntelliSense* functions. Thus during input listboxes are automatically displayed offering for your selection all possible completions of the input—in the current context. In the input of functions and methods their parameter lists are displayed, and so on.

IntelliSense has brought with it some new keyboard shortcuts: When no listbox is displayed, you can use Ctrl+spacebar to complete the input with the given keyword (or variable name). If there is more than one option, then the listbox automatically appears.

Once the listbox has been displayed, you can select the desired input with the cursor key. The Tab (not Return!) key completes the selection. With Esc you can avoid having to select from the listbox and can complete the input manually (for example, for input of a variable name that has yet to be defined).

Definition of New Procedures

There are many ways of writing a new procedure. For general procedures (subroutines, functions) you can create a template for a new procedure with a click of the mouse using Insert|Procedure. (The meaning of the keywords *Sub, Function, Property, Public, Private,* and *Static* will be described in detail in Chapter 4, in the section on procedural programming.)

Once you have acquired some facility with Visual Basic, you will be able to carry out the definition of new procedures more quickly by typing the instructions *Function Name* or *Sub Name* in the code window. Visual Basic completes the procedure definition automatically with *End Function* or *End Sub.*

Cursor Movement in the Program Code Window

The text cursor can be moved within a subprogram or function as usual with the cursor keys. Page Up and Page Down move the text cursor horizontally through the procedure. When the cursor reaches the start or end of the subprogram, the previous or following procedure is shown. (The sequence of procedures is arranged in the order in which they were defined.)

Ctrl+↑ and Ctrl + Page Up, Ctrl +↓ and Ctrl+ Page Down point independently of the current position of the cursor to the previous or next subprogram. F6 changes the active region if the window is split.

Shift+F2 moves the cursor to the procedure on whose name the cursor is currently located (command View|Definition). If the procedure in question was defined in another file of the project, Visual Basic automatically shifts into the relevant code window. Ctrl+Shift+F2 shifts back to the previous position. In this connection Visual Basic manages a multilevel buffer for return positioning.

For quickly jumping to another part of the program you can also use the object browser, in which (among other things) all procedures that you have programmed are visible. (See the next section.)

Indenting

To make program code easier to read, blocks of code within branches and loops are generally indented (as in all the program listings in this book). This indentation does not occur automatically, but must be done with the space bar or tab key. If later you alter the structure of the program (for example, by an additional "If" test), it is then necessary to change the indentation pattern on large numbers of lines. Instead of doing this manually for each line, you can ask Visual Basic to help: Select the entire block of lines with the mouse, and then press Tab or Shift+Tab. Visual Basic then moves the entire block either in or out by one tab position.

The tab width can be set in the options window (TOOLS|OPTIONS|EDITOR) up to a single character. The default setting is four characters, though in this book we use two, which leads to more compact program code. (Visual Basic works with genuine tabs. The tab width setting indicates only how many spaces are passed over by Tab.)

Declaration of Variables

In empty modules there is usually to be found the instruction *Option Explicit* in the first line. The effect of this instruction is to require that all variables be declared before they are used. If this instruction does not automatically appear, then go at once to the TOOLS|OPTIONS|EDITOR window and activate "Require Variable Declaration." Excel then adds the instruction to newly created modules. (In modules currently open you will have to type in the keywords yourself.)

Commentary

The apostrophe (') is used to introduce a comment. Comments are allowed both at the start of a line and after an instruction. The comment symbol can be used, for example, temporarily to transform lines of code containing errors into comment lines. Comments are usually shown in green.

> **NOTE** *During the testing phase of program development it is often practical to deactivate certain lines of code temporarily by prefixing them with the comment symbol. The development environment has designated two tools in the* EDIT *toolbar, but no menu command, for commenting out a number of lines and for undoing this command. You can remedy this lack with* VIEW|TOOLBARS|CUSTOMIZE.

Multiline Instructions

Long instructions can be divided over several lines. To accomplish this simply type anywhere (except *within* a keyword) a space followed by the underscore (_) symbol. For example:

```
Selection.Sort Key1:=Range("A3"), Order1:= xlAscending, _
  Header:=xlGuess, OrderCustom:=1, MatchCase:=False, _
  Orientation:=xlTopToBottom
```

NOTE *Variables can be declared to be accessible only within a given procedure or within an entire module or even within the entire program (global variables). Details on the range of effect of variables can be found in Chapter 4.*

If you provide multiline instructions with comments, you can do so only in the last line of the instruction. The following instruction is syntactically incorrect:

```
Selection.Sort Key1:=Range("A3"), _    'not allowed!
  Order1:= xlAscending, _              'not allowed!
  Header:=xlGuess                      'this comment is ok
```

Undoing Changes

If you inadvertently delete a selected region of cells or wish to undo a change in program code, you can restore the previous state of the program with the command EDIT|UNDO or with Alt+Backspace. With EDIT|REDO or Ctrl+Z you can undo the effect of the undo command. The undo and redo functions are multilevel functions; that is, you can take back several changes.

Automatic Saves

Excel is a stable program by and large, but the occasional crash is not unheard of. Therefore, you should save your workbook as often as possible! You can also activate the add-in extension "autosave" to save your workbook at regular intervals. To do this, execute in Excel (not the development environment) TOOLS|ADD-INS and activate the option AUTOSAVE ADD-IN. Now every ten minutes you will be asked whether you wish to save unsaved files.

Executing Macros

It has already been mentioned above that you can easily call up the macro in whose code the cursor is located via F5. However, this way of executing a macro is available only in the development environment. In general, one uses the command TOOLS|MACRO, which is available both in Excel and in the development environment. With it you can run parameterless macros defined in any currently open file.

There are also a number of elegant methods for running macros:

- You can associate a keyboard shortcut of the form Ctrl+first letter of the macro to a macro by clicking on the OPTIONS button Ctrl+first letter in the form TOOLS|MACRO|MACROS. For some strange reason this OPTIONS button is available only in Excel, not in the development environment. Go figure.

- Macros can be associated with event routines. Then when a certain event occurs (such as when a certain amount of time has passed or the activation of a worksheet) it is automatically activated. There is an entire section devoted to events in Chapter 4.

- With the command VIEW|TOOLBARS|CUSTOMIZE|COMMANDS (still in Excel) you can insert the menu entry "Custom Menu Item" or "Custom Button" (both in the group "macros") to a menu or toolbar. Then you can alter the menu text or tool with the associated pop-up menu. By clicking on the entry or tool for the first time you can select the macro to which the entry will be associated in the future. More information on individual menus and toolbars is to be found in Chapter 8.

These methods hold for procedural macros, those introduced with the keyword *Sub*, which we shall call subprograms. Function macros (keyword *Function*) are, on the other hand, not designed to be called directly. They can be placed within other macros or inserted as calculating functions in the formula of a worksheet cell.

Interrupting Macros

All macros can be stopped at any time with Ctrl+Break. If you then select the button DEBUG in the form that appears after you hit Ctrl+Break, you can edit the code. You can also examine individual variables and then continue execution of the macro with F5.

The Immediate Window (Test Window)

The immediate window is an aid for testing new procedures and for debugging. (In earlier versions the immediate window was called the test window.) The instruction *Debug.Print* places output in the immediate window, which is activated via View|Immediate Window or with Ctrl+G.

The immediate window contains the last two hundred outputs implemented by *Debug.Print*. Inz the immediate window you can input instructions that are executed immediately when Return is pressed. The immediate window is particularly useful for testing variables or properties, for example by instructions such as *?varname* or *?Application.ActiveSheet.Name* (outputs the name of the active worksheet). The question mark is an abbreviation for the *Print* method. Floating point numbers are generally displayed in the immediate window to at most eight places beyond the decimal point, even when sixteen places exist.

In the immediate window it is also possible to assign values to variables or properties or to start macros by giving their name. In the immediate window you can introduce new variables without a previous declaration (even if *Option Explicit* is in force in the program code).

"Watches" make it possible to define conditional halting points and the continuous display of the content of various properties or variables in its own watch window. How to use the watch window will be described in full in Chapter 6, where debugging is discussed. There we will also describe the window for the display of all active procedures.

Recording Macros

In principle, there are two possibilities for creating macros. You can either input the macro at the keyboard, or you can use the command Tools|Macro|Record New Macro to record the sequence of some Excel commands in the form of VBA instructions. In reality, the most frequent way of creating macros is a mixture of the two variants. First you use the macro recorder to create the basic form of the macro, and then you edit the details of the macro with keyboard input.

The great advantage in recording macros is that you are spared the endless search for the correct keywords. Even if the recorded macro represents your ultimate goal only in bare outline, at least the objects, properties, and methods that the recording produces will be useful.

The disadvantages of macro recording are, among others, that Excel often produces unnecessarily elaborate code. In the recording of dialog input, for example, *all* input possibilities are given (even if only one setting was changed).

Starting and Ending Macros

The recording of macros normally begins in a worksheet with the New Macro command mentioned above. Then you must give the name of the macro to be recorded and into which workbook the macro is to be recorded (usually in "this workbook").

The macro recording is terminated with Tools|Macro|Stop Recording or by clicking on the corresponding tool (the small square).

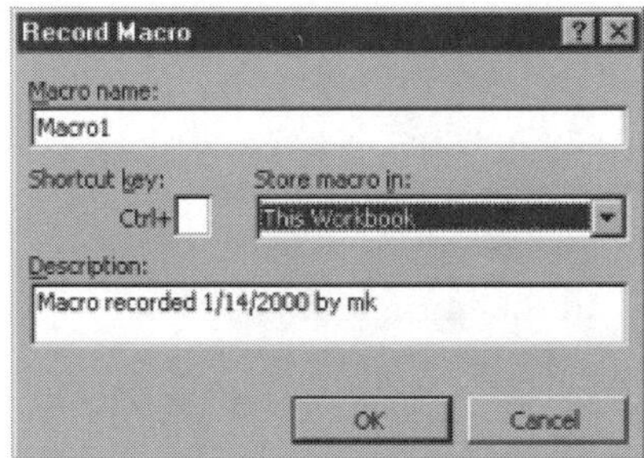

Figure 3.3. The beginning of macro recording

In recording a macro, Excel usually produces a new module. After the recording is done, you can cut and paste the macro's code, if you wish, into another module sheet (via the clipboard) and then delete the now empty module.

NOTE *As opposed to what was available in Excel 5 and 7, it is no longer possible to record macro code in an already existing procedure. But hey, no problem! Simply record the code in a new procedure and then copy it to wherever you need it.*

The Personal Macro Workbook

Macros that are to belong to a particular workbook should always be recorded in "this workbook." Macros that are to be universally available (for example, for general improvement of Excel's operation or for special tools) should, on the other hand, be saved in the "personal macro workbook." This workbook is saved under the name `Personal.xls` in the user directory `Application Data\Microsoft\Excel\Xlstart` and is loaded automatically when Excel is launched. The macros in this file are therefore always available.

Frequently, the personal macro workbook's window is kept hidden, so as not to take up valuable monitor real estate. This has the additional benefit of protecting this workbook against accidental changes. The workbook can be made visible via WINDOW|UNHIDE.

Absolute and Relative Macro Recording

During macro recording cell references can be made either relative to the start position or with an absolute address. Which of these two variants is to be chosen depends on the use to which your macro will be put. To switch between the two modes you must use the tool RELATIVE/ABSOLUTE REFERENCE on the "Stop Recording" toolbar.

One can switch back and forth between these two macro recording settings as many times as one wishes. The wrong choice of setting is often the reason that a previously recorded macro does not function properly!

Keyboard Shortcuts

This section provides an overview of the most important keyboard shortcuts that are used during program development. We shall not go into keyboard shortcuts that hold generally under Windows (such as Ctrl+C to copy to the clipboard). The keyboard shortcuts have been organized by the uses to which they are most frequently put.

Changing the Active Window

Alt+F11	switches between Excel and the development environment
Ctrl+Tab	switches among all Visual Basic windows
Alt+F6	switches between the last two active windows
Ctrl+G	switches into the immediate window (debug window)
Ctrl+R	switches to the project explorer
F2	switches into the object browser
F4	switches to the properties window
F7	switches to the code window

Properties Window

Shift+Tab	jumps to the object list field
Ctrl+Shift+X	jumps to the property whose name begins with the letter *X*

Program Execution

F5	start the program
Ctrl+Break	program interrupt
F8	execute a single command (single step execution)
Shift+F8	execute a command or call a procedure (procedure step execution)
Ctrl+F8	execute a procedure up to the cursor position
Ctrl+Shift+F8	execute the current procedure to the end
F9	set a breakpoint
Ctrl+F9	determine the location of the next command

Code Window

Tab	indent the selected block of lines
Shift+Tab	unindent the selected block of lines
Ctrl+Y	delete lines
Alt+Backspace	undo changes
Ctrl+Z	redo changes
Ctrl+↑/↓	move the cursor to the next or previous procedure
Shift+F2	move to procedure definition or variable declaration
Ctrl+Shift+F2	return to previous cursor position (undo Shift+F2)
F6	change code sector (in split windows)
Ctrl+F	find
F3	find again
Ctrl+H	find and replace
Ctrl+spacebar	complete keyword or variable name
Tab	complete selection in IntelliSense listbox
Esc	exit IntelliSense listbox

CHAPTER 4

VBA Concepts

This chapter describes the language features of VBA and provides the theoretical background for programming in VBA. The themes dealt with here include the use of variables, procedural programming (loops, branches), and the management of objects and events. It is in the nature of the subject that this chapter is rather dry. But the information contained here is absolutely necessary for successful macro programming.

Chapter Overview

Variables and Fields

> **NOTE** *All example programs in this chapter can be found in the file* VBA-Concepts.xls.

Managing Variables

Variables are placeholders for numbers, characters, or other data. Variables are used to store data during the execution of a program and to carry out computations with these data. The following example program shows a trivial application of variables:

```
' Example file VBA-Concepts.xls, Module "Variables"
Option Explicit
Sub macro1()
  Dim length, width, area
  length = 3
  width = 4
  area = length * width
  Debug.Print area
End Sub
```

The variables *length* and *width* store the length and width of a rectangle, and from these data the area of the rectangle is computed and stored in the variable *area.* The result of the computation is then output via *Debug.Print* into the immediate window, where it can be viewed via Ctrl+G.

The instructions *Sub macro1()* and *End Sub* are necessary because VBA can execute program code only if it is contained within one or more procedures. More detail on this theme can be found in the following section. On the other hand, for the management of variables, the lines *Option Explicit* and *Dim length, width, area* are relevant.

Definition of Variables

If the instruction *Option Explicit* appears at the beginning of a module, then all variables must be defined via the command ***Dim*** before they can be used. At first glance this seems an undue burden, but in reality it is an important and effective protection against typographical errors. Namely, Excel refuses to execute a procedure until it knows about all the variables appearing in it.

> **NOTE** *When you activate the option* Require Variable Declaration *in* Tools|Options|Editor, *Excel adds* Option Explicit *to every module.*
>
> *Variables can be declared in such a way that they can be used only in a particular procedure, in an entire module, or in the entire workbook. In the following section we shall discuss more fully the scope of variables and the keyword* Static.

Naming Variables

A variable name must begin with a letter, be of length less than 256 characters, and contain no blank spaces, periods, or any of a number of other special characters. Variable names are not case sensitive, and they may not coincide with predefined VBA keywords, such as *Sub, Function, End, For, To, Next, Dim, As.*

> **NOTE** *Names of objects, methods, and properties are* not *as a rule considered keywords, and can therefore be used as names of variables. VBA generally has no problem with this duplication and can determine from context whether what is meant is a variable, on the one hand, or a property or method, on the other. (In the case of properties or methods in which object specification is optional, if there is a variable of the same name, then the specification is no longer optional. See the section after next for more on the theme of objects.) In any case, variable names that duplicate those of objects, methods, or properties can lead to confusion in reading or analysis and for this reason are best avoided.*

Variable Types (Data Types)

In the example above three variables were defined using *Dim*, but no variable type was specified. This is permissible in VBA—the program then automatically chooses a suitable type. Nonetheless, it is a good idea if you know the variable types provided by VBA to define variables with the desired type included in the definition. In this way you will reduce the amount of time expended in editing, the amount of space required for the program, and the probability of introducing errors.

VBA VARIABLE TYPES

	Byte: whole number between 0 and 255; requires 1 byte of storage
	Boolean: truth value (*True, False*); 2 bytes
%	*Integer*: whole number between –32768 and +32767; 2 bytes
&	*Long*: whole number between –2147483648 and +2147483647; 4 bytes
@	*Currency*: fixed point number with 15 places before and four after the decimal point; 8 bytes
	Decimal: This is not an independent data type, but a subtype of *Variant*; the precision is 28 places; the number of places to the right of the decimal point depends on the size of the number: A number whose integer part is ten digits will have the remaining 18 places to the right of the decimal point; the allowed range of numbers is $\pm 10^{28}$; 12 bytes
#	*Double*: floating point number with 16-place accuracy; 8 bytes
!	*Single*: floating point number with 8-place accuracy; 4 bytes
	Date: for dates and times; the date is limited to the period between 1/1/100 and 12/31/9999, the time to the range 00:00 to 23:59:59; 8 bytes
$	*String*: a character string; the number of characters is limited only by the amount of RAM (up to 2,147,483,647 characters); 10 bytes plus 2 bytes per character
	Object: objects; the variable stores a pointer to an object; 4 bytes
	Variant: Default variable type, assumes one of the above variable types according to what is required (with automatic conversion); the memory requirement is at least 16 bytes, and with character strings 22 bytes plus 2 bytes per character

In addition to the data types listed here, variables can be defined in all objects defined in Excel (for example, as a *Chart* or *Worksheet*). In this case the variable will be considered an object variable. Working with objects is discussed in greater detail later in this chapter.

In the definition of variables with *Dim* the variable type can be determined either by placing the label directly after the variable name or via the *As data type*.

CAUTION *It is syntactically allowed to place several variables between* Dim *and* As. *However, only the last variable is given the desired variable type, and all remaining variables will be considered* Variant *variables!*

```
Dim a, b, c As Integer  'only c is an integer; a and b 'have the
                         data type Variant!
```

With the keywords *DefBool, DefCur, DefDbl, DefDate, DefInt, DefLng, DefObj, DefSng, DefStr*, and *DefVar* the default data type for variables with certain initial letters can be preset. The commands must be given at the beginning of a module (before the beginning of the first procedure), and they hold for the entire module. The effect is best understood by means of an example.

```
DefSng a-f
DefLng g, h
```

All variables that begin with the letters a, b, c, d, e, f will have data type *Single*, while those beginning with g or h will be of type *Long*. The default data type holds for all variables that are not bound to a different data type by a *Dim* command.

The Data Type Variant

By far the most universal data type is *Variant*. It is a preset type for all variables whose type is not explicitly given. Variables of type *Variant* adjust themselves automatically to the data stored within them, and can thus contain integers, floating point numbers, text, data, or Excel objects. However, the administrative overhead for *Variant* variables is the greatest among all the data types.

Variables of type *Variant*, in contrast to other variables, can contain error codes as well as two special values: *Empty* (indicates that the variable is empty; *Empty* is not the same as 0 or an empty character string) and *Null* (indicates that no space is reserved in memory for the variable). The data type currently in residence in a *Variant* variable can be determined via the functions *VarType, IsObject, IsError, IsEmpty,* and *IsNull.* The functions *IsNumeric* and *IsDate* determine whether the content of variables can be transformed into a number or into a data value.

CAUTION *The comparison* x = Null *is syntactically correct, but is handled incorrectly. Even when* x *is actually* Null, *the comparison returns* Null *instead of* True *as its result! Therefore, always use* IsNull(x)*!*

Computing with Whole Numbers

There are certain difficulties associated with computing with whole numbers in VBA. The following example results in an overflow error. Such an error usually occurs when the allowed range of values for the number is exceeded. The multiplication below produces the value 65280, which actually can be stored easily in a *Long* variable (see above).

```
Sub macro_overflow()
  Dim l As Long
  l = 255 * 256    ' here an overflow error occurs
End Sub
```

The problem with this example is that in the multiplication of 255 and 256 , Excel internally interprets the two numbers as *Integer* numbers and thus invokes its routine for the multiplication of numbers of type *Integer*. The result exceeds the permissible range for numbers of type *Integer* and thus leads to an error before the definition of *l*. A remedy exists in the form of the symbol "&", which must be placed after one of the two numbers. This signals Excel that the multiplication routine for *Long* numbers should be invoked:

```
Sub macro_no_overflow()
  Dim l As Long
  l = 255& * 256  'now it works!
End Sub
```

Links Between Differing Data Types

VBA normally carries out type conversion automatically. Depending on the format of the target variable, this can lead to loss of data. If you associate a *Variant* variable with the value 3.6 to an *Integer* variable, then the value 4 will be stored. *Date* values are transformed by such linkages into floating point numbers whose fractional part becomes the time and whose integer part is transformed into the date.

Definition of Custom Data Types

Using the predefined data types in Excel you can create your own custom data types. Such data types (which in other programming languages are known as structures, records, or something similar) can be used to organize data to facilitate their management.

The definition of a new data type is introduced by the command ***Type*** and ended by ***End Type***. Within the data type one can place as many separate variables as one wishes in the form *name As vartype* (each on its own line). For character strings the keyword *String*, an asterisk, and a number can be placed at the end. In this case the length of the string is limited to the given value.

In the example below the data type *article* is defined, in which the name and price of an article of merchandise can be stored. In real-world applications you will probably wish to plan for additional elements such as article number and supplier. The *macro* here shows the use of the data type: Access to individual elements is made through affixing the element's name.

```
'example file VBA-Concepts.xls, Module "Type_Article"
Option Explicit
Type article
  artname As String
```

```
  price As Currency
End Type
Sub macro()
  Dim a As article, b As article
  a.artname = "nuclear minireactor"
  a.price = 3.5
  b = a
  Debug.Print b.price
End Sub
```

Data types are normally valid only within the module in which they are defined. However, you can prefix the keyword with the keyword *Type Public.* Then the data type is valid for all modules in the workbook. The possible scopes of variables are discussed further in the following section. Fields are allowed within a custom data type. Fields, too, will be explained in the following section.

Constants

If you use symbols whose value will not change during the entire course of program execution, such symbols should be declared as constants by means of the keyword ***Const.*** You can give a data type to a constant just as with normal variables:

```
Const maxsize = 3
Const Pi2 As Double = 1.570796327  'Pi/2
```

In VBA there are countless constants already defined. In addition to the values *True* and *False* and the *Variant* values *Null* and *Empty,* there are various other values that can be used for setting properties or for evaluating methods. These constants begin with the letters *vb* (for Visual Basic constant) or *xl* (for Excel constant). The constant *Pi* is defined only as a method of *Application* and therefore must be written in the form *Application.Pi.*

Fields

Fields are lists of variables of the same name that are referenced by one or more index values. Fields are always used when several similar pieces of information (for example, the entries in a matrix) are to be manipulated.

Dimensioning Fields

Before a field can be used, it has to be defined. For this the command *Dim* is used, where after the field name the greatest permitted index is given in parentheses. The data type of the field is given as in the case of variables with a label or with the keyword *As*.

NOTE *In the case of large fields you should think carefully about which data type is required. When you give no data type, VBA automatically selects* Variant *variables, which require by far the most space. With a field of 1000 elements it makes a significant difference whether 2 or 16 bytes per element are required.*

```
Dim a(10) As Integer
```

Access to a field is always accomplished by giving an index. The example below also demonstrates that two instructions can be given on the same line if they are separated by a colon.

```
a(4) = 10: a(5) = a(4)/2
```

The index must lie within the range 0 to *max_index* (unless you select *Option Base 1*; see below). With *Dim a(10)*, then, a field with eleven elements is generated. If you wish, you can set the range of the field within an arbitrary interval, such as between –5 and +7:

```
Dim a(-5 To 7) As Integer
```

Visual Basic also permits the defining of multidimensional fields, such as in the following:

```
Dim a(10, 20) As Integer
```

This defines a field with 11 times 21 elements. With multidimensional fields, too, indices can be given as arbitrary intervals.

With the instruction *Option Base 1* at the start of a module you make the index 0 impermissible. All fields will thereby become a bit smaller. *Option Base* has no influence on the indices of enumeration methods predefined by Excel. (Usually, the smallest index is in any case 1.)

Dynamic Fields

Visual Basic also supports fields whose size can vary during program execution. Such fields must first be dimensioned without explicit indices, as in the following example:

```
Dim a() As Integer
```

At the place in a program where the field is required to have a certain size, the command ***ReDim*** is given, as in the following example:

```
ReDim a(size)
```

The size of the field can later by changed with a further *ReDim* command. If you append the keyword ***Preserve***, then the contents of the field are preserved:

```
ReDim Preserve a(size + 10)
```

Fields can be defined to be arbitrarily large and to have arbitrarily many dimensions. The only limitation comes from the amount of memory available.

Deleting Fields

The instruction ***Erase*** deletes the contents of the elements of static fields (that is, values are reset to zero, strings to the empty string, *Variant* variables to *Empty*). With dynamic fields *Erase* deletes the entire field, and the reserved memory is freed. Before further use the field must be redimensioned via *ReDim*.

Index Range

The functions ***LBound*** and ***UBound*** return the smallest and greatest permitted index of a field. In the case of multidimensional fields the dimension whose index bound is to be returned must be given in the optional second parameter. An example of the application of these two functions appears in the next section, where, among other things, the passing of fields to procedures is handled.

Data Fields

As if normal fields weren't enough, Microsoft has promoted in VBA the concept of the "data field." Data fields are stored internally in individual *Variant* variables, even though they outwardly behave like fields. Many operations are possible only with normal fields, others only with data fields, and others with both types. There are no transformation functions to mediate between the two types of fields.

Data fields are created with the command *Array*, in which the individual field elements are listed. The *Array* expression is then linked to the *Variant* variables. The first element has, depending on the setting of *Option Base*, the index 0 or 1.

In practice, data fields have the advantage over normal fields that they are easier to initialize. With normal fields every element has to be defined individually, for example *a(0)=1: a(1)=7: a(2)=3*. But with data fields one can simply define *a= Array(1, 7, 3)*. The keyword *Array* cannot, alas, be used for defining normal fields.

```
Dim x
x = Array(10, 11, 12)
Debug.Print x(1)          ' returns 11
```

In the example above, *x* actually represents a *Variant* field. In contrast to a normal field, which is declared with *Dim x(2)*, here *x* can be passed as a field to a procedure without an empty pair of parentheses being given.

Data fields (again in contrast to normal fields) can also be used as parameters for many Excel methods. In the first example that follows the worksheets declared as a data field are selected, while in the second example four adjacent cells of "Table 1" are filled with values:

```
Sheets(Array("Table1", "Table2", "Table3")).Select
Sheets("Table1").[a1:d1] = Array("abc", "def", 1, 4)
```

NOTE *It is not always quite clear when a data field is supported and when not. If you were to replace* `[a1:d1]` *by* `[a1:a4]` *in the previous example, that is, to change four adjacent cells, the definition would no longer function! The correct instruction would now be as follows:*

```
Sheets("Table1").[a1:a4] = _
  Array(Array("abc"), Array("def"), Array(1), Array(4))
```

Thus a two-dimensional (nested) data field is required. In this case it is easier to fill in the fields individually.

POINTER *As the above examples have already indicated, data fields are suitable for, among other things, efficiently transferring midsize ranges of cells between worksheets and program code. (It is an order of magnitude faster than accessing each individual cell!) More information about this can be found in Chapter 5.*

Syntax Summary

Variable Types (Data Types)

$	*String*	character string
%	*Integer*	whole number (–32768 to +32767)
&	*Long*	whole number (–2^31 to +2^31)
!	*Single*	floating point number with 8 significant digits
#	*Double*	floating point number with 16 significant digits
@	*Currency*	fixed point number with 15 places before the decimal point and 4 after
	Date	date and time value
	Boolean	true or false
	Object	pointer to an object
	Variant	arbitrary data

Declaration of Variables and Constants

Option Explicit
Dim var1, var2%, var3 As type
Const const1, const2#, const3 As type

Predefined Constants

True	*Empty*	*vbXxx*
False	*Null*	*xlXxx*

Using Variant Variables

IsNumeric(variable)	test whether conversion to a number is possible
IsDate(variable)	test whether conversion to a date or time is possible
IsObject(variable)	test whether is a pointer to an object
IsError(variable)	test whether is an error value
IsEmpty(variable)	test whether is empty
IsNull(variable)	test whether is not initialized
VarType(variable)	numerical value representing the data type
TypeName(variable)	character string describing the data or object type

---

Custom Data Types

Type newtype
  element1 As type
  element2 As type
  ...
End Type

FIELDS

Option Base 1	smallest allowed index is 1 (instead of the default 0)
Dim field1(5), field2(10,10)	one- and two-dimensional fields
Dim field(-3 through 3)	field with negative indices
Dim field()	temporarily empty field
Redim field4(10)	dynamic redimensioning
Redim Preserve field4(20)	as above, but data are not erased
Erase field()	erases the field
LBound(field())	returns the smallest permitted index
UBound(field())	returns the largest permitted index
L/UBound(field(), n)	as above, but for the *n*th dimension

DATA FIELDS

Dim x	normal variant variable
x = Array(x1, x2, ...)	definition

Procedural Programming

Procedural programming languages are distinguished by the fact that program code is written in small, separate units. These program units (procedures) can be called by one another, and parameters can be passed between them. Almost all of the currently popular programming languages, such as Pascal, C, and modern dialects of Basic, belong to the family of procedural programming languages (unlike, say, the languages LISP and Prolog).

This section describes the characteristic commands of a procedural language for controlling the execution of a program and for the division of the program into functions and procedures.

Procedures and Parameters

The two general syntax variants for procedures have already been revealed in the previous examples: ***Sub*** *name()* ... ***End Sub*** defines a *subprogram* (=macro, ="procedural macro"). Procedures of this type can carry out certain actions (for example, save the current workbook), but they do not return a value. For this reason there exists a second type of procedure, the *function* (=function macro, =user-defined function). Functions are introduced by the keyword ***Function*** *name()* and are terminated by ***End Function***. Before a function is exited, that is, at the very latest in the last line, the value that the function is to return must be specified by giving a value to the function's name, *name*.

Note that procedures can call one another. If you wish to program a new command, the procedure defining the command can call other subprograms and functions. Procedures also serve to break up complex programming tasks into small, bite-size modules.

The easiest way to understand the concepts of subprogram and function is by means of an example. The subprogram *macro* calls the function *func* twice. In *func* it is tested whether the first parameter is larger than the second. If that is the case, the function calculates the difference between the two parameters and returns this value. If not, the function returns the product of the two values. After *macro* finishes execution the two values 12 (= 3*4) and 1 (= 7–6) are shown in the immediate window.

```
' example file VBA-Concepts.xls, Module "Procedures"
Sub macro()
  Dim result1, result2
  result1 = func(3, 4)
  result2 = func(7, 6)
  Debug.Print result1, result2
End Sub
Function func(a, b)
  If a > b Then func = a - b: Exit Function
  func = a * b
End Function
```

The function *func* can also be used in worksheets: Input arbitrary values into A1 and B1, and in C1 place the formula *=func(A1,B1)*. You will see that the function thus defined is executed without further ado. (Note that in worksheet formulas, parameters are separated by a comma.) In INSERT|FUNCTION the function *func* is placed in the category USER DEFINED (though without on-line help). Practical examples for user-defined functions can be found in Chapter 5.

Names of Procedures

The names of procedures are subject to the same restrictions as those for variables: The name must begin with a letter, may be at most 255 characters long, and should contain no special characters other than the underscore "_". The name may not be the same as that of a predefined keyword (see the VBA on-line help under "naming rules." Names of objects, properties, and methods are as a rule *not* considered keywords and can therefore also be used as the names of procedures. It is allowed, for example, to define a procedure with the name *Add*, even though many objects exist with a method of that name. VBA knows from the object's specification whether its *Add* method or your *Add* procedure is meant.

It is not allowed to give the same name to two procedures residing in the same module. Procedures with the same name in different modules are, however, allowed, but then when the procedure is called, the name of the module must be prefixed to it. (More on this below.)

Premature Exiting of Procedures

The example *func* above contains the keywords ***Exit Function***. When this instruction is encountered, the function is exited prematurely, that is, before reaching *End Function*. *Exit Function* can be placed anywhere within the function. However, the return value of the function must have been previously determined by a reference to the function's name (otherwise, the function will return, depending on its data type, 0, the empty character string, *False*, or *Empty*). Subprograms can be exited at any time via the instruction ***Exit Sub***. There is no return value to worry about for this type of procedure.

The Data Type of the Value Returned by the Function

Functions are distinguished from other subprograms by their return value. The data type of the return value should be defined as in the case of defining a variable. In the example above no data type was defined, and *func* therefore returns its result in the default data type *Variant*. The two lines below demonstrate the two different ways in which the function *func* can be defined to return a value of type *Double*.

```
Function func(a, b) As Double
Function func#(a, b)
```

The Parameter List

The rules that hold for the definition of the data type of a variable and a function hold, naturally, as well for the parameters of subprograms and functions. For reasons of efficiency and reliability, data types should be given for all the parameters of a procedure. If both parameters of the function *func* are declared as *Double*, then the two definition options look as follows:

```
Function func(a As Double, b As Double) As Double
Function func#(a#, b#)
```

It can be seen from this example that the use of such type declaration characters leads to clearer and shorter definitions.

Value and Return Parameters

Normally, parameters in VBA procedures are return parameters. This means that their content can be changed by the procedure and that this change affects the variable in the calling procedure. Let us consider an example to demonstrate this principle:

```
Sub array_macro1()
  Dim a%, b%
  a = 4: b = 6
  array_macro2 a, b
  Debug.Print a, b
End Sub

Sub array_macro2(x%, y%)
  x = x * 2
  y = y / 2
End Sub
```

After *array_macro1* has finished executing, the values 8 and 3 have been output to the direct window. Thus *array_macro2* has altered the values of the two variables *a* and *b* from *array_macro1*. The parameters *x* and *y* in *array_macro2* are called return parameters because the change in the variables is returned to its origin, the calling procedure. (In more sophisticated programming languages such parameter passing is called "by reference" or "by pointer," because not the data themselves are passed, but a pointer, or reference, to the memory location allocated to the variable in question.) A return value is then possible only if at the time the procedure is called, the actual name of a variable is given. In the macro call *array_macro2 1,2* no value can be returned (1 and 2 are constants), nor can it happen in the case of compound expressions like *array_macro2 a+1,b/c*.

If you wish to avoid the possibility that a procedure can change the variables sent to it, then you must append the keyword ***ByVal*** in the parameter list of the procedure's definition. These parameters then are value parameters and behave within the called procedure like independent variables. A change in a parameter within the called procedure has no effect on the variables outside of that procedure:

```
Sub array_macro2(ByVal x%, ByVal y%)
```

Passing of Fields

Not only can single values be passed to a procedure, but fields as well. For this the parameter must be identified as a field in the parameter list (append an empty pair of parentheses). Fields are always return parameters, and the keyword *ByVal* is not allowed.

The variable type of a field that is given when a procedure is called must coincide with the variable type of the procedure's parameters. Thus it is not allowed to pass an *Integer* field to a procedure whose parameter is defined as a *Variant* field. (This is different from the case of normal parameters: You can send an *Integer* number to a procedure that expects a *Variant* value; it will be automatically converted.)

The example below shows a loop in which all of the elements of the field are output to the immediate window. In the case of multidimensional fields, in this loop first the first index is varied (that is, the sequence *f(0,0), f(1,0), ...; f(0,1), f(1,1), ...*; etc.). This behavior is not documented, and it is possible that in future versions of VBA this will change. The *For* loop will be discussed more fully below:

```
Sub array_macro3(arr())
  Dim var
  For Each var In arr()
    Debug.Print var
  Next var
End Sub
```

Within a procedure you can use the functions *LBound* and *UBound* to determine the admissible index ranges within the different dimensions of a field. There is, however, no function that determines the number of dimensions of the passed field. You can determine the number of dimensions relatively easily, though, if you construct a simple error-handling routine.

In the example below three fields are dimensioned; the first is empty, the second has three dimensions, and the third has two. The procedure *array_macro4* calls the procedure *arraytest* for each of these fields and passes as parameters the individual fields. In *arraytest* first a loop is run that deliberately causes en error as soon as *UBound* is executed for a nonexistent dimension. (This is the only way to determine the number of dimensions of a field!)

This error is caught in the program unit *arraytest_error*, and the procedure is continued with *arraytest_continue*. In the following loop the index limits are given for each dimension.

> **POINTER** *Information on* For *loops can be found below in this section. The mechanisms of error handling will be described in Chapter 6.*

```
' example file VBA-Concepts.xls, Module "Procedures"
Sub array_macro4()
  Dim array1()
  Dim array2(4, 5, 6)
  Dim array3(-2 To 2, 1 To 4)
  array2(1, 2, 3) = 4
  arraytest array1()
  arraytest array2()
  arraytest array3()
End Sub

Sub arraytest(arr())
  Dim i, dimensions
  On Error GoTo arraytest_error
  For i = 1 To 10: dimensions = UBound(arr, i): Next i
arraytest_continue:
  dimensions = i - 1
  Debug.Print dimensions, " Dimensions"
  For i = 1 To dimensions
    Debug.Print "Dimension "; i; ": "; LBound(arr, i);
    Debug.Print " to "; UBound(arr, i)
  Next i
  Exit Sub
arraytest_error:
' this code is executed as soon as the program tries to access a nonexistent
' dimension
  Resume arraytest_continue
End Sub
```

array_macro4 produces the following output in the immediate window:

```
 0            dimensions
 3            dimensions
Dimension  1 :  0  to  4
Dimension  2 :  0  to  5
Dimension  3 :  0  to  6
 2            dimensions
Dimension  1 : -2  to  2
Dimension  2 :  1  to  4
```

Matrices as Parameters

Excel matrices can be passed as parameters to procedures. Matrices are linked regions of cells in Excel worksheets. Excel has its own worksheet functions, such as *LINEST*, that return not a single value, but a matrix containing several values. See also Chapter 5, where the use of the function *LINEST* and the programming of custom matrix functions are described.

Excel automatically converts matrices into one- or two-dimensional fields. Nonetheless, matrix parameters must be given in the form of normal *Variant* variables in the parameter list, and not, say (which would be more logical), as field parameters. (Internally, matrices are not treated like normal fields, but as data fields (arrays).) Within a procedure individual elements of a matrix can be accessed as in the case of a field (*matrix(n)* for a one-dimensional matrix and *matrix(n,m)* for a two-dimensional matrix).

The following example shows a function that returns the number of matrix elements. Within the worksheet you can call this function with *=matrix_func(D17:D19)*, provided that D17:D19 is formatted as a matrix (select the region of cells, input formulas or numbers, and close with Shift+Ctrl+Return). The function returns the result 3; *=matrix_func(LINEST(...))* returns the number of resultant cells that the function *LINEST* returns:

```
Function matrix_func(matrix)
  Dim x
  For Each x In matrix
    matrix_func = matrix_func + 1
  Next x
End Function
```

Optional Parameters

Under normal circumstances, when a procedure is called it has passed all the parameters defined in the procedure. With the keyword ***Optional*** it is not necessary to pass such a parameter. Within the procedure you must, however, test with ***IsMissing*** whether such parameters have been passed in the procedure call.

As soon as a parameter has been designated as *Optional*, all further parameters will be so declared. (That is, it is necessary first to define all the nonoptional parameters and then the optional ones in the parameter list.)

The following procedure increases the value of the parameter *x* either by 1 or, in the event that the second parameter has been passed, by *y*.

```
Sub increment(x, Optional y)
  If IsMissing(y) Then
    x = x + 1
  Else
    x = x + y
  End If
End Sub
```

> **NOTE** *Starting with Excel 97 optional parameters can be of any data type. (Previously, only the type* Variant *was allowed.) However,* IsMissing *functions only for* Variant *parameters. If you use another variable type, the parameter contains simply 0, or an empty character string when no parameter is passed.*

Variable Number of Parameters

Optional parameters have the disadvantage that the number of them is predetermined. If you wish to formulate a procedure to which an arbitrary number of parameters can be passed, then you must use the keyword ***ParamArray*** and use a *Variant* field. Then arbitrarily many parameters can be passed to the procedure, which can then be evaluated in a *For–Each* loop. *ParamArray* is not compatible with *Optional*: You must decide between optional parameters and a variable number of parameters. Note further that all parameters of a *ParamArray* are value parameters. A change in the original variables is thus not possible.

The example below shows the function *sum*, which forms the sum of all the parameters passed to it. The *For* loop is dealt with further below. You can refer to the individual parameters with *x(0), x(1), x(2)*; the problem is that VBA provides no possibility of determining the number of parameters (see above).

```
Function sum(ParamArray x())
  Dim var
  For Each var In x()
    sum = sum + var
  Next var
End Function
```

Calling a Procedure

In calling a procedure a distinction must be made between subprograms and functions. With subprograms one simply writes the name of the procedure followed by the list of parameters. With functions the parameters must be placed within parentheses, and the return value must be applied in some way (for example, in a definition of a variable or as the parameter to another function):

```
macro1                          ' subprogram without parameters
macro2 para1, para2             ' subprogram  with two parameters
result = func1()                ' function without parameters
result = func2(para1, para2)    ' function with two parameters
```

Named Parameters

With procedures having many optional parameters the form of parameter passing described above often leads to very unclear instructions. For example, if the first, second, and eighth parameters are given, the call looks something like this:

```
macro para1, para2, , , , , , para8
```

It now requires careful counting to establish what meaning the parameter *para8* actually possesses. For this reason there exists an alternative form of parameter passing, under which only those parameters that are really necessary need be given. So that VBA can know what meaning the parameter names have, the parameter name must be given as well.

The concept can be easily understood with the help of an example. Assume that you have written the following program as part of a database application:

```
Sub insertRecord(name, address, Optional telNr, _
       Optional birthdate, Optional email)
```

When this procedure is called you must give at least the name and address. If you furthermore wish to give the birthdate, then both calling variants, first the traditional one, then the one with named parameters, look as follows:

```
insertRecord "Polsky,  Ned", "143 West 4th Street, New York, NY 10012, ", , _
  #10/20/1928#
insertRecord name:="Polsky,  Ned", _
  address:="143 West 4th Street, New York, NY 10012", birthdate:=#10/20/1928#
```

Although it is nowhere documented, there is also the possibility of combining both forms of parameter passing. You can give the first *n* parameters as unnamed, and the rest named. Thus there is a third variant of *insertRecord,* one that is shorter and clearer than the two other variants:

```
insertRecord "Polsky, Ned", "143 West 4th Street, New York, NY 10012", _
  birthdate:=#10/20/1928#
```

When you are working with named parameters, the order of the parameters is irrelevant. However, it is always necessary that all nonoptional parameters be given. The concept of named parameters holds, of course, for all VBA methods and functions. The automatic macro recording process uses named parameters intensively, which can lead to instructions like the following:

```
ActiveChart.ChartWizard Source:=Range("A1:A4"), Gallery:=xlColumn, _
  Format:=6, PlotBy:=xlColumns, CategoryLabels:=0, SeriesLabels:=0, _
  HasLegend:=1
```

Recursion

A subprogram or function is called "recursive" if it calls itself. With recursive subprograms or functions certain programming problems, particularly those involving complex data structures, can often be solved simply and elegantly. The simplest and best-known example of a recursive function is the calculation of the factorial function. The factorial of a nonnegative integer n is defined to be the product of all integers between 1 and n. The factorial of 5, for example, is 1*2*3*4*5=120. The recursive possibilities arise from the observation that $n! = n*(n-1)!$ for $n \geq 1$.

```
' example file, vba-concepts.xls, Module "procedures"
Public Sub testrecur()
  Debug.Print recur(3)
End Sub
' recursive procedure for calculating the factorial of x
Function recur(x)
  If x <= 1 Then
    recur = 1
  Else
    recur = x * recur(x - 1)
  End If
End Function
```

The execution of the program for calculating the factorial of 3 runs as follows: The function *recur* is called; *x* has the value 3. In the *If* conditional, therefore, the *Else* block is executed. There *recur* is called again, this time with *x*=2. Again, the *Else* block is executed, now with *x*=1. Now the *If* condition is satisfied, and the third call returns the value 1. The program execution now finds itself back at the second level, in which *x*=2. The result is then multiplied by the returned value 1 (yielding 2), which is returned to the first level, where *x*=3. There the return value 2 is multiplied by *x*=3 and returned to the *Print* method in *restrecur*, where the calculation was begun.

In the course of this calculation there were therefore three simultaneous variables *x* all with different values. With each new invocation of the function a new (local) variable *x* is defined. (See also the following section for a discussion of the scope of a variable.)

If this foray into the factorial function is your first contact with recursive functions, then you have probably been having a rough time grasping all the details of the program's execution. Add the following as the first and last lines to the factorial function:

```
MsgBox "x=" & x & " recur=" & recur
```

You can then better follow the path of the program as it runs. *MsgBox* displays the text from the character strings "x=" and "recur=" and the values of the associated variables in a small dialog window, which you must acknowledge with OK.

> **NOTE** *You can also use Visual Basic's debugging facilities to follow the calculation better (see Chapter 6).*

Realm of Validity of Variables and Procedures

All variables and procedures can be used only in a particular realm of validity. This realm is the region of program code or in Excel in which a variable can be read and changed, or a procedure called. VBA recognizes, according to the setting, three or four realms of validity:

- within a procedure (local variable)
- within a module (module variable)
- within a workbook (global variable)
- within Excel (thus valid for several Excel files)

For variables all four levels exist, while for procedures only the last three are valid.

Variables and Constants

Variables that are defined at the start of a module (though outside a procedure) with ***Dim*** can be used throughout the module, and therefore in all procedures defined within the module. Module variables thus make possible the use of common data in several procedures and simplify the efficient exchange of data.

In contradistinction to these there exist variables that are defined within a procedure. These "local" variables can be used only within the code of the procedure in which they are defined.

This concept makes it possible to use variables with the same name in different procedures without them influencing one another. If both a local variable and a module variable with the same name exist, then within the procedure the local variable is valid, and outside it (that is, in all other procedures), it is the module variable that holds sway.

Public (= Global) Variables

Instead of the keyword *Dim* at the level of a module (outside of procedures) the keyword ***Public*** can be used. *Public* has the same syntax as *Dim* (see above).

If you wish to access a public variable defined in one workbook in a second workbook, then in the second workbook you must construct a reference to the first workbook (command TOOLS|REFERENCES; see also the following section, on the subject of object libraries and references).

If at the beginning of a module the instruction ***Option Private Module*** is given, then the variables defined therein can be accessed only from within the workbook. Without the instruction (that is, in the standard situation) global variables can be used from other workbooks.

Module Variables

All variables defined outside of a procedure with *Private* or *Dim* are considered module variables. Here *Private* functions the same as *Dim*, but it is perhaps clearer (since the realm of validity of the variable is so unambiguous).

Local Variables

Local variables are defined with *Dim*. The command must be used within a procedure. (*Private* and *Public* cannot be used within a procedure).

Static Variables

Local variables are normally deleted when a procedure has finished executing and the memory that has been allocated to them is released. If you wish to preserve the value of a variable that it had the last time a procedure was called, you must then define the variable to be "static." For this you use ***Static*** instead of *Dim*.

If you apply the keyword *Static* in a procedure definition before *Sub* or *Function*, then *all* variables of the procedure will be defined as static.

Procedure Parameters

Parameters of procedures act locally (defined by *Dim*) within a procedure. In recursive procedure calls *ByVal* parameters act like static variables; that is, their old values remain available for use after the recursive return.

Combined Variable Names

When you wish to access variables of the same name outside of the current module or procedure level, you must prefix the name of the module and if necessary the name of the workbook as well, yielding something like the following:

```
modulename.variablenname
[WORKBOOK.XLS].modulename.variablename
```

Life Span of Variables

Normally, the content of variables is saved only as long as the code in the valid realm is being executed. For example, a local variable loses its validity (and its content) as soon as the procedure's code has finished executing. The only exceptions to this rule are the static variables (keyword *Static*), which are saved after a procedure has terminated until the file is closed.

Global variables that are defined in modules have the same life span as static variables: Their value is preserved until the file is closed.

Regardless of the type, the contents of all variables are erased when the program code is edited (and therefore recompiled).

> **NOTE** *The content of a variable, whether local, global, or static, is never saved in the Excel file of the workbook. If you wish to do so, you must copy the content of the variable into the cell of a worksheet before it is saved, and when the file is opened the value can then be read. For automatic execution of the necessary code you can use event procedures (see the section after next one).*

Constants

In general, what holds for variables holds for constants as well. Constants that are to be valid in all the modules of a workbook must be preceded by the keyword *Public.*

Procedures

Procedures are generally categorized as public, that is, they can be used in all modules of the same workbook. If a procedure is to be used in other workbooks as well, then in every workbook a reference must be made to the workbook in which the procedure is defined (with the command TOOLS|REFERENCES; see also the next section, on the theme of object libraries and references).

If procedures of the same name exist within a workbook, then the module name must be prefixed to the procedure call. Procedures of the same name in different workbooks must be identified uniquely by the file name of the workbook.

```
modulename.macro                    ' within the current workbook
[WORKBOOK.XLS].macro                ' in another workbook
[WORKBOOK.XLS].module name.macro    ' in another workbook
```

If you wish to prevent the use of a procedure outside of the module in which it is defined, then you must write ***Private*** before the keyword *Sub* or *Function.* This should be done for all procedures that are designed to be used only within a particular module. The declaration "private" not only prevents accidental and therefore erroneous use, but also simplifies the selection of macros in TOOLS|MACROS and INSERT|FUNCTION.

When you employ the instruction *Option Private Module* at the beginning of a module, then *all* procedures of that module will be closed outside of that worksheet. The option is confusingly formulated: The procedures can be used in other modules of the same workbook. This option is therefore less restrictive than the keyword *Private.*

As with *Private,* you can prefix a procedure with the keyword *Public.* This keyword has no effect, however, since procedures are public by default. The program code will, however, be somewhat clearer.

> **NOTE** *When you declare a procedure as* Private, *this has the advantage that this procedure will not be listed in the forms "macro" and "assign macro." This makes these forms easier to read (especially in the case of large projects or when several workbooks are open).*

Add-Ins

Excel programs that were saved as add-ins (see Chapter 14) differ in one respect from normal workbooks: The procedure name need not be prefixed with a file name, even when the procedure is used outside of the add-in.

Accessing Variables and Procedures in Another Workbook

To access variables and procedures belonging to another workbook from within a workbook, two conditions must be fulfilled: First, the variables in the other workbook must be declared as *Public*, and procedures may not be declared as *Private*. Second, a reference (via TOOLS|REFERENCES) must be made to the workbook whose variables or procedures are to be used. If like-named variables or procedures exist, then the variable names must be preceded by the module or file name (see above).

Internal Management of Variables

Excel stores the names of all variables and procedures that appear during the course of program development in an invisible table. Experience has shown that variable names change frequently during the programming process, and many test procedures are deleted. Therefore, the internal name table becomes full of data trash over time, resulting in bloated Excel files. The only method of clearing this invisible table consists in saving all modules as text files, then deleting all modules, and finally creating new modules out of the text files. This convoluted method really makes sense only if you wish to pass along the application in the form of an add-in.

Summary of Keywords

Dim var	defines local procedure or module variables.
Private var	has the same effect as *Dim* in variable declaration.
Public var	defines global variables (possible only at the module level); the realm of validity (scope) depends on the setting of *Option Private Module*.
Static var	defines local static variables (possible only at the level of a procedure).

Sub/Function	defines public procedures; scope depends on *Option Private Module.*
Private Sub/Function	defines local procedures, usable only within a module.
Public Sub/Function	like normal *Sub/Function,* that is, also public.
Static Sub/Function	defines all *Variables* of the procedure as static.
Option Private Module	limits the scope of public variables and procedures to the current workbook. Without this option the variables and procedures can also be used in other workbooks, to the extent that references have been made.

Branching (Tests)

Branching with If-Then-Else

With ***If*** tests it is possible to execute particular program segments according to whether certain conditions are met. The program code "branches" into several pieces, of which only one will be executed.

The following example demonstrates the form of an *If* test: *InputBox* (for details see Chapter 7) calls for the input of a number. The input will then be evaluated: The first *If* test checks whether instead of a number, text was input. If that is the case, then the message "This is not a number!" appears. Otherwise, with *ElseIf* the further distinction is made as to whether the number is greater than 10.

```
' example file VBA-Concepts.xls, Module "LoopsAndConditions"
Sub macro_if()
  Dim number
  number = InputBox("Type in a number, please!")
  If Not IsNumeric(number) Then
    MsgBox "This is not a number!"
  ElseIf number > 10 Then
    MsgBox "The number is larger than 10"
  Else
    MsgBox "The number is greater than or equal to 10"
  End If
End Sub
```

This example illustrates just about everything there is to explain about *If* tests. The general syntax is introduced by *If condition Then* and terminated by *End If.* In between there can be a simple piece of code (one or more lines), which will then be executed only if the condition is satisfied. Additionally, after *Else* another piece of code can appear, which will be executed if all the previous conditions were not fulfilled. And finally, before *Else* there can appear an arbitrary number of *ElseIf–condition–Then* blocks to distinguish different cases.

Every block following *Then* or *Else* can itself contain further procedural structures (including further branches or loops). In addition to the multiline *If* syntax there exists a one-line version. This, however, is suitable only for simple tests:

```
If nr > 10 Then MsgBox "…"
If nr < 5 Then nr = nr * 2 Else MsgBox "…"
```

Formulating and Evaluating Logical Conditionals

In *If* branches and in loops (see the following section) you must always formulate logical conditionals. For this purpose you have available the comparison operators =, <>, <, >, <=, and >=, by means of which you can determine whether two expressions are equal, or whether one of the two expressions is less than, less than or equal to, etc., the other. For comparing two character strings there is the additional operator *Like,* with which you can recognize the form of a character string ("T*son" for "Thompson", "Thomson", or "Tomson").

The result of a comparison is a truth value. In the binary system of a computer there are only the two values *True* and *False.* For the two keywords *True* and *False* VBA uses the values –1 and 0 internally. In logical conditionals every value unequal to 0 is considered to be *True,* that is, in the instruction *If 3 Then,* the *If* condition is satisfied (is true, since nonzero).

In addition to conditionals various functions can also return a truth value, such as the *IsXxx* functions, which determine whether an expression corresponds to a particular data type (*IsNumeric, IsDate* etc.).

In VBA you can join several comparisons together. In this case as well the result of the entire expression is a truth value. The first example below tests whether *a* is less than 5 or greater than 10, while the second example tests whether *a* is between these two values. In the third example the goal is to exclude the possibility that *a* contains the value *Null* or has not yet been allocated.

```
If a < 5 Or a > 10 Then …
'
If a > 5 And a < 10 Then …
'
If Not (IsEmpty(a) Or IsNull(a)) Then …
```

The joining operators are *And* and *Or* as well as the less frequently used *Xor*, *Imp*, and *Eqv*. With *Not* a truth value can be inverted (analogous to the minus sign for addition or reciprocal for multiplication).

CAUTION *VBA does no optimization in evaluating conditionals. A test of the form* If x>=0 And Sqr(x)<3 *leads in the case of negative* x *to an error. (In many programming languages the second part of the conditional is not evaluated if the first part evaluates to false, since in the case of an* And *conditional the result is* False *if even one part is* False.*)*

POINTER *Later in this chapter we give an overview of the operators defined in VBA. For information on working with character strings (including the comparison of strings), see Chapter 5.*

Branching with Select Case

An alternative to the *If* test is another branching structure, introduced by the keyword ***Select Case.*** This variant can lead in many cases to the formulation of more easily readable branching code. This branching structure is also most easily understood by means of an example, one that also determines the range of values of an input number. Note that this time it is not tested whether the input is actually a number. If you input the character "x", then VBA will respond with an error message (since the character "x" cannot be compared with a number).

```
Sub macro_select()
  Dim number
  number = InputBox("Type in a number, please!")
  Select Case number
  Case 1, 2, 3
    MsgBox "1, 2 or 3"
  Case 4 To 10
    MsgBox "Between 4 and 10"
  Case Is > 10
    MsgBox "Greater than 10"
  Case Else
    MsgBox "Less than 1"
  End Select
End Sub
```

The syntax of *Select Case* can be easily understood from this example. Following *Select Case* the expression to be analyzed must be given. This holds for the entire branching structure (which in comparison to *If* branching represents a limitation). In the following *Case* branches, conditions must be formulated that the expression is to satisfy. These can be individual values, ranges indicated by the keyword *To*, or *Is* conditionals similar to what occurs in an *If* branch. Here *Is* represents a reference to the expression given at the start of the *Select Case*.

Loops

Loops serve the purpose of allowing program code to be executed repeatedly. VBA has three such structures: *For–Next*, *Do–Loop*, and *While–Wend*.

Loops with For-Next

The simplest type of loop is constructed with the commands *For* and *Next*. Here initial and terminal values are given to a variable at the start of the loop. The initial value is increased each time the loop is executed, until finally the terminal value is reached.

The following example shows the simplest variant of a ***For*** loop. The variable *i* runs over the values from 1 to 5.

```
Sub macro_loop1()
  Dim i
  For i = 1 To 10
    If i > 5 Then Exit For
    Debug.Print i
  Next i
End Sub
```

With the optional keyword *Step* a value can be given by which the loop variable is to be increased each time through the loop (the default value, without *Step*, is 1). In the example below the loop runs from –0.3 to +0.3 with step size 0.1. For the loop variable *i* the data type *Double* has been given.

```
Sub macro_loop2()
  Dim i As Double
  For i = -0.3 To 0.3 Step 0.1
    Debug.Print i
  Next i
End Sub
```

However, the result of this loop is not completely convincing. In the immediate window the following values are output:

```
-0.3
-0.2
-0.1
 2.77555756156289E-17
 0.1
 0.2
```

The repeated addition of 0.1 has resulted in round-off error. This round-off error results not only in the rather unattractive display of 2.77555756156289E-17, but also in the sad fact that the terminal value 0.3 is never reached. (At the end of the loop *i* has the value 0.30000000000000006. This value is minimally greater than 0.3 and leads to the loop being broken off prematurely.) The problem can be solved by a more careful formulation of the loop condition:

```
For i = -0.3 To 0.300000001 Step 0.1
```

> **NOTE** *Round-off error in floating point numbers is one of the characteristics of* all *programming languages. They are not a particular weakness of VBA (even if there are, in fact, programming languages in which the above error does not occur). As a programmer you should always be aware of this problem.*

The design of a *For* loop is such that it may not be executed even once. That is because even before the first pass through the loop it is checked whether the loop conditions are valid. A loop that begins *For i=5 To 1* will thus not be executed even once (unless a negative step size is assigned with *Step*). At the end of the *For* loop the loop variable contains the value for which the loop condition first failed to be satisfied. After the loop *For i=1 To 10,* for example, the variable *i* contains the value 11.

For loops can be prematurely exited with ***Exit For.*** In the following example the values 1, 2, 3, 4, 5 are output. With *For i=6,* the *If* condition is fulfilled, which leads to a premature exit from the loop

```
For i = 1 To 10
  If i > 5 Then Exit For
  Debug.Print i
Next i
```

Loops with For Each-Next

In VBA there exists a special form of the *For* loop that is designed especially for working with fields and enumeration methods. (Enumeration methods will be expounded in the next section. With them you can access associated objects in a group, such as all sheets of a workbook or all tools on a toolbar.) The example below outputs the names of all the worksheets in the current workbook:

```
Sub macro_loop3()
  Dim w As Worksheet
  For Each w In ThisWorkbook.Worksheets
    Debug.Print w.Name
  Next w
End Sub
```

The syntax is somewhat different from that of normal *For* loops: The variable is given after ***For Each***, and the collection object after the keyword *In*. During the processing of the loop the collection object can be accessed directly via the loop variable.

In using a *For-Each* loop you should not assume that the elements will be processed in a particular order. It is not documented in what order the elements are associated to a loop variable. However, with most collection objects instead of a *For-Each* loop you can use a traditional loop and access the individual elements with indices as in the case of fields.

```
Sub macro_loop4()
  Dim i
  For i = 1 To ThisWorkbook.Worksheets.Count
    Debug.Print ThisWorkbook.Worksheets(i).Name
  Next i
End Sub
```

Loops with Do-Loop

For loops are in one respect inflexible: It is determined at the outset how many times the loop will execute. The keywords ***Do*** and ***Loop*** assist in the formulation of more general loops. In their simplest form these two commands can be used to create an infinite loop:

```
Sub macro_loop5()
  Do
    Debug.Print "and so on"
  Loop
End Sub
```

Once you have started such a loop, you can interrupt it only with the keyboard combination Ctrl+Break. Infinite loops are seldom useful in practice. Therefore, there are two ways in which the above loop can be programmatically terminated: By the command *Exit*, which we have already encountered in the *For* loop, which here must follow the keyword *Do* (and not *Loop*), or by providing a condition at the beginning or end of the loop. Conditions can be given either in the form *While* or *Until*. In the first case the loop is executed until the given condition is satisfied. In the second case the effect is the opposite: The loop is executed until the condition becomes true (or, alternatively, while the condition is *not* satisfied).

Although it may seem at first glance that it makes no difference whether the condition is given at the beginning or at the end, this is not the case: If you give the condition *While*, then it can happen that the loop will, in fact, never execute even once. If, on the other hand, the condition is formulated with *Loop*, the loop must execute at least once.

In the example below, the variable *i* is increased by 1 each time through the loop until it is broken off when the value 11 is reached.

```
Sub macro_loop6()
  Dim i As Integer
  i = 1
  Do
    Debug.Print i
    i = i + 1
  Loop Until i > 10
End Sub
```

Loops with While-Wend

Loops with ***While...Wend*** offer nothing new with respect to the loops with *Do ... Loop*. The only difference is that there is now the possibility of terminating the loop prematurely with *Exit*.

```
While i < 10
  i = i + 1: Debug.Print i
Wend
'
Do While i < 10    ' the same loop [[?]]
  i = i + 1: Debug.Print i
Loop
```

Syntax Summary

Below, square brackets enclose optional commands, which may be given but do not have to be.

Definition of Procedure

Sub macro([parameterlist])	
...	
[Exit Sub]	exit program prematurely
...	
End Sub	
Function func([parameterlist]) [As data type]	
...	
[func = ...: Exit Function]	exit function prematurely
...	
func = ...	
End Function	

Definition of the Parameter List

para1, para2, para3	3 parameters in default data type *Variant*
para As datatype	parameters in given data type
para() [As datatype]	Field
ByVal para [As datatype]	value parameter
Optional para [As datatype]	optional parameter
ParamArray para()	List with variable number of parameters

Evaluation of Parameter in Procedure Code

true_false = IsMissing(para)	test whether an optional parameter was passed
For Each x In para()	loop through all parameters of an argument list
...	
Next x	

Procedure Call

macro x1, x2, x3	traditional input of all parameters (subprogram)
result = function(x1, x2, x3)	traditional input of all parameters (function)
macro para1:=x1, para3:=x3	named parameters (subprogram)
result = function (para1:=x1)	named parameters (function)

Definition of Variables at the Module Level

Dim var	module variable
Private var	module variable (same effect as *Dim*)
Public var	public variable (all modules)
Option Private Module	public variable accessible only within the workbook (also with reference)

Definition of Variables at the Procedure Level

Dim var	local variable, usable only in the procedure
Static var	as above, but retains the value
Static Sub/Function name()	all variables of the procedure are static

Definition of Procedures

Sub/Function name()	public, for all worksheets
Private Sub/Function name()	usable only in the current module
Option Private Module	public procedures usable only with the workbook (also with reference)

Branching with If – Then

If condition Then command	one-line variant
If condition Then k1 Else k2	one-line variant with *Else*
If condition Then	multiline variant
commands	
ElseIf condition Then	optional, arbitrarily many cases
commands	
Else	optional
commands	
End If	

Branches with Select – Case

Select Case expression	
Case possibility1	arbitrarily many cases
commands	
Case Else	optional
commands	
End Select	

Possibilities in Select – Case

value	single value
value1, value2, value3	enumeration
value 1To value2	range of values
Is operator comparison value	comparison condition with =, <, or >

Loops with While – Wend

```
While condition
  commands
Wend
```

Loops with For – Next

```
For var=start To end [Step value]
  commands
  [If condition Then Exit For]
  commands
Next var
```

Loops with For Each – Next

For Each var In enumeration method or *field()*
  commands
  [If condition Then Exit For]
  commands
Next *var*

Loops with Do – Loop

Do [While condition or *Until condition]*
  commands
  [If condition Then Exit Do]
  commands
Loop
	variant 1

Do
  commands
  [If condition Then Exit Do]
  commands
Loop [While condition or *Until condition]*
	variant 2

Objects

Working with Objects, Methods, and Properties

Objects

In VBA elements of Excel are called objects. The following list enumerates the most common objects: *Application* (the Excel application in its entirety), *PageSetup* (page setup for printing), *Workbook* (Excel workbook), *Window* (an Excel window), *Worksheet* (Excel worksheet), *Range* (a range of cells in a worksheet), *Chart* (Excel chart), *ChartArea* (background of a chart), *Axis* (coordinate axis of a chart), *Line* (line for the visual display of charts, forms, etc.), *Oval* (circle or ellipse).

There are about 150 objects altogether defined in Excel (to this are added still more objects from other libraries; but more on that later). These objects are organized hierarchically. At the highest level is the *Application* object. For the properties of this object one can access loaded workbooks (*Workbooks*), and for their properties the individual sheets (*Chart* and *Worksheet*) of the workbook. Chapter 15 contains a reference to all objects defined in Excel and gives an overview of the object hierarchy.

Accessing objects in Excel is useful only if the programmer can read and edit an object's specific data and add and delete new objects. To make this possible, each object possesses a number of properties and methods.

Properties

Properties determine the characteristics of an object, such as the background color of a chart, the alignment of a worksheet cell, the many options of Excel, or the parameters of a page (such as header and footer). For the programmer properties look like predefined variables. The only formal difference is that almost without exception, before the property name the object name must be given (for example, *Application.DisplayFullScreen*). Most properties can be read and edited.

```
' tells whether Excel is in full screen mode (True) or (False)
Debug.Print Application.DisplayFullScreen
' activates full screen mode
Application.DisplayFullScreen = True
' changes the mode
Application.DisplayFullScreen = Not Application.DisplayFullScreen
```

A further difference between variables and properties is that the result of changing a property is in most cases immediately visible. When in the above example you change the property *DisplayFullScreen*, this has the same effect as executing the menu command VIEW|FULL SCREEN. Excel thus reacts immediately to changes in properties.

Methods

While properties are most nearly analogous to variables, methods are closer to procedures. With methods you can execute instructions, for example save the current workbook under a new name, delete a chart, or create a new toolbar. Methods make possible the accessing of other objects. For example, *Sheets(n)* or *Sheets("sheetname")* returns a particular sheet of the workbook.

There exist two types of methods: those that correspond to a subprogram and do not have a return value (*Select, Activate, Delete,* etc.), and those that correspond to functions and return a concrete result. Many methods can be used either with or without a return value, such as the *Add* method.

Enumeration Methods and Objects

A special role is played by the so-called enumeration methods, which end in the plural "s" (such as *Sheets, Windows*). With these methods a group of similar subobjects can be accessed (by "subobject" is meant an object ordered lower on the object hierarchy, such as *Window* with respect to *Application*). Enumeration methods can also be used as the starting point for loops with *For Each.*

When enumeration methods are used without parameters, they refer for the most part to enumeration objects of the same name. An enumeration object thus means, then, the totality of several similar objects. For these objects there exists, independently of their content, a number of coinciding properties and methods: *Count* gives the number of objects at hand. With *Add* and *Delete* the listing can be extended or shortened.

On the other hand, when the *Objects* method is used with a parameter, then it refers to the elements with the given name (*Sheets("name")*) or to the *n*th element (*Sheets(n)*), thus in each case to a single object. The index of the first element is always 1 (never 0). This way of giving parameters is actually a shorthand form. The full syntax would be *Sheets.Item("name").*

Default Objects

In general, every property and method must be supplied with the object to which the property or method is associated. That is necessary not least because there are many properties and methods (in part with varying syntax) that can work with a number of different objects. (With *Add* you can, depending on the object, create a new chart, a new menu item, or a new workbook, for example.)

However, there are some properties and methods that have default objects associated with them. If these properties or methods are used without giving the object, then they automatically assume that the default object is meant. The property *ActiveSheet* refers automatically to the default object *Application.* This property can also refer to a window or to a workbook. In that case the object must be given.

> **NOTE** Application *is the default object in all normal modules, but not in class modules! There the object described by the module is the default object. In the class modules such as "ThisWorkbook" or "Table1" the default objects are thus* Workbook *and, respectively,* Worksheets(...).

Default Properties

For many objects there exist default properties. This means that you can read or change such a property without naming it in your code. For this reason the following two instructions have the same effect:

```
Debug.Print Application
Debug.Print Application.Value
```

In the above example *Value* is the default property of *Application*. (In this case *Value* returns a character string with the content *"Microsoft Excel"*.) Default properties have two disadvantages: First, they make code unclear, and second, they are not documented.

Differences Between Objects, Properties, and Methods

To distinguish between methods and properties we have the following rule of thumb: Keyword with parameter means method; keyword without parameter means property. Enumeration objects such as *Sheets* represent an exception, since they can be used both with and without parameters.

It is not always possible to distinguish methods and properties from their internal aspects: Many actions that are carried out in VBA by methods could be managed just as well by differently formulated properties, and vice versa. In the end, it is the folks at Microsoft who have determined what is a method and what a property. We leave it to you to judge whether there is madness to their methods!

To distinguish between objects and both methods and properties the following rule might be formulated: Objects almost never appear directly in the instructions of program code. Even if it often seems as though objects are being named directly, it is always a like-named method or property that is at issue. There is an important exception to this rule: In the declaration of object variables, objects (more precisely, object classes) are named directly.

Example 1

The following instruction appends a blank chart sheet to the current workbook. This example demonstrates several aspects of dealing with objects: the interplay of objects, methods, and properties; the use of named parameters; the use of predefined constants:

```
Application.ActiveWorkbook.Sheets.Add Type:=xlChart
```

Application gives the root object (the application program Excel). *ActiveWorkbook* is a property of the object *Application* and refers to a *Workbook* object. *Sheets* is a method (even if it looks like a property) that refers to a *Sheets* object. *Add* is again a method of *Sheets* and makes possible the addition of new worksheets. *Add* recognizes four named parameters, all of which are optional. When no parameter is given, the method generates a new worksheet, which is appended in front of the currently active sheet. By means of the four parameters one can determine the insertion point, the type of sheet (such as chart, table, module, macro template), and the number of sheets to be added. In the example above only the type was specified, and in that case with the predefined constant *xlChart*.

The property *ActiveSheet* and the method *Sheets* refer automatically to the active workbook of Excel (the active workbook is the default object). For this reason, in the above instruction it is allowed not to mention the object: *Application.ActiveWorkbook*. In the three following instructions this input simplification will be taken into account.

The name of the new sheet cannot be set with *Add*. Following the *Add* method, the new sheet is the active sheet. The name can thus be set without problem in a further instruction by changing the *Name* property.

```
Sheets.Add Type:=xlChart
ActiveSheet.Name = "My Chart"
```

Instead of the two lines above a single somewhat longer line will suffice:

```
Sheets.Add(Type:=xlChart).Name = "My Chart"
```

The method *Add* will now be used not as a subprogram without return value, but as a function. For this reason the parameter now appears in parentheses. The result of the method (namely a reference to the new *Chart* object) will be further modified with the property *Name*.

Example 2

Many methods are equipped with a huge number of parameters. A noteworthy example from this viewpoint is the method *ChartWizard*, with no fewer than 11 parameters (all optional). This method is suitable for creating new charts as well as for the rapid modification of existing charts. (See also Chapter 10, which is devoted to charts.)

When you work with such complex methods as *ChartWizard*, you can save much time and grief if you first use the macro recorder. You thereby start off with some code that actually runs, code that you can alter by degrees until it accomplishes exactly what you want it to do.

In the example below a new chart object is created in the active worksheet. The four numerical values give the position and size of the chart within the worksheet and result from the selection of a rectangular frame during the recording of the macro. (The position values are given in units of points, a point being about 1/72 inch.) The method *Add* is used here as a function (and not as above as a command): The parameters are enclosed in parentheses. The result of the method is further operated on with *Select* and made into the active chart. In the following the method *ChartWizard* refers to this object (the active chart):

```
' example file VBA-Concepts.xls, Module "CreateChart"
Sub CreateChart()
  Sheets("Tab1").Activate
  ActiveSheet.ChartObjects.Add(184.5, 110.25, 187.5, 69.75).Select
  ActiveChart.ChartWizard Source:=Range("B3:B7"), _
    Gallery:=xlColumn, Format:=6, PlotBy:=xlColumns, _
    CategoryLabels:=0, SeriesLabels:=0, _
    HasLegend:=1
End Sub
```

Access to Active Objects

Excel recognizes a number of "active" objects, meaning marked or selected parts of Excel—the active window, the selected sheet within it, the selected cells within it, for instance. Access to these objects is accomplished by means of various *ActiveXxx* or *SelectXxx* properties. Most of these properties are defined for the *Application* object, which must be supplied additionally (since *Application* is the default object). Some of the properties can, however, also be applied specifically to another object. For example, *ActiveSheet* produces automatically the current sheet of the active workbook. *ActiveSheet* can, however, also be prefixed by the name of another workbook or a *Window* object. Then the property yields a reference to the currently active sheet of the currently active workbook or window.

Special mention should be made of the property *ThisWorkbook*. This property refers to the workbook in which the VBA code that is currently being executed is located. This workbook does not have to be the same as the *ActiveWorkbook*. In fact, with the code of one workbook a worksheet of another can be worked on.

In modules associated with worksheets and forms as well as in class modules the keyword *Me* can be used to refer to the related object. In a worksheet module *Me* refers to a *Worksheet* object, in a form module to a *UserForm* object, and so on.

Properties for Accessing Active Objects

ActiveCell	active cell in a worksheet
ActiveChart	active chart in a worksheet/window/workbook/Excel
ActiveMenuBar	active (currently visible) menu bar in Excel
ActivePane	active pane of a window
ActivePrinter	selected printer in Excel
ActiveSheet	active sheet in a window/workbook/Excel
ActiveWorkbook	active workbook in Excel
SelectedSheets	selected sheets of a window

Selection	selected objects in a sheet/window/workbook/Excel; the property can refer to quite different objects depending on the selection; most frequently, *Selection* is used to access the selected cells of a worksheet
ThisWorkbook	workbook whose code is currently being executed
Me	the object belonging to the module (for example, *Worksheet*, *UserForm*)

The Object Browser (References)

An inseparable assistant in working with objects, methods, and properties is the object browser. The object browser is a form that can be invoked via VIEW|OBJECT BROWSER or, more conveniently, with F2. This form has already been described in Chapter 3.

In the browser are to be found all (well, almost all) currently available objects, methods, and properties, including user-defined procedures. The entries in the object browser are ordered by libraries. The two most important are the VBA and Excel libraries.

The *VBA library* contains all instructions and functions that belong to the VBA programming language except for those that concern special features of Excel. Among other things, in the VBA library you will find commands for working with character strings, for managing files, and for working with dates and times. The VBA library is, unfortunately, incomplete. For instance, all the keywords for procedural programming are lacking. (This restriction is perhaps determined by the system; that is, it may be that this type of keyword cannot be integrated into the browser. It would, of course, be nice if the documentation gave some indication of this situation, but that, alas, is not the case.) Also, there are none of the normal functions that are easy to forget (such as the string function *InStr*).

The *Excel library* is a complete reference for all defined objects (about 150 of them), the associated properties and methods, and the predefined constants. The object browser also represents an important interface to the on-line help: After selecting a keyword, you can get help on that word with the "?" button.

Also contained in the object browser are libraries of the currently loaded workbooks and add-ins. By the library of a workbook is meant the directory of all modules and the procedures contained therein. (Constants defined within workbooks are not shown.)

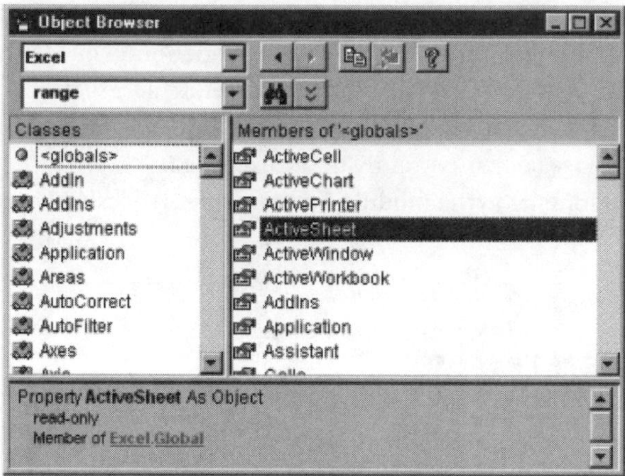

Figure 4.1. The Object Browser

Excel Object Libraries

With Excel are included the following object libraries (among others):

`StdOle2.tlb` basic functions for ActiveX automation (Windows system directory)

`Vbe6.dll` VBA object library (directory `Common Files\Microsoft Shared\VBA\VBA6\`)

`Excel9.olb` Excel object library (directory `Office2000\Office`)

`Mso9.dll` MS-Office object library with the objects common to all Office components (directory `Office2000\Office`)

`Fm20.dll` MS Forms library for creating “intelligent worksheets” (Windows system directory)

`Scrrun.dll` MS-Scripting runtime library with FSO objects for convenient access to data (Windows system directory)

`Msado15.dll` ADO 2.1 object library for database programming (directory `Common Files\System\Ado`)

Usually, the first four of the libraries listed above are active. The MS Forms library is automatically activated as soon as you add a form to an Excel file. The ADO library must be activated manually via TOOLS|REFERENCES if you wish to employ database functions in VBA code.

> **POINTER** *The VBA and Excel libraries are so extensive that their description has been distributed throughout the entire book. Thus most of the objects of the Scripting library are described in Chapter 5, those of the MS Forms library in Chapter 7, those of the Office library in Chapter 8, and those of the ADO library in Chapter 12.*

Packaged with Excel are a number of add-in files, in the directory `Office2000\Office\Library` and its subdirectories. Some of these files contain functions that can be used in VBA, such as `Analysis\Atpvbaen.xla`, `Solver\Solver.xla`, and `MSQuery\Xlquery.xla`. You will have to search out the particular file with TOOLS|REFERENCES|BROWSE. (That is, it is not sufficient to activate the appropriate add-in with the add-in manager, TOOLS|ADD-INS.) In the past, the use of these add-in libraries led to numerous problems, which occurred particularly when an application was given to another user.

Finally, the object model can be extended by means of external libraries that in and of themselves have nothing to do with Excel. In this way external programs—such as Word or Access—can be controlled from within Excel. More information on these control mechanisms can be found in Chapter14 under the heading ActiveX automation.

Providing References to Object Libraries

Before the functions, objects, methods, and properties in external object libraries can be used, a reference to them must be activated via TOOLS|REFERENCES.

If the name of the required object library is not yet displayed in the REFERENCES form, you can select and add the file using the BROWSE button. Only those files that have been registered (that is, a key has been inserted into the Windows Registration database) are shown automatically. The files that are considered active are those marked with a check. It is not sufficient that the file merely be shown in the REFERENCES form.

The information as to which references are active is stored separately for each workbook. Even if an object library has been activated in one workbook, this library is considered inactive in another workbook until it is activated there.

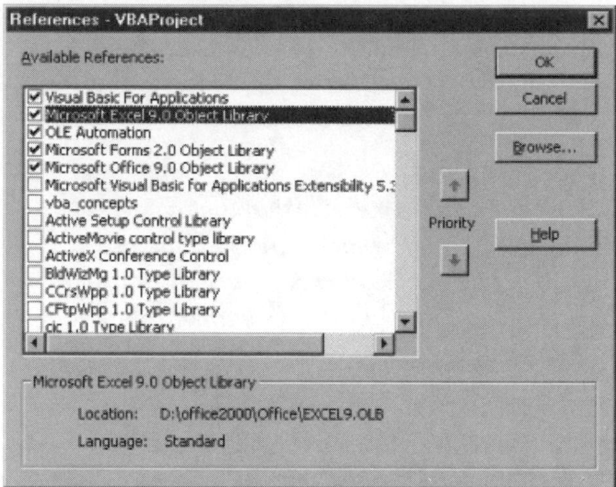

Figure 4.2. The References form

References to files that are no longer needed can be deleted simply by unchecking them. References to the Excel, Office, and VBA libraries are always needed and for that reason cannot be deactivated.

References to Other Workbooks

Just as you can set up references to object libraries, you can also set up references to other workbooks. For this purpose, in the REFERENCES form are listed the file names of all active object libraries. (The name of the currently active workbook is not listed, since this workbook does not require a reference to itself.)

Establishing a reference to another workbook has the advantage that you can use its public procedures and variables in the currently active workbook as well. (Public variables must be defined with *Public*. Procedures are automatically considered public if they have not been privatized with the keyword *Private*.)

References belong to the data of the currently active workbook and are saved with it. When the workbook is again opened, Excel is then in a position, since it has these references, to activate the referenced workbooks and libraries.

Accessing Objects Clarified with Keyword `With`

The examples given in previous sections have already shown that you often end up with an endless jumble of nested properties and methods, each of which provides the object for the next property or method. By the time you get to the object that you actually want to refer to, the input line is full.

With the keyword combination ***With...End With*** you can temporarily latch onto a particular object and then set properties or execute methods without having to list the entire reference to the object each time.

An example will make things clear. In the first variant the individual instructions are so long that they must be split over two lines. In the second example the object (namely, the first tool on the toolbar "new toolbar," is fixed by means of *With*. Note that within the keywords *With* and *End With* all instructions that relate to the fixed object must begin with a period.

```
' traditional
CommandBars("New toolbar").Controls("File").Controls(1). _
  Caption = "End"
CommandBars("New Toolbar").Controls("File").Controls(1). _
  OnAction = "Menu_Quit"
' with the keyword "With"
With CommandBars("New Toolbar").Controls("File").Controls(1)
  .Caption = "End"
  .OnAction = "Menu_Quit"
End With
```

With can also be nested. In the example below the first *With* is used to fix the toolbar, and the second *With* is used to fix first the first tool and then the second.

```
With Toolbars("New Toolbar")
  With .ToolbarButtons(1)
    .PasteFace
    .OnAction = "Button1_Click"
  End With
  With .ToolbarButtons(2)
    .PasteFace
    .OnAction = "Button2_Click"
  End With
End With
```

Within *With* constructs "normal" VBA instructions are also allowed, those that do not refer to the current object (and therefore do not begin with a period). In the following example new images are copied from the clipboard to all icons on the toolbar. Moreover, the macros *Buttoni_Click* are linked to the icons, where *i* is replaced by the current content of the loop variable.

```
Dim i
With Toolbars("New Toolbar")
  For i=1 To .Count
    With ToolbarButtons(i)
      .PasteFace
      .OnAction = "Button" & i & "_Click"
    End With
   Next i
End With
```

An alternative to *With* is a process involving object variables (see the next subsection) that also makes it possible to avoid complex referencing of objects.

Object Variables

Normally, numbers and character strings are stored in variables. However, variables can also refer to objects. The definition of object variables is not accomplished with the definition operator "=" but by means of the keyword ***Set.***

The following example demonstrates how one works with object variables. The variable *w* of object type *Window* is defined in *objvar1*. A reference to the active window is stored in this variable, and then the subprogram *objvar2* is called. There the title of the window of the object variable *x* is changed. The example shows that object variables can be passed as parameters to subprograms and functions.

```
' example file vba-concepts.xls, Module "Objects"
Sub objvar1()
  Dim w As Window
  Set w = Application.ActiveWindow
  objvar2 w
End Sub
Sub objvar2(w As Window)
  w.Caption = "new window title"
End Sub
```

Many objects can also be declared with *Dim x As **New Object***. In this case the corresponding object is created immediately. This syntax is normally possible only with object classes that are made available through external libraries (ActiveX server) or are defined by Excel class modules (see the following section).

Above all, object variables are used to make a more readable organization of program code. When you wish to access an object, you do not have to give an often endless chain of methods and properties every time, but you can refer to the object by means of an object variable (see the example below). This way of proceeding is more flexible than the use of *With* (see the previous section), since a number of object variables can be used in parallel. The possibility of passing object variables as parameters leads to a better modularization of program code.

```
' traditional
CommandBars("New Toolbar").Controls(1).CopyFace
CommandBars("New Toolbar"). _
  Controls(1).OnAction = "Button1_Click"
' with object variables
Dim cbc As CommandBarControl
Set cbc = CommandBars("New Toolbar").Controls(1)
cbc.CopyFace
cbc.OnAction = "Button1_Click"
```

Object variables differ from normal variables in that only a reference to the object is saved and not a copy. The object variable thus points to an object whose further management is the responsibility of Excel. The programmer has no possibility of creating *new* objects (except with methods that we have seen previously such as *Add*).

A number of object variables can point to the same object. A change in the object's properties effected by one variable thus affects all the object variables.

The reference to an object can be deleted by means of *Set var* = ***Nothing***. (There is no effect on the object itself!) Object variables can be defined as a particular object type with *Dim*, *Private*, or *Public* and are then explicitly limited to this object type (for example, *Dim w As Window*). Less restrictive is the definition as a general object variable (*Dim o As Object*), since then *o* can accept references to objects, but not normal variable contents (numbers, character strings). It also suffices to make a general declaration as a *Variant* variable (*Dim v*). The variable then automatically assumes the appropriate type. Sometimes, VBA reacts to definitions of the wrong type as though it were highly allergic to them (namely, with a crash). Thus it can be useful to give a general definition as an *Object* or *Variant* variable rather than as a concrete object type.

Object variables also appear implicitly in *For–Each* loops (previous section). The following two loops have the same effect, giving the names of all pages of the active workbook:

```
Sub objvar3()
  Dim s As Object, i As Long
  For Each s In Sheets
    Debug.Print s.Name
  Next s
  For i = 1 To Sheets.Count
    Set s = Sheets(i)
    Debug.Print s.Name
  Next i
End Sub
```

> **NOTE** *There is no* Sheet *object in the Excel library. The above enumeration of* Sheets *can refer equally well to objects of type* WorkSheet *and* Chart. *Thus in the example,* s *must be defined with the generally valid* Object.

With the operator ***Is*** it is possible to compare two object variables. The result is *True* if both variables refer to the same object.

With the function ***TypeName*** you can determine the type of an object variable. *TypeName* returns a character string, such as *"Window"* or *"Workbook"*.

```
Sub obtest()
  Dim a, b
  Set a = Sheets(1)
  Set b = Sheets(1)
  If a Is b Then Debug.Print "a and b refer to the same object"
  Debug.Print TypeName(a), TypeName(b)  ' returns "Worksheet" each time
  Debug.Print a.Name, b.Name            ' returns the sheet name
End Sub
```

Syntax Summary

Methods and Properties

result = object.property	read property
object. property = ...	change property
object.Method para1, para2	method without return value
erg = object.Method(para1, para2)	method with return value
obj.Method(para1, para2).Method	immediate further processing with another method

Accessing Active Objects

ActiveCell	active cell in a worksheet
ActiveChart	active chart
ActiveMenuBar	active (viewable) menu bar
ActivePane	active pane of a window
ActivePrinter	selected printer
ActiveSheet	active sheet in window/workbook/Excel
ActiveWorkbook	active workbook
SelectedSheets	selected sheets of a window
Selection	selected objects in sheet/window/workbook
ThisWorkbook	workbook whose code is currently being executed

Enumeration Methods and Objects

Objects	the plural refers to an enumeration; for example, *Axes, Sheets, Windows*
Objects(n)	refers to the *n*th object
Objects("name")	refers to the object named
Objects.Count	gives the number of objects
Objects.Add obj	adds a new object to the list
obj.Delete	deletes the object from the list

Accessing Objects via With

With object	fixes the object
.property = ...	the period refers to the fixed object
.methods para1, para2	
End With	

Object Variables

Dim var As objecttype	placeholder for objects
Dim var As New objecttyp	generate an object immediately
Set var = object	*var* refers to the given object
Set var = Nothing	deletes the reference (not the object)
name = TypeName(var)	determines the name of the object

Events

VBA is an event-oriented programming language. By this is meant that macros are automatically executed by Excel in reaction to certain events. When you click on a tool, say, or select a menu entry, Excel executes the corresponding procedure on its own. Events are thus triggered by the user via input from the mouse or keyboard. (In traditional programming languages you would be compelled, for example in an infinite loop, to wait continuously for the occurrence of an event, evaluate this event, and in response thereto call the appropriate procedure. This task is taken over by Excel by means of the concept of an event.) The following events can lead to user-defined procedures being called:

- The selection of a macro via TOOLS|MACROS.
- The selection of a custom menu item or tool to which a macro is linked (see Chapter 8).

- Clicking on a control (independent of whether these are located in a form or directly in a worksheet).
- The recalculation of a worksheet (when user-defined functions are used within it).
- Opening, saving, and closing a workbook; activating and deactivating a worksheet; exceeding a certain period of time; pressing a key; double clicking on a worksheet, etc.

> **POINTER** *Clicking on* Ctrl+Break *usually leads to a program interrupt. This event is not handled in VBA in the framework of event procedures, but rather is treated as an error. Chapter 6 contains a description of how a program interrupt can be responded to.*

Automatic Opening of Excel Files

All files located in the directory `Xlstart` are automatically opened when Excel is launched. In conjunction with an *Auto_Open* or *Workbook_Open* event procedure this can be used to carry out various settings when Excel is launched. A particular role within the `Xlstart` files is played by the "personal" workbook `Personal.xls`. This file is designed as the location for saving such items as macros, tools, and menu entries that are supposed to be always ready for use. Further information on the precise location of the `xlstart` directory as well as the individual configuration of Excel by files stored in that directory can be found in Chapter 5.

Event Procedures

Events in Excel 97/2000/...

Starting with Excel 97 explicit procedures have been defined for most objects, which are listed as such in the object browser and are indicated by a yellow lightning bolt. The name of the event procedure is predetermined, being composed of the object name and the event name together, such as *Worksheet_Activate*. When an analogously named procedure exists, it will be executed automatically by Excel. Therefore, it is no longer necessary to set *OnEventXxx* properties, as was necessary in Excel 5/7.

This concept can be most easily explained by an example. Open a new workbook, switch into the development environment, and open the module "This Workbook."

To have a procedure executed every time the Excel file is opened, first select in the first listbox the object *Workbook* and then in the second listbox the event *Open*. The development environment then automatically generates a code template consisting of *Sub* and *End-Sub* instructions. You now need only type in the desired code.

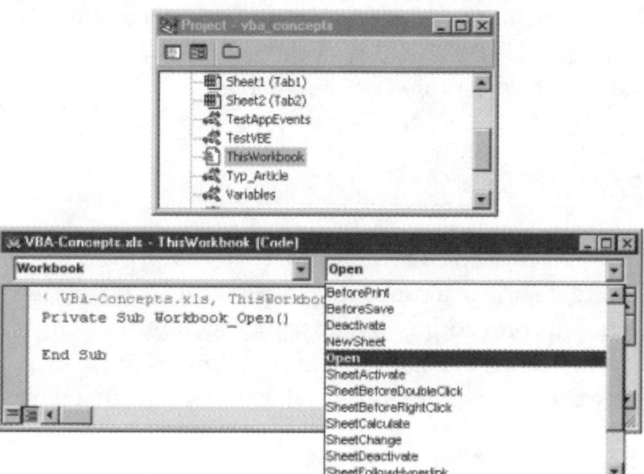

Figure 4.3. Selecting the Worksheet event procedure in the code window

The example given here shrinks all other visible Excel windows of other workbooks into icons.

```
' example file VBA-Concepts.xls, Module "This Workbook"
Private Sub Workbook_Open()
  Dim w As Window
  MsgBox "Executing the event procedure Workbook_Open."
  For Each w In Application.Windows
    If w.Parent.Name <> ActiveWorkbook.Name And w.Visible Then
      w.WindowState = xlMinimized
    End If
  Next
End Sub
```

The processing of events of worksheets and of the workbook is particularly easy, since in the development environment there is a class module with code templates for the event procedures assigned to each of these objects. Other objects as well can trigger events. Their reception, however, is somewhat more complicated, and this will be discussed further below.

> **CAUTION** *In normal modules* Application *is considered a default object, in that all methods and properties derived from it can be used without* Application *being explicitly named. In modules associated to Excel objects (such as "This Workbook," worksheets, chart sheets), on the other hand, the object on which the class is based is considered the default object, such as* Workbook *in the module "This Workbook" or* Worksheet(...) *in a module for a worksheet. For this reason you must give* Application *explicitly in class modules if you wish to use these properties or methods.*

Events in Excel 5/7

In Excel versions 5 and 7 the event concept was quite different: For an event to be triggered, you first had to link the name of a procedure to *OnEventXxx* properties or methods of various objects. This procedure was subsequently automatically called when the indicated event occurred. Let us look at an example: The instruction below results in the procedure *MacroXy* being called whenever the first worksheet is activated.

```
Worksheets(1).OnSheetActivate = "MacroXy"
```

The automatic invocation of the procedure is halted by linking an empty character string "" to the respective property:

```
Worksheets(1).OnSheetActivate = ""
```

The actual event procedure can be located in any module:

```
Public Sub MacroXy()
  MsgBox "Even procedure Excel 5/7"
End Sub
```

> **NOTE** *Beginning with Excel 97 most of the* OnEventXxx *methods and properties were replaced by new events. However, four keywords have remained unchanged:* OnKey, OnRepeat, OnTime, *and* OnUndo. *These four methods are described together with important Excel events in the next section.*

> **CAUTION** *For reasons of compatibility, all* OnEventXxx *procedures can still be used. Note, however, that since Excel 97 all* OnEventXxx *settings are stored in the Excel file and are available when it is opened again. In and of itself this is not a bad idea. The problem is that this behavior is incompatible with Excel 5/7. Many Excel 5/7 programs depend on all the* OnEventXxx *properties being empty at the time the file is loaded into memory. Yet that is no longer the case.*

Auto Procedures in Excel 5/7

Conceptually even older than event procedures are the so-called auto procedures: Whenever a procedure with the name ***Auto_Open*** exists in a given module of an Excel file, this procedure will be automatically executed when the file is opened. Analogously, there is an ***Auto_Close*** procedure, which is executed when the file is closed (that is, before Excel terminates execution, at the latest).

> **NOTE** *Since Excel 97 the auto procedures exist only for reasons of compatibility. The "correct" way of proceeding is instead of* Auto_Open *or* Auto _Close *to use the events* **Open** *and* **BeforeClose** *of the* Workbook *object (Excel object "This Workbook" in the project explorer).*

> **NOTE** *Auto procedures are not executed if the opening or closing of an Excel file is carried out by VBA code (that is, by the* Workbook *methods* Open *and* Close*). For the procedures to be executed anyhow, you must execute the method* RunAutoMacros *for the affected workbook.*

Auto Procedures in Excel-4 Macros

There was even the possibility in the old macro language to set up *Auto* macros: When a workbook is opened, Excel executes—even in the current version—all macros whose name begins with *Auto_Open*; for example, *Auto_Open*, *Auto_Open_Test*. Analogously, when the file is closed, activated, or deactivated, all macros are executed whose names begin with *Auto_Close*, *Auto_Activate*, or *Auto_Deactivate*.

Deactivating Event Procedures

The one serious disadvantage of the new way that events have been conceived since Excel 97 is that activating and deactivating events using program code is difficult. For example, if you wish temporarily to deactivate the call to a specific event procedure, you have to employ the following code:

```
' in the class module of a worksheet
Public activateEvents
Private Sub Worksheet_Activate()
  If activateEvents <> True Then Exit Sub
  MsgBox "Worksheet_Activate " & Me.Name
End Sub
```

Using the variable *activateEvents* one can control whether events are processed (*True*) or not (*False*). Note that to change *activateEvents* you must prefix it with the internal name of the worksheet, for example, *Table1.activateEvents=True.* (This name must not coincide with the name listed in the sheet tabs. The correct name is the one shown in the project window and that can be changed in the properties window.)

If you wish to deactivate all event procedures temporarily (and not simply one procedure as in the example above), you can set the property ***EnableEvents*** for the *Application* object to *False.* This can make sense in procedures, for example, whose VBA code instructions would normally trigger events.

Overview of Important Excel Events

About fifty events have been defined in the object model of Excel. Many events are even multiply defined. For example, the *Worksheet* object has an *Activate* event, while the *Workbook* object and the *Application* object each have a *SheetActivate* event. This dualism is intentional. For example, if you wish to activate every sheet of a workbook with an event procedure, you do not have to equip each *Worksheet* object with an *Activate* procedure. It suffices to supply a single *Workbook_SheetActivate* procedure, which then is called with each change of sheet. A reference to the corresponding sheet is passed to the procedure as a parameter. If instead of this you set up an event procedure for *SheetActivate* of the *Application* object (see the next section), then this procedure will actually be called for every sheet of *every* workbook.

The following description is limited to the most important events of the objects *Workbook* and *Worksheet,* which are particularly simple to execute in the development environment. Furthermore, the four still-supported *OnEventXxx* events will be treated here in accordance with the old event concept. The syntax summary at the end of this section lists all events for several important Excel objects.

Open and Close File (Events Open/BeforeClose*)*

After an Excel file has been loaded, the procedure *Workbook_Open* is executed if it exists. Analogously, when a workbook is closed (that is, when Excel is terminated), *Workbook_Close* is executed if this procedure in the module "This Workbook" contains code. These procedures constitute an alternative to the procedures *Auto_Open* and *Auto _Close*, which were described above.

Save/Print a File (Events BeforeSave/BeforePrint*)*

Before a file is saved, the event procedure *Workbook_BeforeSave* is executed. This makes it possible to update various sorts of information in the workbook immediately before saving, such as to copy the contents of variables into a worksheet. Two parameters are passed to the procedure: *SaveAsUI* indicates whether the form SAVE AS has been selected. *Cancel* makes it possible to interrupt the saving process (for example, to give the user the possibility of correcting errors in the workbook that may still exist).

The event procedure *Workbook_BeforePrint*, which is called whenever part of the workbook is printed, functions similarly. (Surprisingly, there is no separate event for printing a particular worksheet or chart. Also, no information as to which data are to be printed is passed to the *BeforePrint* procedure.)

Changing Sheets (Events Activate/Deactivate*)*

A change of sheets occurs when a user activates another sheet within a workbook. Possible reactions in the event procedure can be a validation control for input or an adaptation of the menu or toolbar to the newly displayed sheet.

Activate and *Deactivate* events can be set for each individual sheet. Furthermore, on the workbook level (*Workbook* object) the *Sheet[De]Activate* can be set if you do not wish to write a separate event procedure for each sheet.

If you do write event procedures for individual sheets as well as for the workbook as a whole, the sequence of procedure calls in the case of a change from worksheet 1 to worksheet 2 will look something like this:

EVENT PROCEDURE	OBJECT
Worksheet_Deactivate	worksheet 1
Workbook_SheetDeactivate	workbook, reference to worksheet 1 as parameter
Worksheet_Activate	worksheet 2
Workbook_SheetActivate	workbook 2, reference to worksheet 2 as parameter

You will be informed about the creation of a new workbook, and this will occur via the *Workbook_NewSheet* event procedure. For some mysterious reason there is no analogous event that is executed before a sheet is deleted.

Changing the Active Workbook (Events Activate/Deactivate*)*

The events *Activate* and *Deactivate* also make an appearance when instead of a sheet within a workbook, a switch is made into the window of another workbook. Otherwise, the functionality is the same as above.

Mouse Events (Events BeforeDoubleClick/BeforeRightClick*)*

The somewhat peculiar names of the two events of this subsection do not mean that the events clairvoyantly execute themselves as you reach for the mouse but before you have clicked. Even Microsoft has not advanced to this level of user friendliness. The *Before* refers, rather, to the fact that the event procedure (for sheets or charts) is executed before Excel reacts to the mouse click.

A *Range* object, which refers to the cell that has been clicked on, is sent as parameter (as in the case of worksheets). By a change in the *Cancel* parameter a possible reaction by Excel to a double click can be thwarted. Before a click of the right mouse button is processed, the entries of a pop-up menu can be changed under some circumstances. For the *Workbook* object the event names are *SheetBeforeDoubleClick* and *SheetBeforeRightClick*.

Changing a Cell (Event Change*)*

The *Change* event for worksheets and the *SheetCalculate* event for the workbook enter the picture *after* a cell is altered or cleared via some input. A *Range* object of the altered range of cells is passed as parameter. Only the change in the content of the cell, by means the formula bar or directly into the cell, is considered an event, but not a change in formatting settings. If a range of cells is shifted by means of the clipboard, then two *Change* events occur.

Changing the Selection (Event SelectionChange*)*

The *SelectionChange* event occurs when the user changes the set of selected cells. The newly selected region of cells is passed as parameter.

Worksheet Recalculation (Event Calculate*)*

The *Calculate* event for worksheets and the *SheetCalculate* event for the workbook make their appearance *after* a worksheet is recalculated (even if only a single cell is affected by the recalculation). It can be used, for example, to bring variables that depend on worksheet data up to date.

Window Events (Events WindowActivate, WindowDeactivate, WindowResize*)*

Surprisingly, the *Window* object has no associated events. Instead, window events are passed to the associated *Workbook* object. A change of window or an alteration in a window's size can be detected with the event procedures of these objects.

Mouse Click (Property OnAction*)*

OnAction was probably the most-used property in Excel 5/7 for linking event procedures to various objects (controls, menu commands, images). Beginning with Excel 97 this property is officially supported only for the *Shape* object and for various *CommandBar* objects. For all other objects it has been replaced by "genuine" events. For reasons of compatibility, however, *OnAction* remains available for these objects as well.

Keyboard Events (Method OnKey*)*

With the method ***OnKey*** a procedure can be defined that will be invoked when a particular key on the keyboard is pressed. Such methods can be established only for the *Application* object, for which reason a reaction to a key being pressed that depends on which workbook or which sheet is currently active is possible only with a certain amount of effort (namely, by the evaluation of the properties *ActiveWorkbook* or *ActiveSheet*).

OnKey is not a property, but a method. This distinction is necessary because no additional parameters (to the input of the key) can be passed to a property. For this reason the activation of the *OnKey* event procedure looks a bit different from what occurs with other events:

```
Application.OnKey "{F4}", "Macro" '<F4> calls the procedure Macro
Application.OnKey "{F4}", ""      'halt automatic calling
```

The syntax for specifying keys can be taken from the on-line help for the *OnKey* method. The result of the example above is that striking the key F4 leads to the procedure *Macro* being called. Please note that defining a procedure to respond to a particular key combination disables the automatic response of Excel to that combination. Normally, the effect of F4 is to repeat the last command. Now, instead of this, *Macro* will be called.

The redefining of keyboard input does not hold in all of Excel's aspects. The usual key conventions hold during the input of a formula or in a form. Thus, F4 can continue to be used in the formula bar for switching between absolute and relative addressing.

A further example of *OnKey* is to be found in the next chapter, where macros are defined for the key combinations Shift+Ctrl+Page Up and Shift+Ctrl+Page Down for jumping to the first, respectively last, sheet of a workbook.

Undo and Repeat (Methods OnUndo, OnRepeat*)*

With the two methods ***OnUndo*** and ***OnRepeat*** one can create procedures that Excel carries out when the user executes the command EDIT|UNDO or EDIT|REPEAT. These two methods are defined only for the *Application* object. The use of these methods is appropriate in macros that the user can execute by carrying out various actions.

Two parameters are passed to these methods: The first gives the text shown in the menu and should take the form "Undo: Xxx", respectively "Repeat: Xxx." The second parameter gives the procedure to be called when the menu command is executed:

```
Application.OnRepeat "Repeat: analyze data", "MacroXxx"
```

The menu texts and procedures provided by these two methods are valid only until the next command is executed (regardless of whether a normal Excel command or a further macro). Thus it is not necessary to clear the entries later by defining an empty string.

The methods must be executed in the last procedure of a chain of procedures. In the course of execution of a *Sub* procedure the settings of *OnUndo*, respectively *OnRepeat*, are cleared upon return to the calling procedure.

If the two methods are *not* used in a macro, Excel shows in the EDIT menu in the spaces provided for "undo " and "repeat" the entries CAN'T UNDO and REPEAT (MACRO NAME) and then executes the macro once more should the repeat option be chosen.

Time Events (Method OnTime*)*

The time event, too, is defined only for the *Application* object. By executing the ***OnTime*** method you can start a procedure at a particular time, say at 12 noon or ten minutes from now. At least two parameters are passed to this method: the time at which the procedure should be started and the name of the procedure. The following instruction starts the macro "Macro" thirty seconds after the execution of the instruction.

```
Application.OnTime Now + TimeValue("0:00:30"), "Macro"
```

With *OnTime* several procedures can be set for various times. VBA automatically manages the list of procedures to be executed. It is even allowed to set several procedures for the same time.

The execution of the procedures so designated can be postponed if Excel is occupied with other things. For example, a procedure cannot be called while, for example, a form is open, a macro is being executed, Excel is waiting for an MS Query query, or OLE data are being processed in Excel.

The *OnTime* method recognizes two optional parameters: In the third parameter can be given the latest time at which the procedure will be started. If this moment passes without Excel having had the chance to call the procedure, then the procedure will not be called at all.

By setting the fourth parameter to *False* a timed procedure can be canceled. For this the planned time as well as the name of the procedure must be given. If VBA does not find the procedure for the given time in the list of such procedures, then an error results.

```
Application.OnTime #8:30#, "Macro"            'set Macro for 8:30
Application.OnTime #8:30#, "Macro", , False   'cancel Macro
```

If you wish to arrange for the periodic calling of a procedure, you need to give a further call with *OnTime* within the procedure. Once it has been started, the following procedure changes the text of the status bar and displays there the current time:

```
Sub statusbar_time()
  Application.OnTime Now + Timevalue("0:00:10"), "statusbar_time"
  Application.Statusbar = Now
End Sub
```

We might mention that it is not particularly easy to stop this procedure once it has been started. Either you can change the name of the procedure (then at the time of the next procedure call, an error will occur with the message that the macro status bar cannot be found), or convert the *OnTime* instruction via " ' " into a comment (then it will end after the next procedure call). If you wish that Excel's normal info text appear in the status bar, you must execute the following instruction in the immediate window:

```
Application.Statusbar = False
```

> **NOTE** *Further information on dealing with the status bar can be found in Chapter 5.*

Receiving Events of Arbitrary Objects

For worksheets and workbooks there are code templates for event procedures available. The programming of such event procedures is therefore quite simple and intuitive.

However, there exist countless other objects that can trigger events (even objects from external libraries, which are activated via TOOLS|REFERENCES). The Excel objects *Application* (21 events) and *Chart* (13) are especially well endowed. In contrast to Visual Basic, where such objects with events can be declared anywhere, in Excel this is possible only in class modules. For this reason the reception of events is, alas, somewhat complicated.

The first step consists in creating a class module (an ordinary module will not suffice) and there defining a public variable of the object class whose events you wish to receive. For this you use the keyword ***WithEvents***. In the listbox of the module window you can thus select all known procedures for this object and add the desired event procedures.

```
' class module "eventclass"
Public WithEvents x As objname
Private Sub x_eventname(parameterlist)
  '… the event procedure
End Sub
```

> **POINTER** *Actually, class modules anticipate the next section of this chapter, which is concerned with programming new classes.*

So that events can actually be received, first an object of the new class and with it an object of the class with the events of interest must be created:

```
' in an arbitrary module
Dim obj As New event class 'obj is an object of the "event class"
Sub startevents()
  Set obj.x = [New] objname    'x is an object of the class "objname"
End Sub
```

After *startevents* has been executed, the event procedure in the class module is executed until *obj.x* or in general *obj* has been cleared (that is, *Set obj = Nothing*).

Example

A concrete example will clarify the situation: The *NewWorkbook* event of the Excel *Application* object is to be used to input some text into cell A1 of the first worksheet of every new workbook. (In practice, a similar procedure could be used to carry out various initialization procedures for every new workbook.)

The code consists of two parts: The event procedure is defined in the class module "ClassAppEvents." A reference to the new *Workbook* object is automatically passed to the procedure *NewWorkbook*.

```
' file VBA-Concepts.xls, class module "ClassAppEvents"
Public WithEvents app As Application
Private Sub app_NewWorkbook(ByVal wb As Excel.Workbook)
  wb.Worksheets(1).[A1] = "This text has been inserted by an " & _
                           " event procedure of the Application object "
End Sub
```

The second part of the test program is located in the module "TestAppEvents." In *InitializeApplicationEvents* the variable *app* of the *ClassAppEvents* object is linked to the *Application* object. If after the execution of this procedure you add a new workbook (FILE|NEW), then *app_NewWorkbook* will be executed for the first time. *StopApplicationEvents* again ends the automatic changing of new workbooks.

```
' File VBA-Concepts.xls, Module "TestAppEvents"
Option Explicit
Dim appObject As New ClassAppEvents
' starts the event procedures
Sub InitializeApplicationEvents()
  Set appObject.app = Application
End Sub
' ends the event procedures again
Sub StopApplicationEvents()
  Set appObject.app = Nothing
End Sub
```

Generating Event Procedures with Program Code

This example shows how a new worksheet is inserted into a workbook and then a *Worksheet_Activate* event procedure is generated for this worksheet. The program makes use of the VBE library, with which the VBA development environment can be controlled. The code is designed specifically for advanced programmers and assumes that you have experience in dealing with objects.

> **POINTER** *Starting with Excel 2000 you can program new classes with their own events (see the next section). The addition of event procedures in Excel files described here has nothing to do with that capability.*

The VBE Library

In this book we are not going to give a detailed description of this library. However, to understand this example it is necessary that you at least know the most important objects:

VBE	start object (access via *Application.VBE*)
└─*VBProject[s]*	projects (Excel files)
└─*VBComponent[s]*	modules, classes, forms of the file, etc.
├─*CodeModule*	code of the components
└─*Properties/Property*	access to an object's properties (properties window)

The most interesting methods for this example, *CreateEventProc* and *InsertLine*, are associated to the *CodeModule*. The problem is how to get to these objects: The *Name* property of an Excel *Workbook* object is, in fact, not identical to the *Name* property of the *VBComponent* object. Further, there are two names, one, which is displayed in Excel in the sheet tab, and a second, which is used in the VBA development environment and can be changed in the properties window. Here the collection of *Properties* helps further:

```
Dim vbc As VBComponent
Set vbc = …
Debug.Print vbc.Name                         ' returns the VBA name
Debug.Print vbc.Properties("Name").Value   ' returns the Excel name
```

With the *Properties* enumeration various object properties can be accessed that come not from the VBE library, but from the underlying object (in this case from a *Workbook* object of the Excel library).

Example

The program code begins with a test, namely, whether a worksheet with the name "new worksheet" already exists. This test is formulated somewhat unusually: The attempt is simply made to read the *Name* property of this *Workbook* object. If no error occurs, then the worksheet in fact exists. (You will learn about *On Error* in Chapter 6. An alternative way to proceed would be to use a loop to test all existing *Workbook* objects as to whether their name is identical to the constant *newname*.)

```
' file VBA-Concepts.xls, Module "TestVBE"
Sub AddWorksheetWithEvents()
  Const newname$ = "new worksheet"
  Dim ws As Worksheet
  Dim vbc As VBComponent
  Dim wsname$, linenr, dummy
  ' test whether a worksheet already exists
  On Error Resume Next
  dummy = ThisWorkbook.Worksheets(newname).Name
  If Err = 0 Then
    MsgBox "The sheet " & newname & " already exists. " & _
           "Please remove this sheet and " & _
           "try again."
    Exit Sub
  End If
  Err = 0
  On Error GoTo 0
```

If the worksheet does not yet exist, then it will be generated by means of *Worksheets.Add.* Then the worksheet will be given the name "new worksheet." The following loop runs through all *VBComponent* objects in the file in order to locate the module whose *Properties("Name")* property is "new worksheet." The VBA internal name of this object is buffered in the variable *wsname.* Here *ThisWorkbook .VBProject* is shorthand for *Application.VBE.VBProjects(ThisWorkbook.Name).*

```
  ' creates a new worksheet
Set ws = ThisWorkbook.Worksheets.Add
  ws.Name = newname
  ' find out the VBE internal name of this sheet
  For Each vbc In ThisWorkbook.VBProject.VBComponents
    If vbc.Properties("Name").Value = newname Then
      wsname = vbc.Name
        Exit For
    End If
  Next
```

Now that access to the worksheet's code has been made possible, the insertion of the event procedure proves to be thoroughly unproblematic: First, the procedure ***CreateEventProc*** is generated. This method returns the line number of the *Sub* instruction. One line further down, the instruction *MsgBox "event procedure"* is added with the method ***InsertLines***.

```
  ' add event procedure
  With ThisWorkbook.VBProject.VBComponents(wsname).CodeModule
    linenr = .CreateEventProc("Activate", "Worksheet")
    .InsertLines linenr + 1, "  MsgBox ""Event procedure"""
  End With
End Sub
```

If you switch into Excel after this macro has been executed and there click on any sheet and then on the new worksheet, the message "Event procedure" will be displayed. It works, by gosh!

Danger of Viruses with Auto Procedures and Events

CAUTION ***Every Excel file that you receive from a friend, acquaintance, or customer might contain a virus!*** *It doesn't matter by what medium the file is transferred, since Excel viruses (or, more generally, Office viruses and VBA viruses) are a part of the file, and can be passed on via diskette, CD-ROM, or even by e-mail. As is usual with viruses, a virus can be transmitted by the sender (perhaps without the individual's knowledge). Therefore, be cautious, even if you know the sender! This section provides some background information on viruses and protection against them.*

Event procedures and the *Auto_Open* and *Auto_Close* procedures are a useful construction. However, they are the key to virus programming in VBA. (The first Excel virus appeared in the summer of 1996, only a few months after I warned about the possibility in the first edition of this book.)

VBA offers all of the essentials for programming a virus:

- The possibility for program code to be executed automatically (*Auto_Open* and *Auto_Close*, as well as countless event procedures).
- The possibility to alter other Excel files (important for the "transplantation" of viruses).

- The possibility to insert new program code or to alter already existing code. (The VBIDE object library included with Excel 97 offers unsuspected new possibilities for virus programmers. Is this really what the inventors had in mind?)

- The possibility of doing damage to the computer in the most various ways. (For example, thanks to DLL support, nearly all of the operating system functions can be called. Thanks to ActiveX automation, every object library installed in the computer can be used. For example, under Windows 2000 the settings in the entire security system can be altered with a few lines of VBA code if the code is executed by a user with *Administrator* status! For example, you can access all e-mail messages and their addresses if the user employs the e-mail client Outlook.)

It would be pointless to go into all the details here. What is important is that you become aware that *any* Excel file can contain a virus, even if the file looks like a completely innocent worksheet. It goes without saying that this holds as well for templates and for add-ins (they are, after all, VBA programs).

Preventing Automatic Execution of Macros

In Tools|Macro|Security there are three options among which to choose:

- High Security: "Only signed macros from trusted sources will be allowed to run. Unsigned macros are automatically disabled." Since it is somewhat difficult to sign macros, this means that the execution of macros is almost entirely prevented. For VBA programmers this is unacceptable, but for many standard users this setting is completely reasonable. Of course, it is then impossible to use Excel applications or templates such as those described in this book.

- Medium Security (default setting): "You can choose whether or not to run potentially unsafe macros." When Excel files are loaded that contain VBA code, a warning appears. You can then enable or disable macros.

- Low Security: All macros will be executed without any warnings. For VBA programmers especially this is the most convenient setting, but it is also the most dangerous!

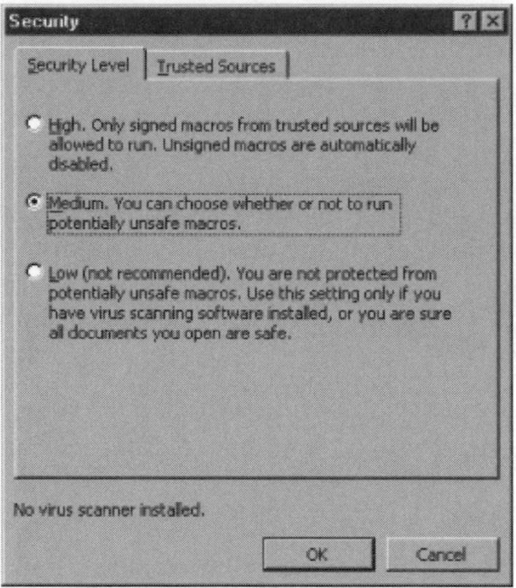

Figure 4.4. The three levels of virus security

NOTE *Even traditional Excel 4 macros (without VBA code) can contain viruses. For reasons that are difficult to comprehend it is impossible to prevent the execution of such macros. When Excel recognizes by means of active virus protection that the Excel file contains traditional macros, it gives notification of this fact. You can then decide whether you wish to open the file anyhow (and take your chances with the macros that might be executed).*

CAUTION *The level of virus protection is stored in the registry. Virus programmers can make use of this fact and change the setting (through another program, such as VBScript code in an e-mail message). Therefore, take a look every now and then at your virus protection setting!*

NOTE *When you pass an Excel file that contains VBA code to someone else, you should advise the recipient of that fact. Otherwise, the recipient may suspect that there may be a virus and deactivate code execution. Information on signing your VBA code can be found in Chapter 14.*

Viruses in Add-Ins and Templates

Templates are the basis on which Excel files are created (for details see Chapter 5 and Chapter 9). Add-ins offer the possibility to expand Excel's front end. Excel recognizes two types of add-ins for this purpose: traditional add-ins (`*.xla`) and COM add-ins (`*.dll`). Details and background information on add-ins are given in Chapter 14.

At this point it is important to note only that templates and both types of add-ins are further playgrounds for viruses. For these files, however, there is another method of protection. In the second tab of the virus protection dialog it is possible to set whether add-ins and templates are to be considered safe in general. Warning: The default setting is to consider them safe! A file installed as an automatic template or a registered COM add-in will be started automatically without question the next time Excel is started.

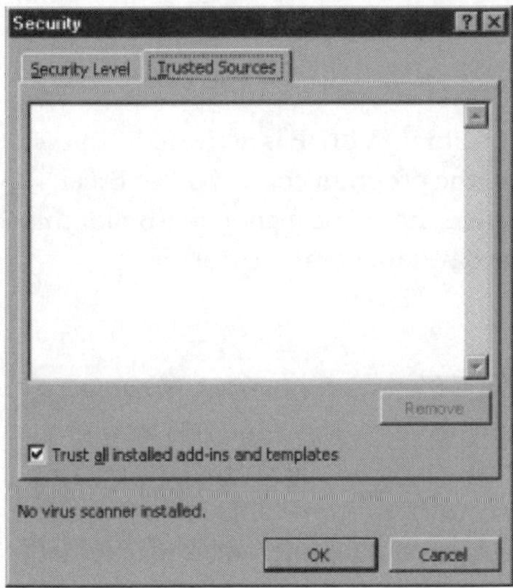

Figure 4.5. Add-ins are considered safe in the default setting

Since add-ins are an integral part of Excel, it is difficult to alter this setting: If you deactivate the option TRUST ALL INSTALLED ADD-INS AND TEMPLATES, then the security level that has been set holds for all add-ins and templates. If you have chosen medium security, then in the future, every time Excel is launched you will be bombarded by numerous virus protection tests (by every one of the countless included add-ins, for example). This leads to the inevitable result that you simply click on ENABLE MACROS, which makes virus protection into an absurdity. (Why Microsoft does not sign its own macros is yet another mystery.)

For this reason the option TRUST ALL INSTALLED ADD-INS AND TEMPLATES is usually activated, leaving add-ins and templates an open door for virus programmers. (Add-ins and template files are more unwieldy than normal Excel files for virus programmers, because they represent a danger only if they are correctly installed. But this hurdle is easily overcome.)

Discovering Viruses on Your Own

If an Excel file appears suspicious to you, then load the file with virus protection activated. Then look at the following code:

- Auto procedures. (Use the command EDIT|FIND and extend the search domain to the entire current project.)
- All event procedures. (Potentially dangerous code can be hidden in an event procedure, which would be called, for example, on saving the file or changing sheets.)
- Test with TOOLS|REFERENCES whether the library VBIDE is activated. This library is the key to the manipulation of the program code of other Excel files. If this library is activated, then there should be a good reason for this, one that has been documented by the developer of the Excel file.

Excel 4 Auto Macros

Even the traditional Excel macro language (up to version 4) had various *Auto* macros, which for reasons of compatibility are executed, right up to the current version. These *Auto* macros are launched by means of *Name* objects whose name begins with "Auto_Open." *Name* objects can also contain references to external files (for example, to add-in files). Furthermore, the *Visible* property of *Name* objects can be set to *False.* If you are suspicious that a virus may be present and can find no *Auto_Open* procedure, then you should have a look at all *Name* objects (for all worksheets as well as for the *Workbook* object). In the immediate window the two instructions look like the following:

```
For Each s In Worksheets: For Each n In s.Names: _
    ?n.Name: Next: Next
For Each n In ActiveWorkbook.Names: ?n.Name: Next
```

Syntax Summary

Receiving Events for Arbitrary Objects

Public WithEvents x As objname	in the class module "eventclass"
Private Sub x_eventname(param)	
'... the event procedure	
End Sub	

Dim obj As New eventclass	in an arbitrary module
Sub startevents	
Set obj.x = [New] objname	from now on events can be received
End Sub	

Auto Procedures

Sub Auto_Open() ... End Sub	launched when the file is opened
Sub Auto_Close() ... End Sub	launched when the file is closed
Sub Auto_Add() ... End Sub	launched when the add-in is entered into the list of the add-in manager (Chapter 14)
Sub Auto_Remove() ... End Sub	launched when the add-in list is removed

Application Events

NewWorkbook	a new workbook is added
SheetActivate	sheet change
SheetBeforeDoubleClick	double click
SheetBeforeRightClick	right mouse button click
SheetCalculate	worksheet was recalculated
SheetChange	cells of the worksheet were changed (content)
SheetDeactivate	sheet change
SheetSelectionChange	selection change
WindowActivate	window change
WindowDeactivate	window change
WindowResize	window resize
WorkbookActivate	change of active workbook
WorkbookAddinInstall	a workbook was installed as an add-in
WorkbookAddinUninstall	a workbook was deinstalled as an add-in
WorkbookBeforeClose	a workbook is about to be closed
WorkbookBeforePrint	a workbook is about to be printed
WorkbookBeforeSave	a workbook is about to be saved
WorkbookDeactivate	change of active workbook
WorkbookNewSheet	new sheet added to the workbook
WorkbookOpen	the workbook was just opened

Workbook *Events*

Activate	the workbook was activated (change of window)
AddinUninstall	the workbook was installed as an add-in
BeforeClose	the workbook is about to be closed
BeforePrint	the workbook is about to be printed
BeforeSave	the workbook is about to be saved
Deactivate	the workbook was activated (change of window)
NewSheet	a new sheet was added
Open	the workbook was just opened
SheetActivate	change of sheet
SheetBeforeDoubleClick	double click in a sheet
SheetBeforeRightClick	right mouse button click in a sheet
SheetCalculate	contents of a sheet were recalculated
SheetChange	input or change to a sheet
SheetDeactivate	sheet change
SheetSelectionChange	change of selection
WindowActivate	change of window
WindowDeactivate	change of window
WindowResize	window resized

Worksheet *Events*

Activate	change of sheet
BeforeDoubleClick	double click
BeforeRightClick	click with the right mouse button
Calculate	contents of sheet were recalculated
Change	input or change to a cell
Deactivate	sheet change
SelectionChange	change of selection

Chart *Events*

Activate	change of sheet (or chart)
BeforeDoubleClick	double click
BeforeRightClick	click with right mouse button
Calculate	chart was redrawn based on changed data
Deactivate	change of sheet (or chart)
DragOver	range of cells dragged over chart (but not yet released)
DragPlot	range of cells was released
MouseDown	mouse button was pressed
MouseMove	mouse was moved
MouseUp	mouse button released

Resize	chart size was altered
Select	chart was selected
SeriesChange	change in selected data series

Events in Excel 5/7

OnAction " macro "	calls the procedure *macro* when the object is clicked
OnKey "key", " macro "	after the pressing of a key
OnUndo "menu text", " macro"	after INPUT|UNDO
OnRepeat " menu text", " macro"	after INPUT|REPEAT
OnTime time, " macro "	at the given time
OnTime time, " macro ", end time	as above, but no later than end time
OnTime time, " macro ", , False	clear previously mentioned macro

Conversion Excel 5/7 → Excel 97, 2000 etc.

OnAction	*Click, Change*, etc.
OnCalculate	*Calculate, SheetCalculate*
OnData	*Change, SheetChange*
OnDoubleClick	*DoubleClick, BeforeDoubleClick, SheetBeforeDoubleClick*
OnEntry	*Change, SheetChange*
OnSheetActivate	*Activate, SheetActivate*
OnSheetDeactivate	*Deactivate, SheetDeactivate*
OnWindow	*Activate, WindowActivate*

Programming Your Own Classes

Up to this point we have described a number of different ways in which Excel objects or objects from external libraries can be used. The mechanisms implemented for this have been relatively stable starting with Excel 5.

New since Excel 97 is the possibility of programming one's own classes. (Classes are the templates for new objects.) Excel 2000 was again enlarged in this respect: Now custom classes can also be derived (*Implements*) and equipped with custom events.

The key to custom classes are the so-called class modules, which in the VBA development environment form their own category (in addition to normal modules and the modules associated to Excel objects). Visually, class modules look just like normal modules, that is, there is nothing to see but a code window. The difference is that the procedures defined in a class module can be used only as properties and methods of the new class. (The name of the class module is simultaneously the name of the class, and thus the correct setting in the properties window is far more important than in the case of normal modules.)

NOTE *The programming of custom classes can be very helpful in large projects to achieve clearer (more object-oriented) code. Furthermore, it represents an opportunity to transmit to others packaged class libraries as an add-in. However, independent of the application, class programming is a rather advanced form of Excel programming. This section gives a first overview. However, it assumes that you are already familiar with the fundamentals and major concepts of object-oriented programming.*

Why Class Modules?

Let us assume that you would like to extend Excel by providing a package of statistical functions: One way to do this is simply to offer a collection of functions that contain the required algorithms. This was already possible in all previous versions of Excel. However, this way of proceeding made it impossible to proceed according to the object-oriented model in a way that also includes the management of statistical data.

Thanks to class modules you can define new objects *XYPoints* and *XYPoint*. *XYPoint* serves for the storing of two-dimensional data points, while *XYPoints* manages an entire group of such objects and makes possible, thanks to various methods and properties, the determination of statistical quantities.

To the user, these two classes might look something like the following:

```
' VBA-Concepts.xls, Module "XYTest"
Sub TestXYStatistics()
  Dim xypts As New XYPoints
  xypts.Add 3, 4
  xypts.Add 7, 2
  xypts.Add 6, 5
  MsgBox xypts.Count & " points have been saved." & _
    "The mean value of the X coordinates is " & _
    xypts.XMean
  Set xypts = Nothing
End Sub
```

The user generates a new object of type *XYPoints* and adds three data points to this object with the method *Add*. Then the number of stored points and their X values are determined via the properties *Count* and *XMean*.

> **NOTE** *As already mentioned, for class modules there is yet another application: You can receive events of external objects. The mechanism assumes that you previously declared an object variable with the keyword* WithEvents. *An example of this can be found in the previous section.*

Class Versus Object

Perhaps the most difficult point in understanding class modules is the difference between classes and objects. A class contains the rules (methods, properties) as well as variables for storing data. An object is an instance of this class. The class is, so to speak, a template for objects. Of course, a number of objects of the same class can be used, whose contents are then independent of one another (although the methods and properties use the same code).

```
Dim a As New XYPoints
Dim b As New XYPoints
```

In the above example *a* and *b* are two object variables that refer to two objects of the class *XYPoints*. The two objects are generated immediately on account of the *New* keyword. The following example is somewhat different:

```
Dim a As New XYPoints
Dim b As XYPoints
Set b = a
```

Here there is only one object, but two variables that refer to it. Any change in *a* has the same effect on *b*.

Custom Methods, Properties, and Events

In defining a new class, in the development environment you execute INSERT|CLASS MODULE. With F4 you now open the properties window and give the new class a name. Then you can equip this class with event procedures and methods. Before we briefly explain these steps, here is some information about what you can do with class modules.

Equipping Classes with Methods

Defining a method for an object class is rather simple: Every procedure that is declared *Public* is considered a method. (Procedures declared as *Private* can be used only within the class module, just as with normal modules.)

You will detect a difference between public procedures in a module and a method in a class module only when they are called: While in normal modules the call is implemented simply by the procedure name, with methods an object variable must be prefixed:

```
Dim a As New XYPoints
Debug.Print a.Count
```

Equipping Classes with Properties

Property procedures are a syntactical variant of normal procedures. In this case we are dealing with procedures that when called behave formally like properties. With property procedures you can define and manage quasi-properties of a module.

> **CAUTION** *To forestall possible misunderstanding we state the following: With property procedures you can neither give new properties to defined Excel objects, nor change properties that already exist. The newly defined properties refer exclusively to a class module. (Theoretically, property procedures are also permitted in normal modules, but there they make no sense.) Moreover, property procedures must not be confused with event procedures, which are described in the next section.*

The most significant difference between normal procedures and property procedures is that precisely two procedures of the same name must be written. One of them is introduced with ***Property Get*** and used to read a property, while the other is introduced by ***Property Let*** and used to link new data to a property.

```
' in the class module
Private mydata
Property Get MyProperty()              ' read property
  MyProperty = mydata
End Property
Property Let MyProperty(newdata)       ' change property
  mydata = newdata
End Property
```

The example above also shows how you save data in class modules, namely, via the declaration of local variables. The access to these variables should occur exclusively through properties or methods. (Globally declared variables behave similarly to properties, but they permit no security mechanism.)

If a property is going to be able to cope with objects, instead of *Property Let*, the related property procedure ***Property Set*** must be defined. Further, for reading the property, *Property Get* is used, though the code must be altered (definition of the return value with *Set*).

```
' in the class module
Dim mydata As ObjectXY
Property Get MyProperty() As ObjectXY        ' read property
  Set MyProperty = mydata
End Property
Property Set MyProperty(newdata As ObjectXY) ' edit property
  Set mydata = newdata
End Property
```

Equipping Classes with Events (New in Excel 2000)

Events are defined similarly to variables in the declaration part of the class with ***Event***. Here the parameters of the event must also be given.

```
' in the class module
Public Event MyEvent(ByVal para As Integer)
```

There are two restrictions in declaring the event procedure: The event procedure is not allowed to be a function (no return value). If you wish to transmit information from the event procedure back to the calling class, you can declare separate parameters with *ByRef* as return parameters. Furthermore, the parameter list may contain neither optional parameters nor a parameter list.

Finally, you can trigger this procedure anywhere in the code of the class with the command ***RaiseEvent.***

```
' likewise in the class module
Public  Sub MyMethod(x, y)
  If x<y Then RaiseEvent MyEvent(57)
  ...
End Sub
```

If the user of the class schedules a *MyEvent* event procedure in the associated code (see below), it is called by the *RaiseEvent* command; otherwise, nothing happens at all. (Unfortunately, the receipt of events in Excel is possible only in class modules; see the previous section.)

The Keyword `Me`

Within the code of a class module you can access the current object with the keyword ***Me***. In custom class modules this is seldom necessary. On the other hand, this keyword is particularly useful in preexisting class modules—for worksheets, for example. For example, in the event procedure *Worksheet_Activate*, which is called whenever the indicated worksheet is activated, you can access the *Worksheet* object of this sheet with *Me*.

`Initialize` *and* `Terminate` *Procedures*

The procedures ***Class_Initialize*** and ***Class_Terminate*** can be defined within class modules. These procedures are automatically executed when an object of the class is generated, respectively when it is later deleted. These procedures can be used only for initialization and cleaning-up tasks.

Class Hierarchies with `Implements` *(New in Excel 2000)*

Often, one would like to define an entire group of associated classes, for example, a superclass *document* and classes *book* and *magazine* derived from it. Unfortunately, VBA does not recognize genuine inheritance, which would make such definitions easier. Instead, VBA supports the so-called polymorphism mechanism with the keyword ***Implements***. With it the use of such superclasses is, in fact, syntactically possible, but the resulting code is so confusing that there are few recognizable advantages for the programmer. (After all, inheritance is supposed to save time and avoid redundancy!) The application of *Implements* is demonstrated in the previous section with an example.

The `Instancing` *Property (New in Excel 2000)*

In the properties window, in addition to the name, a further property is listed, namely, *Instancing*. The default setting is *Private*. This means that the class can be used only within the active Excel file and not in other Excel files (even if there is a reference to it).

If you set *Instancing* to *PublicNonCreatable*, then the class will be public. As soon as a reference to the file has been established, the class becomes visible in the object browser. However, this is still not sufficient to generate an object of this class. In other words, even when you declare a class to be *PublicNonCreatable* and create a reference in another Excel file, the following instructions are not permissible:

```
' attempt to generate in project B an object that is
' declared in the Excel file A
Dim x As New myClass                        ' not allowed
Set x = New myClass                         ' not allowed
Set x = CreateObject("myProject.myClass")   ' not allowed
```

You are probably wondering now (as did your author at the outset) how you can possibly use objects from project *A* in another Excel project *B*. The solution is simple: You declare a public function that returns the desired object.

```
' in project A, where myClass is defined
Public Function newMyClass() As myClass
  Set newMyClass = New myClass
End Function
```

In project *B* the new function *newMyClass* can now be placed:

```
' in project B, where myClass is to be used
Dim x As myClass
Set x = newMyClass()
```

Collection *Object*

The ***Collection*** object is particularly well suited for class programming. However, it can be used only in normal modules and is often a convenient alternative to fields. It makes possible the definition of custom lists (enumeration objects). You can thus use the same mechanism that is so often used in the Excel library for listing objects (*Workbooks, Windows*, etc.).

It is very easy to use the *Collection* object. You must generate a new object of type *Collection* using *Dim New*. Then you can add, with the *Add* method, variables, fields, object references, and even further *Collection* objects to the list. In contrast to fields, elements of a *Collection* can be of differing types.

As a second parameter you must give a character string to be used as a key to accessing the object. This string must be unique, and so may not coincide with an already existing string. As with variables, there is no distinction between uppercase and lowercase letters for keys.

```
Dim c As New Collection
c.Add entry, "key"
```

Objects are accessed just as with all listings: by giving an index value (between 1 and *c.Count*) or by giving the character string that was used with *Add* as a key. With the property *Count* you can determine how many elements the listing contains. With *Remove* you can again remove individual objects.

```
Dim c As New Collection
c.Add "a character string", "abc"
c.Add 123123, "def"
Debug.Print c.Count              ' returns 2
Debug.Print c(1)                 ' as above (Item is the default method)
Debug.Print c("def")             ' returns 123123
```

In the above example "abc" and "def" are the keys with which the elements can be accessed. If you use an already employed string as a key for a new element, then you will receive error 457: "This key is already associated with an element of this collection." As expected, the elements of a collection can be addressed in a *For–Each* loop. Then *element* has the type of the current element. If you save data of various types in a *Collection*, then you must establish the type with *TypeName* and provide a corresponding case distinction.

```
Dim element As Object
For Each element In c
  ...
Next
```

The *Dictionary* object is a competitive alternative to the *Collection* object. It makes possible a subsequent alteration of existing entries and makes some additional methods available. (Note, however, that even with identically named methods of *Collection* and *Dictionary* there is sometimes a different ordering of the parameters. You can thus not automatically convert existing code from *Collection* to *Dictionary*.)

> **NOTE** *The* Dictionary *Object is not defined in the VBA library, but in the* Scripting *library. In order to use* Dictionary *you must activate the library* Microsoft Scripting Runtime *with* TOOLS|REFERENCES.

Example for a Class Module

This example consists of the two class modules *XYPoint* and *XYPoints* of the statistical library mentioned above. The class *XYPoint* proves that a class can be defined without creating a large amount of code. The two global variables *x* and *y* represent the only data elements of the class (a two-dimensional point). Access is accomplished directly (without the detour via property procedures) by means of *objectname.x* and *objectname.y*.

```
' File VBA-Concepts.xls, Class "XYPoint"
Public x As Double, y As Double
```

There is more interesting code to be found in the enumeration class *XYPoints*, which serves both for managing a number of *XYPoint* objects and for their statistical evaluation. The management of data is accomplished by means of the local variable *points*, which refers to a *Collection* object that is generated automatically for every new *XYPoints* object.

The *Add* method makes possible the addition of a new point to the list. For this purpose an *XYPoint* object is generated and *x* and *y* stored within it. Then this object is added to the *Collection points*. The method returns the new *XYPoint* object.

The implementation of the *Count* property is extremely simple: It must simply be passed back to the like-named property of the *Collection* object *points*. The property procedure is defined to be read-only. It would make no sense to change the *Count* property.

In the property procedure *XMean* (also for read-only access) the mean value of all *x* values of all stored *XYPoint* objects is calculated and returned.

```
' file vba-concepts.xls, Class "XYPoints"
Private points As New Collection
Public Function Add(x, y) As XYPoint
  Dim xyp As New XYPoint
  xyp.x = x
  xyp.y = y
  points.Add xyp
  Set Add = xyp
End Function
Property Get Count()
  Count = points.Count
End Property
Property Get XMean()
  Dim p, xm
  If points.Count = 0 Then XMean = 0: Exit Property
  For Each p In points
    xm = xm + p.x
  Next
  xm = xm / points.Count
  XMean = xm
End Property
```

Example for Derived Classes (Implements)

The purpose of this example is first to define a superclass *Document* and then two classes derived from it, *Book* and *Magazine.* Since the example is relatively complicated, it has been included in its own example file (`Implements.xls`). To try out the code, in the development environment launch the procedure *Test_Classes* in the module *TestClasses.* As a result, four lines are output in the immediate window:

```
Title: Linux
Publishing year: 1/1/1999
Title: Linux Magazine 1/2000
Publishing year: 1/1/2000
```

Application of the Object Classes

Before the code for these classes can be explained, we have a few words to say about the application of these classes. In the following lines two objects of type *Book* and *Magazine* are initialized. The only thing that is really interesting is, in fact, the call from *Print_Info.* To this procedure, whose only parameter is declared as *Document,* are passed a *Book* object the first time and a *Magazine* object the second. That is possible syntactically only because both *Book* and *Magazine* are based on the same superclass *Document.*

```
' example file Implements.xls, Module "TestClasses"
Dim mybook As Book
Dim mymagazine As Magazine
Private Sub Test_Classes()  ' Execute this procedure with F5!
  Init_Data
  Show_Data
End Sub
Private Sub Init_Data()
  Set mybook = New Book
  mybook.Title = "Linux"
  mybook.PublishingYear = #1/1/1999#
  mybook.Author = "Kofler, Michael"
  Set mymagazine = New Magazine
  mymagazine.Title = "Linux Magazine 1/2000"
  mymagazine.PublishingYear = #1/1/2000#
End Sub
Private Sub Show_Data()
  Print_Info mybook
  Print_Info mymagazine
```

```
End Sub
Private Sub Print_Info(x As Document)
  Debug.Print "Title: " & x.Title
  Debug.Print "Publishing year: " & x.PublishingYear
End Sub
```

The Superclass Document

There is nothing special about the class module *Document.* Within it are defined the two properties *PublishingYear* and *Title* as well as the method *ShowInfo.*

```
' example file Implements.xls, Class Module "Document"
' two properties: Title, PublishingYear
' one method: ShowInfo
Private docYear As Date
Private docTitle As String
Public Property Get PublishingYear() As Date
  PublishingYear = docYear
End Property
Public Property Let PublishingYear(ByVal date As Date)
  docYear = date
End Property
Public Property Get Title() As String
  Title = docTitle
End Property
Public Property Let Title(ByVal title As String)
  docTitle = title
End Property
Public Sub ShowInfo()
  MsgBox "Title: " & docTitle & ", year of publication: " & docYear
End Sub
```

The Derived Class Book

With the line *Implements Book* the class *Book* is derived from *Document.* This means that all the methods and properties of *Document* must be defined in *Book* in exactly the same way.

In order to use already existing code from *Document* we will need to do a bit of juggling. First of all, within the *Book* class an object of type *Document* must be generated. For this the event procedures *Class_Initialize* and *Class _Terminate* will be employed.

```
' example file Implements.xls, class module Book
' three properties:  Title (of Document)
'                    PublishingYear (of Document)
'                    Author (new)
' one method:        ShowInfo (of Document)
Implements Document
Private mydoc As Document
Private bookAuthor As String
Private Sub Class_Initialize()
  Set mydoc = New Document
End Sub
Private Sub Class_Terminate()
  Set mydoc = Nothing
End Sub
```

Second, procedures for all events and methods of *Document* must be newly implemented. Here, however, you may make use of the events and methods of the *mydoc* object. Note that the names of the procedures are composed of the superclass (that is, *Document*) and the name of the property or method.

```
' Code for the properties of Document
' (relies on the Document properties)
Private Property Get Document_PublishingYear() As Date
  Document_PublishingYear = mydoc.PublishingYear
End Property
Private Property Let Document_PublishingYear(ByVal date As Date)
  mydoc.PublishingYear = date
End Property
Private Property Get Document_Title() As String
  Document_Title = mydoc.Title
End Property
Private Property Let Document_Title(ByVal title As String)
  mydoc.Title = title
End Property
Private Sub Document_ShowInfo()
  mydoc.ShowInfo
End Sub
```

Third (and this is hardly believable!), you must now make the *Document* properties available to the *Book* object as well. (The second step had only the function of being able to use the *Document* code further internally. Therefore, the procedures were declared as *Private*.)

```
' Code, to make the Document properties available to
' the book object as well
Public Property Get Title() As String
  Title = Document_Title
End Property
Public Property Let Title(ByVal title As String)
  Document_Title = title
End Property
Public Property Get PublishingYear() As Date
  PublishingYear = Document_PublishingYear
End Property
Public Property Let PublishingYear(ByVal date As Date)
  Document_PublishingYear = date
End Property
Public Sub ShowInfo()
  Document_ShowInfo
End Sub
```

This means the following: For each property from a superclass that you wish to use in the future unchanged, you need four (!) procedures, while for each method you still need only two.

At long last, the *Book* class should be extended by the additional property *Author*.

```
' code for the additional property
' (specific to the Book object)
Property Get Author() As String
  Author = bookAuthor
End Property
Property Let Author(author As String)
  bookAuthor = author
End Property
```

The Derived Class Magazine

The class *Magazine* as well is derived from *Document*, and this class, too, was extended with an additional property, called *Articles*. In contrast to *Book*, the properties *Title* and *PublishingYear* were newly implemented, in order to demonstrate a second method of programming derived classes. For this reason, no *mydoc* object is needed (as in *Book*).

```
' example file Implements.xls, Class Module "Book"
' three properties:
'   Title          (Definition as in Document, but newly implemented)
'   PublishingYear (Definition as in Document, but newly implemented)
'   Articles       (new)
' one method:
'   ShowInfo       (Definition as in Document, but newly implemented)
Option Explicit
Implements Document
Private magazineYear As Date
Private magazineTitle As String
Private magazineArticles As String
' code for the properties and methods from Document
' (newly implemented for this class)
Private Property Get Document_PublishingYear() As Date
  Document_PublishingYear = magazineYear
End Property
Private Property Let Document_PublishingYear(ByVal date As Date)
  magazineYear = date
End Property
Private Property Get Document_Title() As String
  Document_Title = magazineTitle
End Property
Private Property Let Document_Title(ByVal title As String)
  magazineTitle = title
End Property
Private Sub Document_ShowInfo()
  MsgBox "Title: " & magazineTitle & _
         ", Year of publication: " & magazineYear & _
         ", Article: " & magazineArticles
End Sub
' Code to make document properties
' available to Magazine objects
Public Property Get Title() As String
  Title = Document_Title
End Property
Public Property Let Title(ByVal title As String)
  Document_Title = title
End Property
Public Property Get PublishingYear() As Date
  PublishingYear = Document_PublishingYear
End Property
Public Property Let PublishingYear(ByVal date As Date)
  Document_PublishingYear = date
```

```
End Property
Public Sub ShowInfo()
  Document_ShowInfo
End Sub
' Code for the additional properties
' (specific to the Magazine object)
Property Get Articles() As String
  Articles = magazineArticles
End Property
Property Let Articles(content As String)
  magazineArticles = content
End Property
```

All in all, the programming of derived classes is rather tedious. This mechanism is really interesting only to professional programmers who wish to create a new class library for Excel (in the form of an add-in).

Syntax Summary

Keyword Me

Me	refers to the current instance of the object

Events Within the Class

Class_Initialize	object of the class is created
Class_Terminate	object of the class is deleted

Programming of Methods

Public Sub/Function myMethod(para)	Method without/with return value
[myMethod = ...]	return value (for functions)
End Sub/Function	

Programming of Property Procedures for Data (Numbers/Character Strings)

Property Get myproperty()	read property
myproperty = ...	
End Property	
Property Let myproperty(data)	edit property
... = data	
End Property	

Programming of Property Procedures for Objects

Property Get myproperty() As Object *Set myproperty = …* *End Property*	read property
Property Set myproperty(obj As Object) *Set … = obj* *End Property*	edit property

Declaring and Triggering Events

Public Event myevent(paralist)	declaration in the class module
RaiseEvent myevent	trigger event

Use of Object Classes (Code Outside of the Class Module)

Dim x As New classname	create object *x* of the class *classname*
x.variable	access global variables of this object
x.property	use property of this object
x.Method	use method of this object
Set x = Nothing	delete object

Collection Object

Dim c As New Collection	*c* contains a new collection
c.Count	returns the number of elements
c.Add data, "index"	add an element
c(n) or *c("index")* or	various syntax variants for access
c!index or *c![index]*	to an element
c.Remove(n) or *("index")*	delete element
Set c = Nothing	delete collection

Operators in VBA

The operators in VBA include symbols such as +, -, *, /, =, >, < as well as keywords such as *And, Or, Not.* Normally, operators do not require a lengthy explanation. This section gives a brief overview as to which operators are available and some of their special characteristics.

Arithmetic operators are used for carrying out calculations. Whereas +, -, *, and / need no further explanation, the operators \ and *Mod* are more interesting: \ carries out whole-number division. The two arguments are first rounded to whole numbers if they are not whole numbers already. Thus 5\2 yields the same result as 5.5\1.5, namely, 2. The operator ***Mod*** likewise carries out whole-number division in the same way that \ does. However, it returns the remainder of the division. Thus, *21 Mod 5* returns the remainder 1.

There are two operators available for the concatenation of character strings: + can deal only with character strings, joining, say, *"ab"+"cd"* to yield *"abcd"*. The operator & can do business with numbers as well, turning them into strings. Thus *"12" & "3"* returns *"123"*.

Among the comparison operators, *Is* and *Like* stand out. The operator ***Is*** serves to compare two object variables, and it should return *True* if both variables refer to the same object. In the current version of Excel, however, *Is* can be used only for a comparison with the keyword *Nothing* (that is, *If x Is Nothing Then …*).

The keyword ***Like*** makes possible the comparison of patterns in character strings. In the search pattern (to the right of *Like*) the wildcards ? (any character) and * (any characters) can be used. Here is an example: *"Mississippi" Like "Mis*pi"* yields *True*.

> **POINTER** *If you are working with large numbers of character strings, the instruction* Option Compare Text *at the beginning of a module is often useful. With it uppercase and lowercase letters are not distinguished in ordinary searches, while special symbols are correctly ordered. See Chapter 5.*

Logical Operators

Logical operators make it possible to link several conditions. The expression *a* ***Or*** *b* returns *True* if at least one of the two component conditions *a* and *b* is *True*. The operator ***And*** is restrictive, requiring that both conditions be *True* simultaneously. The operator *Xor* (exclusive or) tests whether one or the other, but not both, of two conditions is true. Thus ***Xor*** returns the result *True* precisely when either *a* is *True* and *b* is *False* or *b* is *True* and *a* is *False*. More seldom used are *Imp* (implication) and *Eqv* (equivalence). ***Imp*** returns *True* unless *a=True* and *b=False*, while ***Eqv*** returns *True* if *a* and *b* have the same truth value.

> **CAUTION** *VBA seems to incorporate no optimization in the evaluation of conditionals. A test of the form* If x>=0 And Sqr(x)<3 *leads in the case of* x *a negative number to an error. (In many programming languages the second part of the test will simply not be carried out if the first part has already tested false, since if on part of an* And *conditional is false, then the whole expressions is false.)*

Many VBA and Excel properties contain bit-coded status information. A typical example is the *Attributes* property of the *File* object in the *Scripting* library (see also the following chapter). Possible attributes are defined in the *FileAttribute* constants:

NAME	VALUE
Normal	0
ReadOnly	1
Hidden	2
System	4
...	...

The values of these constants correspond to the powers of 2 (2^0, 2^1, 2^2, 2^3, etc.), that is, in binary representation, (0001, 0010, 0100, 1000). In a hidden, write-protected system file, *Attributes* has the value 7 (that is, 1 + 2 + 4).

The operators *And* and *Or* are ideally suited for working with such constants. For example, if you wish to set several attributes simultaneously, you simply join the constants with *Or* (alternatively, you could simply use the operator +):

```
myfile.Attributes = ReadOnly Or System
```

If you wish to test whether a particular attribute has been set, then use *And*:

```
If (myfile.Attributes And System) <> 0 Then ' it is a system file
```

Operator Hierarchy

The operators do not all have the same precedence. In the expression *a+b*c* first *b*c* is computed and then the summation with *a*. At the highest level of the operator hierarchy are the arithmetic operators for numbers and the concatenation operators for character strings. After them come the comparison operators, and finally the logical operators. The two definition operators play no role in the evaluation of expressions. A fully ranked listing of all operators can be found in the on-line help under "Operators: Calculation operators in formulas."

Syntax Summary

Arithmetic Operators

-	minus sign
+ - * /	basic operations
^	exponentiation (3^2 yields 9)
\	integer division
Mod	modulo operator (remainder under integer division)

Operators for Concatenating Character Strings

+	only for strings of characters
&	numbers are automatically converted into characters

Comparison Operators

=	equal to
<>	unequal
< <=	less than, less than or equal to
> >=	greater than, greater than or equal to
Is	refer to the same object
Like	pattern comparison

Logical Operators

And	logical And
Or	logical Or
Xor	exclusive Or (*a* or *b*, but not both)
Imp	implication (if *a* is true, then *b* must also be true)
Eqv	equivalence (*a* and *b* must be the same)
Not	logical negation

Definition Operators

=	allocation of variables and properties
:=	allocation of named parameters in procedure calls

CHAPTER 5

Techniques of Programming

This chapter provides answers to a host of everyday questions about programming: How do I access tables, cells, and regions of cells? How do I carry out calculations with dates and times? How are character strings processed? How are new worksheet functions defined?

Chapter Overview

Cells and Ranges of Cells

Accessing individual cells or entire groups of cells belonging to different worksheets is a bit confusing, because Excel distinguishes among numerous similar objects and concepts. In many cases there are, in fact, several correct ways to proceed.

We first describe all the important objects, methods, and properties that provide for accessing ranges of cells. Then we introduce concrete techniques for applying these keywords to such tasks as editing individual cells of a range of cells and carrying out multiple selection. We then explore the possibilities of data transfer via the clipboard.

Objects, Methods, Properties

The **active cell** (*ActiveCell*) is the cell of a worksheet in which the cell pointer is located. At this location it is possible to input data via the keyboard. (With program code you can edit inactive cells as well.) A **Range** (*Range*) is a group of cells. A **selection** (*Selection*) encompasses the currently selected range. Selection is possible only in an active workbook.

Here is an example to illustrate these concepts: If you select several cells in a worksheet, then these cells are considered a selection. One cell in this selection is the active cell. The selection represents *one* of infinitely many possible ranges.

The Range *Object (Range of Cells)*

Range: This keyword can refer to the *Range* object as well as to the like-named method (see below). The *Range* object is the central object of this section. A range can consist of individual cells or a group of cells. Even an entire row or column can be a range. Although in general, Excel can also work with three-dimensional ranges (for example, *=SUM(Sheet1:Sheet2!A1:B2)* forms the sum over eight fields), the *Range* object in the present version of Excel is limited to ranges of cells in a *single* worksheet.

VBA does not recognize an object for a single cell. Cells are considered a special case of a range (with *Range.Count*=1). Numerous properties of ranges can be applied to the special case of a single-celled region, for example, *Formula* (returns or alters the formula of a cell).

It is possible to edit a range either directly or via the detour of selection. In the first variant the properties and methods of a range are executed immediately after the *Range* method is executed, as in, for example, *Range("A1:B2").Count*. In the second variant a range is first made the "active selection" by means of the methods *Select* or *Activate*. Then the range is accessed via *ActiveCell* or *Selection*, with *Selection.Count*, say.

Instead of the long-winded *Range("A1:B2")* for selecting the range A1:B2, the shorthand *[A1:B2]* is allowed. It is also possible in *Range* as well as in the shorthand notation to give a named range of cells. Thus with *[profit]* you can access cell C20 if this cell has previously been associated with the name "profit" by means of INSERT|NAME|DEFINE.

If now the cells of this range are to be edited individually, each cell of the range can be accessed by means of *Cells*. (*Cells* again returns *Range* objects!)

Ranges of cells composed of several rectangular regions (manually selected with the mouse and Ctrl) frequently cause difficulties: Most properties and methods that refer to a *Range* object take into account only the first rectangular segment of the range! To work through all the parts of the range the method *Areas* is available, which will be discussed below in greater detail.

In many cases, ***Evaluate*** can be used instead of *Range*. *Evaluate* evaluates a character string passed to it and returns the associated object. *Range("A1")* corresponds to *Evaluate("A1")*, and that corresponds in turn to the shorthand *[A1]*. All three variants return a *Range* object as result. Furthermore, with *Range* and *Evaluate* it is permitted to express the range by means of a string variable, which in the shorthand notation is not possible.

Moreover, *Evaluate* does not have precisely the same function as *Range*, even if at first glance that seems to be the case. While *Range* is suitable exclusively for ranges of cells, *Evaluate* can also be used with other named objects (such as drawing elements). For almost all applications of *Evaluate* the shorthand notation with square brackets can be used.

Access to Selected Ranges of Cells

ActiveCell: This property points to the active cell of the application or of a window (that is, to the cell in which the cell pointer is located). *ActiveCell* can be read, but it cannot be changed. If you wish to move the cell pointer into another cell, you have to use the method *Activate*, *Select*, or *Offset*.

ActiveCell returns *Nothing* if no worksheet is displayed in the active window (for the *Application* object) or in the given window. *ActiveCell* cannot be used for a particular worksheet. (This property is defined only for the *Application* object and the *Window* object.) If you wish to determine the active cell of a worksheet that is not currently active, you must first make this worksheet the active sheet of the current window with *Worksheets(...).Activate*.

Selection: This property is, like *ActiveCell*, defined only on the *Application* and *Window* levels. It refers to the object that has just been selected in the current window. It can be related to a single cell, a selection of cells, or even a chart or button. (You can establish the object type by means of *Typename(Selection)*.) This property can only be read; it cannot be altered directly. The selected object can, rather, be manipulated by means of the method *Select Activate*.

RangeSelection: This property is a variation on *Selection*. It returns the selected range of cells even when another object (such as a chart or button) is active.

UsedRange: This property returns the range of a worksheet whose cells are actually being used. In contrast to *Selection*, this property can be used with worksheets (not only windows).

Selection of a Range

Range: The *Range* method returns a *Range* object. A *Range* represents a group of worksheet cells (in the simplest case only a single cell). Examples: *Range("A1")*, *Range("A1:B3")*, *Range("Table2!B7")*.

Range usually refers to the active worksheet. If *Range* is applied to another *Range* object, then the cell references are considered to be relative to the upper left corner of the range. Example: *Range("B3:D4").Select: Selection.Range("B1")* returns a reference to cell C3. (Thus in this example B1 means, "column plus 1, same row," and refers to the starting point B3.)

In program code it is often awkward to give references to cells in the form "A1". The reason is that within *Range*, *Cells(row,column)* can be used. *Range(Cells(1,1), Cells(4,2))* corresponds to *Range("A1:B4")*. The advantage of writing things this way with *Cells* is that *Cells* expects numerical parameters and therefore can easily be placed within a loop.

> **TIP** Cells *automatically refers to the active worksheet. If you want to access cells of another sheet, then the correct way of writing it is not* Worksheets(n).Range(Cells(...), Cells(...)), *but rather* Range(Worksheets(n).Cells(...), Worksheets(n).Cells(...))*!*

Note that with *Range(Cells(...), Cells(...))* only simple rectangular ranges can be defined. Ranges of a complex form must be constructed out of several rectangular ranges with *Union*. For individual cells the expression *Range(Cells(z,s))* is not allowed—in this case, however, *Range* can simply be avoided, since *Cells* directly delivers a single cell.

Offset: This method returns a range that is offset to the range given as object. Thus, for example, *[A1].Offset(3,1)* returns a reference to the cell B4. This method does not change the active range (in contrast to *Select* and *Activate*). The instruction *ActiveCell.Offset(0,1).Select* moves the cell pointer one cell to the right.

> **CAUTION** *Both* Offset *and* Cell *expect the parameters in the order* (row, column). *This is the opposite of the usual order in the way that cells are named (such as B5, where first column B is given and then row 5), as well as the mathematical custom by which first the* x *and then the* y *coordinate is given.*

Select and ***Activate***: The first of these two methods selects the given object, while the second activates it. Both methods are used without parameters and do not return a direct result. They merely change properties such as *ActiveCell* and *Selection*.

According to the on-line help, *Activate* is intended for individual cells and *Select* for ranges of cells. In fact, there is no concrete difference between the two methods. Regardless of whether you select the range *Range("A1:B3")* via *Activate* or *Select*, A1 becomes the active cell and A1:B3 the active range.

With both methods only cells or cell ranges in the active worksheet can be selected. *Range("Table2!A1").Activate* leads to an error if at the time *Table1* is the active worksheet.

GoTo: This method selects a range, and is thus comparable in its effect with *Select*. However, the syntax is quite different from that of *Select*—the range to be selected is given not as an object (via *Range*) but in a parameter: *GoTo Worksheets(n).Range("C10")*. It is allowed for the range of cells to be located in another worksheet (this worksheet will then be automatically activated). With the optional scrolling parameter it is possible to set the scroll bars in such a way that the range that is selected is, in fact, visible. This does not always happen automatically.

Access to Cells and Ranges of Cells

Cells: With the method *Cells* it is possible to access an individual cell of a worksheet or of a rectangular range of cells. One may give two-dimensional input in the form *Cells(row, column)* or by a sequential number: *Cells(n)*. In the second variant the cells are numbered row by row. When an entire worksheet is used as object, then 1 corresponds to cell A1, 2 to cell B1, 256 to cell IV1, 257 to cell A2, and so on. (Note that 256 is the maximum number of columns allowed. It is possible that a future version of Excel would allow more than 256 columns!)

The row-by-row numbering also holds for ranges of cells: *Range("A1:C2").Cells(4)* refers to cell A2. The cell given by *Cells* can lie outside the given range, for example, *Range("A1:C3").Cells(10)* for A4 or *Range("C3:D4").Cells(4,5)* for G6. (G is the fifth column if numbering begins with C, while 6 is the fourth row if the numbering begins with 3.)

TIP *You can try out the addressing of cells in the immediate window of the development environment. Just use the property* Address, *which gives the resultant address of a range of cells:*

```
?Range("a1:c2").Cells(4).Address
$A$2
```

TIP *In ranges composed of several rectangular blocks, only the first block can be accessed with* Cells. *To access all the ranges the method* Areas *must be used.*

Areas: This method is similar to *Cells*, but it returns connected (rectangular) ranges of cells. The application of *Areas* is necessary for working on ranges that comprise several rectangular ranges (for example, after several uses of Ctrl).

Row, Column: These properties return the row and column number of a cell (or the number of the first row or column of a range).

Columns, Rows: These two methods enable convenient access to required columns or rows of a range of cells. The number of columns or rows of a range can be determined with *range.Columns.Count* or *range.Rows.Count*.

EntireColumn, EntireRow: These two properties return the columns or rows in which the given range is located. Rows and columns are not treated as actual objects, but as normal ranges of cells.

Offset, Resize: ***Offset*** returns a range offset by a number of rows or columns from the given range. For example, *[A1].Offset(3,1)* returns the cell B4. With ***Resize*** you can alter the size of a range. The desired number of rows and columns is passed as parameter. Thus *[A1].Resize(2,3)* returns the result A1:C2.

Union and ***Intersect***: The first of these two methods forms a single range out of several individual ranges (their union), while the second returns the range of cells common to all the given ranges (their intersection). For experienced programmers: *Union* corresponds to logical "or," *Intersect* to logical "and." *Intersect* is suitable, for example, to select from a range of cells all those cells that lie in a particular row or column. With *Union* you can form a multiarea range out of several rectangular ranges.

SpecialCells, RowDifferences, ColumnDifferences, CurrentRegion, CurrentArray, [Direct]Precedents, [Direct]Dependents: With these methods and properties particular cells of a region can be referenced: for example, all empty cells, all visible cells, all connected cells. These keywords make it possible to access all regions that can be selected with EDIT|GO TO| SPECIAL.

CAUTION *The methods* SpecialCells *and* CurrentRegion *do not work if they appear in the execution of user-defined worksheet functions. Instead of using these methods, you must recreate these functions using loops, which is tedious to program and slow in execution. In this regard see the user-defined function* Holiday, *which is described later in this chapter.*

Determining the Address of a Range of Cells

Address: This method returns the address of a range in the form of a character string. If the range A1:B4 is selected, then *Selection.Address* returns the string *"$A$1:$B$4"*. By means of various parameters one can control the transformation into a string (such as absolute vs. relative address, A1 or R1C1 format, local vs. external reference). ***AddressLocal*** functions like *Address* in that it returns addresses, but it does so in the regional format of the language of the particular country .

If you have an address, whether in A1 or R1C1 format, you can work with the address further with the *Application* method *ConvertFormula*, which makes possible, among other things, a conversion between A1 and R1C1 notation and between absolute and relative addressing.

TIP *In the "R1C1 notation" (R for "row," C for "column"), cells are specified by row and column numbers. In "A1 notation" the column letter is followed by the row number. The A1 notation is default in Excel, but you may use the R1C1 notation instead:* TOOLS|OPTIONS|GENERAL|R1C1 REFERENCE STYLE.

Named Ranges

Names: This method of the currently active worksheet makes it possible to access named ranges of cells. With *Add* a new name can be defined or an already existing name changed. What is important is that the range of cells is given absolutely and with a prefixed equal sign, say, *Names.Add "rangename", "=d5"*. In what follows, named ranges can be used with *Range* or in the shorthand form *[rangename]*. *Names("rangename").Delete* deletes the definition of a name. With the method *Goto* you can quickly move the cell pointer into a named cell or region.

TIP *Many short programming examples related to named ranges can be found in the example file* `Names.xls`.

Furthermore, *Name* objects can be used not only for naming ranges of cells, but also for other tasks. For example, the additional program MS-Query saves its query parameters in a palette of *Name* objects. Here the *Visible* property of the objects is set to *False*, so that these objects do not appear in the form INSERT|NAME|APPLY. The contents of the parameter can be obtained from the *Value* property.

> **CAUTION** *Microsoft was apparently not clear as to whether the definition of a new named range should be associated to the workbook or to a special worksheet: On the one hand, it should be possible to use the same name in every worksheet without one instance of the name interfering with another. On the other hand, it is also desirable that a name that has been globally defined be available in all worksheets.*
>
> *The result is that the first time a name is defined, its definition is valid for the entire workbook. If the same name is used again in another worksheet, then this definition is local for this worksheet. The old definition is valid for all other worksheets. The consequence is that it is sometimes extremely difficult to determine whether a definition of a name must be invoked by* ActiveWorkbook.Names(...) *or by* ActiveSheet.Names(...). *In case of doubt, decide in favor of the first variant. There the* Names *listing contains all local definitions (of the currently active worksheet) as well as all global definitions that are overlaid by the current worksheet.*

Notes/Comments

Every cell can have a note stored with it. Setting or retrieving it is accomplished with the method ***NoteText***. Since with Excel methods character strings to be passed as parameters can have a maximum of 255 characters, this method has two parameters by which the start and end position within the note can be given. These parameters make it possible to read or edit notes that are longer than 255 characters.

Starting with Excel 97 notes are also called comments. They are controlled by the new *Comment* object. (However, *NoteText* may still be used.) With the method *AddComment* new comments can be defined. *ClearComment* deletes existing comments. The listing of *Comments* for the *WorkSheet* object helps in tracking down all comments in a worksheet.

Adding and Deleting Ranges of Cells

There are five methods available for deleting cells: ***ClearContents*** deletes only the contents of cells, leaving the format intact. ***ClearFormats*** has the opposite effect, clearing only the formatting. ***ClearNotes*** deletes the notes associated to the cells. ***Clear*** deletes both the formatting and the contents. A quite different effect is exhibited by ***Delete***. With it the cells of a worksheet are made to disappear; the cells to the right or below are promoted to the vacated location(s) (this corresponds to the command EDIT|DELETE).

For inserting new cells into the worksheet there exists the method ***Insert***. It is similar to *Delete* in that with an optional parameter you can determine whether cells should be shifted to the right or downwards. (When no parameter is given, Excel attempts to figure out the more logical choice.)

Content and Format of Cells

The following paragraphs describe the most important properties of the *Range* object for setting the content and format of cells. Most of the properties listed in what follows will be used in the usual way in single-celled ranges. Reading the properties in multicelled ranges leads to various results (such as an error or setting the first cell of the range). More standard is the reaction in changing the properties of multicelled ranges. Here the settings of *all* affected cells are changed.

Value: This property contains the value of the cell (in the case of formulas, the result). Empty cells can be determined with *IsEmpty(obj.Value)*. With the definition of the *Value* property the content of cells can be changed. Formulas are input as character strings that begin with an equal sign: *obj.Value= "=A4"*. The *Value* property is the default property. This means that the shorthand *obj="=A4"* is also permissible. ***Value2*** differs from *Value* in that dates and currency values are not identified in the formats of *Date* and *Currency*, but as floating point numbers. In many cases this simplifies further processing.

Text: This property contains the content of a cell as a character string. *Text* is distinguished from *Value* by two particular features: With values, *Text* returns an appropriately formatted string (while *Value* returns the value directly, as a number or a date); furthermore, *Text* can only be read (and not changed). References to cells must be handled with *Value*.

Characters: With this method one can access individual characters of a text constant in a cell (for example, in order to set the type characteristics of a single character).

FormulaLocal and ***FormulaR1C1Local***: These properties return the formula of a cell in the A1 or R1C1 format (see below) in the local language. In the case of empty cells an empty string is returned, while with formulas with constants the values of the constants are returned. For example, if A5 contains the formula *=SUM(A1:A4),* then in Germany, say, *[A1].FormulaLocal* returns the string *=SUMME(A1:A4),* while *[A1].FormulaR1C1Local* returns *=SUMME(Z(-4)S:Z(-1)S).*

Formula, FormulaR1C1: These two related properties return formulas in international (that is, English) syntax in the A1 or R1C1 format. *[A1].Formula* returns the string *=SUM(A1:A4),* while *[A1].FormulaR1C1* returns *=SUM(R[-4]C:R[-1]C).*

Formula returns or expects the formula in English. The formula is also saved internally in this format and is displayed with the properties of the local language only in the Excel interface. A formula that is displayed in German Excel in a worksheet as *=Euroconvert(1,2; "DEM"; "EUR"; WAHR)* corresponds to the *Formula* character string *"=Euroconvert(1.2, "DEM", "EUR", TRUE)"* (period instead of comma for the decimal point, commas instead of semicolons as separators, *TRUE* instead of *WAHR*).

HasFormula: This property tells whether a formula exists in a cell (*True* or *False*).

Font: This property refers to the *Font* object, which determines a number of properties of the typeface in a cell, such as *Name* (of the font), *Size, Bold, Italic.*

Orientation, HorizontalAlignment, VerticalAlignment, WrapText: These properties determine the orientation of the text (horizontal or vertical), the justification (left/centered/right/justified or top/middle/bottom), and line breaking (true or false). New in Excel 97 was the possibility of using *Orientation* to give an angle in the range –90° to 90° for the orientation of text. Zero degrees corresponds to normal horizontal text, with the angle being determined from this position in the counterclockwise direction (the standard in mathematics). With 45 the text runs diagonally up from left to right, while –45 yields text running down and to the right.

With ***IndentLevel*** one can determine how far to the right the content of a cell should be shifted (the permissible range is 0 to 15).

ColumnWidth, RowHeight: These properties determine the width of the entire column and the height of the entire row.

Borders: This method refers to six *Border* objects (left/right/above/below and diagonally up and down) whose properties control the appearance of the border: *LineStyle, Weight, Color.*

BorderAround: With this method the entire border can be set.

*Formatting of Numbers (*NumberFormat, NumberFormatLocal, *and* Style*)*

NumberFormat returns the number format of the cell as a character string. *NumberFormatLocal* carries out the same task, but the string returned conforms to the conventions of the local language. Finally, *Style* refers to a formatting template (*Style* object).

To obtain a fuller understanding of the situation it would be a good idea to begin with styles. As was shown already in the introductory example back in Chapter 1, a style can be used to set a number of format characteristics of a cell, such as the font, text orientation, and color. Most formatting instructions are easily understood, and so in this section we shall limit ourselves to a discussion of number formats.

In VBA, styles are invoked as ***Style*** objects. Every Excel file (*Workbook* object) can use *Styles* to access available styles in the file. Some format templates are predefined (*Builtin=True*) and are thus always available for use. The following loop returns a table of all such styles.

```
Dim s As Style
For Each s In ThisWorkbook.Styles
  If s.BuiltIn = True Then
    Debug.Print s.Name, s.NumberFormat
  End If
Next
```

Predefined Styles

NAME	NUMBERFORMAT
Comma	`_(* #,##0.00_);_(* (#,##0.00);_(* "-"??_);_(*@_)`
Comma [0]	`_(* #,##0_);_(* (#,##0);_(* "-"_);_(*@_)`
Currency	`_($* #,##0.00_);_($* (#,##0.00);_($* "-"??_);_(*@_)`
Currency [0]	`_($* #,##0_);_($* (#,##0);_($* "-"_);_(*@_)`
Normal	`General`
Percent	`0%`

TIP *In the English version of Excel the properties* Name *and* NameLocal *as well as* NumberFormat *and* NumberFormatLocal *contain identical character strings. However, in international versions this is not the case. There the* Local *properties contain the region-specific settings, which take precedence over the international settings. For example, in the German version* NameLocal *contains* "Währung" *instead of* "Currency". *The connection between basic properties and their* Local *variants is unfortunately extremely poorly documented.*

The difference between *Comma* and *Comma [0]* and between *Currency* and *Currency [0]* is that in each case the first variant displays two places to the right of the decimal point, while the [0] variant displays none.

All cells that are not otherwise explicitly formatted are automatically formatted with the style *Styles("normal")*. It is not possible to define the *Style* property of a cell to be *Nothing*. Every cell must be formatted with one style or another.

When you format a cell directly, this format takes precedence over the settings of the overall style. However, the style remains valid for all formatting that is not directly altered.

With the currency, percent, and comma style buttons in the formatting toolbar the style in the affected cell can be changed to *Comma*, *Currency*, or *Percent*.

> **TIP** *If you use the euro add-in, then a further style is defined.* Euro *is used for* Name *and* NameLocal. *The* NumberFormat[Local] *character strings look as follows:*
>
> ```
> _-* #.##0,00 [$€-1]_-;-* #.##0,00 [$€-1]_-;_-* "-"?? [$€-1]_-
> ```

Let us proceed to the property ***NumberFormat***, which is used for styles (*Style* object) as well as for direct cell formatting (*Range* object). In the case of an unformatted cell, *NumberFormat* contains the character string *"General"*, which is based on the style *Normal*. However, *"General"* is an exception. As a rule, *NumberFormat* is set by a rather horrifying string.

Here is some brief information on constructing this string. It normally consists of four parts, separated by semicolons:

```
positive;negative;zero;strings
```

The first part is concerned with positive numbers, the second with negative numbers, the third with the value zero, and the fourth with character strings. If you provide only the first part, then all numbers will be formatted according to this format. Strings will be formatted in the standard way (flush left, without indentation).

The following list describes the meaning of the most important symbols in *NumberFormat*:

;	separates the four parts of the string
#	placeholder for a digit or for all significant digits
0	placeholder for a digit; if the place is not significant, then instead a 0 is shown. For example, 123.00 or 0.12 is obtained from *#0.00*
?	placeholder for a digit; if the place is not significant, then a space character is displayed

. decimal point (displayed according to the local format. In Germany, for example, a comma is displayed; in any case, in *NumberFormat* a period must be given)

, thousands separator

% placeholder for a number in percent format (0.1 is transformed to 10%)

`_x` leaves blank space in the size of the following character x; this character itself is not shown; _(means, for example, that a space the size of a parenthesis is left

_ is often inserted to ensure that numbers are displayed aligned and in fact, independently of whether they are positive or negative (enclosed in parentheses) or whether they are displayed with or without the currency symbol

`"x"` indicates a character string between the quotation marks

`*x` fills the remaining space with the symbol `x`; `*x` can be used only once in each part of the *NumberFormat* character string

`*-#` means that before the number enough hyphens are inserted so that the cell is completely filled, for example, "———— 123"

`"DM"* #` means that the symbol DM (the symbol for German marks) appears flush left and the number flush right, with the necessary number of blank characters in between

$ placeholder for the currency symbol defined in the system settings (for example DM or €); this placeholder $ is unfortunately not documented

`*@` placeholder for a character string (for the fourth part of *NumberFormat*)

TIP *In addition to the symbols defined here there are numerous additional symbols for formatting of dates, times, fractions, exponentials, and so on. Further information about these symbols can be found in the Excel on-line help under "Create a custom number format." (If you have opened the VBA on-line help, then you have to close it, switch to Excel, and summon the Excel on-line help. This is the only way to open the correct help file! The on-line help for* NumberFormat *is useless.)*

In most cases the easiest way to achieve a correct NumberFormat *character string is to set a format with* FORMAT|CELLS *and view the resulting string in the immediate window with* Debug.Print ActiveCell.NumberFormat.

The last property left to be explained is ***NumberFormatLocal***. This property's documentation is practically nonexistent. Experiments with the German version of Excel has shown that there is no simple one-to-one translation of code into the local format. For example, the position of the currency symbol is shifted. With the format *Currency* positive numbers are formatted, according to *NumberFormat* `_($* #,##0.00_)` (that is, with the currency symbol before the number). However, according to *NumberFormatLocal* they are formatted with `_-* #.##0,00 €_-` (that is, with the currency symbol at the end). *NumberFormatLocal* has precedence over *NumberFormat*.

For this reason an attempt to change *NumberFormat* with program code can lead to curious results. Let us suppose that we have formatted the number 1234 as currency (*1.234,00 €*). If the instruction

```
ActiveCell.NumberFormat = _
  Replace(ActiveCell.NumberFormat, "$", """DEM""")
```

is carried out, to replace the system-setting currency symbol with the string `"DEM"`, then *1.234,00 €* is suddenly turned into *DEM 1.234,00* , that is, the currency sign has been moved from the back to the front. To achieve the desired result you have to execute the following instruction instead:

```
ActiveCell.NumberFormatLocal = _
  Replace(ActiveCell.NumberFormatLocal, "€", """DEM""")
```

However, the direct editing of *NumberFormatLocal* is not an optimal solution, because your program code becomes country-specific, which leads to unexpected (and seldom correct) results with Excel versions in other languages.

Let us consider one more example. You set *NumberFormatLocal="T.M.JJJJ"* (which returns, for example, 1.12.1999, which is a date in German format; T, M, and J are abbreviations for *Tag* (day), *Monat* (month), and *Jahr* (year)). If you now select *NumberFormat*, then you get *"d/m/yyyy"*, which is more or less in one-to-one correspondence, even if written with slashes instead of periods.

On the other hand, if you set *NumberFormatLocal="TT.MM.JJJJ"* (which returns 01.12.1999), then you get *NumberFormat="m/d/yy"*! The order of month and day has been switched! (The reason is perhaps that Excel recognizes *"TT.MM.JJJJ"* as a predefined German format and has a table of international correspondences. Perhaps *"T.M.JJJJ"* does not appear in this table, and the transformation for *NumberFormat* is accomplished by some other mechanism. All in all, there are many open questions in connection to *NumberFormatLocal*, questions that could be answered only by Microsoft, which for some reason known perhaps only to its chairman has neglected to provide adequate on-line documentation.)

A1 Versus R1C1 Notation

In general, cell references are given in the A1 notation. *Range("R1C1")* is not permitted. In program code it is often more practical to set cell references with *Cells*. This method expects numeric parameters as input of the row and column numbers and therefore corresponds to the R1C1 syntax.

Formulas in worksheets represent a special case. With the property *Formula* the formula of a cell in the A1 format can be read or edited, while *FormulaR1C1* does the same for the R1C1 notation, and *FormulaR1C1Local* in, for example, the Z1S1 notation in the German version (*Zeile* = row, *Spalte* = column).

The property *Application.ReferenceStyle* determines how cell references are displayed in Excel. This property can exhibit either of the values *xlA1* or *xlR1C1*. The format in which the cell reference will be shown can also be set in TOOLS|OPTIONS|GENERAL.

Programming Techniques

Setting and Moving the Active Cell

```
Range("B1").Select             ' activates B1
[B1].Select                    ' likewise activates B1
Cells(1,2).Select              ' likewise activates B1
ActiveCell.Range("A2").Select ' activates the cell one row down
ActiveCell.Offset(1,0).Select ' activates the cell one row down
```

> **TIP** *All of the lengthier examples of this section can be found in the example file* `Cells.xls`.

Selecting and Editing Ranges of Cells

As a rule, the macro recorder leads to code that looks something like that in the example below.

```
Range("D11:F14").Select
With Selection.Font
  .Name = "Courier New"
  .Bold = True
End With
```

The pattern that generally prevails in macro recording—first select a range of cells, then execute various settings—is not compulsory. The following example code fulfills the same task without altering the current position of the cell pointer or the current range of selected cells:

```
With Range("D11:F14").Font
  .Name = "Courier New"
  .Bold = True
End With
```

In many cases the use of *With* leads to more readable and efficient code, but it is not compulsory, as our last example shows:

```
Range("D11:F14").Font.Name = "Courier New"
Range("D11:F14").Font..Bold = True
```

However, giving cell references in the A1 form is, on the one hand, difficult to read, and on the other, extremely inflexible in changing the structure of the worksheet. If you were to add a row or column to the worksheet, you would have to alter the code of the entire macro!

For this reason you should provide names for frequently used ranges of cells, which can be done via INSERT|NAME|DEFINE. Then you can use these names in your code: *Range("Name")*. (The macro recorder is, unfortunately, not able to use predefined names automatically. You have to massage the code that it generates.)

Copying and Moving Cells

Selecting More Complex Ranges of Cells

In practice, it happens frequently that you wish to select associated ranges of cells whose sizes are variable. You often select such ranges via the keyboard with End, Shift+Cursor key. In VBA code you can use the method *End(xlXxx)* to select a single cell at the end of a block of cells. With *Range* you can then access a range of cells between two corner cells. (The macro recorder does not use this method, sad to say, and instead produces inflexible cell references. The macro thus created is thus unable to cope with an altered worksheet structure and so must be changed manually.)

Sometimes, the properties *CurrentRegion* and *CurrentArray* or the Method *SpecialCells* can be of assistance. However, in user-defined worksheet functions these functions often cause trouble. If necessary, you must work through the range in question cell by cell to find the positions of the initial and terminal cells.

The sample procedure *SelectRow* selects—beginning with the current position of the cell pointer—all connected cells of a row. By this we do not mean the entire row of a worksheet, but only a group of occupied (not empty) cells.

This procedure merely shows how such a selection is made. However, the two cells *cell1* and *cell2* could more easily be determined with *End* instructions.

First a few words about how the procedure functions: The starting point is the active cell *startcell.* If this cell is empty, then the procedure is exited at once. Otherwise, in a *For* loop a search is made for the last nonempty cell to the left of the current cell. With *Set* a reference to this cell is stored in *cell1*. The *If* test at the end of the loop takes care of the special case that the row contains values all the way to the first column, in which case the loop terminates without a reference being stored in *cell1*.

```
' example file Cells.xls
' selects a connected range of cells within a row
Sub SelectRow()
  Dim startCell As Range, cell1 As Range, cell2 As Range
  Dim rowNr&, colNr&
  Set startCell = ActiveCell
  rowNr = startCell.Row: colNr = startCell.Column
  If IsEmpty(startCell) Then Exit Sub
  ' look for left end of row; store end cell in cell1
  For colNr = startCell.Column To 1 Step -1
    If IsEmpty(Cells(rowNr, colNr).Value) Then
      Set cell1 = Cells(rowNr, colNr + 1)
      Exit For
    End If
  Next colNr
  If cell1 Is Nothing Then Set cell1 = Cells(rowNr, 1)
  ' search for right end of row; end cell stored in cell2
  For colNr = startCell.Column To 256
    If IsEmpty(Cells(rowNr, colNr).Value) Then
      Set cell2 = Cells(rowNr, colNr - 1)
      Exit For
    End If
  Next colNr
  If cell2 Is Nothing Then Set cell2 = Cells(rowNr, 256)
  ' select the range between cell1 and cell2
  Range(cell1, cell2).Select
End Sub
```

In analogy to the first loop, in the second loop the last nonempty cell to the right is sought and then stored in *cell2*. Finally, the range between *cell1* and *cell2* is selected.

Combining Ranges (Union and Intersection)

The method *Union* is used to combine several ranges of cells into a composite range. The resulting range does not have to be connected. To edit such a disconnected range requires the *Areas* object (see below).

In the first example *Union* is used to enlarge a preexisting selection to include the cell A4 (corresponds to clicking on A4 while holding down the Ctrl key).

```
Union(Selection, Range("A4")).Select
```

In the second example first the range A1:D4 is selected. Then *Intersect* is used to select that part of the range that is contained in column A. The new selection thus comprises the range A1:A4.

```
Range("A1:D4").Select
Intersect(Selection, Range("A:A")).Select
```

> **CAUTION** *If you join two overlapping* Range *objects with* Union, *the cells common to both objects are multiply contained in the united object. The effect is the same as that obtained by selecting overlapping ranges of cells with the mouse while holding down the* Ctrl *key (see Figure 5.1).*

Editing All Cells of a Rectangular Range

With the method *Cells* you can access all the cells of a rectangular range. The example below shows a concrete application: The macro *IncreaseFontSize* sets a 2-point larger typeface for all cells of the current selection. Therefore, the macro has a similar function to that of the INCREASE FONT SIZE tool.

The significant difference is that the macro edits each cell individually, while clicking on the tool results in the font size of all the selected cells being determined by the font size of the first selected cell.

The test *If Selection Is Nothing* is necessary to avoid an error in the case that the macro is inadvertently launched in a chart of a module sheet. (There are no cells in this case whose font can be changed.)

```
Sub IncreaseFontSize()
  Dim cell As Range
  If Selection Is Nothing Then Exit Sub
  For Each cell In Selection.Cells
    cell.Font.Size = cell.Font.Size + 2
  Next cell
End Sub
```

The loop could have been formulated differently (though less elegantly):

```
Dim i As Integer
If Selection Is Nothing Then Exit Sub
For i = 1 To Selection.Cells.Count
  Selection.Cells(i).Font.Size = _
    Selection.Cells(i).Font.Size + 2
Next Cell
```

Edit All Cells of a Compound Range

The example above has one shortcoming: It does not work with compound ranges of cells. Such ranges result when you select several ranges with the Ctrl key or when you create ranges using *Union* or *Intersect*. In such a case the above macro changes only the cells of the first rectangle. In order that all cells be changed, the individual component ranges must be accessed via the *Areas* method:

```
' example file Cells.xls
Sub IncreaseFontSize()
  Dim rng As Range, ar As Range
  If Selection Is Nothing Then Exit Sub
  For Each ar In Selection.Areas
    For Each rng In ar
      rng.Font.Size = rng.Font.Size + 2
    Next rng
  Next ar
End Sub
```

CAUTION *If a user first selects D3:D10 and then B6:F6 using* Ctrl *(see Figure 5.1), then cell D6 is contained in both ranges, and is therefore doubly selected! With the procedure* IncreaseFontSize *above this would result in the font of cell D6 being increased not by 2 points like all the others, but by 4 points.*

There can exist applications in which a multiple editing of the same cell must be excluded. In such cases a list must be kept of all cells that have already been edited. The following adapted version of IncreaseFontSize *demonstrates one possible way of proceeding.*

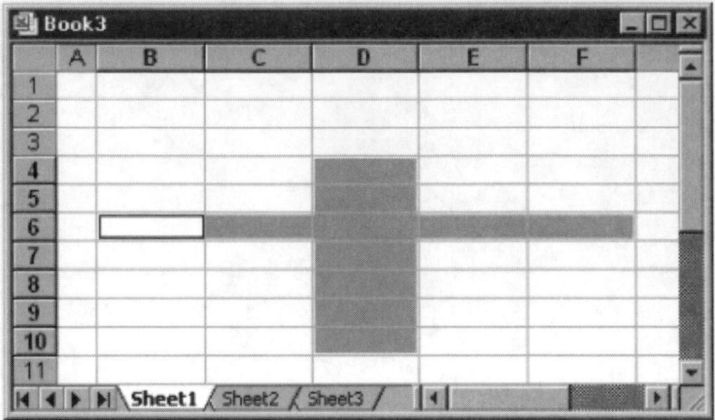

Figure 5.1. Cell D6 is doubly selected

```
' in cellsDone is kept an address list of all cells
' that have already been edited in order to avoid
' a possible multiple editing of the same cell
Sub IncreaseFontSize()
  Dim rng As Range, ar As Range
  Dim cellsDone$, thisCell$
  If Selection Is Nothing Then Exit Sub
  For Each ar In Selection.Areas
    For Each rng In ar
      thisCell = "[" + rng.Address + "]"
      If InStr(cellsDone, thisCell) = 0 Then
        rng.Font.Size = rng.Font.Size + 2
        cellsDone = cellsDone + thisCell + " "
      End If
    Next rng
  Next ar
End Sub
```

Setting a Font

Setting the font of an entire cell can be accomplished simply by changing the properties of the *Font* object.

```
With Selection.Font
  .Name = "Courier New"
  .Bold = True
  .Size = 10
```

```
  .Strikethrough = False
  ' etc.
End With
```

It is more complicated to edit the font characteristics of individual letters than those of the entire cell. In general, this is possible only if the cell contains a text constant (not a number, not a formula). Access to individual characters is accomplished with the method *Characters*. The example macro below formats the characters of a cell with increasingly larger fonts; that is, the first letter is set to 10 points, the second to 11, and so on.

```
Sub SpecialFont()
  Dim i&
  If IsEmpty(ActiveCell.Value) Or ActiveCell.HasFormula Then Exit Sub
  If IsNumeric(ActiveCell.Value) Then Exit Sub
  For i = 1 To ActiveCell.Characters.Count
    ActiveCell.Characters(i, 1).Font.Size = 9 + i
  Next i
End Sub
```

Our last example is a bit more practical. It changes the text style of the selected cells among the styles normal, bold, italic, and bold italic. Each time it is called, the text is transformed into the next style. The macro can then be assigned to a new tool in the toolbar. This tool can replace the two existing tools BOLD and ITALIC, while occupying only half of the high-priced real estate on the toolbar, which is always too small for everything that you want to put on it.

```
' shifts among normal, bold, italic, and bold italic.
Sub ItalicBold()
  Dim bld As Boolean, ital As Boolean
  If Selection Is Nothing Then Exit Sub
  bld = Selection.Font.Bold: ital = Selection.Font.Italic
  If Not bld And Not ital Then
    bld = True
  ElseIf bld And Not ital Then
    ital = True: bld = False
  ElseIf Not bld And ital Then
    bld = True
  Else
    bld = False: ital = False
  End If
  Selection.Font.Bold = bld: Selection.Font.Italic = ital
End Sub
```

Borders

For each cell, Excel manages six *Border* objects, which describe the left, right, upper, and lower borders of the cell and the diagonal lines within the cell. You can access the individual border objects with *Cell.Borders(n)*, where *n* can be replaced by any of the following constants:

xlEdgeTop	upper
xlEdgeBottom	lower
xlEdgeLeft	left
xlEdgeRight	right
xlDiagonalDown	diagonal from upper left to lower right
xlDiagonalUp	diagonal from upper right to lower left
xlInsideHorizontal	horizontal lines within a group of cells
xlInsideVertical	vertical lines within a group of cells

xlInsideVertical and *xlInsideVertical* can be used to draw lines in ranges that stretch over several cells. They cause a change in the affected *Top/Bottom/Left/Right* borders. Internally, however, for each cell only six border lines are managed (corresponding to the first six constants in the above table).

TIP *For some strange reason the loop* For Each b In rng.Borders *does not always encompass all the borders of a cell or region of cells. Instead, use the following:*

```
For Each i In Array(xlEdgeTop, xlEdgeBottom, xlEdgeLeft, _
xlEdgeRight, xlDiagonalDown, xlDiagonalUp)
```

Here i *must be declared a* Variant *variable.*

CAUTION *When in Excel a border line between two cells lying one above the other is visible, there are three possibilities: It is the lower border of the top cell, the upper border of the lower cell, or both of these. When you use* FORMAT|CELLS|BORDER *in interactive mode, then when a border is removed, Excel acts automatically on the neighboring cells to remove all affected borders. In changing a border with VBA code you must take care of this yourself. The following example shows the correct way to proceed.*

The following macro offers a solution. It removes *all* borders of the previously selected cells, even if the borders actually belong to a neighboring cell:

```
' example file Cells.xls
Sub RemoveAllBorders()
  Dim calcMode&, updateMode&, i
  Dim rng As Range, ar As Range
  Dim brd As Border
  If Selection Is Nothing Then Exit Sub
  ' speed optimization
  calcModue = Application.Calculation
  updateModue = Application.ScreenUpdating
  Application.Calculation = xlManual
  Application.ScreenUpdating = False
  '
  For Each ar In Selection.Areas   ' for each region of cells
    For Each rng In ar             ' for each cell
      ' delete all borders of the current cell
      For Each i In Array(xlEdgeTop, xlEdgeBottom, xlEdgeLeft, _
                    xlEdgeRight, xlDiagonalDown, xlDiagonalUp)
        rng.Borders(i).LineStyle = xlLineStyleNone
      Next i
      ' remove the right border of the cell bordering on the left
      If rng.Column > 1 Then
        rng.Offset(0, -1).Borders(xlRight).LineStyle = xlLineStyleNone
      End If
      ' remove the left border of the cell bordering on the right
      If rng.Column < 256 Then
         rng.Offset(0, 1).Borders(xlLeft).LineStyle = xlLineStyleNone
      End If
      ' remove the lower border of the cell above
      If rng.Row > 1 Then
        rng.Offset(-1, 0).Borders(xlBottom).LineStyle = xlLineStyleNone
      End If
      ' remove the upper border of the cell below
      If rng.Row < 65536 Then
         rng.Offset(1, 0).Borders(xlTop).LineStyle = xlLineStyleNone
      End If
    Next rng
  Next ar
  ' end speed optimization
  Application.Calculation = calcMode
  Application.ScreenUpdating = updateMode
End Sub
```

Speed Optimization

The execution of a procedure that makes extensive changes in a worksheet can be quite slow. Two possible reasons for this are the time it takes for constant updating of the display and the time required for recalculating the worksheet after each change. You can improve the performance of your macros dramatically if you deactivate screen updating and worksheet recalculation during execution. To do this you have to set the *Application* properties *ScreenUpdating* and *Calculation* at the beginning and end of the procedure.

The procedure *RemoveAllBorders* (see the example above) saves the current values of both properties at the start, and then sets them to *False* and *xlManual*, respectively. At the end of the procedure the original values are restored.

Syntax Summary

Access to Selected Ranges of Cells

ActiveCell	active cell (position of the cell pointer)
Selection	selected range or selected object in the window
RangeSelection	selected range (even when additionally another object was selected)
UsedRange	range used in the worksheet

Selection of Ranges

Range("A3")	a cell
Range("A3:B5")	a range of cells
Range("A3:B5,C7")	disconnected ranges
Range("name")	access to a named range
Evaluate("name")	access to a named range; second variant
[A3] or *[A3:B5]* or *[name]*	shorthand for *Range*, respectively *Evaluate*
Range(range1, range2)	range between two cells; *range1* and *range2* can also be given by *Cells*
range.Offset(r, c)	returns a range displaced by *r* rows and *c* columns
range.Resize(r, c)	changes the size of the range to *r* rows and *c* columns
range.Select	selects the given range
range.Activate	as above
GoTorange	selects the given range
GoTorange, True	as above, but also scrolls as necessary to make the range visible
Union(range1, range2,..)	union of the given ranges
Intersect(range1, range2,..)	intersection of the given ranges

Accessing Particular Cells

range.Cells	enumeration object of all cells
range.Cells(n)	*n*th cell (1 = A1, 2 = B1, 257 = A2, etc.)
range.Cells(r, c)	cell of the *r*th row and *c*th column
range.Areas	enumeration object of all rectangular ranges
range.Areas(n)	*n*th rectangular range
range.EntireColumn	rows in which the range is located
range.EntireRow	as above for rows
range.Columns(n)	access to individual columns
range.Rows(n)	access to individual rows
range.SpecialCells(type)	access to empty, visible, subordinate, etc., cells
range.End(xlXxx)	access to the last cell in a direction
range.CurrentRegion	access to a connected range of cells
range.[Direct]Precedents	access to preceding cells (raw data)
range.[Direct]Dependents	access to following cells (formulas)
range.ListHeaderRows	returns the number of header rows

Named Ranges, Addresses of Ranges

Names.Add "test", "=d5"	defines the name "test" with reference to cell D5
[test].Select	selects the range "test"
Names("test").RefersTo	returns address of a range (e.g., *"=Table1!$F$4:$G$6"*)
Names("test").RefersToR1C1	as above, but in R1C1 notation
Names("test").RefersToR1C1Local	as above but in local language format
Names("test").Delete	deletes the name "test"
range.Address(..)	returns a string containing the address of the range
range.AddressLocal(..)	as above, but in local language format

Inserting and Deleting Data in Cells

range.ClearContents	clear content of cells
range.ClearFormats	clear formatting of cells
range.Clear	clear content and formatting
range.ClearNotes	clear notes
range.Delete [xlToLeft or *xlUp]*	delete cells
range.Insert [xlToRight or *xlDown]*	insert cells

Content and Format of Individual Cells

range.Value	value of a cell
range.Text	formatted string with content of the cell (read-only)
range.Characters(start, number)	individual characters of text
range.Formula	cell formula in A1 format, English function names
range.FormulaR1C1	formula in R1C1 format, English function names
range.FormulaLocal	cell formula in A1 format, local language names
range.FormulaR1C1Local	formula in local format, local function names
range.HasFormula	tells whether the cell contains a formula
range.NoteText(text, start, end)	reads or changes up to 255 characters of a cell note
range.Font	refers to a font object
range.VerticalAlignment	vertical alignment (left/right/center/justified)
range.HorizontalAlignment	horizontal alignment (upper/lower/middle)
range.Orientation	text orientation (horizontal/vertical)
range.WrapText	text wrap
range.ColumnWidth	width of an entire column
range.RowHeight	height of an entire row
range.NumberFormat	string with number format
range.Style	string with style name
range.BorderAround style, weight	sets the entire border
range.Borders	reference to border object
range.Row	row number of the cell
range.Column	column number of the cell

Workbooks, Windows, and Worksheets

This section deals with workbooks, windows, and worksheets. All three of these concepts are represented by objects, where an additional distinction is made among types of worksheets (tables, charts, and forms). We first describe all important methods and properties for working with these objects, and then give several examples of their application.

Objects, Methods, and Properties

Application Object

Application represents the basic object within Excel. *Application* does not refer to a particular Excel file, but to the program Excel as a whole. The properties and methods of *Application* thus influence for the most part settings that hold for all open files (general options, for instance). In this section the object *Application* is of great importance to the extent that it is the starting point for practically all methods and properties used to control workbooks, windows, and worksheets. In this respect *Application* is frequently the default object: When methods such as *Worksheets* are used without an object being specified, then *Application* is automatically supplied as the object.

Workbooks

Workbooks (the *Workbook* object) are synonymous with Excel files. A workbook generally comprises several sheets and is displayed in one or more windows. There is also the possibility that the windows of a workbook are invisible. Though such a workbooks may be invisible, its data are present, and procedures defined therein can be executed. There are three methods and properties for accessing open workbooks, all of which return as result a *Workbook* object.

Workbooks: This method enables access to all open workbooks. Individual workbooks can be accessed by supplying a numerical index (1 to *Count*) or by providing the file name. If no workbook is open, then *Count* returns the value 0.

ActiveWorkbook: This method refers to the currently active workbook. The active workbook is the workbook that is located in the front window and can accept input.

ThisWorkbook: This property refers to the workbook that contains the code that is currently being executed. This workbook is not necessarily the same as the *ActiveWorkbook*, since a procedure in workbook *A* can process a sheet in workbook *B*. In particular, this property must be used when the code in question is located in an invisible workbook, since in this case it is always another workbook that is considered "active."

Methods for Processing Workbooks

Activate: This method transforms the given workbook into the active workbook. Note that the equivalent method ***Select*** used with other objects cannot be used here.

Add: This method must be used on *Workbooks*, and it returns a new, empty, workbook. An optional sheet type (such as *xlChart*) can be given, in which case the new workbook will contain only one sheet.

Close: This method closes the workbook given as object. If the workbook contains unsaved data, then an alert automatically appears. (This alert can be eliminated with *Application.DisplayAlerts=False.*)

Open: This method must be used on *Workbooks*. It loads the workbook given by its file name. A host of optional parameters control a number of loading variants (such as transforming from another data format, password protection, read-only format).

Save: This method saves the given workbook (or the active workbook if *Application* is given as object) under its current name. If the file does not have a name, then a file-selection dialog box opens automatically.

SaveAs: As above, but now a valid file name must be given. If the file name already exists, then an alert appears that asks whether that file should be overwritten. *SaveAs* cannot be applied to the *Application* object, but rather to individual tables and charts.

SaveCopyAs: As above, but this method does not change the file name of the workbook. It is for *Workbook* objects only.

GetOpenFilename: This method displays the form for file selection. When a valid file name is selected, this name is returned by the method; otherwise, it returns the Boolean value *False*. However, the selected file is not opened. This method must be applied to the *Application* object.

GetSaveAsFilename: As above, but in this case an as yet nonexistent file name can be given.

Important Properties of Workbooks

Name*, *Path*, *FullName: These three properties give respectively the file name without the path, only the path, and, finally, the full file name with path. *Path* contains an empty character string if the workbook has not yet been saved and thus has no file name.

Saved: This property tells whether the file has been changed since the last time it was saved (*True*) or whether it must be saved (*False*).

Windows

Windows are provided for the display of workbooks, where the possibility exists of opening several windows for the same workbook. Even invisible windows or windows that have been reduced to icons are considered "normal" windows by Excel. They differ from visible windows only in the properties *Visible* and *WindowState*. The management of windows is similar to that of workbooks.

Windows: This method enables access to individual windows, which are given by an index number or by name. Note that this method also returns windows that have been reduced to icons or have been rendered invisible. When *Application* is given as the object, then *Windows* returns an enumeration object of *all* windows. However, this method can also be applied to a *Workbook* object, and then it returns only the windows of this workbook.

ActiveWindow: This property of the *Application* object refers to the active window.

Methods for Processing Windows

Activate: This method activates the window given as object. Note that the often equivalent method ***Select*** cannot be used on windows.

ActivatePrevious, ActivateNext: These methods activate the previous and next windows, respectively, and place the window given as object at the end of the list of windows.

Close: This method closes the given window. If the window in question is the last window of the workbook and this workbook contains data that have not yet been saved, then an alert appears automatically to ask whether the workbook should be saved.

NewWindow: This method (applied to an existing window or to a *Workbook* object) creates a new window. This window contains a copy of the given window or, respectively, of the active window of the workbook. Note that the method *Add* is, in fact, defined for almost all other objects, but not for windows!

Important Properties of Windows

WindowState: This property determines the appearance of a window. Possible values are *xlMaximized, xlMinimized* (icon), *xlNormal.*

Visible: This property tells whether the window is visible (*True*) or invisible (*False*). Invisible windows are said to be "hidden" (command WINDOW|HIDE).

Caption: This property gives the title of the window.

DisplayGridlines, DisplayHeadings: These properties determine whether the gridlines, respectively row and column headings, should be displayed.

Zoom: This property determines the zoom factor (10 to 400 percent).

ScrollColumn, ScrollRow: These properties determine the column and row numbers in the upper left-hand corner of the window.

Split, FreezePanes: These properties tell whether the window is split and whether the division is fixed.

SplitRow, SplitColumn: These properties determine the position of the window division lines.

Width, Height, Left, Top: These properties give the size and position of a window in points (1 point = 1/72 inch).

UsableWidth, UsableHeight: These properties give the internal dimensions of a window (without window border, title bar, scroll bars, and so on).

Windowpanes

Divided windows can exhibit up to four sections (panes). Windowpanes are controlled with individual *Pane* objects. Access to these objects is made either with the *Window* property ***ActivePane*** or with the *Window* method *Panes.ActivePane*. The enumeration of *Panes* can also be done with unsplit windows, though in this case there exists only a single pane.

The currently active pane can be altered with *Activate*. The two most important properties of a *Pane* object are *LineColumn* and *SplitColumn*, which are defined similarly to windows.

Worksheets

Access to sheets is accomplished with enumeration methods and with individual *ActiveXxx* properties. Excel recognizes three types of sheets: worksheets (also for saving Excel 4 macros), charts, and forms in the format of Excel 5/7.

TIP *To be precise, there is also a fourth type of sheet, which, however, has not been supported since Excel 97: module sheets (object type* Module*). Modules were displayed in Excel 5/7 as worksheets, but since Excel 97 they can be edited only in the VBA development environment. Note, however, that in the loop* For Each s In Sheets *all modules will be run through, even though this object type supposedly no longer exists.*

Sheets: enables access to all sheets of a workbook, or all sheets of the currently active workbook when the *Application* object is given. This method returns the result as, depending on the type of sheet, a *Worksheet, Chart,* or *DialogSheet* object.

CAUTION *There is no general object type for sheets (thus no* Sheet *object). If* x *is defined, as in the following example, as a* Worksheet *(instead of a more general object variable), then an error will result if another sheet type is assigned to the variable. Solution: Define* ws *as a general* Object *and fix the object type of the variable with* Typename.

```
' Warning, this example produces an error if the workbook
' contains sheets other than worksheets!
Dim ws As Worksheet
For Each ws In ActiveWorkbook.Sheets
  Debug.Print ws.Name
Next ws
```

Worksheets, Charts, DialogSheets, Excel4MacroSheets, Excel4IntlMacro-Sheets: These are like *Sheets*, but these six methods return sheets only of the given type.

SelectedSheets: This enables access to all selected sheets of a window. This method is useful for working with groups of sheets, that is, after several sheets have been simultaneously selected.

ActiveSheet, ActiveChart, ActiveDialog: These three properties refer to the currently active sheet of the corresponding type. (In the case of the first property, all three sheet types are possible.)

Methods for Working with Sheets

Select, Activate: These two methods activate the given sheet. As long as only one sheet is being processed, the two methods are equivalent. With *Select*, however, it is possible to set an optional parameter to *False*. The selected sheet then does not replace the sheet that has been active up to now. Rather, there results a multiple selection. In this way groups of sheets can be worked on together.

Add: This method inserts a new, empty, sheet. The position, number, and type of new sheets can be set with four optional parameters. Without these optional parameters, VBA inserts an empty worksheet in front of the currently active worksheet. The new sheet is made into the active sheet. The name of the worksheet can be set with the property *Name*.

Copy: This method copies the sheet given as an object into a new, otherwise empty, workbook. If a sheet is given in *Copy* in an optional parameter, then the new sheet will be inserted before this sheet. In this way the new sheet can also be duplicated within the workbook. Together with the sheet, all objects contained within it and all program code belonging to it are copied as well.

> **CAUTION** *In copying an Excel 97 worksheet with embedded MS Forms controls these controls will indeed be copied, but they receive new names (*CommandButton1, CommandButton2, *etc.). However, the program code is not correspondingly changed, for which reason the link between controls and code is lost.*
>
> *In the case of controls that were inserted in Excel 2000 into a worksheet this problem no longer occurs. On the other hand, if you use an existing Excel 97 file under Excel 2000, then this error is present as before. Solution: Under Excel 2000 change the names of all controls. Then Excel will "notice" this change. (The best thing to do is to change the names twice. The second time you simply restore the original name. Then you will not have to change the code.)*

Delete: This deletes the sheet specified as object. There appears an alert, in which the user must confirm that the sheet is really to be deleted. In the current version this box cannot be prevented from appearing! In the following section we shall show how with *SendKeys* the message can be acknowledged at once without action on the part of the user.

The Most Important Sheet Properties

Name: This property determines the name of the sheet.

Visible: This property tells whether a sheet is visible or hidden. Hidden sheets can be made visible with the program code (*Sheets(...).Visible=True*). There is no equivalent menu command for this operation! Invisible sheets cannot be activated with *Select*.

Programming Techniques

Obtaining File Names and Opening Workbooks

VBA offers two methods for obtaining a file name, namely, *GetOpenFilename* and *GetSaveAsFilename*. These methods lead to the display of a dialog box for selecting a file, and then they return the file name or *False*. The only difference between the two methods is that with *GetSaveAsFilename* it is permissible to give the name of a file that does not yet exist.

The following example code requests the user to select an Excel file, which then is opened. The parameter of *GetOpenFilename* gives the file filter; in the dialog box only those file names are displayed that match the pattern `*.xl?`. Further details on dealing with *GetOpenFilename* and *GetSaveAsFilename* are to be found later in this chapter.

```
' example file Sheets.xls
Sub LoadExcelFile()
  Dim result
  result = Application.GetOpenFilename("Excel files,*.xl?", 1)
  If result = False Then Exit Sub
  Workbooks.Open result
End Sub
```

Transforming Windows into Icons

If you can no longer see what is going on due to a superfluity of windows, then it can be advantageous to shrink all windows to icons at the push of a button. The only thing special in the following example is the test *If win.Visible*. This prevents the attempt at making invisible windows become smaller (which would lead to an error).

```
' example file Sheets.xls
Sub ShowWindowsAsIcons()
  Dim win As Object
  For Each win In Windows
    If win.Visible Then win.WindowState = xlMinimized
  Next win
End Sub
```

Splitting Windows at the Current Position of the Cell Pointer

The following example program splits a window at the current position of the cell pointer. If the division of the window was previously fixed, then it will again be fixed in the new division. We will use *win* as an abbreviation for accessing the active window. The location at which the window is split is a result of the row and column difference between the active cell and the cell visible in the upper left-hand corner (whose position is determined with the window properties *ScrollRow* and *ScrollColumn*).

```
' example file Sheets.xls
Sub SplitWindow()
  Dim freezeMode, win As Window
  If TypeName(ActiveSheet) <> "Worksheet" Then Exit Sub
  Set win = ActiveWindow
  freezeMode = win.FreezePanes
  win.FreezePanes = False      ' otherwise, the division
                               ' cannot be changed
  If win.Split Then win.Split = False: Exit Sub  ' join split parts
  ' set new split position
  win.SplitRow = ActiveCell.Row - win.ScrollRow
  win.SplitColumn = ActiveCell.Column - win.ScrollColumn
  win.FreezePanes = freezeMode   ' reinstitute freezing
End Sub
```

With the *TypeName* test, the macro is immediately exited if no worksheet is currently active. (Splitting of a window is possible only with worksheets.)

Turning Gridlines and Cell Headings On and Off

There are two window properties that are used particularly often in daily work with tables: showing gridlines and showing row and column headings. The program below tests the current state of both settings and changes into the next mode from among the four possible modes: both window elements visible, only gridlines, only cell headings, neither of them.

The macro can be linked to a new tool in the toolbar. Then with a single tool (once again saving toolbar space) it is possible to switch among four different settings. Even if you have to click three times to achieve the desired mode, this is still more convenient than using the command TOOLS|OPTIONS|VIEW.

```
' example file Sheets.xls
Sub ToggleHeadingsGrids()
  Dim gridMode&, headingsMode&
  On Error Resume Next
  headingsMode = ActiveWindow.DisplayHeadings
  gridMode = ActiveWindow.DisplayGridlines
  If headingsMode And Not gridMode Then
    headingsMode = False
  ElseIf Not headingsMode And Not gridMode Then
    gridMode = True
  ElseIf Not headingsMode And gridMode Then
    headingsMode = True
  Else
    gridMode = False
  End If
  ActiveWindow.DisplayHeadings = headingsMode
  ActiveWindow.DisplayGridlines = gridMode
End Sub
```

> **TIP** *With* On Error Resume Next *the macro can be executed without the error message that would appear if no worksheet were present (and therefore the macro makes no sense).*

Deleting a Sheet

For deleting a sheet, all that is necessary is to execute the *Delete* method. The problem is in the safety alerts that Excel displays before deletion. In some applications it could be an irritant to the user to be confronted suddenly with an alert generated not by the user, but by the program. For this reason the property *DisplayAlerts* can be used to deactivate such alerts during macro execution.

```
Sub DeleteActiveSheet()
  Application.DisplayAlerts = False
  ActiveSheet.Delete
  Application.DisplayAlerts = True
End Sub
```

One final suggestion: This procedure is not able to delete a single module sheet. If you launch the procedure in a module with F5, then nothing happens. VBA is equipped with a security mechanism that prohibits a sheet with executing code from being deleted.

Jumping from the First to the Last Sheet of a List

With the keyboard combinations Ctrl+Page Up and Ctrl+Page Down you can switch to the next or previous sheet. However, there is no keyboard combination for jumping to the first or last worksheet. The following four procedures, which you may copy into your personal workbook `Personal.xls` (see also the section on configuration files below), use the keyboard combinations Ctrl+Shift+Page Up and Ctrl+Shift+Page Down.

In the procedure *Workbook_Open*, which is automatically executed when a file is loaded, the event procedures for these keyboard combinations are recorded (see Chapter 4 on the subject of auto and event procedures). *Workbook_BeforeClose* then deactivates both macros when the file is closed. *GotoFirstSheet* and *GotoLast-Sheet* are more complicated than seems at first glance necessary. The instructions

```
Sheets(1).Select              ' select first sheet
Sheets(Sheets.Count).Select   ' select last sheet
```

would suffice for most situations. However, they have the disadvantage that they lead to an error if the first, respectively last, sheet is hidden. Furthermore, it is necessary to test that the sheet to be activated is not a module sheet, which can occur in the *Sheets* listing, but since Excel 97 is no longer considered a regular sheet.

```
' Sheets.xls, "This Workbook"
Private Sub Workbook_Open()
  Application.OnKey "+^{PGUP}", "GotoFirstSheet"
  Application.OnKey "+^{PGDN}", "GotoLastSheet"
End Sub
' executed automatically when the file is closed
Private Sub Workbook_BeforeClose(Cancel As Boolean)
  Application.OnKey "+^{PGDN}", ""
  Application.OnKey "+^{PGUP}", ""
End Sub
```

```
' Sheets.xls, "Module1"
Sub GotoFirstSheet()' activates the first sheet
  Dim i&
  For i = 1 To Sheets.Count
    If Sheets(i).Visible And TypeName(Sheets(i)) <> "Module" Then
      Sheets(i).Select
      Exit Sub
    End If
  Next i
End Sub
Sub GotoLastSheet()      'activates the last sheet
  Dim i&
  For i = Sheets.Count To 1 Step -1
    If Sheets(i).Visible And TypeName(Sheets(i)) <> "Module" Then
      Sheets(i).Select
      Exit Sub
    End If
  Next i
End Sub
```

Syntax Summary

All of these methods and properties can refer to the *Application* object, some of them also to *Workbook* or *Window* objects.

Access to Workbooks, Windows, and Sheets

Workbooks	access to all workbooks
Windows	access to all windows
Sheets	access to all sheets of a workbook
SelectedSheets	access to groups of sheets (with multiple selection)
Worksheets	access only to worksheets
Charts	access only to chart sheets
DialogSheets	access only to form sheets
Modules	access only to module sheets
Excel4MacroSheets	access only to Excel 4 macro sheets
Excel4IntlMacroSheets	access to international macro sheets
ActiveWorkbook	currently active workbook
ThisWorkbook	workbook in which the code is located
ActiveWindow	active window
ActiveSheet	active sheet of a window/workbook/application
ActiveChart	active chart of a window/workbook/application
ActiveDialog	active form of a window/workbook/application

Working with Workbooks

workbk.Activate	determines the active workbook
Workbooks.Add	adds a new, empty, workbook
workbk.Close	closes the workbook
workbk.Open "filename"	opens the specified file
workbk.Save	saves the workbook
workbk.SaveAs "filename"	as above, but under the given name
workbk.SaveCopyAs "dn"	as above, without changing the name of the workbook
workbk.Name	contains the file name without the path name
workbk.Path	only the path
workbk.FullName	path plus file name
workbk.Saved	tells whether the workbook has been saved
Application.GetOpenFilename	select an existing file name
Application.GetSaveAsFilename	select a new file name

Working with Windows

win.Activate	activates the specified window
win.ActivatePrevious	activates the previously active window
win.ActivateNext	activates the next window in the list
win.Close	closes the specified window
win.NewWindow	creates a new window
win.WindowState	*xlMaximized/xlMinimized/xlNormal*
win.Visible	makes visible or invisible (*True/False*)
win.Caption	gives the window caption
win.DisplayGridlines	show gridlines (*True/False*)
win.DisplayHeadings	display row and column headings (*True/False*)
win.Zoom	zoom factor (10-400 percent)
win.ScrollColumn	visible column number on the left border
win.ScrollRow	visible row number on the upper border
win.Split	tells whether a window is split (*True/False*)
win.FreezePanes	tells whether a window division is fixed
win.SplitRow	determines the number of rows in the upper pane
win.SplitColumn	determines the number of columns in the left pane
win.Width/Height	outside dimensions in points (1/72 inch)
win.UsableWidth/UsableHeight	internal dimensions in points
win.Left, win.Top	position in points

Working with Windowpanes

win.Panes	access all panes of a window
win.ActivePane	access the active pane of a window
pane.Activate	determines the active pane
pane.SplitColumn	row number on the upper border
pane.SplitRow	column number on the left border

Working with Worksheets

sheet.Activate	selects a sheet
sheet.Select False	multiple selection
workbk.Add	adds an empty worksheet
workbk.Add before:= , type:=	as above, plus position type and sheet type
sheet.Copy	copies a sheet into a new workbook
sheet1.Copy sheet2	copies sheet 1 and inserts it before sheet 2
sheet.Delete	deletes the sheet (with alert)
sheet.Name	name of a sheet
sheet.Visible	make visible or invisible

Data Transfer via the Clipboard

Copying, Cutting, and Pasting Ranges of Cells

If you wish to relocate or copy a range of cells, your best bet is to use the clipboard, just as in using Excel manually. The following methods are designed for data transfer to and from the clipboard.

Copy: This method copies the range of cells specified as object to the clipboard. If the method is used with an optional parameter, then the data are not copied to the clipboard, but directly to the given range.

Cut: This method functions like *Copy*, but the original data are deleted. If a range is given with the optional parameter "destination," then the cells will be shifted to that location. For this reason there is no method specifically for shifting cells.

Paste: This method inserts data from the clipboard. A worksheet must be given as object. If the destination is not given in an optional parameter, then the current selection in the worksheet will be the destination.

PasteSpecial: This method enables more complex editing with the command EDIT|PASTE SPECIAL, such as the insertion of values (instead of formulas) or carrying out calculations. This method recognizes numerous optional parameters, which are described in the on-line help. In particular, with the help of these parameters you can shift to the right or below those cells that were overwritten by the insertion.

Two properties of the object *Application* give additional information about the current contents of the clipboard and the current copy or cut mode:

CutCopyMode: This property tells whether Excel is currently in copy or cut mode. Possible values are *False, xlCut,* and *xlCopy.* With a specification of *False* an operation of cutting or copying that has already begun can be interrupted. With this the blinking frame around the copied or cut data disappears.

ClipboardFormats: This enumeration property tells which formats are exhibited by the data in the clipboard. This property is organized as a field, since the clipboard can contain data in several formats simultaneously. Possible formats are *xlClipboardFormatText* and *xlClipboardFormatBitmap* (see the on-line help).

TIP *Starting with Office 2000, Excel, Word, and the like possess not merely one clipboard, but twelve. In other words, the last twelve cut or copied data are in temporary storage and can be restored as needed. For this you need to make the toolbar "Clipboard" visible.*

However, this new feature is not accessible to VBA programmers. The commands described in this section are valid only for the last piece of data added to the clipboard. The up to eleven remaining clipboard items cannot be accessed by code.

Copying a Range of Cells into Another Sheet

The following instructions copy the data of the current region in which the cell pointer is located from table 1 to table 2. With *SpecialCells(xlVisible)* only visible data are copied. This restriction makes sense, for example, in database applications in which only the filtered data are to be transferred. If you simply wish to transfer the selected data, then the instruction *Selection.Copy* suffices.

Note that when *Paste* is invoked, although the active sheet is specified as object, the data beginning with cell A1 are copied into table 2.

```
' copy visible data to the clipboard
Selection.CurrentRegion.SpecialCells(xlVisible).Copy
' insert data beginning with A1 into table 2
ActiveSheet.Paste Range("Table2!A1")
' cancel copy mode (blinking border)
Application.CutCopyMode = False
```

Linking and Inserting Data

Depending on the origin of the data, it is possible in inserting data from the clipboard to create a link to the program from which the data originate. Then when the original program is changed, the data will also be updated in Excel.

Data linking is used most frequently within Excel, namely, when data from one file are needed in another. In using Excel in manual mode you copy data in the first file and then paste it into the second file with EDIT|PASTE SPECIAL|PASTE LINK.

For this action in program code you do not use the method *PasteSpecial*, but the method *Paste* introduced in the previous example. However, you must now employ the optional parameter *Link:=True*. Moreover, the destination must coincide with the active selection. In the example above, therefore, table 2 must be activated before the insertion and the cell pointer inserted into A1.

```
' copy visible data to the clipboard
Selection.CurrentRegion.SpecialCells(xlVisible).Copy
' insert and link data beginning with A1 into table 2
Worksheets("table2").Select
Range("A1").Select
ActiveSheet.Paste Link:=True
Worksheets("table1").Select
' cancel copy mode (blinking border)
Application.CutCopyMode = False
```

Access to the Clipboard with the DataObject

The MS Forms library offers a *DataObject* that can be used to write text to the clipboard and read text from it. (If your Excel application has no user-defined forms, insert a new form to activate the library. You may delete the unused form, and the library stays active.)

The *DataObject* is an object independent of the clipboard, which can be declared in program code as follows:

```
Dim dataobj As New DataObject
```

You can then copy the contents of the clipboard into this object with the method *GetFromClipboard*. Conversely, you can use *PutInClipboard* to transfer the contents of *dataobj* to the clipboard. To read a character string from the clipboard, the following two commands are necessary:

```
Dim cliptext$
dataobj.GetFromClipboard
cliptext = dataobj.GetText()
```

The other direction, that is, copying a text to the clipboard, goes as follows:

```
dataobj.SetText "abc"
dataobj.PutInClipboard
```

If you wish to delete the contents of the clipboard, you should execute the following two commands:

```
dataobj.Clear
dataobj.PutInClipboard
```

NOTE *As an example of programming an ActiveX library that can be used from within Excel, a program will be introduced in Chapter 14 that makes the* Clipboard *object of the programming language Visual Basic usable in Excel as well.*

Syntax Summary

Copying/Cutting/Inserting Ranges of Cells

range.Copy	copy a range to the clipboard
range1.Copy range2	copy data from *range1* to *range2*
range.Cut	as with copy, but *range* is deleted
range1.Cut range2	shift data from *range1* to *range2*
wsheet.Paste	inserts data into a worksheet
wsheet.Paste Link:=True	as above, but with a link
wsheet.Paste range	inserts data into the given range
wsheet.PasteSpecial format	inserts data in the specified format
Application.CutCopyMode	gives the current mode
Application.ClipboardFormats(n)	contains information about data in the clipboard

MSForms.DataObject—Methods

Clear	deletes content of object
GetFromClipboard	reads content of object from the clipboard
PutInClipboard	transfer the contents of the object to the clipboard
GetFormat	determines data format (like *ClipboardFormats*)
GetText	read text from object
SetText	store text in object

Working with Numbers and Character Strings

Numerical Functions, Random Numbers

There is a general problem with numerical functions in that they are to some extent defined twice, once in the VBA programming language and again as worksheet functions in Excel. For this reason it can transpire that there exist several functions for the solution of a problem that look similar but do not function in exactly the same way.

The focus of this section is the many functions for rounding off numbers, not least because there are many similar functions, and this turns rounding into a very confusing business indeed.

Using Excel Worksheet Functions

In VBA you can use all Excel worksheet functions. Many functions, for instance the trigonometric functions, are defined in Excel as well as in VBA and can be used without additional keywords, say *Sin(0.7)*. Worksheet functions that are not represented in VBA must be preceded by *Application.WorksheetFunction*, for example, *Application.WorksheetFunction.Sum(...)* to use the *SUM* function.

Even when an international version of Excel is used, the English function names must be given (see the object catalog for the *WorksheetFunction* object). If you do not know the foreign equivalent to the English name, it's tough luck for you. You will have to consult a bilingual dictionary, since the on-line help is of no use whatsoever in this regard.

> **TIP** *In Excel 5/7, worksheet functions were invoked directly with* Application.Name(), *that is, without the property* WorksheetFunction, *first introduced in Excel 97, which refers to the like-named object with a list of all worksheet functions. The greatest advance in* WorksheetFunctions *consists in the fact that now more worksheet functions than previously can be used in VBA.*
>
> *The shorthand* Application.Name() *is still permitted for reasons of compatibility, but the functions are not shown in the object catalog. In new code you should use* WorksheetFunction *to avoid potential compatibility problems in future versions of Excel.*

Rounding Numbers

In Excel and in VBA there are numerous functions that supposedly "round." However, not a single one of these functions adheres to the simple mathematical formula whereby a number with fractional part 0.5 is rounded up to the nearest integer. The functions *CLng* and *Application.WorksheetFunction.Round* come the closest.

CInt and ***CLng*** round up if the fractional part is greater than 0.5, and they round down if the fractional part is less than 0.5. Strange things begin to happen, however, when the fractional part is exactly 0.5. In this case the functions round to the nearest even integer! Thus 1.5 as well as 2.5 are rounded to 2. (Why is this so? So that the sum of a sequence of rounded random numbers will be as close as possible to the sum of the unrounded numbers.)

CInt and *CLng* differ from all the other functions named here in two further particulars: First, a character string can be given as parameter, and second, the functions return an error if the range of the variable type *Integer* (±32,767), respectively *Long* (±2^31 = ± 2,147,483,648), is exceeded.

The worksheet function *Application.WorksheetFunction.**Round*** comes fairly close to the mathematical rounding function, although it rounds negative numbers with fractional part equal to 0.5 down instead of up. Furthermore, the function requires a second parameter, which gives the desired number of decimal places. Thus *Round(1.5, 0)* returns 2; *Round(-1.5, 0)* returns –2; *Round(1.57, 1)* returns 1.6; *Round(157, -1)* returns 160.

Int generally rounds floating point numbers down: 1.9 becomes 1, while –1.9 becomes –2. The worksheet function *Application.WorksheetFunction.**RoundDown*** functions quite similarly, though as with *Round* there is a second parameter, which contains the desired number of decimal places. Thus *RoundDown(1.98, 1)* returns 1.9. Analogously, *Application.WorksheetFunction.**RoundUp*** rounds up for a desired number of decimal places.

Fix simply slices off the fractional part of the number: 1.9 is truncated to 1, while –1.9 becomes –1.

*Application.WorksheetFunction.**Even*** and *Application.WorksheetFunction.**Odd*** round to the next even, respectively odd, integer, whereby the rounding is up for positive integers and down for negative. Thus *Even(0.1)* returns 2, while *Even(-0.1)* returns –2. *Application.WorksheetFunction.**Ceiling*** and *Application.WorksheetFunction.**Floor*** round (up for ceiling and down for floor) to a multiple of the second parameter. Thus *Ceiling(1.55, 0.3)* returns 1.8. Both of these functions are defined only for positive arguments.

Fractional Part, Modulo

The instruction *x-Fix(x)* returns the fractional part of a number, where the sign is that of ***x***. You may use *Abs* to eliminate the sign.

With the modulo operator you can determine a remainder after division. Thus *x Mod 60* returns the remainder when *x* is divided by 60, that is, the number of minutes that will not fit in a whole hour (the result with *x=70* is 10, while it is 50 with *x=230*). However, the modulo operator functions only with integers.

You can easily define a modulo function for floating point numbers using *Ceiling*. *Modf(2.1, 0.5)* defined below returns 0.1, while *Modf(0.123, 0.1)* returns 0.023. The function thus defined can also be used in worksheets.

```
Function Modf(a, b)
  Modf = Abs(a) - Application.WorksheetFunction.Ceiling(Abs(a), Abs(b))
End Function
```

Sign, Absolute Value

Abs returns the absolute value of a number; thus negative numbers are turned into positive numbers. ***Sgn*** (this abbreviation stands for signum) returns –1 for negative numbers, +1 for positive numbers, and 0 for 0.

Trigonometric, Exponential, and Logarithmic Functions

VBA recognizes all of the basic trigonometric functions as well as the exponential and the square root functions, namely, ***Sin***, ***Cos***, ***Tan***, ***Atn***, ***Log***, ***Exp***, and ***Sqr***. In the on-line help under "derived functions" you can find information about how you can form other functions from these basic functions (such as Sinh or ArcCos).

Random Numbers

Rnd returns a sixteen-place random number between 0 (inclusive) and 1 (exclusive). If you require random numbers in a different range, you need to process the result of *Rnd* a bit further. Here are two examples

```
a + Rnd * (b-a)           ' returns random decimal numbers between
                          ' a (inclusive) and b (exclusive)
Int(a + Rnd * (b-a+1))    ' returns integer random numbers between
                          ' a (inclusive) and b (inclusive)
```

If you wish to avoid VBA generating the same sequence of random numbers each time that Excel is launched, you should execute ***Randomize*** in your program.

Special Functions

Aside from the functions defined in Excel and VBA (which we have by no means completely described) there are numerous additional functions in the file `Office2000\Office\Library\Analysis\Atpvbaen.xla`. Unfortunately, this poorly documented library causes so many problems in its application that its use cannot be recommended.

Character Strings

Character strings are necessary for processing information in text format. Character strings in VBA must be enclosed in double quotation marks, for example, *"abc"*. In order for a character string to be stored in a variable, it must be defined as type *Variant* or *String*. Beginning with Excel 7, the length of a character string is limited only by available memory.

> **TIP** *In certain situations many functions and properties that return a character string can return the* Variant *special value* Null. *The further processing of this value using character string functions can lead to errors. Such errors can be avoided by making a preemptive test with the function* IsNull.

> **NOTE** *Character strings are stored internally in Unicode format, that is, with two bytes per character. Unicode format is a worldwide universal character string format that is able to encode the many characters of Asian languages. If you are using Office in a country that uses the Latin alphabet, you will not notice the presence of Unicode format. All character string functions work as they always did when character strings were still stored in ANSI format, with one byte per character.*

Functions for Working with Character Strings

The three most important character string functions are *Left, Right,* and *Mid.* ***Left*** returns the first *n* characters of a string, while ***Right*** returns the last *n* characters. With ***Mid*** it is possible to read and edit an arbitrary segment of the string. Some examples: *Left("abcde",2)* returns *"ab"*, *Right("abcde",3)* returns *"cde"*, and *Mid("abcde",3,2)* reads two characters starting with the third, and thus returns *"cd"*. If *Mid* is used without the optional third parameter, then the function returns all characters starting with the one in the given position. Thus *Mid("abcde",4)* returns *"de"*.

Mid can also be used as an instruction, in which capacity it changes that part of the character string that would otherwise have been read. Here is an example, which can be executed in the immediate window.

```
s="abcde"           'variable s is given the value "abcde"
Mid(s, 3, 1)="x"    'change the third character in s
?s                  'result is "abxde"
```

Another function that gets a frequent workout is ***Len***. It returns the number of characters in a character string. Thus *Len("abcde")* returns 5.

The three functions *UCase, LCase,* and *Trim* simplify the evaluation of user-provided input: ***UCase*** changes all letters in a character string to uppercase, while ***LCase*** returns all lowercase letters. Thus *LCase("aAäÄ")* returns "aaää". The function ***Trim*** eliminates space characters at the beginning and end of a character string.

For searching character strings the function ***InStr*** is provided. This function returns the position at which one character string is to be found within another. If the search fails to find the character string, then *InStr* returns the value 0. For example, *InStr("abcde","cd")* returns 3. With an optional parameter at the beginning, *InStr* can be told at which position to begin the search. The following loop can be tried out in the immediate window; it gives all positions at which "ab" is to be found in the character string "abcdeababcd" (result: 1, 6, 8).

```
p=0
Do: p=InStr(p+1,"abcdeababcd","ab"): ?p: Loop Until p=0
```

If the value 1 is given in the optional fourth parameter of *InStr*, then in its search Excel ignores possible differences in upper- and lowercase letters.

String generates a character string made up of a given number of repetitions of a given string. Thus *String(4,"a")* returns *"aaaa"*. ***Space*** is designed especially for empty characters. For example, *Space(2)* returns " " (that is, a character string consisting of two empty spaces).

New Character String Functions in Excel 2000

With VBA 6, which is a part of Office 2000, Microsoft has blessed programmers with some new character string functions. (These are not really new at all. VBScript programmers have had these functions available for a long time.)

Split lives up to its name and splits a character string into a one-dimensional data array. In this way one or more arbitrary separation characters can be given (the default is a space character).

```
a = "abc efg"
b = Split(a)       'returns b(0)="abc", b(1)="efg"
```

> **TIP** vbCrLf *is allowed as a separation character. This will split a multi-line character string (for example, a text file) into individual lines.*

The inverse function of *Split* is ***Join***, which joins individual strings together.

```
c = Join(b)     'returns c="abc efg"
```

An aid to processing data arrays is the function ***Filter***. This function expects a one-dimensional array with character strings in its first parameter, while the second parameter should contain a search character string. The result is a new array with all character strings in which the search character string was found. The size of the resulting array can be determined with *UBound* and *LBound*.

```
Dim x, y
x = Array("abc", "ebg", "hij")
y = Filter(x, "b")          ' returns y(0)="abc", y(1)="ebg"
```

StrReverse reverses a character string (the first character becomes the last). ***InstrRev*** functions like *Instr*, but it searches starting from the end of the string.

```
x = StrReverse("abcde")                 ' returns "edcba"
n = InstrRev("abcababc","ab")           ' returns 6
```

Replace replaces a search expression in a character string with another expression. Complex search patterns such as are possible in Perl or Unix are not permitted, but for simple applications *Replace* is useful. In the following example commas are replaced by periods.

```
x = Replace("12,3 17,5 18,3", ",", ".")    ' returns "12.3 17.5 18.3"
```

The Concatenation Operator &

Several character strings can be joined together with the operator "+". For example, . *"ab"+"cde"* returns our old friend "abcde". However, the operator "&" is considerably more flexible. It automatically transforms numerical values into character strings. For example, *"ab" & 1/3* returns *"ab 0.3333333"*.

Comparison of Character Strings

Character strings, like numbers, can be compared with the assistance of the operators =, <, and > and combinations thereof (see also the overview of operators in Chapter 4). In comparing character strings, however, there are several features to note.

VBA generally compares the binary encoding of characters; that is, in comparing two character strings the code of the individual characters is compared. Therefore, uppercase letters are always "less than" lowercase letters. For example, *"Z"<"a"* is true. Furthermore, most accented letters are "greater than" all other letters, and so, for example, *"ä">"b"*.

Instead of using the comparison operators you can use the function ***StrComp***. This function returns –1 if the first character string is less than the second, 0 if both strings are equal, and 1 if the first character string is greater than the second. Thus *StrComp("a","b")* returns –1.

An example of the application of character string comparison, namely a procedure that determines the file names of the current folder and sorts them, can be found in this chapter, under the heading "Working with Files."

Country-Specific Features

With the instruction ***Option Compare Text***, which must be given at the beginning of a module and which then remains valid for the entire module, you can activate a different comparison mode. This mode takes into account the particularities of the local country's language installed under Windows. In particular, uppercase and lowercase letters now have equal values. The characters "ä" and "Ä" are now located between "A" and "B", "ß" is between "S" and "T", and so on.

Option Compare Text affects not only the comparison operators, but also the operator *Like* (see below) and the function *InStr*. With the function *StrComp* the comparison mode can be given independent of the chosen comparison option (0: binary, 1: country-specific).

The Euro Symbol €

Starting with Excel 2000 the euro sign can be effortlessly input with Alt-E and also printed on most printers. In earlier versions of Office the euro symbol was available only if a special update was installed.

> **TIP** *If you wish to use the euro sign as the default currency symbol, then you must change the country setup in the control panel. Then* Format *and* FormatCurrency *will automatically use € instead of the previously set currency symbol.*

Internally, this symbol is represented by the Unicode 8364 (hexadecimal 20AC) as well as by the ANSII code 128. (Thus it is possible to store the euro sign in ANSI files). For this reason the standard function *Asc* (gives the ANSI code of a character string) and the variant *AscW* (for the Unicode) two different values.

```
euro="€"
?Asc(euro), AscW(euro)
 128           8364
```

> **TIP** *More information on the subject of the euro and Excel can be found later in this chapter. There the euro add-in with the function* EuroConvert *is described. Furthermore, you will find there several macros to help you in the conversion of your tables to the euro.*

Pattern-Matching

The operator ***Like*** is used for pattern matching. Here "?" and "*" are wildcards that stand for an unknown character, respectively for arbitrarily many (including none) unknown characters. For example, *"Polsky" Like "*l*y"* returns *True.*

String Comparison in the Immediate Window

You can try out the principles of character string comparison in the immediate window. For example, if you input *?"a"<"b"*, then VBA answers *True.* In general, *Option Compare Binary* is valid in the immediate window unless a procedure from a module with *Option Compare Binary* has been interrupted. This situation can be most easily arrived at by typing the following four lines into a module and then executing *comp*:

```
Option Compare Text
Sub comp()
  Stop
End Sub
```

Character Strings: Input and Output

In contrast to many traditional programming languages, in VBA there exists no simple commands of the form *Print* or *Input*, commands with which a character string can be output to the display. *Debug.Print* enables output to the immediate window, but this output is invisible unless the immediate window is opened.

If you wish to deliver some information to the user of an Excel program, then your best bet is to use the command ***MsgBox***. VBA then displays a dialog box with the given text and an OK button. *MsgBox* can be used as a function for simple decisions (YES/NO or OK/CANCEL). The following program lines show the two application variants. The parameters and return values of *MsgBox* are described extensively in the on-line help.

```
MsgBox "short message"
result = MsgBox("Should this file be saved?", vbYesNo)
```

The function ***InputBox*** functions similarly to *MsgBox*, but it enables the input of a character string. The dialog box is equipped with the buttons OK and CANCEL. If the user terminates the dialog with CANCEL, then the function returns an empty string.

```
result = InputBox("Please input a number")
```

> **TIP** *In addition to* MsgBox *and* InputBox *there exists the Excel-specific variant* Application.InputBox, *which enables the input of formulas and cell references. More on this topic can be found in Chapter 7.*

Transformation Functions

This section discusses numerous functions for transforming character strings into numbers and vice versa. We shall consider the so-called information functions, by means of which the data type of a variable or property can be established. Transformation functions for date and time values can be found in the next section, which covers the topic "Date and Time."

Transforming Character Strings into Numbers

The simplest way to convert a character string into a numeric format is to use one of the functions ***CInt***, ***CLng***, ***CSng***, ***CDbl***, and ***CCur***. These functions take as argument character strings as well as numbers in an arbitrary *Variant* format and return a number in the corresponding variable type. Thus *CSng* returns single-precision floating point numbers (data type *Single*), while *CInt* and *CLng* round the result (see the beginning of this section).

With all five of these functions an error message is encountered if the range of numbers of the associated variable type is exceeded, or if the argument does not denote a valid number (for example, *CInt("abc")*). These functions expect a period (or a comma in some country-specific versions) as separator between the integer and fractional part of a number. Similarly, a comma is interpreted in the English-language version as the thousands separator and is ignored when the string is interpreted, while in other versions a period serves this function. (This is true also in the English VBA variant of Excel 7. The conversion functions do not orient themselves according to the settings of the development language via TOOLS|OPTIONS|MODULE GENERAL, but rather only according to the system-wide country setting.)

These functions also process data and time values. For example, *CDbl(#12/31/95#)* returns 35064 . Details on dates and times are to be found in the next section.

The function ***Val*** is quite different from the functions discussed above. The most important difference is that in all cases a period must separate the integer and fractional parts of the number. The function returns its result automatically in the appropriate data type, and thus behaves like a *Variant* variable. *Val* is much less allergic to invalid input. For instance, *Val("abc")* simply returns 0. *Val("1.2abc")* returns 1.2, and *Val("1,2")* returns 1 (since the comma is interpreted as just another text symbol). *Val* cannot accept numbers, dates, or times.

Asc returns the ANSI code of the first character. This code governs the internal representation of letters under Windows. *Asc("A")* returns 65, because Windows represents the character "A" with the code 65.

Transforming Numbers into Character Strings

CStr takes as its argument an arbitrary numerical value, a date, or a time and returns a character string derived from it. (The function uses a period as the decimal point in the English-language version, a comma in some other versions.) Thus *CStr(1/3)* returns *"0.333333"*.

The function ***Str*** is similar to the *Val* function to the extent that a period is used as the decimal separator. Hence. *Str(1/3)* returns *".333333"*. This function does not work with dates. *Str* is especially useful for the further processing of character strings that are read from text files.

Chr is the inverse function of *Asc. Chr(65)* returns *"A"*. This function can be used, for example, in order to print vertical double quotation marks (") via *Chr(34)*.

Format Functions

Much more flexible than *Str* is the function ***Format***, which transforms a format character string. Two examples will serve to indicate how this function can be used: *Format(1/3, "Scientific")* returns 3,33E-01, while *Format(1234.5678, "#,##0.##")* returns 1,234.57. Here # serves as a placeholder for an optional digit, 0 as a placeholder for digits or 0 (that is, making the placement of leading zeros possible: *Format(1234.5678, "000,##0.##")* yields 001,234.57), the period as a placeholder for the decimal point, and the comma for the thousands indicator.

> **TIP** *The enormous number of predefined formats and placeholder symbols (for dates and times as well) for defining various formats is documented in the on-line help under* Format. *(Click on* FORMAT FUNCTION EXAMPLE.*)*

New in Excel 2000 are the functions ***FormatNumber***, ***FormatCurrency***, and ***FormatPercent*** for formatting numbers, and ***FormatDateTime*** for formatting dates and times (see the next section). While these functions are less flexible than *Format*, they make up for this lack of flexibility by being easier to use. These functions use optional parameters, of which the first usually gives the number of digits to the right of the decimal point. The basic settings are taken, as with *Format*, from the system settings (such as the currency symbol). Here are some examples:

```
?FormatPercent(0.123456)            ' returns 12.35%
?FormatPercent(0.123456, 1)         ' returns 12.3%
?FormatCurrency(12345678)           ' returns $12,345,678.00
?FormatNumber(123456.789012)        ' returns 123,456.79
?FormatNumber(123456.789012, 4)     ' returns 123,456.7890
```

Determining Data Type

With the function *IsXxx* already mentioned in Chapter 4 (subject variable types) you can determine whether an as yet unknown expression (usually a *Variant* result) is of a particular data type, or whether it can be converted into that type. The most important such functions are ***IsNumeric***, ***IsDate***, ***IsEmpty***, and ***IsNull***. Note that *IsNumeric* and *IsDate* do not determine whether the argument is a number or a date, but whether the argument can be converted into this type. *IsNumeric(1)* returns *True*, but so does *IsNumeric("1")*! On the other hand, *IsNumeric("ab")* gives the result *False*.

A direct test of whether a Variant variable contains a character string is possible only with ***VarType***. This function returns for each data type a specific code number. For character strings this code number is 8.

Syntax Summary

All functions prefixed by the keyword *Application* are Excel worksheet functions. All other functions belong to the VBA language. The parameters *v*, *f*, *n*, and *s* represent *Variant* values, floating-point numbers, whole numbers, and character strings (*String*).

Rounding	
CInt(v)	rounds to nearest even integer at 0.5
CLng(v)	rounds to nearest even integer at 0.5
Int(f)	always rounds down
Fix(f)	deletes the digits to the right of the decimal point
WorksheetFunction.Round(f, n)	rounds up at 0.5, to *n* digits to right of decimal point
WorksheetFunction.RoundDown(f, n)	always rounds down (*n* decimal digits)
WorksheetFunction.RoundUp(f, n)	always rounds up (*n* decimal digits)
WorksheetFunction.Even(f)	rounds to the next even number, up or down depending on the sign
WorksheetFunction.Odd(f)	rounds to the next odd number, up or down depending on the sign
WorksheetFunction.Ceiling(f1, f2)	rounds up to a multiple of *f2*
WorksheetFunction.Floor(f1, f2)	rounds down to a multiple of *f2*

Other Numeric Functions	
Abs(f)	removes the sign
Sgn(f)	returns, according to sign –1, 0, 1
Sqr(f)	square root
Sin(f), Cos(f), Tan(f)	trigonometric functions
Atn(f)	inverse tangent
Log(f), Exp(f)	logarithmic and exponential functions
Rnd	random number between 0 and 1
Randomize	initializes the random number generator

Character Strings

Left(s, n)	returns the first *n* characters
Right(s, n)	returns the last *n* characters
Mid(s, n)	returns all characters from the *n*th on
Mid(s, n1, n2)	returns *n2* characters from the *n1*th character
Mid(s1, n1, n2) = s2	inserts *s2* into *s1*
Len(s)	returns the length of the character string
InStr(s1, s2)	searches for *s2* in *s1*; result: position or 0
InStr(n, s1, s2)	as above, but search begins with the *n*th character
InStr(n, s1, s2, 1)	as above, but case-insensitive
InStrRev(s1, s2 [,n])	like *InStr*, but search from back to front
Split(s, "x")	splits *s* at the location of the character *"x"*; returns array
Join(array, "x")	joins an array of character strings (with *"x"* inserted at the joins)
Filter(array, "x")	returns array of all character strings that contain *"x"*
Replace(s, "x", "y")	replaces all *"x"* in *s* with *"y"*
UCase(s)	changes all lowercase to uppercase
LCase(s)	changes all uppercase to lowercase
Trim(s)	deletes spaces at beginning and end
String(n, "x")	returns the character string *"x"* repeated *n* times
Space(n)	returns *n* spaces
Option Compare Text	then *"a"="A"* and *"A"<"Ä"<"B"*
StrComp(s1, s2)	–1 if *s1<s2*, 0 if *s1=s2*, else +1
StrComp(s1, s2, 0)	as above, but always binary comparison
StrComp(s1, s2, 1)	as above, but always country-specific comparison
MsgBox "text"	displays the text in a dialog box
MsgBox("text", buttons)	as above; enables a choice to be made
InputBox("text")	enables the input of a character string

Transformation Functions

CInt(v)	returns an integer
CLng(v)	as above, but a long integer, thus within a greater range
CSng(v)	simple floating point number
CDbl(v)	double floating point number
CCur(v)	number in currency format

CBool(v)	Boolean value (*True/False*)
CDate(v)	date/time
CStr(v)	character string
Val(s)	returns the value of the character string
Str(v)	transforms a number into a character string
Format(v, s)	returns a character string, where the format instruction in *s* is applied
FormatNumber(v, n)	formats *x* as a number with *n* decimal places
FormatCurrency(v, n)	formats *x* as a currency value with *n* decimal places
FormatPercent(v, n)	formats *x* as a percentage with *n* decimal places
Asc(s)	returns the ANSI code of the first character
AscW(s)	returns the Unicode of the first character
Chr(n)	returns the character with code *n* (0–255)

Determining Data Type

IsNumeric(variable)	test whether conversion to a number is possible
IsDate(variable)	test whether conversion to a date or time is possible
IsArray(variable)	test whether not a variable, but a field
IsError(variable)	test whether error value
IsMissing(variable)	test whether optional parameter is missing
IsEmpty(variable)	test whether empty
IsNull(variable)	test whether uninitialized
IsObject(variable)	test whether reference to an object
VarType(variable)	numeric value given by the data type
TypeName(variable)	character string that describes the data or object type

Working with Dates and Times

Working with dates and times has always been a task that is more difficult than it appears to be at first glance. With its host of date and time functions, Microsoft has done little to improve the situation.

Excel and the Year 2000

Let me state at once that Excel has no difficulty with representing the year 2000 correctly. A possible source of problems, however, is the automatic addition of the century when only the last two digits of a year are given. Usually, a window of time is applied; that is, two-digit years are automatically attributed to the period from 1930 to 2029. It is readily admitted that this interval is not a constant of nature, and it could change in the future (with a different operating system or version of Office). With Windows 98 and Windows 2000, in fact, this interval can be set by the user (Control Panel/Regional Settings/Date), which can open the floodgates to untold trouble. You would do well not to rely on these settings.

In general, in your program code you should represent all years with four digits, without exception. (Fortunately, beginning with Excel 2000, dates input in the form *#12/31/1999#* are automatically represented with four digits. In Excel 97 this was impossible for some unexplained reason.) If you permit input into a form in two-digit format (it's less work ...), then you should immediately convert this input to four-digit representation so that the user receives, while still interacting with the form, a reply showing how the input date has been interpreted internally.

> **TIP** *Dates in worksheets are usually represented with only two digits. The reason for this is that for formatting it frequently happens that the "short date format" predefined by the system setting is used, and this contains only two digits. You can change this setting globally in the local settings by using* yyyy *instead of simply* yy *(Figure 5.2). The new setting then holds in all programs that use this format (and also, by the way, for the VBA functions* Format *and* FormatDateTime*).*

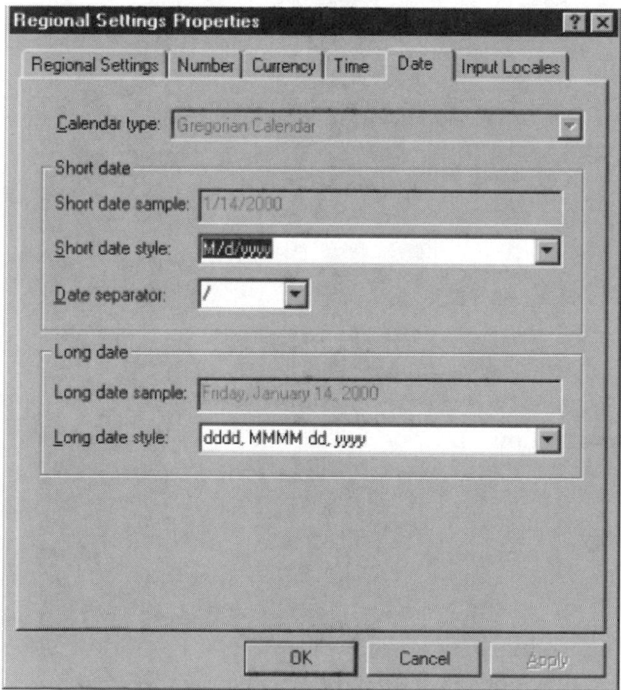

Figure 5.2. Four-digit years as the global default setting

Dates and Times in Program Code

In VBA procedures dates and times are enclosed between two # signs, for example, *#12/31/1999#* or *#17:30#* or even the combined *#12/31/1999 17:30#*. Sad to say, Excel turns *#17:30#* into *#5:30:00 PM#*, whether you want it to or not, but at least it accepts *#17:30#* as valid input. However, *#31.12.1997#* is not permitted, and it leads to an error message. Dates must be input in American format (month/day/year).

American notation for dates and times is required only in VBA code. In conversion from or to character strings, VBA conforms to the regional setting under Windows. Thus it is only you as the programmer who is confronted with the requirement of American format, not the user of your VBA program. In the German regional setting, for example, *MsgBox "Datum: " & #12/31/1999#* displays the character string *"Datum: 31.12.1999"*. Similarly, the character string *"31.12.1999"* is properly processed by most functions.

If you wish to use an international format in program code as well, then you can declare dates and times as character strings in the *Cdate* function, say, *CDate("31.12.1999")* instead of *#12/31/1999#* or *CDate("17:30")* instead of *#5:30:00 PM#*. These time inputs will be correctly converted according to the Windows regional setting. However, this form of time declaration has two drawbacks: First, the code runs (minimally) slower, and second, the code is not portable (since the results of *CDate* depend on the regional settings of the computer on which the code is executed).

A further alternative for declaration of dates and times is offered by the functions *DateSerial(year, month, day)* and *TimeSerial(hour, minute, second)*. This does not look like particularly compact code, but at least it is unambiguous and independent of the regional setting.

Internal Representation of Dates and Times

Date and time are represented internally by floating point numbers. The number 0 corresponds to the date 1 January 1900, 2 to 2 January 1900, etc. The time is stored in the digits to the right of the decimal point. Thus 0.25 corresponds to 1 January 1900, 6:00 A.M., while 34335.75 corresponds to 1 January 1994 at 6:00 P.M.

> **NOTE** *In worksheets, floating point numbers are represented as a date or time only if the cell in question has been set to contain a date or time format. If a date or time is input at the keyboard, then Excel automatically chooses a suitable format. On the other hand, if you carry out calculations with dates and times, you yourself are responsible for the correct formatting of the result cell.*

As far as Excel is concerned, dates and times are just ordinary numbers that can be employed in calculations without further processing. Therefore, you can effortlessly calculate the difference between two dates or two times or add a given number of days to a particular date.

In Excel tables the valid range of dates is from 1 January 1900 to 31 December 2078. In VBA procedures in which the variable type *Date* is used, dates are allowed between 1 January 100 and 31 December 9999. In this case, dates before 1 January 1900 are represented as negative numbers.

To achieve compatibility with the Macintosh version of Excel there is the option, under TOOLS|OPPTIONS|CALCULATION, to use the 1904 date system, in which the number 0 corresponds to 1 January 1904. This change is valid in both worksheets and VBA procedures.

Errors

Dates between 1/1/1900 and 2/28/1900 are incorrectly converted between VBA and Excel tables. If you execute the instruction *Worksheets(1).[A1]=#1/1/1900#*, you will find in cell A1 the date 1/2/1900! If you directly type 1/1/1900 into cell A1 and then execute the VBA instruction *?Worksheets(1).[A1]*, then the result is 12/31/1899.

The cause of the error is easy to establish. In Excel worksheets the leap day 2/29/1900 is allowed, but not in VBA. (VBA is correct!) In the year 2000, which is the critical one, both date functions work correctly and accept 2/29/2000 as a valid date.

The result is that within Excel tables dates before 3/1/1900 cause trouble. Since the entire range of validity for dates begins only with 1/1/1900, the problem is restricted to a period of two months. The VBA date function seems to function entirely correctly (at least all attempts to find an error have failed).

For the interested reader, here is the background: According to the Gregorian calendar, which is the calendar used in most of the world today, every year that is divisible by 4 is, in general, a leap year, such as the years 1988, 1992, and 1996. However, if a year is divisible by 100, then it is not a leap year, unless it is also divisible by 400, in which case it is. Therefore, 1700, 1800, and 1900 are not leap years, but 1600 and 2000 are.

Overview of the Remainder of the Section

The numerous functions for dates and times constitute a veritable Tower of Babel. There are functions that can be used only in worksheets, others that can be used only in VBA procedures, and still others that are doubly defined for both VBA and worksheets, those that can be used in VBA code only if prefixed by *Application.WorksheetFunction*, and so on.

So that you do not lose your overview entirely, the following description goes subsection by subsection. First are described the functions that can be employed in VBA code. Then worksheet functions are described, with like-named functions referred to in the first section. We then go on to demonstrate application techniques in both worksheets and VBA code. The next subsection goes especially into the problem of holidays, which vary from country to country and thus cannot be provided independently by Excel. The last subsection provides the usual denouement: a syntax summary.

VBA Functions

The functions described below can be used only in VBA code, not in worksheets. However, for each of these functions there exist equivalent worksheet functions.

Date returns the current date, while ***Time*** returns the current time. These two keywords (and these only, not the keywords *Now, Timer,* etc. described below) can also be used in variable assignments, and then they change the computer system's date and time. Here both character strings and *Date* values can be defined, such as *Time= #8:30#: Date=#12/31/97#.* The function ***Now*** returns the current date and time. ***Timer*** returns the number of seconds since midnight.

Please note that the three properties *Date, Time,* and *Now* are accurate only to the second. *Timer* has a somewhat finer division, changing 17 times per second under Windows 9x , and 100 times under Windows NT.

DateValue and ***TimeValue*** take as argument a character string in the language set under Windows and return their result in Excel's *Date* format. Thus *DateValue("31 December 1999")* returns 12/31/1999.

DateSerial and ***TimeSerial*** each take three arguments, *year, month, day* or *hour, minute, second.* The result is again a *Date* value. *DateSerial(1997,12,31)* returns 12/31/1997. These functions are extremely flexible in the evaluation of the parameter. Thus *DateSerial(1997,13,1)* returns 1/1/1998 , *DateSerial(1997, 2,31)* returns 3/3/1998, *DateSerial(1998,0,-1)* returns 11/29/1997. Analogously, *TimeSerial (4,-5,0)* returns 3:55 (that is, five minutes before 4:00). In carrying out calculations (such as the current date plus one month) this flexibility is quite valuable.

Hour, ***Minute***, and ***Second*** return the components of the time. *Minute(#6:45:33#)* returns 45. The time can also be given as a *Date* value or as a character string.

Year, ***Month***, and ***Day*** are the equivalent functions for year, month (1–12), and day (1–31) of a date. Hence *Month("1 April 1999")* returns 4.

WeekDay functions like *Day* and returns the day of the week (1 = Sunday through 7 = Saturday). Alternatively, you can use the worksheet function *Application.WorksheetFunction.WeekDay.* This function is distinguished from the like-named VBA function by a second optional parameter for the mode *m.* For *m*=2 the function returns the values 1 through 7 for Monday through Sunday, for *m*=3 the values 0 though 6. (See also the on-line help under *Weekday*.)

For calculations based on a 360-day year, which is used in some applications, there exists the function *Application.WorksheetFunction.**Days360***. This worksheet function returns the number of days between two dates on the basis of twelve months of thirty days each. If an optional third parameter *False* is given, then the function calculates according to the European method, otherwise (the default) according to the American. Details on this function can be found in the on-line help under *Days360*. An example showing a result different from that obtained by direct subtraction of dates is *Days360(#4/30/1999#, #5/31/1999#, False)*: Calling this function returns the value 30, although there are 31 days between the ends of the two months.

For transformation of character strings and numbers into *Date* values and vice versa we have the functions ***CDate***, ***CStr***, ***CSng***, and ***CDbl***, defined in the previous section. *CDate* corresponds essentially to a combination of *DateValue* and *TimeValue* (since date and time are considered together). Here are two examples: *CDate(34418.4)* returns 3/25/1994 at 09:36 a.m., while *CDbl(#31/12/1995 11:30#)* returns 35064.479.

Calculating with Dates

The functions *DateAdd*, *DateDiff*, and *DatePart*, which have been available since Excel 4, have also made their way into VBA. ***DateAdd*** is used for adding one or more intervals of time to a time or date. The interval is given in the form of a character string: *"yyyy"* for years, *"q"* for quarters, *"m"* for months, *"ww"* for weeks, *"y"*, *"w"*, or *"d"* for days, *"h"* for hours, *"m"* for minutes, and *"s"* for seconds. The second parameter tells how often the interval should be added (with negative numbers you can even count backwards. However, only whole-number intervals are possible; half and quarter hours must be given in minutes.) The third parameter contains the starting time:

```
DateAdd("yyyy", 1, Now)     ' date and time a year from now
DateAdd("h", -2, Now)       ' date and time two hours ago
```

If invalid dates result from addition (such as 4/31), then Visual Basic returns the first valid previous date (4/30). Note that *DateSerial* behaves differently in such a situation, since *DateSerial(1998,4,31)* gives 5/1/1998!

With ***DateDiff*** you have a simple method of determining how many time intervals there are between two dates or times. The interval is given in *DateAdd* with a character string. The on-line help describes in detail how this function works. (In general, calculation is done in terms of the given interval. Therefore, the time difference between 1/31 and 2/1 is considered an entire month, while the much longer difference between 1/1 and 1/31 in considered 0 months.

```
DateDiff("m", Now, "1/1/1998")  ' number of months until/from 1/1/1998
```

DatePart determines the number of periods for a particular point in time: In the case of years the calculation is from year 0, while with quarters, months, weeks, week of the year (*"ww"*), and day of the year (*"y"*) it is from 1/1 of the year. Then there is day of the month (*"d"*) (without the optional parameter this is Sunday) and day of the week (*"w"*). In the case of hours, calculation is from 0:00, while with minutes and seconds the calculation is from the last complete hour or minute. Thus *DatePart* in most cases fulfills the same functions as the already mentioned functions *Year, Month, Day, Weekday*, and so on.

```
DatePart("m", Now)               ' number of months since 1/1
DatePart("y", Now)               ' number of days since 1/1
DatePart("d", Now)               ' number of days so far this month
DatePart("w", Now)               ' number of days so far this week
```

Character Strings for Date and Time

The functions ***MonthName*** and ***WeekdayName*** are quite practical (new in Office 2000), returning character strings according to the regional setting of the local computer. For example, *MonthName(2)* returns the character string *"February"*, while *WeekdayName(1)* gives the result *"Monday"*.

With ***FormatDateTime*** the optional parameter yields the desired format (*vbGeneralDate, vbLongDate, vbShortDate, vbLongTime, vbShortTime*). In the USA standard setting for dates one has the following results:

```
For i=0 To 4: ?FormatDateTime(Now, i): Next
  1/14/2000 3:11:05 PM
  Friday, January 14, 2000
  1/14/2000
  3:11:05 PM
  15:11
```

> **TIP** *In the above example the year has four digits even in the case of* vbShortDate. *This is not always so, depending as it does on the system setting. They look this way on the author's computer, where years are always formatted with four digits.*

Worksheet Functions

The worksheet functions described below, apart from the exceptions *Days360* and *WeekDay,* can be used only in worksheets. They correspond to various VBA functions described above, but in some cases have somewhat different names.

TODAY and *NOW* correspond to the VBA functions *Date* and *Now,* and they return the current date and, respectively, a combination of the current date and time.

DATE and *TIME* correspond to *DateSerial* and *TimeSerial* and form a date and a time from three values: year/month/day, and, respectively, hour/minute/second.

TIMEVALUE and *DATEVALUE* correspond to the like-named VBA functions. They transform character strings (such as *"3-Aug-1978"*) into times and dates. If no year is given, then Excel automatically uses the current year. (This feature holds only for worksheet functions, not for VBA functions.)

YEAR, MONTH, DAY, HOUR, MINUTE, and *SECOND* as well as *WEEKDAY* and *DAYS360* correspond to the VBA functions *Year, Month,* etc.

> **TIP** *The functions* TODAY, NOW, DATE, DATEVALUE, TIME, *and* TIMEVALUE *return numbers as their result. From these values a date or time is displayed in a cell only once that cell has been formatted in date or time format.*

One can give numerical date values (such as 34393.72917) or character strings (such as ("28-February-1994 5:30") to these functions. (In worksheets the regional setting generally holds.) *DATEVALUE* and *TIMEVALUE* pay attention only to the information relevant to them. If date and time are to be read from a character string, then the formula *DATEVALUE(x)+TIMEVALUE(x)* is required.

> **TIP** *The input of dates into cells can be in the form 2/1/00 or even 2/1, if 2/1/2000 is meant and the current year is 2000. These input forms have the advantage that they can be used without the* Shift *key.*

Application and Programming Techniques

This section describes the application of the functions just introduced to both worksheets and VBA code. Sometimes the worksheet function will be given, and at others the equivalent function in VBA syntax. The worksheet functions for the techniques here described can be found in the example file `DateTime.xls`.

In general, dates and times can be used in a "normal" fashion. That is, dates can be compared, added, and subtracted. Note that Excel automatically inserts a date format into a cell containing a function that returns a date as result. This is usually practical, but it can be annoying, for example, when instead of the result 31 (a difference in times) the date 1/31/1900 is displayed. In such cases you will have to change the format of the cell. In the examples below, "d" represents a date.

Adding a Week to a Date

```
=d+7
```

Adding a Month to a Date

```
=DATE(YEAR(d),MONTH(d)+1,DAY(d))           ' worksheet formula
DateSerial(Year(d), Month(d)+1, Day(d))    ' VBA
```

The above formula, for example, takes 3/23/1999 and returns 4/23/1999. There are exceptions to this rule when invalid dates come into the picture. From 1/31/1996 the result will be 3/2/1996 (because there is no 2/31/1996 in spite of the leap year).

Adding a Year to a Date

```
=DATE(YEAR(d)+1, MONTH(d), DAY(d))
DateSerial(Year(d)+1, Month(d), Day(d))
```

Number of Days in the Current Month

```
=DATE(YEAR(d), MONTH(d)+1,1) - DATE(YEAR(d), MONTH(d),1)
DateSerial(Year(d),Month(d)+1,1) - DateSerial(Year(d),Month(d),1)
```

Number of Days in the Current Year

```
=DATE(YEAR(d)+1,1,1) - DATE(YEAR(d),1,1)
DateSerial(Year(d)+1,1,1) - DateSerial(Year(d),1,1)
```

Number of Days in the Year Until a Given Date

```
=1+d-DATE(YEAR(d),1,1)
1 + d - DateSerial(Year(d),1,1)
```

Date of the Last Day of the Month

```
=DATE(YEAR(d), MONTH(d)+1, 0)            ' worksheet
DateSerial(Year(d), Month(d)+1, 0)        ' VBA
```

Time Difference in Years (Age Calculation)

The formula *Year(d2)-Year(d1))* is unsatisfactory for calculating a person's age. For example, *Year("1/1/1999")-Year("7/1/1950")* returns the result 49, even though the person is only 48 years old on 1/1/1999.

The solution to this problem is somewhat complex, but a simpler solution does not seem to be available. The difference will be corrected by 1 if the current date *d2* is smaller than the birth date *d1* (ignoring the year). To get the year out of the comparison, the year of date *d1* is set to the same value as in *d2*. Thus only month and day matter, not the year.

Returning to the example above, the difference in years amounts first to 49, but since 1/1/1999 is "less than" 7/1/1999, this value must be reduced by 1.

```
=YEAR(d2)-YEAR(d1)-IF(d2<DATE(YEAR(d2), MONTH(d1) ,DAY(d1)), 1, 0)
```

The formulation in VBA is somewhat more complicated, but in exchange it is easier to read:

```
diff = Year(d2) - Year(d1)
If d2 < DateSerial(Year(d2), Month(d1), Day(d1)) Then
  diff = diff - 1
End If
```

Time Difference in Months

The same problem appears in calculating with months. If the time difference between 1/25/1994 and 3/3/1994 is to be considered as two months, then you can use the first, simpler, formula. If the difference is to be considered as two months only from 3/25/1994, then you have to use the second formula (floating date boundaries):

```
=(YEAR(d2)-YEAR(d1))*12 + MONTH(d2)-MONTH(d1)     ' month boundary at the 1st
=(YEAR(d2)-YEAR(d1))*12 + MONTH(d2) - MONTH(d1)-   ' month border
  IF(d2<DATE(YEAR(d2), MONTH(d2), DAY(d1)), 1, 0)  ' as in d1
```

Date of the Next Monday

One is often faced with the problem that one is given a particular date, and from it one needs to calculate the date of the following Monday (or some other day of the week). The VBA formula for calculating the next Monday is as follows:

```
d = d + (9 - WeekDay(d)) Mod 7
```

Here is an example: Suppose that *d* is a Wednesday. Then *WeekDay* returns the value 4. Since *(9 - 4) Mod 7* returns 5, an additional five days are added to the current date. If *d* was already a Monday, then the date does not change. If you wish to change the formula so that the following Tuesday, Wednesday, and so on should be calculated, then simply replace the number 9 by 10, 11, and so on.

Calculating with Times

In calculating with times you must consider whether you are dealing with a pure time between 00:00 and 23:59 (thus a numerical value between 0 and 1) or with a time value that also contains a date. In Excel's time format both times are displayed the same way, although in the first case only times on the day 1/1/1900 are considered, while in the second case the time can be on any date.

This difference has an effect, for example, if you wish to calculate the number of minutes since midnight. If you simply multiply the time value by 24*60, you will in the first case obtain the correct result, while in the second you have the number of minutes since 1/1/1900! The correct formula is thus *=(x-TRUNC(x)) *24*60*, or, in VBA, *(x-Fix(x))*24*60*.

Cell Formats for Times Larger Than 24 Hours / 60 Minutes / 60 Seconds

The integer part of a time is also problematic when the result of a calculation is to be expressed in hours/minutes/seconds, with results greater than 24 hours/60 minutes/60 seconds allowed. Thus 30 hours is represented internally as 1.24, and in the usual time format as 6:00. In such cases you must use a time format in which the format character for hours/minutes/seconds is placed in square brackets. The brackets cancel the otherwise valid time limits (24 h, 60 m, 60 s). Possible format strings are *[h]:mm:ss*, *[m]:ss*, and *[s]*. Square brackets for days and months are not allowed.

Time Differences Spanning Midnight

The calculation of the difference between two times that span midnight, say from 20:30 to 6:40, produces a negative value. This problem can be solved by the addition of 1 (corresponding to 24 hours):

```
=IF(t2<t1, 1+t2-t1, t2-t1)
```

If the date as well is stored in *t1* and *t2* (such as 3/30/1994 , 20:30 to 3/31/1994, 6:40), then a simple difference suffices. However, the above formula presents no difficulties in this case, since in any case *t2>t1*.

Holidays

A topic worthy of a separate discussion is holidays. In addition to all the other problems of working with dates, here we have the additional difficulty that the dates of many holidays change each year! For many planning tasks it is necessary that holidays be able to be calculated easily. The example file `Holidays.xls` contains the function *Holiday(datum)*, which tests whether a given day is a holiday, and in that case returns the name of the holiday. If the date is not a holiday, then an empty character string is returned.

First some preliminaries: From an algorithmic point of view there are three types of holidays:

- those that occur on the same date each year (such as Christmas)
- those whose date depends on Easter (such as Pentecost, which is the seventh Sunday after Easter)
- those whose date depends on another formula (such as Thanksgiving Day, which occurs on the fourth Thursday in November)

Every country has its own set of holidays. Furthermore, individual states, counties, or towns may celebrate their own holidays or have a special set of bank or school holidays. It is relatively easy using the program presented here to define a custom set of rules for holidays and to calculate these for each year anew.

The determination of Easter is a special case to be dealt with. (The occurrence of Easter Sunday depends on both the solar and lunar calendars. It occurs on the first Sunday after the first full moon after the vernal equinox!) Many mathematicians have already turned their attention to this problem. The following function calculates the date of Easter for an arbitrary year using an algorithm due to Gauss. Allegedly, this algorithm works correctly for dates through 2078 (I have not checked it; for the next several years it does indeed work).

```
' example file Holidays.xls
Function EasterDate(calcYear&) As Date
  Dim zr1&, zr2&, zr3&, zr4&, zr5&, zr6&, zr7&
  zr1 = calcYear Mod 19 + 1
  zr2 = Fix(calcYear / 100) + 1
  zr3 = Fix(3 * zr2 / 4) - 12
  zr4 = Fix((8 * zr2 + 5) / 25) - 5
  zr5 = Fix(5 * calcYear / 4) - zr3 - 10
  zr6 = (11 * zr1 + 20 + zr4 - zr3) Mod 30
  If (zr6 = 25 And zr1 > 11) Or zr6 = 24 Then zr6 = zr6 + 1
  zr7 = 44 - zr6
  If zr7 < 21 Then zr7 = zr7 + 30
  zr7 = zr7 + 7
  zr7 = zr7 - (zr5 + zr7) Mod 7
  If zr7 <= 31 Then
    EasterDate = DateSerial(calcYear, 3, zr7)
  Else
    EasterDate = DateSerial(calcYear, 4, zr7 - 31)
  End If
End Function
```

The second supplementary function is called *NumberedWeekday*. It calculates for a given year and month the first, second, third, fourth, last, second to last, weekday, say, the first Monday in May or the fourth Thursday in November. The algorithm is easy to understand. Beginning with the first or last day of the month, at most 28 days are run through forward or backward. If the weekday for this date coincides with the desired weekday, then *dayCounter* is increased by 1, respectively reduced by 1. If *dayCounter* coincides with the desired number of the weekday in question, then the day that was sought has been found.

```
Function NumberedWeekday(calcYear&, calcMonth&, calcWeekday&, _
    number&) As Date
  Dim startdate As Date
  Dim i&
  Dim dayCounter&
  If number = 0 Then
    MsgBox "Invalid parameter in NumberedWeekday."
    Exit Function
  End If
  If number >= 1 Then
    'first, second, third … weekday in a month
    startdate = DateSerial(calcYear, calcMonth, 1) '1st day of month
    For i = 0 To 27
```

```
      If Weekday(startdate + i) = calcWeekday Then
        dayCounter = dayCounter + 1
        If dayCounter = number Then
          NumberedWeekday = startdate + i
        End If
      End If
    Next
  Else
    ' last, next to last … weekday in a month
    startdate = DateSerial(calcYear, calcMonth + 1, 0) 'last day of m.
     For i = 0 To 27
      If Weekday(startdate - i) = calcWeekday Then
        dayCounter = dayCounter - 1
        If dayCounter = number Then
          NumberedWeekday = startdate - i
        End If
      End If
    Next
  End If
End Function
```

HolidayTable(year) creates a list of all holidays for the given year and stores their dates and names in the two fields *holidayDate* and *holidayName*. These fields are then available to the *Holiday* function and need to be recalculated only when the year changes.

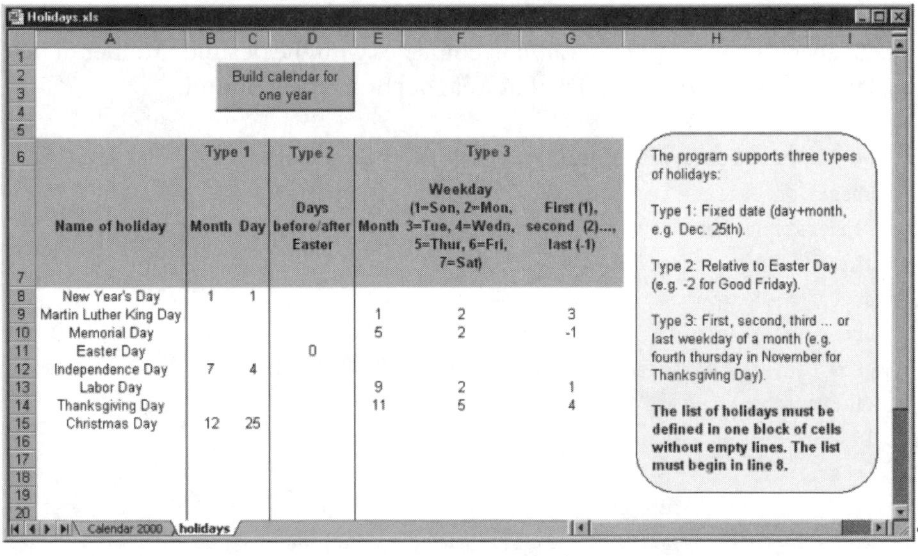

Holidays.xls

Build calendar for one year

	Type 1		Type 2	Type 3		
Name of holiday	**Month**	**Day**	**Days before/after Easter**	**Month**	**Weekday (1=Son, 2=Mon, 3=Tue, 4=Wedn, 5=Thur, 6=Fri, 7=Sat)**	**First (1), second (2)..., last (-1)**
New Year's Day	1	1				
Martin Luther King Day				1	2	3
Memorial Day				5	2	-1
Easter Day			0			
Independence Day	7	4				
Labor Day				9	2	1
Thanksgiving Day				11	5	4
Christmas Day	12	25				

The program supports three types of holidays:

Type 1: Fixed date (day+month, e.g. Dec. 25th).

Type 2: Relative to Easter Day (e.g. -2 for Good Friday).

Type 3: First, second, third ... or last weekday of a month (e.g. fourth thursday in November for Thanksgiving Day).

The list of holidays must be defined in one block of cells without empty lines. The list must begin in line 8.

Calendar 2000 | holidays

Figure 5.3. The calculational basis for the holiday function

The calculation of this table of holidays is based on the worksheet function "holidays." This worksheet contains a list of all holidays, where the date must be given as an absolute date, a date relative to Easter, or the *n*th particular weekday of a given month. The holiday table can be easily altered to account for peculiarities of various countries or if some regulation changes the date of a particular holiday.

The majority of the code of the function *HolidayTable* is thus responsible for reading the holiday block beginning in cell A8. Since the properties *CurrentRegion* and *SpecialCells* do not function when *HolidayTable* is executed via *Holiday* during calculation in a worksheet, the size of the block must be determined in a *For–Next* loop. Otherwise, the example shows how the program can be kept readable by the use of object variables (such as *holidaysRng* for the range of cells with information on the holidays, *rowRng* for a column of this range).

```
Private Sub HolidayTable(calcYear&)
  Dim easter As Date
  Dim holidaysRng As Range, rowRng As Range
  Dim upperleft As Range, lowerleft As Range
  Dim ws As Worksheet
  Dim i&
  If Not IsNumeric(calcYear) Then Exit Sub
  ' holiday table has already been calculated
  If lastcalcYear = calcYear Then Exit Sub
  ' Easter formula is defined for this range
  If calcYear < 1900 Or calcYear > 2078 Then
    MsgBox "The algorithms for this program work only between " & _
      "1900 and 2078."
    Exit Sub
  End If
  easter = EasterDate(calcYear)
  ' the sheet with the holiday data must be named "holidays"
  Set ws = ThisWorkbook.Sheets("holidays")
  ' the list of holidays starts at A8
  Set upperleft = ws.[A8]
  ' but where does it end?
  ' SpecialCells may not be used out of a
  ' worksheet function (for unknown reason);
  ' therefore, we need a loop to find the end
  For i = 1 To 300  'there are certainly less holidays …
    If upperleft.Offset(i, 0).Text = "" Then
      Set lowerleft = upperleft.Offset(i - 1, 0)
      Exit For
    End If
  Next
  Set holidaysRng = ws.Range(upperleft, lowerleft)
```

```
  ' loop for all lines of the holiday list
  ReDim holidayDate(holidaysRng.Rows.Count - 1)
  ReDim holidayName(holidaysRng.Rows.Count - 1)
  i = 0
  For Each rowRng In holidaysRng.Rows
    holidayName(i) = rowRng.Cells(1, 1)
    If rowRng.Cells(1, 2).Text <> "" Then
      ' type 1: fixed date
      holidayDate(i) = DateSerial(calcYear, rowRng.Cells(1, 2), _
        rowRng.Cells(1, 3))
    ElseIf rowRng.Cells(1, 4).Text <> "" Then
      ' type 2: date relative to Easter Sunday
      holidayDate(i) = CDate(CDbl(easter) + rowRng.Cells(1, 4))
    Else
      ' type 3: first/second/… weekday of month
      holidayDate(i) = NumberedWeekday(calcYear, rowRng.Cells(1, 5), _
        rowRng.Cells(1, 6), rowRng.Cells(1, 7))
    End If
    i = i + 1
  Next rowRng
  ' save calcYear; thus, the holiday table has to be recalculated only
  ' if the year changes
  lastcalcYear = calcYear
End Sub
```

Once the fields *holidaysDate* and *holidaysName* exist, determining a holiday becomes child's play. All dates of the *holidaysDate* field are simply compared in a loop with the given date. If a match is found, the function returns the name of the corresponding holiday. Note the construction *CDate(Int(dat))*: It accomplishes the eventual separation of the time from the date; the digits to the right of the decimal point are deleted, and then the resulting integer is again converted to a date.

```
Function Holiday(ByVal dat As Date)
  Dim i%
  If Year(dat) <> lastcalcYear Then HolidayTable Year(dat)
  dat = CDate(Int(dat))  ' eliminate the time
  For i = 0 To UBound(holidayDate())
    If dat = holidayDate(i) Then
      Holiday = holidayName(i): Exit Function
    End If
  Next
  ' it is not a holiday
  Holiday = ""
End Function
```

Calendar Generation

The function *Holiday* can be employed as a user-defined worksheet function as well as inserted into other VBA procedures. The procedure *CreateCalendar* shows how a new worksheet is introduced into the currently active workbook and a calendar inserted within it. A considerable part of the code is simply responsible for the formatting of the calendar. The procedure makes intensive use of *With*, in order to make access to individual cells more efficient and to make the code easier to read. With *Application.ScreenUpdating = False* is achieved that the screen is updated only at the end of the procedure. This speeds up the creation of the calendar. If the construction or formatting of calendars doesn't appeal to you, you can use the ideas of this procedure as a starting point for your own calendar procedures.

```
Sub CreateCalendar()
  Dim i&, calcYear&, calcMonth&, calcDay&
  Dim holid$
  Dim ws As Worksheet
  Dim start As Range
  Dim d As Date
  calcYear = InputBox("Please type in the year for the calendar!", _
    "Create calendar", Year(Now))
  Application.ScreenUpdating = False
  If Not IsNumeric(calcYear) Then Exit Sub
  ' create new worksheet in current workbook
  Set ws = Worksheets.Add()
  ws.Name = "Calendar " & calcYear
  ActiveWindow.DisplayGridlines = False
  Set start = ws.[A3]
  With start
    .Formula = calcYear
    .Font.Bold = True
    .Font.Size = 18
    .HorizontalAlignment = xlLeft
  End With
  ' add month captions
  With start.Offset(1, 0)
    For i = 1 To 12
      d = DateSerial(calcYear, i, 1)
      .Offset(0, i - 1).Formula = Format(d, "mmmm")
    Next
  End With
  ' format captions
```

```
  With Range(start.Offset(1, 0), start.Offset(1, 11))
    .Font.Bold = True
    .Font.Size = 14
    .Interior.Pattern = xlSolid
    .Interior.PatternColor = RGB(196, 196, 196)
    .HorizontalAlignment = xlLeft
    .Borders(xlTop).Weight = xlThin
    .Borders(xlBottom).Weight = xlThin
    .Interior.ColorIndex = 15
    .Interior.Pattern = xlSolid
    .Interior.PatternColorIndex = 15
    .ColumnWidth = 15
  End With
  ' add dates
  For calcMonth = 1 To 12
    For calcDay = 1 To Day(DateSerial(calcYear, calcMonth + 1, 0))
      With start.Offset(calcDay + 1, calcMonth - 1)
        d = DateSerial(calcYear, calcMonth, calcDay)
        holid = Holiday(d)
        If holid = "" Then
          .Value = calcDay
        Else
          .Value = holid
        End If
        'saturdays, Sundays, and holidays bold
        If holid  "" Or Weekday(d) = 1 Or Weekday(d) = 7 Then
          .Font.Bold = True
        End If
        'saturdays and sundays with grey background
        If Weekday(d) = 1 Or Weekday(d) = 7 Then
          .Interior.ColorIndex = 15
          .Interior.Pattern = xlSolid
          .Interior.PatternColorIndex = 15
        End If
      End With
    Next
  Next
  ' left alingment for all dates
  With Range(start.Offset(2, 0), start.Offset(32, 11))
    .HorizontalAlignment = xlLeft
  End With
End Sub
```

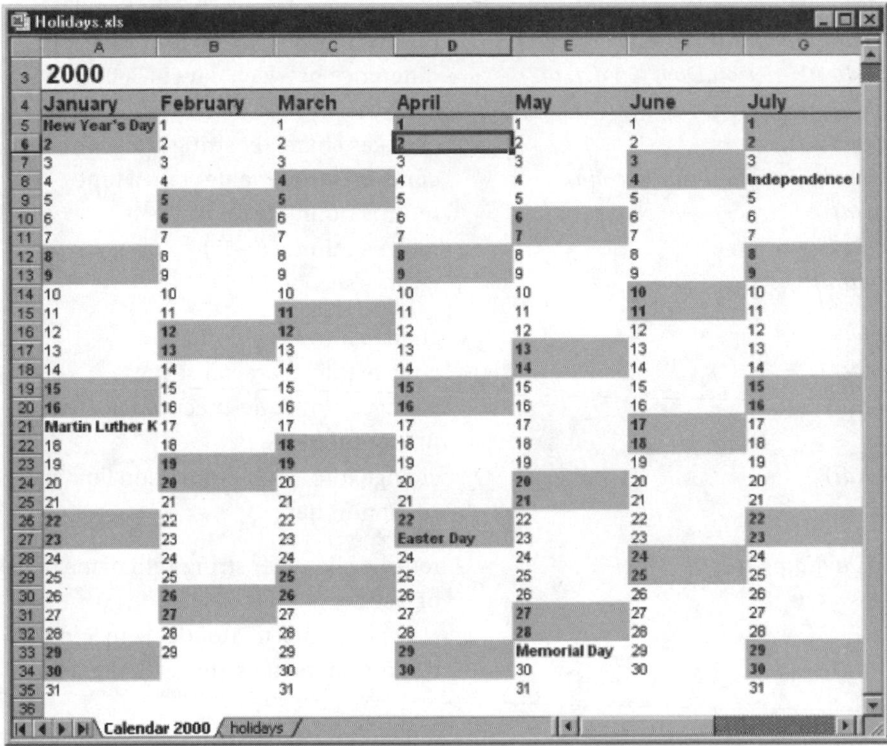

	A	B	C	D	E	F	G
3	2000						
4	January	February	March	April	May	June	July
5	New Year's Day	1	1	1	1	1	1
6	2	2	2	2	2	2	2
7	3	3	3	3	3	3	3
8	4	4	4	4	4	4	Independence I
9	5	5	5	5	5	5	5
10	6	6	6	6	6	6	6
11	7	7	7	7	7	7	7
12	8	8	8	8	8	8	8
13	9	9	9	9	9	9	9
14	10	10	10	10	10	10	10
15	11	11	11	11	11	11	11
16	12	12	12	12	12	12	12
17	13	13	13	13	13	13	13
18	14	14	14	14	14	14	14
19	15	15	15	15	15	15	15
20	16	16	16	16	16	16	16
21	Martin Luther K	17	17	17	17	17	17
22	18	18	18	18	18	18	18
23	19	19	19	19	19	19	19
24	20	20	20	20	20	20	20
25	21	21	21	21	21	21	21
26	22	22	22	22	22	22	22
27	23	23	23	Easter Day	23	23	23
28	24	24	24	24	24	24	24
29	25	25	25	25	25	25	25
30	26	26	26	26	26	26	26
31	27	27	27	27	27	27	27
32	28	28	28	28	28	28	28
33	29	29	29	29	Memorial Day	29	29
34	30		30	30	30	30	30
35	31		31		31		31
36							

Figure 5.4. The calendar for the year 2000

Syntax Summary

In the following lines *dt* stands for a date or a time (variable type *Date*), and *str* for a character string.

VBA Functions

Date	returns the current date
Date = dt	changes the system date
Time	returns the current time
Time = dt	changes the system time
Now	returns date and time
Timer	returns seconds since 00:00
DateValue(str)	transforms character string into a date
DateSerial(year, month, day)	combines three values into a date
Year(dt)	returns the year
Month(dt)	returns the month (1–12)
Day(dt)	returns the day (1–31)
WeekDay(dt)	returns day of week (1–7 for Sun–Sat)

WorksheetFunction.WeekDay(dt, 2)	returns day of week (1–7 for Sun–Sat)
WorksheetFunction.WeekDay(dt, 3)	returns day of week (0–6 for Mon–Sun)
WorksheetFunction.Days360(dt1, dt2)	difference between days in 360-day year
WorksheetFunction.Days360(dt1, dt2, False)	as above, European mode
TimeValue(str)	changes character string into a time
TimeSerial(hour, minute, second)	combines three values into a time
Hour(dt)	returns hour (0–23)
Minute(dt)	returns minute (0–59)
Second(dt)	returns second (0–59)
CDate(v)	change into *Date*-Format
CStr(dt)	change into character string
CSng(dt)	change into single-precision floating point number
CDbl(dt)	change into double-precision floating point number
WeekdayName(n)	returns character string with name of day of week (1 corresponds to Monday, 7 to Sunday)
MonthName(n) month	returns character string with name of
FormatDateTime(d, type)	returns character string with date or time (*type=vbGeneralDate / vbLongDate / vbShortDate / vbLongTime / vbShortTime)*

Worksheet Functions

TODAY()	current date
NOW()	current time
DATE(year, mon, day)	combines three values into a date
DATEVALUE(str)	changes a character string into a date
YEAR(dt)	returns year
MONTH(dt)	returns month (1–12)
DAY(dt)	returns day (1–31)
WEEKDAY(dt)	returns day of week (1–7 for Sun–Mon)
WEEKDAY(dt, 2)	returns day of week (1–7 for Mon–Sun)
WEEKDAY(dt, 3)	returns day of week (0–6 for Mon–Sun)
DAYS360(dt1, dt2)	difference between dates in 360-day year
DAYS360(dt1, dt2, False)	as above, European mode
TIME(st, min, sek)	combines three values into a time
TIMEVALUE(str)	combines three values into a time
HOUR(dt)	returns hour (0–23)
MINUTE(dt)	returns minute (0–59)
SECOND(dt)	returns second (0–59)

Working with Files; Text Import and Export

This section describes commands and techniques for working with files. The need to read from or write to files appears in practice when you wish to exchange data with external programs.

The commands, methods, and properties in Excel programming for manipulation of files come from three different libraries, which explains a great deal of the resulting confusion.

- The *Microsoft Scripting Library* makes possible object-oriented access to files, directories, and text files with *File System Objects* (FSO). This library is available to programmers for the first time with Excel 2000. (Those who also work with the programming language Visual Basic or with the Windows Scripting Host have known about this library for a longer time.)

- Since Excel 5 the commands integrated into the VBA library, with which not only text files but binary files as well can be processed, have been available.

- Finally, there is also a host of methods and properties that are Excel specific and therefore belong to Excel. To these also belong the functions for the importation of text files.

To round things off we shall introduce a procedure with which you can save a range of cells in *Mathematica*'s list format. In the process we shall present some useful programming techniques that you can use in programming your own export filters.

File System Objects: An Overview

After a long time during which the commands for working with files and directories did not change, beginning with Office 2000, *File System Objects* (FSO for short) are available for use. The significant advantage of these object classes is that they offer modern, clear, and object-oriented access to most of the functions that are needed for the analysis of file systems and for reading from and writing to files. In contrast to the traditional commands, text files in Unicode format can now be read from and written to.

We shall not be silent about the disadvantages: For one, the new objects do not constitute an integral part of VBA, but rather are located in the *Scripting Runtime* library. Therefore, you must create a reference to this library. Moreover, this library is not complete. In particular, there are no functions for reading from and writing to binary and random access files. The upshot is that in many programs the result is an unavoidable ugly and error-prone mélange of traditional commands and FSO methods.

> **TIP** *In this section the new* File System Objects *take center stage. The traditional commands will be extensively described only to the extent that they offer functionality that is lacking in the new objects. (The syntax summary at the end of this section is, however, complete.)*

Using the FSO Library

If you wish to use the FSO library in your program, you must first activate the *Microsoft Scripting Runtime* library via TOOLS|REFERENCES. The base object of this library is the ***FileSystemObject***. This object is the starting point for various methods by which *Drive[s], File[s], Folder[s],* and *TextStream* objects can be generated. For this reason it is often useful to define a global *FileSystemObject* variable with *Dim As New.* Then this variable is available whenever FSO functions are needed.

```
Public fso As New FileSystemObject
```

Starting with *fso* you can generate new objects. The following two commands, for example, generate a *Folder* object, which refers to the existing root folder in `C:`.

```
Dim f As Folder
Set f = fso.GetFolder("c:\")
```

Now with *f.Files* you can access all files in this folder, with *f.SubFolders* all directories, and so on. With properties like *Attributes, Name, Path,* and *Size* you can determine various features of the addressed files and directories.

> **TIP** *In contrast to most other enumerations, with* Drives, Files, *and* Folders *access to individual elements via* Files(n) *is not possible. As index only the name of the particular object can be used. Since as a rule this is not known in advance, you* must *work with a* For–Each *loop.*

Methods for generating or editing new directories and files are directly subordinate to the *FileSystemObject,* for example, *CopyFile, CreateFolder, DeleteFile.*

FileSystemObject : Object Hierarchy

FileSystemObject	top of the object hierarchy
└ *Drives*	listing of drives and partitions
└ *Drive*	Drive object for describing the drive

Drive: Object Hierarchy

```
Drive                    Drive object
└─RootFolder             refers to drive's root folder (directory)
   └─Folder              Folder object
```

Folder: Object Hierarchy

```
Folder                   Folder object
├─Drive                  Drive object
├─Files                  listing of all files in folder
│  └─File                File object with the attributes of a file
├─ParentFolder           parent folder
│  └─Folder              Folder object of the parent folder
└─SubFolders             Folders listing
   └─Folder              Folder object with the attributes of the subfolder
```

File: Object Hierarchy

```
File File object
└─ParentFolder           parent folder
   └─Folder              Folder object of the parent folder
```

Drives, Folders, and Files

Properties of Drives (Drive Object)

A list of all available drives can easily be obtained via the enumeration *fso.**Drives***. The properties of the associated ***Drive*** objects give information about the characteristics of the drive: ***VolumeName*** (name), ***ShareName*** (name under which the drive is known in a network), ***TotalSize*** and ***FreeSpace*** (total and free space), ***FileSystem*** (the file system type as a character string, such as *"FAT"*, *"NTFS"*, or *"CDFS"*), and ***DriveType*** (*Fixed, Remote, Removeable,* etc.).

> **TIP** *The* Drives *listing contains only local drives (and network drives associated with the drive's letter). On the other hand, possibly accessible network directories are not included.*

The sample program below shows the most important information for all accessible drives. If in drive `A:` there is no diskette, then this drive is skipped, thanks to *On Error*.

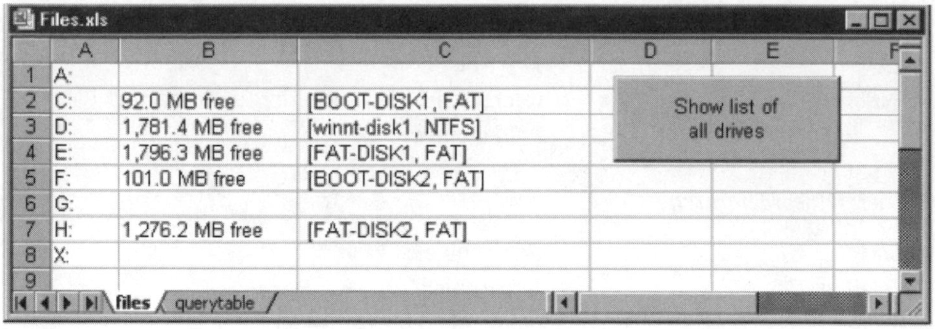

Files.xls

	A	B	C	D	E
1	A:				
2	C:	92.0 MB free	[BOOT-DISK1, FAT]	Show list of all drives	
3	D:	1,781.4 MB free	[winnt-disk1, NTFS]		
4	E:	1,796.3 MB free	[FAT-DISK1, FAT]		
5	F:	101.0 MB free	[BOOT-DISK2, FAT]		
6	G:				
7	H:	1,276.2 MB free	[FAT-DISK2, FAT]		
8	X:				
9					

files / querytable

Figure 5.5. Information on all accessible drives

```
' example file Files.xls, Module1
Public fso As New FileSystemObject
' example file Files.xls, worksheet "drives"
' display list of all drives and accessible storage devices
Private Sub btnShowDrives_Click()
  Dim dr As Drive
  Dim rng As Range
  Dim i&
  Set rng = Me.[a1]
  rng.CurrentRegion.Clear
  On Error Resume Next
  i = 1
  For Each dr In fso.Drives
    rng.Cells(i, 1) = dr
    rng.Cells(i, 2) = FormatNumber(dr.AvailableSpace / 1024 ^ 2, 1) & _
      " MB free"
    rng.Cells(i, 3) = " [" & dr.VolumeName & ", " & _
       dr.FileSystem & "] "
    i = i + 1
  Next
End Sub
```

The Current Directory

Although you will search in vain among the FSO objects for a *CurrentDir* property, this program information is considered, for example, in the method *GetFolder*. Thus *fso.GetFolder(".").Path* returns the path of the current directory (for example, `H:\WINNT4\Profiles\Administrator\Personal`).

To change the current drive and folder you must, however, still resort to the traditional commands: ***ChDrive*** changes the current drive, ***ChDir*** changes the current directory, and ***CurDir*** returns the current directory (together with the drive).

CAUTION *To change the current directory,* ChDir *is usually insufficient. The drive must also be changed. Therefore, the usual sequence of commands is as follows:*

```
path = "d:\backup"
ChDrive path
ChDir path
```

However, if path *points to a network directory (*`\\server\share\`*), then there are problems.* ChDrive *does not work with network directories and triggers an error. (This can easily be overcome with* On Error Resume Next.*) Indeed,* ChDir *changes the current directory, but only when the network directory is considered the current drive (for example, at the start of a compiled Visual Basic program that resides on a network server). If that is not the case, then there exists under Visual Basic no possibility to make a network directory the current directory!*

TIP *In addition to the current directory there is a host of Excel-specific directories whose paths can be determined by means of various properties of the Excel* Application *object. See below under Excel-specific methods and properties.*

Temporary Folder

It often happens that you wish in a program to create a temporary file (that is, a file that you use during program execution and afterwards delete). Under Windows there exists a directory designed for precisely this purpose. Normally, this is the subfolder `temp` in the Windows folder. The associated *Folder* object can easily be generated with *fso.**GetSpecialFolder**(TemporaryFolder)*. (Visual Basic recognizes two further folders: the Windows folder and the Windows system folder. Access is via *GetSpecialFolder*. As parameter you use *WindowsFolder*, respectively *SystemFolder*.)

TIP *You can, moreover, easily determine the location of the temporary folder without FSO objects: The path to this folder is contained in the system variable* TEMP. *You can access this variable via the VBA function* Environ("temp") *(for example,* `C:\WinNT4\Temp`*). Similarly with* Environ("windir")*, you can easily determine the Windows directory (for example,* `C:\WinNT4`*).*

> **TIP** *If you need not only the name of the temporary folder but also a suggestion for a valid (not already used) file name within it, you simply use* fso.**GetTempName**(). *However, this method returns only the name; you still must determine the associated directory via* GetSpecialFolder.

Properties of Folders (Folder Object)

In the FSO object model, access to folders is accomplished with the ***Folder*** object. If this is not already derivable from another FSO object, it can be easily created with ***GetFolder***. (This method also works without problems with network directories.)

```
Dim f As Folder
Set f = fso.GetFolder("c:\windows\system32")
```

Now a number of properties can be accessed: ***Name*** contains the name of the folder (in the example above, *"system32"*), while the default property ***Path*** contains the complete path, including the drive. If communication with old DOS or Windows 3.1 program names according to the 8+3 character convention is necessary, these can be determined with *ShortName* and *ShortPath*.

DateCreated, ***DateLastAccessed***, and ***DateLastModified*** give information about when the folder was created and when it was last accessed or modified. ***Attributes*** contains a binary combination of several attributes (such as *Compressed, Hidden, ReadOnly*). ***Type*** returns a character string with a description of the folder type, for example, "File Folder" for a folder. Please note that the type string depends on the system language of the operating system. For a German version of Windows, *Type* would give the string "Dateiordner". (The *Type* property is more useful with *File*, where with known file extensions the data type is given.)

Drive refers to a drive object. (In the case of network directories, *f.Drive* also returns, as expected, the server and sharing name in the usual syntax `\\server\share`.)

With ***IsRootFolder*** one can determine whether a given directory is a root directory (such as `C:\`). Only when that is not the case can the parent directory (again a *Folder* object) be determined by means of ***ParentFolder***. ***SubFolders*** refers to a *Folders* enumeration of all subfolders of a given folder (to the extent that there are any; if not, then *SubFolders.Count=0*). The folder names in a *Folders* enumeration are not sorted!

Files refers to all the files within a folder. In contrast to the traditional *Dir* command, neither subfolders nor the pseudofiles *"."* and *".."* are included.

Size determines the space requirement of a folder and recursively goes through all subfolders. For this reason the determination of this property can take considerable time. Do not use this property unnecessarily!

TIP *The resulting value contains the sum of the number of bytes of all files. In fact, the space on the hard drive is usually larger, because files are always saved in sectors. (A file containing three bytes thus requires, depending on the file system, one or more kilobytes of hard drive capacity.) However, the actual space requirement can also be smaller, namely, when the files (for example, in an NT file system) are compressed. Therefore, take the result of* Size *with a grain of salt!*

TIP *Most of these properties are* read-only, *and cannot be altered. The only exceptions are* Attributes *and* Name.

Properties of Files (File Object)

As already mentioned, with the instruction ***Files*** of the *Folder* object you can access all files of a given folder. As with the *Folders* enumeration, the files are not sorted! In contrast to the function *Dir*, here there is no possibility of searching for files of a particular type (for example, `*.txt`) or with particular attributes. You must make such tests yourself inside a loop.

*Files.**Count*** returns the number of files, but the files themselves can be processed only in a *For–Each* loop. These ***File*** objects for the most part exhibit the same properties as *Folder* objects: *[Short]Name, [Short]Path, Drive, ParentFolder, Attributes, DateXxx, Size, Type.*

The only difference worthy of mention relates to *Type*: This property contains a character string, which depends on the file extension that describes the file, such as *"Microsoft Word Document"* for a `*.doc`. This is the same character string that also is displayed in Explorer in the type column.

Creating, Moving, Copying, and Deleting Files and Folders

With *fso.**CreateFolder*** you can create a new folder. This method expects as parameter a character string with the complete path of the folder. The FSO library is less flexible with files. As of now, you can create only text files (not binary files). The method ***CreateTextStream*** will be described in detail in the section after next.

The methods ***Copy***, ***Move***, and ***Delete*** can be applied to both *Folder* and *File* objects. Alternatively, you also use *fso.CopyFile/-Folder* and *fso.DeleteFile/-Folder*, as well as *fso.MoveFile/-Folder*. In this case you have to provide the full folder or file name as a character string.

With the *Copy* operations you can use an optional parameter *Overwrite* to declare whether existing files and folders are to be overwritten. Caution: The default setting is *True*, meaning that existing files and folders will be overwritten without further ado! If you give the value *False*, then you will encounter error 58 (file already exists), which you can intercept with *On Error*.

The *Move* methods can likewise be used to change the name of a file or folder, or to move the object to another location (even to another drive). This operation will be carried out only if the target file or folder does not already exist. (This security feature cannot be changed with optional parameters.)

For *Delete* operations there again exists an optional parameter *Force*, which determines whether *Delete* should ignore the read-only attribute. The default setting is *False*, meaning that read-only files and folders are not changed; instead, error 70 (permission denied) is the result.

One should exercise caution in dealing with files. If access rights are in order, they will be deleted without further query together with all their contents.

Recursively Processing the Directory Tree

It often happens that instead of working on all files within a given folder (search, copy, and so on), you wish to process all files in all subdirectories. In general, it then makes sense to formulate a recursive procedure that first processes all files in the current folder and calls itself with the paths of all subfolders.

```
Sub processFile(fld As Folder)
  Dim subfld As Folder, fil As File
  For Each fil In fld.Files
    ' process files
  Next
  For Each subfld In fld.SubFolders
    processFile subfld  ' recursive call for all subfolders
  Next
End Sub
```

Additional Helpful Functions

With the *fso* object various methods can be invoked that are helpful in the analysis and synthesis of file names. All the methods described here expect character strings as parameters and return a character string as result (thus they do not return *File* or *Folder* objects).

***BuildPath**(path, name)*	forms a complete file name from path and name
***GetAbsolutePath**(name)*	returns the complete file name when only a name relative to the current folder is given
***GetBaseName**(name)*	returns the simple file name (without folder or drive)
***GetDriveName**(name)*	returns the drive name
***GetFileName**(name)*	like *GetBaseName*
***GetParentFolderName**(name)*	returns the directory (including the drive but without the file name)

With the following three functions you can test whether a particular drive, folder, or file already exists:

***DriveExists**(name)*	tests whether drive exists (*True / False*)
***FileExists**(name)*	tests whether file exists
***FolderExists**(name)*	tests whether folder exists

Text Files (TextStream)

The ***TextStream*** object assists in reading from and writing to data files, either in ANSI or Unicode. The following list contains the methods with which *TextStream* objects can be created:

```
Dim ts As TextStream
Set ts = fso.CreateTextFile(name$ [, overwrite, unicode])
Set ts = fso.OpenTextFile(name$ [, mode, unicode])
Set ts = folder.CreateTextFile(name$ [, overwrite, unicode])
Set ts = file.OpenAsTextStream([mode, unicode])
```

A word about the meaning of the optional parameters: *overwrite* (default *True*) determines whether a possibly already existing like-named file will be overwritten.

The parameter *mode* tells whether the file is open for reading (*ForReading*, default setting), writing (*ForWriting*), or appending (*ForAppending*). In the case of *ForWriting* a preexisting file will be deleted. With *ForAppending* such a file will be preserved, with new writing appended to the end of the file.

Finally, it is a bit strange the way text formats (ANSI or Unicode) are selected. In both *Create* methods the selection is made with a *Boolean* value: *False* for ANSI (default setting) or *True* for Unicode. With the *Open* methods the parameter can take three values: *TristateFalse* for ANSI (default setting), *TristateTrue* for Unicode, or *TristateDefault* (depends on the system default setting).

Access to a file is accomplished by means of the properties and methods of the *TextStream* object. For reading files we have ***Read***, ***ReadLine***, and ***ReadAll***. With these a given number of characters, a line, or the entire text is read and returned as a character string. With ***Skip*** and ***SkipLine*** you can skip over individual characters or an entire line. With ***AtEndOfLine*** and ***AtEndOfStream*** you can determine whether the end of a line or the end of the file has been reached. ***Line*** and ***Column*** give the current line and column numbers.

For writing text we have ***Write*** and ***WriteLine***. The only difference between these two methods is that with ***WriteLine*** an end of line character is automatically inserted. ***WriteBlankLines*** creates a number of blank lines.

File operations should be terminated with ***Close***. (At the end of a program or when the *TextStream* object ceases to exists, this occurs automatically. As a rule, though, it is preferable to close files explicitly. This also makes the program code easier to understand.)

Example

CreateTextFile creates a temporary text file. *ReadTextFile* reads the file line by line and shows the contents in a *MsgBox*. *DeleteTextFile* then deletes the file.

```
' example file Files.xls, Module1
Option Explicit
Public fso As New FileSystemObject
Dim filname$
' create text file
Private Sub CreateTextFile()
  Dim i&, tstream As TextStream
  With fso
    filname = .BuildPath(.GetSpecialFolder(TemporaryFolder), _
       .GetTempName)
    Set tstream = .CreateTextFile(filname)
  End With
  With tstream
    .Write "a character string; "
    .WriteLine "another character string with newline character"
    .WriteBlankLines 3   '3 blank lines
    For i = 1 To 5
      .WriteLine i
    Next
    .WriteLine "end of the file"
    .Close
  End With
  MsgBox "temporary file " & filname
```

```
End Sub
' read text file
Private Sub ReadTextFile()
  Dim tstream As TextStream
  Dim txt$
  If filname = "" Then Exit Sub
  Set tstream = fso.OpenTextFile(filname)
  With tstream
    While Not .AtEndOfStream
      txt = txt + .ReadLine() + vbCrLf
    Wend
  End With
  MsgBox "content of the file:" & vbCrLf & txt
End Sub
' end of program; delete temporary file
Private Sub DeleteTextFile()
  If filname = "" Then Exit Sub
  fso.DeleteFile filname
End Sub
```

Binary Files (Open)

The *TextStream* object works very well in operating on text files. But there are times when one needs to work with binary files. The current version of the Scripting library does not offer any such functions, alas. For this reason, this section provides an overview of the traditional Visual Basic commands that fulfill this purpose, where for the sake of completeness the commands for working with text files are also described.

Data Channel

Traditional file access is made not with objects, but with so-called data channels. A data channel is a connection to a file identified by a number. This number is usually called a *file handle*. First, the command *Open* is used to access a file. Then the channel can be used for reading and writing data. Working with data channels is supported by a large number of commands and functions:

Open	open file
Close	close file
Reset	close all open files
FreeFile	returns the next free file handle
Print, Write	write data in text mode

Input, Line Input	read data in text mode
Put	write data in binary or random access mode
Get	read data in binary or random access mode
LOF	returns length of file
EOF	tells whether end of file has been reached
Loc	location—gives the current position of the file pointer
Seek	changes or reads the current position of the file pointer

In executing ***Open*** the purpose of the file access must be given in addition to the file name and file handle. *Input, Output,* and *Append* refer to text files and imply by their names the type of access (*Input*: read-only; *Output*: write only; *Append*: read/write). *Binary* is intended for access to binary data and enables both reading and writing of data. Optionally, with *Binary* you can restrict the type of access to read or write. The following seven lines demonstrate the useful variants of the *Open* command.

```
Open "datname" For Input As #1                    '(1)
Open "datname" For Output As #1                   '(2)
Open "datname" For Append As #1                   '(3)
Open "datname" For Binary As #1                   '(4)
Open "datname" For Binary Access Read As #1       '(5)
Open "datname" For Binary Access Write As #1      '(6)
Open "datname" For Random …                       '(7)
```

Example (1) opens a text file from which data are read. An accidental alteration of the file is excluded. Example (2) opens a file for writing. If the file already exists, it will be deleted! Example (3) opens a file for both reading and writing. If a like-named file already exists, it will not be closed. Read and write operations will normally be carried out at the end of the file (in contrast to all other variants, in which the data are read or overwritten from the beginning of the file). See also *DPos* somewhat further below.

Examples (4) to (6) open a binary file. With (4) both reading and writing are allowed, with (5) reading only, and with (6) writing only. A preexisting file will not be deleted. Example (7) opens a random access file (see below for details).

If several files are to be opened at the same time, then each file must be given a unique file handle. The permissible range is from 1 to 511. The function ***FreeFile*** returns an available file handle.

After a file has been processed, it must be closed. It is only after the file has been closed that writing operations have been effectively completed. The file can then be used by other programs. It is a good idea to close files as soon as possible after they are no longer being used. The command for this purpose is ***Close***, where the file handle must be given. ***Reset*** closes all open files.

We proceed now to the commands that can be executed once a valid file handle is at hand. ***LOF*** (length of file) tells the size of the file. The function ***Loc*** (location) gives the current position of the file pointer, whether for reading or writing. This position locates which byte of the file is the next to be read or changed. (The smallest value is 1, not 0). *Loc* can also be used in definitions, and then it determines a new position. Alternatively, the current position in the file can be changed with ***Seek***. ***EOF*** (end of file) determines whether the end of the file has been reached (in which case *Loc* and *LOF* coincide).

Text Files

Text files are sometimes also known as sequential files, because access to the data is achieved byte by byte, that is, sequentially. In the following lines the temporary file `example.txt` will be created. With the *Open* command the file handle 1 will be used. All further access to this file will be achieved with this file handle. To store data as ANSI text the command *Print #* will be used (*Print* with a file handle is a command, not a method). After two text lines have been input, the file will be closed with *Close*.

```
Open Environ("temp") + "\example.txt" For Output As #1
Print #1, "Text"
Print #1, "yet more text"
Close #1
```

If you wish to read this text file, you must access it again with *Open*, though this time in *Input* mode, in order to exclude the possibility of changing the file. In a *While–Wend* loop the file is read line by line with *Line Input* until the end of the file is encountered (tested with the function *EOF*).

```
Dim lineOfTxt$
Open Environ("temp") + "\example.txt" For Input As #1
While Not EOF(1)
  Line Input #1, lineOfTxt
  Print lineOfTxt
Wend
Close #1
```

In addition to the command *Line Input* text data can also be read with *Input*. However, *Input* reads only up to the next comma. That is, lines containing commas are read in several pieces. Thus the *Input* command is particularly suitable for reading numbers into numeric variables.

> **TIP** *Although Visual Basic has used Unicode internally since Version 4, the traditional file operations have been carried out in ANSI format (with one byte per character). The conversion between Unicode and ANSI takes place automatically; Unicode characters for which there is no ANSI code cause problems, as could be expected. For reading and writing of Unicode files you should therefore use the* TextStream *object.*

Binary Files

In the above example numbers and text were stored in text format. But there is also the possibility of storing numbers in Visual Basic's internal format. This format is considerably more efficient for floating point numbers. Moreover, with this format each individual byte of a file can be read, written, and changed. This is particularly important in working with files created by other programs.

The construction of the following example program is quite similar to that of the program above. In *CreateBinaryFile* the binary file is opened, and in *LoadBinaryFile* it is read. In the binary file square roots of numbers between 1 and 100 are stored as *Double* values. In *LoadBinaryFile* three values are read from the file (the square roots of 15, 16, and 17).

```
' example file Files.xls, Module2
' example for traditional commands for working with files
' create temporary binary file test.bin
Private Sub CreateBinaryFile()
  Dim sq As Double, i
  Open Environ("temp") + "\test.bin" For Binary As #1
  For i = 1 To 100
    sq = Sqr(i)
    Put #1, , sq
  Next i
  Close #1
End Sub
' open file, display the first three values in the immediate window
Private Sub LoadBinaryFile()
  Dim dbl As Double, i
  Open Environ("temp") + "\test.bin" For Binary As #1
  Seek #1, 8 * 14 + 1
  For i = 1 To 3
    Get #1, , dbl
    Debug.Print dbl
  Next i
```

```
  Close
End Sub
' delete file
Private Sub DeleteBinaryFile()
  Kill Environ("temp") + "\test.bin"
End Sub
```

For loading and storing data in binary format we have the commands *Get* and *Put*. ***Put*** stores a number or a character string. Here the file handle must be given as the first parameter and the variable to be stored as the third. The second parameter is optional, giving the position in the file at which the data are to be stored. If the second parameter is omitted, then Visual Basic begins at the location of the last access. Thus with several *Put* commands the data are written sequentially into the file. At the end of *CreateBinaryFile* the file `Test.bin` has length 800 bytes (100 numerical values of eight bytes each, which is what is required for a *Double* number).

Similar to *Put* is ***Get***. In *LoadBinaryFile* the read position within the file is set with *Seek* to the 113th byte. With this the first 14 numerical values, of 8 bytes each, are passed over. In the sequel three *Double* values are read from the file into the variable *dbl* and output to the screen.

Variant Variables in Binary Files

With *Boolean* (two bytes), *Byte*, *Int*, *Long*, *Single*, *Double*, and *Currency* variables the number of bytes that are written with *Put* or read with *Get* are determined uniquely by the data type. This is not the case with *Variant* variables. Now the storage requirement depends on the type of the data just stored. Therefore, with *Put* first two bytes with type information are written. Then follow the actual data, whose number of bytes depends on the format.

The result is that you should avoid using *Variant* variables if you wish to use *Get* and *Put*. The file is now enlarged by two bytes for each variant variable, in addition to the overhead for internal storage. (If you are storing primarily integer numbers, then two bytes is quite a bit, representing an increase of 50 or 100 percent!)

Character Strings in Binary Files

With character strings the problem arises that *Put* stores only the content, and not the length. *Get* can therefore not know where the character string to be read ends. For this reason *Get* reads exactly as many characters as at that moment are to be found in the variable. That, however, is no solution to the problem.

The correct way to proceed with the binary storage of character strings with variable length is first to store the length of the character string as a *Long* variable and then to store the content of the character string.

```
Dim strlen&, mystr$
mystr = "123"
strlen = Len(mystr)
Put #1, ,strlen
Put #1, ,mystr
```

In loading you determine first the length of the character string and then initialize the character string before you execute *Get*:

```
Get #1, , strlen
mystr = Space(strlen)
Get #1, , mystr
```

If character strings appear in fields or in user-defined data types, then *Get* and *Put* incidentally take care of these administrative details themselves. *Put* stores the length of the character string, *Get* takes note of this information without the character string being previously initialized. So it works, hurray! (See the next section.)

User-Defined Data Types and Fields in Binary Files

You can also use *Get* and *Put* for the efficient storage of fields and user-defined data types. In the case of fields, particularly, there seems to be a possible increase in program speed (over the previously necessary storage of each element individually).

Excel-Specific Methods and Properties

Excel Folders

The Excel object model offers a host of properties for accessing various folders. The following list offers a sampling of these.

- *ActiveWorkbook.**Path*** determines the path of the current Excel file, *ActiveWorkbook.* Name its file name.
- *Application.**Path*** determines the path to the Excel program file: `C:\Office2000\Office`

- *Application.**DefaultFilePath*** determines the path to the Excel folder that is considered the current directory after the program has been launched:
  `C:\WINNT4\Profiles\Administrator\Personal`

- *Application.**LibraryPath*** returns the path of the `Library` folder of Excel:
  `C:\Office2000\Office\Library`

- *Application.**TemplatesPath*** returns the path to the personal template folder. For some unexplained reason this property returns the path with a terminal \ character, in contrast to all other *Path* properties mentioned here. Go figure.
  `C:\WINNT4\Profiles\Administrator\Application Data\Microsoft`
  `\Templates\`

- *Application.**StartupPath*** returns the personal `XLStart` folder:
  `C:\WINNT4\Profiles\Administrator\Application Data\Microsoft`
  `\Excel\XLStart`

- *Application.**AltStartupPath*** returns the path to the additional autostart folder (which can be set with TOOLS|OPTIONS).

- *Application.**UserLibraryPath*** (new in Excel 2000) returns the path to the personal folder with add-in files:
  `H:\WINNT4\Profiles\Administrator\Application Data\Microsoft\AddIns\`

CAUTION *The meaning of* TemplatesPath *and* StartupPath *has changed in Excel 2000 from that of previous versions. In Excel 97 these two properties returned the path to the global templates and the path to the* `Xlstart` *directories. However, in Excel 2000 these properties refer to the personal directories.*

Unfortunately, there are no new properties to provide the global `Xlstart` *folder that is simultaneously valid as global template folder. The following instruction has the drawback that it is region-specific (and in this form functions only for the English version of Excel; in the German version, for example, the* `Library` *directory has the name* `Makro`*):*

```
globalxlstart = Replace(LCase(Application.LibraryPath), _
"library", "xlstart")
```

TIP *You will find an overview of the meaning of the Excel configuration files in the section on configuration files.*

File Selection Form

The two methods ***GetOpenFilename*** and ***GetSaveAsFilename*** display a dialog box to select an already existing file, respectively to name a new file. *GetOpenFilename* can be used only to select an existing file, while *GetSaveAsFilename* also can be used to specify a new file name. In an optional parameter a list of possible file filters (such as `*.xl?`) can be given as a character string. The filter list contains, pairwise and separated by commas, the description of the file and the matching filter (normally a file extension, such as *.txt). In the following example, which can be executed in the immediate window, the filter list contains an entry for both text files and Excel files. The second parameter defines which of the two filters is used at the beginning

```
?Application.GetOpenFilename( _
  "Textfiles (*.txt), *.txt,Excel-files (*.xl?), *.xl?", 2)
```

With *GetSaveAsFilename* a default file name can be placed before the two filter parameters:

```
?Application.GetSaveAsFilename("name.xls", _
  "Textfiles (*.txt), *.txt,Excel-files (*.xl?), *.xl?", 2)
```

TIP GetOpen- *and* GetSaveAsFilename *determine only one file name. However, no Excel file is opened or saved. For this there exist some methods that have already been introduced in this chapter under the subject of workbooks.*

Importing and Exporting Text Files

It frequently happens that the files to be processed in Excel do not yet exist as Excel worksheets, but have been saved by some other program as ASCII text. The importation of such data usually causes trouble, since each program has its own ideas as to how the decimal point is to be saved (period or the European comma), how dates and times are represented, how individual entries in the table are separated (space, tab, comma, or some other symbol), and how character strings are denoted (for example, in quotation marks).

> **TIP** *If your external data are not located in a text file, but in a database, then you should have a look at Chapter 12. This chapter describes, among other things, the ADO library, with which you can establish a link to database data and database servers in order to automate the import and export of data.*

Text Import Wizard for Interactive Importing

Aid in reading such files is offered by the text import wizard. This assistant appears automatically as soon as you select a text file with FILE|OPEN. In three steps you indicate how the columns of the text file are separated and in what format the data of each column appear.

In the following program two three-column files will be imported. The file `german.txt` contains numbers that are formatted in the style used in Germany—period for the thousands separator, comma as decimal point. (You may feel that the Germans have it backwards, but they probably think the same about you.) In the text column the character strings are not designated as such. The column separator is a space

```
123.456,23  text without quotes (but with special characters äöü)
 23.456,23  text
 -3.456,23  text
```

The file `scientific.txt` is more computer friendly. The column separator is now the tab, and numbers have a period as decimal point and no thousands separator.

```
12.3   12/31/1999  17:30 "text"
.33    1/2/2000    11:20 "several words in quotes"
-1e3   1/3/2000     0:13 "text"
```

The importation of both files proceeds smoothly with the import wizard. In the case of `german.txt` the data type "fixed width" must be given. (The column separator then orients itself according to the position of the character within the line.) The number of blanks between the data columns can be different in each line, depending on the length of the previous item. Therefore, the import wizard must not count blanks. Instead, the second column always starts at a certain position—here the sixteenth character of the line. In the second step the positions must be given at which the columns begin (Figure 5.6). In the third step you must push the button ADVANCED to tell whether settings other than period for decimal point and comma for thousands separator are being used.

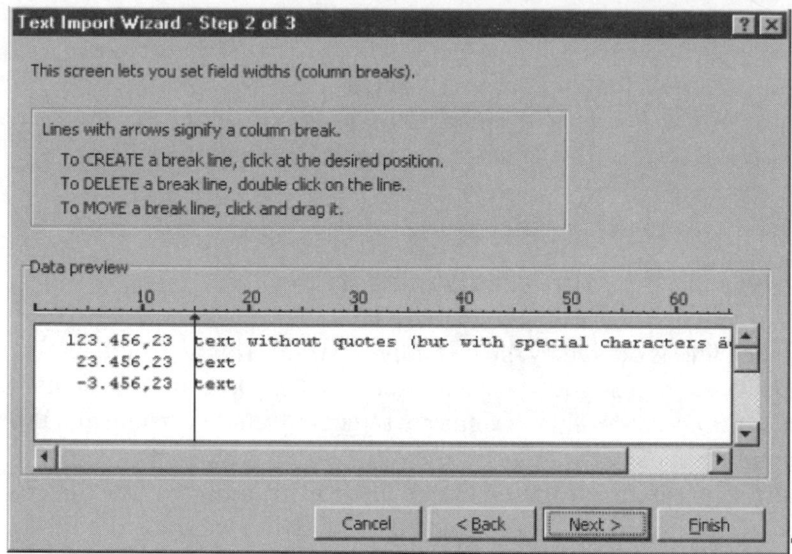

Figure 5.6. Input of the column breakpoints in the text import wizard for importing the file german.txt

For `scientific.txt` the wizard knows all by itself that the columns are separated by tabs. In the third step the date format must be set according to the region. The wizard recognizes various date formats, which vary in the order of day, month, and year (Figure 5.7).

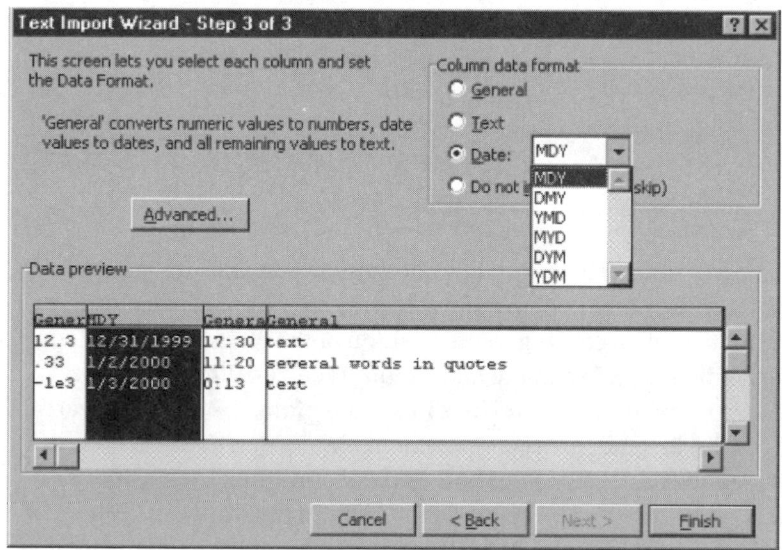

Figure 5.7. Setting the date format in importing scientific.txt

german.txt

	A	B	C	D	E	F
1	123,456.23	text without quotes (but with special characters äöü)				
2	23,456.23	text				
3	-3,456.23	text				
4						

german

scientific.txt

	A	B	C	D	E	F
1	12.3	12/31/1999	17:30	text		
2	0.33	1/2/2000	11:20	several words in quotes		
3	-1.00E+03	1/3/2000	0:13	text		
4						

scientific

Figure 5.8. The result of the importation

Importing Text, Variant 2

The importing we have done thus far is based on importation via File|Open. It is interesting to note that the command Data|Get External Data|Import Text File offers a second option. Here the same wizard appears as before, so that one has the impression that internally the same commands are being executed, commands accessible from two different menus. This impression is incorrect:

- Variant 2 imports data not into a new file, but to an arbitrary location in a worksheet.

- Variant 2 remembers the import parameters (through an internal *QueryTable* object) and thus one is in a position to repeat the text importation at a later time without reentering all parameters and options (command Data|Refresh Data). This is particularly attractive if the content of the text file regularly changes and the file must be repeatedly imported anew.

This second variant is thus more attractive than the first for many applications. The use (other than the location in the menu) is identical, though the programming is different.

The Method OpenText *(Text Import, Variant 1)*

The method ***OpenText*** of the object *Workbooks* is the counterpart of the text import wizard. However, the setting of the many optional parameters is no trivial task. Therefore, it is particularly recommended to obtain a first approximation with the macro recorder.

> **CAUTION** *With the macro recorder only those settings that differ from the current default settings will be written in code. If the procedure is later to be executed on another computer, where possibly a different default setting is in force, this can lead to problems. To ensure that the code is portable, you will usually have to enlarge the code.*

During the importation of `german.txt` the macro recorder produced the following code:

```
Workbooks.OpenText Filename:="D:\code\Xl-2000-engl\german.txt", _
  Origin:=xlWindows, StartRow:=1, DataType:=xlFixedWidth, _
  FieldInfo:=Array(Array(0, 1), Array(15, 1)), _
  DecimalSeparator:=",", ThousandsSeparator:="."
```

For `scientific.txt` the command looks like this:

```
Workbooks.OpenText Filename:="D:\code\Xl-2000-engl\scientific.txt", _
  Origin:=xlWindows, StartRow:=1, DataType:=xlDelimited, _
  TextQualifier:=xlDoubleQuote, ConsecutiveDelimiter:=False, _
  Tab:=True, Semicolon:=False, Comma:=False, Space:=False, _
  Other:=False, _
  FieldInfo:=Array(Array(1, 1), Array(2, 3), Array(3, 1), Array(4, 1))
```

To make these cryptic lines understandable, a few words about the many parameters are perhaps in order:

Filename	expects a character string with the file name.
Origin	gives the format of the text (of line division, etc.). Possibilities are *xlMacintosh, xlWindows,* and *xlMSDOS.*
StartRow	tells at which line importation should begin. The default is 1. If you wish to skip over several header lines, simply give a correspondingly higher value. Some tables begin with one or more header lines, which may or may not be needed after the importation; *StartRow* helps to drop such lines.
DataType	tells how the data are organized: *xlDelimited* means that the columns are delimited by a unique symbol (such as tab); *xlFixedWidth* means that the columns begin at a fixed position (and any extra space is filled with the space character).

Tab	tells whether the columns are tab delimited (*True/False*, only with *DataType:=xlDelimited*).
Semicolon	as above, but column separator is the semicolon.
Comma	as above, but column separator is the comma.
Space	as above, but column separator is the space.
Other	as above, but column separator is given by some other character specified by *OtherChar*.
OtherChar	gives the column separator explicitly (only with *DataType:= xlDelimited* and *Other:=True*).
ConsecutiveDelimiter	tells whether several column delimiters together are to be regarded as a unit. This usually makes sense only if the column separator is a space. The default setting is *False*.
TextQualifier	tells how character strings are indicated: by double quotation marks (*xlTextQualifierDoubleQuote*), single quotation marks (*xlTextQualifierSingleQuote*), or nothing at all (*xlTextQualifierNone*).
DecimalSeparator	gives the decimal point character (for example, "."). Warning: If no character is given, then the system setting is used!
ThousandsSeparator	gives the character for the thousands separator (for example, ",").
FieldInfo	expects as argument an encapsulated data field (*Array*). Each column is specified with *Array(n, opt)*; *n* gives either the column number (*DataType:=xlDelimited*) or the column position (*DataType:=xlFixedWidth*); *opt* denotes the data type of the column. Possibilities are as follows: *xlGeneralFormat (1)*: standard *xlTextFormat (2)*: text *xlSkipColumn (9)*: skip column *xlMDYFormat (3), xlDMYFormat (4)*, etc.: data format

If *OpenText* is executed without error, then the result is a new Excel file whose name coincides with the file name. If instead you wish to import data into a previously existing (and already loaded) file, then use *ActiveWorkbook* to refer to the new workbook and copy its single worksheet (or only several cells) into the desired file. Then you can close *ActiveWorkbook* (that is, the new Excel file with the imported results).

Note that with *Worksheets.Copy* the active Excel file is changed. *ActiveWorkbook* now refers to the target file! To close the import file you must use an object variable.

```
' example file Files.xls, Module3
' Import / Export
Sub ImportScientific()
  Dim fname$
  Dim newworkb As Workbook
  fname = ThisWorkbook.Path + "\scientific.txt"
  Workbooks.OpenText Filename:=fname, …
  Set newworkb = ActiveWorkbook
  newworkb.Worksheets(1).Copy after:=ThisWorkbook.Worksheets(1)
  newworkb.Close False
End Sub
```

TIP *With the macro recorder only those import settings are shown that are different from the default setting (regional setting!) If the code is later executed on a computer with a different regional setting, then unexpected problems could arise, since other default settings might be in use. If your code is designed for international use, you have to give all relevant settings explicitly, even those that are not automatically recorded by the macro recorder!*

TIP *If all the many settings available with* OpenText *are insufficient for importing a text file correctly, then you will have to program an importation procedure yourself. Essentially, you have to open the text file, read it into a character string variable line by line, and there analyze it. This might require some effort, but it is by no means all that complicated.*

The Object QueryTable *(Text Import, Variant 2)*

In addition to FILE|OPEN you can also use in Excel the command DATA|GET EXTERNAL DATA|IMPORT TEXT FILE. The importation is then carried out by the ***QueryTable*** object. This object is generally used by Excel to describe the import parameters of external data, which includes not only text files, but databases and web sites as well.

POINTER *Here we are dealing only with importing text. Additional background information and a detailed description of database importation can be found in Chapter 12. Some special features of HTML importation are described in Chapter 14.*

The first time you import via code, you must attach a new *QueryTable* object to the worksheet with *Add*. You then set a number of properties for this object. A large proportion of these properties correspond to the above-described parameters of *OpenText*. Worthy of note is the property *Name*: It determines not only the name of the *QueryTable* object, but during the importation of data a named range is defined that includes the import range and has the same name. This named range is absolutely necessary for the internal management of the *QueryTable* object and makes possible the later updating of the data.

After the many *QueryTable* properties have been set, you then carry out the actual importing with the method *Refresh*. The following code was originally created with the macro recorder and then manually optimized and formatted for readability. That is generally a reasonable way to achieve rapid results.

```
Sub ImportNewText()       'Files.xls, Module4
  Dim qt As QueryTable, ws As Worksheet
  Dim fname$
  fname = ThisWorkbook.Path + "\scientific.txt"
  Set ws = Worksheets("QueryTable")
  ws.Activate
  Set qt = ws.QueryTables.Add("Text;" + fname, [A1])
  With qt
    .Name = "scientific"
    .FieldNames = True
    .RowNumbers = False
    .FillAdjacentFormulas = False
    .PreserveFormatting = True
    .RefreshOnFileOpen = False
    .RefreshStyle = xlInsertDeleteCells
    .SavePassword = False
    .SaveData = True
    .AdjustColumnWidth = True
    .RefreshPeriod = 0
    .TextFilePromptOnRefresh = False
    .TextFilePlatform = xlWindows
    .TextFileStartRow = 1
    .TextFileParseType = xlDelimited
    .TextFileTextQualifier = xlTextQualifierDoubleQuote
    .TextFileConsecutiveDelimiter = False
    .TextFileTabDelimiter = True
    .TextFileSemicolonDelimiter = False
    .TextFileCommaDelimiter = False
    .TextFileSpaceDelimiter = False
    .TextFileColumnDataTypes = Array(1, 3, 1, 1)
    .TextFileDecimalSeparator = "."
```

```
    .TextFileThousandsSeparator = ","
    .Refresh BackgroundQuery:=False   'here the importing is triggered
  End With
End Sub
```

To repeat the importation at a later time, you need only execute *Refresh* for the existing *QueryTable* object. The property *TextFilePromptOnRefresh* governs whether the file-selection dialog will again be displayed.

```
Sub RefreshImport()
  Dim ws As Worksheet
  Set ws = Worksheets("QueryTable")
  ws.Activate
  With ws.QueryTables("scientific")
    .TextFilePromptOnRefresh = False
    .Refresh
  End With
End Sub
```

Exporting Text Files

In the long list of file formats in the form "Save As" you will find two text formats that are suitable for the exportation of a worksheet into a text file: "Text (Tab delimited)" and CSV (Comma delimited). The essential difference between these two formats is that in the first, a tab character is inserted, while in the second, it is commas that come into play. In both cases only a worksheet can be saved (not the whole file).

> **TIP** *There are many other formats for saving a file or worksheet, such as HTML document, Unicode file, or database (dBase format).*

If you wish to carry out the export through VBA code, then you have available the method ***SaveAs***, which can be applied to a *Workbook* object as well as to a *Worksheet* object.

```
ActiveWorkbook.ActiveSheet.SaveAs _
  Filename:="c:\sample-file.csv", FileFormat:=xlCSV
```

An unpleasant side effect of *SaveAs* is that the active name of the current file changes. For example, `Files.xls` is turned into `Files.csv`. If you then wish to save the entire file again as an Excel file, you must again use SAVE AS (or *SaveAs*) and specify that you again wish to save in the standard Excel format. By means of *DisplayAlerts=False* we avoid an alert asking whether the file may be overwritten.

The following procedure first saves the current worksheet in CSV format. Then the entire file (that is, the *Workbook*) is saved under its original name and file type.

```
' Files.xls, Module3
Sub ExportActiveWorksheet()
  Dim oldname$, oldpath$, oldformat
  With ActiveWorkbook
    oldname = .Name
    oldpath = .Path
    oldformat = .FileFormat
    .ActiveSheet.SaveAs _
      Filename:="c:\sample-file.csv", FileFormat:=xlCSV
    Application.DisplayAlerts = False  ' avoid alert
    .SaveAs Filename:=oldpath + "\" + oldname, FileFormat:=oldformat
    Application.DisplayAlerts = True
  End With
End Sub
```

The built-in export mechanisms are much less flexible than *OpenText*. You cannot control the details of formatting, nor is there the possibility of saving a selected range of text. Therefore, if you have more stringent requirements, you will have to give Microsoft a hand, as the following example demonstrates.

Text Exportation for Mathematica Lists

The procedure *SaveRangeAsMmaFile* saves a previously selected range of cells in a text file, using the list format of *Mathematica*, which can later use the file. (*Mathematica* is a program for processing mathematical data and formulas. For example, it can be used to represent Excel data graphically. In particular, for the three-dimensional representation of data *Mathematica* offers commands that are much more efficient and flexible than those of Excel.)

The procedure demonstrates several generally valid processes that appear over and over in similar tasks, such as selecting a file name, creating a backup copy, dealing with the situation in which the selected file already exists, writing a text file, selection of a three-dimensional range of cells (across several worksheets).

Specific to *Mathematica* are only the formatting symbols in the text file: In *Mathematica* associated data (such as those of a row) must be grouped in curly braces. A two-dimensional field with 2*2 elements might be represented in *Mathematica* as *{{a,b},{c,d}}*.

If you wish to transmit Excel data to another program, you will have to change only those parts of the procedure that provide these braces. According to the program, some other format will be required, such as tabs (*Chr(9)*), linefeed (*Chr(10)*), and/or carriage return (*Chr(13)*).

Testing the Macro

To test the procedure, load `Mma.xls`, use Shift to select the worksheets Table1 and Table2, and within them select the cells B4:N6. (You have thereby selected a three-dimensional range of cells, comprising the cells B4:B6 in both worksheets.) Then execute the procedure *SaveRangeAsMmaFile* with TOOLS|MACROS or simply click on the tool in the new *Mathematica* toolbar. You will be asked for a file name under which the selected range of cells is to be saved. Call it `Test.dat`. The file saved in this way can now be used in *Mathematica* with the command *Get*:

```
list1 = Get["C:\\test.dat"]
```

Data Selection with SelectFilename

The procedure *SaveRangeAsMmaFile* begins with a test whether in fact, a range of several cells has been selected. The procedure will not function correctly with ranges made up of several partial regions. This case is handled in the third *If* test.

If a valid range has been selected, then the method *GetSaveAsFilename* is executed in the function *SelectFilename*. A dialog box appears for selecting a file name. If the name of an existing file is chosen, then the program displays an alert in a *MsgBox*. The user must affirm the overwriting of the file by clicking YES. The file selection is placed in a loop so that the user has the possibility of selecting a new file name. The loop is executed until the user has selected a valid file name or has canceled the selection process.

The following program lines again test whether the given file already exists. If that is the case, then this file is given a new name with the extension `*.bak`. An existing backup copy will first be deleted.

```
' mma.xls, Module1
' Select file name, create backup file
Function SelectFilename(filenam$) As String
  Dim pos&, result&
  Dim file, backupfile$
  Do   ' loop until valid file name or cancel
    file = Application.GetSaveAsFilename(filenam, , , _
      "Save as Mathematica List")
    If file = False Then file = ""
```

```
    If file = "" Then Exit Function
    result = vbYes
    If Dir(file) <> "" Then   ' Warning, file already exists
      result = MsgBox( _
        "The file " & file & " already exists! Overwrite?", _
        vbYesNoCancel)
      If result = vbCancel Then Exit Function
    End If
  Loop Until result = vbYes
  ' if file already exists: create backup copy
  If Dir(file) <> "" Then      ' the file already exists
    backupfile = file + ".bak"
    ' delete existing backup
    If Dir(backupfile) <> "" Then Kill backupfile
    ' rename existing file
    Name file As backupfile
  End If
  SelectFilename = CStr(file)
End Function
```

Saving Data in SaveRangeAsMmaFile

The function *SelectFilename* returns the file name to the procedure SaveRangeAsMmaFile. There the name is stored in the static variable *filename*. If the procedure is called again, this name is displayed in the form for file selection.

Open creates a data channel to the selected file. (That is, the traditional file processing command is used, not the *File System Object*.) Note the use of the function *FreeFile* for determining a new, unused, channel number! This way of proceeding is particularly recommended if the procedure can be called from other locations in an Excel program. If you simply give #1 as channel number, you run the risk of an error in the execution of the procedure. This error occurs if #1 is already being used in another place in the program.

```
Public Sub SaveRangeAsMmaFile()
  Dim sh As Worksheet, shList As Object   ' worksheets
  Dim sh1 As Worksheet, sh2 As Worksheet
  Dim shCount&
  Dim rw&, rw1&, rw2&                     ' rows
  Dim cl&, cl1&, cl2&                     ' columns
  Dim dataitem, filechannel&              ' other variables
  Static filenam$, file$
  ' On Error Resume Next
  If Selection Is Nothing Then _
```

```
  MsgBox "Select a range of cells!": Exit Sub
If Selection.Cells.Count = 1 Then _
  MsgBox " Select a range of cells!":  Exit Sub
If Selection.Areas.Count > 1 Then _
  MsgBox "Mma.xls supports only a single range of cells.": Exit Sub
' select file name
file = SelectFilename(filenam)
If file = "" Then Exit Sub Else filenam = file
filechannel = FreeFile()
Open file For Output As #filechannel
```

Processing the Group of Worksheets

The procedure saves a normal range of cells in the form *{{a,b...},{c,d...}...}*, that is, in nested curly braces. However, the procedure also works with a three-dimensional range of cells, stretching over several worksheets. Three-dimensional ranges are selected by first selecting the range in *one* sheet and then clicking on additional worksheets with Ctrl or Shift. The program saves three-dimensional ranges in the form *{{{a1,b1}, {c1,d1}}, {{a2,b2}, {c2,d2}}}*, that is, nested to three levels.

In the program *ActiveWindow.SelectedSheets.Count* determines how many sheets have been selected. In the procedure the variable *shList* is used as a reference to the group of sheets, in order to save typing effort and to make the program easier to write. In *sh1* and *sh2* references to the first and second sheets are stored. Note that the variables *shList, sh1, sh2* cannot be assigned with normal assignment statements. The content of the variable is a pointer to an object, which can be set only with *Set*.

```
' Initialization
Set shList = ActiveWindow.SelectedSheets
shCount = shList.Count
Set sh1 = shList(1)
Set sh2 = shList(shList.Count)
rw1 = Selection.Row
rw2 = rw1 + Selection.Rows.Count - 1
cl1 = Selection.Column
cl2 = cl1 + Selection.Columns.Count - 1
```

Saving Data in Text Format

The initialization of *rw*1, *rw2, cl1,* and *cl2* is easy to understand. With *Row* and *Column* the first line and column of the selected range are returned. *Rows.Count* and *Columns.Count* determine the number of selected rows and columns.

Now three nested loops begin in which the three-dimensional range of cells is read element by element and stored with *Print #* in the text file. If the range is only two-dimensional (in a single worksheet), then *shCount* has the value 1. In that case, the *Print* command for the outer level of braces is not executed. The outer loop selects the currently active worksheet.

Then after following element is placed either a comma (for separating two elements) or a curly brace (as termination for the elements of a row). Note the closing semicolon with the *Print* method. These have the effect that *Print* does not begin a new line with each output. The file thus created will therefore be much more readable.

```
If shCount > 1 Then Print #filechannel, "{"
For Each sh In shList                  ' loop for all worksheets
  Print #filechannel, "{";
  For rw = rw1 To rw2                  ' loop for all rows
    Print #filechannel, "{";
    For cl = cl1 To cl2                ' loop for all columns
      dataitem = sh.Cells(rw, cl)
      If IsNumeric(dataitem) Then    ' number or string?
        Print #filechannel, Scientific(Str(dataitem));
      Else
        Print #filechannel, Chr(34); dataitem; Chr(34);
      End If
      If cl = cl2 Then
        Print #filechannel, "}";
      Else
        Print #filechannel, ", ";
      End If
    Next cl
    If rw = rw2 Then
      Print #filechannel, "}"
    Else
      Print #filechannel, ","
    End If
  Next rw
  ' comma or } between list entries
  If shCount > 1 Then
    If sh.Name = sh2.Name Then
```

```
        Print #filechannel, "}"
      Else
        Print #filechannel, ","
      End If
    End If
  Next sh
  Close #filechannel
End Sub
```

Formatting of Numbers

Each element is tested to determine whether it is text or a number. In the former case the text is placed in quotation marks. These are produced with *Chr(34)*. (The character " has ANSI code 34. *Chr* returns the character having the given code.)

Numbers are changed into character strings with *Str*. This transformation function has the advantage that it generates a period for the decimal point (and not a comma), which almost every international version prescribes.

The character string produced by *Str* must, however, be further processed with the auxiliary function *Scientific*, because *Mathematica* does not recognize the notation *1.2E-03*. Such numbers are transformed into the form *1.2*10^-03*.

```
Function Scientific(s As String) As String
  Dim pos%
  pos = InStr(s, "E")
  If pos Then
    Scientific = Left(s, pos - 1) + "*10^" + Mid(s, pos + 1)
  Else
    Scientific = s
  End If
End Function
```

Syntax Summary

File System Objects

FileSystemObject—Property

Drives	refers to a list of all drives

FileSystemObject—Methods

CopyFile/-Folder	copy file or folder
DeleteFile/-Folder	delete file or folder
DriveExists(name)	tests whether drive exists
FileExists(name)	tests whether file exists
FolderExists(name)	tests whether folder exists
GetAbsolutePath(relname)	creates complete file name (from relative input)
GetBaseName(name)	returns simple name (without folder/drive)
GetDrive	returns *Drive* object
GetDriveName(name)	returns drive name
GetFile	returns *File* object
GetFileName(name)	like *GetBaseName*
GetFolder	returns *Folder* object
GetParentFolderName(name)	returns folder name (with drive)
GetSpecialFolder	returns *Folder* object for Windows (System)folder
GetTempName	returns name for temporary file (without folder!)
MoveFile / -Folder	move or rename file or folder
OpenTextFile	opens a text file

Drive—Properties

AvailableSpace	free drive capacity
DriveType	drive type (e.g., *Remote, CDRom*)
FileSystem	file system (e.g., *"NTFS", "FAT"*)
FreeSpace	like *AvailableSpace*
IsReady	ready (used with A: Disk)
Path	character string of the path without \ (e.g., *"C:"*)
RootFolder	reference to *Folder* object
ShareName	drive name on network
TotalSize	total capacity
VolumeName	volume name

File / Folder—Common Properties

Attributes	attributes (write protected, compromised, etc.)
DateCreated	date and time of creation
DateLastAccessed	date and time of last access
DateLastChanged	date and time of last change
Drive	reference to drive (*Drive* object)
Files	list of all contained files (only *Folder*)
IsRootFolder	*True*, if root folder (only *Folder*)
Name	name (without folder / drive)

ParentFolder	pointer to folder one level up (*Folder* object)
Path	character string with complete name (including folder/drive)
ShortName	name in 8+3 convention (DOS/Windows 3.1)
ShortPath	path in 8+3 convention (DOS/Windows 3.1)
Size	file size or sum over contained files
SubFolders	list of all subfolders (only *Folder*)
Type	name of file type

File / Folder—Common Methods

Copy	copy file / folder
CreateTextFile	create text file (only *Folder*)
Delete	delete file / folder
Move	rename or move file / folder
OpenAsStream	open as text file (only *File*)

TextStream—Properties

AtEndOfLine	end of line reached?
AtEndOfStream	end of file reached?
Column	current position within a line
Line	current line number

TextStream—Methods

Close	close file
Read	read *n* characters
ReadAll	read entire file into a character string
ReadLine	read next line
Skip	skip *n* characters
SkipLine	skip lines
Write	write character string (without line break character)
WriteLine	write one line (with line break character)
WriteBlankLines	write *n* blank lines

VBA Commands

In the syntax boxes *n* stands for data input (such as *"test.dat"*) and *k* for channel number.

Managing Files and Folders

CurDir	returns current folder
Environ("Temp")	returns folder for temporary file
ChDir n	changes current folder
ChDrive drv	changes current drive
MkDir n	creates new folder
RmDir n	deletes empty folder
Name n1 As n2	gives *n1* the new name *n2*
FileCopy n1, n2	copies *n1* to *n2*
Kill n	deletes the given file(s)
Dir(n [,attribute])	returns the first file that corresponds to the search pattern
Dir	returns the next file or an empty character string
FileLen(n)	returns the length of *n* in bytes
FileDateTime(n)	returns date and time of last change
GetAttr(n)	returns the attribute (read-only, etc.) of *n*
SetAttr n, attr	changes the attribute of *n*

Open Data Channel

f = FreeFile	returns free data channel number
	open data channel to:
Open d For Input As #f	... read text file
Open d For Output As #f	... write text file
Open d For Append As #f	... read and write text file
Open d For Binary As #f	... read and write binary file
Open d For Binary Access Read As #f	... read-only binary file
Open d For Binary Access Write As #f	... write-only binary file
Open d For Random As #f Len=l	... read and write random access file

Process Files via Data Channel

Close #f	close data channel
Reset	close all open data channels
EOF(n)	reached end of file?
LOF(n)	determine size of file

Loc(n)	determine current position of file pointer
Seek #f, position	change file pointer
Print #f, var1, var2	write line in text format
Write #f, var1, var2	as above, but with format character " and ,
Input #f, var1, var2	read variables
Line Input #f, var	read entire line
var = Input(n, #f)	read *n* characters
var = InputB(n, #f)	read *n* bytes
Put #f, , var	variable / field / etc. store as binary
Get #f, , var	read variable as binary

Excel-Specific Methods and Properties

Drives and Folders

ActiveWorkbook.Path	path of active workbook
ActiveWorkbook.Name	file name of active workbook
Application.Path	path to `Excel.exe`
Application.DefaultFilePath	path to workbook
Application.LibraryPath	path to global `Library` directory (folder)
Application.UserLibraryPath	path to personal add-in directory
Application.StartupPath	path to personal `XLStart` directory
Application.TemplatesPath	path to personal template directory
Application.AltStartupPath	path to additional autostart directory (can be set with TOOLS|OPTIONS)

File Selection

Application.GetOpenFilename	file selection (open file, existing files only)
Application.GetSaveAsFilename	file selection (save file, with alert)

Import / Export

Workbooks.OpenText	import text file, variant 1
Worksheets(...).QueryTables.Add	import text file, variant 2
Worksheets(...).SaveAs	save worksheet in various formats

User-Defined Worksheet Functions

Fundamentals

Excel has available a large assortment of predefined worksheet functions, the most well known and important of which is *SUM*. For more complex applications the function *IF* plays an important role as well. *IF* allows for case testing within worksheet formulas. However, in complex situations *IF* formulas can be so opaque that their application is practically impossible (or extremely error-prone). There are also situations in which the demands made on the formula's syntax are simply too great.

For such situations Excel offers the possibility of defining your own functions in VBA. These functions are then known as user-defined worksheet functions. An important advantage of such user-defined functions is that the function need be defined only once in a VBA module. It is then easy to make changes in such a function. (In contrast, worksheet formulas must be copied into all cells. When subsequent changes are made, all affected cells must also be changed.)

The programming of user-defined functions is often much easier than writing "genuine" Excel programs. In most cases they use no objects, methods, or properties. Indeed, often simple *If–Then* tests suffice.

> **TIP** *The calculation of a user-defined worksheet function is always incomparably slower than the use of a predefined Excel function. Before you begin to program a new worksheet function, look first in the on-line help to see whether there exists a predefined function that meets your needs.*

Defining Your Own Functions

You may already have guessed that a user-defined worksheet function is defined by a garden-variety VBA function. (The function definition may not be declared as *Private*; that would restrict the domain of validity to the current module!)

Let us look at an example: The function *Discount* calculates the final price, given the unit price and the number of pieces. If ten or more pieces are purchased, then a five percent discount is applied.

The function can be placed in a worksheet just like a predefined worksheet function. It is allowed to take as input actual numbers as well as cell references.

```
=Discount(8, 12)        ' returns 91.2
=Discount(A1, B1)
' Function.xls
Function Discount(unitprice, pieces)
```

```
  If pieces >= 10 Then
    Discount = pieces * unitprice * 0.95
  Else
    Discount = pieces * unitprice
  End If
End Function
```

> **CAUTION** *As in previous versions, Excel does not feel obliged to recalculate the affected cells automatically when there is a change in the VBA code of a worksheet function. The explicit request for recalculation with* F9 *usually functions properly, but is not always completely reliable. (This problem has plagued Excel since version 5.) In particularly stubborn cases it usually helps to add and then delete a new row or column above, respectively to the left of, the affected cells.*

Short Description of Functions for Inserting a Function

In the form INSERT|FUNCTION (in previous versions this was the function assistant) a short description of all functions is displayed. For user-defined functions you can provide such a description if you select this function in the object browser and select the command PROPERTIES with the right mouse button. The form MEMBER OPTIONS that appears gives an impression of incompleteness, but it fulfills its mission.

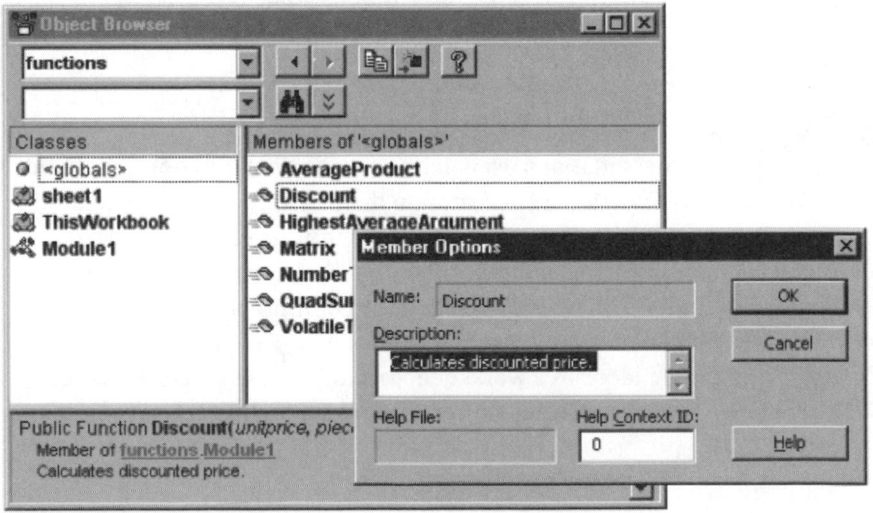

Figure 5.9. Short description of the Discount function

Function Categories

In Excel 5/7 user-defined worksheet functions could be put into various categories, such as "financial" and "date and time." Starting with Excel 97, the form MEMBER OPTIONS no longer offers this possibility, and all user-defined functions belong to the category "User Defined" in the PASTE FUNCTION form. However, if you wish to assign your functions to another category, you must give an instruction in the immediate window like the following:

```
Application.MacroOptions Macro:="Discount", Category:=1
```

The function will then be permanently associated to the group "Financial" (that is, the setting for this function will be stored together with the Excel file). The following list gives the numbers of the most important categories:

Category	*Category Name*
1	Finance
2	Date & Time
3	Math & Trig
4	Statistical
5	Lookup & Reference
6	Database
7	Text
8	Logical
9	Information
14	User Defined

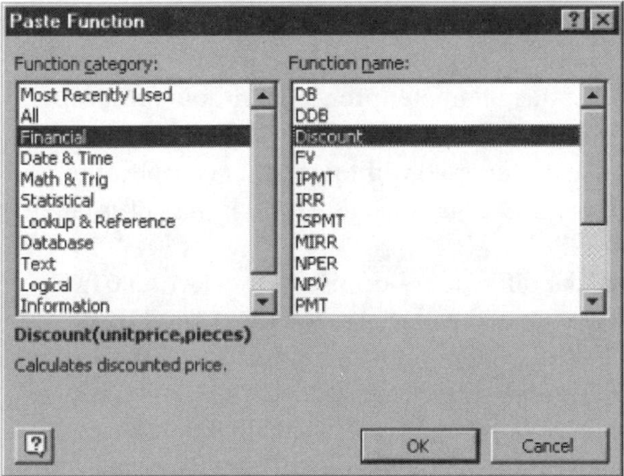

Figure 5.10. The user-defined function "Discount" has been associated with the function category "Financial"

Using User-Defined Functions in Other Workbooks

The function *Discount* can be used only in worksheets of the workbook in whose module it is defined. If you wish to use *Discount* in other workbooks as well, then you must provide the name of the workbook in which the function is defined, that is, *=Function.xls!Discount(8,12)*. Alternatively, you can create a reference to `Function.xls` in the current workbook with TOOLS|REFERENCES. Then it can be used without the prefixed file name. (The command TOOLS|REFERENCES can be used only when a module sheet is active.)

> **TIP** *Please note that Excel distinguishes between the use of user-defined functions in worksheets and in VBA code. If you wish to use* Discount *in the VBA code of another workbook, then you always have to supply a reference. The prefixing of the file name is not possible in VBA code.*

User-Defined Functions in Add-Ins

You can compile a workbook with the definitions of several user-defined functions into an add-in. These functions then are available in all workbooks once this add-in has been activated. In contrast to the definition of functions in normal workbooks, neither a prefixed file name when the function is called nor the provision of a reference is required. Extensive information on creating your own add-ins can be found in Chapter 14.

Cell Ranges as Parameters

If a user-defined function is called with a cell reference (such as *=Discount(A1,B1)*), then a *Range* object is passed to the function. In the case of a single cell, the further evaluation of the parameter proceeds without any problems: The *Value* property of the *Range* object is considered the default property, whence the contents of the cell can be accessed without further complication. Things get more difficult when a range of cells (such as A1:A3) is passed as parameter.

The situation presents particular difficulties because in Excel A1:A3,C1:C3 usually means a range of cells made up of the partial ranges A1:A3 and C1:C3. But "A1:A3,C1:C3" could as well indicate *two* arguments (for a function with two parameters). If ranges are given in this form, then Excel indeed interprets this as two arguments. However, when the entire range of cells is placed in parentheses (that is, (A1:A3,C1:C3) or when the range is stored under a name, then Excel considers the argument a single parameter.

For this reason the programming of functions that are meant to work with any number of combined ranges of cells is a bit complicated. The function *QuadSum* sums the squares of the values of all input cells. Here the parameter of the function is defined as a *ParamArray*, so that arbitrarily many parameters can be passed. For each of these parameters all cells of the partial range are squared and summed into *result*. Then, thanks to the test *TypeName(var)="Range"*, the function *QuadSum* works also with numeric parameters. Thus *QuadSum(1, 2, 3)* returns 14.

```
' Function.xls, "Module1"
' returns the sum of the squares of all input cells
Function QuadSum(ParamArray x())
  Dim var As Variant, result As Double
  Dim a As Range, c As Range
  For Each var In x()
    If TypeName(var) = "Range" Then
      For Each a In var.Areas   ' all partial ranges
        For Each c In a.Cells   ' all cells of the partial range
          result = result + c ^ 2
        Next c
      Next a
    Else
      result = result + var ^ 2
    End If
  Next var
  QuadSum = result
End Function
```

Error Checking

If you wish to program a function that is *not* conceived for ranges of cells, but exclusively for individual values, you should use an error check to exclude the possibility of invalid parameters being passed. The function *Discount* thus protected would look something like the following:

```
Function Discount(unitprice, pieces)
  On Error Resume Next
  If TypeName(unitprice) = "Range" Then
    If unitprice.Count > 1 Then
      Discount = CVErr(xlErrValue): Exit Function
    End If
  End If
```

```
  If TypeName(pieces) = "Range" Then
    If pieces.Count > 1 Then
      Discount = CVErr(xlErrValue): Exit Function
    End If
  End If
  If pieces >= 10 Then
    Discount = pieces * unitprice * 0.95
  Else
    Discount = pieces * unitprice
  End If
  If Err Then Discount = CVErr(xlErrValue)
End Function
```

CVErr(xlErrValue) returns a variant data type of subtype Error containing an error number. In a worksheet, you see #VALUE in the cell in which the function is used. More information on the subject of error checking can be found in Chapter 6.

Matrix Functions

Excel recognizes so-called matrix functions. Since these functions seldom occur in the everyday use of Excel, we first present an example of the application of a matrix function that is part of Excel. The function *LINEST* calculates the slope m and y-intercept b for the line that is the best least squares approximation to a given set of points (arrays of y-values and x-values are passed as parameters). If there are several ranges of x-values, then instead of a single value m the values m_1, m_2, ... are returned corresponding to the equation $y = m_1x_1 + m_2x_2 + \ldots + b$. (Extensive information on *LINEST* can be found in the on-line help.)

The function *LINEST* is interesting for us here because it returns a matrix (namely, in the sequence ..., m_3, m_2, m_1, b). Since only one result can be displayed in a cell, matrix functions must be divided over several cells. Moreover, matrix formulas must be so identified. Excel has a rather complex input form for them:

You must first select, with the mouse or with Shift and the cursor keys, as a range all cells in which the results of the matrix function are to be displayed. Then you press F2 to input the function into the active cell of the range (it doesn't matter in which cell of the range). Finally, the input must be terminated with Ctrl+Shift+Return. With this, the formula is copied into all cells of the range. The entire range is now considered to be a matrix.

Furthermore, you can transform a normal formula into a matrix formula: Move the cell pointer into the cell that contains the formula, beginning with it select the remaining cells, press F2, and confirm the unchanged formula with Ctrl+Shift+Return. It is not possible to convert individual cells into a matrix. You can carry out changes only with Ctrl+Shift+Return. Then they again hold for all cells of the matrix. It is also impossible to delete individual cells. You can delete only the entire matrix.

Programming Matrix Functions

Programming matrix functions is simpler (from a purely formal point of view) than placing a matrix formula into a worksheet. The only difference from normal functions is that the result is not a single value, but rather must be returned as a field. The following example shows a matrix function that takes no parameters and returns a 2*2 matrix with the values 1, 2, 3, and 4. This function demonstrates only the syntax of a matrix function, without accomplishing anything useful.

```
Function Matrix()
  Dim x(1, 1)
  x(0, 0) = 1: x(0, 1) = 2
  x(1, 0) = 3: x(1, 1) = 4
  Matrix = x()
End Function
```

The Volatile Method

With the instruction *Application.**Volatile*** a user-defined function can be set as "volatile." (Normally, functions are recalculated only when their precursor, or precedent, cells change. This is usually sufficient and certainly much more efficient.)

```
Public Function VolatileTest()
  Application.Volatile True
  VolatileTest = Rnd
End Function
```

If you input the formula *=VolatileTest()* into a cell, the indicated value will change whenever any cell in the worksheet is changed or recalculated.

Peculiarities and Problems

Basically, the same rules apply to the code of user-defined functions as for all other procedures. However, there are a few exceptions:

- It is not possible to change ranges of cells in the worksheet directly with user-defined functions that are used within a worksheet. (For example, you cannot write a function that will color the cell green or red according to its content. However, you can accomplish this by another route, namely, with the *FormatCondition* object, described at the beginning of Chapter 9.)

  Not only that: Even if you do not wish to change ranges of cells, many Excel methods and properties, such as *SpecialCells* and *CurrentRegion,* do not work in accessing associated ranges of cells.

  Note that in testing such a function in the immediate window everything works just as you would wish. (The changing of ranges of cells is permitted with VBA code.) But when you use the function in a worksheet, then errors occur. These restrictions are nowhere documented, and thus it is difficult to say how many methods and properties are affected.

- If an error occurs in a user-defined function (such as division by 0), then in the result cell the error message *#VALUE!* is displayed. There is no VBA error message, however. The same things holds when an error occurs in the passing of parameters (such as an incorrect data type). This behavior makes it much more difficult to detect errors in user-defined functions. The solution is to attempt to run the function in the immediate window with comparable parameters.

- Since Excel 5 there have been continuing problems with the automatic recalculation of cells. Earlier Excel versions occasionally did not recalculate all cells after a change in the worksheet structure, and thus there were old, and hence false, results to be seen. Many of these problems appeared only with user-defined functions, while others occurred exclusively with built-in functions.

  In this regard, the information police in the hallowed halls of Microsoft have been more than reticent (to formulate it politely). The problems appearing in Excel 97 were solved only in a series of updates. The best source of information around this issue was

  `http://www.wopr.com/wow/wowarch.shtml.`

  The reliability of the calculation functions of Excel 2000 is difficult to estimate. There is an apparent problem that fortunately appears only during code development: After the VBA code of a user-defined function has been changed, the affected cells are not automatically recalculated. The recalculation must be accomplished explicitly with F9. Other than that, during the course of preparing this book no calculational problems occurred.

Examples

In this section you will find some additional user-defined functions. A more complex function has been introduced previously: *Holiday(date)* tests whether a given day is a holiday and returns the name of the holiday if it is.

NumberToText

The following example is suited above all for applications in the world of banking (for example, for check writing). Given a number, the function *NumberToText* returns a character string in which each digit is given as text. For example, given 12.34 the function returns the character string "—— one two point three four ——". The function works within the range ±9999999999.99. At most two decimal places are returned. Numbers between –0.005 and 0.005 are represented by "——zero ——".

The function first tests whether the parameter *x* contains a valid number for being converted. If that is the case, then the number is converted to a character string with *Format*. So that this character string can be more easily further processed, as many space characters as necessary so that the character strings are of a uniform length are added with *Space*. If the character string ends with ".00", the last three characters of the string are ignored in the conversion to the text of digits.

```
Function NumberToText(x)
  Dim i&, result, character$, lastchar&
  Dim digit$(9)
  digit(0) = "zero": digit(1) = "one": digit(2) = "two"
  digit(3) = "three": digit(4) = "four": digit(5) = "five"
  digit(6) = "six": digit(7) = "seven": digit(8) = "eight"
  digit(9) = "nine"
  If isEmpty(x) Then NumberToText = "": Exit Sub
  If x >= 10000000000# Or x <= -10000000000# Then
    NumberToText = "number too big or too small"
    Exit Function
  End If
  If x < 0 Then result = "minus ": x = -x
  x = Format$(x, "0.00")
  x =
  x = Space(13 - Len(x)) + x
  If Right(x, 3) = ".00" Then lastchar = 10 Else lastchar = 13
```

```
  For i = 1 To lastchar
    character = Mid(x, i, 1)
    If character >= "0" And character <= "9" Then
      result = result + digit(Val(character)) + " "
    ElseIf character = "." Then
      result = result + "point "
    End If
  Next i
  NumberToText = "— " + Trim(result) + " —"
End Function
```

AverageProduct

Most problems in the programming of new functions, such as for statistical applications, are caused by their parameters, say if two ranges of cells are to be passed that must be exactly the same size, or if the number of ranges should be variable. In the following two examples you should therefore pay attention to the evaluation of the list of parameters.

AverageProduct expects two ranges as parameters. These ranges are not permitted to be formed of partial ranges (control with *Area.Count*) and must have the same number of cells (control with *Cells.Count*). If that is the case, then the first cell of the first range is multiplied by the first cell of the second range. Similarly, products are taken of the corresponding second, third, and so on, cells, and these products are then summed. Finally, this sum is divided by the number of cells in each range. A correct call to the function looks like this: *=AverageProduct(F19:F22, G19:G22).*

```
Public Function AverageProduct(p As Range, q As Range)
  Dim i&, result
  If p.Areas.Count > 1 Or q.Areas.Count > 1 Then
    AverageProduct = CVErr(xlErrRef): Exit Function
  End If
  If p.Cells.Count <> q.Cells.Count Then
    AverageProduct = CVErr(xlErrRef): Exit Function
  End If
  For i = 1 To p.Cells.Count
    result = result + p.Cells(i) * q.Cells(i)
  Next
  AverageProduct = result / p.Cells.Count
End Function
```

HighestAverageArgument

The function *HighestAverageArgument* expects as parameter an arbitrary number of ranges of cells, which can be of various sizes. For each range an average is computed. The function returns the number of the range whose average value is the greatest. (In the case of two or more ranges with the same average, the function returns the number of the first range.) A possible function call is the following:

=HighestAverageArgument(F25:F27, G25:G26, H25:H28).

Because of the use of *ParamArray*, it is impossible to declare *p* as a *Range*. Therefore, the correct passing of the ranges is tested in program code with a *TypeName* test. As in the example above, multipartite ranges are rejected. Likewise, the function is ensured against a range of cells containing only text (no numbers), in which case calculating the average value with the function *Average* leads to an error (test with *IsNumeric* for the result of *Average*).

```
Public Function HighestAverageArgument(ParamArray p())
  Dim nrOfRanges&, i&, maxnr&
  Dim averg(), tmp
  nrOfRanges = UBound(p())     'UBound returns 2, if 3 parameters
  ReDim averg(nrOfRanges)      '   are passed
  ' calculate average value for all ranges of cells
  ' and store in a field
  For i = 0 To nrOfRanges
    If TypeName(p(i)) <> "Range" Then
      HighestAverageArgument = CVErr(xlErrValue): Exit Function
    End If
    If p(i).Areas.Count > 1 Then
      HighestAverageArgument = CVErr(xlErrRef): Exit Function
    End If
    averg(i) = WorksheetFunction.Average(p(i))
    If Not IsNumeric(averg(i)) Then
      HighestAverageArgument = CVErr(xlErrValue): Exit Function
    End If
  Next
  ' find highest value
  For i = 0 To nrOfRanges
    If averg(i) > tmp Then
      tmp = averg(i)
      maxnr = i
    End If
```

```
  Next
  ' return result; plus 1, thus 1 for the first range
  ' (and not 0)
  HighestAverageArgument = maxnr + 1
End Function
```

Configuration Files, Custom Configuration

There are numerous ways in which Excel can be configured to the user's specifications:

- custom toolbars,
- changing and extending the menu system,
- changing general options,
- use of templates,
- extension of Excel by macros in the personal macro workbook and/or add-ins.

This section describes how to carry out and save such configuration settings.

Options

The appearance and behavior of Excel is influenced by countless options. You can set a large fraction of these options with the menu command Tools|Options, others with various other commands. This section discusses briefly some of the most important options (both manual changes and changes via program code). Please observe that in spite of their centrally located setting through Tools|Options, options have various realms of validity (Excel as a whole, a workbook, a window) and are stored in various files! (Details on configuration files appear in the next section.)

What Can Be Set with the Command Options?

With the menu command TOOLS|OPTIONS you open a form with eight tabs, in which numerous Excel options can be set. The meaning of most of these settings is obvious or can be read about in the on-line help, so that here we do not need an extensive discussion.

Other Settings

The form for setting the **printing options** is hidden within the menu command FILE|PAGE SETUP. This setting normally holds only for the active worksheet. (However, several worksheets can be selected and then set simultaneously.)

With FILE|SAVE AS|TOOLS|GENERAL OPTIONS you can set various **save options** (password, write protection, backup file). The command FILE|SAVE AS|TOOLS|WEB OPTIONS opens up a further form with a host of options that govern the conversion of a document to HTML format.

> **NOTE** *The file and print options hold only for the active file. Unlike Word, Excel cannot easily be given such default settings as always to make a backup copy when a file is saved or to maintain a particular page format. One possible solution to this problem is the use of templates (see Chapter 9).*

Window options are to be found, with one exception, in TOOLS|OPTIONS|VIEW. The exception is the zoom factor, which is found in VIEW|ZOOM. Window options are valid only for the currently active window (and not for the entire workbook or in general for Excel). Options for the display of **toolbars** are set with VIEW|TOOLBARS|CUSTOMIZE. (For details see Chapter 8.)

> **TIP** *Office 2000 has the peculiarity of at first displaying incomplete menus. The missing entries appear only after a while. It seems that in its benevolence Microsoft believes that this arrangement simplifies the life of the user. However, you can undo this nonsense by deactivating the option* MENUS SHOW RECENTLY USED COMMANDS FIRST *in the form* VIEW|TOOLBARS|CUSTOMIZE|OPTIONS.

Some **virus protection options** are hidden in the form TOOLS|MACRO|SECURITY. Where these settings are stored is fortunately not documented (in any case, not in the form just described). A change in these options by VBA code was not planned for. (But there are doubtless inventive programmers who will figure it out, who will also manage to pull it off with calls to certain API functions.)

Setting Options with Program Code

Most Excel options are set with numerous properties of the *Application* object. Options that do not affect Excel as a whole, but only a file, a window, or a chart, for example, can be changed via the properties of the corresponding object (*Worksheet, Window,* etc.), where the association is not always logical.

The settings for the page format, headers and footers, and so on, are carried out with the *PageSetup* object, which is set for every sheet object (*WorkSheet*, *Chart*, etc.) and can also be addressed with the *Window* object. It is not possible to change all at once the page format of several sheets through program code. (Execute a loop over the sheets in question and change *PageSetup* for each individual object.)

The active printer, on the other hand, is set with the *ActivePrinter* property of the *Application* object. However, there is no possibility of using VBA code to obtain a list of all available printers.

The following tables give an overview of the most important properties and methods.

Application Object (General Options)

ActivePrinter	set the currently active printer
AddIns(...)	access to add-ins
Calculation	recalculation of worksheets automatic/manual
CommandBars(...)	access to menu bars and toolbars (see Chapter 8)
DisplayAlerts	display alerts
DisplayFormulaBar	formula bar on/off (*True*/*False*)
DisplayFullScreen	full screen mode on/off
DisplayNoteIndicators	red markings in cells to indicate notes
DisplayStatusBar	status bar
MoveAfterReturn	cursor moves on Return into the next cell of a table
MoveAfterReturnDirection	direction of cursor movement on Return
OnEvent ...	various event procedures (see Chapter 4)
PromptForSummaryInformation	form for input of information on saving
ScreenUpdating	update screen during macro execution
SheetsInNewWorkbook	number of empty worksheets in a new file
StandardFont	name of the default font in worksheets
StandardFontsize	size of the default font in worksheets

Workbook Object (File-Specific Options)

ChangeFileAccess	change access privileges
Colors	access file's color palette (56 colors)
CreateBackup	create backup file on saving
DisplayDrawingObjects	display drawing objects
Protect	turn write protection on and off
Styles(...)	access to templates
Visible	file visible/invisible (hidden)

Worksheet Object (Worksheet-Specific Options)

DisplayAutomaticPageBreaks	display page breaks in worksheets
EnableAutoFilter	enables display of autofilters
EnableOutlining	enables display of grouping
EnablePivotTable	enables the creation of pivot tables
FilterMode	autofilter on/off
PageSetup	access to page and printer settings
SetBackgroundPicture	set background picture
Visible	worksheet is visible/invisible

Window Object (Window-Specific Options)

DisplayFormulas	display formulas instead of results
DisplayGridlines	display gridlines
DisplayHeadings	display row and column headings
DisplayHorizontalScrollbar	display horizontal scroll bar
DisplayOutline	display grouping
DisplayZeros	display 0 values (or display empty cell)
DisplayVerticalScrollbar	display vertical scroll bar
DisplayWorkbookTabs	display workbook tabs
FreezePanes	split window frozen/unfrozen
GridLineColor	set color (RGB value) of gridlines
GridLineColorIndex	color of gridlines from the color palette (0 to 55)
PageSetup	access to page and printer settings
Split	window split/not split
SplitColumn	column in which the window is split
SplitRow	row in which the window is split
TabRatio	ratio of tab area to horizontal scroll bar
Zoom	zoom factor

PageSetup Object (Page Layout, Set Separately for Each Sheet)

BlackAndWhite	print in black and white
BottomMargin	bottom margin, in points (1/72 inch ≈ 0.35 mm)
CenterFooter	footer, central part
CenterHeader	header, central part
CenterHorizontal	print horizontally centered
CenterVertical	print vertically centered
FirstPageNumber	start value for pagination
FooterMargin	size of footer
HeaderMargin	size of header
LeftFooter	footer, left part

LeftHeader	header, left part
LeftMargin	left margin in points (≈1/72 inch ≈ 0.35 mm)
Orientation	print in vertical or horizontal format
PaperSize	paper size
PrintArea	area of page to be printed
PrintTitleColumns	column title (printed on each page)
PrintTitleRows	row title (printed on each page)
RightFooter	footer, right side
RightHeader	header, right side
RightMargin	right margin in points (≈1/72 inch ≈ 0.35 mm)
TopMargin	top margin in points (≈1/72 inch ≈ 0.35 mm)

DefaultWebOptions (Excel Global) / WebOptions (File-Specific)

AllowPNG	encode pictures in PNG format
DownloadComponents	download missing web components.
Encoding	desired character set for web browser
LocationOfComponents	location to which web components are to be saved
OrganizeInFolder	save pictures, etc., in their own folder
RelyOnCSS	use *Cascading Style Sheets*
RelyOnVML	use *Vector Markup Language*

Configuration Files

Basics

Most current operating systems—with the exception of the first versions of Windows 95—are automatically configured in such a way that a personal directory (folder) is available to each user (that is, for each login name or each account). The location of this folder depends on both the operating system and the individual configuration.

For example, if you are logged in as the administrator under Windows NT 4, the personal folder is `C:\Windows\Profiles\Administrator`. (Perhaps you are more familiar with the subfolder `C:\Windows\Profiles\Administrator\Personal`.) This folder is recommended as the location to save your personal files.

Of course, there is a reason for describing the fundamentals of Windows in such detail: The user-specific configuration files of Excel are stored in subdirectories of the personal folder. For the remainder of this section this folder will be abbreviated as **`Userprofile`**.

Some additional configuration files are stored relative to the installation folder of Office 2000. This folder will hereinafter be abbreviated as **`Office2000`**.

Overview of Excel Configuration Files

Excel strews information about the current configuration and the setting of options all over the hard drive. The abundance of configuration files becomes more and more difficult to keep track of with each new version.

- Some individual settings are saved in the Windows registry.
- Information on the individual content and placement of toolbars is located in `Userprofile\Application Data\Microsoft\Excel\`**`Excel.xlb`**.
- The personal macro workbook is stored in `Userprofile\Application Data\Microsoft\Excel\Xlstart\Personal.xls`.
- Globally available macros can be stored in arbitrary files in the folder `Office2000\Office\`**`Xlstart`**.
- Personal templates are stored in `Userprofile\Application Data \Microsoft\`**`Templates`**.
- The appropriate folder for storing global templates is `Office2000 \Office\`**`Xlstart`**. (The folder `Office2000\Templates\n`, which is apparently the template folder for other Office programs, has nothing to do with Excel 2000, at least not in the current version. Here *n* is a language code; for example, it is 1031 for the German version.)
- Global add-in files are stored in `Office2000\Office\`**`Library`**.
- Personal add-in files, however, are located in `Userprofile\Application Data\Microsoft\`**`AddIns`**.
- Predefined (that is, included with Excel) chart templates are stored in `Office2000\Office\`*`n`*`\`**`Xl8galry.xls`**. Here *n* is again the language code.
- User-defined chart templates are stored in `Userprofile\Application Data\Microsoft\Excel\`**`Xlusrgal.xls`**.
- All remaining settings are file-specific and are stored in their own Excel files.

> **TIP** *File names and paths of configuration files change with every version, not least to avoid conflicts with the simultaneous use of several versions of Office. If you wish to create portable Excel applications, you should not rely on the configuration files being located in any particular place.*

> **TIP** *You can find an overview of Excel properties for accessing most of the above-mentioned folders, in the section of Excel-specific methods and properties.*

Settings in the Office Registry

The Microsoft Office registry contains an entry in the folder

HKeyLocalMachine\Software\Microsoft\Office\9.0\Excel\InstallRoot

that identifies the Office installation directory on the hard drive (that is, the folder that is usually denoted in this book by `Office2000`). Furthermore, various individual settings are stored in the registry, and in fact, in the following location:

HKey_Current_User\Software\Microsoft\Office\9.0\Excel\Options

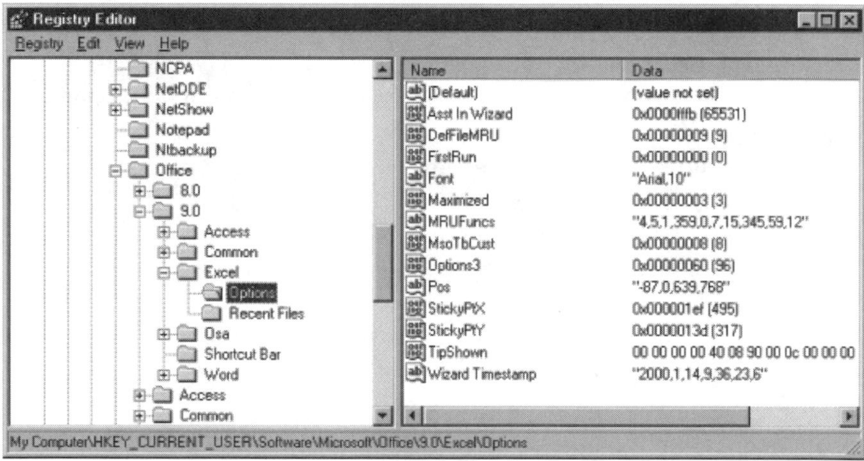

Figure 5:11. The registry editor in Windows NT

These settings can be edited with the program `RegEdit.exe`. (However, it is not recommended to do so unless you know what you are doing. By changing the registry you can screw up Office and even Windows to such an extent that they will have to be reinstalled.)

Information on Toolbars in Excel.xlb

The file `Userprofile\Application Data\Microsoft\Excel\`**`Excel.xlb`** is automatically created for each user the first time a change in a toolbar is made. The file contains information on the arrangement of the toolbars and the office assistant for making changes in the given toolbars, paths to the associated macro functions, and new toolbars that were available the last time Excel was exited.

`*.xlb` files can be opened with FILE|OPEN and then be used to change the current state of the toolbars. The last valid state when Excel is exited will automatically be saved. However, there is no way of saving the file in a menu command or a macro without simultaneously leaving Excel.

> **TIP** *It is possible to store user-defined toolbars directly in an Excel file with* VIEW|TOOLBARS|CUSTOMIZE|TOOLBARS|ATTACH. *This makes sense when the toolbar is to made available to other users (possibly on another computer).*

Macro Templates in the Xlstart Folder

Starting with Excel 2000 the "personal macro workbook" is justly named, since every user actually receives his own version. (In earlier versions of Excel all users of a particular computer had to share this workbook.) For this reason there is no longer just one, but two `Xlstart` folders:

```
Userprofile\Application Data\Microsoft\Excel\Xlstart     personal
Office2000\Office\Xlstart                                global
```

When it is launched, Excel first loads all `*.xls` files from the personal `Xlstart` folder, then all `*.xls` files from the global `Xlstart` folder. The personal macro workbook with the name `Personal.xls` is not given any preference. So far as I have been able to determine, Excel simply loads all files in alphabetical order (but always first the personal, then the global files). The order is not documented, so do not depend on it.

To be precise, in addition to the two `Xlstart` folders just referred to, there is a third folder whose `*.xls` files are automatically loaded upon launch of Excel. The location of this folder is not predetermined, but can be set with TOOLS|OPTIONS|GENERAL|ALTERNATE STARTUP FILE LOCATION.

This location is of particular interest if global macro files are to be shared across a network. In that case a network directory can be given here. The information about this additional start directory is stored in the registry.

In practice, the `Xlstart` directories are used primarily to load automatically VBA code that is meant to be always available. Of course, VBA can automatically be executed, for example with a *Workbook_Open* event procedure. Files in the directory `Xlstart` can thus also be used to carry out extensions or changes in the menu structure.

Workbooks from the `Xlstart` folders are usually stored in a "hidden" state, so that they are not visible on the screen and appear only in the VBA development environment. Invisible files can be made visible with WINDOW|UNHIDE.

A special place within the personal `Xlstart` files is held by the personal macro workbook `Personal.xls`. In this workbook all newly recorded macros are automatically stored if in the options for macro recording the entry "personal macro workbook" has been activated. If you never use user-created macros, then this file does not even exist.

CAUTION *Excel normally displays a virus warning before files with VBA code are loaded. However, this does not automatically hold for files that come from the* `Xlstart` *folder. The reason for this is the option* TRUST ALL INSTALLED ADD-INS AND TEMPLATES, *which is the default. You can change this in* TOOLS|MACRO|SECURITY|TRUSTED SOURCES.

This default setting makes sense, of course. It would be a pain in any one of a number of places if every time Excel was launched it asked permission to run the macros that you personally had stored in `Personal.xls` *and other* `Xlstart` *folders. On the other hand, one could imagine that a virus programmer would take delight in this breach of security in Excel.*

TIP *If you wish to launch Excel without having certain files open automatically, you may use the command line option* `/s`. *Thus execute* START|RUN *and input* `excel /s`.

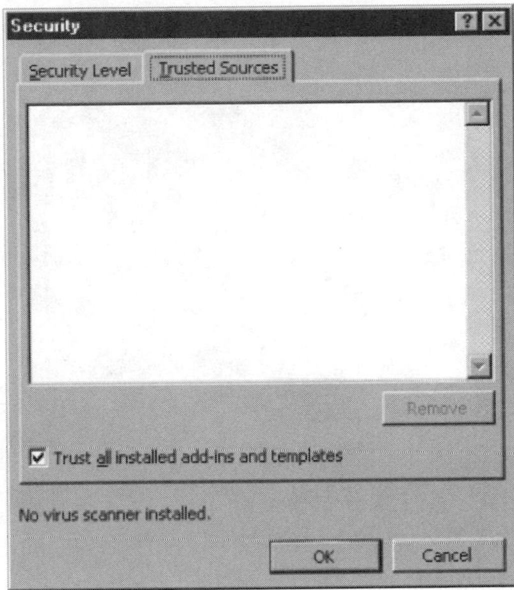

Figure 5.12. Files in the Xlstart folder are considered safe

Templates

Templates are Excel files with the file extension `*.xlt`, which serves as the model for new worksheets, charts, and workbooks. These are in principle normal Excel files for which the file type "Template" was given in SAVE UNDER.

In order for templates to appear as selections in the form FILE|NEW, you must have saved them in one of the following folders:

`Userprofile\Application Data\Microsoft\Templates` personal
`Office2000\Office\Xlstart` global
`additional start folder` depending on setting

If one of the two `Xlstart` folders or the additional start folder contains files with the names `Book.xlt`, `Sheet.xlt`, and `Chart.xlt`, these files are considered the automatic templates and will be used (without asking) as templates when new workbooks are created with the tool NEW or when new worksheets or chart sheets are appended to preexisting worksheets.

`Sheet.xlt` and `Chart.xlt` can contain only a worksheet or chart sheet. `Book.xlt` can contain an arbitrary combination of sheets. The number of worksheets contained in `Book.xlt` has priority over the setting of the number of empty worksheets in TOOLS|OPTIONS|GENERAL.

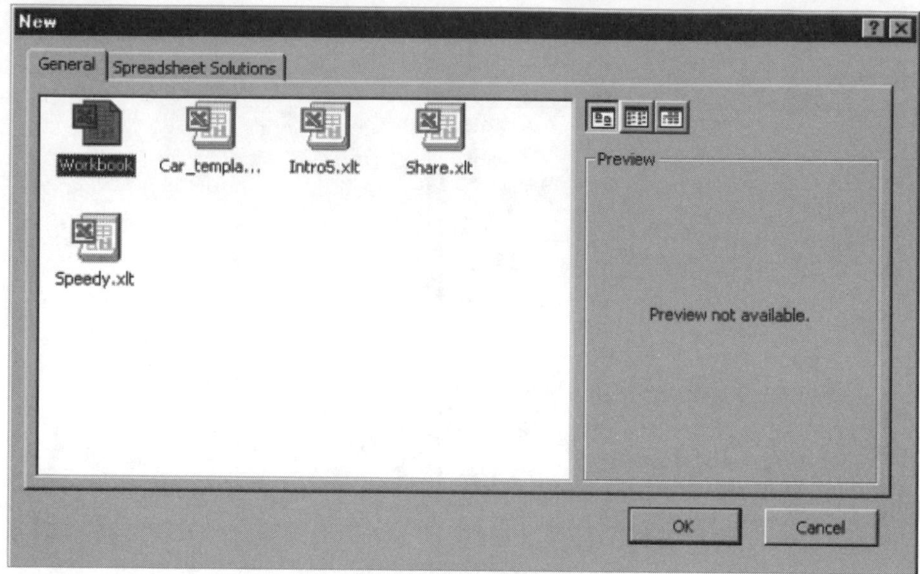

Figure 5.13. Selection from the installed templates

`Book.xlt` and `Sheet.xlt` can be used to set a host of options that otherwise would have to be set in every sheet, causing much unnecessary work, such as print format templates, settings for page layout including headers and footers, and window options (gridlines, zoom factor, form of the row and column headings).

> **TIP** *Templates and their extensive possibilities are described more fully in Chapter 9. There the support of input of formulas by VBA code (intelligent forms) will be explained.*

Chart Templates

In principle, charts can also be saved as templates. For charts Excel prefers a more practical variant: user-defined formats (previously autoformats). These chart templates are stored in the file `Office2000\Office\n\Xl8galry.xls`. The chart types thus defined can be accessed with the command CHART TYPE|CUSTOM TYPES of the chart context (pop-up) menu.

To save your custom chart templates you first create a chart according to your specifications. Then select the above-mentioned command and click on the button ADD. You can now give a name to your chart type as well as a short description. The chart template will be saved in `Xl8galry.xls` and is available in the future whenever Excel is launched.

Saving Configuration Data in Their Own Excel Files

A large part of all configuration data is stored (independently of whatever templates are later used) directly in individual Excel files, such as information on the arrangement of windows for that file, window options (such as gridlines, zoom factor, for of row and column headers), type styles, and page setup (printing parameters).

The place for storing these data is at once practical and impractical: practical, because most Excel options can be set individually for each file (to some extent for each individual worksheet and window); and impractical because often the same settings (such as relate to headers and footers) have to be set over and over again. This is burdensome, and one would rather not have to do it. You can minimize this formatting task by using automatic templates, but then you cannot later make changes. (Changes in templates affect only new Excel files, not those that already exist.)

Add-In Files

As you can read in Chapter 14 in full detail, Excel recognizes two types of add-ins. Traditional add-ins are in principle normal Excel files, which, however, are stored as add-in files with the file extension `*.xla`. On the other hand, COM add-ins are ActiveX DLLs with the extension `*.dll`. COM add-ins can be created only with Office Developer.

So that traditional add-in files are recognized as such and can be activated in the add-in manager (TOOLS|ADD-INS) they have to be installed in one of the following two folders:

userprofile`\Application Data\Microsoft\AddIns`	global
`Office2000\Office\Library`	personal

In the case of COM add-ins the installation location can be anywhere on the hard drive. What is important is that the COM add-ins be correctly registered in the registry. This task is usually handled by a separate installation program.

Excel Meets the Euro

Considering the fact that in the next few years possibly millions of Excel files will need to be converted to deal with the euro, it must be said that Microsoft has not expended excessive effort in this direction. Essentially, there are two new functions:

- Starting with Excel 2000 the euro symbol can finally be input—via Alt+0128 (U.S. keyboard: type numbers on the numeric keypad with Num Lock on),

AltGr+4 in the UK, and for other countries see the on-line help under "euro"—without installing one or another update.

- The so-called euro add-in (file `Eurotool.xla`) offers a euro conversion function as well as a button with which a currency amount can be represented in euros. (Here only the cell format is changed.)

Any tools that might have been of help in reconfiguring existing worksheets to include the euro are completely lacking. And even the *Euroconvert* function is not without its problems.

> **TIP** *You can set the currency symbol in the control panel in the country-specific settings. This symbol will be used as the default in the formatting of currency amounts. It probably is not a good idea to change this setting to the euro, since then many amounts will be displayed as euros that really should be in pounds sterling, or German marks, for example. It makes more sense to format explicitly for the euro in new documents and tables that are being converted.*

The Euroconvert Function

If the *Euroconvert* Function is inserted into a worksheet, the syntax looks as follows:

=Euroconvert(number, source, target [, full_precision, triangulation_precision])

The source and target currencies are passed as character strings. Here the ISO currency codes are used, such as *"DEM"* for the German mark, *"ATS"* for the Austrian schilling, *"IEP"* for the Irish pound, and *"EUR"* for the euro. (A complete table appears in the Excel on-line help.)

Here are some examples:

Formula	*Result*	*Notes*
=Euroconvert(100, "EUR", "DEM")	195.58	100 € = 195.58 DM
=Euroconvert(100, "DEM", "EUR")	51.13	100 DM = 51.13 €
=Euroconvert(100, "EUR", "ATS")	1376.03	100 € = 1376 ATS
=Euroconvert(100, "ATS", "EUR")	7.27	100 ATS = 7.27 €
=Euroconvert(100, "DEM", "ATS")	703.55	100 DM = 703.55 ATS
=Euroconvert(100, "ATS", "DEM")	14.21	100 ATS = 14.21 DM

In general, *Euroconvert* returns only two decimal places. If you are converting small amounts, the result will be zero. (Note that not only is 0 displayed, it is the value stored internally, even if you then multiply the result by 1000.) For example, if you wished to convert 1 Austrian groschen into euros, the result will be 0 *(Euroconvert(0.01, "ATS", "EUR")*.

According to the on-line documentation, this behavior corresponds to the currency-specific rounding rules. However that may be, if you give *TRUE* as the fourth parameter, then this noteworthy rounding mode will be ignored, and instead, calculations will be made to full accuracy. *Euroconvert(0.01, "ATS", "EUR", TRUE)* demonstrates that an Austrian groschen is, in fact, worth a whopping 0.0007267283416786 euro.

It remains only to explain *Euroconvert*'s fifth parameter. It comes into play only when neither the source *x* nor target *y* is the euro. In such calculations, first *x* is converted to euros, and then this intermediate result is converted into *y*. The fifth parameter of *Euroconvert* determines the number of decimal places to which the intermediate result (not the final result) is to be rounded. If the parameter is omitted, then *Euroconvert* does not round the intermediate result, and thus calculates with maximum precision.

Installing Euroconvert *in VBA Code*

The *Euroconvert* function is, of course, available in VBA code. You have merely to set up a reference to the *Eurotool* library (Figure 5.14).

```
Sub eurotest()
  MsgBox EUROCONVERT(100, "DEM", "EUR")
End Sub
```

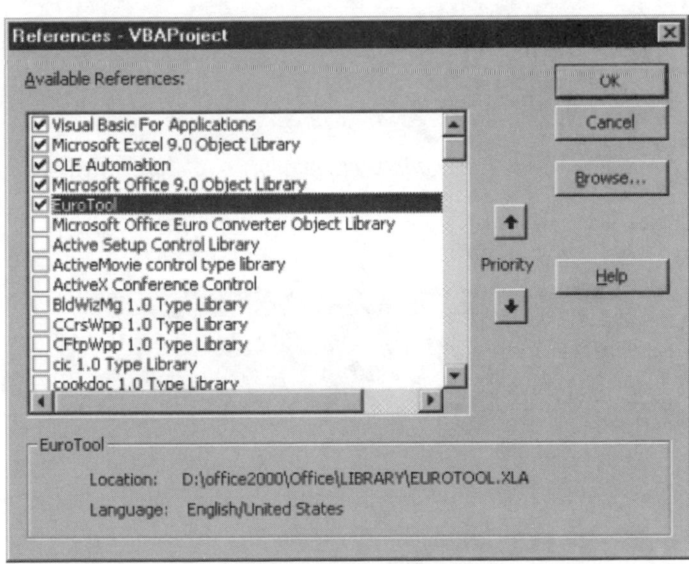

Figure 5.14. A reference to the EuroTool add-in

The *Eurotool* library provides a second function: *ApplyEuroformatting* formats all previously selected cells of the active worksheet into euro currency format (thousands separator, two decimal places, postfixed _-Symbol).

Problems with Euroconvert as a Worksheet Function

As already mentioned, the Euroconvert function is available only if the euro add-in has been activated. The biggest problem with the use of add-ins is that when you pass Excel files to other users, you do not know whether the user has activated the add-in. Why such an important function whose code takes up only a few kilobytes of storage could not be integrated directly into Excel is a secret known only to Microsoft. (Perhaps the reason is that an add-in can be more easily brought up to date, for example, if the UK decides to join the euro zone.)

If the individual receiving your file in which you have used the *Euroconvert* function has not activated the euro add-in, then when the file is loaded two error alerts will appear. First, Excel announces in a rather cryptic way (Figure 5.15) that certain links to other workbooks need to be updated. (What is meant is the add-in file `Eurotool.xla` , but how on earth is the user supposed to know that?) If the user is lucky and chooses YES, then the result will be a confrontation with yet another alert, in which Excel maintains that the function *Euroconvert* was not found in `Eurotool.xla`. (Figure 5.16).

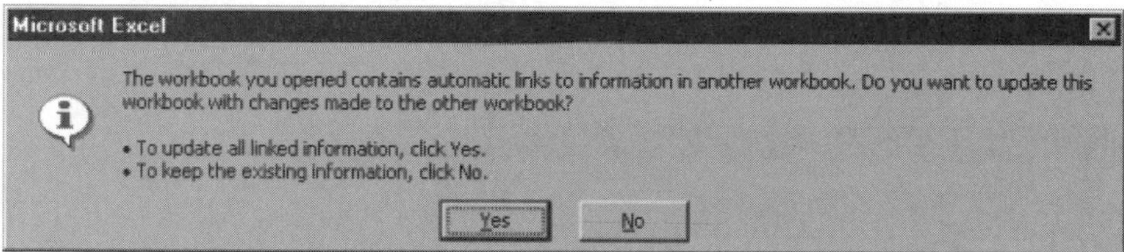

Figure 5.15. Excel asks somewhat cryptically whether the workbook with the euro add-in should be loaded

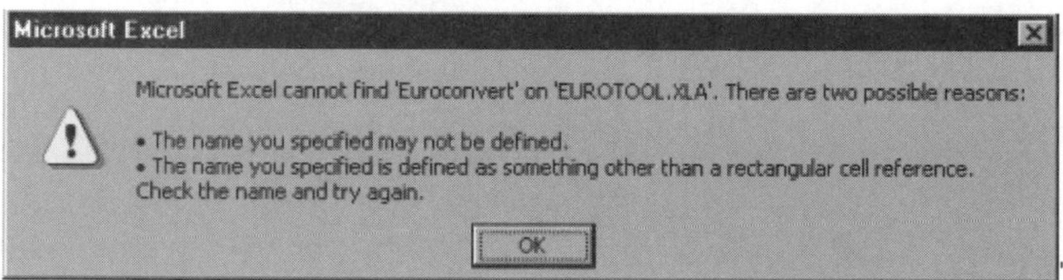

Figure 5.16. Excel maintains that Euroconvert is not defined in Eurotool.xla

The reason for the second error alert remains completely opaque. Fortunately, however, there is a simple solution: Before passing on your file, switch into the development environment with Alt+F11 and establish a reference to *EuroTool.* (This library will be displayed automatically once the euro add-in has been activated; see Figure 5.14.)

If the file thus prepared is now opened on a computer on which the euro add-in has not been activated, everything functions correctly anyhow. (To be sure, the add-in remains inactive, but the add-in file is nonetheless loaded, and the *Euroconvert* function is available both in the worksheet and as VBA code.)

The only requirement is that the euro add-in be installed on the computer. If that is not the case, then there appears, alas, not the question whether the add-in should be installed, but an error alert, which gives no indication as to the cause of the trouble (Figure 5.17).

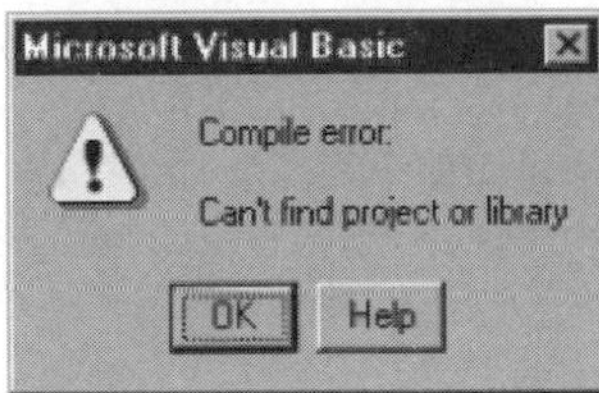

Figure 5.17. Error alert if the euro add-in has not been installed

Thus you have no choice but to advise the user somewhere at the beginning of the worksheet that this file uses the euro add-in and that the user should install it and preferably activate it. Welcome to the brave (sort of) new world of Microsoft meets the euro!

The Microsoft Office Euro Converter Mystery

In addition to the Excel euro add-in, one can discover in the REFERENCES form of the VBA development environment the *Microsoft Office Euro Converter Object Library.* This library is defined in the file `Program Files\Common Files\Microsoft Shared\Euro\MSOEuro.DLL` and has the abbreviation *MsoEuro.* The object catalog reveals that the library contains the object *Converter,* which in turn is equipped with the two properties *Convert* and *Version. Convert* has the same parameters as *EuroConvert.*

However, all attempts to use this *Convert* function fail. *Convert* is not defined as a global method—therefore, a *Converter* object must be created before *Convert* can be used. The instruction leads, however, to an unfathomable syntax error ("invalid use of keyword New").

What is this library for, then? How was it installed? Was it installed automatically with Office 2000? Is it always installed, or is it optional? Is it in only the European versions, or in all versions? Many questions, but no answers, because the library has not been documented as of the writing of this book, and because all attempts to use the library have thus far ended in failure.

This library would be a most attractive alternative to the euro add-in with all of its problems, if only one could use it and could rely on its existence. Furthermore, this library would provide the possibility of programming COM add-ins for euro conversion. (In COM add-ins no functions can be used that are defined in normal Excel add-ins. Therefore, *EuroConvert* cannot be placed there. Information on COM add-ins can be found in Chapter 14.)

Converting Excel Files to the Euro

By this time you are probably wishing that I would offer you a macro that at the push of a button would convert marks, pounds, and francs into euros. Unfortunately, that is impossible. The conversion of currency continues to be "made by hand" and accomplished only with the help of a participating human intelligence. The macros presented here, which are to be found in the file `Euro.xls`, should at least lighten your burden and speed you on your way.

Basics

In Figure 5.18 you see two tiny worksheets whose contents are equivalent: A price is calculated from a price per piece, number of pieces, and discount percentage. The difference in the two tables is in the formatting—one of them has formatting for currency values, while the other does not.

To convert both of these tables into euros, the value of only one cell (B3) needs to be changed. In Table 1 the format of cells B3 and E3 must be changed.

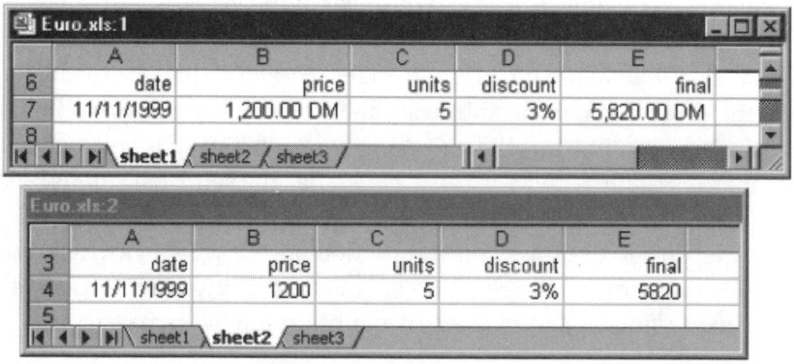

Euro.xls:1

	A	B	C	D	E
6	date	price	units	discount	final
7	11/11/1999	1,200.00 DM	5	3%	5,820.00 DM
8					

sheet1 / sheet2 / sheet3

Euro.xls:2

	A	B	C	D	E
3	date	price	units	discount	final
4	11/11/1999	1200	5	3%	5820
5					

sheet1 / sheet2 / sheet3

Figure 5.18. Two worksheets before euro conversion

In Table 1 it should be theoretically possible to carry out an automatic euro conversion. The process would look something like this:

- Search through all cells that contain a number (not a formula, date, character string) and are formatted as a currency value. Carry out the conversion from the given units into euros and change the formatting as required.

- Search through all cells that contain a formula and that are formatted as a currency value. Change the formatting. (The formula itself, E3 in Figure 5.18, does not need to be altered. The result is automatically in euros if all base cells are euro values or valueless factors.)

Let us now proceed to some of the numerous reasons that a fully automated conversion will not work in practice:

- In only a very few worksheets are all currency values formatted as such. Many tables look more like Table 2 in Figure 5.18 either to save space or simply for convenience. No program would be able to tell what needed to be converted and what not.

- In many tables there are cells in which the source number is input not as a number (such as *1200*), but as a formula (say, *=1000+200*). Even if in general no changes in formulas need to be made, such formulas are the exception.

- Sometimes, currency values are used directly in formulas. For example, suppose that in Figure 5.18 there was no column for unit price. Then the formula for the final price would look like this: *=C3*1200*(1-D3)*. This formula, too, would have to be altered.

- In many tables values appear in a variety of currencies, some that are not euro currencies. This complexity exceeds the "intelligence" of every conversion program.

- Many tables that unite date from several years should not be converted wholesale. Instead, only a part needs to be converted into euros, those entries later than a certain date (such as 1/1/1999).

In short, an automatic conversion is a pleasant dream, but it will not survive a reality check. The following macros should at least make the work a bit easier.

Converting Individual Cells

If a cell contains a currency value as a number, there are several options for conversion:

- You can calculate the value in euros in a VBA program and insert the value directly into the cell:

  ```
  cell.Value = EUROCONVERT(cell.Value, currencyIso, "EUR", True)
  ```

- In a VBA program you can create the character string for a formula that inserts the *Euroconvert* worksheet function. The VBA instruction for this looks a bit complex:

  ```
  cell.Formula = "=Euroconvert(" & Str(cell.Value) & _
                 ", ""DEM"", ""EUR"", True)"
  ```

  The resulting formula looks as follows:

  =Euroconvert(1200, "DEM", "EUR", TRUE)

  For international versions you may expect some differences. Here is the German version:

  =Euroconvert(1200; "DEM"; "EUR"; WAHR)

  Note that the property *Formula* expects the formula in the English-language fashion (period for decimal point, comma for thousands separator, *True* instead of *WAHR*, etc.), regardless of the Excel version used. For this reason *cell.Value* is changed into a character string with *Str.* It is only when you look at the formula in an international version of Excel that you will notice that country-specific features are in fact represented.

  The advantage of this option are that later one can reconstruct how the conversion can be carried out. The original amount is part of the formula, that is, the conversion can be carried out repeatedly if necessary without rounding error (for example, if you notice that you were working in the wrong cell). However, there is also a disadvantage: The converted worksheet is now dependent for all time on the *Euroconvert* function. As mentioned above, this can lead to problems if you give the file to someone else who has not activated the euro add-in.

- A third variant consists in constructing a formula that multiplies the given number by the conversion factor. The advantage is that the resulting worksheet is independent of *Euroconvert*. The disadvantage is that the rounding options that *Euroconvert* offers cannot be utilized. The VBA code looks like this:

```
cell.Formula = "=" & Str(cell.Value) & "*" & _
               Str(EUROCONVERT(1, "DEM", "EUR", True))
```

= 1200 * 0.511291881196218

Instead of multiplying by *Euroconvert(1, "DEM", "EUR", False)*, you could also divide by *Euroconvert(1, "EUR", "DEM", False)*. The advantage is that in the resulting formula there will be only five decimal places, because the official conversion rate has been set with this degree of precision. The result should be the same in the limits of Excel's precision (16 places), but the resulting formula is easier to read. First the VBA code:

```
cell.Formula = "=" & Str(cell.Value) & "/" & _
               Str(EUROCONVERT(1, "EUR", "DEM", True))
```

And here is the resulting formula:

= 1200 / 1.95583

If the cell contains a formula instead of a number, then the first of the three variants above is, of course, impossible. The other variants look as follows (with results based on the assumption that the starting formula is =1000+200*):*

- ```
  cell.Formula = "=Euroconvert(" & Mid(cell.Formula, 2) & _
                 ", ""DEM"", ""EUR"", True)"
  ```

  =Euroconvert(1000+200, "DEM", "EUR", TRUE)

- ```
  cell.Formula = "=(" & Mid(cell.Formula, 2) & ") * " & _
                 Str(EUROCONVERT(1, "DEM", "EUR", True))
  ```

  *=(1000+200) * 0.511291881196218*

  or:

  ```
  cell.Formula = "=(" & Mid(cell.Formula, 2) & ") / " & _
                 Str(EUROCONVERT(1, "EUR", "DEM", True))
  ```

  =(1000+200) / 1.95583

Euro Formatting

There are many ways in which currency values can be formatted: with or without decimal places, with or without thousands separator, with red text to represent negative numbers, with the explicit display of the currency symbol either before or after the number (or none at all, since it is often clear that the value represents currency, or somewhere in the table is the text "values in thousands of U.S. dollars"), and so on.

The tool for euro formatting that is part of the Microsoft euro add-in pays no attention to any previous formatting of a cell, but simply replaces the format with another predefined format. The probability that precisely this format meets your requirements is small.

A more intelligent way of proceeding is to take into account the previous formatting of a cell and to adapt it. For this the property *NumberFormatLocal* must be used. If the old currency symbol is found in the formatting character string, then it is replaced with the euro symbol. The necessary code takes care of the situation in which the currency symbol appears in the formatting character string within quotation marks (which could be the case).

If the cell has not previously been formatted, then the number of decimal places will be limited to two. (This makes sense because otherwise, hitherto whole-number amounts would acquire upon euro conversion a large number of decimal places, making their representation unreadable.) The example here is for conversion of German marks to euros.

```
Dim tmp$
If cell.NumberFormat = "General" Then
  If IsNumeric(cell.Value) Then
    cell.NumberFormat = "0.00"
  End If
ElseIf InStr(cell.NumberFormatLocal, "DM") <> 0 Then
  tmp = cell.NumberFormatLocal
  tmp = Replace(tmp, "DM", "€")
  tmp = Replace(tmp, """DM""", "€")
  cell.NumberFormatLocal = tmp
End If
```

> **TIP** *Working directly with* NumberFormatLocal *is not without its problems, not least because this property is most unsatisfactorily documented, so that one can only guess what effect a change in format will have. The procedure described here has proven effective in both the German and English versions of Excel, but it is difficult to say whether it will work in other current versions or in future versions. Background information on the property* NumberFormatLocal *and the related property* NumberFormat *can be found in the first section of Chapter 5.*

Using the Euro Conversion Machine

- The first step consists in opening the file `Euro.xls` and customizing it to your requirements. For this purpose, in Module1 there are three constants whose preset values are as follows:

```
' example file Euro.xls, Module1
Const currencyIso = "DEM"           ' Iso currency code for euro con-
                                      version
Const currencyFormat = "DM"         ' currency symbol for NumberFormat
Const convertOnlyCurrency = True ' for TestAndMarkForEuroConversion
```

  This setting means that the program will carry out a conversion from German marks (DM) into euros, that in converting number formatting it searches for the character string *DM,* and that the marking function (see below) it marks only those numerical values that are formatted in *DM.* It also assumes a table like that in Figure 5.18 above. If your table is formatted as in Figure 5.18 but without a currency symbol, then you must set *convertOnlyCurrency* to *False.* (Then, however, cells such as C3 will also be marked for conversion, that is, some manual labor is going to be required.)

- If these preliminary tasks have been accomplished, open the file to be converted and save it at once under a new name. (This is to ensure that the changes hold for the new file only, while the original file, if only as a control reference, remains as it was.)

- Select the entire worksheet (mouse click on the upper left corner of the row and column labels). Then click on the first symbol in the euro toolbar. The program now attempts to recognize all cells suitable for conversion to euros and marks them with a red diagonal line. (The actual conversion does yet take place.)

In Figure 5.19 you can see what the little example table looks like after this step. Only cell B3 has been marked for the conversion to come.

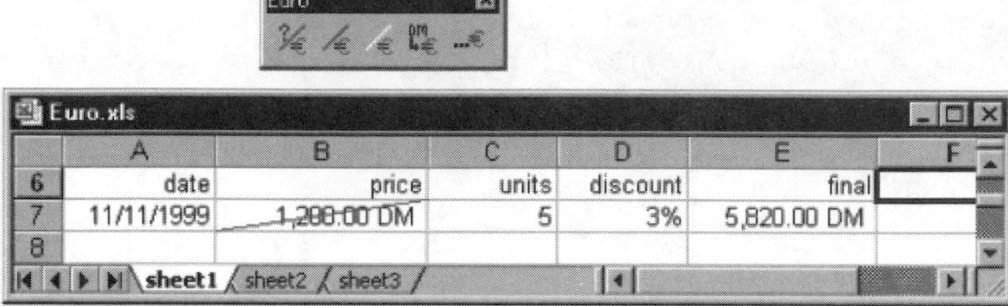

Figure 5.19. Only cell has been marked for subsequent conversion to euros

- Now the real work begins. You have to decide whether the selection made by the program is adequate. If too few cells have been marked, then you must select additional cells with the mouse and then mark with the second button on the euro toolbar. On the other hand, if too many cells have been marked, you need to select these cells and cancel their marking with the third button.

  Note that as described at the outset, only cells with currency values need to be converted. In the case of cells with formulas the euro conversion proceeds automatically. For this reason E3 must *not* be marked.

- When you are sure that the proper cells have been marked, click on the fourth button. Now all marked cells will be converted to euros. Simultaneously, the formatting of these cells will be changed.

Euro.xls

	A	B	C	D	E	F
6	date	price	units	discount	final	
7	11/11/1999	613.55 €	5	3%	2,975.72 DM	
8						

sheet1 sheet2 sheet3

Figure 5.20. The table after euro conversion

- If you in fact marked the correct cells, then the euro conversion is complete. (If you neglected to mark some cells, then simply repeat the above process: first mark cells, then convert them.)

  However, in the last step result cells like E3 must be formatted. The correct amount in euros appears, but it is formatted as for German marks. The fifth button on the euro toolbar changes the format of all cells previously marked with the mouse. (Please note that with this button what takes place is merely an exchange of currency symbol (that is, *DM* → €). In the case of cells that are not formatted in *DM*, nothing changes (except that in the case of cells that have not been formatted, the number of decimal places will be limited to 2).

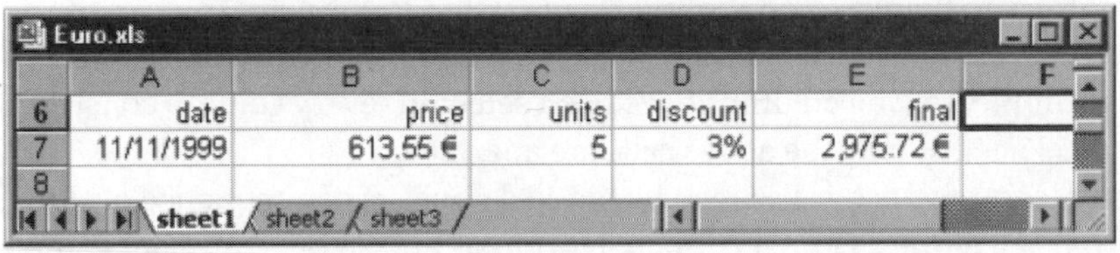

Euro.xls

	A	B	C	D	E	F
6	date	price	units	discount	final	
7	11/11/1999	613.55 €	5	3%	2,975.72 €	
8						

sheet1 / sheet2 / sheet3

Figure 5.21. The table after formatting is complete

NOTE *Do not expect that euro conversion will always proceed so effortlessly as in this example. In reality, Excel tables are much more complicated, and euro conversion can take a great deal of time. The most important step is to compare the old and new tables after conversion is complete and ensure that indeed not too many, but also not too few, cells have been converted.*

Program Code

TestAndMarkForEuroConversion is invoked by the first button on the euro toolbar. In the procedure a test is made as to whether any cells at all have been selected. If none have, then the procedure exits at once.

The following lines are for speed optimization. They deactivate the automatic recalculation of the worksheet after every change as well as screen updating (details in the last section of this chapter).

```
' tests for all previously selected cells whether
' a conversion is possible; if yes,
' they are marked for conversion by a red diagonal line
Sub TestAndMarkForEuroConversion()
  Dim ar As Range, cell As Range
  Dim usedrng As Range
  Dim calcMode&, updateMode&
  If Selection Is Nothing Then Exit Sub
  If TypeName(Selection) <> "Range" Then Exit Sub
  ' speed optimization
  calcMode = Application.Calculation
```

```
updateMode = Application.ScreenUpdating
Application.Calculation = xlManual
Application.ScreenUpdating = False
```

The loops over *Areas* and *Cells* ensure that indeed every selected cell is analyzed, even if with Ctrl a multipartite range of cells was selected.

With *Intersect* the range to be analyzed is restricted to the actual area of the worksheet that is being used. Here again it is a question of speed optimization. Even if, for example, several columns have been selected (every column consists, after all, of 65536 cells), only the active cells are analyzed.

The actual test of which cells are to be marked consists of a sequence of simple tests. Is the cell empty? Does it contain a formula? and so on. Only if all criteria are fulfilled (or not fulfilled in the case of *Not*) will the cell be marked. For this the auxiliary procedure *MarkRangeForEuroConversion* is called. (By the way, the program code is not, as is usual, indented for every *If* test, simply because the width of the pages of this book is insufficient. Since VBA tests are not optimized with *And*, the nested *If* construction is faster than a combination of conditionals with *And* together with a single *If* test.)

NOTE *To give you an idea of how fast (or slow) the program is, here is an example: The analysis of 25,000 filled cells (100 columns, 250 rows) takes 15 seconds on a Pentium II 400. Therefore, every attempt to optimize the program is worth making.*

```
Set usedrng = Selection.Worksheet.UsedRange
' loop over all cells
For Each ar In Intersect(Selection, usedrng).Areas
  For Each cell In ar.Cells
    If Not IsEmpty(cell) Then                   ' not empty
    If Not cell.HasFormula Then                 ' not a formula
    If Not TypeName(cell.Value) = "Date" Then   ' not a date
    If Not TypeName(cell.Value) = "String" Then ' not a character string
    If InStr(cell.NumberFormat, "%") = 0 Then   ' not a % format
    ' only cells with DM format
    If convertOnlyCurrency Then
      If InStr(cell.NumberFormatLocal, currencyFormat)  0 Then
        MarkRangeForEuroConversion cell
      End If
    Else
      MarkRangeForEuroConversion cell
    End If
    End If
```

```
      End If
      End If
      End If
      End If
    Next
  Next
  Application.Calculation = calcMode
  Application.ScreenUpdating = updateMode
End Sub
' mark for conversion (red diagonal line) for range of cells
Sub MarkRangeForEuroConversion(rng As Range)
  Dim ar As Range, cell As Range
  For Each ar In rng
    For Each cell In ar.Cells
      cell.Borders(xlDiagonalUp).LineStyle = xlContinuous
      cell.Borders(xlDiagonalUp).Color = vbRed
    Next
  Next
End Sub
```

The second button has associated to it the procedure *MarkSelectionForEuroConversion*. With it the previously selected cells are marked for conversion without a lengthy test. The procedure calls *MarkRangeForEuroConversion* after the above-described security test and speed optimization.

```
Sub MarkSelectionForEuroConversion()
  Dim calcMode&, updateMode&
  If Selection Is Nothing Then Exit Sub
  If TypeName(Selection)  "Range" Then Exit Sub
  ' speed optimization
  calcMode = Application.Calculation
  updateMode = Application.ScreenUpdating
  Application.Calculation = xlManual
  Application.ScreenUpdating = False
  MarkRangeForEuroConversion Intersect(Selection, _
    Selection.Worksheet.UsedRange)
  Application.Calculation = calcMode
  Application.ScreenUpdating = updateMode
End Sub
```

The procedure *UnMarkSelectionForEuroConversion* is assigned to the third button. It looks very similar to the procedure above. The actual work then takes place in *UnMarkRangeForEuroConversion*:

```
' to unmark cells for conversion
Sub UnMarkRangeForEuroConversion(rng As Range)
  Dim ar As Range, cell As Range
  For Each ar In rng
    For Each cell In ar.Cells
      cell.Borders(xlDiagonalUp).LineStyle = xlLineStyleNone
    Next
  Next
End Sub
```

The actual euro conversion takes place in *ConvertNumberIntoEuro*. This procedure tests, for all cells of the currently active worksheet, whether the cell has been marked for conversion (that is, with a red diagonal line). It you wish, you can restrict the test to a previously selected region of cells

```
Sub ConvertNumberIntoEuro()
  Dim calcMode&, updateMode&
  Dim cell As Range
  If TypeName(ActiveWindow.ActiveSheet) <> "Worksheet" Then Exit Sub
  ' speed optimization
  calcMode = Application.Calculation
  updateMode = Application.ScreenUpdating
  Application.Calculation = xlManual
  Application.ScreenUpdating = False
  ' for all cells of the worksheet
  For Each cell In ActiveWindow.ActiveSheet.UsedRange
    If Not IsEmpty(cell) Then
      If cell.Borders(xlDiagonalUp).LineStyle = xlContinuous Then
        If cell.Borders(xlDiagonalUp).Color = vbRed Then
```

If a cell is encountered that is to be converted, the program then differentiates between formulas and numerical values. In the case of formulas the expression is placed in parentheses and divided by the *Euroconvert* conversion value for the respective currency. For numbers, a formula is constructed with an appropriate division. In each case this process produces a clear formula, which can effortlessly be transformed back to its original form. For the cell in question the conversion marking is then erased and a formatting in euros carried out.

```
          If cell.HasFormula Then
            cell.Formula = "=(" & Mid(cell.Formula, 2) & ") / " & _
              Str(EUROCONVERT(1, "EUR", currencyIso, True))
            UnMarkRangeForEuroConversion cell
            EuroNumberFormatRange cell
          ElseIf IsNumeric(cell.Value) Then
```

```
          cell.Formula = "=" & Str(cell.Value) & "/" & _
            Str(EUROCONVERT(1, "EUR", currencyIso, True))
          UnMarkRangeForEuroConversion cell
          EuroNumberFormatRange cell
        End If
      End If
    End If
  End If
Next
Application.Calculation = calcMode
Application.ScreenUpdating = updateMode
End Sub
```

The euro formatting procedure *EuroNumberFormatRange* tests whether the affected cells are formatted at all (*NumberFormat = "General"*). If they are not, then a formatting with two decimal places is executed. Cells that are already formatted will have their previous currency symbol changed to the euro symbol by *NumberFormatLocal*. Cells in which up to now no currency has been displayed retain their formatting.

```
Sub EuroNumberFormatRange(rng As Range)
  Dim tmp$
  Dim ar As Range, cell As Range
  For Each ar In rng.Areas
    For Each cell In ar.Cells
      If cell.NumberFormat = "General" Then
        If IsNumeric(cell.Value) Then
          cell.NumberFormat = "0.00"
        End If
      ElseIf InStr(cell.NumberFormatLocal, currencyFormat) <> 0 Then
        tmp = cell.NumberFormatLocal
        tmp = Replace(tmp, currencyFormat, "€")
        tmp = Replace(tmp, """" + currencyFormat + """", "€")
        cell.NumberFormatLocal = tmp
      End If
    Next
  Next
End Sub
```

The fifth button on the euro toolbar is assigned to *EuroNumberFormat*, whose only purpose in life is to call *EuroNumberFormatRange* after the usual process of speed optimization to carry out the formatting for the current selection.

```
Sub EuroNumberFormat()
  ... speed optimization
  EuroNumberFormatRange Intersect(Selection, _
    Selection.Worksheet.UsedRange)
  ... speed optimization
End Sub
```

Room for Improvement

If `Euro.xls` were a commercial product, then there would be some work left to be done:

- To supplement the five buttons on the toolbar, corresponding menu entries would be added.
- Every conversion step would have to be reversible (Undo function).
- Configuration details should be able to be set via a form.
- There is no on-line help.
- The mark for a cell to be converted—a red diagonal line—is arbitrary. (Not quite: The advantage of this method is that the marked cells are easily recognizable, and the content of the cell can be easily read.) For the unlikely case that in a table somewhere diagonal red lines have been used already, an alternative marking method should be made available.

However, the goal of this section was not to put euro tool programmers out of business, but to discuss some programming techniques. So, as a starting point for further development, these examples should suffice.

Tips and Tricks

In this section we collect some useful tips and tricks that somehow didn't fit into the earlier sections of this chapter, yet have such an elementary character that they belong here. The example programs can be found in the file `miscellaneous.xls`.

Speed Optimization

Procedures that make extensive changes to a worksheet can run very slowly. Two possible reasons for this are the time expended on constant updating of the screen and recalculation of the table after every change. You can make a significant improvement in the speed of your macro if during its execution you deactivate screen updating and worksheet recalculation. For this you need to set the *Application* properties ***ScreenUpdating*** and ***Calculation*** at the beginning and end of the procedure.

```
Sub HighSpeed()
  Dim calcMode, updateMode
  '
  ' begin speed optimization
  calcMode = Application.Calculation
  updateMode = Application.ScreenUpdating
  Application.Calculation = xlManual
  Application.ScreenUpdating = False
  '
  ' here place the actual code of the macro
  '
  ' end speed optimization
  Application.Calculation = calcMode
  Application.ScreenUpdating = updateMode
  Application.Calculate    ' recalculate everything (if necessary)
End Sub
```

The procedure *HighSpeed* saves the current values of both properties at the outset and then sets them to *False* and *xlManual,* respectively. At the end of the procedure the original values are reset.

If it becomes necessary during the course of the procedure to recalculate the table or even just a range thereof, you can entrust that task to the method *Calculate.*

> **NOTE** *If you use the command* Exit Sub *in your procedure, you must not forget first to reset* Calculation *to its previous setting. It is less critical that the property* ScreenUpdating *be reset, since it is automatically set to* True *by VBA after the macro finishes its execution. The instruction with* True *is necessary only if you wish to update the screen during execution of the macro.*

Time-Intensive Calculations

Infotext in the Status Bar

While lengthy calculations are underway you should notify the user of the progress of the calculation by means of a message in the status bar. This gives the user some feedback and indicates that the computer has not (yet) crashed. The status bar should at least give information as to what the computer is up to at the moment. Even better would be an indication of progress, in the form of a percentage of the calculation completed, though this is not always possible, of course.

The text of the status bar is set with *Application.**StatusBar***. Once the property is set to *False*, Excel concerns itself again with displaying its own text in the status bar (for example, during menu selection).

The property ***DisplayStatusBar*** determines whether the status bar is displayed. If it is not currently displayed, you can display it temporarily and then make it disappear at the end of the procedure.

> **NOTE** *Unfortunately, in Excel, as always, there is no possibility of displaying the state of a lengthy calculation with a progress bar (with small blue squares). Excel itself uses this layout object frequently, such as during opening and closing of files. However, there are no VBA methods for control of the progress bar.*

The following example shows how a lengthy calculation can be carried out in such a way that makes it bearable for the user of the program. The procedure begins by storing the current state of the status bar (visible or not) in *status*. Then the status bar is activated if it was invisible.

In the *For* loop for the calculation there are two *If* tests built in. The first tests whether the current value of the loop variable is a multiple of 50. The purpose of this is merely to ensure that the following, relatively expensive, time comparison is not executed too often. The second test determines whether more than one second has passed since the previous updating of the status bar. If that is the case, then the display in the status bar is updated and the variable *nextUpdateTime* is increased by one second. The overhead for managing the status bar increases the calculation time of the procedure by about five percent.

The part of the procedure that carries out the actual calculations is only an example, and it does not do anything useful. At the end of the procedure the text in the status bar is erased with the setting *False*. This has the effect of returning control of the status bar text to Excel. Moreover, the status bar is deactivated if that was the case at the start of the procedure.

Real-world calculations do not usually take the form of a simple loop as sketched in this example. If you wish to set a rather substantial procedure to run in the background, you can store both *If* tests in a procedure. Then you will have to define *nextUpdateTime* as a module variable outside of the procedure. Such external storage has the advantage that you can carry out the tests by means of a simple procedure call from several locations within the main procedure.

```
' miscellaneous.xls, Module1
Sub slowcode()
  Const loopEnd = 1000000
  Dim statusMode&, nextUpdateTime As Date
  Dim i, x, result&
  Application.EnableCancelKey = xlErrorHandler
  On Error GoTo slow_error
  nextUpdateTime = Now
  statusMode = Application.DisplayStatusBar ' save state of the status bar
  Application.DisplayStatusBar = True       ' show status bar
  '
  For i = 1 To loopEnd                      ' calculation loop
    If i Mod 50 = 0 Then                    ' test only once every 50 loops
      If Now > nextUpdateTime Then          ' update status bar
        nextUpdateTime = Now + TimeSerial(0, 0, 1)
        Application.StatusBar = "calculation " & _
            CInt(i / loopEnd * 100) & " percent complete"
      End If
    End If
    '
    x = Sin(i) * Cos(i) ^ 3 * Sqr(i)        ' simulate a calculation
    x = Sin(i) * Cos(i) ^ 3 * Sqr(i)
    x = Sin(i) * Cos(i) ^ 3 * Sqr(i)
    x = Sin(i) * Cos(i) ^ 3 * Sqr(i)
  Next i
  '
  Application.StatusBar = False             ' return control to Excel
  Application.DisplayStatusBar = statusMode ' restore old setting
  Exit Sub
slow_error:
  If Err = 18 Then
    result = MsgBox("Continue the program?", vbYesNo)
    If result = vbYes Then Resume Next
  End If
  ' otherwise, stop procedure
  Application.StatusBar = False             ' return control to Excel
  Application.DisplayStatusBar = statusMode ' restore old setting
  If Err = 18 Then Exit Sub
  Error Err                                 ' error message
End Sub
```

Program Interrupts

The above example begins and ends with several lines that ensure the orderly termination of the program if an error occurs or the user presses Ctrl+Break. Here the property ***EnableCancelKey*** plays an important role, one that controls the behavior of Excel when Ctrl+Break is pressed. If *EnableCancelKey* is set to *xlErrorHandler*, then in reaction to Ctrl+Break an error with the number 18 occurs, which can be caught in an error-handling routine. Details on the subject of error handling and program interrupts can be found in Chapter 6.

Warnings

Excel displays the same warnings during the execution of macros as it does during normal operation. This can be burdensome. An execution of a macro free from interruption can be achieved by setting the *Application* property Display-Alerts to *False*.

Blocking Input

By setting the property *Application.**Interactive*** to *False*, you can block Excel from receiving any input (keyboard and mouse). As a rule, that is not necessary, since Excel does not accept input during the execution of a macro.

> **CAUTION** *The property* Interactive *must be set to* True *at the end of the procedure, even if the procedure is prematurely exited by means of* Exit Sub. *The procedure must be protected against possible errors (see Chapter 6), so that even in the case of an error that property is reset. There is no way of resetting the property outside of VBA code. Not only will Excel be blocked by this property, the program will not even be able to be ended! In the end, unsaved data will be lost.*

DoEvents

Under Windows 3.1 the problem frequently occurred with complicated calculations that not only Excel, but all other running programs, were blocked. A solution was offered by the regular execution of *DoEvents* in VBA program code.

Since Windows 95 the execution of *DoEvents* is no longer necessary for this purpose. The parallel execution of several programs is now possible without *DoEvents*.

In some (very rare) cases, however, it is possible to react to certain events in parallel to the execution of VBA code. For example, you start a procedure with one button and you want to allow the user to interrupt the procedure by clicking a second button. In this case you must use *DoEvents* in the procedure of button 1 to allow event processing for button 2. This works only beginning with Excel 2000, and the possible range of applications making use of this feature is small, since Excel 200 does not allow real multitasking within VBA code.

Working Efficiently with Worksheets

It is in the nature of Excel applications that in many cases their main purpose in life is to process enormous worksheets (read or write values, change them, analyze them, and so on). This section covers various programming techniques that can make working with worksheets more efficient.

Efficient Processing of Ranges of Cells

If your VBA code has to process a large number of cells, then the easiest (but alas the slowest) method consists in addressing each cell individually. Even *ScreenUpdating = False* and *Calculation = xlManual* do not gain you much in the way of efficiency. The following lines show how 10,000 cells can be filled with numbers.

```
' example file miscellaneous.xls, Module1
' the simplest yet slowest variant: ca. 10 seconds
Sub SlowFill()
  Dim i#, j#, k#, r As Range
  Set r = Worksheets(1).[a1]
  Sheets(1).Activate
  r.CurrentRegion.Clear
  Application.ScreenUpdating = False
  Application.Calculation = xlManual
  For i = 0 To 199     ' rows
    For j = 0 To 199   ' columns
      k = i * 200 + j
      r.Offset(i, j) = k
    Next
  Next
  Application.Calculation = xlAutomatic
  Application.ScreenUpdating = True: Beep
End Sub
```

If you would like to speed things up, you have several options:

- Use predefined Excel methods, that is, work with methods such as *AutoFill* (fill cells automatically), *PasteSpecial* (insert contents and execute operations such as subtraction, and multiplication) *Copy* (copy ranges of cells). Of course, these methods are not suitable for every purpose. But if they do meet your needs, then they are *very* fast in comparison to traditional programming.

- Work with fields: Accessing field elements proceeds much more rapidly than accessing cells. Fields can have all their calculations carried out and then copied as a unit into a range of cells.

- Work with data fields: Data fields have many disadvantages as compared with normal fields, but they have a decisive advantage, namely, they can transfer entire ranges of cells into a data field all at once. (With normal fields the wholesale transport of data is possible only in one direction.)

- Work with the clipboard: With the clipboard an efficient transport of data in both directions is possible, that is, from the worksheet and then back into it.

Working with Normal Fields

It is little known that the contents of one- and two-dimensional fields can be simply copied by a simple assignment into a range of cells. Consider an example:

```
Dim y(3)                            '4 Elemente
y(i) = ...
Worksheets(1).Range("a1:d1") = y    'changes A1:D1

Dim x(9, 4)                         '10*5 Elemente
x(i,j) = ...
Worksheets(1).Range("a1:e10") = x   'changes cells A1:E10
```

In working with cells attention must be paid to certain details:

- The target range must be specified exactly. If it is smaller than the field, then correspondingly fewer elements will be transferred. If it is too large, then the excess cells will be filled with the error value *#NV*.

- One-dimensional fields can be assigned only to a horizontal cell block, not a vertical one.

- In the case of two-dimensional fields the first index gives the row, the second the column (that is, *field(row,column)*). This corresponds to the format familiar from *Offset*, though intuitively, one might expect the reversed order (that is, *field(x,y)*).

- The transfer of data is possible only in the direction field _table. Reading from cells into a field is not possible (or, more precisely, only with data fields; see below).

The code for filling in 10,000 cells with the help of a data field is not much more complicated than direct entry of data into the cells, but it is an order of magnitude faster:

```
' fast variant, under 1 second
Sub FastFill()  Dim i#, j#, k#
  Dim r As Range, r1 As Range, r2 As Range
  Dim cells(199, 199)
  Worksheets(1).Activate
  Worksheets(1).[a1].CurrentRegion.Clear
  Application.ScreenUpdating = False
  Application.Calculation = xlManual
  For i = 0 To 199           ' rows
    For j = 0 To 199         ' columns
      k = i * 200 + j
      cells(i, j) = k
    Next
  Next
  'return goal range
  Set r1 = Worksheets(1).[a1]
  Set r2 = r1.Offset(199, 199)
  Set r = Worksheets(1).Range(r1, r2)
  r = cells
  Application.Calculation = xlAutomatic
  Application.ScreenUpdating = True
End Sub
```

TIP *In Excel 7 only ranges up to a maximum of 5200 cells can be changed. The above program would have to be changed in such a way that cells would be changed in blocks (say, of 10 rows).*

Working with Data Fields

Data fields are a rather peculiar invention. Actually, they offer nothing that ordinary fields cannot do, but they have a different internal organization. Their advantage is that data fields can be used together with user-defined Excel methods that for normal fields are incompatible (for one reason or another). Most of what was said above for normal fields holds as well for data fields. What is new is that now data transport from a range of cells into a data field is possible.

```
Dim x As Variant
x = Worksheets(1).[a1:b4]          'read 8 elements...
                                   'process
Worksheets(1).[c1:d4] = x          'change 8 cells
```

Now individual elements can be accessed in the form *x(1,1)* to *x(4,2)* (for B4). The following differences with respect to ordinary fields should be noted:

- Access to the first field begins with index 1. (Normally, this is 0 for fields. Only if you use *Option Base 1* does indexing begin with 1.)

- The size of data fields cannot be set with *Dim*. The number of elements is revealed only when cells are copied from the worksheet. Therefore, data fields are suitable most of all when a group of already defined cells needs to be changed or analyzed. On the other hand, normal fields are more practical when data have only to be written into the worksheet.

Protection Mechanisms

In setting up Excel tables and applications it frequently happens that you wish to protect parts of the workbook from unintentional changes (or from curious eyes). This section discusses the most important methods that Excel offers for this purpose.

However, please note that most of the protection mechanisms presented here represent protection only against "normal" Excel users. Any protection that you can later undo can also be undone by a professional Excel hacker. The only protection functions that are relatively secure are those that require a password (and even these can be hacked). In this respect only COM add-ins are truly perfect, which are passed as binary DLL. But they have many other drawbacks (see Chapter 14).

Hiding Rows and Columns of Worksheets

The simplest way of protecting data from access by the user is to hide them. In program code this is accomplished simply by changing the ***Hidden*** property (for rows or columns) or the ***Visible*** property (for sheets). Possible settings for both properties are *True* and *False*; *Visible* can also be given the value *xlVeryHidden*, in which case the sheet no longer appears in the unhide list and can be made visible only via program code.

Shrinking a Worksheet's Visible Area

A worksheet can be up to 256 columns wide and more then 65,000 cells high. Only very rarely will you make use of the full theoretical capacity of a worksheet. If you use a smaller area you can hide the unused rows and columns. In this way you make it impossible for the user to wander accidentally into a uncharted regions of the worksheet and proceed to input values, either intentionally or unintentionally.

If the range of cells is to be strictly predefined, you can hide rows and columns interactively. Simply select the rows and columns in question and execute the command HIDE from the pop-up menu.

However, if the size of the region to be used can vary dynamically, then you will have to let program code do the work of hiding and unhiding. To do this, simply set the *Hidden* property of rows or columns to *False* (to unhide) or *True* (to hide). The following lines of code will leave rows 1 to 10 unhidden while hiding all other rows. If instead of *Rows* and *EntireRow* you use the properties *Column* and *EntireColumn*, then the same thing happens, only for columns. With the *Protect* method you can ensure that the user does not unhide the hidden rows or columns.

```
Dim ws As Worksheet, i&
Set ws = Sheets(1)
i = 10
ws.Unprotect
ws.Rows("1:" & i).EntireRow.Hidden = False
ws.Rows(i + 1 & ":16384").EntireRow.Hidden = True
ws.Protect
```

Restricting the Area of Activity

Another possibility to restrict the user to a particular region of the worksheet is offered by the property ***ScrollArea***: With it you can limit the range in which the user can operate (with the cursor keys or the mouse). The rest of the table remains, however, visible.

```
ws.ScrollArea = "A1:E10"    ' cell pointer can be moved only in A1:E10
ws.ScrollArea = ""          ' unrestricted movement
```

> **TIP** *The* ScrollArea *setting is not stored with the Excel file. Thus if you wish to ensure that a region is restricted as soon as a file is reopened, you need to execute the instruction* ScrollArea *assignment in* Workbook_Open()

Protecting Cells and Worksheets from Changes

Excel has taken care to provide protection at the level of cells, worksheets, and entire workbooks. The protection of cells is accomplished in two steps. The first step consists in formatting the affected cells with the attributes "Locked" and "FormulaHidden" (FORMAT|CELLS|PROTECTION). Normally, Excel cells are locked. However, the attribute "Hidden" is inactive.

In program code, cells can be locked by changing the ***Locked*** property. *Locked* can be applied not only to *Range* objects, but also to drawing objects, controls (such as buttons and text fields), charts, and OLE objects, to protect these objects from being changed. To make formulas invisible, ***FormulaHidden*** must be set to *True.*

In the second step the command TOOLS|PROTECTION|PROTECT SHEET is executed. It is only now that the protection of cells has become active. This means that you have to format explicitly as "unlocked" those cells that in spite of this sheet protection should be able to be changed. If you wish to keep secret the construction of the table (that is, how the formulas are used), then you should format all cells of the table with the attribute "FormulaHidden."

With VBA code, sheet protection can be activated and deactivated with the methods ***Protect*** and ***Unprotect***. These methods can be applied to objects of type *WorkSheet, Chart,* and *DialogSheet.* Five optional parameters can be passed to *Protect,* options that determine the degree of protection. Here is information on the meaning of the named parameters: The parameter *password* contains a character string that must be given again with *Unprotect* in order to lift the protection. If this parameter is not given, then protection is applied without a password, and thus it can be lifted again without any difficulty.

drawingObject specifies whether drawing objects (included are also controls and OLE objects) are protected against changes (default setting is *True*).

The parameter *contents* tells whether the contents of the sheet are protected. By this is meant cells in the case of worksheets, code in the case of modules, and in the case of forms and charts, their structure and formatting (default setting *True*).

scenarios tells whether scenarios are protected against changes (default setting is *True*).

userInterfaceOnly determines whether the elements of the interface of an application (such as formatting, size, and placement of objects) is to be protected but not the program code (default setting is *False*). The three properties ***EnableAutoFilter***, ***EnableOutlining***, and ***EnablePivotTable*** determine the degree of protection. However, in spite of several experiments, the application of these three properties (which were new in version 7) is not fully clear.

The current state of sheet protection can be read from the properties ***ProtectContents***, ***ProtectScenarios***, and ***ProtectDrawingObjects***. These properties can only be read. A change can be effected only through the *Protect* method.

Protecting the Entire Workbook

With TOOLS|PROTECTION|PROTECT WORKBOOK you can protect the sequence of sheets in a workbook and/or the arrangement of windows. With the second of these you can fix the distribution of available screen space. Although this may seem tempting for many applications, you would do well to resist the temptation. The optimal distribution of screen space depends on factors that you cannot always foresee, such as screen resolution and selection of system fonts.

Workbook protection is independent of the protection of individual worksheets. Even if workbook protection is active, you can still change the cells of the worksheets of this workbook if these have not been secured by sheet protection.

The protection of a workbook is carried out in program code by the method ***Protect***. If this method is applied to *WorkSheet* objects, it recognizes three named parameters:

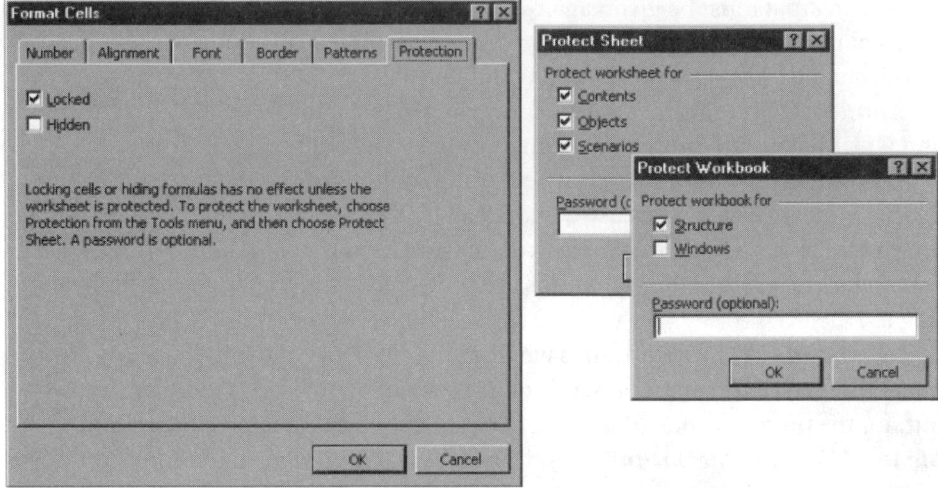

Figure 5.22. The three levels of protection (cells, sheet, workbook)

The parameter *password* provides the password for lifting protection (see above). The parameter *structure* tells whether the sequence of sheets should be protected (default setting is *False*). The parameter *windows* tells whether the arrangement of windows is to be protected (default setting is *False*).

> **TIP** *Since the default setting of the named parameters is* False, *a* Protect *call without parameters will have no effect. At least one of the parameters* structure *and* windows *must be set to* True.

The current state of the protection function can be read from the two properties ***ProtectStructure*** and ***ProtectWindows***. These properties can only be read. A change can be effected only via the *Protect* method.

Protection Mechanism for Shared Workbooks

Since Excel 97 it has been possible to save an Excel file in a special file-sharing format. In this way all changes made by various users can be managed by a change protocol. To activate this mode, execute Tools|Share Workbook|Editing and activate the option Allow changes by more than one user at the same time. You will then be asked to save the file anew. (It would have been more logical to have placed this option in the Save As form.)

The Excel file is now considered a "shared" file. In the Tools protocol just cited you can make various settings that determine how changes are tracked, updated, and sorted out when conflicting changes are made. If you wish to deactivate sharing, execute TOOLS|SHARE WORKBOOK|EDITING and deactivate the option CHANGES BY MORE THAN ONE USER.

If you wish to prevent another user from changing the sharing status, execute TOOLS|PROTECTION|PROTECT AND SHARE WORKBOOK and activate the option SHARING WITH TRACK CHANGES. This is the top level of the protection mechanism in Excel workbooks. As long as sharing protection is active, the underlying protection mechanism cannot be changed. Sharing protection is an aid for the administrator of an Excel file. This form of protection can be set via program code with the method ***ProtectSharing*** and again lifted with ***UnprotectSharing***.

> **NOTE** *As long as a file is being shared, VBA modules can neither be seen nor changed. (The macros can, however, be executed.) Most sharing functions including making settings and executing changes can be controlled with several* Workbook *properties and methods.*

Protecting ToolBars

To protect toolbars and user-defined menus from being changed you can set the ***Protection*** property of the *CommandBar* object. There are eight possible values to be set, by which the content, position, and visibility of the object can be protected from changes (*msoBarNoProtection, msoBarNoCustomize, msoBarNoResize, msoBarNoMove, msoBarNoChangeVisible, msoBarNoChangeDock, msoBarNoVerticalDock*, and *msoBarNoHorizontalDock*). These protection functions are available only via the object model. A manual change of the protection setting is impossible.

Protecting Program Code

Just as confusing as the protection mechanisms in Excel are those in the VBA editor. If you wish to prevent another user from looking at or altering your code, then execute TOOLS|VBAPROJECT PROPERTIES|PROTECTION, activate the option LOCK PROJECT FOR VIEWING, and provide and then confirm a password. When you later open the file, the module can be viewed only after the password has been entered.

If you do not activate the locking option in the protection form, the only effect of the password is that you will have to provide it in order to view the VBA project properties form again. In spite of the password it is possible to view and change VBA code. Therefore, for the protection mechanism to work the option must always be activated! A deactivation is necessary only if you wish to lift the protection and eliminate the password.

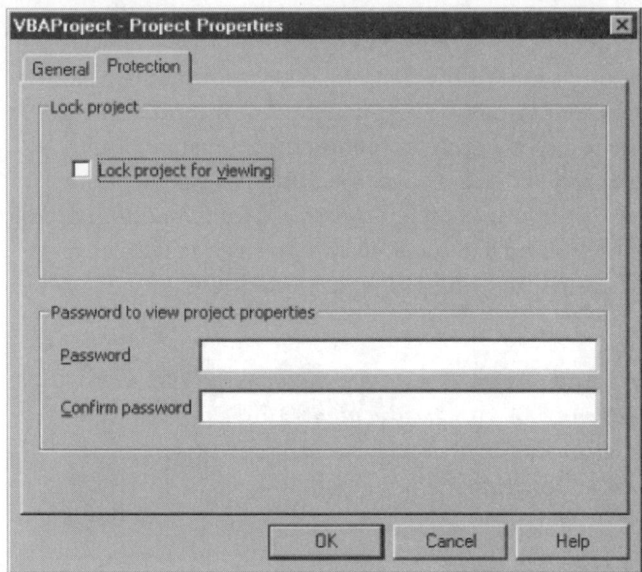

Figure 5.23. Protection of VBA code from prying eyes and unwanted changes

CAUTION *The value that Microsoft places on password protection in Excel is apparent from the change from Excel 7 to Excel 97. Modules that were invisible and password protected in Excel 7 were immediately accessible to users of Excel 97. Thus if you gave Excel workbooks to other users or purchased some yourself, your code is now accessible to any interested programmer.*

The password protection of Excel 2000 is somewhat better, but has already been cracked. There are commercial tools for recovering "lost" passwords or replacing them with another password (see `http://soft4you.com/mso/vba.htm`*). The solution to this problem is not to rely on the protection mechanisms outlined above. What is truly secure is to have your code available as a COM add-in (see Chapter 14).*

Interplay with Excel-4 Macros

There is no way to convert traditional macros to VBA macros at the touch of a button. You can, however, continue to use traditional macros without problems. Functions and procedures created in VBA modules can be called in worksheets and macro sheets directly by name (=*Macro1()*). Conversely, traditional macros can continue to be used in VBA programs with the method *Run*.

```
Run "macroname1"
Run "macroname2", parameter1, parameter2
```

Calling Macro Functions in VBA Code

Even individual macro commands can be executed directly in VBA. For this the entire command is passed as a character string, without the prefixed equal sign, to the method *ExecuteExcel4Macro.* Note that the command name must be given in the regional language.

```
ExecuteExcel4Macro "functionname(...)"
```

TIP *We repeat once more how Excel worksheet functions are used in VBA code: with the English function name and prefixed by* WorksheetFunction *(a property of the* Application *object),*

WorksheetFunction.Sum(Range("A1:A3")).

Determining the Version of Excel

If you wish to use VBA code to determine which version of Excel is executing a procedure, evaluate *Application.Version* (the return value is a character string). The main version number can be determined most easily with *Val(...)*. For the last four versions the following relation holds:

Excel version	*contents of* ***Version***
Excel 5	5.0
Excel 7 alias 95	7.0
Excel 97	8.0 (8.0a, 8.0b etc., according to service release)
Excel 2000	9.0

If you wish to program Excel applications that can be executed in older versions of Excel, you will have to restrict yourself to the weakest link in the chain.

TIP *The differences between Excel 2000 and Excel 97 are relatively slight. Avoid ADO and FSO, and then things cannot go too far wrong. However, the differences between these and earlier versions are large. Among other things, the format of* `*.xls` *files has been changed.*

Helping You to Help Yourself

This chapter has dealt with some particularly important and elementary techniques for programming in Excel. But there is still enough that we have not discussed to prolong this chapter for as long as we might wish. Some things will be discussed in other chapters, for example, programming charts (Chapter 10) or database programming (Chapters 11 through 13). Other subjects have been shortchanged in this book. There just is not enough space!

Of course, it would be much preferred if this book could be lengthened by exactly those twenty pages that are necessary for the problem that you, dear reader, are currently trying to solve. But every Excel user has different priorities, and to add those twenty pages for many users would have meant doubling the size of the book, doubling its cost, and delaying its publication. And by then the hope of producing a readable introductory book would have gone to the dogs. The long and short of it is that you will not be spared the opportunity to do a bit of experimenting yourself.

Use the On-Line Documentation

A glance at the on-line help cannot hurt. Unfortunately, the on-line help provided with Office 2000 has been completely redone, in some ways a bit better, but in many ways much worse. Most distressing are the diminished search options.

> **TIP** *The quickest way to your goal is often the object catalog. There you can select a keyword and press* `F1`.

In general, your search for detailed information will improve the more you get to know Excel and VBA. For this reason it might be a good idea to glance once through the object reference in Chapter 15. This reference provides a good overview of the objects that are frequently used in Excel programming. Even if you cannot memorize everything, perhaps what will remain lodged in your memory is that you can find the keyword once again in the object catalog.

If you are working with Office Developer or have access to a programming language in the Visual Studio family (Professional or Enterprise version), then in addition to the normal on-line help you have the MSDN library at your disposal. That is an enormous collection of on-line documentation with excellent search options. Among other things, you have access to the "knowledge base," a collection of solutions to problems that have arisen in the course of many user queries.

> **TIP** *The MSDN library is available as a stand-alone product. If you subscribe, you receive a set of CDs (or a DVD) four times per year with the current version. In my opinion, this library is indispensable for developers.*
>
> *If you need such information only occasionally, you can also access without charge the on-line version (registration required). However, there the search options are less useful.*
>
> `http://msdn.microsoft.com`

Experiment in the Immediate Window

Sometimes, you have no choice but simply to experiment with unfamiliar properties or methods. The easiest way to do this is in the immediate window. A large monitor is helpful in this case. Then you have enough room to place the VBA and Excel windows next to each other or one above the other.

Within the immediate window you can use almost all the language structures of VBA, even loops! The one condition is that the entire instruction must fit on a single line (or on several lines if they are joined with "_"). You may use as many variables as you like (directly, without *Dim*).

In the analysis of unfamiliar data or properties the functions *VarType* and *TypeName* are very useful. *VarType* returns a numerical value that gives the data type of a *Variant* value or of a variable. A list of possible values can be found in the on-line help. *TypeName* returns the name of an object type: for example, *Worksheet*, *Window*, or *Nothing*. This provides you with a keyword for searching in the on-line help. Furthermore, from the immediate window you can very easily get some concrete help by setting the input cursor within a keyword and pressing F1.

Use the Macro Recorder to Hunt for Keywords

When you are programming procedures that simplify or automate the operation of Excel, then the macro recorder often provides the shortest path to a workable macro. Even if the code thus produced can seldom be used as is, it nonetheless usually contains the correct keywords.

Syntax Summary

All properties and methods apply, if not otherwise stated, to the object *Application.*

Background Calculation, Options for Program Execution

Interactive = True/False	allow input
EnableCancelKey = xlDisabled	no reaction to Ctrl+Break
... = xlErrorHandler	error 18 on Ctrl+Break
DisplayAlerts = True/False	alert during macro execution
DisplayStatusBar = True/False	display status bar
StatusBar = "infotext"/False	place text in the status bar

Speed Optimization

ScreenUpdating = True/False	screen updating on/off
Calculation = xlAutomatic/xlManual	automatic/manual calculation
object.Calculate	recalculate range/sheet/entire application

Below, *rc* stands for row or column (*Row* or *Column* object), *ws* for a worksheet (*WorkSheet*), *obj* for a range of cells or a drawing object (including controls and OLE objects), *rng* for a range of cells (*Range* object), *cb* for a command bar (*CommandBar* object), and *wb* for a workbook (*Workbook* object).

Protection Functions

rc.Hidden = True/False	rows/columns hide or unhide
ws.ScrollArea = "a1:e10"	reduce scroll area
ws.Visible = True/False/xlVeryHidden	hide or unhide sheets
obj.Locked = True/False	protect object (only in combination with *Protect*)
rng.FormulaHidden = True/False	hide formulas
ws.Protect ...	protect worksheet (except for objects with *Locked=False*)
ws.Unprotect	lift worksheet protection
wb.Protect ...	protect workbook structure
wb.Unprotect	lift protection
cb.Protection = ...	protect toolbar (CommandBar object)

Excel-4 Macros and Worksheet Functions

Run "macroname" [,para1, para2 ...]	execute Excel-4 macro
ExecuteExcel4Macro "KOMMANDO(...)"	execute Excel-4 macro command (German)
WorksheetFunction.Function()	execute worksheet function (English)

Excel Version Number

Application.Version	character string with Excel version number

CHAPTER 6

Debugging, Protection When Errors Arise

Where there is programming, there are errors. This rule has proved itself true over the course of the past half century. Even in programs that have been maintained for years, new errors are always being discovered. (We shall pass over in silence such programs as Excel and Word, where the implementation of new functions appears to have priority over the debugging process.) The purpose of this chapter is not, however, to quibble about the quality of the software at hand, but to show you how you can make yours better. Perhaps you will even come to appreciate that even Microsoft is not perfect.

This chapter is divided into two sections. The first describes the possibilities for analyzing programs with bugs in them. For this purpose VBA offers an excellent work environment, which among other things allows for step-by-step execution of programs, conditional breakpoints, and keeping track of variables. The second section of this chapter shows how you can protect your program against going out of control when an error does occur (for example, when the user uses the program incorrectly).

Chapter Overview

Debugging Aids

Syntax Control

Errors Reported Before Program Execution

VBA will refuse to execute a procedure as long as there exist syntactical errors in the code. VBA recognizes errors such as variables that have been incorrectly declared or not declared at all (see below), the incorrect use of keywords as variables or procedure names, the attempt to call a nonexistent procedure, multiply defined procedures, and the use of the semicolon where a comma should be used. Most of these errors are easy to recognize and fix with little effort.

Many errors, such as typographical errors in naming methods and properties, can be caught only at compilation time (and sometimes not until the code is executed). However, in the default setting only those parts of the program are compiled that are actually needed. Thus it can happen that syntactical errors will not be discovered for a long time, that is, until the procedure in question is executed.

> **NOTE** *It is generally a good idea to uncover all syntactical errors before the program is executed. For this you can either convert the entire project to pseudocode with* `Debug|Compile VBA Project` *or deactivate both compiler settings in* `Tools|Options`.

Errors in Variable Declaration

If the instruction *Option Explicit* appears at the beginning of your module, then every variable must be declared before its use with *Dim, Private,* or *Public.* This may appear to be unnecessary extra work, but it is an important and efficient mechanism for avoiding typographical errors. It is precisely in the unpleasant and longwinded keywords (such as the method *ToolbarButtons*) that typos are practically preprogrammed. *Without* the option *Explicit* VBA generally interprets an incorrectly written keyword as an undeclared *Variant* variable. It can thus happen that such a program will be syntactically correct! The program will then be launched without difficulty, and perhaps an error will be detected only when the procedure in question fails to perform as expected.

Therefore, always use the option *Explicit.* If you click on the option REQUIRE VARIABLE DECLARATION in the form TOOLS|OPTIONS| EDITOR, then VBA automatically adds the instruction *Option Explicit* to every new module. (This option has no effect on preexisting modules.)

If you give the type of your parameters explicitly in your procedures (and you should), then this type must match exactly the type of the variable passed when the procedure is called. Otherwise, an error alert will result.

Reaction to Errors

In TOOLS|OPTIONS|GENERAL you can select from among three error-trapping options to determine how Visual Basic reacts to errors during code execution.

The option BREAK ON ALL ERRORS means that every error leads to a program break even if this error is caught by *On Error*. (Information on programming error-handling routines appears in the next section.) This option is very useful to the extent that often errors that you had not even thought of during program development remain hidden by *On-Error* routines. Thus the option BREAK ON ALL ERRORS deactivates all *On-Error* instructions.

With thc other options (BREAK IN CLASS MODULE, BREAK ON UNHANDLED ERRORS) an error leads to a break only if there is no error-handling routine. These two options differ only when you are testing class modules.

> **TIP** *When program execution is interrupted, the content of variables is automatically shown in the code windows when the mouse is passed over the variable name.*

> **TIP** *When program execution in the development environment is interrupted, several commands and functions in Excel are locked. This can be annoying, since in Excel the cause of the blocking is invisible. If you do not wish to continue execution of the faulty procedure, execute* RUN|RESET *in the development environment.*

The Immediate Window as a Debugging Tool

An important assistant in debugging is the immediate window. You can open the immediate window before a procedure is launched with VIEW|IMMEDIATE WINDOW (or Ctrl+G) and then execute the procedure with an instruction in the immediate window. For a subprogram without parameters it suffices merely to give the name of the procedure and hit Return. If parameters are required, then you will have to input some valid values. In the case of functions you must note that the parameters are placed in parentheses and that the return value of the function will be calculated. The easiest way to proceed is to prefix the function call by "?" (the abbreviation for *Print*): VBA then prints the result on the next line of the immediate window.

List of Procedures (Call Stack)

With Ctrl+L or the menu command VIEW|CALL STACK you open a dialog that lists the procedures whose execution has led to the current procedure being called. The list is sorted in reverse order: At the top is the current procedure, and below it the procedure from which the current procedure was called, and so on down the list. In the case of recursive procedures (those that call themselves) it can happen that the same procedure name will occur repeatedly in the call stack. Thus the CALL STACK dialog allows you to determine how the current procedure came to be called. A double click on one of the procedures alters the current context for variables in the immediate window.

In Figure 6.1 you can see the list of procedure calls that resulted after the launch of *testrecur* in the module *Procedures* of the example file `VBA-Concepts.xls`. After *recur* was executed the first time by *testrecur*, the two further *recur* entries in the list resulted from recursive calls.

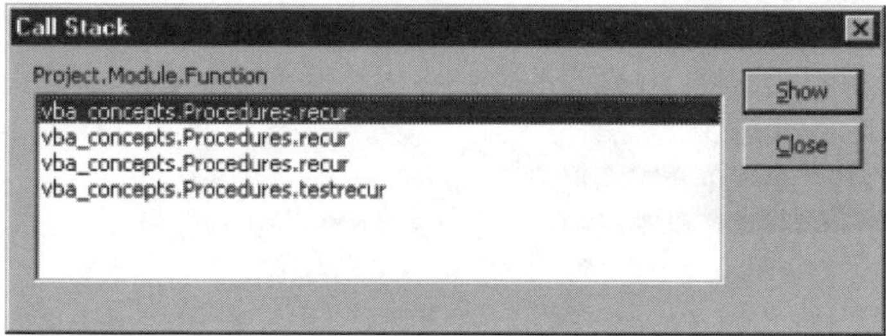

Figure 6.1. The call stack

```
' file VBA-Concepts.xls, Module Procedures
Public Sub testrecur()
  Debug.Print recur(3)
End Sub
' recursive procedure for calculating the factorial of x
Function recur(x)
  If x <= 1 Then
    recur = 1
    Stop    ' here the execution is interrupted
  Else
    recur = x * recur(x - 1)
  End If
End Function
```

Program Changes in a Running Program

Since Excel 97 it has been possible to make changes in a running program and then continue execution. Needless to say, this is a very practical method of debugging. However, continuing the program is not possible if the structure of the program changes, such as in the declaration of a parameter of a currently active procedure. If you activated the option NOTIFY BEFORE STATE LOSS in TOOLS|OPTIONS|GENERAL, the development environment warns you about such changes.

> **TIP** *You can interrupt a running program (which is perhaps lost in an infinite loop) with* Ctrl+Break.

Continuing Execution

Interrupted programs can be continued with F5 or F8 (single step mode). This holds as well for programs in which an error has occurred. However, a continuation makes sense only if the cause of the error can be eliminated (which is seldom the case). An example: A division by zero occurs in a program from the instruction *a=b/c*. You can execute *c=1* in the immediate window and then continue with F5.

Control Output in the Program

In many cases it is useful to have the program output control information. For this there are two possibilities:

- You can use the command *MsgBox* to output an arbitrary (short) text in a small window. As soon as you press the OK button of this window, execution continues.
- You can use the *Print* method for the *Debug* object to output text or values of variables into the immediate window

Controlled Program Execution

With F8 or the menu command DEBUG|STEP INTO you can run the program one line at a time (or instruction by instruction if more than one instruction appears on a line). Visual Basic executes the next instruction and then interrupts execution automatically. With this command you can follow program execution in detail (for example, in nested loops, branches, or event procedures). At any time you can inspect the contents of different variables and thus reconstruct individual steps in a calculation. F8 can be used to start a new procedure in single step mode as well as to continue a running program that has been interrupted.

There are several variants to single step mode:

- DEBUG|STEP OVER or Shift+F8 normally executes only a single instruction. However, if in this instruction a function or procedure is called, then this procedure will be executed in its entirety.

- DEBUG|STEP OUT or Ctrl+Shift+F8 executes all intructions up to the end of the current procedure. If in the process other procedures are called, these will also be executed to the end.

- DEBUG|RUN TO CURSOR or Ctrl+F8 works similarly, but execution is again interrupted at the line of the current procedure in which the cursor is located. This command is frequently useful to avoid the necessity of setting a breakpoint.

Skipping or Repeating Instructions

A program is generally executed instruction by instruction. If program execution is interrupted (for example, at a breakpoint or in single step mode), you can then use the command DEBUG|SET NEXT STATEMENT or Ctrl+F9 to determine the line at which execution will continue. It is not possible to select a line located outside of the current procedure. The command SET NEXT STATEMENT is particularly suitable for executing program lines that have already been executed or for skipping over program lines.

Program Interruption with Breakpoints

Before a program is started or while program execution has been interrupted you can hit F9 or execute the menu command DEBUG|TOGGLE BREAKPOINT to mark particular program lines as breakpoints. Breakpoints are indicated in the program code by a special color (in the standard setting a red background). Visual Basic interrupts execution automatically at each breakpoint (in fact, just *before* this line is executed).

Breakpoints are of great use in checking critical program segments. Simply set a breakpoint in the first line of a procedure in which you suspect an error to be lurking. As soon as this procedure is reached in the course of program execution, Visual Basic interrupts execution. You can now investigate variables in the immediate window or continue the program in single step mode.

Program Interruption with Watch Expressions

A clever possibility for defining breakpoints is offered by watch expressions. These are usually based on a simple variable or property whose state you wish to watch. (But simple compound expressions are also allowed.) The input of a watch expression is most simply done in code windows by clicking on the right mouse button over the variable in question and then executing ADD WATCH. There then appears the form shown in Figure 6.2.

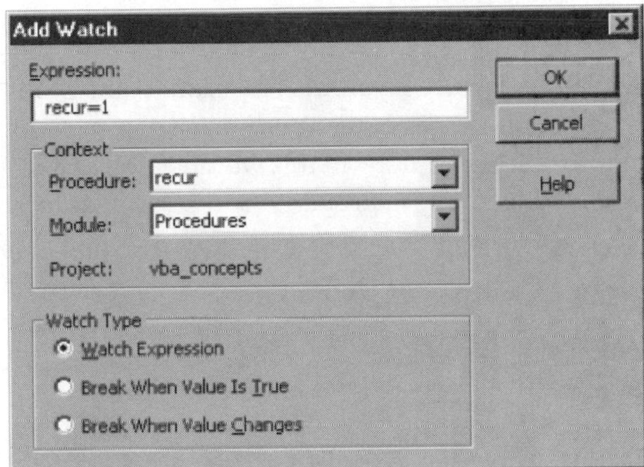

Figure 6.2. Defining a watch expression

You then choose from among three forms of watching. The simplest variant is WATCH EXPRESSION, by which Visual Basic indicates the current value of the variable in the immediate window. With the other two modes the program is interrupted when the entire expression assumes the value *True* or when its value changes. You can thus use watch expressions to interrupt a program automatically when the value of a variable is, say, greater than 100.

In the ADD WATCH form you can also determine from what context the variable is to be read (that is, which module, which procedure; this question is important, since there can exist like-named variables in different contexts). All defined watch expressions are shown in the Watches window.

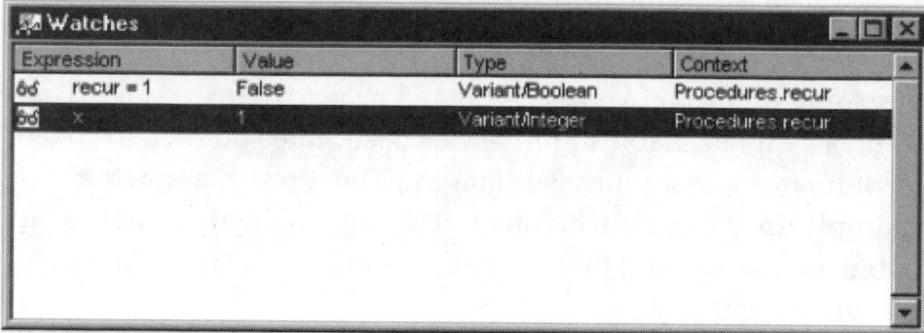

Figure 6.3. The Watches window

The ADD WATCH form is particularly attractive if you wish to examine the properties of objects. Figure 6.4 shows some properties of the *Application* object. Note that you can move through the entire object hierarchy in this window. The property *ActiveWindow* leads to a *Window* object, whose property *ActiveCell* leads to a *Range* object, and so on.

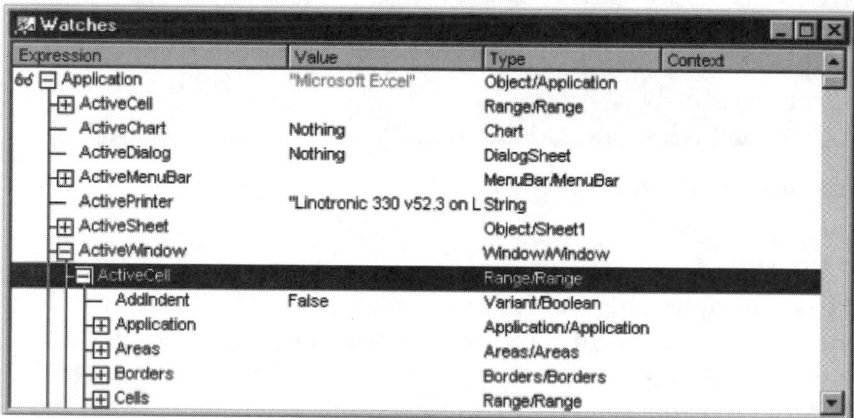

Figure 6.4. The Application object in the Watches window

Error-Tolerant Behavior of Programs

Normally, an error causes an interrupt. VBA displays a dialog box by means of which program execution can be terminated or the code analyzed in the immediate window. A continuation of the program is essentially never possible. During program development interrupts due to errors are unavoidable. However, a user who uses an Excel program developed by you should never encounter a dialog box with the words "macro error."

But since even in a well-developed program it is not impossible that under certain circumstances an error will occur (blatantly incorrect program operation, lack of memory, hard drive full, and so on), the command *On Error* provides a controlled continuation of the program in the event of an error.

The Command On Error

The command ***On Error*** determines how the program should behave when an error occurs. There are three variants for the use of this command:

```
On Error Resume Next        '(1) execute the next instruction
On Error GoTo label         '(2) call error handling routine
On Error GoTo 0             '(3) normal: macro error dialog
```

Variant (1): On Error Resume Next

Variant (1) represents the most convenient way to suppress error alerts: The program will simply continue with the next instruction. Since the instructions of a program build as a rule one on the other, there is a great probability that another error will soon occur. This error, however, will be met the same way as the previous one, so that the procedure will sooner or later come to an end. It is rather obvious that in this case the procedure will not have accomplished its intended purpose.

Thus it is generally the case that variant (1) does not represent a reasonable reaction to errors. There are exceptions, though. Consider, for example, the procedure *test_resume_next*. This procedure changes the display of row and column headers in the currently active window.

Of course, the execution of this procedure makes sense only if a worksheet is currently being displayed. If another sheet happens to be active, then an error occurs (since a chart sheet, say, that is, the object *Chart*, does not recognize the property *DisplayHeadings*). Instead of thinking long and hard about how one might test whether the active sheet is in fact a worksheet, it is easier simply to insert the instruction *On Error Resume Next* into the procedure. Problem solved!

```
Sub test_resume_next()
  On Error Resume Next
  ActiveWindow.DisplayHeadings = _
    Not ActiveWindow.DisplayHeadings
End Sub
```

Within the procedure the occurrence of an error can be verified with *Err*. This function contains the number of the most recently occurring error (even if this error did not lead to an error alert due to *On Error Resume Next*). The instruction *On Error* resets *Err* to 0.

Variant (2): On Error Goto Label

Variant (2) enables the programming of "genuine" error-handling routines. VBA branches on the occurrence of an error into the part of the procedure indicated by a *label.* There a response to the error can take place (for example, display an error alert, save unsaved data, and so on). Then the procedure can be exited or continued with *Resume.*

For understanding the *Goto* command it is necessary first to understand the notion of a label. A label is a program line consisting only of a name followed by a colon. Within a procedure a label can be jumped to with the *Goto* command, that is, the execution of the program is continued on the line after the label. Jumps using *Goto* can have the effect of making the syntax of a function or procedure difficult to decipher and therefore are to be avoided in structured programming. The command *Goto* should therefore never be used (*except in conjunction with OnError*). (There is also no need. All the examples in this book have been formulated without *Goto.*)

But let us return to error handling in which labels and jumps are not only allowed, but are absolutely necessary. On an error VBA jumps to the location given by the label. The label must be located within the current procedure. Normally, the error-handling routine is placed at the end of the procedure. To avoid the error-handling routine being executed in the normal course of the procedure, *Exit Sub* or *Exit Function* is usually placed just before the label.

Within the error-handling routine you can determine the number of the error that has occurred with *Err()* and reply accordingly. A list of error numbers used by VBA can be found in the on-line help under the topic "error number." The response to an error can include calling other procedures (for example, to save data).

Note, however, that it is possible for errors to occur both within the error-handling routine and in other procedures called. Variant (2) of *On Error* holds only for a *single* error! The next error triggers again the normal behavior (that is, the display of the "macro error" form). You can avoid this by executing *On Error xxx* within the error-handling routine.

The Command Resume

The faulty procedure can be continued from the error-handling routine with ***Resume*** or ended with *Exit Sub/Function.* If the end of the error-handling routine is reached without *Resume* being encountered, then the procedure is considered to have ended and the error as having been dealt with. There are three variants of the *Resume* command:

```
Resume              ' reexecutes the instruction on which the error occurred
Resume Next         ' resumes the procedure with the next instruction
Resume label        ' resumes the procedure at label
```

In all three cases the program is continued within the procedure in which the error-handling routine is located. It is impossible to use *Resume* to jump into another procedure. To make possible a controlled response in the case of further errors, a new (or perhaps the same) error-handling routine should be erected at the latest before *Resume*. (Take care, however, to avoid an infinite loop by continual repetition of a faulty program segment.)

Example of Variant (2)

A procedure with an error-handling routine can be constructed along the lines of the procedure *test_resume*: In the normal case, that is, when no error occurs, the procedure will continue to the instruction *Exit Sub*. If an error occurs, then then program will be continued on the line after *test_resume_error*. If the error handling is successful, then the procedure is continued at *test_resume_cont*; otherwise, it is interrupted. If a second error occurs, then a branch to *test_resume_another_error* occurs. At that point there is no further attempt to continue the procedure. Depending on the application, here an alert can be displayed, data saved, or some other action taken.

Do not depend on your error-handling routine to succeed in actually removing the error. Consider the possibility of an error occurring in the error-handling routine itself. Avoid at all cost an infinite loop! (An error leads to a call to the error-handling routine, from there the procedure is continued, the error appears again, a new call to the error-handling routine, and so on, and so on.)

From the point of view of the user one thing is most important: It matters not how, when, or where an error occurred, but in no case should data be lost.

```
Sub test_resume()
  On Error Resume test_resume_error
  ...
test_resume_cont:             ' here the procedure is continued after an error
  ...
  Exit Sub                    ' End of the procedure
test_resume_error:            ' error-handling routine begins here
  If Err()=... Then
    On Error Resume test_resume_another_error
    ...                       ' response to a recognized error
    Resume test_resume_cont ' resume procedure
  End If
test_resume_another_error:    ' unknown error or a second error
  ...                         ' error alert, save data, etc.
End Sub
```

Variant (3): On Error GoTo 0

The third variant of *On Error* serves to deactivate previously erected error-handling routines. After *On Error GoTo 0* the "normal" behavior of VBA is again in force, that is, the display of MACRO ERROR forms.

Error Handling in Nested Procedures

Suppose that by clicking on a tool procedure A is called; A calls B, and B calls C. If an error occurs in C, the error-handling routine belonging to C will be called. If there is no error-handling routine in C, then control is returned to B. If there is no error-handling routine in B, then control is passed back to A. Only if there is no error-handling routine in A does the MACRO ERROR form appear.

Visual Basic thus searches through all of the mutually called subprograms in reverse order for a suitable error-handling routine. Only when there is none even in the original calling procedure does Visual Basic display an error alert and interrupt program execution.

The two commands *Resume* and *Resume Next* are always valid for procedures in which they are placed. If an error occurs in procedure C but is dealt with only in the error-handling routine of procedure A, then the program is resumed with *Resume* at the indicated location in A. It is impossible to jump with *Resume* to the current procedure (for example, to the instruction in C on which the error occurred).

The Functions Err, Error( ), CVErr, and the Command Error

Err returns an identification number of the error that has occurred. The range of possible error numbers is given in the on-line help. ***Error()*** returns the error text of the most recently occurring error. *Error(n)* returns the error text of error number *n*.

The comand ***Error*** can be used to simulate an error. This would make sense, for example, in testing an error-handling routine. The instruction *Error n* leads to the display of the macro error form and can thus be reasonably placed at the end of an error-handling routine for the case that the error was not removed.

With the function ***CVErr*** you can create an error value for a *Variant* variable. This function can, for example, be used in a user-defined worksheet function to return an error value instead of a result.

```
result = CVErr(xlErrValue)
```

A list of predefined error constants for this purpose can be found in the online help under "error values in cells." An example for the application of *CVErr* can be found in Chapter 5 (in the variant of the user-defined *Discount* function).

Application Example

The following example was introduced already in Chapter 4, where the issue there was to determine the number of dimensions of a field that was to be passsed as a parameter to a procedure. Since there is no suitable function to accomplish this purpose, the upper index limit up to dimension 10 is determined in the first *For* loop with *UBound*. Since one may assume that the field does not have so many dimensions, sooner or later an error will occur. The error is, in fact, planned for! In the error-handling routine the number of dimensions is determined from the current value of *i* that led to an error in *UBound*.

```
' example file VBA-Concepts.xls, Module Procedures
Sub arraytest(arr())
  Dim i, dimensions
  On Error GoTo arraytest_error
  For i = 1 To 10: dimensions = UBound(arr, i): Next i
arraytest_continue:
  dimensions = i - 1
  Debug.Print dimensions, " Dimensions"
  For i = 1 To dimensions
    Debug.Print "Dimension "; i; ": "; LBound(arr, i); " Bis "; UBound(arr, i)
  Next i
  Exit Sub
arraytest_error:
  ' this program segment is called as soon as a nonexistent arrdimension is
  ' accessed in the loop
  Resume arraytest_continue
End Sub
```

Response to Program Interrupts

VBA programs can usually be interrupted with Ctrl+Break. During the test phase of program development this is a great convenience, but in finished applications such program interrupts are usually unwelcome. If you wish to make it impossible for the user to interrupt your program with Ctrl+Break, then you have two options:

- With *Application.**EnableCancelKey** = xlDisabled* you achieve the result that Ctrl+Break has no effect whatsoever. The advantage of this measure is that only one instruction (in the *Auto_Open* procedure) is necessary.

- On the other hand, if you set the constant *xlErrorHandler* with *EnableCancelKey*, then each time the user hits Ctrl+Break an error with error number 18 occurs. You can catch this "error" just as you would catch any other error. The disadvantage is obvious: Each procedure must be equipped with an error-handling routine. Another variant consists in allowing interrupts only in those program segments in which very time-intensive calculations are carried out.

The "normal" reaction to interrupts, that is, the display of an alert, can be reinstated with the instruction *EnableCancelKey=xlInterrupt*.

Example

```
' example file miscellaneous.xls, Module1
Sub slowcode()
  Application.EnableCancelKey = xlErrorHandler
  On Error GoTo slow_error
  '
  ' ... the actual procedure
  '
  Exit Sub
slow_error:
  If Err = 18 Then
    result = MsgBox("Should the program be continued?", vbYesNo)
    If result = vbYes Then Resume Next
  End If
  ' otherwise, interrupt procedure
  '
  ' .. cleanup tasks
End Sub
```

The above code segment from the example file `miscellaneous.xls` shows how an orderly response to Ctrl+Break can be achieved. The complete program code, which also demonstrates the control of the status bar and execution of background calculations, can be found in the last section of Chapter 5.

Syntax Summary

Debugging

Debug.Print ...	output to immediate window
MsgBox ...	output to alert box
Stop	program interrupt

Response to Program Errors

On Error Resume Next	execute next instruction
On Error GoTo label	call error-handling routine
On Error GoTo 0	normal reaction: macro error form

Commands and Functions in the Error-Handling Routine

Resume	reexecutes error-causing instruction
Resume Next	resumes at the next instruction
Resume label	resumes at label
Err	returns the current error number
Error(n)	returns the text of error number *n*
Error n	simulates an error
CVErr(n)	transforms *n* into an error value (for return)

Response to Program Interrupts

Application._	determines the reaction to Ctrl+Break
EnableCancelKey = ...	allowed values: *xlInterrupt, xlDisabled,* *xlErrorHandler*

CHAPTER 7

Forms (Microsoft Forms Library)

Forms are free-standing windows in which various items can be placed. Excel recognizes countless predefined forms, such as forms for file selection or for setting options. Additionally, you can create forms or set up worksheets to act like forms with an entire palette of controls.

Chapter Overview

Predefined Dialogs

Standard Excel Dialogs

Excel is equipped with a huge number of predefined dialog objects. These dialogs are used by Excel for its everyday tasks, such as for selecting a file name, input of a search text, setting options of Paste Special. The dialogs appear automatically as soon as the corresponding menu or keyboard command is executed.

In a VBA program you can select these forms with the *Application* method ***Dialogs*** and use ***Show*** to display and execute them. With the command given below a dialog box appears for the arrangement of windows. You can now input the desired state of the windows (overlapping, split, and so on). As soon as you click on Ok, the windows will indeed be positioned as you indicated. As a programmer you need not concern yourself with the evaluation of the dialog box.

```
Application.Dialogs(xlDialogArrangeAll).Show
```

The execution of the *Show* method is possible only when a suitable sheet is active or a suitable object has been selected. Thus, for example, it is not possible to display the dialog for setting the border of a cell (*xlDialogBorder*) while a chart sheet is active.

The method *Show* can be used both as a command and as a function. In the latter case it returns *True* if the dialog was exited normally with Ok, and *False* if the dialog was ended with Cancel, Esc, or the window's close box.

```
result = Application.Dialogs(xlDialogArrangeAll).Show
```

Predefined standard dialogs cannot be altered. If you have need of a dialog box that is similar to one that already exists, you will have to define it from scratch. User-defined forms are handled in the next section.

Passing Parameters to a Dialog

A list of all *xlDialog* constants can be found in the object browser (library: Excel; object: *xlBuiltinDialogs*). Up to thirty parameters can be passed to the method *Show*, with which settings can be set in the dialog box. A description of the parameters can be found in the on-line help under the link "Built-In Dialog Box Argument Lists." But even so, the passing of parameters remains a tedious and difficult undertaking. This will become clear from the following example: The dialog box for opening an Excel file (*xlDialogOpen*) is described as follows in the on-line help:

xlDialogOpen	*file_text, update_links, read_only, format, prot_pwd, write_res_pwd, ignore_rorec, file_origin, custom_delimit, add_logical, editable, file_access, notify_logical, converter*

That this is a dialog for opening a file (and not, say, a window or a workbook) you can figure out. But more difficult is figuring out what the parameters mean, unless you can immediately understand what values *add_logical* expects and what effect it has.

Let us proceed now to parameter passing: Like all other VBA methods, *Show* uses the mechanism of named parameters. However, since *Show* must deal with many different dialogs, the parameter names are rather simple: *Arg1, Arg2, Arg3,* etc. If you wish in opening a file to activate the option button OPEN READ-ONLY, the corresponding instruction looks as follows:

```
result = Application.Dialogs(xlDialogOpen).Show(Arg3:=True)
```

Thus you must count to obtain the number of the parameter that you need. It is clear that the program code will not be very self-explanatory.

Simulating Keyboard Input in Dialogs

Show displays a dialog box, but the input of parameters is left to the user of your program. It can often be useful to simulate keyboard input. For this you have available the *Application* method *SendKeys.* Note that in using this method it must be executed *before* the dialog box is displayed, which seems unlogical. The reason is that Windows saved the simulated key sequence in a keyboard buffer and executes the keyboard input only when it has the chance—after the appearance of the dialog box.

The following example shows once again the dialog box for arranging windows, but it has selected the option "Horizontal" with Alt+O.The user needs only to confirm the dialog with Return.

```
SendKeys "%o"
Application.Dialogs(xlDialogArrangeAll).Show
```

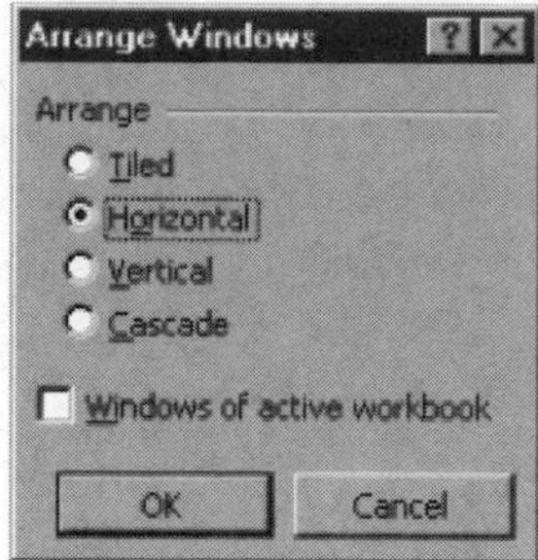

Figure 7.1. Dialog box for arranging windows

The syntax of the character string in which the simulated keyboard input is given in *SendKeys* is described extensively in the on-line help for this method. In principle, it is also possible with *SendKeys* to terminate the input in the dialog at once with Ok (that is, by simulating Return). In this way you can execute various Excel commands directly via the detour of a dialog box. If the property *ScreenUpdating* is set to *False*, then the user of your program doesn't even see the dialog box. Nonetheless, this method is not to be recommended, for the following three reasons:

- By executing the appropriate methods the same result can be achieved usually more simply and always significantly faster. (However, it is not always completely simple to find the right method. This problem has no doubt already made itself known to you. In the case of window arrangement the suitable method is *Arrange*, and it is used by the *Windows* enumeration.)

- The necessary keyboard inputs are naturally dependent on the regional version of Excel. That is, their code in not usable internationally.

- If Microsoft changes the construction of individual dialogs in a future version of Excel, your program will most likely no longer operate correctly, if at all. (The simulation of keyboard input is indeed based on the fact that individual elements of the dialog box can be accessed with Alt+Key.)

Dialogs for File Selection

You can execute the dialog for file selection via *Dialogs* with the constant *xlDialogOpen* or *xlDialogSaveAs*. Then the operation (opening or saving) will be executed at once.

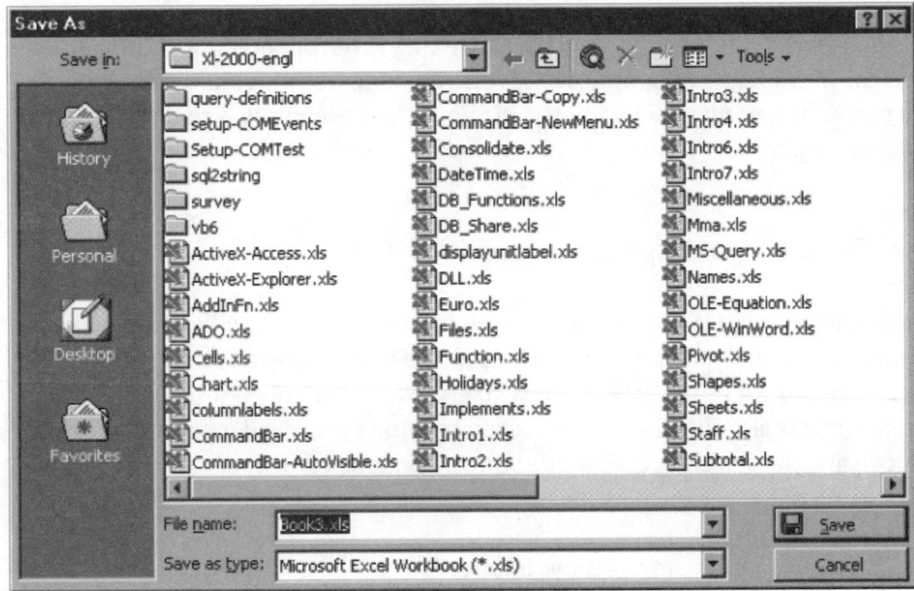

Figure 7.2. Save As dialog (GetSaveAsFilename)

Instead of this you can also use the two methods *GetOpenFilename* and *GetSaveAsFilename*. Then the file selection dialog box will be displayed, but only the selected file name will be returned (without opening or saving a file). Therefore, you have more flexibility with these methods with regard to further response.

```
filename = Application.GetSaveAsFilename
```

The Database Form

The dialog for selecting, changing, and input of data records is not invoked with *Dialogs(...).Show*, but with *ShowDataForm*. The use of the database mask is described in Chapter 11.

Since Excel 5 it has no longer been possible to change the database form. If you wish to set up your own database form, you will have to program all the elements of the database form yourself. However, this requires considerable effort.

Warnings

Many unwanted forms can appear during the execution of methods. Usually, these are in the form of warnings that advise against the consequences of the operation (such as loss of data). For example, with the instruction *Sheets(...).Delete* for the deletion of a sheet of a workbook there appears an alert asking whether you really (cannot be undone) want to delete it.

While in the normal use of Excel such warnings are quite practical, they are a nuisance in the running of a program, since they interrupt execution and confront the user of the program with a cryptic warning. To get around this problem you can set the *Application* property *DisplayAlerts* in such a way that no warnings at all are displayed.

The Functions MsgBox and InputBox

The two functions *MsgBox* and *InputBox* have already been briefly described in conjunction with character strings (Chapter 5). *MsgBox* displays a text in a small window that must be acknowledged with Ok. With a suitable setting of the second parameter it is also possible to have several buttons displayed (such as Yes, No, Cancel) and the selection evaluated. *InputBox* enables the input of a simple character string that is returned by the function.

```
result = Inputbox("Please type in your name:")
result = MsgBox("Do you really want to delete this file?", _
  vbYesNo + vbQuestion)
If ergebnis = vbYes Then ...
```

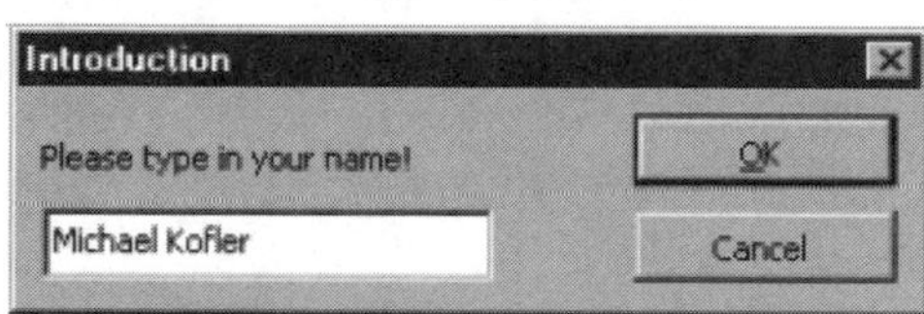

Figure 7.3. VBA input box

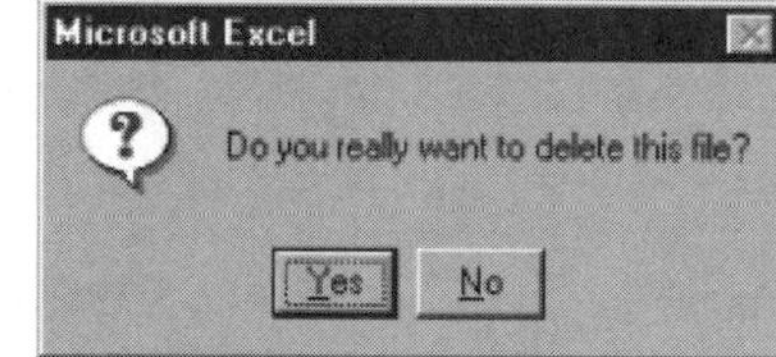

Figure 7.4. Message box

The Method Application.InputBox

Although the function *InputBox* described above is available from the VBA library (and thus can be used in the same form in Word, Acces, etc.), the Excel library offers a second, like-named, variant that is realized as a method of the *Application* object. In contrast to the traditional *InputBox*, the function *Application.InputBox* can also be used for input of formulas and ranges of cells. Furthermore, the position at which the input window appears can be determined in advance.

Decisive for the application of *Application.InputBox* is the last parameter, by which the type of input can be set, as long as no text input is to be given. The most important values for this parameter are 0 (formula), 1 (number), 8 (range), 64 (matrix of cells).

If type 1 (number) is given in *Application.InputBox*, then the user is also permitted to input a formula in the form "= 2 + 3." The formula will be automatically evaluated, and *InputBox* returns the value 5. With *Type:=8* the user can select a range of cells with the mouse. The user can even select another window or another sheet—actions that are not permitted in normal Windows dialog boxes.

In calling this function you give the first parameter in the usual way, and the eighth by name:

```
Dim b As Range
Set b = Application.InputBox("Please input a range of cells", _
  Type:=8)
```

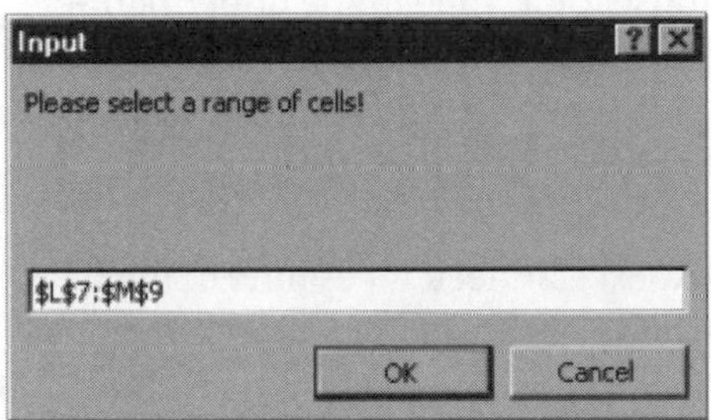

Figure 7.5. Excel input box

InputBox returns the affected selection in the format determined by the *Type* parameter. If the user ends input by pressing Cancel, then the method returns the Boolean value *False*. This situation makes the evaluation of the input for *Type:=8* somewhat complicated: Since the result is normally a *Range* object, the assignment of the result must take place via *Set*. But this leads to an error if *InputBox* returns only the Boolean value *False* instead of a *Range* object. Therefore, properly written code would look like this:

```
Dim b As Range
On Error Resume Next
Set b = Application.InputBox("Please input a range of cells", _
  Type:=8)
If Err > 0 Then  'an error occurs
  MsgBox "That was not a range of cells"
End If
```

In the case of type 64 (matrix) *InputBox* returns a *Variant* field with the values of the given range (for example, a 3 × 2 field for the range A1:B3).

> **POINTER** *A rather advanced example of the use of* InputBox *can be found in Chapter 11 under the heading "editing a preexisting invoice." There the command is used to select a row of a worksheet. The user can click on a cell with the mouse , and the program takes takes the row number of the formula returned by* InputBox.

Positioning of Dialog Boxes

Forms that are not invoked from a pop-up menu but via the keyboard or the main menu usually appear precisely where they are the least useful. If you execute the command WINDOW|ARRANGE and place the mouse for a while in the upper right-hand corner of the screen, it could happen that on its own the dialog box appears in the lower left-hand corner of the screen. This is particularly irritating when you are working with a large monitor and have to move a long distance with the mouse to complete the input.

If you move the window of the dialog box, Excel indeed takes note of the new position. But at a later point in time this can be as unsatisfactory as the previous position. Furthermore, apparently it is not the last position of each dialog that is stored individually, but for all dialog boxes together.

In many cases it would be best if the dialog box would appear where the mouse is located. (This is precisely the case with all dialog boxes that are invoked by context menus.) But in the current version there is no opportunity for the programmer to influence the position at which the box appears in the case of predefined dialogs. An exception is *InputBox*, where the fourth and fifth parameters (*Left* and *Top*) control the position of the box. With a bit of programming effort you can use these parameters to ensure that the dialog box does not appear over the currently selected cells. (Their position on the screen can be determined with the *Range* properties *Left* and *Top*.)

User-Defined Forms

Overview

The purpose of user-defined forms is to make the operation of custom Excel applications as clear and simple as possible. Forms can be used for the input of parameters of a calculation, for setting various options, for selecting elements of lists, for selecting various program components, and so on. Excel's predefined dialogs (forms) show most vividly the enormous application spectrum of forms.

The subject of user-defined forms is rather extensive, for which reason it has been divided into several parts. This section provides an introduction on using user-defined forms. With the help of a simple example it introduces the essential principles for defining and managing forms.

The following sections then go into some particular topics in greater detail. First we describe how to use the forms editor. Then we provide an overview of controls that can be used in forms. Following that, we demonstrate that individual form elements can also be placed directly in worksheets (that is, without a form) and discuss the various advantages and drawbacks of such a process. Finally, we introduce programming techniques for managing forms, for example, using forms whose structure can be changed dynamically.

In all the sections you will find numerous examples for using forms. These examples are to be found in the file `Userform.xls`. Further examples, closer approximations to what you might see in real life, appear in the following chapters, where forms are placed in the framework of "genuine" application examples.

Changes with Respect to Excel 5/7

Beginning with Excel 97 forms have been completely reconceptualized. Their development no longer takes place in an Excel dialog sheet but in a *UserForm* object of the VBA development environment.

The *UserForm* object is one of the many objects in the so-called MS Forms library. This library also contains an object for every control. The unusual feature of the MS Forms library is that it can be used not only in Excel, but in other Office components (such as Word), in Internet Explorer, and in Visual Basic.

In contrast to other changes, the old Excel 5/7 dialogs are still completely supported. Not only can old dialogs be used in most cases without any changes (there are only a few compatibility problems, such as in the association of a *Range* object to a listbox). Additionally, the dialog editor is still available for editing existing dialogs.

In this book all of the examples using forms have been transposed to the new MS Forms library, and this chapter also treats exclusively the new *UserForm* forms. There are several reasons for this:

- MS Forms make possible more precise management of the controls in a form (more properties, more events).

- It is possible to maintain more sheets in a form (such as the form TOOLS|OPTIONS).

- In addition to the controls provided with Office, external ActiveX controls can also be used. Such controls can provide a particular functionality for special applications. With Visual Basic 6 (thus not with VBA, but with the free-standing programming language) you can even program new ActiveX controls yourself that are then usable in Excel.

- Finally, it is uncertain how long dialogs based on Excel 5/7 will continue to be supported.

Of course, in comparison to Excel 5/7 there are some drawbacks as well.

- MS Forms cannot be ornamented with characters, text boxes, or other Office objects. In this connection there are fewer visual formatting options than existed with the dialogs of Excel 5/7.

- The use of MS Forms controls frequently leads to problems if the keyboard focus remains in the control. With buttons, that can be avoided with *TakeFocusOnClick=False,* but with other controls the focus must be firmly placed via program code into a particular cell before further instructions can be executed.

Tips for Upgrading

If you already have experience with dialogs in Excel 5/7, here you will find some some tips for upgrading. (An automatic conversion of preexisting Excel 5/7 dialogs into MS Forms is not possible! It is also impossible to mix controls in a form. You will have to decide between the old and new formats.)

- Any procedure can be linked to controls in Excel 5/7 dialogs. With MS Forms, on the other hand, the event procedure is predetermined by the conjunction of element name and event name.

- Event procedures associated to forms are automatically linked to their own form module. They can no longer be placed in an arbitrary module. (This sounds like a restriction, but in reality it has the effect of making large projects more readable.)

- The button option Close no longer exists (nor an equivalent property). If in response to a button click you wish to terminate the form, in the event procedure you must call *Unload Me* or *Hide.* (*Unload* removes the form with all its variables from memory, while *Hide* only hides it. At first sight the result appears in both cases the same; however, with *Hide* the form's settings remain and are available in the case of a future *Show.* With *Unload,* however, the uninitialized form is shown anew. In this case less RAM is taken up.)

- Forms are objects. Calling one therefore occurs with *dialogname.Show* instead of as previously with *Dialogs("dialogname").Show.* The access to the control has also been simplified: *dialogname.controlname* without brackets. In the form event procedure the shorthand *controlname* is even allowed, since the form module is a class module and within it the form is the default object. Thus the repeated naming of *ActiveDialog* has become unnecessary.

- The method *Show* for invoking the form no longer returns a result. In general, however, you should know whether the form was ended with OK or Cancel. For this you should define a variable in the form module as *Public.* To this variable you give values in the *Button* event procedures (for example, 0 if the dialog was ended with Cancel, –1 if it was ended with OK). Then the variable can be evaluated in VBA code.

- The MS Forms library is not automatically activated with Excel 5/7 files. When the first *UserForm* form is inserted there a query automatically appears. However, you can also activate the Microsoft Forms Object Library directly with TOOLS|REFERENCES.

- The operation of the new form editor does not give the impression of having achieved full maturity. The response to a double click is seldom the one that you would expect; the continually appearing and disappearing toolbox is irritating; the broad border around the selected control makes exact positioning difficult, and so on.

Introductory Example

To create a new form, shift into the development environment with Alt+F11 and there insert a blank form with INSERT|USERFORM. When the form window is active, so is the "Toolbox" window with its controls. From this window you can select individual controls and add them to the form with the mouse. For the form in Figure 7.6 two buttons, a label box, and a text box were added.

Controls are thus components of forms. They provide labels for the form and they accept input. Input can take the form of simply clicking with the mouse (on a button, for example), the input of text (in a text box), shifting an element (in the scroll bar), or the selection from a list (listbox). Controls are also called form elements or form fields.

The texts in controls can be edited directly in the form. To do this, click twice slowly on the control (not so fast that the action is evaluated as a double click). The first click activates the control; the second reveals the input (I-beam) cursor.

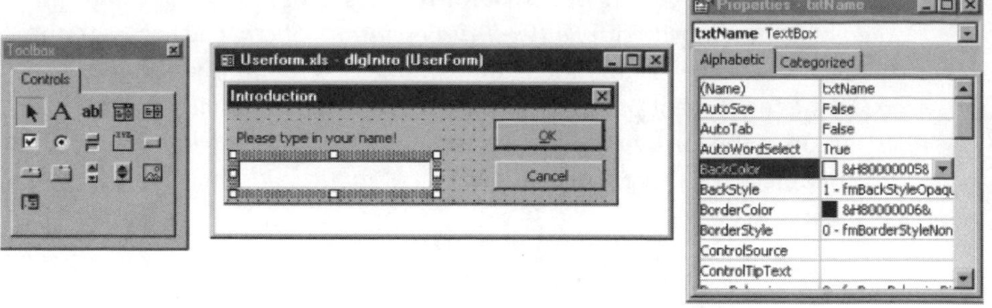

Figure 7.6. The creation of our first form

Naming Controls

Upon insertion into the form a control is automatically given a name (such as CommandButton1, CommandButton2). Since these names are also used in event procedures and in other parts of the program code, it is a good idea at this point to select names with greater mnemonic value. To do this, open the property window with F4 and edit the character string in the field "Name." A popular naming technique is to use the first three letters to describe the type of control, such as *btn* for buttons and *txt* for text boxes. The remaining letters describe the purpose of the control. One then arrives at names like *txtName* and *btnOK*.

The form as a whole has a name, and this, too, can be changed when the form is selected (and not a particular control). Again, it is recommended that you select a meaningful name. For our example form the name *dlgIntro* was chosen. The title of the form is independent of its internal name and is set with the *Caption* property.

Testing the Form

Once the first control has been added you can test the form: Simply press F5. The form appears as an independent window . (At the same time Excel is activated.) The form is functional; that is, you can input text to the text box, click the buttons, and so on. However, there is no response to the clicking, because there are as yet no associated event procedures. To close the form, click on the close box in the upper right corner of the window.

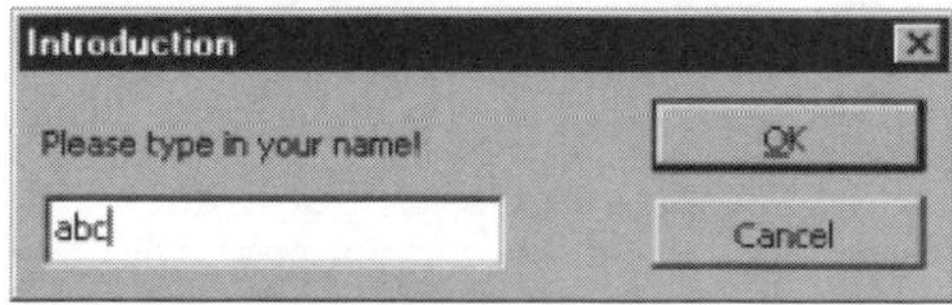

Figure 7.7. The first test

You can also launch the form with program code: For this apply the *Show* method to the new form object that you have made by creating the form. You must give the form name as object name.

```
dlgIntro.Show
```

Properties of Controls

Controls are equipped with countless properties, which are set in the properties window. In addition to the elementary properties *Name* (the internal name of the object) and *Caption* (the title), you there are properties for controlling the appearance and functionality of the control.

OK and Cancel Buttons

Almost every form is equipped with OK and Cancel buttons. To ensure that the form behaves like other forms to which you are accustomed, you should set the property *Default* to *True* for the OK Button. For the Cancel button you should set the property *Cancel* to *True*. With this you achieve that the buttons can be selected not only with the mouse, but also with Return and Esc, respectively.

Event Procedures

In order to make the form usable, at least two event procedures are required: When either button is clicked the form must be made invisible with *Hide*. Moreover, there must be saved in a global variable how the form was terminated (with OK or with Cancel). In most correct applications, there is also a validation control within the event procedure to test whether inputs were admissible.

The most convenient way to proceed is to double click on the control, which brings you into a module window for input of an event procedure. At the same time, a code template is created for the most important event associated to this control. If you wish to write a procedure for another event, simply select another event in the right listbox of the code window and then delete the empty template for the standard procedure.

```
' File Userform.xls, UserForm "dlgIntro"
Public result As Boolean
Private Sub btnOK_Click()
  result = True
  Hide
End Sub
```

```
Private Sub btnCancel_Click()
  result = False
  Hide
End Sub
```

> **NOTE** *If you close the form with* Unload Me *instead of with* Hide, *then not only is the form released from memory, but all variables defined in the associated module (in this example,* result*) are lost.*

Invoking and Evaluating Forms

A form can be called from any procedure. In the file `Userform.xls` it is an event procedure associated to a button in sheet 1. (Information on using controls directly in worksheets, as opposed to forms, can be found later in this chapter.) The invocation is accomplished with *Show*. The program execution in *btnIntro_Click* is interrupted until the form is closed. Then it is tested with *dlgIntro.result* as to whether the form was ended with Cancel or OK. In the latter case the character string in the text box is accessed with *dlgIntro.txtName*. (This is a shorthand for *dlgIntro.txtName.Text*. As you may have guessed, *Text* is the default property for text boxes and thus does not have to be written out.)

```
' file Userform.xls, Class module "mainmenu"
Private Sub btnIntro_Click()
  dlgIntro.Show
  If dlgIntro.result = False Then
    MsgBox "Cancel"
  Else
    MsgBox "Input: " & dlgIntro.txtName
  End If
End Sub
```

> **NOTE** *New in Excel 2000 is the possibility to give the optional parameter* vbModeless *with* Show. *With this you achieve that the form is shown with the property set to modeless. This means that the user can continue working in Excel without having first to exit the form. A possible application would be a form displaying a help text.* Show vbModeless *should not be used in forms with the* RefEdit *control (form box). In Excel 2000 this can lead to massive difficulties.*

The Form Editor

A first introduction to working with the form editor—which is an integral part of the VBA development environment—has been given already in the previous section. In this section you will find additional information to help you in the efficient development of intelligent forms.

Setting Properties

Most of the time spent in the form editor is lost in setting countless properties. You can save some time by working on several controls at once. Select the controls by clicking with Shift or Ctrl, or draw a frame around all the elements you want to work on by drag-clicking. Then you can set all the properties common to the selected controls in the properties window.

Changing the Size and Position of Controls

Controls can be clicked on with the mouse and dragged to a new position. In positioning the tool it will snap to the grid displayed in the form. The size of this grid can be set with TOOLS|OPTIONS|GENERAL. (There the grid alignment can be turned off as well.)

The form editor offers a host of commands by which several controls can be aligned. These commands are invoked via the FORMAT menu. (The most important of these are also available in the pop-up menu.) With them you can, for instance, align several controls along their top, bottom, left, or right borders, or make them the same height or width.

Copying Tools

If you are going to use several controls of the same type, you can first insert a single control of that type, set its properties, and then with the Ctrl key held down drag-click with the mouse. With this the control is copied to the new position and automatically acquires in the process a new name; all other properties are transferred intact from the first control to the second. (In contrast to Visual Basic 5, it is not possible in *UserForm* forms to give several controls the same name and manage them as a single control box.)

Setting the Access Key

In most Excel forms you can direct the input focus into a particular control with ALT+LETTER. In user-defined forms you have to input the required letter in the ***Accelerator*** property of the control. The letter will autmatically appear, underlined, in the associated caption text (if that letter appears in the caption).

Setting the Activation Sequence

The tab order is the order in which the focus shifts from one control to the next. The user can press the Tab key to move the input focus to the next control, or Shift+Tab to move to the previous one. The tab order should be set up in such a way that the individual controls are run through in a logical order (spatially or functionally). At the head of the tab order should stand the first input box. At the end should be the buttons for exiting the form.

The tab order initially corresponds to the sequence in which the controls were placed in the form. However, it can later be changed with the property ***TabIndex.*** This property has the value 0 for the first control in the tab order, 1 for the next, and so on. Instead of changing these values directly it is more convenient to set the tab order with its associated form, invoked by VIEW|TAB ORDER. In this form you select one or more elements (CTRL click to select nonadjacent elements) and then move them up or down in the hierarchy.

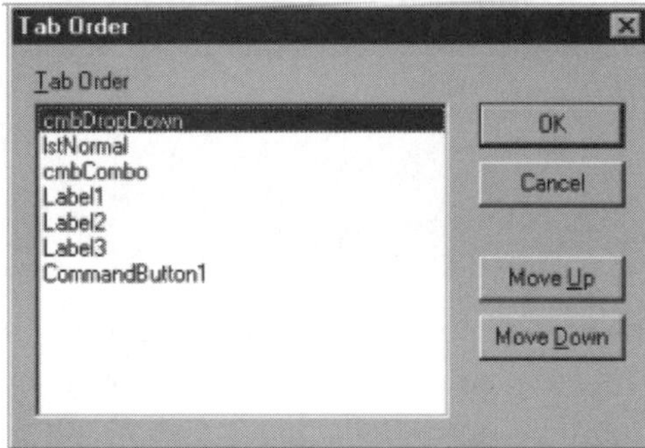

Figure 7.8. The form for setting the tab order

If you wish to remove certain controls from the tab order, you simply set their ***TabStop*** property to *False.*

The input focus can not only be changed by the user using Tab or by clicking on individual elements, but also via program code using the method ***SetFocus:***

```
formname.controlname.SetFocus
```

Visual Appearance of Forms

You have a number of possibilities for setting the visual apearance of your forms:

- You can change the color of the controls (*BackColor, ForeColor*).
- You can group several controls by setting them on an *Image* box and emphasize this box by means of another color or a frame.
- You can store a bit-mapped file in most controls. (But please consider the memory requirements for this!) If several controls overlap, you can move them forward or backward with FORMAT|ORDER.

In contrast to Excel 5/7 it is no longer possible to use the numerous drawing elements in Excel to adorn your forms.

Additional Controls (ActiveX Controls)

Fifteen MS Forms controls are displayed in the toolbox window. If you are working with Office Developer or have installed other programs in addition to Office, then you have a host of additional controls at your command. Namely, in MS Forms forms you can use all ActiveX controls that have been installed on your computer.

A list of controls at your disposal can be obtained by the pop-up menu command ADDITIONAL CONTROLS, which you can invoke from the toolbox window.

To use these controls you must click on them in the form pictured above. The controls will then be displayed in the toolbox just like that for the MS Forms controls. At the same time, the associated object library is activated, so that you can manage the controls like MS Forms elements by means of methods and properties. If there are entries in the on-line help for a particular ActiveX control, this can be beamed up through the help feature of the object browser.

If you use very many additional controls, you can divide the toolbox window into several pages. The necessary command for this can be found in the pop-up menu that pops up when you click on the sheet tab (labeled "Controls") in the toolbox window.

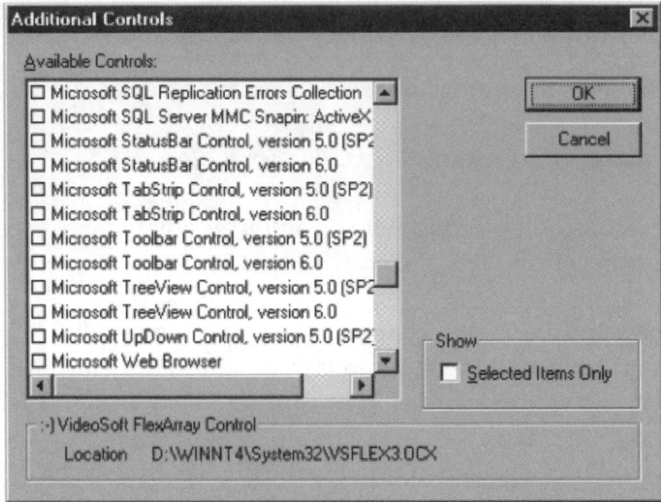

Figure 7.9. List of additional controls installed on the author's computer

NOTE *Although the associated object library is automatically activated when a control is selected, when you remove the control again, the library reference remains. You should deactivate the reference explicitly with* TOOLS|REFERENCES.

NOTE *If you wish to pass your Excel application on to someone else, take care that you use only those controls that you are certain are available on your client's computer. Only if you are working with Office Developer can you include additional controls together with a setup program (and this, of course, only to the extent permitted by your license).*

Building New Controls

Just as you can move controls from the toolbox window into the form window, there is the converse possibility of moving controls in the opposite direction. Indeed, you can even move several controls together (as a group) into the toolbox window. These controls will be represented in the toolbox window by a new symbol. You can then bring up the pop-up menu for this symbol, in which you can edit the symbol and give the control a new name.

The next time you create a form you can add this new entry into your form as if it were an ordinary control. In this way you save the trouble of repeatedly setting the same properties. For example, you could define a group consisting of an OK button and a CANCEL button: This group is needed in almost every form.

> **NOTE** *The toolbox window accepts only the controls with their properties, and not program code. If you wish to save program code as well, you can export entire forms. For example, you could export the framework of a form consisting of an* OK *button and a* Cancel *button together with the required program code, and in this way accelerate even more the creation of new forms.*
>
> *If you own Visual Basic 6 and are an experienced programmer, you can program "truly" new controls yourself, that is, independent of the limits associated with the MS Forms library.*

The MS Forms Controls

The following subsections describe one after the other the predefined controls in the MS Forms library. The section titles relate to the texts that are shown when you let the mouse linger over one of the symbols in the toolbox window. Further examples on the use of individual controls and associated programming techniques are to be found in the two sections following.

Common Features

The MS Forms controls have a number of common properties, methods, and events that we describe here in order to avoid excessive repetition. These and some further common features can be found in the object browser under the MS Forms *Control* object.

The properties ***Cancel*** and ***Default*** identify the controls of a form that can be selected with Esc and Return, respectively (normally with the Cancel and OK buttons). The properties can be set to *True* only for a single control in a form. (The form editor automatically resets the property to *False* for all other controls.)

With ***ControlSource*** you can link the contents of a control with the contents of a cell. Changes in the table then are reflected automatically in the content of the control. (In the case of listboxes ***RowSource*** can be used to synchronize the entire list with a range of cells in a worksheet.)

The ***Tag*** property usually is of help in managing controls. A character string can be stored in the control that is not displayed.

The ***Visible*** property governs the visibility of the control. This property can be used to make individual controls appear and disappear as needed.

Common Properties

Cancel	*True* if a control can be selected by means of Esc
ControlTipText	yellow infotext (tooltip text)
ControlSource	creates the linkage to a cell in a worksheet
Default	*True* if the control can be selected by Return
RowSource	creates the linkage to a range of cells (for listboxes)
TabIndex	the number in the tab order
TabStop	*True* if the control can be selected by Tab
Tag	invisible supplementary information that may help in control management
Visible	*True* if the control is visible

Common Methods

SetFocus	moves the input focus to a control

Common Events

Enter	the control has received the input focus
Error	an error has occurred
Exit	the control has given up the input focus

Label

The label box, true to its name, provides labels for the form. A label is normally placed next to or above other controls, and it should offer a hint as to their function or the type of input that is expected. The text is set with the property *Caption* and can extend over several lines, in which case *WordWrap* must be set to *True*. The text can be aligned left, center, or right (*TextAlign*). If *AutoSize* is set to *True*, then the size of the label box is automatically adjusted to fit the length of the text.

In contrast to the Excel 5/7 label box, the font and color can be freely set with the properties *Font, BackColor*, and *ForeColor*. Further options exist for the border (*BorderStyle, BorderColor*), and the property *SpecialEffect* governs the type of 3-D effect the buttons have. Finally, a bitmap can be displayed in the label (*Picture, PicturePosition*).

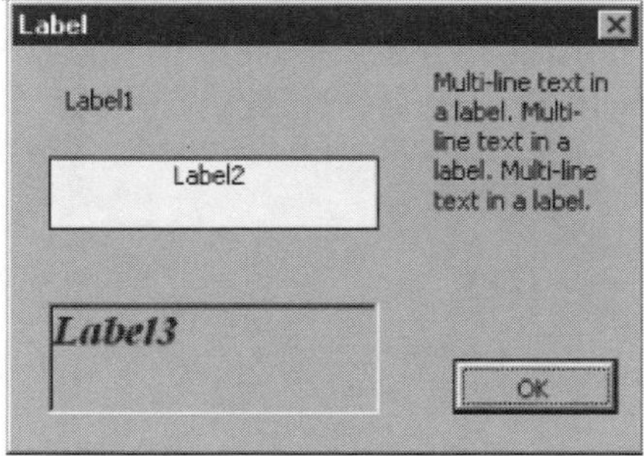

Figure 7.10. Some representative forms of the label box

Label	*Properties*
AutoSize	size of the control fits the text
BackColor	background color
BorderColor	border color
BorderStyle	border yes/no
Caption	the displayed text
Font	font style
ForeColor	text color
Picture	bitmap
PicturePosition	position at which the bitmap is displayed
SpecialEffect	3-D effect
TextAlign	text alignment (left, right, center)
WordWrap	line breaking

Label	*Event*
Click	the label box was clicked

TextBox

Text boxes make possible the input of text. In contrast to the text box of Excel 5/7, the input of cell references is not permitted. For this purpose the *RefEdit* control is provided in Excel. This is described below.

Many of the properties of the text box are identical to those of the label box, so we may avoid covering that ground here. Access to the displayed text is achieved with *Text*. The number of characters can be determined with *Len(textfield.Text)*, the number of lines with the property *LineCount*, and the current line with *CurLine*.

With the properties *MultiLine* and *Scrollbars* a multiline text input is made possible, with the display of scroll bars if applicable. With *PasswordChar* you can set a character (usually *) that is shown instead of the input text. In this way you can accept the input of a password without any curious passersby looking over the user's shoulder seeing what is being input.

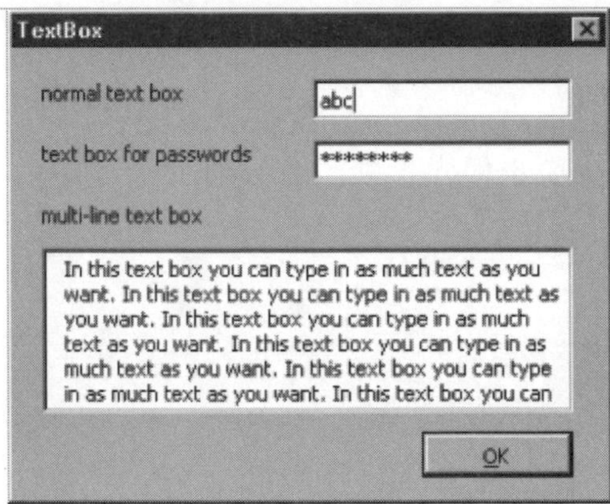

Figure 7.11. Various forms of text boxes

With *EnterFieldBehavior=0* you achieve that when a text box is activated the entire contents are automatically selected. This makes it convenient for new input and is especially practical with one-line text boxes.

EnterKeyBehavior governs the behavior of the field when Return is pressed. If the property is set to *True,* then Return allows the input of a new line. If, however, it is set to *False,* then Return selects the button with the setting *Default=True.* In that case a new line is input by pressing the combination Ctrl+Return. The meaning of *TabKeyBehavior* is analogous: The property tells whether in the control Tab the tab key can be used for input or whether that key is reserved for changing controls by moving through the tab order.

> **TIP** *If you use a text box for short input texts, you will observe the appearance of an irritatingly large empty space at the left edge of the text box. This space is governed by the default setting* SelectionMargin=True. *This setting makes it easy to select entire lines, but it makes sense only for multiline text boxes. If you set* SelectionMargin *to* False, *the space at the left margin obligingly disappears.*

Selected Text, Clipboard

Accessing selected text is accomplished via *SelText*. The properties *SelStart* and *SelLength* give the first character of the selected text and the length of the selection, respectively. The following lines demonstrate how these properties can be used.

```
With textbx
  .SelLength = 0                 ' cancel selection
  .SelStart = 0: .SelLenght = 5  ' select the first five characters
  .SelText = ""                  ' delete the selected text
  .SelStart = 10                 ' input cursor to new position
  .SelText = "abc"               ' there insert three characters
End With
```

With the methods *Copy* and *Cut* you can copy or cut text that has been selected into the clipboard. *Paste* replaces the currently selected text with the contents of the clipboard.

Events

The most important event is *Change*. It always appears when the content of a text box changes (that is, at each input or deleted character). This event occurs very frequently when text is input, so see to it that the event procedure can be processed very quickly.

The events *KeyDown*, *KeyUp*, and *KeyPress* enable a precise evaluation of keyboard events:

- *KeyPress*: This event occurs when an alphanumeric key is pressed. The ANSI code for the input character is passed to the event procedure. In addition to the alphanumeric characters, the keys Return and Esc, as well as Ctrl combinations, are reported. *KeyPress* does not occur when the user presses cursor or function keys, or keys such as Insert and Delete, and thus it is not sufficient for general control of the keyboard.

- *KeyDown*: This event occurs when any key is pressed. The internal keyboard code of the pressed key as well as the position code for the shift key are passed to the event procedure. *KeyPress* occurs not only when cursor or function keys are pressed, but also when only the Shift or Ctrl key is pressed.

- *KeyUp*: This event is the complement to *KeyDown*. It occurs when a key is released. The same parameters are passed as those for *KeyUp*.

When an alphanumeric key is pressed, Visual Basic first calls the *KeyDown* event procedure, then *KeyPress*, and finally *KeyUp*. If the key remains held down for a while, then the *KeyDown* and *KeyPress* event procedures are called several times (auto-repeat). The three events do not occur when the user does any of the following:

- uses Tab to change controls
- uses Esc to select a button for which *Cancel=True*
- uses Return to select a button for which *Default=True*.

When the *KeyPress* occurs, you have the possibility to change the ASCII code, upon which the text box will contain another character. This possibility could be used, for example, by the input of numbers to change every comma to a decimal point:

```
Private Sub TextBox1_KeyPress(ByVal KeyAscii As MSForms.ReturnInteger)
  If Chr$(KeyAscii) = "," Then KeyAscii = Asc(".")
End Sub
```

Further applications: With the function *UCase* you could transform lowercase letters into uppercase; you could respond to Return by executing a different part of the program.

TextBox	*Properties*
CurLine	current line number
EnterFieldBehavior	*0* if the entire contents are selected upon activation
EnterKeyBehavior	*True* if upon Return a new line can be input
LineCount	number of lines
MultiLine	*True* if several text lines are used
PasswordChar	placeholder character for text
Scrollbars	tells whether scroll bars are to be shown with long texts
SelectionMargin	*True* if a space appears at the left margin, facilitating selection of whole lines of text
SelLength	Length of selected text
SetStart	beginning of selected text
SetText	selected text
TabKeyBehaviour	*True* if Tab can be used to input a tab character
Text	content of the text box

TextBox	*Methods*
Copy	copy selected text to the clipboard
Cut	cut selected text to the clipboard
Paste	insert text from the clipboard to replace selected text

TextBox	*Events*
Change	text box contents have changed
KeyDown	a key was pressed
KeyPress	keyboard input
KeyUp	a key was released

ListBox and ComboBox

The MS Forms library recognizes three types of listboxes, which look different from one another but which have many similarities in their programming:

- Normal listbox (*ListBox*): The list is displayed in a rectangular field whose size is fixed when the form is created. If not all elements can be shown at once, a scroll bar appears automatically.

- Dropdown listbox (*ComboBox* with *Style=fmStyleDropDownList*): As above, but the list can be unfolded. In its folded state the control takes up much less space. This form of the listbox is probably the one most frequently used, but it is not the default setting. Do not forget to set *Style* in the properties window.

- Dropdown combination listbox (*ComboBox* with *Style=fmStyleDropDownCombo*): It is this variant that gives the ComboBox its name: The unfoldable listbox is combined with a text box in which text can be input that does not correspond to any of the list entries. This listbox thus makes possible the extension of a list through user input.

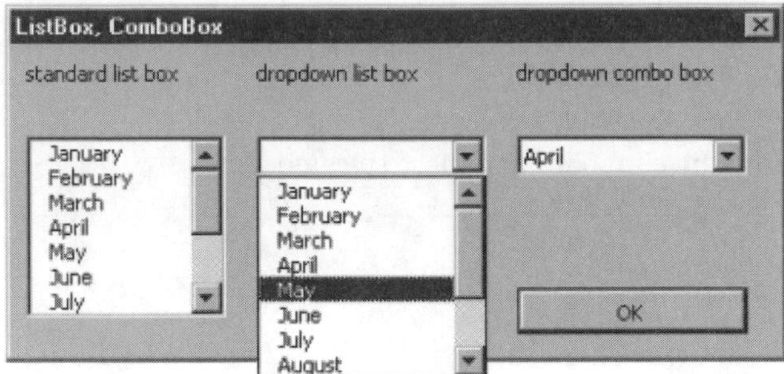

Figure 7.12. The three types of listbox

With both of these controls you can achieve an alternative representation with *ListStyle=**fmListStyleOption**:* Every list entry will now appear with an option button or check box. This setting has no effect on the function of the listbox.

TIP *Using listboxes is not difficult in principle. The problem is rather that first various options must be set correctly, and the default settings are usually unsatisfactory. The following list gives the four most frequent sources of problems in creating a useful setting. A detailed description of the properties follows below.*

BoundColumn	*0, so that* Value *contains the number of the list entry*
RowSource	*source data from a table, e.g.,* "Sheet2!A1:A5"
SelectMargin	True, *so that input is shown without the left margin*
Style	fmStyleDropDownList, *so that no text input is possible*

Access to List Elements

The individual entries of a list are passed to the control with the method *AddItem* (see the example program). Access to the list elements is achieved with the property *List(n)*. *ListIndex* gives the last selected entry (or –1 if no entry has been selected); *ListCount* gives the number of entries in the list. With *RemoveItem* individual list entries can be removed. *Clear* deletes the entire list.

The three listboxes that appear in Figure 7.12 are initialized in the following manner when the form is displayed:

```
Private Sub UserForm_Initialize()
Dim i
  For i = 1 To 12
    lstNormal.AddItem MonthName(i)
    cmbDropDown.AddItem MonthName(i)
    cmbCombo.AddItem MonthName(i)
  Next i
End Sub
```

The number of the currently selected list element is accessible via the property *ListIndex*. (The numbering begins, as with all properties of the listbox, with 0.) *Value* normally contains the same value as *ListIndex* (provided that *BoundColumn* has been left in its default state; see below). The *Text* property contains the contents of the selected element.

TIP *For some unexplained reason a selection border has been provided in the text area of the combination listbox as it is in a text box. The default setting of* SelectionMargin *is* True *(although in the text area of this control only one line can be shown). Set this property to* False *if you wish to get rid of the annoying margin.*

Multiple Selection

In normal listboxes several entries can be selected simulaneously if the property *MultiSelect* is set to *fmMultiSelectMulti (1)* or *fmMultiSelectExtended (2)*. For evaluation you have to test all the *Selected(i)* properties in a loop in order to determine which list entries were selected. (The multiple selection is accomplished via Shift-clicking or Ctrl-clicking.)

Multicolumn ListBoxes

Several columns can be displayed simultaneously in a listbox. For this to happen *ColumnCount* must be set to a value greater than 1. Access to individual list entries is achieved with *List(row, column)*, where the numbering begins with 0. References to *List* can also be made directly by means of a two-dimensional field, that is, *List=field()*. However, this is not possible in the reverse direction.

If *ColumnHead* is set to *True*, then a place for an additional header line is provided. It does not seem to be possible to achieve direct access to these entries. The headers are read automatically from an Excel table if *RowSource* has been used to set up a link to a range of cells. In the listbox in Figure 7.13 we have *RowSouce="Sheet2!B2:D6"*.

The column headers from B1:D1 are read by the listbox. With *ControlSource* an additional worksheet cell can be given that contains the number of the current column.

The widths of the columns are governed by *ColumnWidths*. In the default setting –1 all columns are the same width. (But at least 95 points; if the listbox is too narrow for this, a horizontal scroll bar is inserted.) With the setting *"2cm;3cm"* the first column will be 2 centimeters wide and the second, 3 centimeters. The width of the third column will be the amount of space remaining.

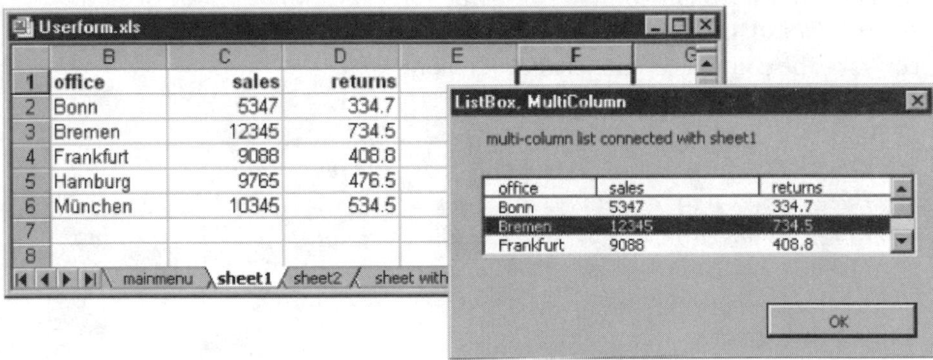

Figure 7.13. A multicolumn listbox whose content is linked to a worksheet

Since our listbox now consists of several columns, there are also several possibilities for the values that the properties *Text* and *Value* should contain when the user selects a particular row. For this purpose *TextColumn* determines which column's contents should appear in the *Text* property. Note, here, that in contrast to all other list properties, the numbering begins with 1, that is, 1 for the first column, and so on. The setting 0 indicates that it is not the contents of the column, but the column number (that is, *ListIndex*) that should appear in the particular property. Furthermore, with *TextColumn* the setting –1 is allowed. In this case *Text* contains the contents of the first column whose width is not equal to zero.

In order that the entire list available in sheet 2 be gone through in the form pictured in Figure 7.13, there is a rather complicated-looking instruction in *btnListBoxMulti_Click*:

```
' file Userform.xls, UserForm "dlgListBoxMultiColumn"
Private Sub btnListBoxMulti_Click()
  With dlgListBoxMultiColumn
    .ListBox1.RowSource = Worksheets(2).name & "!" & _
      Intersect(Worksheets(2).[b2].CurrentRegion, _
                Worksheets(2).[b2:d1000]).Address
    .Show
  End With
End Sub
```

Worksheets(2).Name returns the name of the second worksheet (that is, *"Sheet2"*).

Worksheets(2).[b2].CurrentRegion returns a *Range* object with all cells belonging to the range beginning with B2. (In Figure 7.13 *CurrentRegion* returns the range A1:D6.)

For the listbox, however, neither cell A1 (in which the index of the selected list entry is displayed) nor the header line (which the listbox determines itself) is needed. Therefore, the *CurrentRegion* range is restricted by *Intersect* to columns B–D and rows 2–1000. Thus *Intersect* forms a range of cells that have the *CurrentRegion* and B2:D1000 in common.

The entire instruction returns the result *sheet1!$B$2:$D$6* for the list in Figure 7.13.

Events

For controlling listboxes there are two events of interest: *Click* (for the selection of a list entry) and *Change* (when the text of a combination listbox is changed by keyboard input). Sometimes, *DblClick* is evaluated in order for this form of selection of an element to be interpreted as a request to exit the form.

With combination listboxes the event *DropButtonClick* is triggered before the drop-down list appears or again disappears. That can be used to build the list dynamically only when it is actually needed.

Example

In Figure 7.14 you see a form with a listbox in which the names of all worksheets of the active Excel file are presented. A double click on one of the names (or selecting a name followed by OK) activates that worksheet.

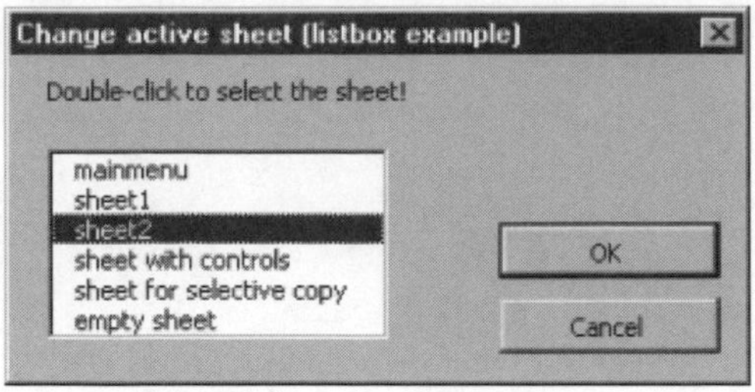

Figure 7.14. A listbox for switching into another worksheet

The programming is a piece of cake: The listbox is initialized in *UserForm_Initialize*. For this purpose a loop is executed over all worksheets (*Worksheets* enumeration). The names of the sheets are transferred into the listbox with *AddItem*.

```
' userform.xls, Userform dlgListWorksheets
' form for changing the active worksheet
' fill listbox with the names of all worksheets
Private Sub UserForm_Initialize()
  Dim wsh As Worksheet
  For Each wsh In Worksheets
    listboxSheets.AddItem wsh.Name
  Next
End Sub
```

In *btnOK_Click* a test is made as to whether a valid selection of a list element exists (that is, *ListIndex>0*). If that is the case, the selected entry (property *ListIndex*) is determined from the control's list (property *List*). The resulting character string is used for selecting a worksheet, which is activated with *Activate*. The procedure is also executed when the user selects a list entry with a double click.

```
' activate selected sheet, close form
Private Sub btnOK_Click()
  If listboxSheets.ListIndex >= 0 Then
    Worksheets(listboxSheets.List(listboxSheets.ListIndex)).Activate
    Unload Me
  Else
    Beep
  End If
End Sub
Private Sub listboxSheets_DblClick(ByVal Cancel As _
                                  MSForms.ReturnBoolean)
  btnOK_Click
End Sub
```

List and ComboBox	*Properties*
BoundColumn	column whose contents are declared in *Value*
ColumnHead	header for multicolumn lists
ColumnWidths	width of the column
ControlSource	cell with the number of the selected element
List(n)	access to list elements
List(row, column)	access for multicolumn lists
ListCount	number of list elements or rows
ListIndex	number of the selected element (beginning with 0)
ListStyle	list entry represented as an option button
MultiSelect	permit multiple selection
RowSource	cell range with list contents (e.g., *"Sheet1!A1:B3"*)
Style	*fmStyleDropDownList* or *fmStyleDropDownCombo* (*ComboBox* only)
Text	text of selected element
TextColumn	column whose contents are declared in *Text*
Value	number or text of the list element (with *BoundColumn>0*)

List and ComboBox	*Methods*
AddItem	expand list
Clear	delete list
RemoveItem	delete list entry

List and ComboBox	*Events*
Change	element selection or text input with *ComboBox*
Click	element selection
DblClick	double click on a list element
DropButtonClick	the dropdown list should be displayed (*ComboBox* only)

Check Box and OptionButton

Check boxes are useful for carrying out yes/no decisions. The current state is indicated by an "x" displayed in a small square.

The state of an option button is indicated by a dot in a round circle. In addition to this visual difference, in comparison to the check box, there is a difference in functionality as well: When one of several option buttons is activated, then all the others are automatically deactivated; that is, only one of the several options can be selected at a given moment. If there are several independent groups of option buttons in a form, then the *GroupName* property of the associated controls must be supplied with identical character strings.

The current state of both controls is taken from the *Value* property. Permitted values are *True, False,* and *Null.* (The setting *Null* denotes an undefined state. That would be useful, for example, in a check box for boldface type when a region of text is selected whose text is only partially in boldface.) When the property *TripleState* is set to *True,* then all three states can be set with the mouse (otherwise, only *True* or *False*).

> **NOTE** *For some mysterious reason it is impossible to preset the* Value *property in the form editor. Rather, you must execute the relevant instruction in* User_Initialize.

```
' file Userform.xls, "dlgOption"
Private Sub UserForm_Initialize()
  OptionButton1.Value = True
End Sub
Private Sub CheckBox1_Click()
  Label1.Font.Bold = CheckBox1.Value
End Sub
Private Sub CheckBox2_Click()
  Label1.Font.Italic = CheckBox2.Value
End Sub
Private Sub OptionButton1_Click()
    Label1.Font.Name = "Arial"
End Sub
Private Sub OptionButton2_Click()
    Label1.Font.Name = "Times New Roman"
End Sub
Private Sub OptionButton3_Click()
    Label1.Font.Name = "Courier New"
End Sub
```

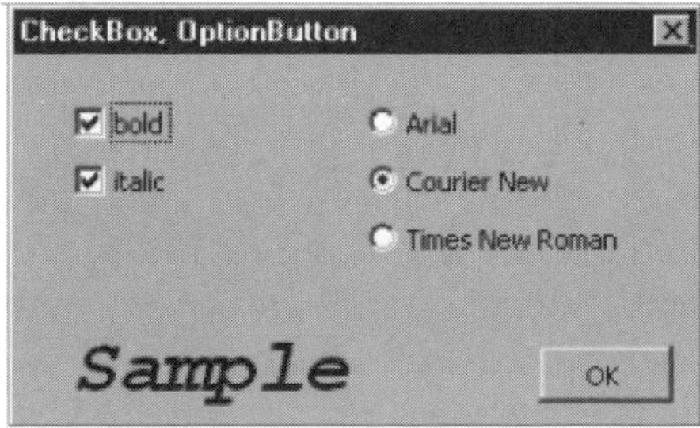

Figure 7.15. Check box and option button

CheckBox, OptionButton	*Properties*
Caption	descriptive text
TripleState	permit "undefined" (*Null*) as input
Value	current state

CheckBox, OptionButton	*Event*
Click	the state has changed

Command Buttons and Toggle Buttons

Using buttons is particularly easy. The caption text is set with *Caption*. An optional graphic image (bitmap) can be displayed in the button, which can be created with the help of the *Picture* property. One can do without a *Caption* text and create a purely graphical button. In this case there should at least be the yellow infotext provided by means of *ControlTipText*.

Toggle buttons are distinguished from normal buttons in that they remain in their pressed-in state and pop back only upon being pressed a second time. The current state can be determined with *Value* (*True/False/Null*) as with option buttons.

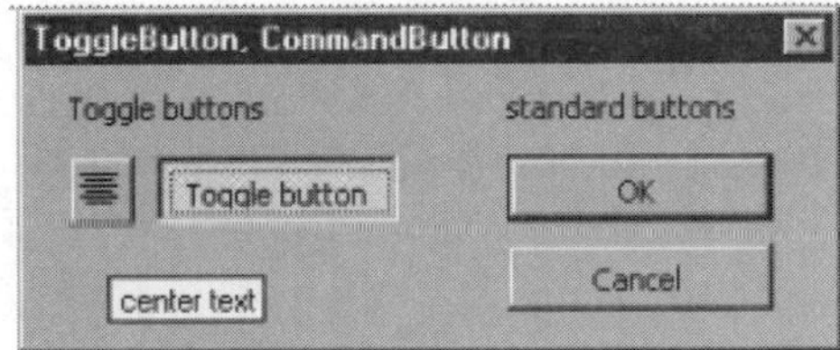

Figure 7.16. MS Forms buttons

> **NOTE** *If you use buttons directly in a worksheet (as opposed to a form), then by all means set the property* TakeFocusOnClick *to* False. *Otherwise, the keyboard focus remains in the button after it is clicked on, thereby blocking a number of other functions until a further mouse click brings the focus again into the worksheet.*

CommandButton, ToggleButton	*Properties*
AutoSize	fit button size to contents (text/graphic)
Cancel	select with Esc
Caption	caption text
ControlTipText	yellow infotext
Default	select with Return
Picture	graphic
PicturePosition	position of the graphic
TakeFocusOnClick	the setting *False* prevents the button from obtaining the input focus when clicked (important in worksheets)
TripleState	permit "undefined" (*Null*) as input
Value	current state

CommandButton, ToggleButton	*Event*
Click	the button was clicked

Frames

The frame has the job of visually collecting associated controls. All of the controls within a frame are considered to be a single unit. If the frame is moved, the controls will move with it.

One feature of frames is that a zoom factor can be given for all of its controls. The controls are correspondingly enlarged or shrunk. In rare cases this feature can be used to represent extensive forms.

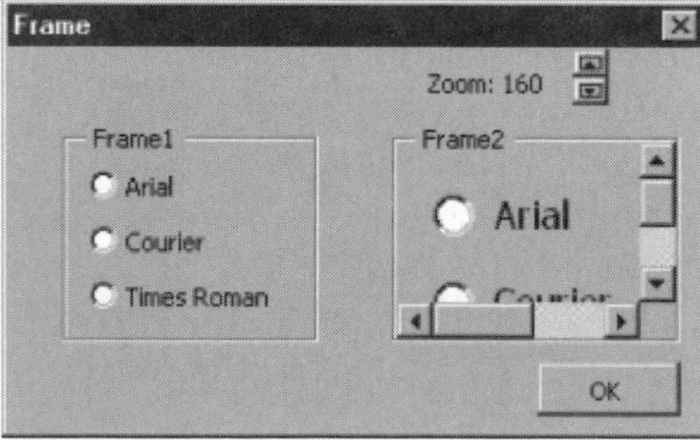

Figure 7.17. Two frames with different zoom factors

The contents of a frame can be equipped with scroll bars. In order for scroll bars to be displayed, *Scrollbars* must be set to *fmScrollbarsBoth*. If you want the scroll bars to disappear when the entire contents of the frame are visible, then you must additionally set *KeepScrollbarsVisible=fmScrollbarsNone*.

In order for the frame to know how large its scrollable contents are, the properties *ScrollWidth* and *ScrollHeight* must also be given values. The appropriate settings usually must be determined in program code (such as in *Form_Load*). The commands in *Form_Initialize* have the effect of making the scrollable region correspond to the currently visible inside dimensions of the frame. (Scoll bars will then be required when either the zoom factor is increased or the frame decreased in size.) *InsideWidth* and *InsideHeight* specify the usable inside dimensions of the frame.

The following lines show the necessary initialization code for displaying scroll bars correctly. The temporary setting of the zoom factor to 100 percent is necessary to ensure that the entire inner region can be displayed.

```
Private Sub UserForm_Initialize()
  With Frame2
    .Zoom = 110
    .ScrollWidth = .InsideWidth
    .ScrollHeight = .InsideHeight
    .Zoom = 100
  End With
End Sub
```

With the *Controls* enumeration you can access all the controls within the frame. *ActiveControl* refers to the active control within the frame. The methods *AddControl* and *RemoveControl* enable the insertion and deletion of controls.

Frame	*Properties*
ActiveControl	active control within a group
Controls	access to the individual controls
InsideWidth/-Height	size of the usable inside area
KeepScrollbarsVisible	always display scroll bars
Scrollbars	specifies whether scroll bars should be used
ScrollLeft/-Top	upper left corner of visible region
ScrollWidth/-Height	size of scrollable region
Zoom	zoom factor for the contents of the region

Frame	*Methods*
AddControl	insert control
RemoveControl	delete control

MultiPage, TabStrip

The controls *MultiPage* and *TabStrip* offer two ways of creating multipage forms. The resulting forms are indistinguishable, but the effort required to set up and program is more difficult in the case of *TabStrip.* (There is really no good reason for *TabStrip* to be in the MS Forms library at all.) Therefore, in this section we restrict our attention to a description of the *MultiPage* control.

Multipage Forms

Multipage forms are often used to allow for a large number of options to be set in a single form (see the Excel OPTIONS dialog). There is, however, the possibility that the user will get lost among too many choices. Take care that your sheets are easily distinguishable one from the other with respect to their function and that the captions make sense. Less can often be more! Forms that have so may sheets that their captions take up several lines constitute an unreasonable demand on the user.

The user should be able to exit a multipage form at any time (independently of the currently visible page). Therefore, place the OK, Cancel, and other such buttons outside the individual sheets!

The MultiPage *Control*

The creation of a multipage form is extremely simple, requiring not a single line of code. You simply insert a *MultiPage* control, activate one of the pages with a mouse click, and there insert the desired controls. The moment you click on the second page, the first disappears into the background and you can proceed at your leisure to insert controls into the second page. With the pop-up menu summoned with a right-click of the mouse you can change the captions and sequence of pages, and insert new pages or delete existing ones.

You will have an easier time with the *MultiPage* control if you understand from the outset that you are working with not one but several controls. When you insert a *MultiPage* control into a form, then at once two *Page* objects are inserted into the *MultiPage* control. The *MultiPage* control is thus primarily a container for *Page* objects. For their part, the *Page* objects then take responsibility for the controls for the individual pages of the form. (To be precise, you are dealing with three rather than two objects: *Pages* is an independent enumeration object, even if this is usually unnoticeable.)

> **NOTE** *In setting the properties, take care that you have activated the correct control. It is almost impossible to click on the* MultiPage *control in the form editor. The editor always activates an embedded* Page *control. Select the* MultiPage *control in the listbox of the properties window. Furthermore, it is impossible to set the properties of several sheets simultaneously, or to copy sheets and insert them via the clipboard.*

One of the most interesting properties of the *MultiPage* object is *TabOrientation*. With this you can specify whether the page caption (the tab) is displayed above, below, on the left, or on the right. If you have very many tabs (which will make for a form that is confusing and difficult to use, such as the options forms in Word), you can set *MultiRow=True* to display the captions over several lines.

Access to the *Page* object is achieved, perhaps not surprisingly, by means of the *Pages* property. This property is also the default property, so that *MultiPage1(1)* can access the first *Page* object. The number of the currently active *Page* object can be retrieved and edited with the *Value* property.

If you wish to insert new pages or delete existing ones in program code, you can use the *Pages* methods *Add* and *Remove*. This leads to an *AddControl*, respectively *RemoveControl*, event for the *MultiPage* object.

Let us now proceed to the properties of the individual pages (that is, those of the *Page* object): These exhibit practically the same events, properties, and methods as the frame. Thus you can equip individual pages with scroll bars, shrink or enlarge with *Zoom*, and so on. What is new are the properties *TransitionEffect* and *TransitionPeriod*, with which imaginative programmers can set fanciful effects for changing pages.

Example

Our example program is once again merely for the purposes of demonstration. To set the type style of a cell in a worksheet a two-page form is summoned. In the first sheet the type attributes can be set (boldface, italic), while in the second sheet five font familes are offered from which to choose. When the form appears, the *Font* object of the cell is analyzed and the corresponding options are shown. (Of course, there is a much more complete, and above all predefined, form for setting the type style; the example here is just to demonstrate the principle.)

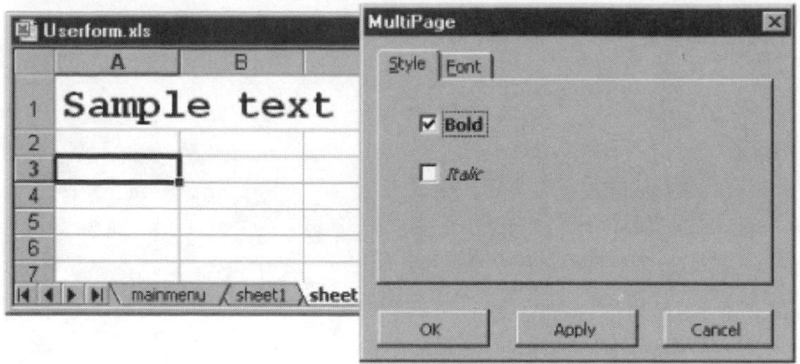

Figure 7.18. A simple multipage form

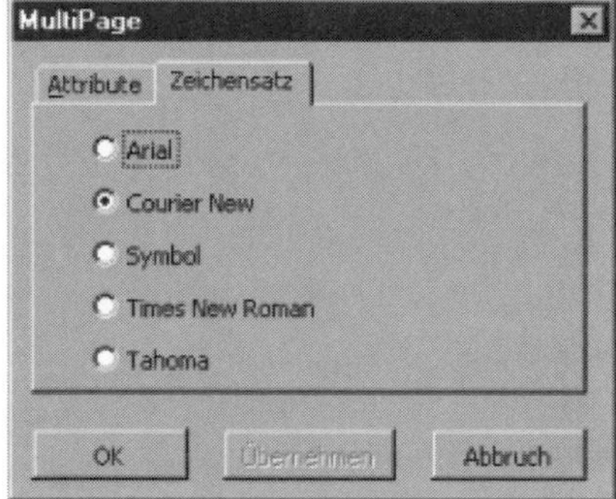

Figure 7.19. The second page of the form

The program code for this form has little to do with the fact that it is dealing with a multipage form. The programming effort is concentrated in editing the *Font* object correctly. Before the form is called, the *Font* object to be edited must be written into the public module variable *fnt*. In the procedure *UserForm_ Activate*, which is executed automatically when the form is displayed, the option buttons and control boxes corresponding to the properties of *fnt* are preset.

```
' Userform.xls, UserForm "dlgMultiPage"
Public fnt As Font
Private Sub OptionButton1_Click() ' as soon as something changes,
  CommandButton2.Enabled = True   ' "Apply" button is activated
End Sub
Private Sub OptionButton2_Click()         ' as above
Private Sub OptionButton3_Click()
Private Sub OptionButton4_Click()
Private Sub OptionButton5_Click()
Private Sub CheckBox1_Click()
Private Sub CheckBox2_Click()
```

The three event procedures for the buttons OK, Apply, and Cancel offer few surprises. According to which button is pressed a change is made or the form is exited.

```
Private Sub CommandButton1_Click()   'OK
  WriteAttributes
  Unload Me
End Sub
Private Sub CommandButton2_Click()   ' Apply
  WriteAttributes
  CommandButton2.Enabled = False
End Sub
Private Sub CommandButton3_Click()   ' Cancel
  Unload Me
End Sub
```

The procedure *ReadAttributes* first tests whether either or both of the properties *Bold* and *Italic* of the *Font* object are set. Depending on the result, one or both of the corresponding control boxes are initialized. Somewhat more original is the loop over all controls in the second page of the *MultiPage.* Here the fact is made use of that the caption text of the option buttons corresponds exactly with the name of the font. If the name of the *fnt* font agrees with that of the control, then the *Value* property of this option button is set to *True.*

Furthermore, the button Apply is deactivated (that is, *Enabled=False*). This button becomes active only when a change is made to the form, that is, when there are actually some data to process. For this reason each control on both pages of the form has an event procedure with *CommandButton2.Enabled = True.*

```
' read data from fnt variable
Sub ReadAttributes()
  Dim c As Control
  If fnt.Bold Then CheckBox1 = True Else CheckBox1 = False
  If fnt.Italic Then CheckBox2 = True Else CheckBox2 = False
  For Each c In MultiPage1("Page2").Controls
    If fnt.Name = c.Caption Then c.Value = True
  Next
  CommandButton2.Enabled = False
End Sub
```

> **NOTE** *Originally, it was planned that* ReadAttributes *would be called in* UserForm_Activate *automatically each time the form was displayed. Because of a bug in Excel 97 the* Activate *event procedure is not reliably executed each time the form is displayed. For this reason* ReadAttributes *must be executed in code for calling the form before* Show *is executed.*

WriteAttributes has precisely the opposite task. There the current state of the control box is evaluated and *Font* correspondingly changed.

```
' write data to the fnt variable
Sub WriteAttributes()
  Dim c As Control
  If CheckBox1 Then fnt.Bold = True Else fnt.Bold = False
  If CheckBox2 Then fnt.Italic = True Else fnt.Italic = False
  For Each c In MultiPage1("Page2").Controls
    If c.Value Then fnt.name = c.Caption
  Next
End Sub
```

The form is called by the following event procedure:

```
' file Userform.xls, "mainmenu" module
Private Sub btnMultipage_Click()
  Worksheets(3).Activate
  With dlgMultiPage
    Set .fnt = Worksheets(3).[a1].Font
    .ReadAttributes
    .Show
  End With
End Sub
```

MultiPage	*Properties*
Pages	refers to the *Pages* enumeration object
Pages(n)	refers to an individual *Page* object
MultiRow	several rows of tabs for page selection
TabOrientation	tabs left/right/above/below

Page	*Properties*
Caption	page caption (tab text)
Scrollbars	specifies whether scroll bars should be used
KeepScrollbarsVisible	always display scroll bars
ScrollWidth/-Height	size of scrollable region
ScrollLeft/-Top	upper left corner of visible region
InsideWidth/-Height	size of usable inside region
Zoom	zoom factor for page contents
TransitionEffect, -Period	effect in changing to another page

Scrollbar and SpinButton

Scroll bars are useful for selecting an integer from a given range of values. In comparison to Excel 5/7 scroll bars, the allowed range of numbers has been extended to the *Long* range (that is, $\pm 2*10^9$). The scroll bar can be used in both the horizontal and vertical directions according to the way you have presented your controls.

A spin button is an emaciated variant of the scroll bar. It consists of two small arrows pointing up and down, or left and right. A spin button does not have a scroll bar.

The most imporant proerties are *Min* (the smallest allowed value), *Max* (largest allowed value), *SmallChange* (size of change when the arrow is clicked), and *Value* (current value). For the scroll bar there is the additional property *LargeChange* for the sideways movement of the scrollable region. *Delay* specifies the time in milliseconds by which the event is delayed and thus controls the maximum speed of change.

In the form displayed in Figure 7.20 the three scroll bars allow the user to set the background color of an image. The code consists of seven identical procedures:

```
' Userform.xls, UserForm "dlgScrollbar"
Private Sub UserForm_Activate()
  Image1.BackColor = RGB(scrR, scrG, scrB)
End Sub
Private Sub scrR_Change() ' as above
Private Sub scrG_Change()
Private Sub scrB_Change()
Private Sub scrR_Scroll()
Private Sub scrG_Scroll()
Private Sub scrB_Scroll()
```

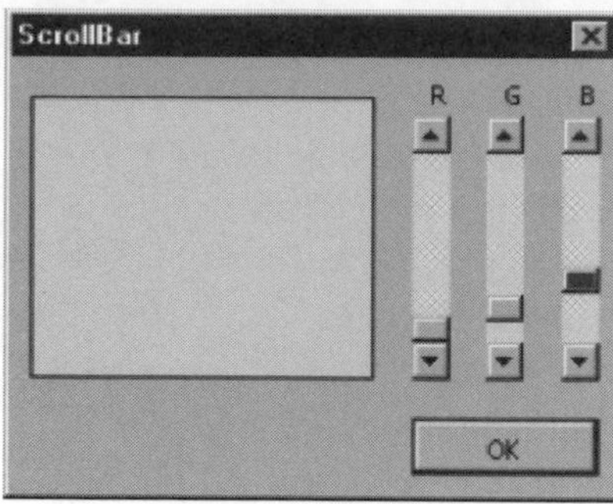

Figure 7.20. Three scroll bars

ScrollBar, SpinButton	*Properties*
Delay	delay between events in milliseconds
LargeChange	sideways change (for *Scrollbar* only)
Min/Max	allowed range of values
Orientation	arrow up/down or left/right
SmallChange	change amount when button is clicked
Value	current value

ScrollBar, SpinButton	*Properties*
Change	*Value* has changed
Scroll	scroll region has been moved (*Scrollbar* only)
SpinDown	lower (right-hand) arrow was selected (*SpinButton* only)
SpinUp	upper (left-hand) arrow was selected (*SpinButton* only)

Image

The *Picture* property is used to display a bitmap file on an object (image field). If a graphic is not placed in the properties window, but is to be loaded by program code, you can use *LoadPicture*:

```
Image1.Picture = LoadPicture("filename")
```

A host of further properties govern the resulting display: *PictureAlignment* specifies how the bitmap is to be positioned if it is larger than the image field image. *PictureSizeMode* tells whether the bitmap should be resized to fit the image field. *PictureTiling* determines whether the bitmap should be repeated horizontally or vertically to make use of the entire available space (as is used for the background bitmap of the Windows screen).

Images with 256 colors are generally displayed in MS Forms forms at lower quality (that is, fewer colors). This seems to depend on the color palette used by Excel.

There are also some properties available that have been discussed previously: *AutoSize=True* has the effect of making the image field fit the bitmap. *Border* controls the border around the image field, while *SpecialEffect* produces 3-D effects for the border. With this, one can give the image field the appearance of a graphical button. With the program that appears in Figure 7.21 you can try out various effects.

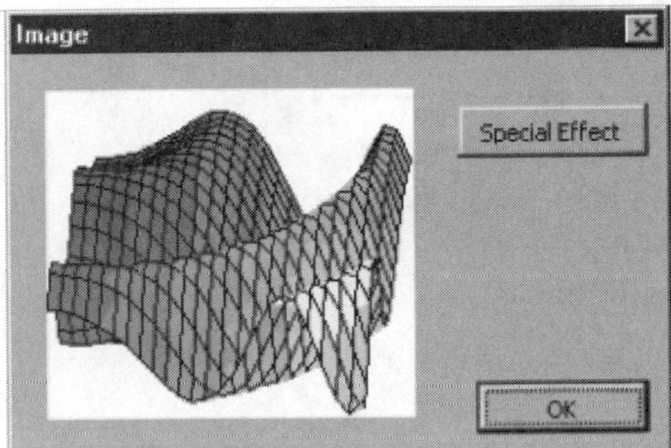

Figure 7.21. Test program for the SpecialEffect property

Image	*Properties*
AutoSize	image field is made to fit the bitmap
Border	border control
Picture	bitmap
PictureAlignment	positions the bitmap
PictureSizeMode	scaling for the bitmap
PictureTiling	*True* if the bitmap is to be repeated horizontally and vertically
SpecialEffect	3-D effect for the border

Image	*Event*
Click	the control was clicked

Formulas (RefEdit)

The *RefEdit* control facilitates input of cell references, that is, addresses of ranges of cells. (In Excel 5/7 this task was performed by the text box when *Edit Validation* was set to *Formula*.) The *RefEdit* control does not belong to the MS Forms library, but is an independent ActiveX control. *RefEdit* has two features that distinguish it from all other controls. First, it is possible to select a range of cells in a worksheet and even to change worksheets while the input cursor is in the control. (With all other controls Excel responds to this bizarre request with a beep.) Second, the entire form shrinks to the size of the *RefEdit* control, so that the form does not take up space needed for selecting the range.

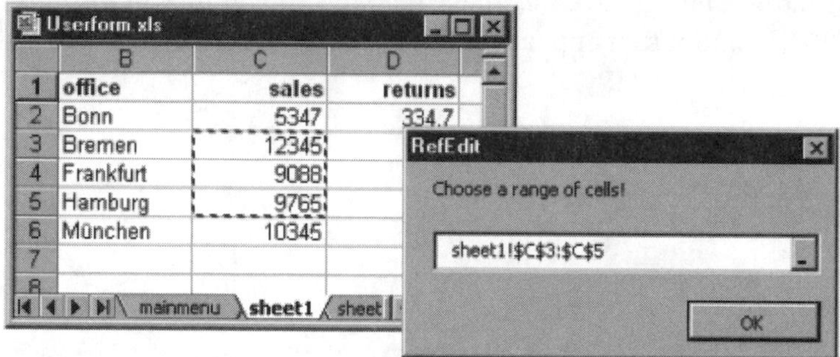

Figure 7.22. Input of a range of cells in a RefEdit control

Figure 7.23. The shrunken control

Figure 7.24. Result of the selection

The *RefEdit* control is provided with a large assortment of properties, methods, and events, most of which you will never need to use. (Many properties are the same as those of the text box.) The *Value* property contains, according to the selection, a character string with the cell reference, for example, *"sheet1!$A$1"* or *"[book2]sheet1!$B$13"*, the latter case for when the range of cells is located in another Excel file.

> **CAUTION** *The RefEdit form does not have about it the air of a finished product. For one, the CPU load climbs frequently (though not always) to 100 percent when a form with a RefEdit control is displayed. Furthermore, the control offers a large number of events, but the only important one, namely* Change, *is not triggered at every change. If you wish to carry out a validation control or a calculation based on what has been input, you can do that only in the event procedure of a button.*

Sad to say, in a *RefEdit* control not only cell references, but an arbitrary character string, can be input. But there is no function that allows you to determine whether the Excel corresponds to a correct cell reference. You should therefore back up the following code with an error-handling routine.

After completion of the example form in Figure 7.24 the formula of the selected range of cells and the sum of numbers in those cells is displayed in an alert form. The requisite code for displaying the alert form is as follows:

```
' Userform.xls, UserForm "dlgRefEdit"
Private Sub CommandButton1_Click()
  On Error Resume Next
  Hide
  MsgBox "You have selected the range " & RefEdit1.Value & _
    ". The sum of these cells is: " & _
    WorksheetFunction.Sum(Range(RefEdit1.Value))
  If Err Then
    MsgBox RefEdit1.Value & " is not a valid range of cells"
  End If
End Sub
```

RefEdit	*Properties*
Value	contains a character string with the cell reference

RefEdit	*Events*
Change	*Value* has changed (unfortunately, the event is not always triggered)

The UserForm Object

Now that we have described all the important controls, we should say a few words about the object for representing the form. All forms are based on the *UserForm* object. This object has a large number of properties that you already know from other controls: how in a frame all controls in a form can be addressed with the enumeration *Controls*; how with *Controls.Add* and *Controls.Remove* additional controls can be added and controls deleted. *ActiveControl* refers to the control that currently exhibits the input focus. With *Zoom* the scaling factor for the inside region of a form can be set between 10 and 400 percent.

The background of the form can be underlaid with a bitmap grahpic. The bitmap is loaded by means of the *Picture* property. All the options for representing graphics that were available for an image field are available here.

Displaying the Form

To display a form you use the method *Show*. Normally, the form is displayed in modal form, that is, the form must be terminated before control is passed back to Excel. Beginning with Excel 2000 there is also the option of displaying the form modeless by specifying the optional parameter *vbModeless*.

```
dlgName.Show                'display form in normal mode
dlgName.Show vbModeless     'display form modeless
```

Posiitoning the Form

It is interesting to note that there are certain *UserForm* properties and methods for which you can search in the object browser in vain. For example, with *StartupPosition* you can set the place at which the form appears on the screen. There are four possibilities:

0 manual positioning via the properties *Left* and *Top*

1 centered in the Excel window: the default

2 centered on the screen

3 Windows default position (upper left corner of the screen)

Completely independent of *StartupPosition* you can have a form appear at an arbitrary place if you set the properties *Left* and *Top* in the *UserForm_Activate* event procedure. The ideal spot, namely in the neighborhood of the actual mouse position, cannot be set without DLL functions.

Closing the Form

There are two ways in which a form can be closed: the method *Hide* and the command *Unload*, to which a reference to the form—the property *Me*—is passed as parameter. This apparent duplication often causes confusion. However, in this case the two commands carry out two completely different operations.

Unload Me closes the form and clears it from memory. All local variables in the module belonging to the form are lost. If the form is later displayed with *Show*, it is reloaded into memory and appears as if for the first time in an uninitialized state.

Hide makes the current form invisible. Visually, the effect is the same as that of *Unload*, but internally the form remains in memory. *Show* shows the form as it was last displayed. This means that earlier text inputs or option settings remain available when the form is shown again.

Thus the decision whether to use *Unload* or *Hide* depends on the use to which it will be put. Usually, *Unload Me* is preferable, because the form is cleared from memory. But if you wish to access the form's properties or variables outside of the module belonging to the form, or if the form's settings are to be preserved from one call to the next, then *Hide* is the better choice.

Events

The *UserForm* object recognizes a number of familiar events, such as *Click*, *DblClick*, *MouseDown*, *MouseMove*, and *MouseUp* for precise control of the mouse, as well as *KeyDown*, *KeyUp*, and *KeyPress* for keyboard events.

For managing the form the events *Activate*, *Deactivate*, *Initialize*, and *Terminate* are helpful: ***Initialize*** occurs when the form is loaded into memory (before it is displayed for the first time). ***Terminate*** occurs when the form is later removed from memory (that is, when the controls and variables contained within are deleted). *Terminate* is triggered both by *Unload Me* and through clicking the Close box (that is, the x in the upper right corner of the form).

Activate occurs (if necessary after *Initialize*) every time the form is displayed. The difference between it and *Terminate* is that *Activate*, for example, also occurs at subsequent displays of a form that was closed with *Hide*. (In this case *Initialize* does not occur again, since the form remains in memory and therefore does not need to be reinitialized.)

Deactivate occurs only when a second form is displayed while the first form remains visible. If the second form is closed (whereby the first becomes again active), another *Activate* event is triggered.

> **CAUTION** *In Excel 97 there were occasional problems with the* Activate *event. This event occurred only at the first display of a form, but not again (or only when the development environment was open). This problem has apparently been solved in Excel 2000. But you should keep your eye on the situation if you wish to program applications that are to run under Excel 97 as well as Excel 2000.*

Avoiding Form Termination via the Close Box

Sometimes, the user is to be prevented from being able to close the form with the x-button in the upper right-hand corner of the form. In this case the event ***QueryClose*** (apparently forgotten about in the Office 2000 documentation) occurs. The parameter *CloseMode* specifies for what reasons the window can be closed:

vbFormControlMenu (0)	close button
vbFormCode (1)	*Unload* instruction in code
vbAppWindow (2)	Windows is terminated (shutdown)
vbAppTaskManager (3)	program end by the task manager

With *Cancel* the attempt to exit the form can be blocked.

```
' Do not exit the form with the close button
Private Sub UserForm_QueryClose(Cancel%, CloseMode%)
  If CloseMode = vbFormControlMenu Then Cancel = True
End Sub
```

UserForm	*Properties*
ActiveControl	active control within the group
Controls	access to controls
InsideWidth/-Height	size of available internal region
KeepScrollbarsVisible	always show scroll bars
Picture	bitmap graphic
PictureAlignment	position of the picture
PictureSizeMode	picture scaling
PictureTiling	*True* if the image should be repeated horizontally and vertically

Scrollbars	determines whether scroll bars are to be used
ScrollLeft/-Top	upper left corner of the visible region
ScrollWidth/-Height	size of the scrollable region
Zoom	zoom factor

UserForm	*Events*
Activate	the form is displayed or reactivated (after *Deactivate*)
Click	the form (not a control) was clicked
Deactivate	the form loses the focus because a subform is displayed
Initialize	the form is loaded into memory (initialization)
QueryClose	the form should be closed (close box)
Terminate	the form is removed from memory (cleanup tasks)

Placing Controls Directly into Worksheets

Most of the controls introduced in the previous section can be used not only in forms, but directly in worksheets and charts. The exceptions are *MultiPage* and *TabStrip* for multipage forms, *RefEdit* for cell references, and *Frame*. Controls in worksheets make it possible to create tables that are very easy to use. Here are a few application examples:

- You can provde a button to save or print the active worksheet or for some other frequently used process.
- With a control box or option button various calculation options within the table can be selected.
- A spin button can be used for conveniently setting the parameters of a calculation.
- A listbox can be inserted for selection from among various calculational models.
- A program can be centrally controlled by means of a group of buttons.

What are the advantages of worksheets with controls? The greatest advantage, in comparison to their use in forms, is that they are much more flexible in worksheets. The user has the possibility of setting the visible range of the table with scroll bars. Problems that can arise with working with a large form on a laptop with 680×480 pixels disappear when the control is in a worksheet.

There is also greater flexibility in the application. While a form must be closed before further work in Excel is possible, a jump from one worksheet to the next is always possible.

A further advantage for worksheets is that all the formatting and calculational features of worksheets can be used in parallel with the controls. For example, a chart can be updated according to the setting of a spin button.

Where there are so many advantages, there must be some drawbacks. The most significant of these is that the controls in worksheets cannot be operated via keyboard input. There is no way of associating a control to a key or to move among controls with Tab. (This drawback should not be underestimated, since is applies precisely to those applications that are used frequently and thus should have maximal efficiency. The only solution is to construct procedures for keyboard management of the controls (property *OnKey*), but that involves considerable programming effort.)

Another disadvantage is that worksheets with controls are unsuitable for being run by add-ins. (Add-ins are generally invisible and are usually run by forms. See Chapter 14.)

Finally, we should mention that lists (databases) can be combined in worksheets with drop-down listboxes. These listboxes, however, are not inserted into the worksheet as controls, but are activated with DATA|FILTER|AUTOFILTER and are managed directly by Excel.

Since with these listboxes we are dealing not with true controls, but with an aid for structuring data, autofilters will be discussed in the chapter on data management, Chapter 11.

> **CAUTION** *In copying an Excel 97 worksheet with embedded MS Forms controls these controls are copied, but they receive new names (*CommandButton1, CommandButton2*, etc.). However, the program code is not changed correspondingly, and thus the connection between controls and code is lost.*
>
> *In the case of controls that have been added to an Excel 2000 worksheet this problem no longer arises. But if you use an existing Excel 97 file under Excel 2000, the problem is still there. The solution is to change under Excel 2000 all the names of controls. Excel thereby "notices" the change. (Your best bet is to change the names twice, the second change being back to the original name. Thus you save the effort of revising your code.)*

Working Techniques

Most of what you have learned about the forms editor you can now forget. It is simply amazing in how many particulars working with controls in tables is inconsistent with the forms editor.

Inserting controls is accomplished as was done with forms. But working with controls is much more difficult, since Excel assumes every time you click on it that you actually wish to use the control. For this reason you can switch between a work mode and design mode with the DESIGN MODE tool. The controls can be worked on only within design mode.

> **TIP** *If you wish to insert controls into a worksheet, you must activate the "control toolbox" toolbar.*
>
> *Take care that you do not accidentally activate the similar-looking "forms" toolbar. This toolbar contains the Excel 5/7 controls, which look the same but behave differently and are programmed differently as well.*

There is no longer a simple mouse click for providing captions for controls. You have to select OPTIONBUTTON OBJECT|EDIT from the pop-up menu. Now you can edit the text (Ctrl+Return adds a new line). The input is ended not with Return, but with Esc! (This goes against all tenets of good practice under Windows.)

Most of the rest of the properties can be set via the properties window. However, not all of the properties known from the forms editor are available. To top it off, many of the properites have different names (such as *LinkedControl* instead of *ControlSource*, and *ListFillRange* instead of *RowSource*).

> **TIP** *The selection of several controls can be accomplished quite easily by drawing a frame about them with the mouse after having first clicked on the* SELECT OBJECTS *button in the "Drawing" toolbar.*

> **TIP** *It often takes considerable effort to place controls: All buttons should be as close to the same size as possible, arranged in a row, and be the same distance apart. Unfortunately, the* FORMAT *commands known from the forms editor are not all available in worksheets. Some of the commands are hidden in the "drawing " toolbar* (ALIGN AND DISTRIBUTE). *If you wish to make several controls the same width or height, select the controls (mouse plus* Shift *instead of the otherwise usual* Ctrl*) and input a numerical value for* Width *or* Height *in the properties window.*
>
> *If in copying a button you wish to move in only horizontally or vertically, you can press the mouse button together with* Shift+Ctrl.

> **POINTER** *You can find examples of worksheets with controls in the sheets "mainmenu" and "sheet with controls" in* `Userform.xls`. *Further application examples can be found in Chapter 1 (literature database) as well as in Chapter 9 (templates): There, for example, a control box is placed to make it possible to switch between internal and external taxation (final amount with or without value-added tax, VAT) or to select one from among several rental car options (with differing price categories). Listboxes come yet again into Excel tables that are conceived as questionnaires. An example for setting up and evaluating such a form can be found in Chapter 12.*

Formatting Controls

While properties specific to MS Forms are set via the properties window, there are some additional Excel-specific properties that can be edited in the dialog FORMAT CONTROL. (To be precise, we are dealing here with properties of the *Shape* object, which is used internally for embedding controls; see below.)

This dialog is invoked by way of the pop-up menu associated to the control. The settings of greatest interest are offered by the page called "Properties," where it can be determined how the size and position of the control change when column width and row height change. Moreover, here one may specify whether the control should be printed together with the rest of the table (the default is to print it).

> **TIP** *Excel automatically uses the font (* Font *property) MS sans serif. This font, however, is very difficult to read when the zoom factor for the worksheet is less than 100 percent. You would be better advised to use the font Arial or Tahoma.*

> **TIP** *Worksheets, unlike forms, are badly protected against (often unintentional) alteration by the user. As soon as the format of a worksheet has been determined, you should protect it against unintentional alterations. To this end first deactivate the default activated protection for all cells and controls that should remain changeable (via the pop-up menu* FORMAT CONTROL *or* FORMAT CELLS, *followed by the dialog sheet "Protection"). Then activate the protection function for the entire sheet with* TOOLS|PROTECTION| PROTECT SHEET.

Properties for Positioning Controls (Shape Object)

The embedding of controls in worksheets is carried out with ***Shape*** objects with *Type=msoOLEControlObject* (see also Chapter 10). The properties for positioning controls are thus based on the *Shape* properties: For each control the upper left corner (*Left* and *Top*) as well as width and height (*Width* and *Height*) are saved. These coordinates relate to the upper left-hand corner of the form or worksheet. *TopLeftCell* and *BottomRightCell* specify, furthermore, the cells beneath the upper left or beneath the lower right corner of the control

Placement determines how the control is to behave when changes to the worksheet are made. The setting *xlMoveAndSize* causes the control to be moved and resized when the worksheet is moved or resized. (The properties *Left, Top, Width,* and *Height* are thus automatically changed.) With the setting *xlMove* the size remains constant, but the location remains variable. With the setting *xlFreeFloating* the size and position are independent of the table's format; thus *Left* and *Top* do not change, regardless of how you may change the rows and columns.

> **TIP** *All the properties listed here are valid not only for controls, but also for all other drawing objects (such as lines, arrows, OLE objects, embedded charts).*

Communication Between Controls and the Worksheet

Communication between controls and the worksheet is carried out by a ***ControlFormat*** object, which can be addressed via the like-named property of the *Shape* object. The *ControlFormat* object is normally transparent. Its properties appear, to the extent that it makes sense, in the properties window of the control, and they can also be employed in program code as control properties (affecting, for example, *LinkedCell, ListFillRange,* and *PrintObject*).

> **CAUTION** *In the default setting a button maintains the input focus after it has been clicked. In forms this is no problem. However, as long as the input focus is within some object of a worksheet, Excel will refuse to carry out all operations. Completely correct code therefore no longer functions correctly, and you can change neither worksheet cells nor the user interface. And on top of everything, the error messages that appear are completely useless.*

Special Features of Buttons

A solution to this problem lies in the property *TakeFocusOnClick=False.* With this even when a button is clicked the focus remains where it was previously, and you can carry out all the operations of the event procedure. Why the default setting for this property is not *False* is a secret maintained by the wizards at Microsoft (or perhaps not).

The property *TakeFocusOnClick* exists, alas, only for buttons, though it is often needed for other controls. For example, if after a control box is clicked you would like the input focus to shift to a cell of the worksheet, you can add the following line to the *Click* event procedure of the control:

```
Me.Range("C1").Activate
```

Me refers here to the worksheet in which the control is located (since the event procedure is located in the class module of the worksheet). C1 is an arbitrary cell. If you wish to move the focus to the cell next to the control, you can use the following command:

```
CheckBox1.TopLeftCell.Activate
```

Special Features of Listboxes

The contents of a listbox can be set with the *ListFillRange* property. The result of the selection is written into the cell specified by *LinkedControl.*

In contrast to the Excel 5/7 listbox, the selected list text and not the index number is transferred to the *ControlSource* cell. Often, however, an index number is needed for further processing of the selection, in which case one should set *BoundColumn* to 0.

But then there is still a difference between the Excel 2000 and Excel 5/7 listboxes: The *ControlSource* cell contains values between 0 and *ListCount-1* (instead of the previous 1 and *ListCount*). You can take this into consideration in the further evaluation of the selection, but it is now no longer possible to distinguish between the first list entry (value 0) and no value at all (value *Null*). The reason for this is that in Excel worksheets *Null* is occasionally interpreted as 0 (and sometimes also as the value *#NV*). Unfortunately, I have no explanation as to why Excel interprets *Null* in different ways as the mood strikes it.

The next feature concerns initialization: When a worksheet with a listbox is loaded, no entry of this control is activated. *ListIndex* has the value –1. If this undefined state is unwished for, then a definite state must be established in *Worksheet_Open* (object "This Workbook"). For example, with *ListIndex=0* the first entry can be activated.

> **CAUTION** *Listboxes with* ListStyle=fmListStylePlain *(that is, in the default setting) are sometimes erroneously displayed; that is, not all list entries are visible. You can solve this problem with* ListStyle=fmListStyleOption, *which displays the list entries as option buttons.*

Program Code

The event procedures associated to the controls are to be found in the module belonging to the associated worksheet. If you click on the tool VIEWCODE or select the like-named command from the pop-up menu, you are transported into the development environment, where the relevant instructions *Sub* and *End Sub* are immediately inserted (in the case of a new control, that is; for a control that has already been programmed, its code is shown).

The Start Menu for Userform.xls

The sheet "mainmenu" in `Userform.xls` is command central for this workbook (see Figure 7.25). Actually, this sheet contains only a few buttons. Its attraction is in the visual formatting of the buttons and the formatting of the background, which leads the user to forget that this sheet is in reality an ordinary worksheet.

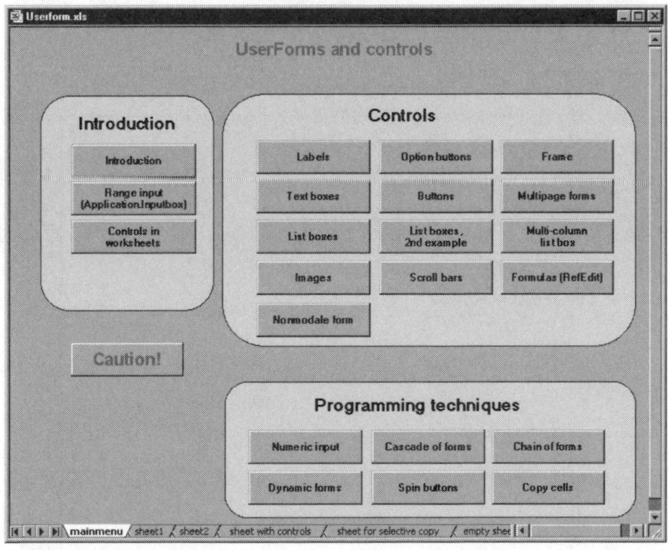

Figure 7.25. Command Central for Userform.xls

The event procedures associated to the buttons are quite simple, so that we have provided here only one example:

```
' Userform.xls, Object "sheet1"
Private Sub btnFrame_Click()
  dlgFrame.Show
End Sub
```

For the visual presentation of the worksheet all cells were simply provided with a background color. Under the buttons was placed a rectangle with rounded corners in a contrasting color. The rectangle was added as an AutoForm object ("Drawing" toolbar) and placed under the buttons with the pop-up menu entry ORDER|SEND TO BACK. Furthermore, with TOOLS|OPTIONS the row and column headers and the gridlines were made invisible.

A Simple Calculational Model with Controls

The sheet "sheet with controls" demonstrates the relationship between a control box and a listbox via a simple table with a chart. The control box is used to determine whether in the table beneath it a discount should be given. The listbox makes possible the selection from among five different discount models.

The worksheet and its associated graphic are updated immediately. The example is rather simple, but it demonstrates rather impressively how just by clicking on a control the calculational result changes.

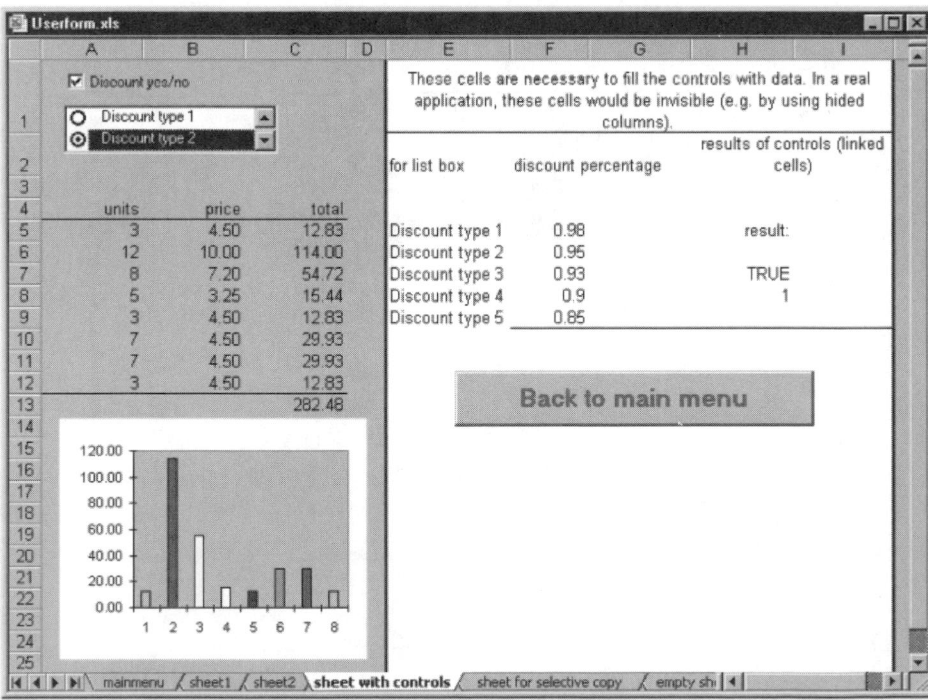

Figure 7.26. A worksheet with integrated controls

The state of the control box is displayed as a *LinkedCell* in H7. The listbox takes its entries from the range E5:E9 and places the number of the active entry in H8. In the cells for the total price (such as C5) the following formula is used:

```
=IF($H$7=FALSE, B5*A5, B5*A5*INDEX($F$5:$F$9,$H$8+1))
```

This formula has the following meaning: When the control box is inactive, then the total price is simply the product of the number of units and the price per unit. However, if the control box has been selected, then this product is multiplied by a discount factor that is taken from the table in cells F5:F9. Access to this factor is accomplished by the worksheet function *Index*, which reads the contents of the *n*th row of this range.

In the event procedure for the *CheckBox* control the listbox is hidden and unhidden.

```
' Userform.xls, class module sheet4 ("sheet with controls")
Private Sub CheckBox1_Click()
  ListBox1.Visible = CheckBox1.Value
  Me.Range("C1").Activate
End Sub
```

In a real application you would make columns E through I invisible (pop-up menu Hide). These columns merely hold the data for internal management of the two controls and are of no interest to the user.

Programming Techniques

Numerical Input

This introductory example displays a form for input of a number between 0 and 100. The form exhibits two features of interest:

- Validity control of the input when OK is pressed.
- Reciprocal updating of the editing field and scolling field when one of these controls is changed.

The transfer of the result is accomplished, as with most examples of this chapter, with the module variable *result*. New in this example is the situation that with this variable the initial state of the form can be set with this variable. To ensure that the required initialization tasks are carried out in spite of the unreliable *UserForm_Activate* event, the form is equipped with a new method, *ShowMe*, which takes over both the initialization and display of the form.

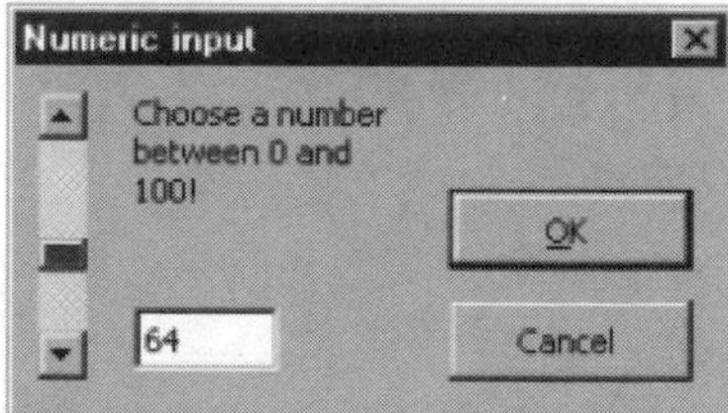

Figure 7.27. Form for the input of a number between 0 and 100

```
' Userform.xls, class module »dlgNumber«
Option Explicit
Public result
Public Sub ShowMe()
  Dim nmb
  nmb = result
  If nmb < 0 Or Not IsNumeric(nmb) Then nmb = 0
  If nmb > 100 Then nmb = 100
  txtNumber = nmb: scrSlider = nmb
  Show
End Sub
```

The synchronization between a text box (*txtNumber*) and scroll bar (*scrSlider*) is accomplished with the event procedures of these two controls.

```
Private Sub scrSlider_Change()
  txtNumber = scrSlider
End Sub
Private Sub scrSlider_Scroll()
  scrSlider_Change
End Sub
Private Sub txtNumber_Change()
  Dim nmb
  nmb = Val(txtNumber)
  If nmb >= 0 And nmb <= 100 And IsNumeric(txtNumber) Then
    scrSlider = nmb
  End If
End Sub
```

If the form is terminated with OK, then *btnOK_Click* checks the contents of the input field. If the value is outside of the valid range, then the user is requested by an alert to mend his ways and input a valid number. At the same time the input focus is placed in the text box (*Focus* method). If the input is correct, the form is terminated (*Hide* method).

```
Private Sub btnOK_Click()
  Dim nmb
  nmb = Val(txtNumber)
  If nmb < 0 Or nmb > 100 Or Not IsNumeric(txtNumber) Then
    MsgBox "Please choose a number between 0 and 100"
    txtNumber.SetFocus
  Else
    result = nmb
    Hide
  End If
End Sub
```

Reciprocal Calling of Forms

There are numerous possible applications of reciprocal calling of forms.

- If the user makes an input error, he can be sent to an error-handling form that explains the error and offers the possibility of fixing it.
- A subdialog can be available for little-used options, summoned by an OPTIONS button. After input of the options the original form would reappear.
- If the input data are so complex that they cannot be conveniently handled in a single form, then an entire chain of forms (such as in the case of the office assistant) can be displayed that take the user step by step through the process of data entry.

Cascades of Forms

Programming cascades of forms presents few difficulties. Essentially, the event procedure for the relevant button must be programmed so that the next form is launched with *Show*. Forms that are active are not influenced by this process, and when the last form is terminated, they become active again. (For Visual Basic pros, the forms are displayed modally, that is, previously launched forms are blocked until the termination of the last form.)

`Userform.xls` contains a three-stage cascade of form pages, "Cascade1" through "Cascade 3," which demonstrates the basic pattern (though without offering the possibility of setting any options). Here as an example is the code for the second form; the event procedures for the first and third forms are similar.

```
' Userform.xls, UserForm »dlgCascade2«
Private Sub btnOK_Click()
  Unload Me
End Sub
Private Sub btnCancel_Click()
  Unload Me
End Sub
Private Sub btnOption_Click()
  dlgCascade3.Show
End Sub
```

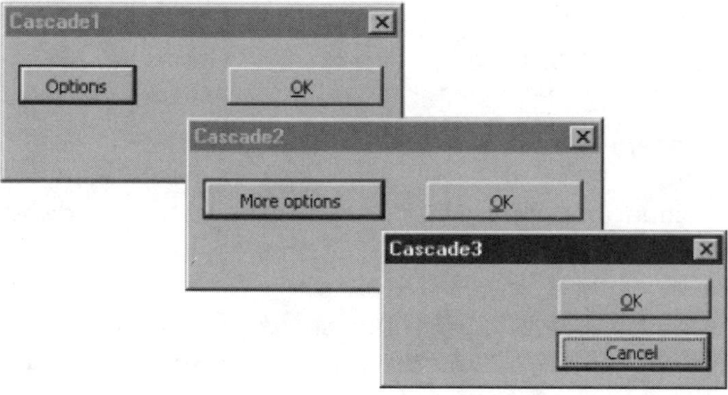

Figure 7.28. A three-step cascade of forms (all three forms can be made visible at one time)

Chain of Forms (Creating Your Own Assistants)

In a chain of forms there are several forms of which only one is visible at a time. The main distinction between a chain and a cascade is that the user must follow the chain to the end except to cancel, while the cascade can be terminated with OK at any stage. With Next and Back buttons you can jump from one form to the following or previous one in the chain, until all input has been taken care of the chain ended in the last form.

The only particular issue in this example is the manual positioning of the forms: When form 1 is moved to another position by the user, forms 2 and 3 appear in the same new position. To enable this feature the property *StartupPosition* must be set manually to (0) in the development environment. Now the position of the forms can be influenced by the properties *Left* and *Top* before the form is displayed via *Show*.

Now to the example: It is merely a chain of forms, without doing anything useful. The event procedures for the second form are as follows:

```
' Userform.xls, UserForm "dlgChain2"
Private Sub btnNext_Click()
  dlgChain3.Left = Left
  dlgChain3.Top = Top
  Hide
  dlgChain3.Show
End Sub
Private Sub btnPrevious_Click()
  dlgChain1.Left = Left
  dlgChain1.Top = Top
  Hide
  dlgChain1.Show
End Sub
Private Sub btnCancel_Click()
  Unload Me
End Sub
```

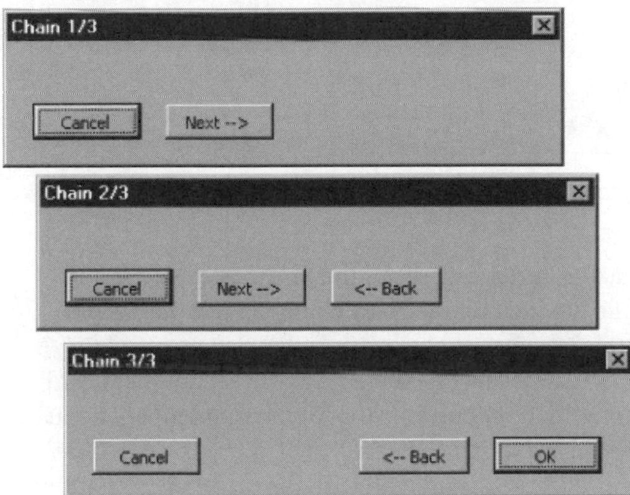

Figure 7.29. A three-stage chain of forms (only one form at a time is visible)

Editing Forms Dynamically

By the dynamic editing of a form we mean that the appearance of the form can be changed while it is being displayed. An example of a predefined dynamic form is the one for finding and replacing. When you execute Edit|Find and then click on Replace, the Find form is extended to include a "replace" field.

Dynamic forms are always used when a form is to be used for several similar cases or when the user might become confused by a large selection of seldom-used setting options.

The simplest way to set dynamic forms is to take into consideration during the development of the form all the controls that you are going to need. In the form's program code you can then make individual controls visible or invisible as the need arises. You can also place several controls one on top of the other, provided that you take care in the code to make only one of these controls visible at a time.

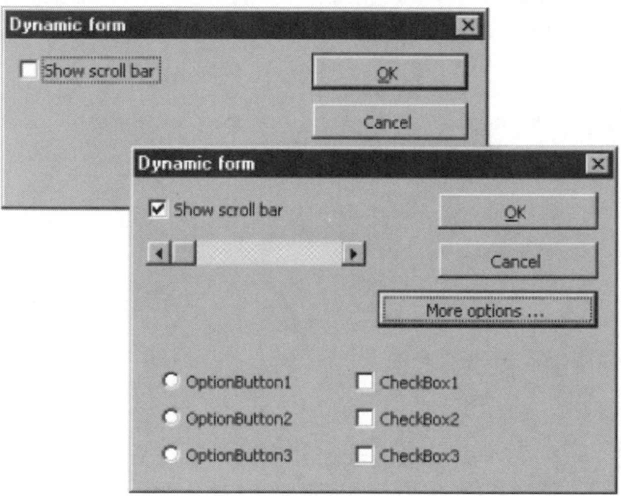

Figure 7.30. A dynamic form; left: in its initial state; right: expanded

Furthermore, you can place controls outside of the form's boundaries and then enlarge the form as needed to include them (by changing the *Height* and *Width* properties). But be careful to ensure that controls that lie outside of the form are nonetheless active and can be accessed (Tab) via the keyboard. Regardless of the actual size of the form field, all controls that at the moment are not usable should have their *Enabled* property set to *False.*

The form shown in Figure 7.30 can be enlarged with the MORE OPTIONS button. The scroll bar is displayed according to the state of the control box. When the form is displayed, there must be in the code for running the form a clearly defined state that is independent of the settings the last time the form was called. For this reason the method *ShowMe* is defined, which must be used to call the form instead of *Show*:

```
' Userform.xls, UserForm "dlgDynamic"
Public Sub ShowMe()
  OptionButton1.Enabled = False
  OptionButton2.Enabled = False
  OptionButton3.Enabled = False
  CheckBox1.Enabled = False
```

```
  CheckBox2.Enabled = False
  CheckBox3.Enabled = False
  Show
End Sub
```

The event procedures for displaying the scroll bar as well as for enlarging the form are less spectacular:

```
Private Sub chkSlider_Click()
  Scrollbar1.Visible = chkSlider
End Sub
Private Sub btnExpand_Click()
  Height = 170
  OptionButton1.Enabled = True
  ...
End Sub
```

Working with Spin Buttons

Spin buttons are a very practical item for the user. By simply clicking on the mouse certain data can be input, such as date and time, without the risk of a syntax error. Figure 7.31 shows a few possible applications.

For the programmer, on the other hand, things are not quite so simple. The main problem is in arranging the various options, dates, or times in order. The task is made easier by the fact that one is no longer restricted, as in Excel 7, to a range between 0 and 30000.

In addition to convenient settings with the mouse, it usually should be possible for direct text input: For this reason the contents of the text field and spin box must be synchronized (see also the introductory example below).

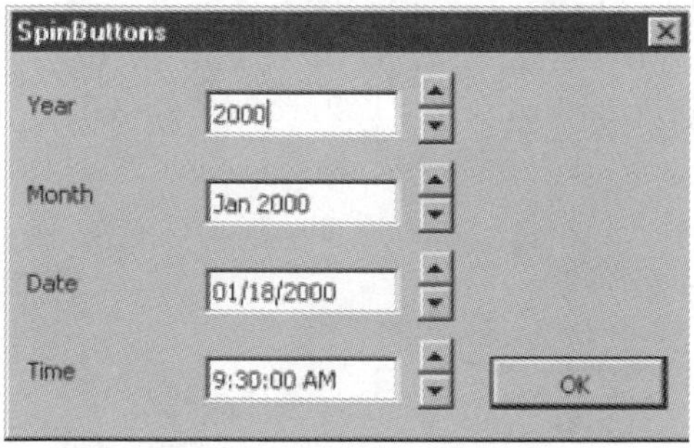

Figure 7.31. Applications of spin buttons

Setting the Year with a Spin Button

The procedures *spnYear_Change* and *txtYear_Change* show how text and spin fields can be synchronized for a simple numerical input. When the spin field is changed, the current value is transformed into a character string and written into the text field. Conversely, when the text field is altered an attempt is made to associate this value to those of the spin field. The upper and lower limits are set with the control options for minimum and maximum values, which are accessible in program code via the properties *Min* and *Max*.

```
' Userform.xls, UserForm "dlgSpin"
Private Sub spnYear_Change()
  txtYear = spnYear
End Sub
Private Sub txtYear_Change()
  Dim y
  y = Val(txtYear)
  If y >= spnYear.Min And y <= spnYear.Max Then
    spnYear = y
  End If
End Sub
```

Setting the Month with a Spin Box

The situation becomes somewhat more complicated when not only the year but also the month is to be set. For changing a number in the spin box to a date the formula *n=year*12+month* is used. The properties *Min* and *Max* for the spin box are set to 0 and 30000, so that dates between January 0000 and December 2499 can be represented. When the spin field is clicked on, the date is calculated and the resulting date transformed with *Format* into a character string, which then is displayed in the text field.

In the converse case, that is, where the date is input into the text field, an attempt is made to use *CDate* to transform the character string into a date. If this fails (on account of a syntax error in the input), the current value of the spin field is left unchanged.

```
Private Sub spnMonth_Change()
  ' n=year*12 + month
  Dim y, m, dat As Date
  y = Int(spnMonth / 12)  'year
  m = spnMonth Mod 12     'month
  dat = DateSerial(y, m, 1)
  txtMonth = Format(dat, "mmm yyyy")
End Sub
Private Sub txtMonth_Change()
  Dim dat As Date
  On Error Resume Next
  dat = CDate(txtMonth)
  If Err <> 0 Then Exit Sub 'input is not a valid date
  spnMonth = Month(dat) + Year(dat) * 12
End Sub
```

Setting the Date in a Spin Box

There is no problem in converting the numbers in the spin box into consecutive dates. Excel's internal representation is used. The preset valid range from 0 to 109574 corresponds to dates between 12/31/1899 and 12/31/2199.

Using *Like "*.*.??**"* to make comparisons, a conversion to a date is attempted only if the input looks like a date. This measure prevents incomplete (and thus erroneous) input from being processed too early.

```
Private Sub spnDate_Change()
  txtDate = Format(spnDate, "mm/dd/yyyy")
End Sub
Private Sub txtDate_Change()
  Dim dat As Date
  On Error Resume Next
  dat = CDate(txtDate)
  If Err <> 0 Then Exit Sub 'invalid input
  spnDate = CLng(dat)
End Sub
```

Setting the Time with a Spin Box

Like dates, times can also be set in a spin box. In the example below the time can be input precisely via the keyboard, or via the spin box in half-hour intervals. The valid range of values for *n* (in half hours) is from 0 to 47.

```
Private Sub spnTime_Change()
  Dim t
  t = CDate(spnTime / 48)
  txtTime = FormatDateTime(t, vbLongTime)
End Sub
Private Sub txtTime_Change()
  Dim tim As Date
  On Error Resume Next
  tim = CDate(txtTime)
  If Err <> 0 Then Exit Sub
  spnTime = Int(CDbl(tim) * 48 + 0.5)
End Sub
```

Initialization

UserForm_Initialize takes care that when the form is first launched, reasonable preset values are displayed.

```
' Initialization
Private Sub UserForm_Initialize()
  txtYear = Year(Now)
  txtYear_Change
  txtMonth = Format(Now, "mmm yyyy")
  txtMonth_Change
  txtDate = FormatDateTime(Now, vbShortDate)
  txtDate_Change
  txtTime = FormatDateTime(Int(Now * 48 + 0.5) / 48, vbLongTime)
  txtTime_Change
End Sub
```

Working with Cell References

In RefEdit forms input can take the form of a cell reference. As a rule this input is carried out with the mouse. That is, the user first moves the input cursor to the RefEdit control and then selects the desired range with the mouse. Although using such a form is not particularly difficult (and is carried out in the same manner in many predefined Excel dialogs), the programming is quite a challenge. The problem is above all to manage the input ranges properly and to protect against possible input errors in the program code.

Selective Copying of Ranges of Cells

The following example demonstrates the programming of a form that expects four ranges of cells as input parameters. The program copies selected parts of a column of data from one table into a second table. The functionality is best understood from looking at Figure 7.32 and Figure 7.33. In the form the range B3:E9 is specified as the source, and within it "Column 3." (This column is specified in the form by cell E3.) The column is to be copied to the target range B13:B16, into "Column A" (cell C13).

Figure 7.32 shows the result of the copying process. Only the data from "Column 1" were copied, and in fact, only for those rows in which the row label corresponds. Just try to carry out such a copying process without VBA programming!

Now let us look at the program code for this form. It consists of only two procedures: the event procedure *btnCopy_Click*, in which a test is made to ensure that the four given cell ranges make sense, and the procedure *SelectiveCopy*, where the actual copying is carried out.

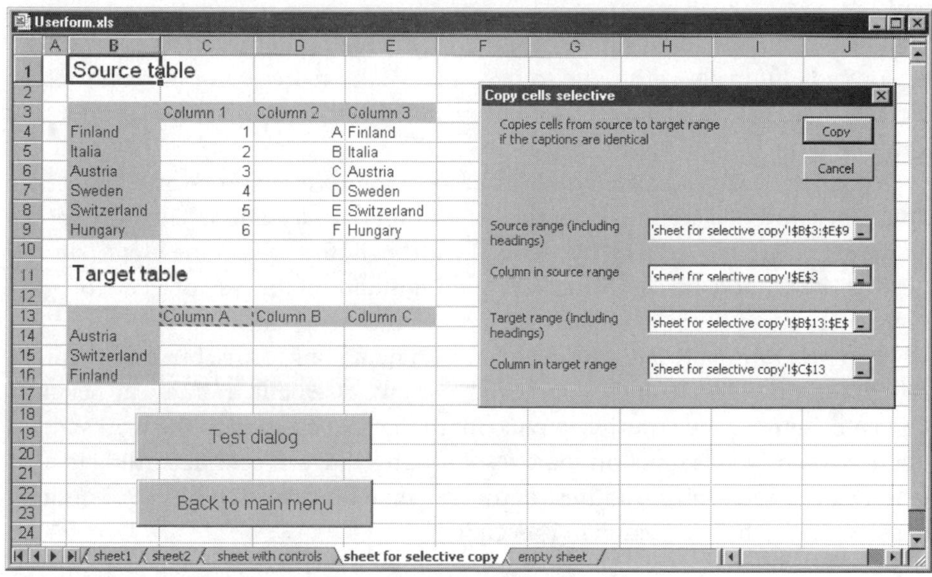

Figure 7.32. The example program copies cells from the source table to the destination table

	Column A	Column B	Column C
Austria	Austria		
Switzerland	Switzerland		
Finland	Finland		

Figure 7.33. The destination table after the execution of the form shown in Figure 7.32

The first thing that *btnCopy_Click* does is to foreclose the possibility of program interruption due to errors. A possible error can occur in the rows in which an attempt is made to transform the input (that is, a text in which an address is specified) into a *Range* object. This transformation works only if a valid range is given:

```
Set source = Range(refSource.Text)
```

If an error occurs in the transformation, the procedure is exited with a warning. The input focus is first set in the corresponding input field, so that the user knows immediately which field was affected.

If a single cell (instead of a block of cells) is given as source range, then the *CurrentRegion* method is used to determine the block of cells in which the selected cell is located. Then a further test is made to determine whether this range contains at least two rows and two columns. If this is not the case, then a meaningful copying is impossible, and the procedure is exited.

A similar approach is taken for the source column. Here, too, first a test is made as to whether an error would occur in the transformation to a *Range* object. If that is not the case, then a test is made with the method *Intersect* as to whether the source column lies within the source range. If the source column was specified as a single cell, then the entire column in which this cell is located is intersected with the source range.

A similar process is carried out with respect to the target range and target column. Since the code is almost identical, it is not reproduced here. Then the source and target ranges are reduced by the top row (that is, the column headers), since these rows are not to be changed. Now nothing stands in the way of a call to *SelectiveCopy* and a termination of the form with *Unload Me.*

SelectiveCopy really has nothing to do with managing forms, but it is an interesting procedure. In a loop the source range is processed line by line. The cell in the first column of each row is searched for in the goal range with the worksheet function *Match.* (This function searches through a range of cells according to a search text and returns the address of the first matching cell that it finds. This address can be further processed in VBA code.)

```
' Userform.xls, UserForm "dlgCopyCells"
Private Sub btnCopy_Click()
  ' source and target range
  Dim source As Range, sourceCol As Range
  Dim dest As Range, destCol As Range
  On Error Resume Next
  ' -----
  ' valid source range?
  Set source = Range(refSource.Text)
  refSource.SetFocus
```

```
  If Err <> 0 Then
    MsgBox "Invalid Source Range."
    Exit Sub
  End If
  ' only one cell selected: include corresponding range
  If source.Count = 1 Then
    Set source = source.CurrentRegion
    refSource.Text = source.Address
  End If
  ' range too small: show error message
  If source.Rows.Count < 2 Or source.Columns.Count < 2 Then
    MsgBox "Source range too small."
    Exit Sub
  End If
  ' -----
  ' valid range for source column?
  Set sourceCol = Range(refSourceCol.Text)
  refSourceCol.SetFocus
  If Err <> 0 Then
    MsgBox "Invalid source column."
    Exit Sub
  End If
  If TypeName(Intersect(source, sourceCol)) = "Nothing" Then
    MsgBox "Source column is not within source range."
    Exit Sub
  End If
  ' only one cell selected: include corresponding range
  If sourceCol.Count = 1 Then
    Set sourceCol = Intersect(source, sourceCol.EntireColumn)
    refSourceCol.Text = sourceCol.Address
  End If
  ' -----
  ' valid target range?
  ...
  ' -----
  ' remove headings from source and target ranges
  Set source = source.Resize(source.Rows.Count - 1)
  Set source = source.Offset(1, 0)
  Set dest = dest.Resize(dest.Rows.Count - 1)
  Set dest = dest.Offset(1, 0)
  ' call SelectiveCopy
  SelectiveCopy source, sourceCol, dest, destCol
  Unload Me
End Sub
```

When a matching row heading was found in the target range, the procedure determines (with *Intersect*) the intersection cell of the current row and the source column and copies the contents of this cell into the target cell, which again is determined with *Intersect* (this time as the interseciton of the row of the found cell and the target column).

```
Sub SelectiveCopy( _
    source As Range, sourceCol As Range, _
    dest As Range, destCol As Range)
  Dim foundLineNr As Variant ' row number
  Dim cellRow As Range       ' for row loop
  Dim insertCell As Range
  Dim copyValue As Variant
  For Each cellRow In source.Rows
    ' use worksheet function Match to find
    ' the correct position (row number)
    foundLineNr = Application.Match(cellRow. _
      Columns(1), dest.Columns(1), 0)
    If Not IsError(foundLineNr) Then
      copyValue = Intersect(cellRow, _
        sourceCol).Value
      Set insertCell = _
        Intersect(dest.Rows(foundLineNr), _
        destCol)
      insertCell.Value = copyValue
    End If
  Next
End Sub
```

CHAPTER 8

Menus and Toolbars

New and customized toolbars and menus help to make life under Excel simpler and more efficient. At the same time, you can use menus and toolbars to equip your applications with a clear and easy-to-use user interface. This chapter describes the many possibilities that the *CommandBar* object offers for this purpose.

Chapter Overview

Menu Bars and Toolbars

Manual Editing of Menus and Toolbars

Placing Toolbars, Hiding and Unhiding

Toolbars can be moved with the mouse and anchored, if desired, to one of the four borders of the screen or placed in their own toolbox windows. Excel keeps track of these settings, independent of the current mode. For example, Excel saves your settings for "full screen" mode.

If you click with the right mouse button on a menu or toolbar, you open a pop-up menu (context menu) in which you can turn the most important toolbars on and off. However, a complete list of all toolbars is available only in the TOOLS|CUSTOMIZE dialog.

The menu bar behaves essentially like a toobar, and like a toolbar it can be moved. However, there are two exceptions. First, no other toolbar can reside on the same row with the menu bar, even if sufficient space is available. Second, it is not permitted to deactivate the standard menu bar and replace it with a custom menu bar.

Changing Existing Menus and Toolbars

When the CUSTOMIZE dialog is displayed you can move or copy individual entries of existing menus with the mouse (hold down the Ctrl key). To delete them drag the entries off the toolbar.

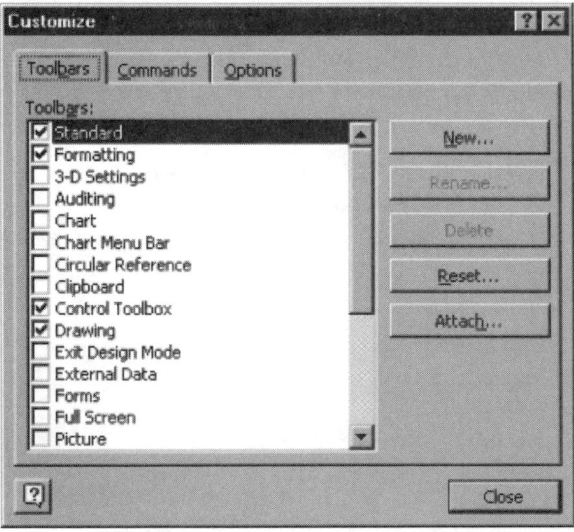

Figure 8.1. Customizing menus and toolbars

If you wish to add new commands or menus, you will find a complete (though confusing) list in the COMMANDS sheet of the CUSTOMIZE dialog. All the commands displayed on the right-hand side of this sheet can be copied directly with the mouse into a menu or toolbar. If you wish to copy a command into a menu (or submenu), you have to open it first. (To make this task more efficient, menus behave differently than they do in normal mode while the CUSTOMIZE dialog is displayed: No commands can be executed, and menus remain visible, even if you click again on the CUSTOMIZE dialog.)

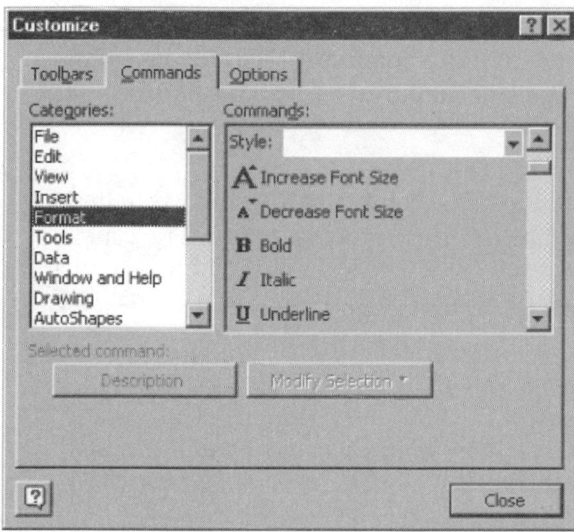

Figure 8.2. The long list of predefined commands

> **TIP** *As we have already mentioned, there are two independent menu bars that are displayed according to whether a worksheet or chart is active. If you wish to insert a new menu command that will be accessible in both cases, you must insert it into both menu bars. To do this you can activate both menu bars simultaneously (only while the* CUSTOMIZE *dialog is visible). If you wish to define a group of commands in a custom menu, you can define this group first for one menu bar and then copy from one menu bar into the other.*

> **TIP** *In the* TOOLBARS *sheet of the* CUSTOMIZE *dialog you can reset all predefined menu bars and toolbars to their original condition. This is particularly practical if you have deleted entries and wish to use them again.*

Creating New Menu Bars and Toolbars

In the TOOLBARS sheet of the CUSTOMIZE dialog you can use NEW to create a new toolbar. Since there is no major difference between toolbars and menu bars (since Office 97), you can use the new bar for menus as well.

You can now copy menu commands and tools from other toolbars into the new bar. The method of doing so is the same as was used for preexisting toolbars. However, you can also create completely new menus and tools and associate them to your own macros.

- New menus: Insert the command (right-hand side) "New Menu" from the like-named category (left-hand side) in the COMMANDS sheet into the toolbar.
- Individual menu commands: Insert the command "Custom Menu Item" from the "Macros" category directly into the toolbar or into a new menu.
- New tools: Insert the command "Custom Button" from the "Macros" category into the toolbar.

> **TIP** *If you are not working with a large monitor, you will find that toolbars take up a great deal of space that you really need for displaying your worksheet. One possible solution is to collect into your own toolbar just those tools that you use most frequently in your daily work. This new toolbar can then replace all the other toolbars.*

Editing Menu Items and Tools

The easiest way to edit menu items and tools is by clicking on them with the right mouse button. A pop-up menu then appears in which you can edit the text of a menu item, the tool, or any one of a number of options. Furthermore, you can associate the tool or menu item to a macro. (The same pop-up menu also appears in the CUSTOMIZE dialog if you click on the button MODIFY SELECTION.)

Menu entries and tools are represented internally by the same object. Four completely confusingly labeled pop-up menu entries make possible the setting of how the object is displayed:

- DEFAULT STYLE: The effect of this setting depends on the location of the object. If it is located directly in a toolbar, then the command is displayed by an image. However, if the object is in a menu, then the text will be shown as well as the image (if one has been defined).

- Text Only (Always): Only the text (no image) is displayed, whether or not the object is located in a menu or in a toolbar.
- Text Only (in Menus): In menus only the text is shown, in toolbars only the image.
- Image and Text: Both text and image are displayed.

Now, wouldn't it have been clearer to have simply provided three entries such as Text/Image/Both?

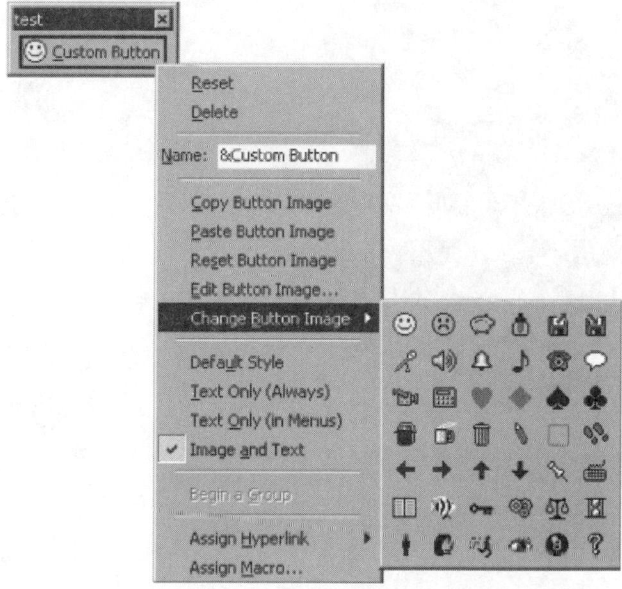

Figure 8.3. Editing menu items and tools via the pop-up menu

Label

The labeling of an entry is accomplished with the pop-up menu entry Name, whose white rectangle can be used as an input box. The text is displayed directly in a menu, while for a tool it is displayed as yellow infotext when the mouse is allowed to linger over the tool. In the case of menu items, an ampersand (&) can prefix a letter, which will then appear in the menu entry underlined, thereby allowing selection of the item via Alt+letter.

Editing Images

Excel offers a collection of predefined images, any of which can be chosen by CHANGE BUTTON IMAGE (see Figure 8.3). Another possibility for obtaining an image quickly is to execute COPY BUTTON IMAGE and then link the image to the new item via PASTE BUTTON IMAGE. Finally, you can summon a primitive editor with EDIT BUTTON IMAGE, with which you may alter the button to your heart's content.

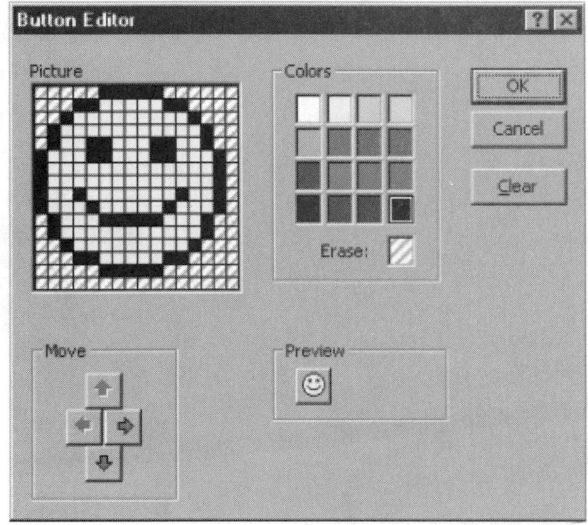

Figure 8.4. The image editor

Groups

Several tools or menu commands can be brought together into a group. To do this, activate the option BEGIN A GROUP for the first entry of the group. A separator bar is then placed in front of, or above, the entry.

Assigning Macros

Each tool and menu item can be assigned to a macro. (In the case of predefined tools the result is that instead of the standard macro for this tool or menu command, the new macro will be executed.) This assignment is normally accomplished by way of the pop-up menu entry ASSIGN MACRO. It is also convenient to use the entry "Custom Menu Item" or "Custom Button" from VIEWS|CUSTOMIZE|COMMANDS, category "Macros." If you click for the first time on such a button or menu item, the ASSIGN MACRO dialog opens automatically.

> **CAUTION** *Excel 2000 frequently crashes when you attempt to assign a macro to a tool (about every third time). Save your work first!*
>
> *If you wish to call a new or recently edited procedure by using a tool, Excel often stubbornly maintains that it cannot find the procedure. The cause is usually a syntax error in the code that prevents the code from being compiled. It is a mystery why Excel is unable (or unwilling, perhaps?) to report this error.*
>
> *A solution is to switch into the development environment. There execute* DEBUG|COMPILE VBA PROJECT *and observe that you receive a syntax error notice, which is the true cause of the problem.*

Defining Extensive Menus

If you have the idea of creating extensive menus in your custom toolbars, you will soon despair at having to go through a large number of mouse clicks to get where you are going. If you wish to save some time, consider the following recommendations:

- In the new toolbar insert first a "New Menu" (of the like-named category) and then into it the entry "Custom Menu Item" (category "Macros").
- Copy this menu item several times within the menu with Ctrl and the mouse. This way you do not have to go back and forth to the CUSTOMIZE dialog.
- Then copy the entire menu with Ctrl and the mouse. This method works for submenus as well.

In this way you can create a menu template with a large number of entries in under a minute. The further steps—that is, naming the entries and creating the individual images—remain labor-intensive.

Saving Changes

In principle, all changes in the toolbars are saved in the file `Userprofile\Application Data\Microsoft\Excel\Excel.xlb`, that is, for every user in his or her own file. This means that each user can have a custom setting independent of those of other users.

Attaching Toolbars

The individual configuration files have the effect that new toolbars are not automatically saved with an Excel file. If you wish to give an Excel file with its own toolbar to another individual (or to use someone else's file on your own computer), you have to "attach" the new toolbar to the file. To do this, click on the Attach button in the dialog VIEW|TOOLBARS|CUSTOMIZE|TOOLBARS. In the dialog that then appears you can copy one or more user-defined toolbars into the currently active Excel file.

> **TIP** *Copying a toolbar copies the current state of the toolbar into the currently active Excel file. Later changes will be saved only in* `Excel.xlb`*, but will not be saved in the current file. To do this you will have first to delete the attached tool bar in the* ATTACH *dialog and then repeat the* COPY *command.*

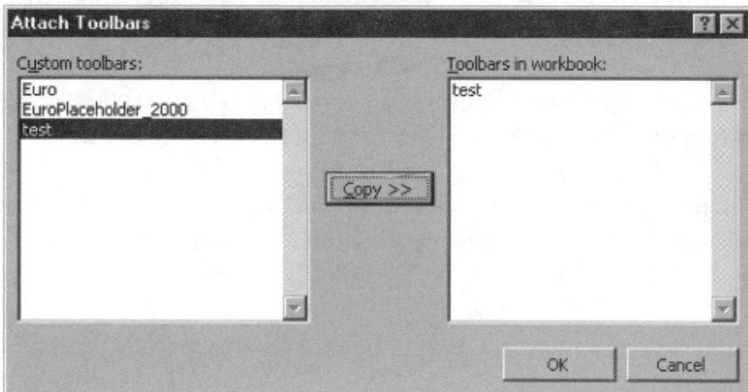

Figure 8.5. The new toolbar "test" has been attached to the current Excel file

> **TIP** *It is indeed possible to attach an entire toolbar, but you cannot save individual changes in preexisting toolbars or menus, such as an additional command in the* TOOLS *menu, so that these changes will be available for other users. The only possibility to transmit these changes is in VBA code that is executed when the file is opened (*Auto_Open *or* Workbook_Open*).*

New Toolbars for All Users

If you wish to make a new toolbar available for all users, simply add it to a file in the folder `Office2000\Office\Xlstart`. Such files are automatically loaded when Excel is launched. With the *Workbook_Open* or *Workbook_BeforeClose* procedure you can also carry out individual changes to standard toolbars in program code.

Object Hierarchy

The *CommandBar* objects are defined in the Office library. The starting point is the *CommandBars* enumeration, which refers to several *CommandBar* objects.

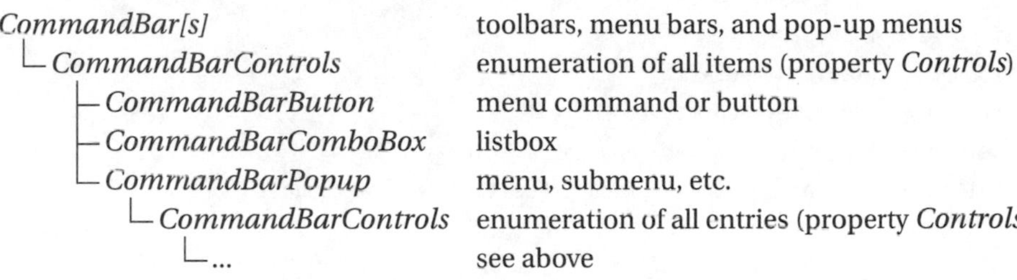

CommandBar[s]	toolbars, menu bars, and pop-up menus
└ *CommandBarControls*	enumeration of all items (property *Controls*)
├ *CommandBarButton*	menu command or button
├ *CommandBarComboBox*	listbox
└ *CommandBarPopup*	menu, submenu, etc.
└ *CommandBarControls*	enumeration of all entries (property *Controls*)
└ ...	see above

Menu Bars and Toolbars (CommandBars)

Access to the ***CommandBars*** is accomplished by means of the like-named *Application* object. The three types of *CommandBar* object—"normal" toolbars, menu bars, and pop-up menus—are identified by the *Type* property: The corresponding settings are *msoBarTypeNormal*, *msoBarTypeMenuBar*, and *msoBarTypePopup*. Visually, the only difference between *msoBarTypeNormal* and *msoBarTypeMenuBar* is that in the first case menus are not identified by a small triangle, while in the second they are.

In accessing objects of the various *CommandBar* enumerations note that they are case-insensitive. Furthermore, any ampersands (&) may be ignored (they appear for individual menu elements; see below). The complete (and very long) list of all toolbars and pop-up menus can be obtained by executing the following procedure:

```
' file Commandbar.cls, Module "Module1"
Sub AnalyseCommandBars()
  Dim c
  For Each c In CommandBars
    If c.BuiltIn Then Debug.Print c.Type, c.Name, c.NameLocal
  Next c
End Sub
```

Every *CommandBar* object can contain buttons, tools, listboxes, or menus. (Menu bars normally contain only *CommandBarPopup* objects, while toolbars in their simplest incarnation contain only *CommandBarButton* objects, and pop-up menus objects of both types.) Access to these elements is accomplished with the property *Controls*, which refers to a *CommandBarControls* object.

With the *Position* property the location of a toolbar can be specified. The toolbar can either be anchored to one of the four screen borders or be left to float freely. In the first case the exact position is determined by *RowIndex*, while in the second the exact position and size are set with *Left*, *Top*, *Width*, and *Height*.

With the *CommandBars.Add* method you can create new toolbars. The optional parameters *Position* and *MenuBar* can be used to distinguish among the three types of toolbar:

```
Dim cb As CommandBar
With Application.CommandBars
  Set cb = .Add(Name:="normal toolbar")
  Set cb = .Add(Name:="proper menu bar", MenuBar:=True)
  Set cb = .Add(Name:="Pop-up  menu", Position:=msoBarPopup)
End With
```

> **CAUTION** *If you attempt to create a new toolbar with* Add *using a name that is already in use, an error occurs. (The most probable cause is that you created the menu earlier and forgot to delete the program code.) You can catch the error either with* On Error Resume Next *(and evaluate* Err *in the following line) or before executing the* Add *command to run a loop through all toolbars to test whether one already exists with the name you wish to use.*

*Menu and Tool Elements (*CommandBarControls*)*

Access to these objects is accomplished with the ***CommandBarControls*** enumeration, which refers to objects of type *CommandBarControl*. Access to this enumeration is not achieved in the usual way via a like-named property, but through the shorthand form *Controls*. ***CommandBarControl*** is a subobject whose properties and methods depend on whether a *CommandBarButton* object, *CommandBarComboBox* object, *CommandBarPopup* object, or some other object is represented. The object type can be determined by the property *Type*. (Although only three types of named objects are provided for in the Office object model, in reality there are considerably more. These additional object types come into play in the built-in menus and toolbars but cannot be used in custom toolbars.)

> **NOTE** *For Visual Basic pros: The* CommandBarControl *object is an example of polymorphism, that is, of an object that serves as a common denominator for special objects derived from it. Polymorphism is a scaled-down version of class inheritance.*
>
> *Since during input of code in the development environment it is unclear which object is actually lurking behind* CommandBarControl, *the automatic expansion of properties and methods functions only for the keywords of* CommandBarControl. *However, depending on the object type (which can be determined in a running program with* Type *or* TypeName*), there exist additional properties, such as* Controls *when one is dealing with a* CommandBarPopup *control. So don't let yourself be irritated by the editor when you are typing in code.*

With *Controls.Add* new tools, menu items, submenus, and listboxes can be added to a menu. With the optional *Type* parameter the type of the menu element can be specified, or with *Id* a predefined command can be used (further information on *Id* follows in the section on programming techniques).

```
Add Id:=123                    'predefined command
Add Type:=msoControlButton     'Button or tool       (CommandBarButton)
Add Type:=msoControlEdit       'text input field     (CommandBarComboBox)
Add Type:=msoControlDropdown   'listbox              (CommandBarComboBox)
Add Type:=msoControlComboBox   'combination list     (CommandBarComboBox)
Add Type:=msoControlPopup      'menu/submenu         (CommandBarPopup)
```

If with *Add* you use the optional parameter *Temporary:=True*, then the new menu item is considered temporary. Such items do not have to be deleted explicitly when the Excel file is closed, since when Excel is terminated they are automatically deleted. (Items without *Temporary:=True* are automatically saved in the file `Excel.xlb`.)

Tools and Menu Items (CommandBarButton)

The most frequently used menu item is certainly ***CommandBarButton.*** According to the setting of the *Style* property (*msoButtonIcon, msoButtonCaption,* or *msoButtonIconAndCaption*) the button is represented as an image, text, or both of these.

Caption determines the displayed text. This text is also used in the case of an image for the yellow infotext if a different text has not been specified with *TooltipText.* There is no property for the image. It can be changed only with the method *PasteFace.* (This method assumes that the bitmap information of an image is located in the clipboard. This information can be copied to the clipboard from another image with *CopyFace*.)

The *OnAction* property specifies the name of the event procedure that will be called when the control is clicked on. (This is necessary only if the event is not to be processed by the *OnClick* event procedure.)

If several menu items or tools are to be collected into a group, then *BeginGroup=True* can be used to display a separator bar above or to the left of such an element.

Text Boxes and Listboxes (CommandBarComboBox)

Text boxes and listboxes can be created only in program code, not with the CUSTOMIZE dialog. (Nonetheless, all listboxes created in code are saved with all other list items in `Excel.xlb`.)

There are three different types of such fields, all of which are represented by the object ***CommandBarComboBox*** (and thereby distinguish themselves from the *Style* properties, which are something else: *msoControlDropdown, msoControlEdit*, or *msoControlComboBox*). Here is a short description: *Dropdown* is a simple listbox; *Edit* is a text input box. The combination of both fields results in a *Combo*, that is, a listbox in which you can add new text in addition to the predefined entry (just like the combination listbox described in the previous chapter). The type that you wish to use is specified in the *Type* parameter of *Add*.

```
Dim cbc As CommandBarComboBox
With CommandBars("...").Controls
  Set cbc = .Add(Type:=msoControlEdit)
  Set cbc = .Add(Type:=msoControlDropdown)
  Set cbc = .Add(Type:=msoControlComboBox)
End With
```

With *AddItem* new entries can be added to a listbox. *RemoveItem* deletes individual entries, while *Clear* deletes all of them. The property *Text* specifies the current contents of the text box or the current selection of a list entry.

The event procedure is set as with *CommandBarButton* via the property *OnAction*. No parameter is passed to the event procedure, that is, the property *Text* must be evaluated there.

In the case of tools Excel automatically displays the *Caption* text as yellow infotext. In the case of listboxes, however, to save space *Caption* texts are frequently not used. In this case you can prescribe an infotext with *TooltipText*. (This property exists for all *CommandBar* elements, but it is seldom used. It takes precedence over any prescribed *Caption* text.)

POINTER *An example of the practical application of the listbox can be found below in the subsection on changing sheets via a toolbar. There it is shown how the listbox can be used to change sheets conveniently in large Excel files.*

Menus and Submenus (CommandBarPopup)

Tools and menu items can be inserted directly into a toolbar or grouped in a menu. Within a menu one may have submenus, and subsubmenus within these. The *CommandBarPopup* object serves to collect menu items into a group. Access to the individual elements is accomplished through the property *Controls*, which refers to a *CommandBarControls* object. With *Controls.Add* new menu elements are added. The menu is labeled using *Caption*.

Accessing Objects

Given the nesting of objects, access to a specific element is often rather difficult. The following lines give some examples:

Access to the standard menu bar (*CommandBar* object):

```
CommandBars("Worksheet Menu Bar")
```

Access to the FILE menu of this menu bar (*CommandBarPopup* object):

```
CommandBars("Worksheet Menu Bar").Controls("File")
```

Access to the item NEW in the FILE menu (*CommandBarButton* object):

```
CommandBars("Worksheet Menu Bar").Controls("File").Controls("New")
```

Access to the submenu FORMAT|SHEET (*CommandBarPopup* object):

```
CommandBars("Worksheet Menu Bar").Controls("Format"). _
  Controls("Sheet")
```

Access to the submenu item FORMAT|SHEET|RENAME (*CommandBarButton*):

```
CommandBars("Worksheet Menu Bar").Controls("Format"). _
  Controls("Sheet").Controls("Rename")
```

Instead of accessing an object directly, in many cases you can make use of the method *FindControl* of the *CommandBar* object. This method searches for the first object in the toolbar that satisfies particular criteria. However, for many applications the criteria are insufficient; for example, you cannot search for the name of an entry. At best, *FindControl* can be used for predefined elements if these elements were linked to a unique *Tag* property.

Programming Techniques

All steps for the manipulation of toolbars described in the introduction can be executed in program code. As a rule, it does not make sense to create entire toolbars in program code, since this can be done more easily manually. However, there is often the necessity to hide or unhide toolbars or individual menu items or to change their text depending on the state of the program. Excel applications with custom toolbars should therefore make sure that these are automatically displayed when the file is opened, and deleted when the file is closed.

> **POINTER** *The next section of this chapter contains a number of further examples of working with menus and toolbars. These examples are all oriented to the question of how programs can best be used to integrate the user interface into Excel.*

Hiding and Unhiding Toolbars

Toolbars can be hidden and unhidden by changing the *Visible* property. The toolbars will be displayed automatically at the last place where they were visible. If a toolbar is attached to an Excel file, you can display it on loading with the following event procedure:

```
' file CommandBar.xls, class module "ThisWorkbook"
Private Sub Workbook_Open()
  Application.CommandBars("new toolbar").Visible = True
End Sub
```

At the end of the program the toolbar can again be made invisible with *Visible=False*. However, the toolbar remains in memory and is saved in the file `Excel.xlb`. To prevent the number of such saved toolbars from growing without bound, it is a good idea to delete the toolbar explicitly with *Delete. Delete* refers here to Excel, not to the workbook: The menu is deleted in Excel, but not in the workbook, and if you load the workbook again, the menu appears again, too. Within the active Excel file the attached toolbar is maintained.

```
Private Sub Workbook_BeforeClose(Cancel As Boolean)
  Application.CommandBars("new toolbar").Visible = False
  Application.CommandBars("new toolbar").Delete
End Sub
```

Adding and Deleting Menu Items via Program Code

The following lines show how when a file is opened a menu item is added to the TOOLS menu of the worksheet toolbar. When the file is closed, the item is deleted.

```
' file CommandBar, class module "ThisWorkbook"
Private Sub Workbook_Open()
  Dim cbb As CommandBarButton
  Set cbb = Application.CommandBars("Worksheet Menu Bar"). _
    Controls("Tools").Controls.Add()
  cbb.Caption = "A new command"
  cbb.BeginGroup = True
  cbb.OnAction = "NewCommand_OnAction"
End Sub
Private Sub Workbook_BeforeClose(Cancel As Boolean)
  Application.CommandBars("Worksheet Menu Bar"). _
    Controls("Tools").Controls("A new command").Delete
End Sub
```

The event procedure was named *object_event* according to the nomenclature in force since Excel 97. But this is not absolutely necessary. You can use whatever name you like. Note, though, that the event procedure must be located in a normal module (not in the module "ThisWorkbook," in which the two above procedures are located).

```
' file CommandBar.xls, Module »Module1«
Sub NewCommand_OnAction()
  MsgBox "Event: NewCommand_OnAction"
End Sub
```

Needless to say, in your own menus you can use one of the countless standard Excel commands. To do so, provide the *Id* value of the command with *Add*. For example, if you wish to insert a SAVE comand in the TOOLS menu, then the instruction is as follows:

```
CommandBars("Worksheet Menu Bar"). _
  Controls("Tools").Controls.Add(Id:=3)  'Id=3 ... save command
```

The problem with the *Id* values is that they seem not to be documented (at least not in one place, in a single table). The following procedure builds the text file `CommandBar-IdList.txt` with about 4,000 entries in the range 2–30426. The program temporarily creates a new toolbar and there as a test inserts each *CommandBarControl* object with *Id* value between 0 and 32000. (Many numbers in this range are invalid and lead to errors. Thanks to *On Error Resume Next* these errors are ignored.) The program could be optimized to evaluate additional properties and thereby determine the type of entry (tool, menu entry, button, listbox).

```
' CommandBar.xls, Module "Module1"
Sub IdList()
  On Error Resume Next
  Dim c As CommandBar, i
  Set c = CommandBars.Add
  Open ThisWorkbook.Path + "\CommandBar-IdList.txt" For Output As #1
  For i = 0 To 32000
    c.Controls.Add Id:=i
    If c.Controls(1).Caption <> "" And _
       c.Controls(1).Caption <> "[Command not available]" And _
       c.Controls(1).Caption <> "custom" Then
      Print #1, i, c.Controls(1).Caption
    End If
    c.Controls(1).Delete
  Next i
  c.Delete
  Close #1
End Sub
```

The first lines of the list look like this:

```
2           &Spelling...
3           &Save
4           &Print...
18          &New...
19          &Copy
```

Checks in Menu Items

It is often desirable to display a check next to a menu item to indicate its current state. This was easy in Excel 5/7 menus. One simply set the property *Checked*. In the versions of Excel starting with Excel 97 such checks are still possible, but the path to them is somewhat long and tortuous.

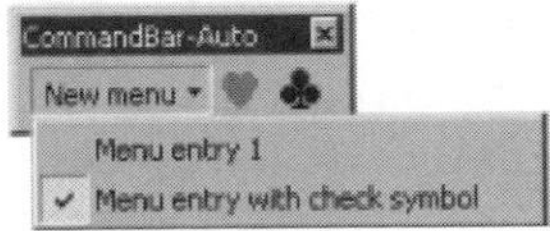

Figure 8.6. A checked menu item

Among the many predefined tools in Excel there is one that represents such a check (*Id=849*). However, it is impossible to create this tool interactively via the CUSTOMIZE dialog. Even a change in the *Id* property of an existing menu entry is not allowed (the property can be read only). Therefore, a menu entry with a check must be created at the start of the program in VBA code.

The way to do this is demonstrated in the example file `CommandBar-AutoVisible .xls` (see also further below). In *Workbook_Open* the toolbar *Commandbar-Auto* is accessed via *With* (see Figure 8.6). Its first *Control* object is a menu, and its second menu entry is to be equipped with a check. First, all menu entries except for the first are deleted (to avoid the menu entry appearing more than once). Then, the new menu entry is created with *Add*. The properties *Caption* and *OnAction* specify the menu text and the event procedure that is to be called when this menu item is selected.

```
' CommandBar-AutoVisible.xls, "ThisWorkbook"
Private Sub Workbook_Open()
  ' create a menu entry with a check symbol
  ' idea: Guido Müller; thank you!
  Dim i&, cbc As CommandBarControl
  ' access menu within the toolbar "Commandbar-Auto"
  With Application.CommandBars("Commandbar-Auto").Controls(1)
    ' delete all entries except the first one
    For i = .Controls.Count To 2 Step -1
      .Controls(i).Delete
    Next
    ' add new menu with check symbol (ID=849)
    Set cbc = .Controls.Add(Type:=msoControlButton, ID:=849)
    cbc.Caption = "Menu entry with check symbol"
    cbc.OnAction = "MenuCommand2_OnAction"
  End With
  ' show toolbar
  Application.CommandBars("Commandbar-Auto").Visible = True
End Sub
```

In the event procedure the property *.State* is moved to between *msoButton-Down* and *msoButtonUp*. In this way the check is hidden and unhidden. It is worth noting in this procedure that the property *ActionControl* is used to refer to the *CommandBarControl* object that has just been chosen.

```
' CommandBar-AutoVisible.xls, Module1
' hide and unhide the check
Sub MenuCommand2_OnAction()
  With CommandBars.ActionControl
    If .State = msoButtonDown Then
      .State = msoButtonUp
    Else
      .State = msoButtonDown
    End If
  End With
End Sub
```

Editing Existing Pop-Up Menus

Since Excel 97 pop-up menus can be edited only in program code. The problem is in finding the name of the given pop-up menu, since in Excel there are no fewer than forty-four pop-up menus defined! The procedure *AnalyseCommandBars* given below can help in the search.

The following lines show how the pop-up menu can be expanded with an entry for editing cells, making possible the convenient invocation of the dialog "Style":

```
' CommandBar.xls, "ThisWorkbook"
Private Sub Workbook_Open()
  Dim cbb As CommandBarButton
  Set cbb = Application.CommandBars("cell").Controls.Add
  cbb.Caption = "St&yle"
  cbb.OnAction = "CellFormat_OnAction"
End Sub
Private Sub Workbook_BeforeClose(Cancel As Boolean)
  Application.CommandBars("cell").Controls("Style").Delete
End Sub
Sub CellFormat_OnAction()
  Application.Dialogs(xlDialogApplyStyle).Show
End Sub
```

Custom Pop-Up Menus

Within worksheets and charts (and only there) you can use the *BeforeRightClick* event procedure to prevent the automatic display of various Excel pop-up menus (depending on which object is currently selected) and in their place to display your own such menu. The first requirement is that you have previously defined such a menu with *Position=msoBarPopup*:

```
' CommandBar.xls, Module "ThisWorkbook"
Private Sub Workbook_Open()
  Dim cb As CommandBar
  Set cb = Application.CommandBars.Add(Name:="NewPopup", _
    Position:=msoBarPopup)
  With cb
     .Controls.Add Id:=3  'Save
     .Controls.Add ...
  End With
End Sub
Private Sub Workbook_BeforeClose(Cancel As Boolean)
  Application.CommandBars("NewPopup").Delete
End Sub
```

Calling this method can take place, in principle, at any place in the code with the method ***ShowPopup***. For the example below the *BeforeRightClick* event procedure of the second worksheet was chosen. The instruction *Cancel=True* ensures that Excel's pop-up menu is not displayed as well.

```
' CommandBar.xls, Module "sheet2"
Private Sub Worksheet_BeforeRightClick(ByVal Target As Excel.Range, _
                                        Cancel As Boolean)
  Application.CommandBars("NewPopup").ShowPopup
  Cancel = True
End Sub
```

Replacing the Standard Menu with a Custom Menu

Initial experiments with the *CommandBar* objects would lead one to believe that since Excel 97 (in contrast to previous versions) it is no longer possible to replace the standard menu with a custom menu. In interactive mode (TOOLBARS|CUSTOMIZE) it is impossible to deactivate the standard menu.

But further experiments have shown that such is indeed possible, though only in program code. The new menu bar must be created with

```
Set c = CommandBars.Add(MenuBar:=True)
```

and it then refers to *Type=msoBarTypeMenuBar* (and not, as for toolbars created with CUSTOMIZE, to *Type=msoBarTypeNormal*). With

```
c.Visible = True
```

the new menu bar is made visible. The standard menu bar automatically disappears (and appears again automatically when *Visible* is again set to *False*). The problem with these menu bars is that they (presumably due to the contrary *Type* setting) cannot be attached to an Excel file.

If you wish to equip an Excel program with a custom menu bar, you must therefore create all of its entries in program code. (The simplest way to do this is certainly to create and attach a normal toolbar interactively. Then in *Workbook_Open* copy in a loop all items in this toolbar into the menu bar created with *CommandBars.Add.*) It is probably more sensible to do without a custom menu bar entirely and instead display the application-specific commands in a supplementary menu in a custom toolbar. (The standard menu thus remains visible.)

If you nevertheless decide to go ahead with your own menu, this should be activated automatically as soon as a sheet of your program is active. Likewise, the standard menu should appear automatically as soon as another sheet or Excel file is activated. You can accomplish this relatively easily by setting the *Visible* property of the menu bar to *True*, respectively *False*, in *Worksheet_(De)Activate.*

Protecting Toolbars Against Changes

With the ***Protection*** property of the *CommandBar* object one can set the degree to which changes in a toolbar are possible: none at all, change position, change size, change contents, and so on. Thus with the appropriate setting you can keep the user from carrying out certain actions with the toolbar.

Changing Sheets via a Toolbar

This section offers a concluding example for the possbilities of using toolbars in your applications: A toolbar is to be equipped with a listbox that enables a smooth change of sheets. When an Excel file grows to contain many sheets, navigation using the sheet tabs becomes rather cumbersome.

The toolbar presented here contains a listbox (*CommandBarComboBox*) that simplifies the task. The crucial task in programming is the synchronization of the listbox with the list of sheets of the currently active workbook. For this, two events of the *Application* object need to be evaluated, which requires a separate class module (see also Chapter 4).

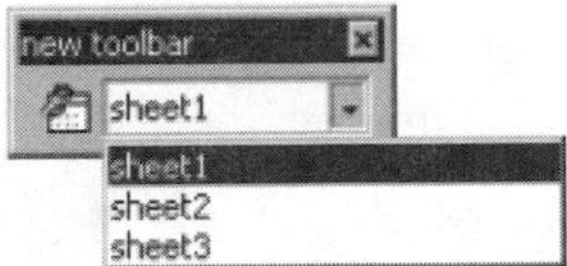

Figure 8.7. A listbox for changing sheets using a toolbar

Creating the Listbox

The listbox can be created only in program code (not interactively). When the file is opened the second time by the same user, it could happen that the listbox still exists in the toolbar. For this reason, a security check is run in *Workbook_Open.*

To save space, the listbox is not given a label (thus no *Caption* text). Instead, a character string is assigned to *TooltipText* in which yellow infotext is shown. Furthermore, the *Tag* property is used, which in other places makes possible the use of the method *FindControl* (see below). The setting of the two properties *DropDownLines* and *DropDownWidth* has the effect of making the listbox appear somewhat larger than it would in the default setting. (This is of benefit in the case of long lists.)

```
' file CommandBar.xls, "ThisWorkbook"
Dim appc As New AppClass the application events
Private Sub Workbook_Open()
  On Error Resume Next
  Dim cb As CommandBar, cbb As CommandBarButton
  Dim cbc As CommandBarControl, cbcb As CommandBarComboBox
  Dim existing As Boolean
  ' new entry in tools menu
  Set cbb = Application.CommandBars("Worksheet Menu Bar"). _
    Controls("Tools").Controls.Add()
  cbb.Caption = "A new command"
  cbb.BeginGroup = True
  cbb.OnAction = "NewCommand_OnAction"
  ' show toolbar "new toolbar"
  Application.CommandBars("new toolbar").Visible = True
  ' add a new command to pop-up menu "cells"
  Set cbb = Application.CommandBars("cell").Controls.Add
```

```
  cbb.Caption = "St&yle"
  cbb.OnAction = "CellFormat_OnAction"
  ' prepare popup menu
  Set cb = Application.CommandBars.Add(Name:="NewPopup", _
    Position:=msoBarPopup)
  With cb
     .Controls.Add Type:=msoControlButton, Id:=3  ' save
  End With
  ' test whether the toolbar "new toolbar" already contains a listbox
  For Each cbc In Application.CommandBars("new toolbar").Controls
    If cbc.Tag = "list of sheets" Then existing = True: Exit For
  Next
  ' add listbox to toolbar "new toolbar"
  If Not existing Then
    Set cbcb = Application.CommandBars("new toolbar").Controls. _
      Add(Type:=msoControlDropdown, Before:=2)
    cbcb.Tag = "list of sheets"
    cbcb.TooltipText = "list of sheets"
    cbcb.OnAction = "SheetCombo_OnAction"
    cbcb.DropDownWidth = 150
    cbcb.DropDownLines = 20
  End If
  ' process events if the active workbook changes
  Set appc.app = Application
End Sub
```

Placing Items in a Listbox

Perhaps in the lines above you missed instructions for giving the sheet names to the list entries. Since the list of sheets can constantly change (in switching between workbooks, opening new files, inserting and deleting sheets), the listbox must be continually supplied with new entries. The required code is found in the class module *AppClass*, which was initialized in the lines presented above (see the *Dim* lines and the last line).

The event procedure *app_SheetActivate* is then called whenever a change of sheets takes place in any open file in Excel. Within the procedure the listbox is first tracked down with *FindControl*. Then the current contents of the list are deleted and replaced with the names of the sheets in the active workbook. (Module sheets, which can still exist in Excel 5/7 files, are not considered.) Finally, the entry in the list that corresponds to the active sheet is activated.

The procedure *app_WorkbookActivate* simply calls *app_SheetActivate*, to update the listbox in the case of a change in workbook.

```
' Commandbar.xls, class "AppClass"
' application events are to be processed
Public WithEvents app As Application
Private Sub app_SheetActivate(ByVal sh As Object)
  Dim cbcb As CommandBarComboBox
  Dim sheet As Object
  Dim i
  Set cbcb = Application.CommandBars.FindControl( _
    Type:=msoControlDropdown, Tag:="list of sheets")
  cbcb.Clear
  For Each sheet In sh.Parent.Sheets
    If TypeName(sheet) <> "Module" Then
      cbcb.AddItem sheet.Name
    End If
  Next
  ' select the correct list entry
  For i = 1 To cbcb.ListCount
    If cbcb.List(i) = sh.Name Then cbcb.ListIndex = i: Exit For
  Next
End Sub
Private Sub app_WorkbookActivate(ByVal wb As Excel.Workbook)
  app_SheetActivate wb.ActiveSheet
End Sub
```

Response to the Selection of a Listbox

The event procedure *SheetCombo_OnAction,* which is executed when the user selects an item in the listbox and thereby indicates the desire to switch to another sheet, is comparatively simple:

```
' CommandBar.xls, Module1
Sub SheetCombo_OnAction()
  Dim cbcb As CommandBarComboBox
  On Error Resume Next
  Set cbcb = CommandBars.FindControl(Type:=msoControlDropdown, _
    Tag:="list of sheets")
  ActiveWorkbook.Sheets(cbcb.Text).Activate
End Sub
```

Differences Compared to Excel 5/7

Starting with Office 97 the toolbars and menu bars have been fundamentally changed. Even if there appear to be similarities with the familiar objects in Excel 5/7, the new objects together with their methods and properties are incompatible. This section assembles the most important differences.

As before, there are predefined standard menus, though now there are only two (instead of the previous four): The worksheet menu bar is displayed when no file is open or when a worksheet is active. The chart menu bar is shown when a chart is active or a chart sheet is displayed.

In general, the new objects are a visual improvement for menus and toolbars (though there is no accounting for taste), and VBA programmers will be disappointed at the unnecessary restrictions:

- The menu editor of version 7, which in any case was poorly conceived, was completely eliminated. The creation of new menus was unfortunately made more complicated than was already the case.

- Pop-up menus can be changed only in program code.

- Changes in predefined menus are no longer saved in the Excel file (but only in the user-specific file `Userprofile\Application Data\Microsoft\Excel\Excel.xlb`).

The greatest advantage in comparison to the old toolbars is less in the improved visual appearance than in the possibility of inserting more than new buttons in a toolbar. If you cast a sharper glance at the toolbars in Excel, you will discover items such as text fields with input possibilities, graphic listboxes, and movable listboxes (which then themselves form a toolbar; see the command CHANGE AUTOSHAPE in the "Drawing" toolbar). Unfortunately, the object model of the Office library provides only for the programming of buttons and text fields; that is, only a part of the features used within Excel can actually be used in VBA code.

> **CAUTION** *Menus and toolbars created in Excel 5/7 can usually continue to be used without restriction. The* Menu *and* Toolbar *objects continue to be supported for compatibility.*
>
> *Problems occur, though, if you wish to alter such preexisting menus. There is no way to transform Excel 5/7 menus or toolbars into* CommandBar *objects. Furthermore, it is impossible to save changes to preexisting menus. (For example, you can assign a new procedure to an existing menu entry. Everything works fine until you save the file and then open it again later. The menu has returned to its original state.) The same restrictions hold when you copy parts of an old menu into a new* CommandBar *object.*
>
> *So, you are faced with a choice: Either leave your old menu exactly as it is, or create a new* CommandBar *menu from the ground up (enjoy!). Especially annoying is that this execrable behavior, already worthy of criticism in Excel 97 (which you may be sure I did!) has not been improved in Excel 2000.*

Syntax Summary

CommandBars	*Methods and Properties*
ActiveMenuBar	refers to a *CommandBar* object with active menu bar
Add	add a new toolbar
FindControls	search for an element in a toolbar

CommandBar	*Methods and Properties*
ActionControl	refers to the previously clicked tool or menu item
BuiltIn	*True* for predefined toolbars
Controls	access to tools and menu items
Delete	delete toolbar
Name	name of the toolbar
NameLocal	name of the toolbar in the regional language
Position	position (anchored or as a toolbox)
Protection	protect against changes by the user
ShowPopup	display as pop-up menu
Visible	visibility of the toolbar

CommandBarControls	*Methods and Properties*
Add	add a tool/menu item/list
Count	number of menu items or tools

CommandBarControl	*Methods and Properties*
BeginGroup	a group begins with the object
BuiltIn	*True* for predefined elements
Caption	label text
Copy	copies an entry from another toolbar
Delete	delete entry
Enabled	*True* if the element can be used
Execute	executes the *OnAction* procedure
OnAction	name of the event procedure
TooltipText	yellow infotext (with *TooltipText=""*, *Caption* is used)
Type	type (for example, *msoControlButton, -ComboBox, -Popup*)

CommandBarButton	*Methods and Properties*
BuiltInFace	*True* if a predefined image
CopyFace	copy image to the clipboard
PasteFace	paste image from the clipboard
Reset	reset entry (useful only when *BuiltIn=True*)

CommandBarComboBox	*Methods and Properties*
AddItem	insert list item
Clear	delete all list items
DropDownLines	desired number of lines for drop-down list
DropDownWidth	desired width for drop-down list
List(n)	access to list items
ListCount	number of list items
ListIndex	index number of selected item
RemoveItem	delete list item
SetFocus	direct input focus to listbox
Text	input text or text of selected item
Type	*msoControlEdit, -Dropdown,* or *-ComboBox*

CommandBarPopup	*Methods and Properties*
Controls	access to elements (refers to *CommandBarControls*)

With the objects *CommandBarButton*, *CommandBarComboBox*, and *CommandBarPopup* only those methods and properties are listed that have already been made available with *CommandBarControl*.

User Interface for Freestanding Excel Applications

This section sets out from the assumption that you want to design an Excel application that can be installed with everything it needs to run on other computers. Basically, there are three possibilitites as to how such applications can behave when opened:

- The application offers, through extensions to the standard menus and toolbars, mechanisms for running the application *in addition to* the normal Excel mechanisms, which remain available for use. The advantage: After the file is loaded, other Excel files can be used as well with no difficulty. The drawback: The new mechanisms can become lost among the normal menus and toolbars.

- The application integrates all operating mechanisms into custom toolbars that are automatically displayed when the file is opened. The advantage: There is no sharp distinction between "normal" Excel elements and additional commands. The drawback: The toolbar requires additional real estate on the monitor. Furthermore, either the items are redundant, or else the user is compelled to move back and forth between the standard menus and toolbars and those specific to the application.

- On startup the application activates its own custom menus and toolbars. The operating elements for the application thus *replace* those of Excel. The advantage: Only those commands are availale that the user needs to operate the application. This is particularly practical for users who are not Excel experts and would be overtaxed by the full spectrum of Excel menus. (Moreover, this lessens the possibility that commands might be accidentally executed that could cause mischief.) The drawback: Excel is now hardly recognizable; all the normal menus and toolbars have vanished. It is possible to work "normally" with other Excel files only if a change of window brings about a reversion to the standard configuration.

Since Excel 97 you can save new toolbars together with an Excel file (via VIEW|TOOLBARS|CUSTOMIZE|TOOLBARS|ATTACH). However, unlike what obtained in Excel 5/7, you cannot save any changes made to predefined menus and toolbars. Such changes are stored only in the file `Excel.xlb`. This file, however, cannot be passed to others. For this reason the second variant is the least problematic of the three. Although there is little concrete information about all of this in the Excel handbooks, one may suppose that this is the variant that Microsoft itself prefers.

The following three sections describe techniques for implementing all three variants. In all the examples care is taken to make the alterations transparent, that is, to restore the standard Excel configuration when the file is closed or the sheet is changed.

Extending the Standard Menu

This section shows how an additional menu can be inserted into the standard menu when an Excel file is opened (in *CommandBars("Worksheet Menu Bar")*). This menu is automatically hidden when a sheet is clicked on that does not belong to the application. Moreover, the menu is deleted when the file is closed. (A similar course of action is available, naturally, for tools that are copied to or deleted from the standard toolbars.)

Copying Menus

There are two ways in which you can add an additional menu to the standard menu bar.

- Carry out all extensions to the standard menu by way of the numerous VBA instructions for creating new items and labels, and assigning event procedures to them. The principal way of doing this is described above in this chapter.

- Save your new menu in an attached toolbar. At the start of your program leave the toolbar invisible, but copy the menu into the standard menu bar. The *CommandBarControl* object uses the ***Copy*** method for this. With the following command the specified object—a single menu entry or even the entire menu (*CommandBarPopup*)—is copied to the location in the target toolbar just ahead of that given by *position*:

  ```
  sourceobject.Copy target toolbar, position
  ```

The second variant has the advantage that the creation of the menu can proceed interactively, and thus it requires much less code. This section is confined to this variant.

> **NOTE** *In both cases you must first test whether the new menu is already in the standard menu bar. Otherwise, it could happen that your menu will appear twice. Furthermore, you should make sure that the menu is deleted when the file is closed.*

Example Program

The toolbar "CommandBar-Copy" is attached to the file `CommandBar-Copy.xls`. In *Workbook_Open* the first menu of this toolbar is copied with *Copy* to the second-to-last place in the standard menu. The menu is made visible with *Visible=True*, while the underlying toolbar is made invisible with *Visible=False*.

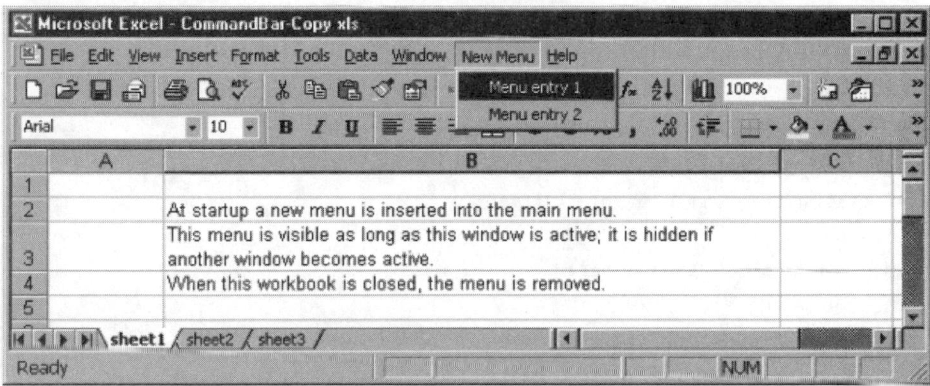

Figure 8.8. A new menu is inserted before the help menu in the main menu bar

```
' CommandBar-Copy.xls, "ThisWorkbook"
Private Sub Workbook_Open()
  Dim standardmenubar As CommandBar
  Dim mycommandbar As CommandBar
  Dim c As CommandBarControl
  Set standardmenubar = Application.CommandBars("worksheet menu bar")
  Set mycommandbar = Application.CommandBars("CommandBar-Copy")
  mycommandbar.Visible = False
  ' test whether menu already exists
```

```
  For Each c In standardmenubar.Controls
    If c.Caption = mycommandbar.Controls(1).Caption Then
      c.Visible = True
      Exit Sub
    End If
  Next
  ' menu does not exist: copy
  Set c = mycommandbar.Controls(1).Copy(standardmenubar, _
    standardmenubar.Controls.Count)
  c.Visible = True
End Sub
```

The procedures *Workbook_Activate* and *Workbook_Deactivate* have the job of making the menu disappear when the focus is shifted to another file; when the workbook is activated once more, the menu reappears.

The instruction *On Error Resume Next* prevents an error when the workbook is closed. In this case first *Workbook_BeforeClose* is executed, and there the new menu is deleted. Then *Workbook_Deactivate* is called, where the menu can no longer be accessed.

```
' activate/deactivate menu
Private Sub Workbook_Activate()
  Application.CommandBars("worksheet menu bar"). _
    Controls("new menu").Visible = True
End Sub
Private Sub Workbook_Deactivate()
  On Error Resume Next
  Application.CommandBars("worksheet menu bar"). _
    Controls("new menu").Visible = False
End Sub
```

When the file is closed, the menu is deleted from the standard menu bar. Furthermore, the toolbar is deleted, so that it is not saved in `Excel.xlb`.

```
Private Sub Workbook_BeforeClose(Cancel As Boolean)
  Dim standardmenubar As CommandBar
  Dim mycommandbar As CommandBar
  Dim c As CommandBarControl
  Set standardmenubar = Application.CommandBars("worksheet menu bar")
  Set mycommandbar = Application.CommandBars("CommandBar-Copy")
  For Each c In standardmenubar.Controls
    If c.Caption = mycommandbar.Controls(1).Caption Then
      c.Delete
    End If
```

```
    Next
    mycommandbar.Delete
End Sub
```

> **NOTE** *This example program deals only with the standard menu. If you wish to alter the menus of charts, you will have to append the additional instructions for* CommandBars("Chart Menu Bar") *and there copy and later delete the new menu.*

Hiding and Unhiding Custom Toolbars

The second variant involves the least effort. In the example file `CommandBar-AutoVisible.xls` the toolbar is made visible, and then it is deleted when the file is closed. Furthermore, the toolbar is automatically hidden and unhidden according to whether a window of the workbook in question, or that of another workbook, is visible .

```
' CommandBar-AutoVisible.xls, Module "ThisWorkbook"
' display toolbar
Private Sub Workbook_Open()
  Application.CommandBars("Commandbar-Auto").Visible = True
End Sub
' delete toolbar
Private Sub Workbook_BeforeClose(Cancel As Boolean)
  Application.CommandBars("Commandbar-Auto").Delete
End Sub
' display toolbar
Private Sub Workbook_Activate()
  Application.CommandBars("Commandbar-Auto").Visible = True
End Sub
' hide toolbar
Private Sub Workbook_Deactivate()
  On Error Resume Next
  Application.CommandBars("Commandbar-Auto").Visible = False
End Sub
```

> **POINTER** *In the example file there is also demonstrated the programming of a menu item with a selection check. The background information and associated code are to be found above, in the subsection on changing sheets via a toolbar.*

Using a Custom Standard Menu

The example program CommandBar-NewMenu.xls carries out a strategy similar to that of CommandBar-Copy.xls: The menu items for the main menu are stored in the toolbar "CommandBar-New," which is never displayed. When the file is opened, a new menu bar, "NewMenu," is created, into which the contents of "CommandBar-New" are copied. As soon as the new menu bar is made visible, the standard menu bar disappears. At program termination both the toolbar and the menu bar are deleted, and the standard menu appears automatically.

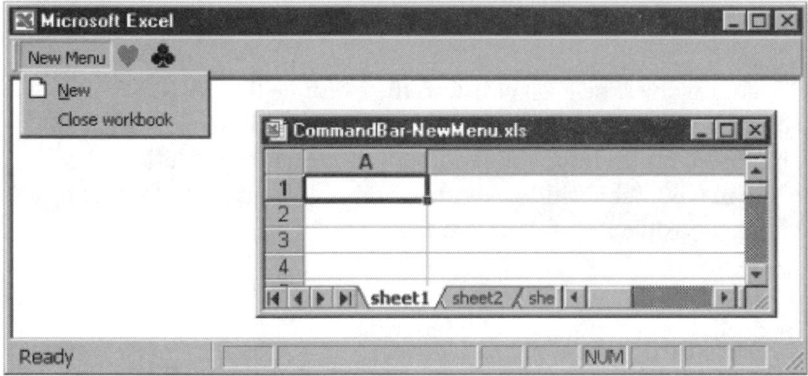

Figure 8.9. The example program has its own standard menu

```
' CommandBar-NewMenu.xls, "ThisWorkbook"
Private Sub Workbook_Open()
  Dim cb As CommandBar, c As CommandBarControl
  ' make toolbar invisible
  Application.CommandBars("Commandbar-New").Visible = False
  ' create new toolbar
  Set cb = Application.CommandBars.Add(Name:="NewMenu", _
    MenuBar:=True, Position:=msoBarTop)
  ' copy all items from "Commandbar-New" to "NewMenu"
  For Each c In Application.CommandBars("Commandbar-New").Controls
    c.Copy cb
  Next
End Sub
Private Sub Workbook_BeforeClose(Cancel As Boolean)
  On Error Resume Next
  ' delete toolbar
  Application.CommandBars("Commandbar-New").Delete
  ' delete new menu (with this the standard menu
```

```
  ' is automatically activated
  Application.CommandBars("NewMenu").Delete
End Sub
```

In this program the procedures *Workbook_Activate* and *Workbook_Deactivate* have the responsibility of seeing that the menu disappears when focus is switched to another file. When the original workbook is again activated, the menu appears again.

In comparison to the two previous programs, here we have something new in dealing with toolbars: As long as `CommandBar-NewMenu.xls` is active, all toolbars are hidden (thus only the new menu is visible). When it makes them invisible, the program saves a list of all visible toolbars in the *Collection* variable *visibleCommandBars*. All toolbars in this list are automatically made visible as soon as another worksheet is activated.

```
Dim visibleCommandBars As New Collection
Private Sub Workbook_Activate()
  Dim cb As CommandBar
  ' make new menu bar visible
  Application.CommandBars("NewMenu").Visible = True
  ' turn off all toolbars
  For Each cb In Application.CommandBars
    If cb.Type = msoBarTypeNormal And cb.Visible = True Then
      visibleCommandBars.Add cb, cb.Name
      cb.Visible = False
    End If
  Next
End Sub
Private Sub Workbook_Deactivate()
  Dim cb As Object
  On Error Resume Next
  Application.CommandBars("NewMenu").Visible = False
  ' make the toolbar visible again
  For Each cb In visibleCommandBars
    cb.Visible = True
  Next
  ' delete Collection list
  Set visibleCommandBars = Nothing
End Sub
```

Part III

Application

CHAPTER 9

Templates, Smart Forms

By smart forms we mean ready-made worksheets that need only to be filled out, ready-to-use templates and spreadsheet solutions, that is, to use Excel's nomenclature.

Templates can be constructed quite easily; they represent simply a layout framework for structuring sequences of operations, applicaton forms, reports, and so on. The templates can me made "intelligent" by a construction that allows them to carry out more or less complex calculations on the input using formulas embedded in the form, or to simplify the printing or saving process with the help of various macros.

Forms of this sort—such as for creating invoices or carrying out frequently occurring calculations—represent an enormous saving of labor in everyday existence. They make it possible even for Excel novices to use complex calculational models and to print out their results in an attractive and standardized form.

Chapter Overview

Fundamentals

In principle, "smart" forms are simply normal Excel tables in which some values have been left open for later input. A key feature is simplicity of operation. That is, it must be clear where input can be made, where not, and what meaning the various inputs have. To ensure against faulty use of the form, all other (noninput) cells must be protected against erroneous changes.

Excel form templates are thus "smarter" than the forms produced by any number of beaurocracies: The user does not have to input results that are a consequence of input already present; these will be calculated and displayed automatically. Perhaps as well, the user will be immediately notified of input errors (such as the input of a number when a date is called for).

In addition to embedded formulas, "smart" forms can have other aids, such as a button to print out and save the form or perhaps other controls that simplify the selection of various options. It is even possible to create a link between the form and a database application.

For creating smart forms it is useful to have templates. Here we are talking about a particular Excel file type (identifier `*.xlt`) that is designed for saving files that are to serve as templates for future Excel files.

In order for templates to be available to the FILE|NEW command, `*.xlt` files must be stored in one of the following three directories (see Chapter 5 for details):

`Userprofile\Application Data\Microsoft\Templates`	personal
`Office2000\Office\Xlstart`	global
`alternative startup file location`	set in TOOLS|OPTIONS|GENERAL

> **TIP** *A so-called template wizard makes it possible to turn a form template into a simple database application without a great deal of programming effort. Below we describe how to use this template wizard and indicate as well some of its limitations.*

Overview

An introductory example on the subject of smart forms can be found way back in Chapter 1. There you will find a form for calculating interest on a savings account with monthly compounding (`Intro5.xlt`). The form is simply structured and does not even use any macros.

In the next subsection we collect information on some typical Excel functions that are useful in creating smart forms: cell protection, *IF* formulas, printing worksheets, and so on. Then we go on to describe the use of the new template wizard and explain how forms are handled internally.

Two more complex examples—the invoice form of the fictive mail-order business "Speedy" and the balance sheet for a car-sharing club—stand at the center of the next two sections. These examples demonstrate the principal representations of smart forms. One could also consider forms for simplifying complex financial calculations (credit repayment, savings accounts, insurance models), for the analysis of measurement data, for evaluating examinations or questionnaires, for organizing data sets, and so on. The templates provided within Excel demonstrate further application possibilities.

The chapter ends with some critical observations, combined with constructive criticism and suggestions for improvement.

Design Elements for Smart Forms

Templates

In principle, templates are normal Excel files that are specified as file type "Template" when saved under the SAVE AS protocol. Templates have the identifier `*.xlt` (instead of `*.xls`). In the SAVE dialog it is automatically suggested that such files be saved in the folder USERPROFILE\APPLICATION DATA\MICROSOFT\TEMPLATES. If you use this directory, then the template can be used only by you (and not by other users with different log-in names).

To open an empty template, the menu command FILE|NEW must be used. In the dialog that appears all existing templates from the three template folders mentioned above are displayed. When you attempt to save the new file, Excel forces you to specify a new file name. In this way you are prevented from accidentally overwritng the template.

> **TIP** *Open templates with* FILE|OPEN *only if you wish to edit the actual template. Only* FILE|NEW *prevents you from accidentally altering the template and saving it as a template file (instead of a creating a normal Excel file based on the template).*
>
> *You may not use the button* NEW *on the standard toolbar in place of* FILE|NEW. *This button creates a new, empty workbook without presenting any templates for your selection.*

Templates are generally used in one of two variants:

- One may create empty worksheets in which merely certain formats are specified. Such templates have the purpose of saving the user effort in creating formats that are used over and over, such as the setting of print parameters and window options or the definition of frequently used styles. In this way it is possible to promote a uniform layout of all Excel worksheets produced by, say, an office or business: company logo on the first page, standardized headers and footers, uniform font, and so on.

- It is such more or less intelligent form templates with integrated VBA code that are the subject of this chapter.

Cell Protection

With Tools|Protection|Protect Sheet you can protect all the cells of a worksheet from being changed. You may generally do without a password, unless you suspect that the user will intentionally make changes to the worksheet. Since it does not make sense to protect all the cells, since then no input could be given at all, before executing the protection command it is necessary to remove protection from the input cells. The dialog for this purpose is invoked with Format|Cells| Protection or the pop-up menu Format Cells|Protection. There you deactivate the option "Locked."

If you frequently change the protection of individual cells, you can add the tool for this to the toolbar. This tool is located under the category "Format." Its image is a padlock.

> **TIP** *Further information on the protection functions available in Excel and the associated properties and methods can be found in Chapter 5.*

Validation of Input Cells

Since Excel 97 you can use DataValidation to formulate validation rules for individual cells or entire ranges of cells (see also the introductory example in Chapter 1). This lets you restrict the format (integer, floating point number, date, text) and the permissible range of values of the input. If you specify text in the dialog pages Input message and Error message, an infotext or error text is automatically displayed whenever the rules for the input are violated. With validation rules you thus ensure the form against incorrect input, and you give the user useful additional information. Validation rules cannot be altered in protected worksheets.

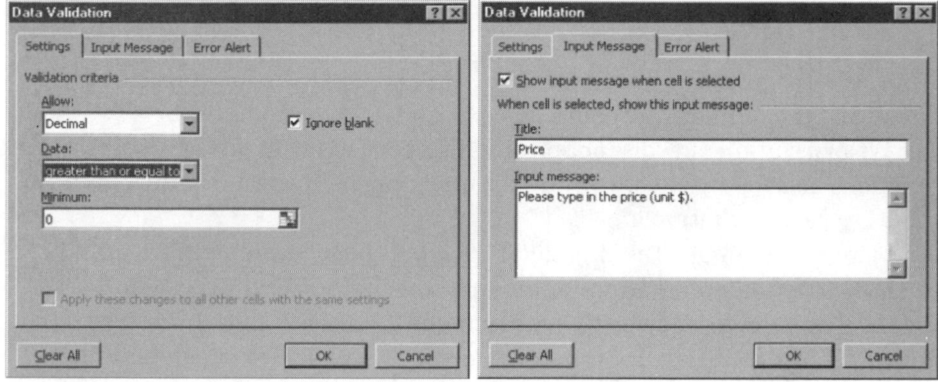

Figure 9.1. Two dialog sheets for data validation

Template Preview

In the dialog File|New there is a place reserved for a preview of the file to be opened. This document preview works only if before the template is saved, File|Properties|Summary is used to activate the Save preview picture. Note, however, that this causes not only the template but all files based on it to increase in size by a certain number of kilobytes.

IF *Formulas*

In order to make a formula template more or less generally usable, the calculational model behind it almost always makes case distinctions. The formulas in a table must determine whether the input is valid. If it is, then there is a result to be calculated. But if not, then a value of 0 or even an empty cell should be displayed. Sometimes, different formulas are required depending on the input values, such as a discount that goes into effect only on a minimum order of goods.

The basis of such case distinctions is the *IF* formulas. The construction of such formulas is simple in principle:

```
=IF(condition, result1, result2)
```

Excel tests in its calculation of the cells in which the *IF* formula is located whether *condition* is satisfied. If it is, then the formula in *result1* is employed for the calculation, and otherwise, the formula in *result2*.

Let us consider an example: Suppose that cell A1 contains a unit price and B1 the number of units. In C1 is to appear the product of the amounts in A1 and B1, with a five percent discount if the number of units is 10 or more. Then the formula in C1 might be as follows:

```
=IF(B1<10, A1*B1, A1*B1*0.95).
```

Nested IF Formula

IF formulas begin to become unreadable when several cases are considered at once or if the conditions are complex.

We first consider the distinction among several cases: In this case several *IF* functions must be nested one within the other; that is, the result of the first *IF* formula is again an *IF* formula.

Here is an example: The situation is like that above (contents of A1, B1, C1), but now we wish to consider the additional case that B1 is empty, in which case the assumption is to be made that the number of units is 1. When A1 is also empty, then no result at all is to be shown (not even 0). The resulting formula might look like this:

```
=IF(A1="", "", IF(B1="", A1, IF(B1<10, A1*B1, A1*B1*0.95))).
```

The contents of the formula can still be easily understood: If A1 if empty, then no result is shown (that is, an empty character string " "). If B1 is empty (and if we have gotten this far, it has been established that A1 is not empty), then the result is simply the contents of A1, which corresponds to a unit count of 1. The third *IF* function comes into play only once it has been established that both A1 and B1 are not empty, and this formula corresponds to that of the first example.

Compound Conditionals

In the foregoing examples the conditions were extremely simple. But frequently, several conditions must be simultaneously fulfilled or perhaps only at least one of several conditions must be satisfied. To this end several conditions can be given within an *AND* or *OR* function. Of course, these functions can be nested as well. The general syntax is as follows:

```
=AND(condition1, condition2, condition3, ...),
=OR(condition1, condition2, condition3, ...).
```

AND returns the Boolean value *TRUE* if all the listed conditions are satisfied (and there can be arbitrarily many of them). *OR* returns *TRUE* if at least one of the conditions is satisfied.

An example of a compound conditional is the following: Values between 0 and 1 should appear in cells A1 and B1. If that is indeed the case, then the following formula computes their product. Otherwise, an error text is displayed:

```
=IF(AND(A1>=0, A1<=1, B1>=0, B1<=1), A1*B1, "incorrect initial values")
```

TIP *With* Shift+Ctrl+A *you can insert the appropriate parentheses and arguments after typing the function name. This input assistance is to be recommended when you are uncertain as to the precise order of the arguments. But you can just as well do without the complicated input assistance provided by Excel (the former function assistant).*

POINTER *Various advanced worksheet functions are described in Chapters 5 (calculations with date and time) and 11 (database worksheet functions). In the case of complex tasks, worksheet formulas can become extremely unreadable. For such situations Excel offers the possibility of defining functions in VBA. Details on creating user-defined functions can be found in Chapter 5.*

Labeling Colored (Red) Error Texts

There is is no way within an *IF* formula to influence the output format (number format, color, alignment, border, and so on) of a cell. By taking the detour of number formatting you can nevertheless manage to get numbers in normal (black) type to be represented in another color.

```
Standard;Standard;Standard;[Red]Standard
```

As an example, with the number format shown above you can display positive and negative numbers as well as 0 in standard format, with texts, however, in red (but otherwise in standard format). In addition to red you can provide in square brackets an additional seven colors: black, blue, cyan, green, magenta, white, and yellow.

POINTER *Of course, you can also define special formats for each of these four cases (number positive, negative, 0 text). A considerable amount of background information can be found in Chapter 5.*

Conditional Formatting

Even more formatting options are offered by so-called conditional formatting. With it three conditions can be formulated that are checked one after the other when the content of a cell changes. Each condition is associated to a format, which in addition to color and font can include border and patterns. The first condtion that is satisfied determines the format for the cell.

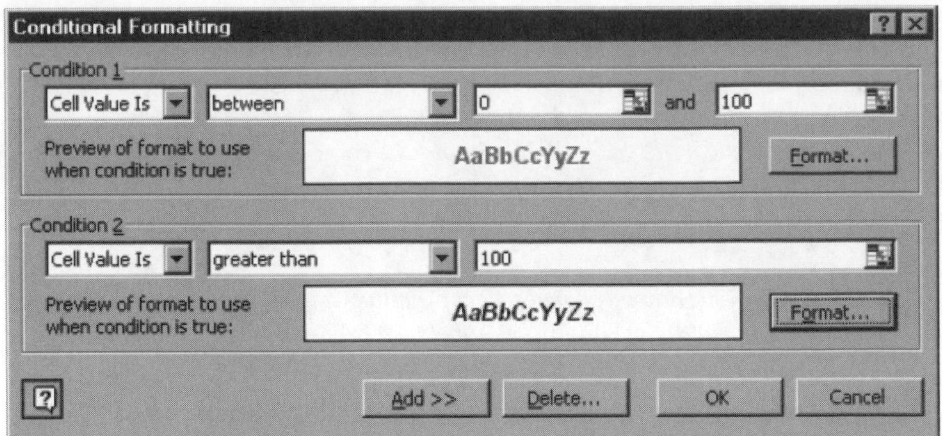

Figure 9.2. Conditional formatting

With conditional formatting you can arrange things, for example, so that numbers exceeding a certain value are highlighted by having their color change. In VBA programming conditional formats can be defined via the object *FormatCondition* (using the *Range* property *FormatConditions(n)*).

Printing the Form

Smart forms are generally conceived in such a way that they can be easily printed. You should plan for this eventuality when you are planning your form and order the document in such a way that it corresponds in a sensible way to the print area of one or more pages.

Headers and Footers

Excel makes provision for worksheets to have no header and footer. For forms these settings are generally not particularly suitable and can be changed or deleted with FILE|PAGE SETUP|HEADER/FOOTER.

Current Date

If the smart form is to contain the current date, you can specify that it appear in any given cell with the formula *=TODAY()*. Alternatively, you can insert the date into the header or footer. In the latter case, however, you have fewer formatting choices in the placement of the date.

With both variants you must beware that when the form is saved and then opened and printed at a later date, the date will have changed (because once again the current date will be inserted). If that is not the desired effect, then a macro must be used to ensure that the date is frozen in time, so to speak, before the file is closed. To this end either the cell with the *TODAY* formula can be changed (EDIT|PASTE SPECIAL, with option VALUES), or else a text string with the current date can be written into the header or footer.

Serial Number

A more challenging task is to equip your smart form with sequential serial numbers, which would be useful, for example, in preparing and printing invoices. A solution to this problem is available only by means of a macro that is executed when the document is printed or immediately before printing. This macro must be able to access the number of the previously printed form. An example is presented in the next section.

Layout of the Form

If you are not satisfied with the layout options offered by Excel, say for the appearance of your firm's logo, you can use an OLE program (such as PaintBrush, WordArt (supplied with Word), or Corel Draw). Graphical objects can be integrated into the worksheet with INSERT|OBJECT or INSERT|PICTURE. If you want to draw a narrow frame around the object, this can easily be done in the pop-up menu for the object. Choose FORMAT PICTURE| COLORS AND LINES.

Color

Colored text, and cells with a colored background, present problems when a document is printed. On the other hand, colors can make the use of a smart form much more user friendly. A way out of this dilemma is to carry out the printing with a macro designed to solve this problem. This macro (which can be easily recorded) eliminates from the printing all background colors and then restores the original format. If this restoration is computationally expensive, you can simply copy the entire worksheet to the clipboard, insert a new worksheet, and there insert the contents of the clipboard, eliminate the background colors, print the worksheet, and then delete it. In this way the original is left untouched. An example of this method appears in the section after next.

Integrating Controls into the Form

The same controls that can be placed in forms (dialogs) (see Chapter 7) can also be placed in worksheets (thus in "smart" forms—note the two unrelated uses of the word "form"): text boxes, buttons, check boxes, option buttons, listboxes, scroll bars, and so on. In practice, the most frequently used of these are the buttons, which can be placed in the worksheet to allow various macros to be run "at the touch of a button."

However, the range of application is much broader. Thus you can insert scroll bars to enable the user to insert a numerical value with the mouse within a prescribed range. Or you can simplify the task of input by using listboxes, by means of which the user can choose an input value from a predefined list of options. With option buttons the user can choose from among various calculational or application variants. An introductory example appears in Chapter 7.

Of particular practicality in connection with controls is the possibility of using the property *PrintObject* to determine whether the particular control will be printed out. The default setting is *True*. If you set the property to *False*, then controls can be placed in a form to facilitate input without ruining the desired appearance of a printout.

Charts in Smart Forms

Form templates can also be used in combination with charts. If the range of a data set is fixed at the start of operations, then a completed chart can be integrated into the worksheet when the form is created. It will then change its appearance as data are entered. On the other hand, if the appearance and data range need to be flexible, then a macro must be used to create a new chart. Programming of charts is discussed in Chapter 10.

Templates Linked to Databases

Excel comes fitted out with a template wizard (command DATA|TEMPLATE WIZARD; if this item does not appear in your menu, you must activate this extension with the add-in manager via TOOLS|ADD-INS; if the add-in manager seems not to know about the template wizard, then you will have to reinstall the wizard). The template wizard creates a link between a template and a database file.

The Template Wizard

To begin you will need a completed template (`*.xlt` file). After having opened this template as a file (not with FILE|NEW but with FILE|OPEN), activate the template wizard with DATA|TEMPLATE WIZARD.

The format of the database file can be set in step 2 of the template wizard. Among the options are Excel worksheets and Access files. Excel worksheets have the advantage of being easily processed within Excel. Access files meet more stringent professional requirements and are particularly suitable for use with large data sets. Furthermore, Access need not be installed for you to be able to read and write Access files under Excel. (See also the next chapter, in which the database capacities and limitations of Excel are described.) After the database file has been defined, select and name in step 3 each input or result cell that you wish to be saved in the database.

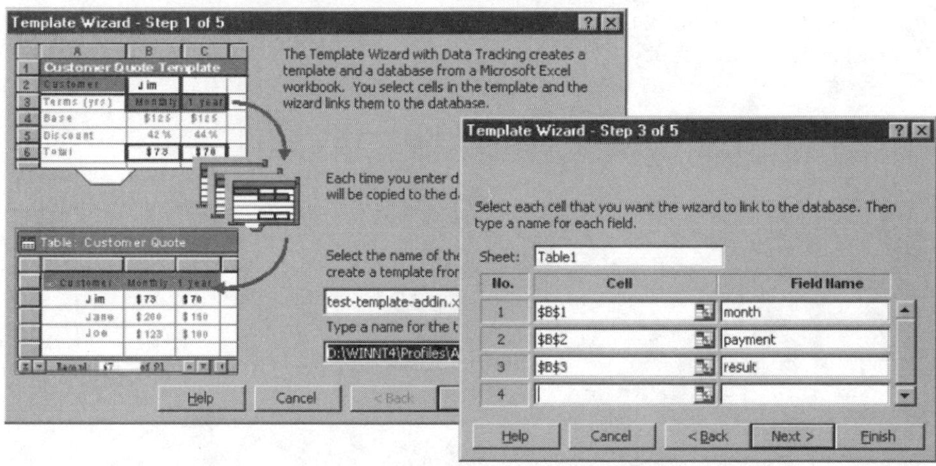

Figure 9.3. The two most important steps of the template wizard

In step 4 you are given the opportunity to add information from existing Excel workbooks whose format corresponds to the template to the database. This makes sense if the template has been used for a while and then later it has been decided to link the template to a database. In the case of new templates, simply answer NO, SKIP IT.

Lastly, in step 5 you can specify e-mail addresses to be placed in a so-called routing list. Each time a new file that has been created based on the template is closed, you are asked whether this file should be sent to the addresses on the routing list. This system functions only if the e-mail client used is Outlook or a sufficiently current version of Outlook Express.

> **TIP** *If an existing file used as the basis of the template is changed, the changed file will not be sent again by e-mail. The changes will, however, certainly be entered in the template database.*

Using a Database Template

Linked templates are used just like normal templates: The user opens the template, fills out the appropriate fields, and saves the file. At this point a dialog automatically appears in which the user is asked whether the data should be saved in the database file. If the user answers in the affirmative (it is hoped), all relevant cells (those previously selected in the template wizard) are entered into a new line or data record of the database.

Unfortunately, this dialog contains no information as to why this duplicate saving is useful or necessary or whether it obviates the need for normal saving. A somewhat more informative text for this dialog and an associated help text would not be an extravagant luxury!

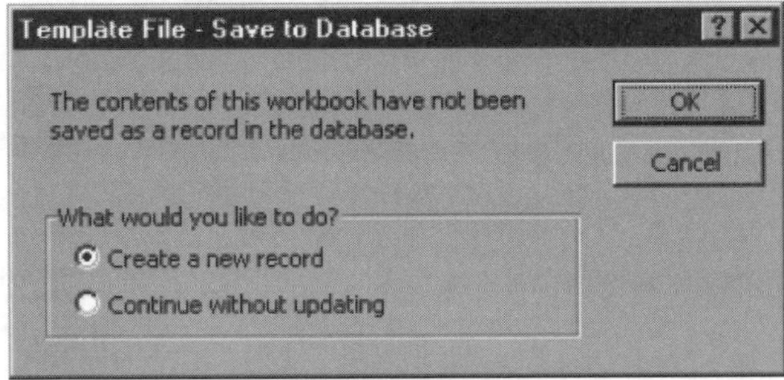

Figure 9.4. Dialog for saving a new file based on a template

In principle, the new template is used as before: fill out, save, print. The only thing that is new is that the data in some selected cells are *additionally* saved in a special file.

Particularly attractive are templates with database linkages in networks. If all users have access to the same template, then all essential data from forms that are created from this template can be automatcally recorded in a centrally managed file.

The evaluation of the database file—whether in Excel, Access, or another file format—is not regulated by the template wizard. If you wish, for example, to create monthly records or transfer data to an invoice database, you will have to write your own VBA macros. A template with database linkage is not a real database program, but at best, a step in this direction.

Internal Affairs

Perhaps you are interested in how a template enhanced by the template wizard functions internally. The template is extended to include two invisible sheets.

- The Excel 4 macro sheet "AutoOpen Stub Data" contains the macro *AutoOpen21*, which is automatically executed when the file is opened. This macro loads the add-in file `Office2000\Office\Library\Vlassist.xla`. The add-in contains the actual VBA program code for the management of the database file. (The separation of template and code into two separate files has the advantage that Excel files resulting from templates are not made unnecessarily large.)

  You can look at the Excel 4 macro code if you first make it visible in the development environment:

  ```
  Sheets("AutoOpen Stub Data").Visible = True
  ```

- The worksheet with the name "TemplateInformation" can likewise be made visible in the development environment:

  ```
  Sheets("TemplateInformation").Visible = True
  ```

  It contains information about which cells of which sheet of the template should be saved where. To prevent an intentional or unintentional manipulation by the user, all rows and columns are hidden. If you wish to have a look, select all cells with Ctrl+A and then execute FORMAT|ROW|UNHIDE and FORMAT|COLUMN|UNHIDE.

> **CAUTION** *The program code in* `Vlassist.xla` *is based on the information in the two sheets described above and responds allergically to changes. Cell A1 of the* TemplateInformation *sheet contains, and with good reason, the text* AutoTemplateWizardDONTMESSWITHIT.

Unfortunately, the source code of the add-in file `Vlassist.xla` is protected by a password and cannot be displayed. However, it is not difficult to guess that in this file an *OnSave* event procedure for templates has been developed such that on each save of a file based on the template, the procedure `Vlassist.xla` is automatically executed.

Deleting the Database Linkage

With DATA|TEMPLATE WIZARD you can create a linkage between a database and a template, but there is no option for breaking this linkage. Furthermore, you will find yourself in trouble if you later wish to change the type of linkage (for example, Access instead of an Excel file). The only solution consists in copying the new Excel file and saving it as a new template.

Templates Included with Excel

A number of templates are included in Excel, for example, for calculating the cost of a trip. These templates do not, alas, offer much in the way of an example for user friendliness and clarity. It is also not clear whether it makes sense to save a file of over 350 kilybytes (which happens each time you fill out a form and save it) every time you calculate the cost of a trip.

Example: The "Speedy" Invoice Form

We shall use the Speedy company as the starting point for our first example of this chapter. This imaginary company has specialized in mail order and has established certain fixed business practices:

- Discount: Ordering ten or more units of an article entitles the purchaser to a 3 percent discount; twenty units increases the discount to 5 percent.
- Packaging: An order of \$50 or less results in a packaging charge of \$3. If the order is more than \$50, this charge is waived.
- Shipping: Orders up to \$50 are charged \$3 for shipping; for larger orders the charge is \$5.
- Value added tax (VAT): This can be optionally added to the total. (This form was conceived for a German firm, for which value added tax is imposed for internal orders—within Germany—and waived for foreign orders. This can be adapted to other systems of taxation.)

Figure 9.5 shows the essential parts of the template for the company's invoice form (file `Speedy.xlt`). The fields for name and address, VAT, product ID, product name, price, and number of units are displayed in yellow on the monitor and indicate the input fields for the user, who must provide the name and address of the purchaser and the identification number of the article purchased, as well as the unit price and number of units. If value added tax is to be imposed, the "VAT" check box must be activated.

> **TIP** *To make* Speedy.xlt *available as a template, the file must first be copied into the folder* USERPROFILE\APPLICATION DATA\MICROSOFT\TEMPLATES. *The file* Speedy.xlt *contains code that causes it to be saved in this location each time the file is saved (regardless of the location where the file was opened).*

Predefined formulas are used to calculate the applicable discount of 3 or 5 percent. The price is calculated from the unit price, number of units, and discount rate. Then the total price is calculated from the individual prices. According to the value of the total order and the VAT field activation, the various surcharges are computed and added in, so that first the net total is computed and finally, if applicable, the value added tax.

The formulas are self-explanatory:

```
Discount (e.g., cell G23):
  =IF(F23<10,"",IF(F23<20,0.03,0.05))
Final price (H23):
  =IF(E23=0,"",IF(F23=0,E23,IF(G23="",E23*F23,E23*F23*(1-G23))))
Packing (H39):
  =IF(H38<50,3,0)
Shipping (H40):
  =IF(H38<50,3,5)
VAT (H42):
  =IF(C20=TRUE,H41*0.16,0)
VAT-label (G42):
  =IF(C20=TRUE,"16 % VAT","no VAT")
```

In the formulas above, the cell references have the following meaning:

```
C20: VAT (the cell is linked to the control box and contains the values
 TRUE or FALSE)
E23: unit price
F23: number of units
G23: discount
H38: subtotal (without packing, shipping, and VAT)
H41: subtotal net (with packing and shipping, but not VAT)
H43: total
```

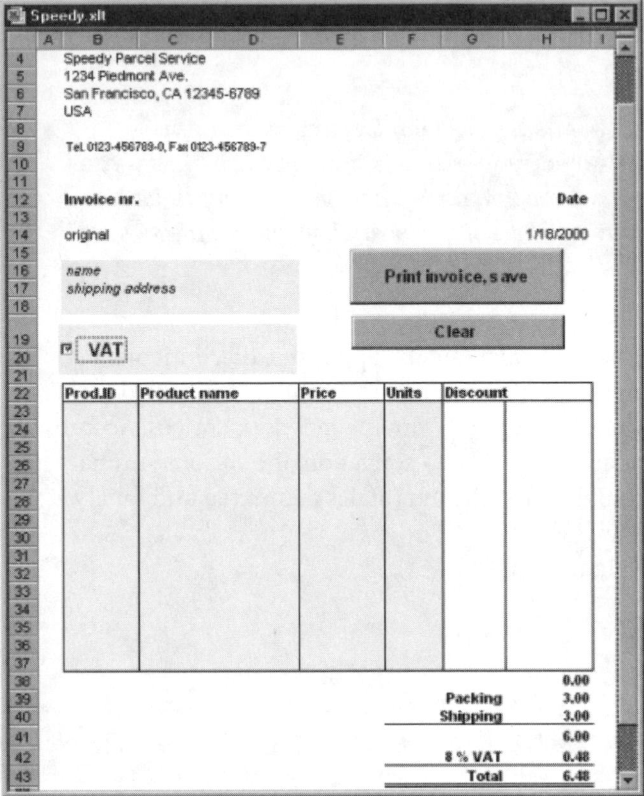

Figure 9.5. Template for the invoice form for the "Speedy" company

Controls

The form is equipped with a spin button by means of which one can set the number of duplicate invoices (0 to 3) that will be printed. The button Clear erases all input data in the form, making possible input for the next form.

With the button labeled Print invoice, save the invoice is printed and saved in a file called `Speedy_nnnnnn.xls`, where nnn is replaced by a running invoice number. In contrast to typical forms, for which the user must take care of the details of saving, this step has been automated by Speedy. The advantage is that the invoice can be saved compactly.

In order for the invoice file to take up as little space as possible, only the numerical values in `Speedy.xlt` are copied (no formulas, no controls, no VBA code). All the cells are locked, and the entire worksheet is protected with the password "speedy." In this way later manipulation of the data in the invoice is avoided.

Features of the Form's Design

In our smart form all the cells in which input values are allowed are colored yellow (see Figure 9.5, where the background is colored gray). Any input outside of these fields is forbidden.

Only the range A1:I47 is printed. The cells in other columns (invoice number, duplication number) are only for the purposes of internal management. For the controls within the printing range the property *PrintObject* is set to *False*. The logo at the top was designed in the program WordArt, which comes bundled with Word. Header and footer in `Speedy.xlt` were set to "none."

The check box `VAT` is linked to cell C20, which, depending on the state of the control box, has the value *TRUE* or *FALSE*. So that this Boolean value does not appear as an irritant, its text color has been set to "white." Therefore, the contents of C20 are invisible.

In `Speedy.xlt` four names for individual cells were defined:

```
printrange:      A1:I47
nrOfCopies:      L19
original_copy:   B14
invoiceNr:       L17
```

These names are used in the procedure *btnPrintAndSave_Click* to refer to the named cells. This makes the program easier to read, but it also has the advantage of giving flexibility to the table structure. For example, if you insert an empty row into the table, then all the affected names are automatically brought up to date. If the program were to refer directly to the individual cells (such as with *Range("L19")* or with the shorthand *[L19]*), then this reference would have to be changed "manually."

Such direct references also appear in program code, and indeed, always when a procedure is created by way of a macro recording (such as *Workbook_Open* or *btnClear_Click*). The macro recorder does not have the ability to place names of regions in the code.

The Program Code

When the file is opened, all input cells of the smart form are cleared in *Workbook_Open* via a call to *btnClear_Click*. The procedure *btnClear_Click* can also be invoked with the button labeled Clear.

```
' Speedy.xlt, "ThisWorkbook"
Private Sub Workbook_Open()
  Worksheets(1).Select
```

```
  Worksheets(1).btnClear_Click
End Sub
' Speedy.xlt, "sheet1"
Public Sub btnClear_Click()
  Worksheets(1).CheckBox1 = False
  Range("B16").FormulaR1C1 = "name"
  Range("B17").FormulaR1C1 = "shipping address"
  Range("B18").FormulaR1C1 = ""
  Range("B23:F37").ClearContents
  Range("B16").Select
End Sub
```

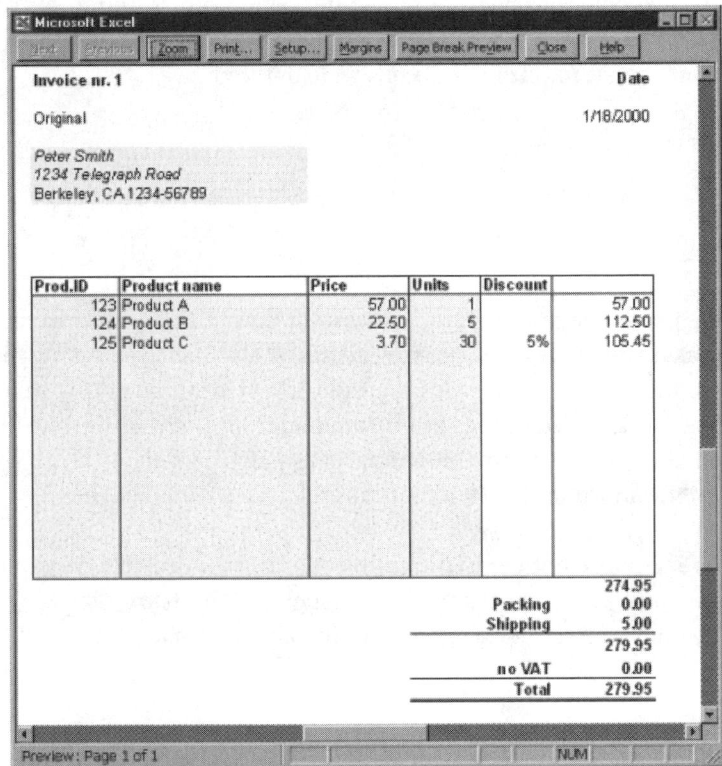

Invoice nr. 1 **Date**

Original 1/18/2000

Peter Smith
1234 Telegraph Road
Berkeley, CA 1234-56789

Prod.ID	Product name	Price	Units	Discount	
123	Product A	57.00	1		57.00
124	Product B	22.50	5		112.50
125	Product C	3.70	30	5%	105.45

	274.95
Packing	0.00
Shipping	5.00
	279.95
no VAT	0.00
Total	279.95

Figure 9.6. Page preview of a "Speedy" invoice

Now let us proceed to the most important part of the program code, the procedure *btnPrintAndSave_Click*. This procedure uses the method *PrintOut* to print first the original invoice and then the desired number of copies. The original and duplicates are identified, not terribly originally, with the words "original" and "duplicate."

Then a new, empty, workbook is opened and into it is copied, via the clipboard, the print region of the form (that is, only the numerical values and the associated formatting). The workbook is saved under the name `Speedy_nnnnnn.xls` in the PERSONAL folder and then closed. Finally, the current invoice number is increased by 1, and `Speedy.xlt` is saved. The greater part of the code is easy to understand, and so we will mention only a few key features here.

Response to Errors

On Error Resume Next ensures that the procedure always terminates. The most likely cause of error is the user interrupting the printing of the invoice. If this interrupt occurs during printing of the original, the procedure is exited at once; the user can alter the invoice and then initiate printing anew. However, if the error occurs only during the printing of a duplicate, the procedure assumes that the invoice has been correctly formulated and that the user simply desires a smaller number of duplicate copies. In this case the printing of all duplicates is terminated, but otherwise, the procedure runs its course to the end.

Displaying the Status Bar

To give the user feedback as to what is happening, in the status bar are displayed first "print invoice" and then "save invoice Speedy_nnnnn." The state of the status bar is restored at the end of the procedure; that is, if the status bar was previously hidden, at the end of the procedure it is again deactivated.

Copying the Invoice into Its Own File

From a technical point of view, the most interesting programming feature of this section is the copying of the print region of `Speedy.xlt` into a new, empty, workbook. After the copying of values and formats by way of two calls to the method *PasteSpecial*, the column width of the first nine columns is correctly set (this information is not transmitted during the copying).

Worksheet Protection

At the start of *btnPrintAndSave_Click* the worksheet protection of `Speedy.xlt` is lifted via the method *Unprotect*, so that the cells *[original_copy]* and *[invoiceNr]* can be changed in the program. This protection is restored at the end of the procedure (without password) with *Protect*. In the invoice file all cells inserted via the clipboard are first locked (property *Locked=True*), and then the entire worksheet is protected with the password "speedy."

```
Private Sub btnPrintAndSave_Click()
  Dim i%, result, filename$, statusbarMode
  Dim ws As Worksheet, newWb As Workbook, wsCopy As Worksheet
  On Error Resume Next
  statusbarMode = Application.DisplayStatusBar
  Application.DisplayStatusBar = True
  Application.StatusBar = "print invoice ..."
  Set ws = Worksheets(1)
  ws.Unprotect
  ' print invoice
  ws.[original_copy] = "Original"
  ws.[printrange].PrintOut Preview:=True
  If Err = 0 Then
    ' print also n duplicates
    For i = 1 To ws.[nrOfCopies]
      ws.[original_copy] = "duplicate " & i
      Application.StatusBar = "print duplicate " & i
      ws.[printrange].PrintOut
      If Err Then Exit For
    Next i
    ' copy sheet in a new workbook and save
    filename = Application.DefaultFilePath & "\Speedy_" & _
      Format(ws.[invoiceNr], "000000")
    Application.StatusBar = "save invoice " & filename & "..."
    Application.ScreenUpdating = False
    ws.[original_copy] = "original"
    ws.[printrange].Copy
    Set newWb = Workbooks.Add
    Set wsCopy = newWb.Worksheets(1)
    ' copy only cells (values, formats), but no controls
    wsCopy.[A1].PasteSpecial xlValues
    wsCopy.[A1].PasteSpecial xlFormats
    ' adjust column width
    For i = 1 To 8
      wsCopy.Cells(1, i).ColumnWidth = ws.Cells(1, i).ColumnWidth
    Next i
    newWb.Windows(1).DisplayGridlines = False
    ' lock sheet, password "speedy"
    wsCopy.[A1:H50].Locked = True
    wsCopy.Protect "speedy"
    ' save as "Speedy_nnnnnn"; n is the invoiceNr
    newWb.SaveAs filename
    newWb.Close
    If Err = 0 Then
```

```
      MsgBox "The invoice has been saved in file " & filename & "."
      ' increment invoiceNr, clear form
      ws.[invoiceNr] = ws.[invoiceNr] + 1
      btnClear_Click
      ' save template
      SaveTemplate
    End If
    Application.ScreenUpdating = True
  End If
  If Err <> 0 Then
    MsgBox "An error has occurred"
  End If
  ws.Protect
  Application.StatusBar = False
  Application.DisplayStatusBar = statusbarMode
End Sub
```

The updated template is stored in the procedure *SaveTemplate.* What has changed is actually only the invoice number, but that change is what necessitates the updating.

```
Private Sub SaveTemplate()
  'don't ask whether existing file may be overwritten (it will)
  Application.DisplayAlerts = False
  ' save file in personal template directory
  ThisWorkbook.SaveAs _
     filename:=Application.TemplatesPath + "Speedy", _
     FileFormat:=xlTemplate
  Application.DisplayAlerts = True
End Sub
```

TIP *With the* SaveAs *method in* SaveTemplate *the file is saved in the personal template directory. If the template is to be available to several users, then instead it must be saved in the global template directory. Unfortunately, since the advent of Excel 2000 there is no longer a property that refers to this folder. You may use the following code, but be aware that it is country-specific. (The* LIBRARY *folder has the name* LIBRARY, *but in the German version, for example, it is called* MAKRO.*)*

```
Dim globalxlstart$
globalxlstart = Replace(LCase(Application.LibraryPath), _
  "library", "xlstart")
ThisWorkbook.SaveAs filename:=globalxlstart + "\Speedy", _
  FileFormat:=xlTemplate
```

Room for Improvement

Speedy.xlt has a number of shortcomings. First, managing the invoice number directly in the template makes it impossible to use the template over a network (since it could happen that two users would print an invoice with the same number). Second, the invoice files Speedy_nnnnn.xls are unnecessarily large by about 20 Kbyte (in consideration of the amount of data stored). And third, making corrections to an invoice that has already been printed is well nigh impossible.

There is a simple solution to the first problem. The invoice number must be located in a central location in its own file. From there the number is read immediately before printing and immediately increased by 1. There is still the possibility that two Excel applications will access the invoice number file simultaneously, but it is most unlikely. A professional solution of the problem would involve managing the invoice number from a central program (preferably through a database application that stores other invoice data).

The second shortcoming can be circumvented by not storing a copy of the entire print area in the invoice file, but only a copy of the input (yellow) cells and the result cells in the lower region of the table. One might also consider whether several invoices might be stored in the same file (for example, in the form of a daily summary, in which all invoices of a given day are stored together).

The solution of the third problem is somewhat more involved. A procedure must be written in which the data of an already saved invoice are read in, changed, and printed. Here, of course, arises the issue of security. Should it be possible, in general, to print out two different invoices with the same invoice number? Or should the first, erroneous, invoice be voided and the corrected invoice be printed as a new invoice with a new number?

All of these suggestions for improvement point in the direction of a database application. This subject will be considered in greater detail in the next chapter, particularly since Excel is not really a database application and is not easily adapted to database programming.

Example: Balance Sheet for a Car-Sharing Club

Our second smart form (example file Share.xlt) manages a balance sheet for a car-sharing club. Members of the club can borrow a car from the club's inventory. In addition to a security deposit and monthly dues, the charges for the use of an automobile might be placed in the following categories, at least for the purposes of this example. These costs will vary depending on the type of car:

hourly rate I (8 am–8 pm)	$ 1.20
hourly rate II (8 pm–2 am, 6 am–8 am)	$ 0.65
hourly rate III (2 am–6 am)	$ 0.00
full day rate (24 hours)	$ 18.00
weekend credit	$ 6.00
charge per mile	$ 0.18

The hourly rate applies to a full hour or a fraction thereof. The daily rate is valid for any 24-hour period, beginning at any time. If the car is borrowed over a weekend, then the charge is reduced by the weekend credit amount. The charge per mile includes gasoline. If the club member fills the tank, then those charges are refunded. These charges should cover all of the club's expenses, including purchase, maintenance, insurance, and taxes.

If the charges seem high, it should be borne in mind that they are conceived for persons who use a car only seldom and for whom it is therefore a more economical alternative to owning and maintaining a car. It should also be taken into account, for urban dwellers at least, that they will not have to pay for parking, which in New York, for example, can easily run to over $30 per day. They also will not have to worry about maintenance, insurance, and so on.

After that short commercial in support of the car-sharing model, let us return to the rigors of Excel. The example file `Share.xlt` contains the form template shown in Figure 9.7. In order to make the template available, it must first be copied into the template directory of the Office package. To open the file, File|New must be used (not File|Open).

For completing the information for a transaction, only relatively few items need to be input: name of the member, type of car (in a listbox), start and end times for the hourly rate or start and end dates for the daily rate, number of miles traveled, and finally, the amount spent on gasoline.

From these few data Excel determines how many hours should be charged to each of the three hourly rates and whether the start and end dates for the daily rate include a weekend. The resulting charges are summed.

The button labled Print invoice initiates printing of the form. The macro thus activated copies the current date and inserts it again as a number so that the invoice will be saved with a fixed date. Then the entire table is copied into a new worksheet. In this worksheet the yellow background (gray in Figure 9.7) is removed. Then the worksheet is printed and afterwards deleted. The resulting printout looks something like the one displayed in Figure 9.8.

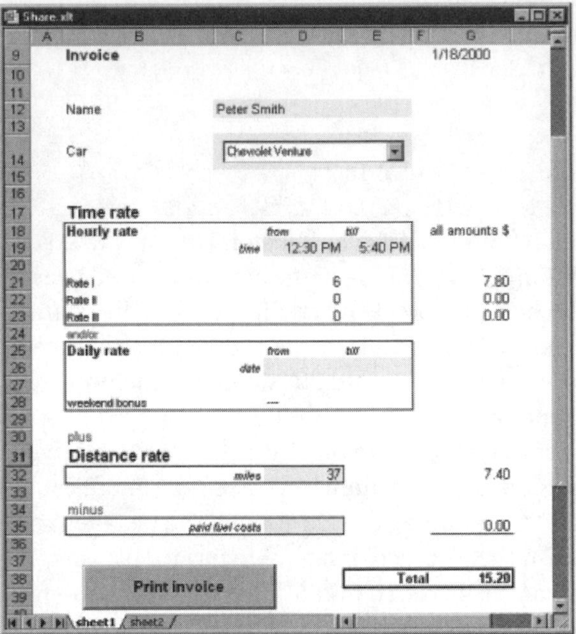

Figure 9.7. Smart form for an invoice of a car-sharing club

In contrast to the invoice form presented in the previous section, where a macro was provided for saving the invoice, here the user must take responsibility for saving. The amount of automation in this example is thus less than that of the previous example.

Constructing the Table

The two input cells for the hourly rate are D19 and E19. Cells D21 through D23 contain the user-defined functions *Rate_I_Hours* through *Rate_III_Hours* (for a description of the code, see below). In G21 through G23 the numbers of hours at each rate are multiplied by the appropriate hourly rate (C45 through C50).

The two input cells for the daily rate are D26 and E26. In G26 the difference between the two dates is multiplied by the daily rate. If E26 is empty, then one day is assumed.

```
G26:  =IF(D26=0,"",IF(E26=0,C48,(E26-D26)*C48))
```

In D28 the function *TestIfWeekend* is used to check whether a weekend is included in the loan period. If that is the case, then the text "OK" is printed in D28;

otherwise, "—-" is shown. The formulas in G28 evaluate D28 and display, if appropriate, the weekend credit value (in C49) as a negative number .

```
G28:  =IF(D28="OK",-C49,"")
```

The button PRINT INVOICE was inserted into the table using the Control Toolbox, then labeled and linked with the macro *btnPrint.*

In the listbox provided for car type one of the three types of automobile in the club's transport fleet can be selected. These types together with the associated tariffs are stored in a second worksheet (the smaller and less expensive the car, the lower the charge). The result of the listbox (a value of 0, 1, or 2) is linked to cell G14. In cell D14, directly beneath the listbox, the type of car is displayed above the index function. This text is normally invisible and becomes visible only when printed (since the listbox itself is not printed).

```
D14:  =INDEX(sheet2!A2:A4,G14+1)
```

The rate range of cells C45:C50 contains *INDEX* formulas, which access the charges in sheet 2 based on the type of auto selected (G14).

```
C45:  =INDEX(sheet2!$B$2:$B$4,$G$14+1)
```

Calculating the Charges

Cells D24 and E24, which contain the start and end dates of the car loan, are passed as arguments to the function *TestIfWeekend.* The code for this function begins with a function declaration together with its two parameters *startDate* and *endDate.* The function's result is given the value "no" at the outset. Three *If* tests check whether values are actually contained in the two parameters and whether the car was borrowed for at least two days (as a condition for receiving the weekend rebate). If one of these conditions is not fulfilled, then the function ends at once, and the result "---" is displayed.

The keyword *For* introduces a loop in which the variable *varDate* runs through all the days from the start date to the day before the end date. To understand this loop it is necessary to know how Excel represents dates and times internally. The number 0 corresponds to the date 1/1/1900 00:00, while 34335.75, for example, represents 1/1/1994 18:00.

The loop tests whether the date in *vardate* is a Saturday (*WeekDay(varDate)=7*). If that is the case, then it must be that the loan period spans a weekend, since the loop runs only to the second-to-last day of the loan period. The result of the function is changed to "OK", and the function is exited. If the loop runs without encountering a Saturday, then at the end of the loop *TestIfWeekend* retains its original value of "---".

```
' file Share.xlt, Module1
Function TestIfWeekend(startDate, endDate)
  Dim varDate
  TestIfWeekend = "---"                          'default result
  If startDate = 0 Then Exit Function            'no start date
  If endDate = 0 Then Exit Function              'no end date
  If endDate - startDate < 2 Then Exit Function  'only one day
  ' weekend between start and end date
  For varDate = startDate To endDate - 1
    If WeekDay(varDate) = 7 Then
      TestIfWeekend = "OK": Exit Function
    End If
  Next varDate
End Function
```

The three functions *Rate_I_Hours* through *Rate_III_Hours* are similarly constructed, and so here a description of only one of these functions will suffice. The function begins with a test as to whether the two parameters are valid values. Note also the use of *IsEmpty*, with which an empty cell can be distinguished from a cell containing the value 0. Thus the value 0:00 as a time is valid.

Next, the two variables *time1* and *time2* are assigned the values of the parameters *startTime* and *endTime*. Note that the case that the car was held beyond midnight (say, from 8:00 pm to 1:30 am) is taken care of.

```
Function Rate_I_Hours(startTime, endTime)
  Dim varTime, time1, time2
  Dim nrOfHours
  If IsEmpty(startTime) Or IsEmpty(endTime) Then Exit Function
  time1 = startTime
  If endTime < startTime Then  'over midnight
    time2 = 1 + endTime
  Else
    time2 = endTime
  End If
  For varTime = time1 To time2 - 1 / 1441 Step 1 / 24
    nrOfHours = Int(varTime * 24) Mod 24  'convert to full hours
    If nrOfHours >= 8 And nrOfHours < 20 Then
      Rate_I_Hours = Rate_I_Hours + 1
    End If
  Next varTime
End Function
```

The loop that now follows runs through the hours (one hour corresponds to 1/24 in Excel's time format) from the start time to exactly one minute before the end time (1 minute corresponds to 1/1440; here 1/1441 is used to exclude possible round-off error). The number of the hour is calculated in the variable *varTime* (for example, 6 for the time 6:30). Then the time is multiplied by 24 (since in Excel 24 hours corresponds to the value 1), rounded, and restricted via the modulo operator to the range 0 to 23. This is necessary for time periods extending over midnight, since in such a case a value greater than 24 could arise.

Finally, a test is made as to whether the current hour is in the range of rate 1. If that is the case, then the resultant value of *Rate_I_Hours* is increased by 1. What is relevant is always the beginning of an hour. The functions *Rate_II_Hours* and *Rate_III_Hours* differ from the function just considered only in the test conditions for the time periods.

Ideas for Improvements in the Rate Calculations

In the model we have chosen, the distinction between hourly and daily rates is irksome. If the car is taken for a day and a half, say, a combination of both rates should be used. The required input of the dates is subject to error. It would be more elegant if the date and time for the start and end of the loan were input. The associated functions would then on their own figure out the minimal cost combination of daily and hourly rates. Clearly, this would require some programming effort.

A further shortcoming in our model is the lack of consideration of holidays (perhaps the club wishes to offer a discount, or perhaps a surcharge, for holiday loans).

Printing the Form

The last macro we wish to describe is *btnPrint_Click*. This macro prints out the car-share form, replaces the current date with a fixed value, and removes the yellow background from the input cells. The whole table is then copied into a new worksheet, which is deleted at the end of the macro.

The main part of the code was generated by the macro recorder with TOOLS|MACRO|RECORD NEW MACRO. Then various changes were made, and the code was commented. The actual printing is accomplished with *PrintOut*, where *Preview:= True* indicates that only a print preview is executed.

The instructions at the start and end of the procedure (*ScreenUpdating=...*) speed up the execution of the macro considerably. They prevent the continual update of the screen while the macro is running. *On Error Resume Next* has the effect that the macro runs to the end even if an error occurs (for example, if the user stops printing with BREAK).

In the penultimate line of the macro the current worksheet (which was created just a few lines above) is deleted. To bypass the alert that asks whether the sheet is truly to be deleted, the property *DisplayAlerts* is set to *False*.

Figure 9.8. Sample printout of an invoice of a car-sharing club

```
' print invoice
Sub btnPrint_Click()
  Application.ScreenUpdating = False
  ' copy varDate, insert as value
  Range("G9").Select
  Selection.Copy
  Selection.PasteSpecial Paste:=xlValues
  Application.CutCopyMode = False
  ' copy entire sheet
  Sheets("sheet1").Select
  Sheets("sheet1").Copy ActiveWorkbook.Sheets(1)
  With Sheets(1)
    ' remove yellow background
    .Cells.Interior.ColorIndex = xlNone
    ' print
    .PrintOut Preview:=True
  End With
```

```
  ' delete new sheet
  Application.DisplayAlerts = False
  ActiveWindow.ActiveSheet.Delete
  Application.DisplayAlerts = True
  ' recalculate sheet 1
  With Sheets(1)
    .Rows(1).Insert Shift:=xlDown
    .Rows(1).Delete Shift:=xlUp
  End With
  Application.ScreenUpdating = True
End Sub
```

The Limits of Smart Forms

Simplifying Use

The two example forms are relatively simple to use, but there is room for improvement. For example, a menu bar that is reduced to only those commands needed to run the form might be useful.

The forms are not well protected against invalid input. If input in incorrect format occurs (for instance, a number instead of a date or time, text instead of a number), the result is incomprehensible error messages, or even completely erroneous results.

A protection against errors in the direct input of values in worksheets (as opposed in forms) is relatively difficult. In general, there are two possibilities: Either have critical values input through a dialog (form), where immediate checking is possible (and the dialog can be terminated only when all input values are syntactically correct), or expand the code of the PRINT or SAVE button with program code that checks over all the input cells of the form to make sure that they are correctly formulated.

Overhead in Saving

The car-sharing smart form requires about 50 kilobytes of storage space. But the significant data can be reduced to ten cells (name, date, type of auto, start time, end time, start date, end date, mileage, gasoline cost, total). All other data are redundant. That is, it would be sufficient to save these data only once, and not in each form. There are several ways of solving this overhead problem:

- One variant consists in separating the template and code into two files. The template needs merely a *Workbook_Open* procedure to be added, in which the code file is loaded and then linked to the template with *OnEvent* procedures. The drawback is that it cannot be avoided that the data file might be transmitted to another computer without the code file. The result would be incomprehensible error messages.

- A second variant was introduced in the Speedy example template. There, a separate "save" macro makes sure that at least only the worksheet (and not the entire VBA code) is saved. The drawback of this way of doing things is that if a file is created on the basis of this template and then later edited, the features of the template that provide ease of input are no longer available.

- The third variant consists in saving only those data that are truly relevant. In principle, this idea is similar to that associated with templates with database linkage via the template wizard; the difference is that the form need no longer be saved in a separate file. For this to happen there must be commands to read previously saved data from the database into the form template for renewed editing. The drawback of this solution is that the template has metamorphosed into a full-fledged database application with all the programming effort involved.

The Danger in Isolated Solutions

Our smart form for creating an invoice is a nice thing to have, but in practice, it is insufficient for a real-world office or business. Normally, invoices from one division are entered in another division, one responsible for entering payments and sending out reminders of overdue payments. Furthermore, orders must be correlated with stock management. Therefore, a clear interface among divisions must be created.

For such complex and interwoven applications it is necessary at least that input data be effortlessly available for further application. For many applications the further processing must happen fully automatically.

Such difficult situations are beyond the capacity of Excel. To be sure, Excel offers a rather extensive suite of database commands, but for full-blown database applications a database program is more suitable.

> **POINTER** *The subject of databases, separate from that of form templates, is discussed in considerable detail in Chapters 11 through 13. The car-sharing template will be expanded into a database application in Chapter 11.*

CHAPTER 10

Charts and Drawing Objects (*Shapes*)

Charts constitute the central feature of many Excel applications. This chapter gives a brief overview of the charts supported by Excel and also shows how you can create and print out your own charts under program control. A lengthy example on the subject of data recording demonstrates various programming techniques.

A further topic of this chapter is that of drawing objects (*Shapes*), available since Excel 97, with which both charts and ordinary worksheets can be ornamented.

Chapter Overview

Charts

Fear not! You are not about to be subjected to an extensive introduction to the use of charts. This topic is exhaustively (in the literal sense of the word) dealt with in countless books on Excel. The goal of this section is rather to describe, without much concern about the details of how they are used, the possibilities for designing charts, and to name the various elements of charts and explain their functions. This information will provide you with the requisite knowledge for entering the world of programming charts, a world swarming with various *ChartXxx* objects.

Fundamentals

Chart Sheets Versus Charts Embedded in Worksheets

In Excel you can either embed charts in worksheets or present them in their own chart sheets. The first variant has the advantage that the chart can be printed out with its associated data. Furthermore, very small charts can be created that take up only part of a page.

The Chart Wizard

Usually, the path to a new chart goes by way of the chart wizard. This wizard is automatically summoned when you create a new chart (with INSERT|CHART or click on the chart wizard tool.)

In the first step of the chart wizard you select the desired chart type. In the second step you choose the data range. Here there is no problem with indicating a range of cells that is the union of other cell ranges. In further steps you can determine various options for the format of the chart. The chart wizard can also be called up to help with preexisting charts if you wish to change certain formatting details.

Further Processing of Charts

Charts that have been created with the chart wizard frequently do not quite meet your requirements. Therefore, the fine details of layout often begin after the chart wizard has been terminated.

In order for you to be able to edit the chart, you have to activate it with a mouse click. As soon as the chart is active, you can click on most of the chart elements within the region of the chart: the legend, the axes, individual data series (which are represented in the form of lines, bars, etc.), the background of the chart, and so on. For each of these chart elements there exists a pop-up menu that usually offers an extensive array of formatting options. You can access the most important setting dialogs with a double click on the corresponding chart element.

If you are working with charts for the first time, you will often encounter the problem that you do not know which element to click on to carry out a specific change. You have two alternatives: Suffering through the user's guide and experimentation.

Chart Types

Although it can seem in working with charts that the number of types of chart is limitless, in reality, there are comparatively few chart types. All possible charts (including the more than seventy predefined chart types (see *Chart Type* in the online help) are derived from these chart types.

- line chart (data placed at equal intervals)
- scatter chart (shows clusters of data)
- bubble chart (a type of scatter chart where the size of the "bubble" indicates the size of a third variable)
- area chart (area under the curve)
- column chart (vertical bars)
- bar chart (horizontal bars)
- pie chart (circular wedges represent the data)
- doughnut (like a pie chart, but for more than one data series)
- radar chart (linear chart in which each category has its own value axis)
- 3D line chart (three-dimensional bands)
- 3D column chart (three-dimensional vertical bars)
- 3D bar chart (three-dimensional horizontal bars)
- 3D area chart (three-dimensional data surface)

- 3D pie chart (three-dimensional wedges)
- 3D cylinder chart (three-dimensional cylinders)
- 3D cone chart (three-dimensional cones)
- 3D pyramid chart (three-dimensional pyramids)

Combination Charts

Combination charts are charts in which several chart types are combined (for example, a line chart and column chart). Combination charts can be created either with the help of a user-defined chart (see below) or by changing the chart type of a single data series (not the entire chart).

Charts can be combined only if they are based on the same coordinate system. Therefore, the range of combination possibilities is relatively narrow. Three-dimensional charts cannot be combined at all.

Pivot Charts

Pivot charts are new in Excel 2000. These are not actually a new chart type, but a new way of linking data between a chart and a pivot table. What is special about pivot charts is that categories for structuring data can be created dynamically (that is, by means of listboxes in charts). The chart is immediately revised. For the chart itself almost all the chart types listed above can be used. Pivot charts will be described within the framework of pivot tables in Chapter 13.

User-Defined Chart Types (Autoformat)

There are two ways to format a chart: You can select one of the eighteen standard types and then carry out the fine formatting on it (such as setting colors, patterns, and the form of the markers) or you can employ a so-called user-defined type (formerly autoformat). Among these types are stored numerous formatting details, so that you can very quickly create a wide variety of different charts. The name "user-defined" is somewhat confusing, since Excel recognizes an entire palette of predefined (integrated) types.

The user-defined formats in Excel give a very good overview as to what is available. The formats are located in `Office2000\Office\n\Xl8galry.xls`, where *n* is a language code (for example, 1033 is the number of the American version).

More important is the possibility of adding your own user-defined formats and using them in the future. For this you format a chart to your specifications, open the "Chart Type" dialog with the right mouse button, switch into the page

"Custom Types," and click on the option button "User-defined." Then click the Add button and save your format as a new chart type. New (personal) chart types are saved in the file `Userprofile\Application Data\Microsoft\Excel\Xlusrgal.xls`.

Chart Elements (Chart Objects) and Formatting Options

For the detailed layout of charts as well as for programming charts it is necessary to know the distinctions made by Excel among various chart objects. Assistance in your experimentation is offered by the chart toolbar. There, in the left listbox is shown the object that was just clicked on, such as "axis *n*," "gridlines *n*," "Series *n*," and so on.

- *Chart Area*: This is the object *ChartArea*, which is responsible for the background of the entire chart (that is, the region that is visible behind the plot area, the legend, and so on). The type style that is input here holds for all text of the chart that is not otherwise specially set.

- *Plot Area*: The plot area (*PlotArea*) represents a rectangle around the graphic region of the chart. The plot area contains the actual chart, but not the title, legend, etc. With most two-dimensional charts even the axes are not part of the plot area. If, for example, you specify the background color green for the plot area and red for the chart area, the labels for the axes will be underlaid with red.

- *Floor, Walls*: These two objects exist only for three-dimensional charts and describe the appearance of the floor and walls of the two vertical border surfaces of the chart. The plot area in this case is considered to be only the rectangular region outside of the chart itself.

- *Corners*: Even the corners exist as an independent object in three-dimensional charts. Corners cannot be formatted. But they can be grabbed with the mouse and turned in three dimensions. This is often more convenient than setting the viewpoint and perspective via the dialog CHART|3D-VIEW.

- *Data Series*: A data series describes a related unit of data (usually the values of a column from the underlying table; only if you select "Series in Rows" in step 2 of the chart wizard will data series be organized by rows). For example, a data series is reprenseted by a line. The formatting data of data series affect the graphic representation of this data series, that is, color, markers, line style, etc.

- *Data Points*: The individual values of a data series are represented by data points. Normally, the format properties of all data points are the same and are preset by the properties of the data series. However, you can set the properties of each data point separately and thereby thrust individual points of a series into prominence, or label points individually, for example. In a pie chart you can shove individual pie slices out from the pie and distinguish them in this way—that, too, affects the property of the data point. Caution: The vertical position of data points in two-dimensional charts can be changed with the mouse, and this changes the underlying value in the data table!

- *Trend Lines*: Data series of two-dimensional charts can be associated with trend lines. The trend lines are drawn in addition to the normal representation of the data. Excel recognizes types of trend lines: best-fit curves (five different types) and averaging curves.

- *Error Bars*: Error bars are another subelement of a data series in two-dimensional charts. They indicate potential error amounts relative to each data marker.

- *Coordinate Axes*: The coordinate axes have a large number of formatting details, which begin with scaling (minimum, maximum, linear or logarithmic) and end with the precise arrangement of the axis labeling (which data points are labeled, which are indicated by a tick marks, whether the tick mark is inside or outside, and so on). New since Excel 97 is the possibility of labeling the coordinate axes with text in any orientation (horizontal, vertical, or slant; FORMAT AXIS|FONT|ALIGNMENT).

  There is also the option to equip a two-dimensional chart with two independent Y-axes, where one is valid for some of the data series and the other for the remaining data series. This is useful when you wish to represent on the same chart two related quantities that have different scales (for example, a voltage and current). In order to employ two Y-axes it is necessary to separate the data series into two groups. The easiest way to accomplish this is by selecting the custom chart type "Lines on 2 Axes."

- *Grid Lines*: The plot area of a two-dimensional chart or the walls and floor of a three-dimensional chart can be combined with grid lines. The position of grid lines is determined by the tick marks on the coordinate axes. The appearance (color, line style) of principal and secondary grid lines can be set separately (but only for normal charts, not composite charts).

- *Title*: A chart can be equipped with several titles (for the chart, the axes, etc.). The position, type style, and alignment can be set independently.

- *Legend*: The legend makes possible a link between the colors used in the chart and the patterns of the data series. The labeling of the legend is taken from the first column or row of the data series. The legend can be placed anywhere in the chart (even beneath the data).

Chart Options in Tools|Options

With TOOLS|OPTIONS|CHART you have access to a few further chart options. These settings concern only the current chart (and can be changed only when the chart is active).

The option "Plot empty cells as" determines how Excel responds to empty cells in the data series. In the setting "not plotted (leave gaps)" there appears a hole in the chart (that is, bars are missing, a line is broken, etc.). The alternatives to this setting are "zero" (then Excel treats empty cells as if they contained the value 0) and "interpolated" (then Excel attempts to interpolate suitable data values for the empty cells).

The check box "Plot visible cells only" determines how Excel deals with hidden rows and columns: If the box is activated, then data in invisible rows or columns are not displayed. In the chart the data are simply ignored (rather than a hole appearing). This setting is of interest primarily when the chart data come from a filtered database.

The check box "Chart sizes with window frame" is of interest only for chart sheets. When the box is activated the chart is fit to the current size of the window. Otherwise, only one print page is shown. To make the entire chart visible, the zoom factor may have to be changed (VIEW|ZOOM).

Trend Lines, Data Smoothing

With line charts you can select the option "Smoothed line" in the formatting settings for the data series. This has the effect of rounding the edges of an otherwise angular course.

Other possibilities for providing a best-fit curve or averaging curve are offered by the command CHART|ADD TRENDLINE. Excel can approximate a data set with five different types of best-fit curves: straight line, polynomial curve (up to sixth degree), logarithmic curve, exponential curve, power curve. With the options in the dialog FORMAT TRENDLINE you can specify whether and to what extent the curve should be extended beyond the current data and whether the formula for the curve should be given.

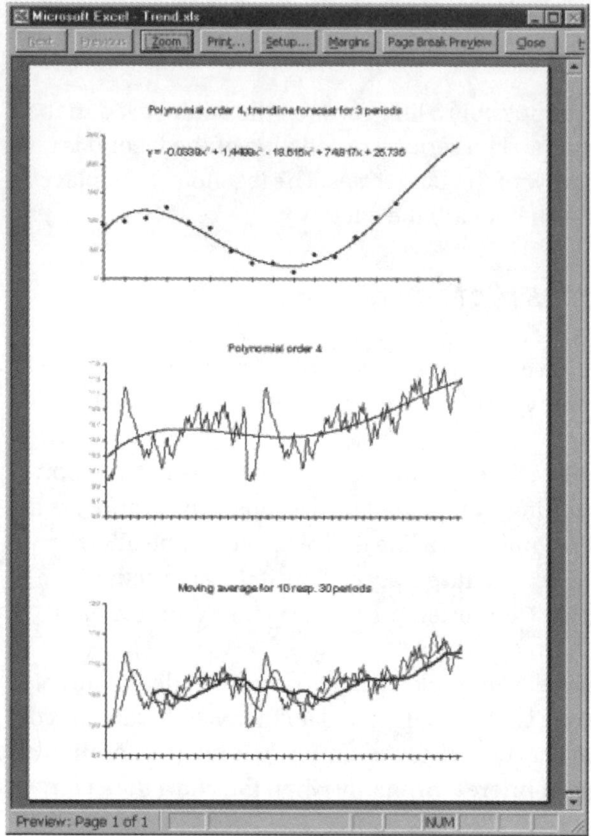

Figure 10.1. Three examples of trend lines

A sixth type of curve can be specified in the TREND LINE dialog: an averaging curve based on a running average. Here every point on the curve is calculated from the average of the *n* preceding points. This has the effect of smoothing statistical errors of measurement. Averaging curves, in contrast to best-fit curves, cannot be extended beyond the range of the data.

Some examples of the application of the trend line function are indicated in Figure 10.1. The associated example file `Trend.xls` is included with the sample files for this book.

Error Indication

Data series in two-dimensional charts can be provided with error indicators (error bars). These are small lines that specify the range in which the actual value of a data point is to be found if statistical error of measurement is taken into account.

Printing

When it comes to printing a chart two variants must be considered: If the chart is embedded in a worksheet, then printing is accomplished by way of printing the worksheet. Here the only problem is that Excel does not give much thought to where page breaks are inserted, and even a small chart might find itself broken into four pieces. It does not hurt to check the page preview before printing. You may find yourself compelled to insert some hard page breaks to optimize printing (INSERT|PAGE BREAK).

On the other hand, if the chart is located in a chart sheet, or if you wish to print an embedded chart that has been selected with a mouse click, then there are some options available in the dialog PAGE SETUP. The most important of these is "Printed chart size" on the CHART page of this dialog. In the standard setting Excel uses the entire page. If the chart does not happen to have the same format as the page, the chart can become completely distorted. Therefore, it is usually better to select the option "Scale to fit page." Excel enlarges the chart only to the extent that the relationship between the length and width does not change (that is, the aspect ratio is preserved). The third variant, "Custom," leaves the size of the chart unchanged.

The option "Print in black and white" allows color charts to be printed on a black and white printer. (Most printers can handle this without the use of this option.) Whether with or without this option, you will achieve usable results on a black and white printer only if you refrain from using color in your chart. Use instead differing line widths and types to distinguish among several data series.

Since the standard and custom chart types are generally extremely color friendly, the creation of a satisfactory black and white substitute usually requires considerable effort (say, about 100 mouse clicks for a typical chart). Therefore, if this is a common situation for you, then save black and white charts as a custom chart type.

Programming Charts

First attempts at programming charts are often very difficult. The reason is that it is not easy to acquire an orientation among the multitude of *Chart* objects, and the association of properties and methods is not always clear.

Here is an example: The method *ClearContents* of the *ChartArea* object clears the data of a chart, but not its formatting. This is strange, in that the *ChartArea* object is actually not responsible for the chart itself, but only for its background. It would have been more logical if chart data were deleted via the *Delete* method of the *Chart* object, but this method returns nothing but an error message in the case of an embedded chart. Apparently, *Delete* is suitable only for deleting chart *sheets*, while the two related methods *ClearContents* and *ClearFormats* of the *ChartArea* object are responsible for the internal affairs of charts.

In constrast to the *ChartArea* object we have the *PlotArea* object. This object also describes the background of the chart, though in this case the area immediately behind the chart lines, bars, and so on.

> **REMARK** *Though at the outset you may feel overwhelmed by the surfeit of objects and their properties, there are positive aspects to the situation: You can truly run almost the entire chart business with program code. Alas, space does permit a full description of this plenitude. For many details you will be referred to the on-line help after finishing this chapter.*

Instead of Searching Fruitlessly, Use the Macro Recorder!

If you would like to know how you can achieve a particular formatting result in program code, then use the macro recorder as your trusted adviser (the examples from the on-line help are practically useless).

The shorter the recording session, the easier it will be for you to interpret the results. Therefore, you should start recording in a chart that already exists, change only a single detail, and then stop recording at once. If you arrange on your monitor one window with program code and a second one with the chart, you can even observe during recording when each line of code is generated.

The code that results from the macro recording usually works (at least no counterexamples appeared during the preparation of this chapter), but it is seldom optimal. In part, the instructions are unnecessarily convoluted, and in part they are completely superfluous. Therefore, the code must be edited after the fact.

Object Hierarchy

The following compilation provides an overview of the object hierarchy for charts. To make the structure clearer, only the most important objects have been included and only the case considered that the chart is embedded in a worksheet (no chart sheets). A complete listing of all chart objects can be found in Chapter 15.

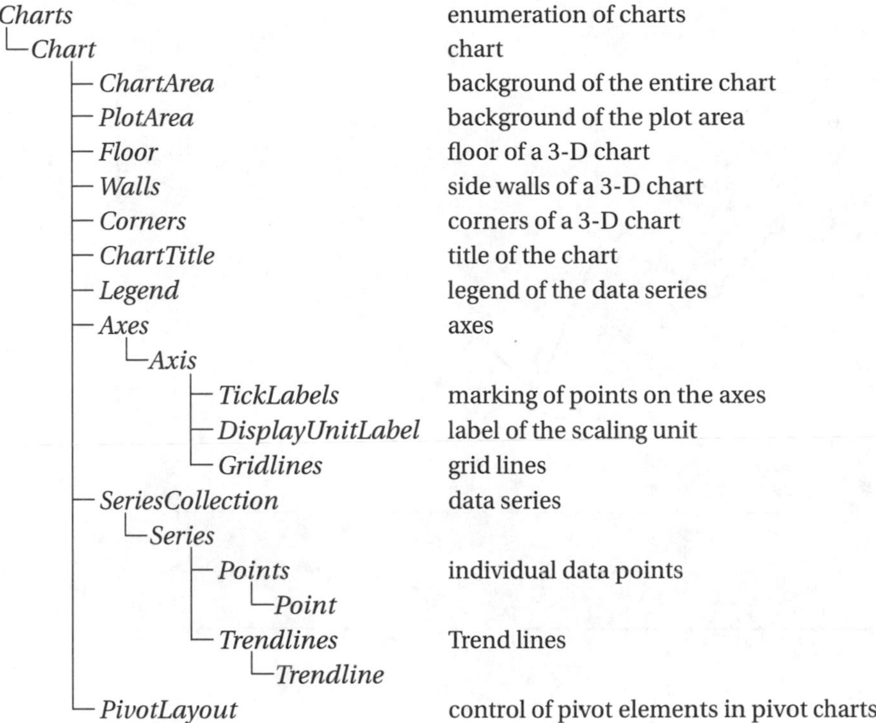

Charts	enumeration of charts
└ *Chart*	chart
├ *ChartArea*	background of the entire chart
├ *PlotArea*	background of the plot area
├ *Floor*	floor of a 3-D chart
├ *Walls*	side walls of a 3-D chart
├ *Corners*	corners of a 3-D chart
├ *ChartTitle*	title of the chart
├ *Legend*	legend of the data series
├ *Axes*	axes
└ *Axis*	
├ *TickLabels*	marking of points on the axes
├ *DisplayUnitLabel*	label of the scaling unit
└ *Gridlines*	grid lines
├ *SeriesCollection*	data series
└ *Series*	
├ *Points*	individual data points
└ *Point*	
└ *Trendlines*	Trend lines
└ *Trendline*	
└ *PivotLayout*	control of pivot elements in pivot charts

A Brief Glossary of Chart Objects

There is enormous confusion surrounding the numerous and often like-named *Chart* and *Plot* objects. Figure 10.2 provides a first overview.

Chart: This is the actual chart; it consists of several data series that are graphically represented, the background, the coordinate axes, the legend, the title, and so on. Access to *Chart* objects is achieved either through the enumeration *Charts*, if the chart is located in a chart sheet, or via *ChartObjects(...).Chart*, if the chart is embedded in a worksheet.

The chart type is set, since Excel 97, with the property ***ChartType*** (formerly *Type* and *SubType*). Over seventy constants have been defined as possible settings (see the on-line help or the object browser).

ChartObject: This is the outer frame (container) of a chart. The *ChartObject* object is necessary only with charts that are embedded in worksheets. It stands between the worksheet and the *Chart* object and determines the position and dimensions of the chart within the worksheet. With the *Worksheet* method *ChartObjects* you can access the list of all chart objects of a worksheet.

You access the associated chart with the *Chart* property of the *ChartObject* object. (Note: In addition to charts a host of other objects can be embedded in worksheets, such as controls, lines, and rectangles. You can access the totality of these objects, including charts, with the method *DrawingObjects*).

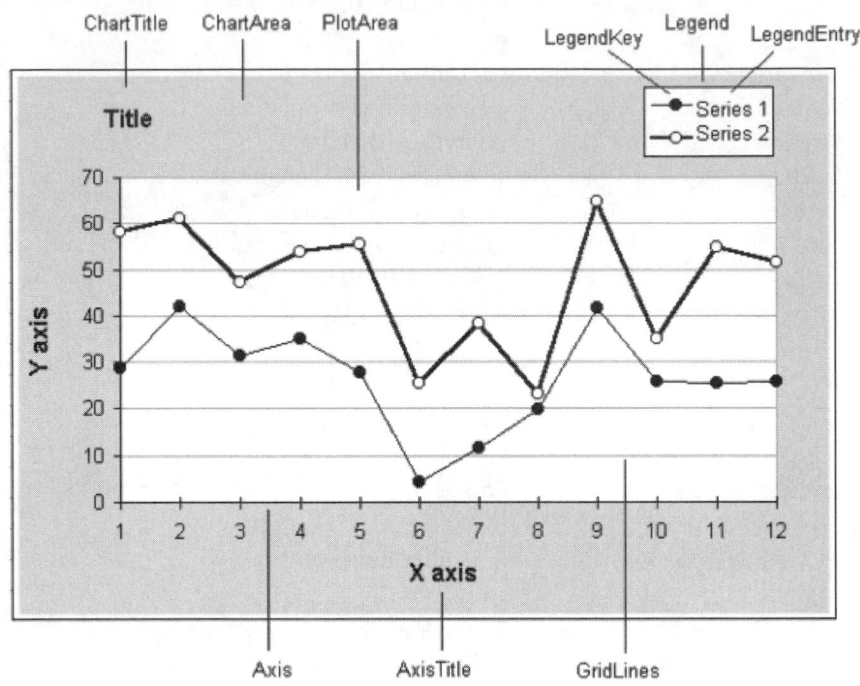

Figure 10.2. The most important objects of a chart

ChartArea: This is the background of the chart. With the properties of this object you can set color, borders, and so on. However, this object has a greater significance insofar as its methods *Copy, Clear, ClearContents,* and *ClearFormats* relate to the actual subordinate *Chart* object (Microsoft alone knows why). In the case of embedded charts the method *Select* can be used only if first the associated *ChartObject* object has beed activated with *Activate.*

ChartGroup: This object groups various chart types within a chart. Normally, a chart possesses only a single chart group. In this case the *ChartGroup* object is irrelevant. This object, then, has significance only when in a composite chart two or more chart types are united (for example, a bar chart and line chart). In this case the chart is managed by several groups with differing chart types (*Type* property).

Charts: The chart object contains the enumeration of all chart *sheets* of a workbook. The like-named method immediately returns the *Chart* object. There is, then, no separate chart sheet object comparable to a worksheet. For chart sheets, no intermediate *ChartObject* is necessary.

Some additional objects do not, in fact, begin with "Chart," but they are nonetheless of interest.

PlotArea: This is the "graphical" area within a chart. The plot area contains the coordinate axes and the actual chart graphic. The main task of this object consists in determining the size and position of this region within the total area of the chart. Other regions in the chart are the legend (***Legend*** object) and the title (***ChartTitle*** object). In the case of three-dimensional charts the objects ***Floor*** and ***Walls*** (as subobjects of *Chart*) are managed independently of *PlotArea*. These two objects are responsible for the visual appearance of the boundary surfaces of a three-dimensional chart.

NOTE *When you execute* PlotArea.Width=n: m=PlotArea.Width, *then* m *is distinctly larger than* n. *The reason is that* PlotArea.Width *actually changes the write-protected property* InsideWidth *introduced in Excel 97, that is, the inside region of* PlotArea. *In addition to this inside region there is an outside region, in which the labeling of the coordinate axes appears. (The same problems occur also with* Height/InsideHeight, *of course). To set the size of the outside region you can usually rely on the following code:*

```
delta = PlotArea.Width - PlotArea.InsideWidth
PlotArea.Width = n + delta
```

This method is not quite exact either, since the size of the label area is not constant. For example, if a chart is greatly reduced in size, Excel simply does without axis labels, and the label area is reduced to size 0.

Series, Point: The *Series* object refers to the data of a data series belonging to a chart. The actual numerical values can be taken from the *Values* property of the *Series* object, which can also be used to change these values. *Series* is a subobject of the *Chart* object. Formatting data that affect not the entire series but only an individual data point are controlled by *Point* objects. These are again a subobject of the *Series* objects.

Axis, Gridlines: The *Axis* object is also a subobject of the *Chart* object. It describes the details of a coordinate axis. The *Gridlines* object is a subobject of the *Axis* object and is addressed via the properties *MajorGridlines* and *MinorGridlines*.

New in Excel 2000 is the ability to specify scaling units for the coordinate axes (for example, "millions"). In this case *Axis.DisplayUnit* must be set with a predefined constant (for example, *xlMillions*). The *DisplayUnitLabel* object specifies how and where this scale unit (that is, in this example *"Millions"*) is displayed in the chart. The property *HasDisplayUnitLabel* specifies whether the axis is scaled.

In addition to the predefined scaling units (10, 100, 1000, up to 1,000,000,000) any other factor can be used. For this, *DisplayUnitCustom* is assigned the desired value (which can also be less than 1, for example, 0.001 to represent thousandths).

```
ActiveChart.Axes(xlValue).DisplayUnitCustom = 0.001
ActiveChart.Axes(xlValue).DisplayUnitLabel.Text = "thousandth part"
```

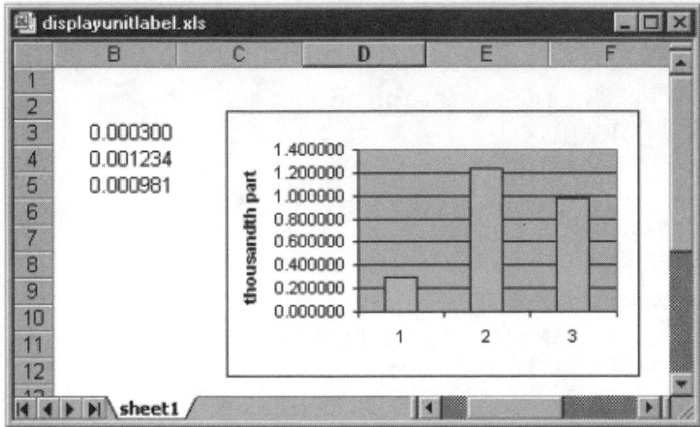

Figure 10.3. The Y-axis uses thousandths as scaling unit

Trendline, ErrorBars: *Trendline* and *ErrorBars* are subobjects of the *Series* object. They describe the details of a trend line of a data series and, respectively, the appearance of the error bars.

> **TIP** *The keywords* Gridlines *and* ErrorBars *appear in the plural, and in contrast to other pluralized Excel objects, they do not refer to enumeration objects.*

> **TIP** *If you do not know the name of a particular object in a chart, you can click on that object (for example, a coordinate axis) and execute* ?TypeName(Selection) *in the immediate window. As result you obtain the object name (in this example,* Axis*).*

Programming Techniques

The Chart Wizard

The method ***ChartWizard*** offers, in general, the fastest route to creating a chart. In order to use this method, you must first generate a *ChartObject* object. You can read all about the infinitude of parameters associated to this method in the on-line help.

```
ActiveSheet.ChartObjects.Add(30, 150, 400, 185).Name = _
  "new chart"
ActiveSheet.ChartObjects("new chart").Activate
ActiveChart.ChartWizard sheet1 .[A3:D99], xlLine, 4, xlColumns, 1, 1
```

Chart Objects: Activate or Select?

With the methods ***Activate*** and ***Select*** Microsoft has blessed us with a certain amount of confusion: Sometimes one method must be used (windows), sometimes the other (worksheets), and sometimes both are allowed (ranges of cells). In the case of *ChartObject* objects not only are both methods allowed, but they lead to different results!

Activate corresponds to a single click on a chart. *Selection* now refers to the object *PlotArea* (thus not to *Chart*)!

Select seemingly also corresponds to a single click on a chart. However, the *Selection* property now refers to a *ChartObject* object. Therefore, use *Select* when you wish to change the position or size of a chart in a worksheet but you do not wish to change features of the actual chart.

```
Sheets(1).ChartObjects(1).Select
```

The two methods have in common that the *Chart* object can then be accessed via *ActiveChart.*

> **CAUTION** *In Excel 97 access to a chart via* ActiveChart *led at times to serious problems. Access the object in question directly instead of first activating it and then altering it via* ActiveChart.

Deactivating Chart Objects

The best way to deactivate a chart is by activating some other object, e.g., Sheets(n).[A1].Select. If you try to record a macro for deactivating a chart, a line like the following is recorded:

```
ActiveWindow.Visible = False    ' deactivate chart
```

However, the chart is only partly deactivated. (There is still a visible frame around the chart, but the size markers are now white instead of black.) Thus, this kind of deactivation, which worked in Excel versions prior to 2000, no longer seems to help.

> **TIP** *When a chart is activated, the property* ActiveSheet *refers to this chart, even if the chart is embedded in a worksheet.*

Deleting, Copying, and Inserting Charts

ChartObject objects can be directly copied together with the chart contained therein with ***Copy*** and then again inserted into the worksheet. After the insertion, the *Selection* property refers to the new *ChartObject* object, so that this can then be named. If you simply wish to duplicate a *ChartObject* object, you can use the method ***Duplicate*** directly instead of *Copy* and *Paste*. With *Delete* you can delete a *ChartObject* object together with all the data contained therein.

```
ActiveSheet.ChartObjects(1).Copy
ActiveSheet.Paste
Selection.Name = "new chart"
' …
ActiveSheet.ChartObjects("new chart").Delete
```

The situation is somewhat different if you wish to delete, copy, or insert only the chart data without altering the *ChartObject* object. In this case the *ChartArea* object takes center stage (since there is no *Copy* method defined for the *Chart* object). Upon insertion into another chart object you must then refer to that *Chart* object.

```
ActiveSheet.ChartObjects(1).Chart.ChartArea.Copy
ActiveSheet.ChartObjects(2).Chart.Paste
```

With deleting chart data, too, you have to access the *ChartArea* object. *Clear* deletes all the chart data, *ClearContents* only the chart's contents (here is meant primarily the data series), and *ClearFormats* only the formatting information.

If you wish to insert an empty *ChartObject* into a worksheet (that is, an empty chart framework), you apply the *Add* method to *ChartObjects*. To this method are passed the position and size specifications (in points: 1 point = 1/72 inch = 0.35 mm). A name can be given at once to the new object:

```
ActiveSheet.ChartObjects.Add(0,0,200,100).Name = "new chart"
```

The bestowal of a name is important, because otherwise, you will later be unable to access the chart. Excel automatically gives the name "Sheet *n* Chart *m*," but normally, you do not know the values of *m* and *n*.

Aligning Several Charts

When you place two or more charts in a worksheet with the mouse, you will soon find out that it is relatively difficult to create two charts of exactly the same size lying one precisely above the other. A very good assistant in this enterprise is the menu of the DRAWING toolbar. With its menu items you can align previously selected objects (including charts). Another variant consists in simply accessing the *Left*, *Top*, *Width*, and *Height* properties of the *ChartObject* object.

The following instructions in the immediate window were used to align the five charts of a monthly report (see the next section) horizontally corresponding to the position and size of the first chart.

```
set wb = Worksheets("MonthlyReport")
For i=2 To 5: wb.ChartObjects(i).Left = _
  wb.ChartObjects(1).Left: Next i
For i=2 To 5: wb.ChartObjects(i).Width = _
  wb.ChartObjects(1).Width: Next i
```

Using Ready-Made Charts or Custom Formats

The complete setting up of a chart with all its formatting details is possible via program code, but this is a laborious and complex programming endeavor. If the appearance of a chart is in any case predetermined (and independent of the data to be processed) it makes more sense to save the completed chart in a worksheet or chart sheet and use program code only to change the data used to draw the chart. The actual formatting of the chart can be carried out directly with the mouse and without programming effort. (The procedure *MonthlyProtocol* in the next section provides an example.)

The use of autoformat requires more than minimal programming, but is still better than programming a chart from scratch. With autoformats, which in turn are derived from charts that you have formatted in the traditional way, you can change practically all the formatting data of a chart generated by program code with a single instruction. Then you need to carry out at most a few instructions for the optimal sizing of individual chart elements. The application of an autoformat to an existing chart is carried out, since Excel 97, with the method ***ApplyCustomType*** (formerly ***AutoFormat***).

```
ActiveChart.ApplyCustomType ChartType:=xlUserDefined, _
  TypeName:="DailyReport"
```

The deployment of autoformats is problematic when you wish to install a complete Excel application on another computer. Personal autoformats are stored in the file `Userprofile\Application Data\Microsoft\Excel\Xlusrgal.xls`. This file cannot be copied to another computer, because you would thereby overwrite the autoformats of another user. Thus the transmission of autoformats in a file is impossible.

However, there is a way around this restriction. You should include in your application a worksheet in which you have embedded a simple example chart for each autoformat used. When the program is launched, activate these example charts one after the other and save their format information as autoformats on the computer on which the application is being run.

```
Application.AddChartAutoFormat Chart:=ActiveChart, _
  Name:= "new autoformat", Description:=""
```

Unfortunately, there is no way to determine which autoformats have already been defined. An object such as *AutoFormats* does not exist in the current version of Excel.

Printing and Exporting Charts

Printing a chart is carried out with the method ***PrintOut***, which can be applied to both *Chart* and *Workbook* objects. Since Excel 97 charts can also be exported into a graphics file in various formats with ***Export***.

```
ActiveChart.Export "test.gif", "GIF"
```

According to the on-line documentation, in the second parameter you can provide all of the graphics formats for which export filters have been installed. What filters exists, what they are called, and how the program can determine whether a particular filter is installed are not revealed in the documentation. Therefore, protect your procedures for exporting with *On Error*. Experiments with *Export* have succeeded with the following formatting character strings:

"GIF", "JPEG", "TIF", "TIFF", "PNG"

On the other hand, *"BMP"* and *"WMF"*, that is, the two standard Microsoft formats for bitmaps and for simple vector graphics, are not supported. If you require charts in these formats, you can use the method ***CopyPicture***, which copies the chart to the clipboard. Unfortunately, the exportation ends there. That is, Excel provides no method to save the contents of the clipboard to a file.

Example: Automatic Data Reporting

The file `Chart.xls` demonstrates the application of Excel to the reporting of measurement data. Data reporting is necessary whenever relatively large data sets need to be documented and perhaps analyzed over an extended period of time. The data source can be just about anything, from the automatically measured amounts of hazardous chemicals in a waste treatment plant to the results of quality control in a factory.

The task of data reporting is to generate informative and readable printouts from the trash heap of numbers consisting of many small, or one large, file or database. It should be clear that charts for data visualization can play an important role in this operation.

Since in the sample files we cannot provide a technological method of data production, the application `Chart.xls` has available the menu command REPORT|CREATE TEST DATA, which creates Excel files with simulated measurement data. In practice, you would need such a command only during the test phase of the program. In general, you would have more genuine measurement data at your disposal than you probably want, and you would not need to increase your data supply with a data simulation program.

Using the Example Program

When the file is opened, a custom menu appears. If you wish to try out the program quickly, execute the following commands in sequence: REPORT|CREATE TEST DATA, |CREATE DAILY REPORT, and |CREATE MONTHLY REPORT. Simply approve with "OK" the forms that appear for data input.

The program then produces for each day of the current month a data file (requiring about 900 kilobytes of storage and half a minute to create on a reasonably modern computer). Then the daily report for the current day and the monthly report for the current month are presented in page view.

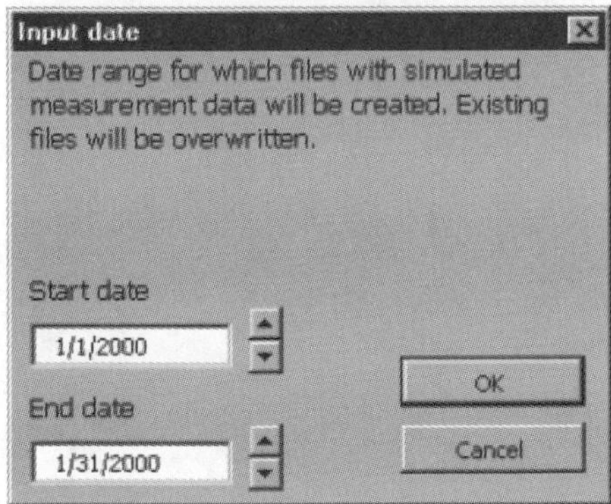

Figure 10.4. The form for input of the data range

Test Data

The menu command REPORT|CREATE TEST DATA leads to the creation, for each day, of files with the names `D_yyyymmdd.xls` (such as `D_19991231.xls` for 12/31/1999). In addition to the actual measurement data (96 values in each of the data series A1, A2, A3, B, C) these files contain six-hour average and maximum values as well as the daily average and maximum (see Figure 10.5). The files `D_yyyymmdd.xls` can be deleted after the program has been tested, of course.

d_20000101.xls

Data for 1/1/2000

Time	A1	A2	A3	B	C
00:00	131.7	96.5	125.7	74.7	152.0
00:15	128.5	97.7	124.6	81.4	150.7
00:30	126.8	97.9	122.2	86.0	150.0
00:45	126.1	99.3	120.0	88.8	148.7
01:00	124.5	103.0	119.8	92.2	146.3
01:15	120.4	108.1	122.1	97.7	143.1
01:30	114.4	112.4	125.0	104.1	140.2
01:45	108.5	115.0	126.5	109.0	138.7
02:00	104.1	117.2	126.3	111.6	138.9
02:15	100.8	121.0	126.0	113.9	139.8
02:30	96.6	127.3	127.5	118.2	140.3
02:45	90.5	134.4	130.6	124.4	139.5
03:00	83.7	140.4	133.4	130.2	137.5
03:15	78.3	144.4	134.0	133.9	135.4
03:30	75.5	147.9	132.9	136.2	134.1
03:45	74.6	152.6	131.9	139.5	134.0
04:00	73.5	159.0	132.7	144.9	134.4
04:15	71.5	165.2	134.8	150.6	134.0
04:30	69.8	169.1	136.3	154.2	131.9

Time	A1	A2	A3	B	C
6 hours average					
00:00 till 6:00	95.5	136.4	129.3	124.1	136.3
6:00 till 12:00	133.4	196.1	102.2	98.9	76.3
12:00 till 18:00	137.8	183.3	141.8	60.8	70.2
18:00 till 24:00	153.9	79.1	193.1	124.2	139.2
6 hours maximum					
00:00 till 6:00	131.7	177.1	136.3	159.6	152.0
6:00 till 12:00	155.3	232.8	136.2	156.7	111.4
12:00 till 18:00	157.7	231.3	179.1	84.2	97.7
18:00 till 24:00	164.6	93.7	221.1	152.8	152.4
Daily average	130.2	148.7	141.6	102.0	105.5
Daily maximum	164.6	232.8	221.1	159.6	152.4

Sheet1

Figure 10.5. The construction of the daily files for the measurement data

In the reporting of the data it is assumed that the dataseries A1, A2, A3 are related. Therefore, these series are presented in a single chart (see Figure 10.6). In the monthly report this was no longer possible due to the complexity of the data, since in the charts for each data series the daily average as well as the daily maximum are presented in their own graph (see Figure 10.7).

Program Code

Overview of the Components of Chart.xls

The Excel file `Chart.xls` consists of the following worksheets:

"Intro":	Worksheet with information about the use of the application.
"DailyReport":	Worksheet in which the daily report is constructed. The charts contained in it are deleted for each new report and constructed anew.
"MonthlyReport":	Worksheet in which the monthly report is constructed. The charts contained in it are final; they are not changed further in program code. In program code only the content of cells B9:M39 is changed.
"DataTemplate":	Worksheet that serves as template for the files with simulated data.

The construction of the worksheets must not be altered, since access to particular cells is carried out directly in program code.

The program code is divided into the following modules:

"ThisWorkbook":	display menu on opening; delete it on closing.
"FormDateInput":	form for input of date range.
"MenuEvents":	event procedures for the menu commands.
"CreateDateFiles":	procedures for generating the test data.
"CreateReports":	procedures for building and printing the daily and monthly reports.

On the following pages the most intesting details of the program code are described. The same order is observed as that for using the program (generate test data, daily report, monthly report). The code not only demonstrates the various possibilities for chart programming, it also shows how you can consolidate data from several Excel files when the Excel function DATA|CONSOLIDATE is too inflexible for your requirements.

Creating the Test Data

The program segment for creating the test data is of little interest to the extent that it would not exist in a real-world application (in which one has genuine data!). In our example *GenerateDailyWorksheet* creates a new Excel file based on the template worksheet in the sheet "DataTemplate." This template contains not only various formatting data, but also some formulas for calculating the six-hour average and maximum values as well as the daily average and maximum values.

The simulated test data are calculated on the basis of six superposed sine curves of various frequencies. The parameters of these functions (amplitude, frequency, and phase) are stored in the global field *rndmat*. The global variable *rndInit* determines whether this field already contains valid values. This avoids the necessity of providing new random numbers for each day. (Random numbers are generated only the first time this procedure is called.)

The random numbers are initialized in the procedure *InitRandomnumbers* (not presented here). Here the attempt is made to choose similar values for the three data series A1, A2, A3. For each day the procedure *DailyRandomnumbers* is called anew. This procedure changes the existing values of the *zfmat* field by a small amount, so that the data do not appear to be too regular.

```
' Chart.xls, Module CreateDataFiles
Dim rndInit          'tests whether random matrix is already initialized
Dim rndmat#(5, 18)   'matrix with random numbers
Const Pi = 3.1415927
' create workbook with (random) measurement data for one day
Function GenerateDailyWorksheet(dat As Date) As Boolean
  Dim filename$            'name of the new workbook
  Dim wb As Workbook       'new workbook
  Dim ws As Worksheet      'sheet in this book
  Dim cell As Range        'first data cell on the sheet
  Dim i%, j%, k%           'loop variables
  Dim x#, z

  filename = ThisWorkbook.Path + "\d_" + _
    Format(dat, "yyyymmdd") + ".xls"
  Application.DisplayAlerts = False
  ' creates new workbook; copies sheet "DataTemplate" from
  ' this workbook into new workbook; deletes all other sheets
  Set wb = Workbooks.Add
  ThisWorkbook.Sheets("DataTemplate").Copy Before:=wb.Sheets(1)
  For i = wb.Sheets.Count To 2 Step -1
    wb.Sheets(i).Delete
  Next i
  wb.Sheets(1).Name = "Sheet1"
  ' insert random numbers into sheet
  Set ws = wb.Worksheets(1)
  Set cell = ws.[A4]
  ws.[a1] = "Data for " & dat
  If Not rndInit Then InitRandomnumbers
  DailyRandomnumbers
  Application.Calculation = xlManual
  For i = 1 To 96                                   '00:00 through 23:45
    z = dat + CDbl(#12:15:00 AM#) * (i - 1)
    cell.Cells(i, 1) = z
    cell.Cells(i, 1).NumberFormat = "hh:mm"
    For j = 1 To 5                                  'five series of data
      x = rndmat(j, 0)
```

```
      For k = 1 To 18 Step 3
        x = x + rndmat(j, k) * (1 + Sin(rndmat(j, k + 1) * z + _
            rndmat(j, k + 2)))
      Next k
      cell.Cells(i, j + 1) = x
    Next j
  Next i
  Application.Calculation = xlAutomatic
  Application.DisplayAlerts = True
  On Error Resume Next
  ' delete existing file
  If Dir(filename)  "" Then Kill filename
  wb.SaveAs filename
  wb.Close False
  If Err = 0 Then
    GenerateDailyWorksheet = True
  Else
    MsgBox "An error has occured: " & Error
    GenerateDailyWorksheet = False
  End If
End Function
```

NOTE *It happens again and again with automated measuring processes that due to some error, data are missing for a period of time (hours, or even days). In the procedure above, error simulation was not implemented. However, the reporting in* DailyReport *and* MonthlyReport *will continue to function if you simply delete some of the data from the generated files. But be careful in the calculation of average values. Missing measurements must not be taken to be zero values. The Excel worksheet function* AVERAGE *behaves admirably in this case and considers only those cells in the given range that are not empty. Only when all of the measurements of an averaging range are missing does it return the error result "division by 0."*

Daily Report

The daily report contains three charts, in which the exact course of the measurements is presented. Here the curves A1, A2, A3 are united in a single chart. So that charts from several days can be compared easily, a uniform scaling is required. For this reason the Y range is set with a fixed range of 0 to 300. (Normally, Excel changes the scaling automatically and fits it to the values that actually occur.) Integrated into the daily report are a tabular overview of the daily average values and the daily maximum of the five curves.

The daily report for a given date is created by the procedure *DailyProtocol.* The charts are created completely in program code and inserted into the worksheet "DailyReport." Any existing charts in this worksheet (from the previous report) are first deleted.

The procedure opens the file with the daily data and copies some basic information (daily average and maximum) from it into the worksheet "DailyReport." Furthermore, the title of the report is extended to include the relevant date.

To generate a new chart, first three empty *ChartObject* frames are placed in the worksheet. Then *ChartWizard* is used to create charts within them corresponding for the most part to the actual requirements. (Some details that are not within control of *ChartWizard* have to be changed later on.) The three *ChartWizard* instructions differ only in that the charts are associated to differing ranges of cells from those of the daily data table.

Then begins the actual detail work of formatting the chart. The three charts can be worked on as a unit in a loop. The procedure ends with the daily data file being closed and the daily report being printed. (On account of the option *Preview:=True* printing takes the form of a page view.)

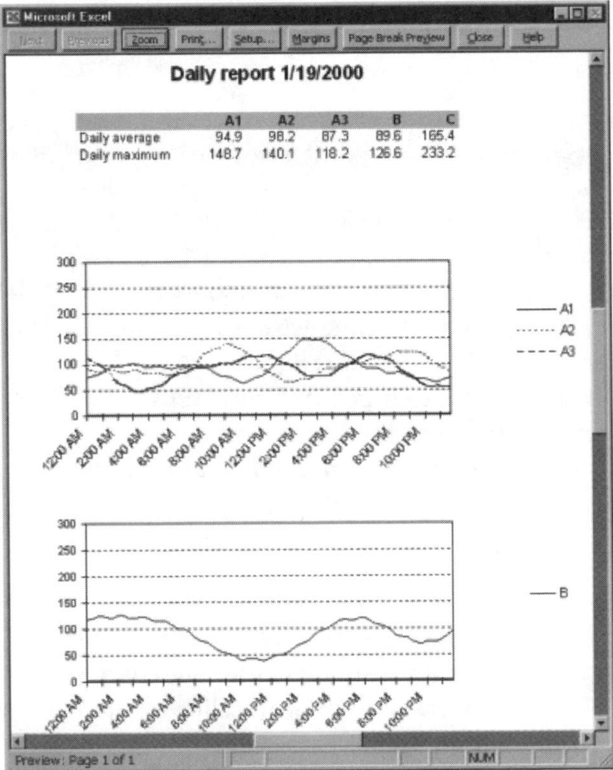

Figure 10.6. A daily report

```
' Chart.xls, Module CreateReports
Sub DailyProtocol(dat As Date)
  Dim filename$                 'report file name
  Dim protWBook As Workbook     'workbook of this file
  Dim protWSheet As Worksheet   'sheet of this book
  Dim protRange As Range        'first data cell in this sheet
  Dim chartWSheet As Worksheet  'reference to sheet with daily data
  Dim i%, chobj As ChartObject  'loop variables
  Application.ScreenUpdating = False
  filename = ThisWorkbook.Path + "\d_" + _
           Format(dat, "yyyymmdd") + ".xls"
  If Dir(filename) = "" Then
    MsgBox "The file " & filename & " does not exist. " & _
      "Please create test data."
    Exit Sub
  End If
  Set protWBook = Workbooks.Open(filename)
  Set protWSheet = protWBook.Worksheets(1)
  Set protRange = protWSheet.[A4]
  Set chartWSheet = ThisWorkbook.Worksheets("DailyReport")
  ' delete all existing charts on this sheet
  For Each chobj In chartWSheet.ChartObjects
    chobj.Delete
  Next chobj
  ' copy caption, daily averages and daily maximum values in table
  chartWSheet.[ReportLabel] = "Daily report " & dat
  protWSheet.[I19:M19].Copy
  chartWSheet.[DailyAverage].PasteSpecial xlValues
  protWSheet.[I21:M21].Copy
  chartWSheet.[DailyMax].PasteSpecial xlValues
  ' create three charts
  For i = 1 To 3
    chartWSheet.ChartObjects.Add(30, 150 + 200 * (i - 1), 400, 185). _
      Name = "Daily data " & i
    chartWSheet.ChartObjects("Daily data " & i).Activate
    If i = 1 Then
      ActiveChart.ChartWizard protWSheet.[A3:D99], _
        xlLine, 4, xlColumns, 1, 1
    ElseIf i = 2 Then
      ActiveChart.ChartWizard protWSheet.[A3:A99,E3:E99], _
        xlLine, 4, xlColumns, 1, 1
    ElseIf i = 3 Then
      ActiveChart.ChartWizard protWSheet.[A3:A99,F3:F99], _
        xlLine, 4, xlColumns, 1, 1
```

```
    End If
  Next i
  ' format charts
  For Each chobj In chartWSheet.ChartObjects
    chobj.Border.LineStyle = xlNone    'no border for entire chart
    With chobj.Chart
      .HasTitle = False                               'no title
      .PlotArea.Border.LineStyle = xlAutomatic        'border
      .PlotArea.Interior.ColorIndex = xlNone          'no pattern/fill
      .Axes(xlCategory).TickLabelSpacing = 8
      .Axes(xlCategory).TickMarkSpacing = 4           'x axis
      .Axes(xlValue).MinimumScale = 0                 'y axis
      .Axes(xlValue).MaximumScale = 300
      .Axes(xlCategory).TickLabels.Orientation = 45  '45 degrees
      .Axes(xlCategory).TickLabels.NumberFormat = "h:mm AM/PM"
      For i = 1 To .SeriesCollection.Count            'format data
        .SeriesCollection(i).Border.ColorIndex = 1    ' series
        .SeriesCollection(i).Border.Weight = xlThin
        .SeriesCollection(i).Border.LineStyle = xlContinuous
        .SeriesCollection(i).MarkerStyle = xlNone
      Next i
      If .SeriesCollection.Count > 2 Then              'distinguish
        .SeriesCollection(2).Border.LineStyle = xlDot  ' 2nd and 3rd
        .SeriesCollection(3).Border.LineStyle = xlDash ' series
      End If
      ' diagram size, legend size
      .PlotArea.Left = 5:    .PlotArea.Top = 5
      .PlotArea.Width = 290
      .PlotArea.Height = 140
      .Legend.Left = 340
      .Legend.Width = 50
      .Legend.Border.LineStyle = xlNone
    End With
  Next chobj
  ActiveWindow.Visible = False  'deactivate chart
  protWBook.Close
  chartWSheet.PrintOut Preview:=True
End Sub
```

Monthly Report

The monthly reports are somewhat more lavishly decked out than the daily reports, taking three pages in all. The first side consists of an overview of all daily average and maximum values as well as the resulting monthly averages and maxima. The next page contains three charts, and the last page sports two charts. These show the progression of the average and maximum values. The curves for the averages have been smoothed (click on the curve, open the pop-up menu FORMAT DATA SERIES|PATTERNS, option SMOOTHED LINE). Figure 10.7 shows the second page of the monthly report with the curves for the measurement values A1 through A3.

For generating the monthly report we have chosen a method completely different from that used for the daily report. The charts were inserted (with the mouse) into the worksheet "MonthlyReport" and are not touched at all by the procedure *MonthlyProtocol*. *MonthlyProtocol* merely changes those data cells that the finished chart accesses.

This way of proceeding has advantages and disadvantages. The advantage is that the programming effort is greatly reduced. Thus you can achieve good results with minimal experience in programming charts. The disadvantages become evident when you attempt to generate five identical charts by mouse click. This is almost as much effort as the programming (even if you first create a chart, and then copy it and change only the ranges of cells of the data series). Furthermore, this way of proceeding is possible only if the chart, as in this example, is to a great extent independent of the data. However, if such items as the number of data series, the number of data points, and the range of values of the data series can vary, then there is no avoiding "real" programming.

REMARKS *The charts assume a month of 31 days. In the case of months with fewer days there are one to three empty data points. Thus the space available for the chart is not used to full capacity, but in exchange there is a distinct advantage: The scaling of the X-axis is independent of the number of days in the month. The charts are thereby more comparable.*

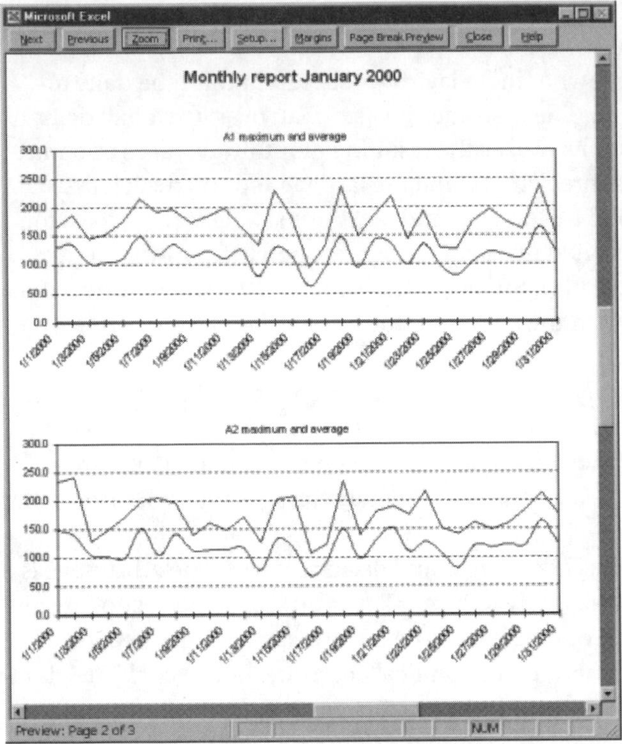

Figure 10.7. A page from the three-page monthly report

Onward to the program code, which for the reasons cited above contains not a single line of instructions that typically apply to charts. The procedure is rather an example of how data from up to 31 files can be consolidated in a single table. The individual files are not opened, but rather direct access to individual cells of other worksheets is made via formulas of type *='C:\Test\[D_20000101.XLS]Sheet1'!$L$19*. This form of data access proceeds surprisingly quickly. The creation of the monthly report takes only a little longer than that of the daily report.

The most complicated part of the procedure relates to the creation of these formulas, which are inserted into the worksheet by changing the *FormulaR1C1* property of the affected cells. The formulas must be created relatively laboriously as character strings. The R1C1 format is better suited for such tasks, because at least there is no transformation from column numbers into letters.

```
Sub MonthlyProtocol(dat As Date)
  Dim sdat, edat, nrdays          'start and end date; nr. of days
  Dim filename$                   'name of report file
  Dim chartWSheet As Worksheet    'sheet of report file
  Dim chartRange As Range         'first data cell
```

```
Dim z, i%, j%                 'loop variables
sdat = DateSerial(Year(dat), Month(dat), 1)
nrdays = DateSerial(Year(dat), Month(dat) + 1, 1) - _
         DateSerial(Year(dat), Month(dat), 1)
edat = dat + nrdays - 1
ThisWorkbook.Activate
Set chartWSheet = ThisWorkbook.Worksheets("MonthlyReport")
chartWSheet.Activate
chartWSheet.[a1].Select
Set chartRange = chartWSheet.[B9]
' build monthly table
Application.Calculation = xlManual
chartWSheet.[B1] = "Monthly report " & Format(dat, "mmmm yyyy")
For i = 1 To nrdays
  z = dat + i - 1
  chartRange.Cells(i, 1) = z
  filename = ThisWorkbook.Path + "\d_" + _
             Format(z, "yyyymmdd") & ".xls"
  If Dir(filename) = "" Then
    For j = 1 To 5
      chartRange.Cells(i, 1 + j).FormulaR1C1 = ""
      chartRange.Cells(i, 7 + j).FormulaR1C1 = ""
    Next j
  Else
    filename = "='" & ThisWorkbook.Path + "\[d_" + _
               Format(z, "yyyymmdd") & ".xls]Sheet1'"
    For j = 1 To 5
      chartRange.Cells(i, 1 + j).FormulaR1C1 = _
        filename & "!R19C" & 8 + j
      chartRange.Cells(i, 7 + j).FormulaR1C1 = _
        filename & "!R21C" & 8 + j
    Next j
  End If
Next i
If nrdays < 31 Then
  For i = nrdays + 1 To 31
    For j = 1 To 12
      chartRange.Cells(i, j).ClearContents
    Next j
  Next i
End If
Application.Calculate
chartWSheet.Range("B9:M39").Copy
chartWSheet.Range("B9:M39").PasteSpecial Paste:=xlValues
```

```
  Application.CutCopyMode = False
  chartWSheet.PrintOut Preview:=True
  Application.Calculation = xlAutomatic
End Sub
```

After all references have been inserted into the worksheet and the worksheet recalculated, the entire range of cells is copied to the clipboard. Then, with *PasteSpecial* only the numerical values (instead of the formulas) are pasted. This process saves memory and increases the speed of further processing. Furthermore, it does not occur to Excel to ask at the next opportunity whether it should update the existing references.

The procedure ends, like *DailyProtocol*, with printing the worksheet together with the five charts contained therein. Furthermore, in the page layout of the worksheet (FILE|PAGE SETUP) "none" is selected for the header, and for the footer the page number is inserted (since the report always contains three pages).

Menu Management

The management of the menus has nothing new about it in comparison to what has been discussed in earlier chapters, for which reason we have not included here the code for the event procedures. The menu is realized as an independent *CommandBar* object. It is made visible in *Workbook_Open* when `Chart.xls` is opened, and is hidden again in *Workbook_BeforeClose*.

Dialog Management

The form *FormDateInput* is used universally for the three commands REPORT|CREATE TEST DATA, ...|DAILY REPORT, and ...|MONTHLY REPORT. The text in the text box *lblInfo* is changed according to the purpose for which it is to be used. With the procedures *ProtocolMenu_GenerateNewFiles*, *_DailyProtocol*, and *_MonthlyProtocol*, of which only one is reproduced here, the texts in the text boxes *txtFrom* and *txtTo* are preset.

The two dates can be increased or decreased with spin buttons. The values are preset to 0, and the permissible range is from –1000 to 1000. Therefore, you can theoretically change the date by ±1000 days. (Theoretically, because you would not have the patience to keep pushing the button. Much quicker is simply to input the date via the keyboard.)

```
' Chart.xls, Module MenuEvents
Sub ChartSampleMenu_MonthlyProtocol()
  Dim dat, lastmonth
  lastmonth = -1
```

```
  With FormDateInput
    .dat1 = DateSerial(Year(Now), Month(Now), 1)
    .dat2 = DateSerial(Year(Now), Month(Now), _
              DateSerial(Year(Now), Month(Now) + 1, 1) - _
              DateSerial(Year(Now), Month(Now), 1))
    .txtFrom = CStr(.dat1)
    .txtTo = CStr(.dat2)
    .spinTo = 0
    .spinFrom = 0
    .lblInfo = "Date range for which monthly reports will be " & _
      "created and printed."
    .Show
    If .result = False Then Exit Sub
    ' create report
    Application.ScreenUpdating = False
    Application.DisplayStatusBar = True
    For dat = CDate(.txtFrom) To CDate(.txtTo)
      If lastmonth  Month(dat) Then
        Application.StatusBar = "Create monthly report for " & _
          Format(dat, "mmmm yyyy")
        MonthlyProtocol CDate(dat)
        lastmonth = Month(dat)
      End If
    Next dat
    Application.StatusBar = False
    Application.DisplayStatusBar = False
  End With
End Sub
```

If the input is terminated with Ok and if in *btnOK_Click* no input error is discovered, then a loop runs through all the days of the date range. Each time the month changes, *MonthlyProtocol* is called. Admittedly, the algorithm has not been overly carefully programmed, but it is surely the simplest solution that functions for arbitrary time intervals (even for more than twelve months). A calculation of the first day of each new month would probably require more time than simply running through all the days. In any case, it would have required more thought in the programming, and programmers are known not always to be in the mood for heavy-duty thinking.

The actual form event procedures turn out to be comparatively short and trivial. Note that the spin button is not synchronized when a new date is input via the keyboard. For this reason it is impossible to input a date via the keyboard and then change it with the spin button.

```
' event procedure for the form for date input
Option Explicit
Public result, dat1, dat2
Private Sub btnCancel_Click()
  result = False
  Hide
End Sub
Private Sub btnOK_Click()
  If IsDate(txtFrom) And IsDate(txtTo) Then
    result = True
    Hide
  Else
    MsgBox "Invalid date!!"
  End If
End Sub
Private Sub spinFrom_Change()
  txtFrom = CStr(dat1 + spinFrom)
End Sub
Private Sub spinTo_Change()
  txtTo = CStr(dat2 + spinTo)
End Sub
```

Syntax Summary for Charts

This section collects almost all the truly important chart objects, methods, and properties. A summary of the object hierarchy of all chart objects appears in Chapter 15. There, all objects are also briefly described. In the following syntax boxes we have used the following abbreviations: *wb* for a *Workbook* object, *ws* for a *Worksheet* object, *chobj* for a *ChartObject* object, and *ch* for a *Chart* object.

Chart Objects

ws.ChartObjects(..)	select embedded chart object
ws.ChartObjects.Add ..	new (empty) chart frame
chobj.Select	corresponds to a single mouse click
chobj.Activate	corresponds to a single mouse click
ActiveWindow.Visible = False	deactivate
chobj.Chart	refers to a chart object
chobj.Copy	copy chart object together with chart
ws.Paste: Selection.Name = ".."	insert chart object together with chart
chobj.Duplicate.Name = ".."	duplicate existing chart object
chobj.Delete	delete chart object together with chart

Charts

ActiveChart	refers to the active chart
wb.Charts(..).Select	selects chart sheet
ch.ChartArea.Copy	copies chart contents
ch.Paste	inserts chart contents
ch.ChartArea.Clear	deletes entire chart
ch.ChartArea.ClearContents	deletes only the data
ch.ChartArea.ClearFormats	deletes only the format
ch.ChartWizard ...	create chart with chart wizard
ch.AutoFormat ...	use autoformat
Application.AddChartAutoFormat ...	save new autoformat
*ch.*CopyPicture	copies chart as graphic or bitmap to the clipboard
ch.Export	saves chart in a graphics file
ch.PrintOut	prints the chart
ch.ChartArea	refers to entire background
ch.PlotArea	refers to background of the graphic
ch.Floor, ch.*Walls*	refers to floor and walls (3-D chart)
ch.ChartTitle	refers to chart title
ch.Legend	refers to legend
ch.Axes(..)	refers to axes
ch.SeriesCollection(..)	refers to data series

Drawing Objects (*Shapes*)

Overview

The ***Shape*** object serves primarily to represent autoshapes (lines, rectangles, arrows, stars, etc.; see the "Drawing" toolbar).

These objects take the place of the various drawing objects in Excel 5/7. However, the large number of related objects can be a source of confusion.

Hierarchy of Shape Objects

```
Worksheet/Chart
 └─Shapes                         all Shape objects within a sheet
    └─Shape                       a Shape object
       ├─ConnectorFormat          connection to other objects
       ├─ControlFormat            additional properties for controls
       ├─FillFormat               background pattern (via Fill property)
       ├─GroupShapes              single object (via GroupItems, if
       │    │                     Type=msoGroup)
```

│ └─*Shape*	
├─*HyperLink*	cross link and internet links
├─*LineFormat*	line properties (via *Line*)
├─*LinkFormat*	additional properties for OLE objects
├─*OLEFormat*	yet more properties for OLE objects
├─*PictureFormat*	properties of picture objects
├─*Range*	anchor cells (via *TopLeft-/BottomRightCell*)
├─*Shadow*	properties for shadow
├─*ShapeNodes*	line segment (via *Nodes*, if *Type*=msoFreeform)
│ └─*ShapeNode*	
├─*ShapeRange*	single ojbects with multiple editing (via *Range*)
│ └─*Shape*	
├─*TextEffectFormat*	properties for WordArt object
├─*TextFrame*	Text box within an autoshape object
└─*ThreeDFormat*	3-D effects (via *ThreeD*)

The *Shapes* enumeration enables access to all *Shape* objects of a worksheet or chart sheet. For the insertion of new drawing objects there is a long list of methods available, such as *AddShape* for autoshapes and *AddLine* for lines.

ShapeRange enables the simultaneous editing of several *Shape* objects (as if these objects were selected with Shift and the mouse).

Freehand shapes (that is, freely drawn line segments) represent a partcular form of *Shape* objects. In this case, the property *ShapeNodes* refers to a like-named enumeration of ***ShapeNode*** objects. These objects contain, among other attributes, coordinate points of the individual line segments.

A *Shape* object is also used for managing a so-called group (in interactive mode: pop-up menu command GROUPING). In this case the property *GroupItems* leads to a ***GroupShape*** object, which, in turn, takes over the management of the group elements. Group elements can include not only *Shape* objects, but also charts and OLE objects, among others.

Finally, *Shape* is used to manage completely foreign objects, such as for MS Forms control objects (*Type=msoOLEControlObject*). In this case, *Shape* stands between the worksheet or chart sheet and the actual object. *Shape* is then concerned, among other things, with the positioning of the control. For communication between the sheet and the control the ***ControlFormat*** object is employed, which is addressed via the like-named property of *Shape*. *ControlFormat* is generally transparent, because its properties appear in the properties window of the control and can be used like control properties.

Shape Properties

AutoShapeType: The two most important properties are surely *Type* and *AutoShapeType.* If *Type=msoAutoShape* is set, then with *AutoShapeType* one of countless autoshape types can be specified (there are more than 130). On the other hand, if no autoshape is represented by the *Shape* object, then the object type is specified by the *msoShapeType* constants. Elements such as *msoChart, msoComment, msoEmbeddedOLEObject, msoFreeForm, msoGroup, msoOLEControlObject,* and *msoTextBox* prove that internally to Excel every object that is located outside of a cell is controlled by *Shape* objects.

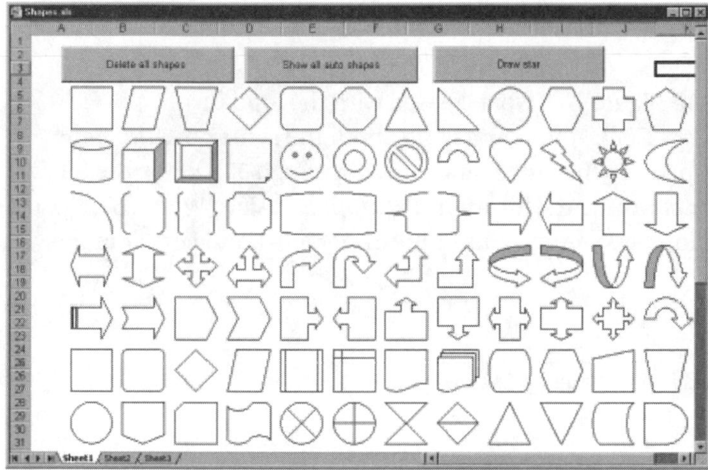

Figure 10.8. Some of the predefined autoshapes

Positioning: For each object is saved the upper left corner (*Left* and *Top*) as well as the width and height (*Width* and *Height*). These coordinates are figured from the upper left-hand corner of the form or worksheet. *TopLeftCell* and *BottomRightCell* specify the cells under the upper left-hand corner and lower right-hand corner. *Placement* determines how the control should behave when the worksheet is changed (*xlMoveAndSize, xlMove,* or *xlFreeFloating*).

Format: The possibilities for visual appearance are practically without bound. Each of the following properties leads to a particular object (whose name is given in parentheses if it is different from that of the property): *Adjustments, Callout (CalloutFormat), Fill (FillFormat), Hyperlink, Line (LineFormat), PictureFormat, Shadow (ShadowFormat), TextEffect (TextEffectFormat), TextFrame,* and *ThreeD (ThreeDFormat).* Perhaps this superfluity of objects is too much of a good thing.

Other: Depending on which objects are represented by *Shape*, there are further properties available: *ConnectorFormat* (if the object is bound to other objects), *ControlFormat* (for controls), *GroupItems* (for object groups), *Nodes* (for freehand objects), as well as *LinkFormat* and *OLEFormat* (for OLE objects).

> **POINTER** *Note that the* Shape *objects are defined in the Excel library, but the associated constants in the Office library. When old Excel 5/7 files are opened, the Office library is not activated under normal circumstances. This must be accomplished with* TOOLS|REFERENCES.

Example

The drawing objects in Figure 10.8 were created with the loop in *btnShowAllAutoShapes_Click*. And now a word about the syntax of *AddShape*: The first parameter specifies the autoshape type (1 through 37), while the following four parameters determine the location (*Left/Top*) and size (*Width/Height*) of the object. The coordinate system begins in the upper left-hand corner of the worksheet.

```
' Shapes.xls, Sheet1
Private Sub btnShowAllAutoShapes_Click()
  Dim i&
  For i = 0 To 136
    ActiveSheet.Shapes.AddShape i + 1, _
      40 + 50 * (i Mod 12), 50 + 50 * (i \ 12), 40, 40
  Next
End Sub
```

To delete the drawing objects the following procedure can be used. The crucial step is the *Type* test: Without it the buttons in the worksheet would be deleted as well!

```
Private Sub btnDeleteShapes_Click()
  Dim s As Shape
  For Each s In ActiveSheet.Shapes
    If s.Type = msoAutoShape Or s.Type = msoLine Then s.Delete
  Next
End Sub
```

The procedure *btnStar_Click* draws a star made up of colored arrows. Note that arrows are not among the autoshapes, but form their own category of *Shape*. For this reason *AddLine* must be used instead of *AddShape*. *ForeColor* refers to a *ColorFormat* object, with which the color of an object can be set.

> **POINTER** *The program code may lead you to believe that Excel offers infinitely many colors for your use. Unfortunately, that is not the case. Rather, there is available a palette of only 56 colors (apparently a relic of earlier versions of Excel). Therefore, a reference to an* RGB *color means only that the closest matching color from this palette is used.*

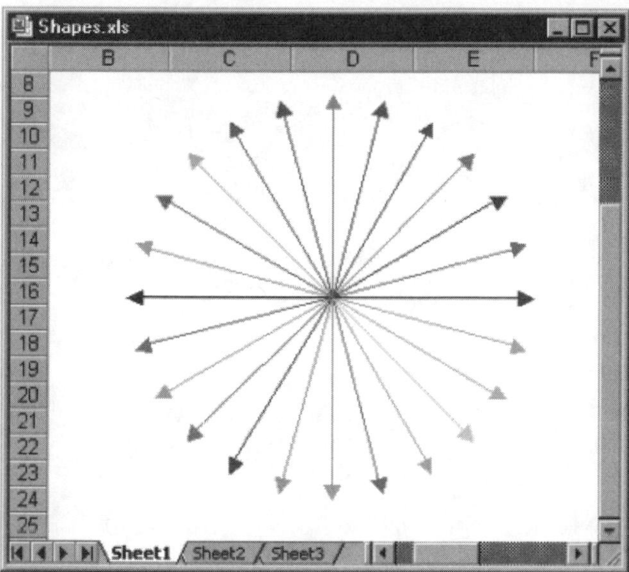

Figure 10.9. A star of colored arrows

```
Private Sub btnStar_Click()
  Dim degree#
  Dim s As Shape
  Const Pi = 3.1415927
  Randomize
  For degree = 0 To 2 * Pi Step Pi / 12
    Set s = ActiveSheet.Shapes.AddLine(200, 200, _
      200 + 100 * Sin(degree), 200 + 100 * Cos(degree))
    s.Line.EndArrowheadStyle = msoArrowheadTriangle
    s.Line.EndArrowheadLength = msoArrowheadLengthMedium
    s.Line.EndArrowheadWidth = msoArrowheadWidthMedium
    s.Line.ForeColor.RGB = RGB(Rnd * 255, Rnd * 255, Rnd * 255)
  Next
End Sub
```

CHAPTER 11

Data Management in Excel

This is the first of three chapters that deal with the extensive and important theme of databases. This chapter begins with a section on fundamentals that ends with the perhaps surprising conclusion that Excel is *not* a database program and should not be entrusted with the management of large data sets.

Knowing that you will nonetheless manage smaller data sets with Excel (and remember my warning only when there is a changeover to a genuine database system that requires an enormous effort), the remainder of the chapter provides information on the functioning of Excel for the management of data in worksheets.

As for the two chapters to follow, there we will consider how from Excel you can access data that reside in an external (genuine) database system. In the midst of all this stands the new ADO library. Finally, the third database chapter is concerned with methods of data analysis (independent of where the data originate). Here pivot tables take center stage.

Chapter Overview

Fundamentals

Experience tells us that the majority of all Excel programs are in reality database programs. Microsoft has taken note of this and has enlarged the repertoire of database functions from version to version. In version 5 this meant revised functions for setting up pivot tables and the supplementary program MS Query. In version 7 we had the template wizard (see Chapter 9) and the DAO library, which for the first time offered programmers full access to the database functions of Access. With Excel 97 DAO was improved (ODBCDirect). Excel 2000 has finally replaced DAO with the totally new ADO library. At the same time, we have the completely revised functions for data import (MS Query and the *QueryTable* object) as well as for data analysis (pivot tables).

This section attempts to collect in as compact a form as possible basic information on the subject of databases. If you wish to use Excel for nothing more than to sort a table of 100 rows quickly (that, too, is a database), you can confidently proceed to the next sections. But if you have more ambitious database applications in mind, then the time that you spend now reading this section is guaranteed to be a good investment.

This section also wishes to warn you against thoughtlessly using Excel (to call a spade a spade, *misusing* Excel) for applications for which it was not designed. The following sections explain why Excel is poorly suited as a database program for advanced applications. Even if you wish to continue to use Excel only to manage smaller data sets, you should be aware of its limitations.

Introduction

What Is a Database?

The concept *database* has unfortunately acquired a number of different meanings depending on the context in which it is used. The lowest common denominator is perhaps that every database is concerned with a collection of associated, ordered data.

- In Excel every table or list can be considered a database. Excel makes available commands for working with such databases in the DATA menu (SORT, GROUP, etc.).

- In database systems such as Access or Oracle a database is stored in its own database file. There, in addition to the data, arranged in several tables, are query functions and perhaps program code. In such database systems large data sets can be processed more securely and efficiently than in Excel.

- Occasionally, the database system will itself be called a database (and not the data stored within it). This shorthand can result in considerable confusion.

Of course, there are great differences among different database systems, relating to the scope of the data to be managed, data security, efficiency over networks, and programming. In essence there are two categories:

- Desktop systems and file server systems. In such systems the data are stored in a network in a directly accessible file. For small database applications this is very convenient and familiar. However, data access in large networks can be very slow. Typical representatives are Access, FoxPro, and Paradox.

- Client/Server systems. In this case there is a separation between the program that manages the data (the server) and the programs that access the data (clients). This separation makes possible significantly greater efficiency and security. However, the programming of clients (that is, of database applications) is more difficult. Popular database servers are Oracle, Microsoft SQL server, IBM DB/2, Informix, and Sybase. For programming of clients Visual Basic or Delphi can be used. As you will see in the next chapter, your Excel application can also be a client for a database server.

POINTER *Please note that the information collected here is greatly abbreviated due to space limitations. If you wish to plunge more deeply into the subject of databases, you will need to consult the literature on the subject. There are good books on Access, but also books that deal with ADO programming under VB and VBA.*

A Small Database Glossary

The following paragraphs describe some important concepts in the world of databases to facilitate unambiguous communication. These definitions are of significance to you above all if you wish to use the supplementary program MS Query for reading external data or the ADO library for database programming.

Databases are usually organized into several **Tables**. A typical table might contain, for example, data on all customers of a business: customer number, name, address, telephone number, etc. Each row of the table is called a **data record**. Individual elements of a row are called **data fields**.

Practically all currently available databases are based on the **relational model**. This model makes it possible to divide the entire range of data into several tables that are linked by relations. This results in a number of advantages in relation to efficiency, data security, and the avoidance of redundancy. The fundamentals of relational databases will be discussed at the beginning of the next chapter, which deals with external data.

Tables usually contain data in unordered form (that is, in the order in which the data were first stored). To make possible the speediest search of the data, there are stored in addition to the actual data certain so-called indexes. An **index**, or **key**, contains essentially the information as to where data are to be found within a table.

To create a sorted list from one or more tables that contain only data that satisfy certain criteria, one employs **queries**. The result of a query is thus a set of data collected according to certain criteria. Queries are processed more quickly than otherwise if the underlying data have been ordered by indexes.

The formulation of queries often proceeds interactively with the database program or in MS Query. Internally or in program code, queries are formulated in **SQL**, which stands for "standard query language" and represents a standard for formulating queries. SQL is thus a programming language.

For programming database applications VB and VBA can be used (among other possibilities). For this reason Excel is also suited for accessing external databases, regardless of whether this is managed with Access, Oracle, or the SQL server. The database-specific functions are made available in the ADO library via objects, methods, and properties (ADO stands for "ActiveX data objects").

Excel Versus Database Systems

Differences Between Worksheet Calculational Programs and Genuine Database Systems

The basic idea of a worksheet calculational program like Excel is that all data (thus the entire Excel file) should be loaded into RAM and reside there for instant access. This has the advantage that data processing goes very quickly, but it has the disadvantage that the size of the data set is limited, as much as by the amount of memory available as by the limits on Excel worksheets, which is currently at 65,000 lines.

A completely different concept is followed by genuine database systems. The data generally reside in a database file. In RAM only the smallest possible portion of the data is loaded. Every change in the data is immediately saved (without an explicit command such as FILE SAVE being required). The advantage is that in this way you can process data sets larger than 100 megabytes. The drawback is that most operations are carried out more slowly than in Excel.

This rather schematic comparison establishes two significant differences between worksheet calculational programs and database programs: First, worksheet programs require a great deal of RAM even to process small amounts of data, while in the case of genuine database systems the data sets can be much larger than available RAM. Second, a worksheet calculational program can save only an entire file, which in the case of large data sets takes so long that it is seldom carried out. In contrast, in a database system each small change is immediately saved. This happens so quickly that you usually don't even notice it. For this reason (and many others as well) data in real database systems are better protected than in Excel.

Features of Genuine Database Systems That Are Lacking in Excel

- **Excel has no indices:** Indices make possible an efficient search in large data sets without having first to sort the data.

- **Excel has no relations:** The relational model offers various advantages with respect to efficiency, data security, and avoiding redundancy.

- **Excel lacks security mechanisms against deletion or alteration of data:** Data security is the most important criterion for a database after speed of access. Every database program is equipped with a set of security mechanisms that prevent the accidental alteration or deletion of data. In Excel such security mechanisms are almost entirely lacking. It is particularly critical in Excel that it is relatively easy to destroy the unity of data series. By this is meant that after the careless insertion or deletion of some cells, for example, the entries no longer match: Next to the name of *X* is now the address of *Y*.

- **Excel has no report generator:** In Excel you can print out large tables, but there is not a sufficiently flexible command to format the printout for a particular purpose. Just try to print labels in Excel sometime!

- **Excel is not designed to manage networked data:** An elementary sign of a database program is its ability to work over a network. The data can be centrally managed on one computer, and several users can access it simultaneously. The database program makes sure that no conflicts arise in this quasi-simultaneous data access. Excel can be run over a network, but the management of central, common data that can be coordinated to be processed on several computers is possible only under severe restrictions.

Why Is Excel Nonetheless Used as a Database System?

- Excel is simple to use. The learning curve with a new database program is steep.
- Excel is available. Another program would first have to be created.
- Excel has elementary database functions available and is therefore quite suitable for simple database applications. (The problem is just that over the course of time most small applications grow larger!)
- In its use as a database system Excel has all of its worksheet functions available. Genuine database systems cannot compete with Excel in this regard.
- Excel is *the* standard spreadsheet calculational program in the office sector. There is no comparable standard in the database sector. For this reason Excel files are excellently suited for data exchange among colleagues within a business or between firms.

For all of these reasons there is hardly an Excel user who would shrink from creating small database applications with Excel. Actually, there is almost no other program that so simply and intuitively can be used to create a small address file.

The Consequence: External Data Storage, Data Analysis with Excel

In spite of the limitations of Excel cited above, it is not necessary that every application involving large amounts of data be realized with a database program. Excel offers a number of advantages that database systems and programming languages lack for the development of database clients.

The optimal solution is often to take the best of both worlds: If you have large data sets, then use a proper database system to store the data. But this does not keep you from carrying out various applications such as data entry, data analysis, and printing of charts in Excel or from creating the needed Excel programs for these tasks. Excel offers optimal conditions for such mixed solutions.

- The auxiliary program MS-Query enables interactive access to almost every database system.
- The object library ADO enables database access via program code as well. With the possibilities offered by MS-Query, the ADO library can also be used to edit data or to store new data series.

When Should Databases Be Used Directly in Excel?

After so many critical observations you are probably at the point of uncertainty as to whether Excel ever should be used for data management. But that would be taking things a bit too far. Excel is completely suited for managing data, under the following circumstances:

- The data sets are small (tables up to 1000 rows are more or less unproblematic).
- The data are simply structured (no necessity for the relational model, minimal redundancy).
- There is no need for simultaneous processing of data over a network.

There is thus (almost) nothing to be said against setting up a small address database, a literature database, or a simple cash account in Excel. However, it is not a good idea to attempt a full-fledged bookkeeping program or an extensive stock management system. And it would be a matter of gross negligence to manage vital information, such as in the field of medicine, in Excel.

Data Management Within Excel

Since many of Excel's data management functions are unknown even to advanced Excel users, this section describes such commands primarily from the point of view of the user. Some brief information on running these functions via VBA code follows in the next section.

> **POINTER** *Please note that the commands described here can generally be used in* any *Excel worksheet. Excel does not distinguish in any systematic way between a worksheet table and a database. Rather, it interprets every associated range of cells as a database.*

Creating a Database in Excel

The database concept in Excel is irresistibly simple: Any table or list can be interpreted as a database. The only condition is that each column must contain information of a single type (such as all addresses in column C, telephone numbers in column D). From this it follows that a unit of associated information (say, that consisiting of a name, address, and telephone number) must reside in a row. This informational unit is frequently called a "data record"or simply "record."

In practice, a database table usually is distinguished by its first row, which contains titles of the various columns. It is a good idea to leave that part of the worksheet below the data entries empty, so that the database can be enlarged as needed. The concept of a workbook in Excel lends itself to placing each database in its own worksheet (and thus clearly separated from other data in a workbook), though this is by no means a requirement. In theory, you can place several databases in a worksheet next to each other or even on top of one another. You can even select an arbitrary range of cells and apply database commands to it (such as DATA|SORT).

Installing a New Database

Creating a new database within Excel is no different from setting up an ordinary worksheet table. You input some data (addresses, say) in the usual way and label the columns. With larger data sets it is useful to divide the window and to fix it so that the row of column labels is always visible.

If some columns have cells containing extensive information, then you should activate the attribute "Wrap text" in FORMAT| CELLS|ALIGNMENT. Excel can then split long entries as needed over several rows (within a cell). Excel will increase the row height automatically. As a rule, this makes the table easier to read than having columns that are too wide. At the same time, the entire table should be aligned vertically from the top (in the same command as above), so that all entries in unusually tall rows begin at the top (and not at the bottom).

> **TIP** *In formatting of cells it is generally a good idea to format entire columns (click on the column head) or even the entire worksheet (click on the corner between the column and row heads) and not individual cells. First of all, from Excel's point of view this is more efficient, and secondly, this formatting is independent of the height of the table; that is, it automatically applies when the table is extended.*

An Employee Database

As an example database, the file `Staff.xls` is available to the staff of a firm, members of a club, or students and faculty of a school, or whatever. In the following paragraphs are presented some details of this minidatabase.

In the first column the individual's gender (m/f) appears, and in the second, the form of address (formal, personal). From this information the third column, salutation, is created, which distinguishes between the formal "Dear Mrs. Pachleitner:" and the personal "Dear Hermann,".

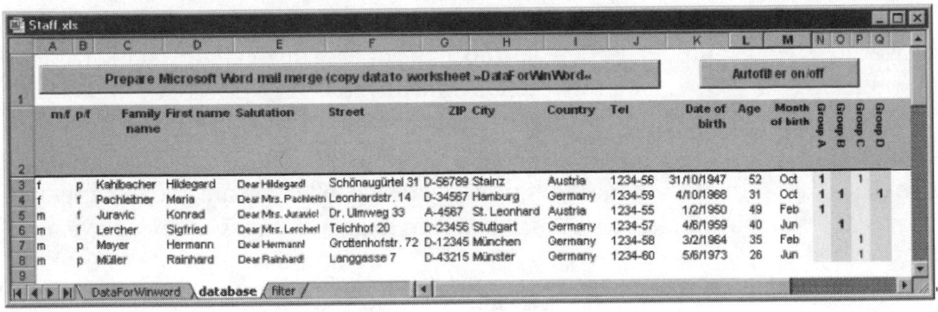

Staff.xls

Prepare Microsoft Word mail merge (copy data to worksheet »DataForWinWord«

Autofilter on/off

m/f	p/f	Family name	First name	Salutation	Street	ZIP	City	Country	Tel	Date of birth	Age	Month of birth	Group A	Group B	Group C	Group D
f	p	Kahlbacher	Hildegard	Dear Hildegard!	Schönaugürtel 31	D-56789	Stainz	Austria	1234-56	31/10/1947	52	Oct	1		1	
f	f	Pachleitner	Maria	Dear Mrs. Pachleitn	Leonhardstr. 14	D-34567	Hamburg	Germany	1234-59	4/10/1968	31	Oct	1	1		1
m	f	Juravic	Konrad	Dear Mrs. Juravic!	Dr. Ulmweg 33	A-4567	St. Leonhard	Austria	1234-55	1/2/1950	49	Feb	1			
m	f	Lercher	Sigfried	Dear Mrs. Lercher!	Teichhof 20	D-23456	Stuttgart	Germany	1234-57	4/6/1959	40	Jun		1		
m	p	Mayer	Hermann	Dear Hermann!	Grottenhofstr. 72	D-12345	München	Germany	1234-58	3/2/1964	35	Feb			1	
m	p	Müller	Rainhard	Dear Rainhard!	Langgasse 7	D-43215	Münster	Germany	1234-60	5/6/1973	26	Jun			1	

DataForWinword | database | filter

Figure 11.1. An employee database

The formation of the salutation takes place in the function *Salutation*. This function takes as parameters the contents of the first four columns. According to the contents of *male_female* and *formal_private* the resulting character string is created and returned as the function result.

```
' example file Staff.xls
Public Function Salutation(male_female, formal_private, _
    last_name, first_name)
  If Left(male_female, 1) = "m" Then
    If LCase(formal_private) = "f" Then
      Salutation = "Dear Mr. " & family_name & ":"
    Else
      Salutation = "Dear " & first_name & ","
    End If
  Else
    If LCase(formal_private) = "f" Then
      Salutation = "Dear Mrs. " & family_name & ":"
    Else
      Salutation = "Dear " & first_name & ","
    End If
  End If
End Function
```

The column labeled "Month of Birth" is created by taking information from the column labeled "Date of Birth." Since the month is formatted as a string of three letters, Excel creates an abbreviation for the month. The only purpose for this column is to be used as a filter criterion. (You will find very few database programs that allow you so easily to find everybody with a birthday in a particular month. You should take note of the way that this is done, that is, the creation of a column that functions as a filter criterion. It is characteristic of databases in Excel.)

In the column "Age" an attempt is made to render the current age of the employee as a whole number. For this purpose the date of birth is subtracted from the current date *NOW()*, and the result is transformed into a number of years with *YEAR()*. Since the reckoning of time in Excel begins with 1900, the result for a twenty-five-year-old is at this point 1925. Therefore, *YEAR(0)* is subtracted off. This formula is simple, but it is not quite exact. Due to leap years, it can happen that one day before or after a birthday can lead to an age that is off by one year.

```
=YEAR(NOW()-K3)-YEAR(0)
```

Finally, the columns "Group A, ..., GroupD" should be mentioned, in which a numeral "1" is used to indicate that an individual belongs to that particular group. (You could as well use a different symbol, such as an "x". The number 1 has the advantage that it can be used for calculations. It would be possible, for example, to create a column of sums that would give the number of groups to which each individual belonged.

> **POINTER** *The database* `Staff.xls` *also possesses the buttons* PREPARE MICROSOFT WORD MAIL MERGE *and* AUTOFILTER ON/OFF. *The associated macros and their functions appear below, in the next section. Background information on calculations with date and time can be found way back in Chapter 5.*

Input, Alteration, and Deletion of Data with the Database Form

In general, databases can be edited directly in the worksheet; that is, data can be altered, deleted, and newly input. An alternative to this, however, is the possibility with the command DATA|FORM to display a so-called database form. In this form is displayed exactly one data record. This data record can be edited or deleted. Database columns containing formulas (rather than input values) cannot be changed in the database form (in Figure 11.1, for example, the birth month, which is provided by the birth date). Accidental changes can be undone with the button Restore. The function EDIT|UNDO is not available after the termination of the database form.

With the button New you can input a new data record. New data records are always inserted at the end of the database. In this case formatting and formulas are taken from the last row of the database. The database is not automatically sorted.

The vertical scrollbar in the database form allows rapid transit through the data records to the one you are looking for. The order in which the records are displayed corresponds to the order of the records in the table—if the data should appear sorted according to some criterion, you must do the sorting before invoking the database form.

The button Criteria in the database form leads to an alternative display of the database form, in which you can provide criteria for the individual fields. Then with FIND PREV or FIND NEXT you can find the next data record (from the current one) that fulfills these criteria. Possible search criteria are *"A*"* (all names that begin with "A") or *">100"* (numbers greater than 100). The syntax for search criteria is treated further on, when filtering of data is discussed.

Working with the database form has both advantages and drawbacks in comparison to working directly in the table. First we discuss the advantages:

- In the database form all data of a data record are displayed in compact form. Database tables are often so wide that you can see only a piece.
- Use of the database form requires no special knowledge of Excel (other than minimal Windows savvy). Database forms are therefore especially suited for input of data by Excel novices.
- It is almost impossible to wreak large-scale havoc among the data. Particular care is required only in the input of new data: The button New must be clicked *before* data input begins. Otherwise, Excel interprets the data not as a new data record, but as a correction to the current data record. (There is also the possibility to edit, via a database form, a database whose window is not visible on the monitor.)

The predefined Excel database form is very convenient to use. However, it has its drawbacks:

- Filter criteria placed in the table (see below) are not taken into account.
- Numerous database commands—such as sorting—cannot be executed unless the form is closed.
- The structure of the form is fixed. The labeling of the data fields corresponds to the labels on the columns of the database, and the same amount of space is just as big (or as small) for one as for another. It is impossible to set up the form so that only selected data fields can be altered.
- An automatic plausibility control over the input (such as whether a valid date has been entered in the birth date field) cannot be instituted.
- A simultaneous processing of several data records (such as to delete all obsolete records) is impossible.
- When the database form is exited, no value is returned to VBA code giving information about the last data record to have been displayed.

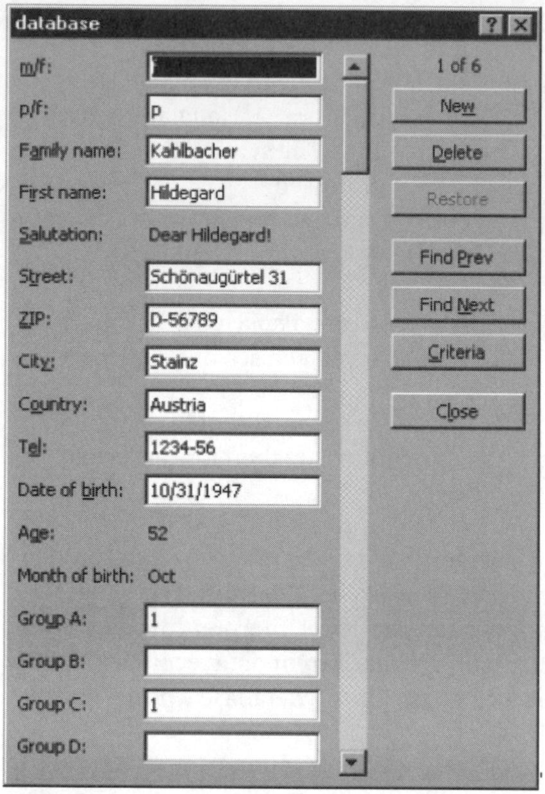

Figure 11.2. The Excel database form

Sorting, Searching, and Filtering Data

Sorting Data

One of the most important database commands is DATA|SORT. This command leads to the dialog displayed in Figure 11.3. There you can input up to three columns of your database according to which you would like the data to be sorted. The input of several sort criteria can be useful, for example, for printing a multiple mailing in which you can save postage costs by sorting first by state and within state by Zip code.

The sort command sorts, as a rule, in the range in which the cell pointer is located. However, the command can also be used to sort cells that have been explicitly selected, independently of whether that particular range of cells is related to a database. In this connection the meaning of the two option buttons "Header row" and "No header row" becomes clear. Normally, in the sorting of a database, Excel selects the entire database including the header row. But the header row is, of course, not sorted along with the database. On the other hand, if a selected range of cells is to be sorted, then such a header usually does not have a header row, and then the option "No header row" must be selected.

Figure 11.3. Dialog for sorting a database

The button Options allows for greater control in the execution of the sort command. First, one may determine whether Excel should distinguish between uppercase and lowercase (which normally, it does not). Second, special sort orders (such as day of the week or month) can be set. The sort lists presented correspond to the lists that can be set with OPTIONS|EXTRAS|CUSTOM LISTS. And finally, you can sort columns instead of rows. A sort by column appears seldom in practice. In database applications it is difficult to imagine a situation in which such a sort would make sense.

The sort command can be undone with an immediate appeal to EDIT|UNDO after it has been executed. Nonetheless, the command should be used with great care. It can destroy the construction of a carefully crafted table.

Particularly critical is the sorting of tables whose formulas relate to cells outside of the data record or tables to whose cells reference is made in other formulas. Upon sorting, Excel changes all relative references that refer within the sorted range to cells outside of the data record. Depending on the construction of the table this can make sense, or it could spell disaster! After executing the sort command check the contents of the table. If the result does not correspond to your expectations, undo the sort command and alter the table's construction by replacing relative references with absolute references (a painful task that cannot be automated) or by replacing formulas by their values (EDIT|COPY, EDIT|PASTE SPECIAL|VALUES).

> **TIP** *When the command* DATA|SORT *is executed while the cell pointer is located in a pivot table, the data fields of the pivot table will be sorted anew. The position of the cell pointer specifies which data are used as the sorting criterion.*

Tracking Down Data

The command EDIT|FIND is actually not a database command, but it can be gainfully employed in databases. The command leads to the dialog exhibited in Figure 11.4. If no range of cells is selected before the command is executed, Excel searches for the search expression in the entire active worksheet. The search is not restricted to the current database. The search phrase can contain either or both of the wildcards * (for an arbitrary number of characters) and ? (for exactly one arbitrary character), but conditions like "> 3" are not allowed.

Let us now examine the options of the FIND dialog, not all of which are equally easy to understand. With the "Search" box you can determine whether the data are seached by row or by column. In particular, in the case of large tables this option can have considerable influence on the search time. (This holds particularly for macro programming if the command is to be employed frequently.) The search begins in the currently active cell.

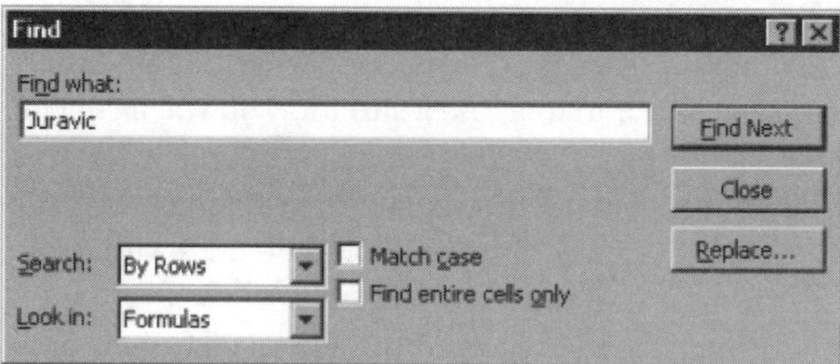

Figure 11.4. Dialog for searching the data

The selection field LOOK IN determines the source of the data: The standard setting "Formulas" means that the search text should be looked for only within a formula (such as the search text "3" in "=A3" or in "=A5+3"). The setting VALUES looks only at results derived from a formula (thus the data displayed in the cell). With the setting COMMENTS you can search for information in the comments attached to cells.

The option MATCH CASE is clear. With "Find entire cells only" is meant that the search phrase must match the entire content of a cell, and not just a part thereof.

Data Filters (Search Criteria)

By filtering data we mean that only those data records of a database are displayed that meet certain criteria. By setting up a filter you can have displayed from among an extensive database only those records that you wish to edit (complete, delete, copy, etc.).

Autofilter

The simplest form of filter is offered by the command DATA|FILTER|AUTOFILTER. It results in the placement of small list selection arrows in the lower right-hand corner of the header cells. Clicking on one of these arrows opens up a list that offers, in addition to all the entries in the particular column of the database, the following settings:

"xyz":	Indicates the records whose data field matches the dummy character string "xyz" exactly.
"(All)":	Displays all data records.
"(Blanks)":	Indicates data records whose field in the current column is empty.
"(NonBlanks)":	Indicates data records whose field in the current column is not empty.
"(Custom)":	Indicates those data records that correspond to the selected criterion in the dialog box (see Figure 11.3).
"(Top 10)":	Indicates those records with the largest or smallest values. It does not necessarily have to be ten records. You can specify the number in an options field. The top-10 variant was new in Excel 7.

As soon as a filter has been selected, Excel displays only those rows of the table whose records match the criterion. The selected filter buttom and the column head are displayed in blue, to indicate that for the moment not all the data are visible.

Several filters can be combined with a logical AND, for example, for selecting all records of the employee database that represent employees belonging to both of groups A and B. (The combination of filter criteria with a logical OR—all employees, say, in Group A or B—is possible only with special filters; see below.)

If data are changed after a filter has been set, this has no influence over whether that particular record will be shown. The decision as to which rows are visible occurs only once, namely, when the filter is set.

The command DATA|FILTER|SHOW ALL restores all of the filters to "All," thus leading to the unfiltered display of all the data records.

Custom Autofilter

With a custom autofilter it is possible to assemble somewhat more complex search criteria. Figure 11.5 shows that a criterion can be assembled from two conditions, which can be joined by a logical AND or OR. However, this combination affects only the conditions for the criterion of the current column, not for several filters in a database. As single conditions one is allowed patterns that are determined by wildcards (such as "*in*ton" for "Clinton" or "Washington") as well as comparisons (such as ">=100" or "<F").

Examples of Autofilters

With autofilters you can create the following groups from the database `Staff.xls`:

- All employees in Group C
- All female employees in Group C
- All employees who live in Tuscaloosa
- All employees who live outside of the Orkney Islands
- All employees whose birthday is in February (birth month = Feb) and are at least fifty years old (age > 50 or, better, date of birth < 3/1/1950, say).

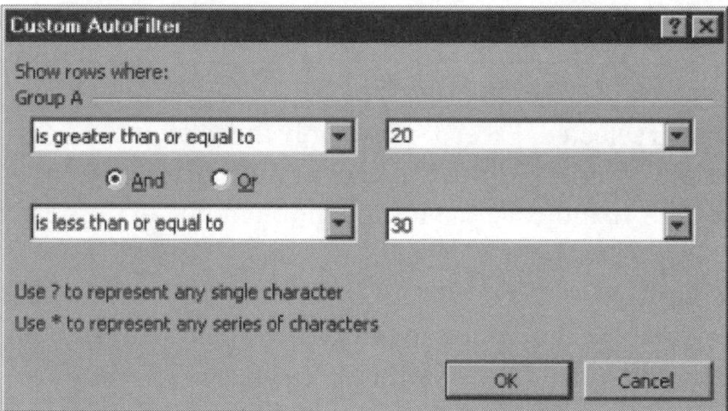

Figure 11.5. Dialog for setting a custom autofilter

Advanced Filters

In addition to the user-friendly autofilters, Excel offers so-called advanced filters. The invocation of DATA|FILTER|ADVANCED FILTER opens up the dialog pictured in Figure 11.6. The effect of an advanced filter is in principle the same as that of an autofilter: Only the data records satisfying the criteria are displayed. (The copying of filtered data is considered a few paragraphs below.) The effect of an advanced filter can be undone, as with an autofilter, with DATA|FILTER| SHOW ALL.

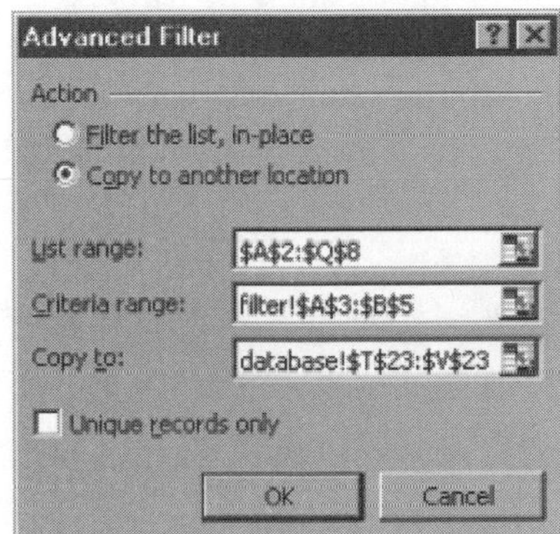

Figure 11.6. Dialog for setting an advanced filter

The decisive characteristic of advanced filters is that the filter criteria must be formulated in a specific range of cells. This range consists of a header row and one or more criterion rows. In the header row are entered all the column headers that are relevant to the search criteria. The headers must match exactly those in the database (including possible blank spaces). The criteria cells contain conditions for the database columns. Several conditions in a row are joined with "and" and must be satisfied simultaneously. When several rows contain criteria, these are joined with "or."

One is allowed to have as conditions, as in the case of autofilters, comparisons such as "*>10*", "*<=5*", or "*>=A*", as well as pattern strings such as "*=M*r*". Note that character comparisons that Excel might interpret as a formula are prefixed by the single-quote character. Otherwise, Excel produces the error message *#Name*, because the character string does not represent a valid cell name.

For many conditions it is required that a column of the database appear twice in the search criteria, such as for all employees whose age is ">=20" and "<=30."

Figure 11.7 shows some examples of possible filter criteria. Please note the difference between OR compounds (in the first example) and AND compounds (in the second and third examples). The criteria in Figure 11.7 are attractively presented with a border and boldface type, but this format serves only better readability and is not a requirement. On the other hand, you must be sure that the column head agrees exactly with that in the database.

In the example file `Staff.xls` the filter criteria have been housed in their own worksheet. This has the advantage that it can be displayed in its own window irrespective of the visible portion of the database table. The ranges of cells with the criteria were given the names "Filter1" through "Filter4" so that the input of a critierion with DATA|FILTER|ADVANCED FILTER can be conveniently carried out: You can set the cell pointer anywhere in the database, execute the above command, and specify "Filter1" through "Filter4" as the criteria range. For this the filter criteria do not have to be visible on the monitor. To try out advanced filters in `Staff.xls`, set the cursor in a cell of the staff list (sheet "database"). Then execute DATA|FILTER|ADVANCED FILTER. Excel automatically selects the entire database as LIST RANGE. You have only to type in "filter1" through "filter4" in the CRITERIA RANGE field and hit OK.

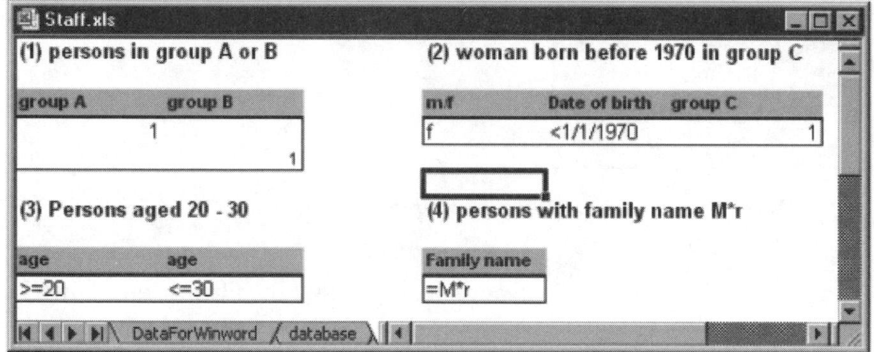

Figure 11.7. Some search criteria for the employee database

> **POINTER** *The database functions introduced in the next section must likewise have criteria specified for them. Here, too, the criteria are formulated in a range of cells. The syntax is the same as with filter criteria.*

Copying and Deleting Advanced Filters

If you wish to copy filtered data to another location in the table, you must select the option COPY TO ANOTHER LOCATION in the ADVANCED FILTER dialog and specify an output range. The output range must be headed (that is, with column heads). At first glance this may seem like unnecessary additional labor, but in fact, it makes possible the selective copying of particular columns of the database. Much more burdensome is the restriction that the output range must be located in the currently active worksheet. It would often be worthwhile (and more readable) to copy the filtered data into another worksheet. In fact, that is possible, but DATA|FILTER|ADVANCED FILTER must be executed while another worksheet is active.

In the example file an output range is defined, beginning with cell T23, that contains only the three columns giving first name, last name, and telephone number. If you would like to try out the copy command, place the cell pointer in the database, select the command DATA|FILTER|ADVANCED FILTER, and in the dialog activate the copy mode. Then give a criteria range of "Filter1" as above (but you must also check the option COPY TO ANOTHER LOCATION and insert this location in the COPY TO field) and a "Copy to" range of T23:V23.

Staff.xls:2

	S	T	U	V
20				
21		**Output advanced filter**		
22				
23		**First name**	**Family name**	**Tel**
24		Hildegard	Kahlbacher	1234-56
25		Maria	Pachleitner	1234-59
26		Konrad	Juravic	1234-55
27		Sigfried	Lercher	1234-57
28				

database / filter

Figure 11.8. The result of copying with an advanced filter

Unfortunately, there is no analogous copy command for autofilters. If you wish to copy selected data records via an autofilter, you must manually select and copy them. Selectively copying only certain columns is achieved only with extra effort—by hiding columns in the database.

Data Processing in VBA Code

Once you have understood how Excel's database function can be used interactively, programming will present few additional problems. It is necessary only that you know what you are doing in working with cells and cell ranges. This topic was discussed quite thoroughly, without reference to database applications, in the first section of Chapter 5.

Programming Techniques

Elementary Database Management in Excel

Most database commands assume that the affected range of cells has been selected or that the cell pointer is located inside the database. Setting out from this cell, the associated table or list can be determined with *CurrentRegion.* (The requirement is that the table have no empty rows or columns, since such would be interpreted as the end of the database.)

With the property *ListHeaderRows* it can be determined how many header rows a table contains. The property attempts to determine whether and how many header lines there are that differ from the remaining structure of the table. (The on-line help, however, contains no information on how headers are recognized. It is thus not certain whether this property can be relied on to function correctly.)

Data Search

With the method *Find* you can search for any text in a range of cells. This method returns a *Range* object with the first cell that contains the search text. If *Find* finds nothing, then the method returns *Nothing* as its result. Here is the syntax of *Find*:

```
rng.Find what, after, lookIn, lookAt, searchOrder, searchDirection, _
       matchCase, matchByte
```

Find is thus applied to a range of cells. The first parameter contains the search text. All the other parameters are optional. The parameter *after* specifies the cell after which the search is to begin. If *after* is not specified, then the search begins in the first cell of the range. The parameter *lookIn* specifies where the search is to take place: in the cell content (xlValues), in a formula, or in cell comments. The paramter *lookAt* determines whether the entire cell content should agree with the search text or whether it suffices if the search text is only part of the character string. The parameter *searchOrder* determines whether the range is searched row by row or column by column, while *searchDirection* specifies whether the search runs forwards or backwards. The parameter *matchcase* determines whether the search is case sensitive.

TIP *Please observe that you must not rely on a default setting for any of the optional parameters. The settings that were last used are the ones that will be used again until they are changed (regardless of whether the search was via VBA code or* EDIT|FIND.

If you wish to repeat the search to find the next matching cell, you can call *Find* once again and specify the last result cell in the parameter *after*. More convenient, however, are the methods ***FindNext*** and ***FindPrevious***, where you need to supply only the one parameter *after*.

> **CAUTION** *As long as there is one cell in the search range that satisfied the search criterion, this will be found, even if this cell is above the parameter* after. *For this reason the following lines lead to an infinite loop if the search range contains a single cell that contains the character string* "xyz".
>
> ```
> Dim obj As Object
> Set obj = [a1].CurrentRegion.Find("xyz")
>  Do Until obj Is Nothing
>    obj.Interior.Color = RGB(196, 196, 196)    'gray background
>    Set obj = [a1].CurrentRegion.FindNext(obj) ' search next cell
>  Loop
> ```

If you wish to search all of the cells once, you need to keep track of the addresses of the already encountered cells. The following lines give an example of this.

```
Dim obj As Object, cellsDone$
Set obj = [a1].CurrentRegion.Find("xyz")
Do Until obj Is Nothing
  If InStr(cellsDone, "[" + obj.Address + "]") Then Exit Do
  obj.Interior.Color = RGB(196, 196, 196)
  cellsDone = cellsDone + " [" + obj.Address + "]"
  Set obj = [a1].CurrentRegion.FindNext(obj)
Loop
```

Sorting Data

When using ***Sort*** you must note that this method normally includes in its sort the first row of the given range. Since this is often a header row, and therefore intended to remain fixed in place, in most cases the optional parameter *Header:=xlNo* must be specified.

Filtering Data

The filter functions are governed by ***AutoFilter*** (to activate an autofilter) and ***AdvancedFilter*** (to activate an advanced filter). In the case of an autofilter (there can only be one autofilter active at any given moment) the property *Filters* results in several ***Filter*** objects that describe the filter criteria for each column of the database. The application of the *Filter* methods causes few problems, and the code can usually be created with the macro recorder.

Displaying the Database Form

ShowDataForm, for calling the predefined database form in Excel, does not, alas, function optimally. The command assumes that the database begins with cell A1, regardless of where the cell pointer is located. You can get around this if you give the range in which the database is located the name "database" and then execute *ShowDataForm*. The example below assumes that A5 is a cell of the database.

```
ActiveSheet.Range("A5").CurrentRegion.Name = "database"
ActiveSheet.ShowDataForm
```

Inserting, Editing, and Deleting Data

Excel provides no command to insert records into an Excel table, or to edit or delete data records. The database form can be called only for the user of the program to take over these tasks. The actions that can be carried out in the database form cannot be executed in a macro program. Changes in the content of the database must therefore be carried out in the tradtional way (see the first section of Chapter 5): Select cells with the *Range* and *Cells* methods, change the content of the cells with the *Value* or *Formula* property, and so on.

> **TIP** *If you have decided to manage the data not within Excel but in an external database, then you have significantly better programming options in the form of the ADO library. More on that in the next chapter.*

Example: A Form Letter in Microsoft Word

Fundamentals

To convert a Word document into a form letter, execute in Word the command TOOLS|MAIL MERGE and in step one use CREATE|FORM LETTERS to transform your document into a so-called main document. Then select in step 2 as data source an Excel file (GET DATA|OPEN DATA SOURCE). You must pay attention to the following rules:

- In the Excel file the addresses should be indicated by a named range.
- If you don't use named ranges, make sure that the sheet with the addresses is the active sheet of the workbook at the time you save the workbook. Fur-

thermore, the address sheet should contain one header row and the data, and nothing else. Data further in the table can annoy Word. (In version 2000, Word somehow fails to offer the possibility of choosing one from among several worksheets, as if multiple worksheets was something entirely new in Excel!)

- The entries in the header row are considered by Word to be "mail merge fields" set in the text as placeholders for the data.

- Any active autofilter criteria for the database in Excel are not considered by Word. Word always reads all of the data that are in the active worksheet. However, you can define similar criteria as in Excel with the Word mail merge manager with the button Query Options. However, the dialog for setting filter criteria is not so convenient or powerful as that in Excel.

Preparing an Excel Table for a Word Form Letter

At the beginning of this chapter the file `Staff.xls` was presented as an example of a small database. To make it possible to send a form letter only to members of a particular group, we can select certain criteria in the example file. By clicking on the button Prepare Microsoft Word mail merge the selected addresses will be copied to a separate worksheet. The range will be named with *WinWordAddresses.*

The code required to make this happen is quite short and is based on elementary Excel methods. The only special feature is the method *SpecialCells(xlVisible),* with which it is achieved that only the visible data records are copied. (If filters are used in the employee database, these filters should also be used for the Word address list.)

```
' Staff.xls, Module "Sheet2"
Private Sub btnWinWord_Click()
  Application.ScreenUpdating = False
  ' clear all cells in sheet "DataForWinword"
  Sheets("DataForWinword").Cells.ClearContents
  ' copy visible data
  Sheets("database").[a2].CurrentRegion.SpecialCells(xlVisible) _
    .Copy Sheets("DataForWinword").[a1]
  ThisWorkbook.Names.Add "WinwordAddresses", "=" & _
    Sheets("DataForWinword").[a1].CurrentRegion. _
    Address(ReferenceStyle:=xlA1, external:=True)
  Application.ScreenUpdating = True
End Sub
```

With *Names.Add* the name "WinWordAddresses" is defined. The cell range of the address list is determined with *CurrentRegion* and is transformed with *Address* into a character string of the form *"='DataForWinword'!$A$1:$Q$5"*. ("DataForWinword" is the name of the worksheet in which the addresses are stored.)

Creating the Word Form Letter

The Word file `Staff.doc` contains a simple schema for a form letter that is constructed using the data in `Staff.xls`. (The Excel file must be located in the same folder; otherwise, the data source must be specified in Word anew.)

The only special feature in `Staff.doc` is the use of conditional text. Conditional text is inserted via INSERT WORD FIELD|IF THEN ELSE. In the dialog that then appears you can input one condition and two texts. The condition must affect the content of a data field. Of the two texts, one is displayed or printed when the condition is met, the other if the condition is not met. In the example below a conditional field for the salutation (Mr. or Ms.) is used based on the content of the database field *m/f*, which for some reason is addressed in the Word formula as *f*:

```
{IF f = "m" "Mr." "Mrs." }
```

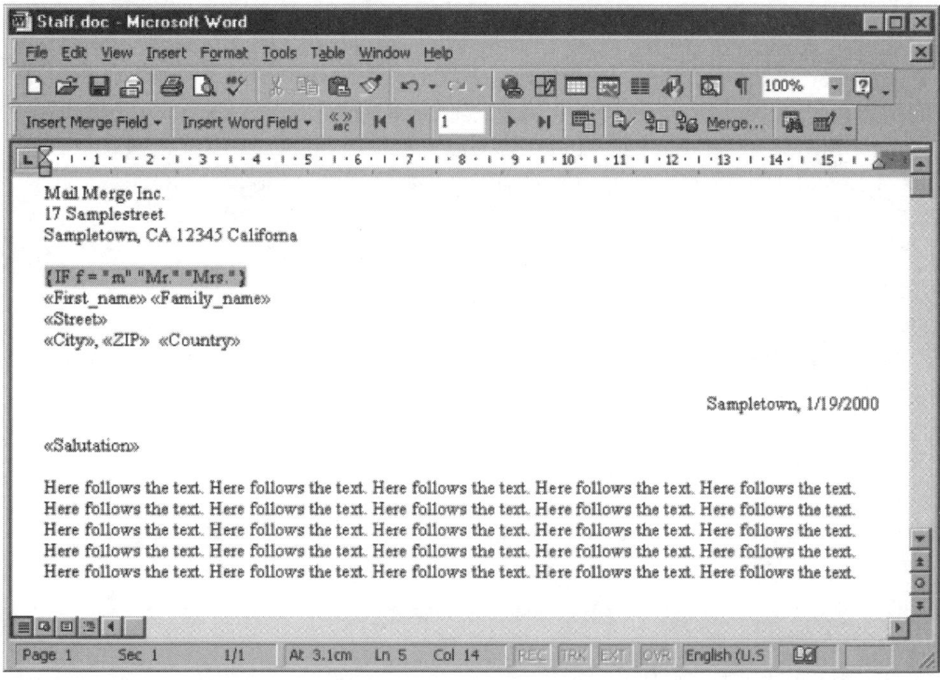

Figure 11.9. A form letter in Word

TIP *Excel cannot respond to requests for data from Word as long as you are editing a cell. If during editing you change from Excel to Word and there you wish to select another data record (by clicking on an arrow in the mail merge toolbar), then Word is blocked, since it is waiting for Excel. The impression that Word has crashed is fortunatetly a false impression. After about half a minute Word replies with an error message. If you do not wish to wait so long, return to Excel and finish your cell input.*

POINTER *Further code examples of data management from within Excel can be found in Chapter 1 (introductory database example) as well as further along in this chapter. The methods for using tables and ranges, which are an elementary requirement for writing your own database programs, are considered in the first two sections of Chapter 5.*

Syntax Summary

In the following tables *wsh* stands for the worksheet containing the database (*WorkSheet* object), *rng* for the range of cells of the database (*Range* object), and "..." for the input of various parameters that are not described here (see the online help).

Database Management in Excel (Sorting, Grouping, etc.)

rng.Name = "database"	names range for *ShowDataForm*
wsh.ShowDataForm	displays the database form
rng.Sort ...	sorts the database
rng.Find ...	searches for data
rng.FindNext	search again
rng.FindPrevious	search backwards
rng.Replace ...	search and replace
rng.Consolidate ...	consolidate several tables

Filter

rng.AutoFilter ...	activate autofilter
rng.AdvancedFilter ...	activate advanced filter
wsh.FilterMode	tells whether the table contains filtered data
wsh.AutoFilter	refers to the *AutoFilter* object
wsh.AutoFilter.Filters(...)	refers to the *Filter* objects (with filter criteria)
wsh.AutoFilterMode	tells whether autofilter is active
wsh.AutoFilterMode = False	deactivates autofilter
wsh.ShowAllData	deletes filter criteria

Database Worksheet Functions

Excel recognizes a variety of so-called database functions. These are worksheet functions that enable complex database calculations, such as the calculation of the average employee salary among those employees who have worked in the company for more than five years (assuming, of course, that the database contains a column with salary information and a second column with the date on which the employee joined the company). Most database functions begin with the letter *D* and feature three parameters: *=Dfunction(database, column, criteria).*

- With the parameter *database* the range of cells is specified, including the header cells. Instead of directly specifying the range, the range's name can be given.

- *column* specifies for which column in the database the calculation is to be carried out (for example, creating an average). The column can be given either by specifying the header cell of this column or by the column name inside quotation marks (e.g., *"LastName"*).

- *criteria* refers to a range of cells with criteria. The database function calculates its result based only on those cells in the database that meet the criteria. (It is precisely this third parameter that distinguishes the database functions from garden-variety worksheet functions.) Criteria are formed as with advanced filters (a header row plus one or more rows with conditions; see the previous section).

Calculational Functions

DCOUNT	returns the number of records that satisfy the criteria
DCOUNTA	as above, but considers only those records whose data field is not empty in the specified column
DMIN / DMAX	returns the smallest/largest value in the specified column
DSUM	sums over the specified column
DPRODUCT	multiplies the data fields of the column

Statistical Functions

DAVERAGE	computes the average value of the column
DSTDEV	computes the estimated standard deviation for a sample (division by `n-1`)
DSTDEVP	computes the true standard deviation for the entire population (division by `n`)
DVAR	computes the variance for a sample
DVARP	computes the variance for the entire population

Other

DGET	returns the contents of a column's data that meets the criteria. The function is useful only if the criteria are so formulated that precisely one data record satisfies them. If several records satisfy the conditions, then the function returns the error value *#VALUE!*.
SUBTOTAL	computes the sum, average, minimum, maximum, etc. of a selected range. The function resembles a database function, but formally it is not one (different syntax, different functionality). It is instituted by the command DATA|SUBTOTALS, but is essentially useless. Functions such as *SUM* and *AVERAGE* can be used much more easily than *SUBTOTAL*.

Even if it was repeated explicitly above, we repeat it here: All these functions with the exception of *SUBTOTAL* operate exclusively on those data records that meet the criteria specified by the third parameter.

> **TIP** *Excel also recognizes some worksheet functions that are similar to a database function, but do not require the planned construction of a database (such as* COUNTIF, SUMIF*).*

Example 1: Stock Management

In Figure 11.10 you see a simple stock management application that can be evaluated with certain database functions. The table is stored in the example file `DB_Functions.xls`.

Most of the examples in Figure 11.10 speak for themselves and require no additional comment. But here are some exceptions: The criterion for the second database formula consists of the header "price" and an additional empty cell. This ensures that all data records are considered, since this pseudocondition is satisfied by all data records. The value 300 in the third criterion is taken from the result of the second database formula. Thus cell A20 contains the formula *=F16.*

Please note that all the results in `DB_Functions.xls` are immediately recalculated as soon as the data on which they are based are altered. This is not at all unusual in Excel worksheets, but there are very few database programs that are capable of this.

DB_Functions.xls

	A	B	C	D	E	F	G
1	**name**	**category**	**quality**	**price**	**stock**	**value**	
2	Artikel 1	a	I	30	21	630	
3	Artikel 8	c	II	30	28	840	
4	Artikel 5	b	I	50	22	1100	
5	Artikel 9	c	II	40	11	440	
6	Artikel 2	a	I	150	34	5100	
7	Artikel 3	a	II	200	20	4000	
8	Artikel 4	b	I	200	24	4800	
9	Artikel 6	c	I	300	26	7800	
10	Artikel 7	c	I	200	11	2200	
11							
12	**criteria**				**purpose**	**result**	**formula**
13	category				Average price of category C	142.5	=DAVERAGE(A1:F10,"price",A13:A14)
14	c						
15							
16	price				highest price	300	=DMAX(A1:F10,"price",A16:A17)
17							
18							
19	price				name of most expensive product	Artikel 6	=DGET(A1:F10,"name",A19:A20)
20	300						
21							
22	quality				value of all articels of quality II	5280	=DSUM(A1:F10,"value",A22:A23)
23	II						

sheet1 / sheet2

Figure 11.10. The application of database functions

Example 2: Frequency Distribution

Figure 11.11 demonstrates an additional application of database functions: From the reaction times of 69 experimental subjects a frequency distribution is determined with a class length of 0.1 seconds. The construction of this table is difficult, despite all of Excel's assistance—seventeen criterion ranges and as many *DCOUNT* formulas have to be input. For example, the formula in E3 is

```
=DCOUNT(A:B,"reaction time",G5:H6)
```

Nonetheless, this schema functions independently of the number of subjects (data items), since all of columns A and B are part of the database (regardless of how many rows actually contain data).

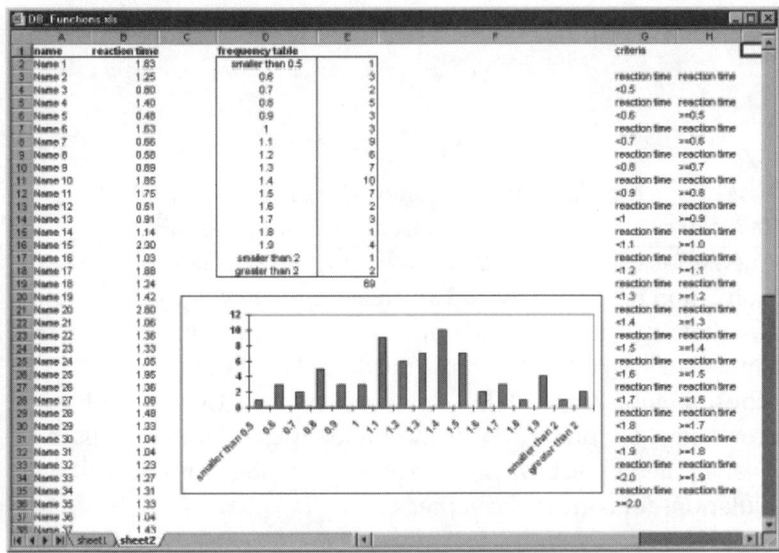

Figure 11.11. Frequency distribution with database functions

Consolidating Tables

Fundamentals

By consolidating tables is meant that the data from several tables are collected into a singe table. This process is most easily understood in the context of a concrete example: Let us suppose that you have four identically formatted Excel files with quarterly reports of certain sales figures, and you wish to create out of them a new Excel file with the annual figures. Or perhaps in the previous weeks measurement reports were created out of which you wish to determine the average values. For such tasks, or similar ones, the command DATA|CONSOLIDATE is useful.

Data consolidation is managed in a dialog in which several references to various cell ranges must be specified. These ranges may be located in the current worksheet, in other worksheets of the current workbook, or in external Excel files. In giving the names of files, wildcards such as *[Name*.xls]Sheet1!A1:C20* are allowed, in which case Excel reads the data from all Excel fields whose first four letters are `Name`.

Excel is less flexible in the selection of worksheets of a file. Here neither wildcards nor ranges (of the form *'Sheet1:Sheet5'!A1:C20*) are allowed. If data are to be consolidated from several worksheets, then all the worksheets must be listed separately, which can be a tiresome occupation.

Excel can execute a number of calculational operations (such as sum, average, variance) in the course of consolidation. The allowable operations are available for selection in the CONSOLIDATE dialog. The operation then holds for all fields in the consolidation range. It is not possible to calculate the sum of some fields and the average value of others.

Options

In the CONSOLIDATE dialog there are three option fields that normally are deactivated. Their effect can scarcely be guessed at from their short texts:

By activating USE LABELS IN TOP ROW and USE LABELS IN LEFT COLUMN a somewhat intelligent consolidation mode is activated: In creating the new table, Excel takes into account the label cells at the left and upper borders of the consolidation region. Excel is capable of correctly assembling the data even if the arrangement of the individual consolidation ranges differs among the tables. (However, it is assumed that all rows and columns are correctly and identically labeled.) If both options are deactivated, then Excel pays no attention to the labels, but simply carries out the calculations for corresponding cells.

By activating the option CREATE LINKS TO SOURCE DATA Excel inserts into the new table countless references to the individual cells in the affected table. These references are then linked together with ordinary Excel formulas. Finally, Excel divides up the table in such a way that only the result cells are visible. This extravagance has an advantage: The consolidation table is continually updated, with every change in the source data reflected in the result table. But this involves two serious drawbacks: The time and memory requirements for this dynamic variant are enormous.

As is clear from the paragraph above, consolidation tables are static as a rule (unless the option CREATE LINKS TO SOURCE DATA has been activated). Sad to say, there is no command, similar to that for pivot tables, by which data might be updated. The only possibility of maintaining current data consists in the repeated application of the consolidation command.

> **TIP** *Excel can save the settings of the* CONSOLIDATE *dialog only once per worksheet. For this reason you should avoid having more than one consolidation table in a worksheet. Otherwise, you will have to input all the references anew upon each updating!*

The consolidation command is seemly inflexible in its application, especially in carrying out complex operations involving several tables. You should therefore consider before using this command whether it might make better sense to work with ordinary Excel formulas, with which references to other tables are also allowed. However, you must allow for the fact that formulas with references to other files are not evaluated quickly. With extensive data sets you could run into time problems.

Altogether, the consolidation of data is a somewhat difficult and error-prone undertaking, one that should be used only by experienced Excel users. An automation of this process with suitable macros is therefore almost a necessity.

Example

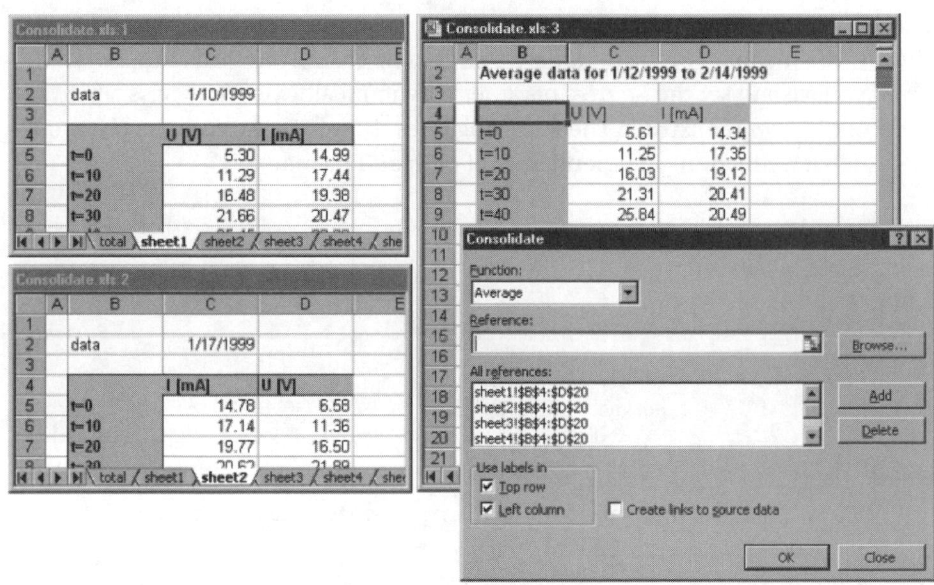

Figure 11.12. Consolidation of measurement data

In Figure 11.12 you may observe three windows: On the left are two (of six altogether) worksheets, in which measurements over six weeks have been entered. To the right is shown the consolidation table, in which the average values of the six measurements appear. This example application can be found on the CD-ROM, in the file `Consolidate.xls`.

Consolidation via VBA Code

If your desires run in the direction of automating consolidation, then the macro recorder can assist you in achieving correct code quickly. For the example above it would look something like the following:

```
Selection.Consolidate Sources:=Array( _
    "'I:\Code\XL-2000\[Consolidate.xls]sheet1'!R4C2:R20C4", _
    "'I:\Code\XL-2000\[Consolidate.xls]sheet2'!R4C2:R20C4", _
    "'I:\Code\XL-2000\[Consolidate.xls]sheet3'!R4C2:R20C4", _
    "'I:\Code\XL-2000\[Consolidate.xls]sheet4'!R4C2:R20C4", _
    "'I:\Code\XL-2000\[Consolidate.xls]sheet5'!R4C2:R20C4", _
    "'I:\Code\XL-2000\[Consolidate.xls]sheet6'!R4C2:R20C4"), _
  Function:=xlAverage, TopRow:=True, _
  LeftColumn:=True, CreateLinks:=False
```

The method *Consolidate* is applied to a *Range* object, which may specify the size of the target range or simply a start cell for the operation ([B4] in the example above). The meaning of the parameters should be clear from the example.

If you wish to set the *Sources* parameter dynamically, you may pass a field instead of the *Array* construct. The following lines show how the code can be modified so that it functions independently of path and file name:

```
' Consolidate.xls, Module1
Sub ConsolidateDate()
  Dim i&, arr$(1 To 6)
  For i = 1 To 6
    arr(i) = "'" & ThisWorkbook.Path & _
             "\[" & ThisWorkbook.Name & "]" & _
             "Sheet" & i & "'!R4C2:R20C4"
  Next
  [B4].Consolidate Sources:=arr(), Function:=xlAverage, TopRow:=True, _
    LeftColumn:=True, CreateLinks:=False
End Sub
```

> **POINTER** *In the previous chapter a program was introduced that creates daily and monthly reports from measurements in the form of daily files. As well there appeared the issue of consolidating data from numerous Excel tables into one new table. However, there the command* DATA|CONSOLIDATE *was not used (too inflexible for this task), but the problem was solved, rather, through a relatively simple VBA procedure (see Chapter 10 under the heading "Monthly Report").*

Example: Balance Sheet of a Car-Sharing Club

The car-sharing example has the character of a complete (and not entirely atypical) Excel application. The application `DB_Share.xls` is derived from the smart form `Share.xls` of the car-sharing club presented in Chapter 9. The program makes it possible to use a smart form to maintain a simply constructed logbook. What is new in comparison to `Share.xls` is the situation that now all trips are logged in a monthly balance sheet, and the administration of the fleet of cars and the usage thereof by the members of the club are integrated into the application. The program is run via a custom menu.

Running the Program

After the file `DB_Share.xls` is opened, the smart form familiar from Chapter 9 appears on the monitor together with a custom menu. Other Excel elements such as the formula and status bars and the toolbars have been deactivated. Little has changed in the operation of the form. New is that the name of the individual who has borrowed a car can now be easily selected in a listbox.

After the form is filled out, it is printed with INVOICE|PRINT AND SAVE and saved in the table of monthly accounts. The input of a second invoice must be effected with INVOICE|NEW. This way the invoice receives a new (running) invoice number and all the input fields of the form are cleared. INVOICE|CORRECT OLD INVOICE OF THIS MONTH enables the selection of an invoice computed in the current month. The data are transferred into the form, and there they can be edited. Finally, the corrected invoice can be printed and saved with INVOICE|PRINT AND SAVE.

With the VIEW menu you obtain access to other sheets of the application: VIEW|MEMBERS DATABASE takes you to the database of club members, where new members can be entered or the data on current members updated. The Sort button can be used to sort the database alphabetically after it has been added to or edited. The sequence of names is reflected in the listbox in the invoice form.

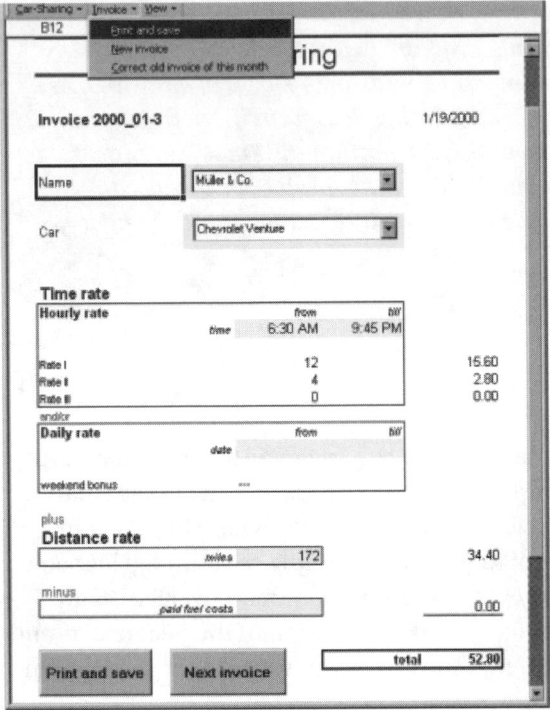

Figure 11.13. The smart form appearing in the application DB_Share.xls

Note in particular the first entry in this database. It is the text " please choose a member" or " please choose a car" that includes a prefixed blank character. This blank character has the effect of placing this entry in the sorted listbox before all the others, enabling the program to achieve a definite starting condition for creating the list or establishing this condition in a query. (In using MS Forms listboxes in worksheets there is no possibility—in contrast to Excel 5/7 listboxes—to distinguish the selection of the first list entry from the condition that no list entry at all has been selected. Both conditions produce the value 0 in the cell specified by *LinkedCell.*)

View|Car database switches into a worksheet for managing the transport fleet. In the table is stored the list of all the cars together with their rate data.

View|Account of this month shows the balance sheet table for the current month. These tables are stored in separate files. The file name contains the year and month: for example, `Car_2000_01.xls` for Januar y 2000. When a new file is created automatically (at the beginning of the month) the template `Car_template.xlt` is accessed, which must be located in the same folder as the application file `DB_Share.xls`.

In the numerous columns of the monthly table are saved the invoice number, invoice date, date and time of the last change in the invoice, name, car, time when the car was used, the number of miles traveled, and so on. The balance sheet table contains all relevant data for the next step, which might be creating a monthly invoice for each member of the club or performing a statistical analysis of automobile usage.

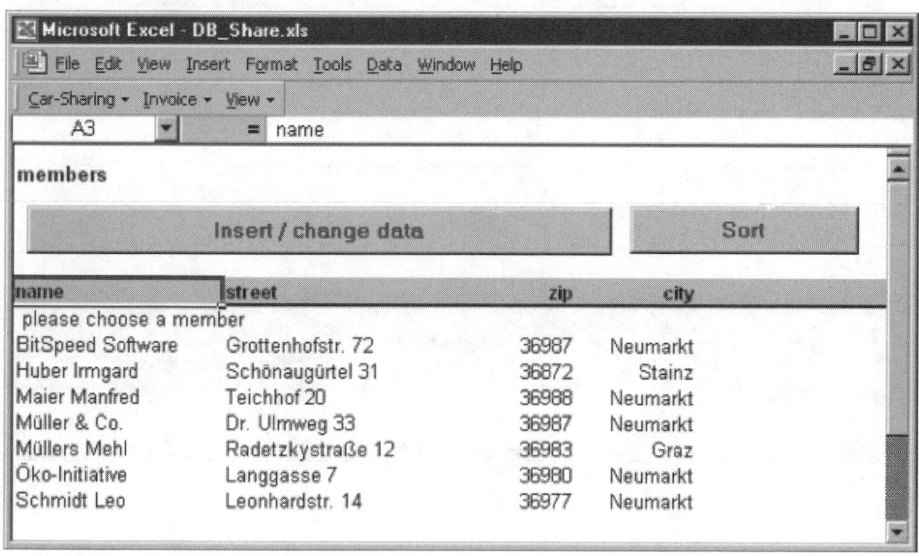

Figure 11.14. Data on club members

The last menu to describe is the CAR-SHARING menu. SAVE, not surprisingly, saves the file `DB_Share.xls`. This ensures, in particular, that the changes in the databases "fleet" and "members" are saved. The monthly balance sheet in the file `Car_yyyy_mm.xls` is completely independent of `DB_Share.xls` and is updated automatically after each change. This costs some time, of course (particularly if the file is large), but from the standpoint of data security it is the only safe way to proceed.

CAR-SHARING|END closes the files `DB_Share.xls` and `Car_yyyy_mm.xls` and removes the Car-Sharing menu. Excel is not itself shut down; that is, END refers only to the application `DB_Share`.

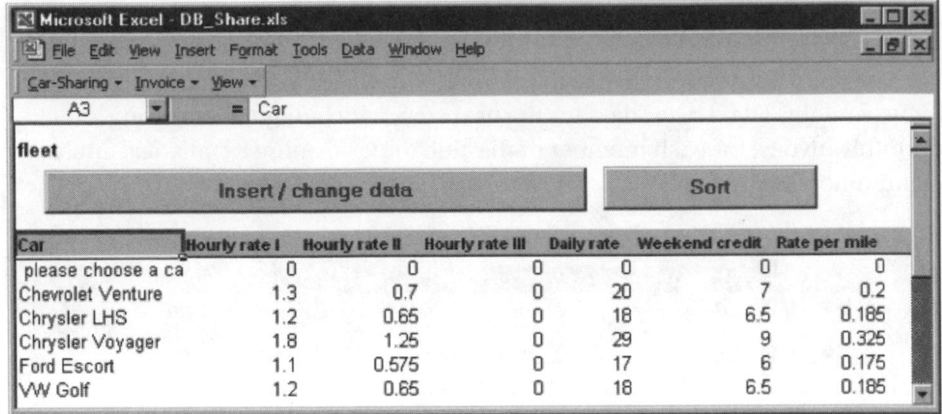

Car	Hourly rate I	Hourly rate II	Hourly rate III	Daily rate	Weekend credit	Rate per mile
please choose a ca	0	0	0	0	0	0
Chevrolet Venture	1.3	0.7	0	20	7	0.2
Chrysler LHS	1.2	0.65	0	18	6.5	0.185
Chrysler Voyager	1.8	1.25	0	29	9	0.325
Ford Escort	1.1	0.575	0	17	6	0.175
VW Golf	1.2	0.65	0	18	6.5	0.185

Figure 11.15. Fleet management

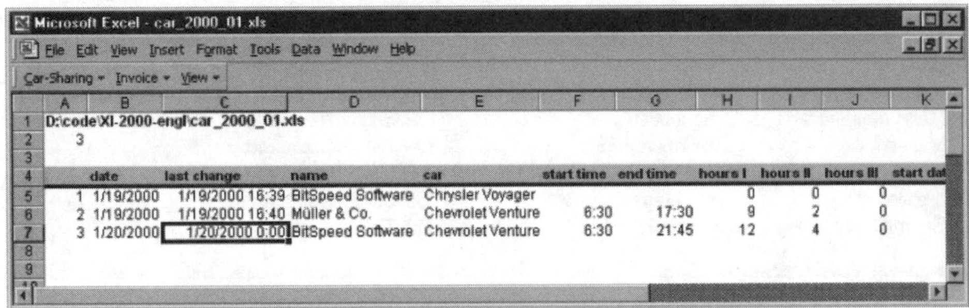

	date	last change	name	car	start time	end time	hours I	hours II	hours III	start dat
1	1/19/2000	1/19/2000 16:39	BitSpeed Software	Chrysler Voyager			0	0	0	
2	1/19/2000	1/19/2000 16:40	Müller & Co.	Chevrolet Venture	6:30	17:30	9	2	0	
3	1/20/2000	1/20/2000 0:00	BitSpeed Software	Chevrolet Venture	6:30	21:45	12	4	0	

Figure 11.16. Monthly balance sheet

Suggestions for Improvements

- In its present form the application is highly susceptible to accidental or intentional abuse. The possibility of changing existing invoices with INVOICE|CORRECT OLD INVOICE or opening and changing the monthly report directly can, of course, be used for dishonest purposes. There are various measures that can be taken to improve the security of the data (for example, the monthly balance sheet could be password protected, or changes in invoices could be marked in the invoice). But complete protection that no Excel pro could crack is unlikely to be obtained.

- The monthly balance sheets could serve as a starting point to send to each member at the end of the month a list of all trips made together with an invoice (instead of billing for each trip individually, which in practice involves too much effort and paperwork). Further, payments could be kept track of, reminders sent, and so on.

- A booking and reservation system could be implemented.

Although it is possible in principle to include these new features using Excel tables, it would be more sensible, and certainly more secure, to store the data in an external database file.

These ideas demonstrate the typical path taken by many Excel applications. From a simple idea (the balance sheet of Chapter 9) a more and more complex database application is developed. The problem that arises is that Excel is really a spreadsheet program and not a database program. Although almost any extension is possible, the ratio of programming effort involved in relation to the benefit gained is an increasing spiral. Before your application starts putting on weight, consider transferring to a database program (and the sooner, the better!).

Overview of the Components of the Application

The application consists of at least two files: `DB_Share.xls` for the program code, the invoice form, and the fleet and member databases; and the template `Car_template.xlt` for the monthly balance sheet. Furthermore, every month in which the program is used produces a file `Car_jjjj_mm.xls` with the monthly statement.

The file `DB_Share.xls` consists of the following sheets and modules:

invoice	worksheet with invoice form
cars	worksheet with car database
members	worksheet with member database
ThisWorkbook	class module with event procedures
moduleMain	code for monthly account report
moduleMenu	code for car-sharing menu
modulefunctions	code with custom worksheet functions (see Chapter 9)

Within the invoice form (that is, in the worksheet *invoice*) most of the input and output cells are named, so that they can be more easily accessed in program code. This makes it possible to avoid having to access cells in the form [H17], the accuracy of which is hard to verify. Here is a list of the names and their addresses:

car	C14
enddate	E26
endtime	E19
fuelcost	D35
hoursI	D21
hoursII	D22
hoursIII	D23
invoicedate	G9
invoicenr	B9
invoicetotal	G38
membername	C12
nrOfMiles	D32
startdate	D26
starttime	D19
weekendbonus	D28

TIP *If you need a list of all named cells for documentation purposes, simply execute in the immediate window*

```
For Each n In ThisWorkbook.Names: ?n.Name, n.RefersTo: Next
```

Both in the invoice form and both database worksheets the row and column headers, gridlines, and sheet tabs are hidden in order to obtain maximal use of the available space.

Program Code

The following pages describe the most interesting details of the program code. The procedures are described in order of appearance, where we have declined to present a repeat of the user-defined worksheet functions (see Chapter 9).

Global Variables

The division of the program code into several modules created the necessity of declaring certain variables as *Public*. These variables can be accessed from any module. With the exception of the variable *accountMonth*, which contains the current year and month as a character string (for example, "2000_05" for May 2000) all other variables relate to the monthly table: *monthReportWb*, *month Report*, and *accountCell* contain references to the workbook, the worksheet, and the first cell of the monthly table. All three variables are initialized in *LoadMonthReport* (see a few pages below).

The constant *pagePreview* specifies whether invoices should be printed or simply presented on the monitor in page view.

```
' DB_Share.xls, moduleMain
Public monthReportWb As Workbook 'workbook with monthly account
Public monthReport As Worksheet  'sheet in monthReportWB
Public accountCell As Range      'first cell in monthReport
Public accountMonth$             'year + date (2000_05 for May 2000)
```

Configuring Excel in Workbook_Open

After the file DB_Cars is opened, the procedure *Workbook*_Open is automatically executed. This procedure makes the invoice form the active sheet. Then with *LoadMonthReport* the monthly table of the current month is opened. *ClearMain-Sheet* takes the current invoice number from this file and inserts it into the invoice form. At the same time, all input fields of the invoice form are cleared. Finally, the additional toolbar "DB_Car_Sharing" with its new menu items is activated.

If you activate lines that have been commented out in the program listing, then at the start all of Excel's toolbars, formula bar, and status bar are deactivated. They are not required for using the program and they just take up space.

```
' DB_Share.xls, "ThisWorkbook"
Private Sub Workbook_Open()
  Dim cb As CommandBar
  Application.ScreenUpdating = False
  ThisWorkbook.Activate
  Sheets("invoice").Select
  ThisWorkbook.Windows(1).DisplayWorkbookTabs = False
  LoadMonthReport                     'load account of this month
  ClearMainSheet                      'clear invoice form
  ' hide formular bar, status bar and toolbars
  '  Application.DisplayFormulaBar = False
  '  Application.DisplayStatusBar = False
```

```
  '  For Each cb In Application.CommandBars
  '    If cb.Type = msoBarTypeNormal Then cb.Visible = False
  '  Next cb
  With Application.CommandBars("DB_Car_Sharing")
    'show toolbar of this application
    .Visible = True
  End With
  ActiveWindow.WindowState = xlMaximized
End Sub
```

Managing Custom Menus

After the application-specific menu has been activated in `Workbook_Open`, the sheet-(de)activation procedures see to it that in the future this menu is deactivated when a worksheet of another Excel file is clicked on and is reactivated when a worksheet of `Share.xls` is clicked. (In *Workbook_Deactivate* the menu remains visible if the invoice table is clicked on.)

```
' Share.xls, class module "ThisWorkbook"
' deactivate menu when another workbook is activated
Private Sub Workbook_Deactivate()
  On Error Resume Next
  If LCase(ActiveWorkbook.Name) <> "car_" + accountMonth + ".xls" Then
    Application.CommandBars("DB_Car_Sharing").Visible = False
  End If
End Sub
' ensure that menu bar is always visible
Private Sub Workbook_Activate()
  Application.CommandBars("DB_Car_Sharing").Visible = True
End Sub
Private Sub Workbook_SheetActivate(ByVal Sh As Object)
  Application.CommandBars("DB_Car_Sharing").Visible = True
End Sub
```

Opening Excel File for Monthly Report

LoadMonthReport is called at various points in the program to ensure that the file with the monthly report is loaded. (It can happen that the user has accidentally closed it.) The procedure first sets the variable *accountMonth* to a character string of the form Form "2000_05" (May 2000) and from it and the path to `DB_Cars` determines the file name of the invoice file (such as `C:\Test\Car_2000_05.xls`). Then a loop is run over all loaded *Workbook* objects. If the monthly file is found, then various variables must be initialized.

On the other hand, if the file is not loaded, then a test is made as to whether the file exists on the hard drive. If it does not exist, which will be the case the first time in the month that the application is run, then a search is made for the template file `Car_Template.xlt`. If this file is found, then the program opens this template file. Otherwise, it opens an empty (unformatted) Excel file. In principle, the program does not complain in this case, but the template file provides the advantage that the monthly table is labeled, the column width is set more or less correctly, and the invidual columns are correctly formatted (date and time format).

In any case, the new file's name is entered into cell A1, and the current invoice number in A2. Then the file is saved under a new name. In the last lines, which are always executed regardless of how the file was found or opened, the window of the file is reduced to an icon.

```
' DB_Share.xls, moduleMain
' load account file for current month
Public Sub LoadMonthReport()
  Dim wb As Workbook
  Dim reportFile$, templateFile$
  Dim loaded
  loaded = False
  accountMonth = CStr(Year(Now)) + "_" + Format(Month(Now), "00")
  reportFile = ThisWorkbook.Path + "\car_" + accountMonth + ".xls"
  'test, if file has already been loaded
  For Each wb In Workbooks
    If UCase(wb.Name) = UCase("car_" + accountMonth + ".xls") Then
      Set monthReportWb = wb: Set monthReport = wb.Worksheets(1)
      loaded = True
      Exit For
    End If
  Next wb
  If Not loaded Then
    If Dir(reportFile) "" Then
      'file does already exist -> load
      Set monthReportWb = Workbooks.Open(reportFile)
      Set monthReport = monthReportWb.Worksheets(1)
    Else
      'file does not exist: open template (if it does exist)
      templateFile = ThisWorkbook.Path + "\car_template.xlt"
      If Dir(templateFile) "" Then
        Set monthReportWb = Workbooks.Open(templateFile)
      Else
        'template is missing also; simply use an empty file instead
        Set monthReportWb = Workbooks.Add
      End If
```

```
      Set monthReport = monthReportWb.Worksheets(1)
      monthReport.[A1] = reportFile  'save filename in A1
      monthReport.[A2] = 0           'save invoice nr in A2
      monthReportWb.SaveAs reportFile
    End If
  End If
  Set accountCell = monthReport.Range("A5")
  monthReportWb.Windows(1).WindowState = xlMinimized
End Sub
```

Initialize Invoice Form

At various places in the program—such as at the start or when the NEXT INVOICE button is clicked—the invoice form must be translated into a defined basic form. That is, all input cells are cleared. These input cells were named in the worksheet "invoice"so that a more readable access is possible in the form *[name]*. Furthermore, the procedure takes the current invoice number from the monthly report (which is located there in cell A2).

In *InitializeListboxes* the source data range (property *ListFillRange*) is set afresh for the listboxes *cmbMembers* and *cmbCars*. Then the listboxes are set to entry 0, so that the first list entry is displayed (that is, "please choose a member" or "please choose a car").

```
Public Sub ClearMainSheet()
  Application.ScreenUpdating = False
  ThisWorkbook.Activate
  Sheets("invoice").Select
  LoadMonthReport
  With ThisWorkbook.Sheets("invoice")
    .[invoicedate].Formula = "=Now()"
    .[startTime] = ""
    .[endTime] = ""
    .[startDate] = ""
    .[endDate] = ""
    .[nrOfMiles] = ""
    .[fuelcost] = ""
    .[invoicenr] = "Invoice " & accountMonth & "-" & _
       monthReport.[A2] + 1
     InitializeListboxes
  End With
End Sub
' reset listboxes in invoice form to 0
Public Sub InitializeListboxes()
```

```
  Dim z1 As Object, z2 As Object
  With ThisWorkbook.Sheets("invoice")
    ' List box members
    Set z1 = [members!A4]
    Set z2 = z1.End(xlDown)
    .cmbMembers.ListFillRange = "members!" + z1.Address + ":" + _
      z2.Address
    .cmbMembers = 0
    ' List box cars
    Set z1 = [cars!A4]
    Set z2 = z1.End(xlDown)
    .cmbCars.ListFillRange = "cars!" + z1.Address + ":" + z2.Address
    .cmbCars = 0
  End With
End Sub
```

Removing Keyboard Focus from Listboxes

There is one further detail in connection with the two listboxes in the invoice worksheet that is worthy of mention: After the selection of a car or a member via the listbox, the input focus is located in the associated listbox. This can block the further execution of VBA code. For this reason, the event procedure *cmbCars_Change* or *cmbMembers_Change* is invoked to switch the keyboard focus immediately back to a nearby cell.

The test *ActiveSheet.Name = Me.Name* ensures that this happens only when the invoice worksheet is the active sheet. (The procedures are also called when the listboxes are changed in program code, and at that time another sheet can be active; the attempt to activate a cell would then lead to an error.)

```
' DB_Share.xls, invoice
Private Sub cmbCars_Change()
  If ActiveSheet.Name = Me.Name Then
    [b14].Activate
  End If
End Sub
Private Sub cmbMembers_Change()
  ' as above
End Sub
```

Event Procedures for the Database Buttons (Database Form, Sorting)

In each of the two worksheets "members" and "cars" there are two buttons, one for displaying the database form and the other for sorting the entries. (Sorting also takes place automatically after the database form has been displayed.)

When the worksheet is exited, the procedure *InitializeListboxes* displayed directly above is executed so that all new entries in the listboxes are taken into account. The code for the two worksheets is identical:

```
' DB_Share.xls, cars
' show database mask
' afterwards sort and reinitialize listbox
Private Sub btnEdit_Click()
  Range("A3").Select
  Range("A3").CurrentRegion.Name = "database"
  ActiveSheet.ShowDataForm
  btnSort_Click
  InitializeListboxes
End Sub
Private Sub btnSort_Click()
  Range("A3").Select
  Selection.Sort Key1:=Range("A4"), Order1:=xlAscending, _
    Header:=xlGuess, OrderCustom:=1, MatchCase:=False, _
    Orientation:=xlTopToBottom
End Sub
Private Sub Worksheet_Deactivate()
  InitializeListboxes
End Sub
```

Event Procedures for Menu Commands

moduleMenu contains short procedures that are called from the commands of the car-sharing menu. Most of these procedures are extremely short; the code should be understandable at a glance, for which reason it is not reproduced here.

Printing the Invoice Form

The procedure *PrintAndSave* is responsible for printing the invoice form. This procedure copies the entire invoice form into a new worksheet, changes the yellow background color to white, and then prints the new worksheet. The analogous procedure *btnPrint_Click* is presented in Chapter 9, where it is described more fully.

What is new in *PrintAndSave* is the call to the function *TestForValidInput*: There a short test is carried out to determine whether the input in the invoice form is valid. If that is not the case, then the function returns an error text that is displayed in an alert box in *PrintAndSave*.

```
Function TestForValidInput()
  Dim errmsg$
  With ThisWorkbook.Sheets("invoice")
    If IsError(.[invoicetotal]) Then
      errmsg = "Invalid total."
    ElseIf .[invoicetotal] = 0 Then
      errmsg = "Total is 0."
    ElseIf .cmbMembers <= 0 Or IsNull(.cmbMembers) Then
      errmsg = "Member name missing."
    ElseIf .cmbCars <= 0 Or IsNull(.cmbCars) Then
      errmsg = "car name missing."
    ElseIf .[startTime] < 0 Or .[startTime] > 1 Or _
          .[endTime] < 0 Or .[endTime] > 1 Then
      errmsg = "Wrong time."
    ElseIf .[startDate]  "" Xor .[endDate]  "" Then
      errmsg = "Incomplete date."
    End If
  End With
  TestForValidInput = errmsg
End Function
```

Saving the Data from the Invoice Form in the Monthly Report

The procedure *PrintAndSave* ends with a call to *SaveAccountData*. This procedure transfers all the basic information of the invoice into the monthly table. The row in which the data are entered is determined from the invoice number of the invoice form, which must be extracted from a character string of the form "Invoice 1999_05\3": *InStr* returns the location of the backslash character, *Mid* reads all characters after this character, and *Val* transforms the resulting character string into a numerical value. After the actual data transfer the invoice number is updated in the monthly table, and then the file is saved.

```
' copy invoice data to month account table
Sub SaveAccountData()
  Dim x
  Dim accountNr%               ' current invoice number
  Dim accountWs As Worksheet   ' reference to account sheet
  On Error Resume Next
  Set accountWs = ThisWorkbook.Sheets("invoice")
  LoadMonthReport
  x = accountWs.[invoicenr]
  accountNr = Val(Mid(x, InStr(x, "-") + 1))
  accountCell.Cells(accountNr, 1) = accountNr
  accountCell.Cells(accountNr, 2) = accountWs.[invoicedate]
  accountCell.Cells(accountNr, 3) = Now
  accountCell.Cells(accountNr, 4) = accountWs.[membername]
  accountCell.Cells(accountNr, 5) = accountWs.[car]
  accountCell.Cells(accountNr, 6) = accountWs.[startTime]
  accountCell.Cells(accountNr, 7) = accountWs.[endTime]
  accountCell.Cells(accountNr, 8) = accountWs.[hoursI]
  accountCell.Cells(accountNr, 9) = accountWs.[hoursII]
  accountCell.Cells(accountNr, 10) = accountWs.[hoursIII]
  accountCell.Cells(accountNr, 11) = accountWs.[startDate]
  accountCell.Cells(accountNr, 12) = accountWs.[endDate]
  accountCell.Cells(accountNr, 13) = accountWs.[weekendbonus]
  accountCell.Cells(accountNr, 14) = accountWs.[nrOfMiles]
  accountCell.Cells(accountNr, 15) = accountWs.[fuelcost]
  accountCell.Cells(accountNr, 16) = accountWs.[invoicetotal]
  If monthReport.[A2] < accountNr Then monthReport.[A2] = accountNr
  monthReportWb.Save       ' save changed file
End Sub
```

Editing a Preexisting Invoice

The procedure *ChangeOldEntry* represents, in principle, the inverse function to *SaveAccountData*: This time data should be transferred out of the monthly report and into the invoice form, so that the invoice can be edited (for example, to correct an error).

The procedure begins with *MenuViewMonthReport_OnClick* displaying the monthly report and inviting the user to use an *InputBox* form to click on the line of the monthly report that contains data to be corrected. For this to happen *InputBox* is given the input type 0 (a formula). The resulting formula looks something like "=R5C7". With *Mid* the equal sign is eliminated. Then the character string is converted with *ConvertFormula* into the A1 format, then with *Range* is transformed into a *Range* object whose row number finally can be read with *Row*.

Since the first four lines of the table are used for headers, the invoice number is determined after subtracting 4.

As soon as the invoice number is known, the actual data transfer can begin. For most of the input cells, data transfer presents no problems. In the case of both listboxes a loop must be used to determine the correct list entry.

Perhaps the many account variables are a bit confusing: `accountWs` refers to the invoice form and `accountCell` to the first data cell in the month table, while `accountNr` contains the invoice number.

```
' copy data of an already existing invoice from the account back
' into invoice form
Sub ChangeOldEntry()
  Dim result, accountNr%, n, i
  Dim accountWs As Object     'invoice form
  ' accountWs cannot be defined as Worksheet; if you try,
  ' Excel complains that the objects cmbMembers and
  ' cmbCars are not known; obviously, the compiler
  ' tries early binding, which is impossible in this case
  Set accountWs = ThisWorkbook.Sheets("invoice")
  On Error Resume Next
  MenuViewMonthReport_OnClick
  result = Application.InputBox("Please choose an invoice nr. " & _
    "You can simply click on the correct line in the account list.", _
    Type:=0)
  MenuViewMain_OnClick
  If result = False Then Exit Sub
  result = Mid(result, 2)   ' »=« remove '=' in result
  If Not IsNumeric(result) Then
    ' extract row number out of formula "R123C123"
    ' and save in result
    result = Range(Application.ConvertFormula(result, xlR1C1, _
       xlA1)).Row - 4
  End If
  If result < 1 Or result > Val(monthReport.[A2]) Then
    MsgBox "Invalid invoice nr.": Exit Sub
  End If
  accountNr = result
  Application.ScreenUpdating = False
  ' change date
  accountWs.[invoicedate] = accountCell.Cells(accountNr, 2)
  ' set member listbox
  For i = 0 To accountWs.cmbMembers.ListCount - 1
    If accountCell.Cells(accountNr, 4) = _
       accountWs.cmbMembers.List(i) Then
```

```
        accountWs.cmbMembers = i
      End If
    Next i
    ' set car listbox
    For i = 0 To accountWs.cmbCars.ListCount - 1
      If accountCell.Cells(accountNr, 5) = accountWs.cmbCars.List(i) Then
        accountWs.cmbCars = i
      End If
    Next i
    ' various input fields
    accountWs.[startTime] = accountCell.Cells(accountNr, 6)
    accountWs.[endTime] = accountCell.Cells(accountNr, 7)
    accountWs.[startDate] = accountCell.Cells(accountNr, 11)
    accountWs.[endDate] = accountCell.Cells(accountNr, 12)
    accountWs.[nrOfMiles] = accountCell.Cells(accountNr, 14)
    accountWs.[fuelcost] = accountCell.Cells(accountNr, 15)
    accountWs.[invoicenr] = "Invoice " & accountMonth & "-" & accountNr
  End Sub
```

CHAPTER 12

Access to External Data

In this chapter we discuss how to access data stored in an external database system from within Excel. There are essentially two ways to accomplish this: One is to use the wizard provided for this purpose, which in turn calls the program MS Query. (This form of data importation can be controlled via the *QueryTable* object.) The alternative is to use the new ADO library, which provides a host of objects for reading and editing data.

Chapter Overview

Fundamental Concepts About Relational Databases

We have already mentioned that Excel does not itself recognize relations. Nevertheless, it is important for you as an Excel programmer to understand the concept of a relational database: Both the supplementary program MS Query and the ADO library enable access to external databases, which almost always are built on the relational database model.

Relational databases are employed when the data are to be used in several tables and when the tables refer to one another. The essential motivation for using relational databases is to avoid redundancy.

> **TIP** *As a starting point for the explanations that follow we shall use the example database* Northwind *(file Nwind.mdb), which Microsoft includes with several of its products, for example with the Office suite, with Visual Basic, and with the SQL server. There are quite a few versions of this database. The file is included with the book's sample files.*

> **NOTE** *This section provides a brief introduction to the relational database model, without going into too much detail. The information provided here should be sufficient for you to understand how to extract data from a relational database. If you wish to construct your own databases, you will need to consult further literature on the subject.*

Sharing Data Among Several Databases

Let us suppose that you have a small business in which orders are entered manually into an order form and kept in this format. The form includes the following fields:

- order data
- name and address of the customer
- name of the seller
- list of ordered articles, consisting of article name, number of items, unit price, total price
- total price of the order
- additional information

Though this way of proceeding is easy to understand, it has several disadvantages:

- If a customer places several orders, his name and address must be written anew each time. If his address changes, all current order forms for this customer must be retrieved and updated. Customer-specific data (such as special arrangements for regular customers) must be stored separately.

- If an article occurs in several orders, its name and price must be written each time, although this is information that in any case is stored centrally (in a price list, say). There is a great danger of typographical errors.

- If a large number of different articles are ordered, then there will be insufficient space on the order form, and several forms will have to be stapled together.

In changing over to a digital system the order form could, of course, be used with little alteration. However, this is not such a good idea, due to the drawbacks mentioned above. Much better would be to partition the data among several tables:

Table *Customers*:	customer number, name, address
Table *Employees*:	employee number, name, etc.
Table *Products*:	article number, name, unit price, possible discounts
Table *Orders*:	order number, date, customer number, salesperson number
Table *Order Details*:	order number, article number, number of units

---

The definition of individual tables for articles, customers, employees (seller), and orders is probably immediately clear. It allows us to avoid the redundancy problem described above.

Conceptually perhaps most confusing is the table *Order Details:* Here are stored all the individual orders. An immediate integration of these individual orders (each order consists of several items: 3 pieces of X, 2 pieces of Y, 10 pieces of Z, say) in the orders table is not possible, since the number of items varies: If there were ten places in the orders table, then for most orders seven or eight items would be left empty (a waste of storage space). With other orders ten lines would be too few, and the order will have to be split (redundancy).

The chosen solution of individual tables therefore seems strange, since it is completely unsuitable for doing things "by hand." It is unthinkable to select from the endless list of items those items that correspond to order number 1234 placed on 5 June 1997. A solution optimized for human capacities would be to store within the order itself at least one reference to the order entries to minimize the task of searching. In a database program this is unnecessary, since the data in *Order Details* can be found rapidly. (Naturally, it is assumed that all access to linked tables is by way of indices. For *Order Details* the combination of order number and article number serves as the primary index.)

Relations Among Several Tables

There exist three basic relations between two tables:

1:1 One-to-one relation between two tables: Each data item in one table corresponds to exactly one data item in the other table. Such relations are rare, because the information of the two tables could as easily be stored in a single table.

1:n A data item in the first table can occur in several data items in the second table (for example, one seller appears in several orders). There cannot exist multiplicity in the other direction, since an order cannot be executed by more than one salesperson (at least not in this example). Occasionally, one speaks of an *n:1* relation that is actually the same as a *1:n* relation (the point of view has merely been shifted).

n:m A data item in one table can appear in several data items in the other table, and conversely (for example, several different articles can occur in one order, while one article can occur in several different orders; another example is that of books and their authors).

In a database the *1:n* relations between tables are created with identification numbers. Each salesperson possesses a unique employee ID number in the employees table. (This number is usually called a primary key. In an order the salesperson is referred to by this number. The field in the orders table is called a foreign key, because it refers to an ID in a different table.

For *n:m* relations a separate, additional, table is necessary, with which the *n:m* relation is reduced to two *1:n* relations. In the following example there exists a single *n:m* relation between orders and products. The order details table serves as the additional table. The primary key of this table is composed of the order and article number (this combination is unique; in a given order a product cannot occur twice). Figure 12.1 clarifies the relations among the tables.

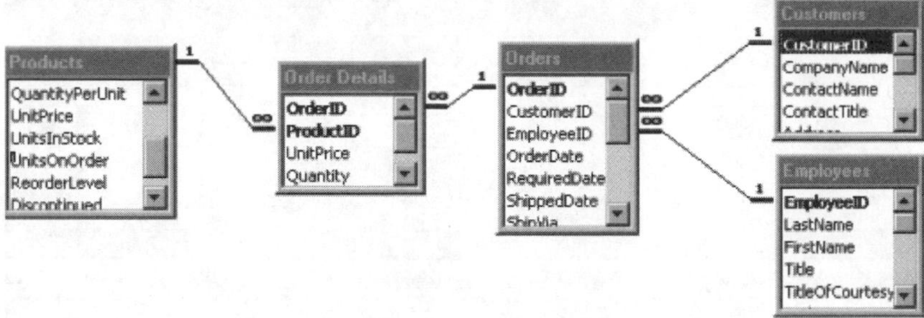

Figure 12.1. Relations for managing the order data

REMARKS *Quite often, when a database is being created, one attempts to give the same name to fields of different tables that later will be linked by a relation. This contributes to clarity, but is not a requirement.*

There are different types of relations, and these differ in their effect and use fundamentally from one another (inner join, outer join, with and without referential integrity). It is beyond the scope of this book to describe these types in any detail.

Relating Data from Different Tables

Figure 12.2 shows, by means of an example, how the data of an order are related: On 7 August 1996, order 10251 was executed. The customer name is stored in the *Orders* table with the ID *VICTE*. The *Customer* table reveals that the customer is, in fact, *Victuailles en stock*.

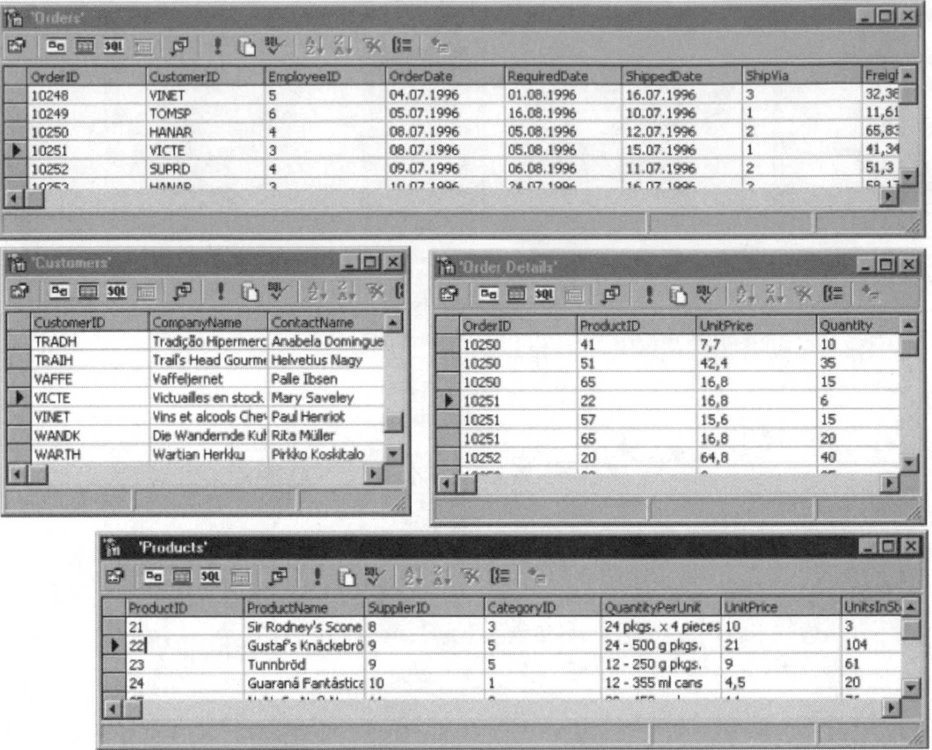

'Orders'

OrderID	CustomerID	EmployeeID	OrderDate	RequiredDate	ShippedDate	ShipVia	Freigl
10248	VINET	5	04.07.1996	01.08.1996	16.07.1996	3	32,38
10249	TOMSP	6	05.07.1996	16.08.1996	10.07.1996	1	11,61
10250	HANAR	4	08.07.1996	05.08.1996	12.07.1996	2	65,83
10251	VICTE	3	08.07.1996	05.08.1996	15.07.1996	1	41,34
10252	SUPRD	4	09.07.1996	06.08.1996	11.07.1996	2	51,3

'Customers'

CustomerID	CompanyName	ContactName
TRADH	Tradição Hipermerc	Anabela Domingue
TRAIH	Trail's Head Gourme	Helvetius Nagy
VAFFE	Vaffeljernet	Palle Ibsen
VICTE	Victuailles en stock	Mary Saveley
VINET	Vins et alcools Che	Paul Henriot
WANDK	Die Wandernde Kuh	Rita Müller
WARTH	Wartian Herkku	Pirkko Koskitalo

'Order Details'

OrderID	ProductID	UnitPrice	Quantity
10250	41	7,7	10
10250	51	42,4	35
10250	65	16,8	15
10251	22	16,8	6
10251	57	15,6	15
10251	65	16,8	20
10252	20	64,8	40

'Products'

ProductID	ProductName	SupplierID	CategoryID	QuantityPerUnit	UnitPrice	UnitsInSt
21	Sir Rodney's Scone	8	3	24 pkgs. x 4 pieces	10	3
22	Gustaf's Knäckebrö	9	5	24 - 500 g pkgs.	21	104
23	Tunnbröd	9	5	12 - 250 g pkgs.	9	61
24	Guaraná Fantástica	10	1	12 - 355 ml cans	4,5	20

Figure 12.2. Data for an order are divided among four tables

What products (and how many of each) has this firm ordered? For this we must search in the table *OrderDetails* for the ordered items with order number 10251. There we find three items: six of product 22, fifteen of product 57, and twenty of product 65. And what might these products be? This information is contained in the table *Products*: Product 22 is *Gustaf's Knäckebröd.*

It may be that this division of data among several tables appears overly elaborate. But in fact, it produces an enormous advantage:

- The most obvious advantage is the result of saving of space: In a real-life application the table *Order Details* would be by far the largest, which for a medium-size business would have about one hundred thousand entries. But for each line only four numerical quantities need to be stored: order ID, product number, number of items, and unit price. Without the relational model you would have to store for each order the product name, name of the salesperson, customer name, and so on. The storage requirement would multiply, without yielding any advantage. A large portion of the data would be merely redundant.

- The relational model helps to avoid errors: If the product name has to be written out for each item each time it is ordered, then it is only a matter of time before typos begin to infiltrate the database.

- The relational model makes possible central editing of data: When the address of a customer changes, only the corresponding entry in the *Customers* table needs to be updated. Without this relational linkage of data you would have to do a global search, which, experience tells us, is fraught with error. (You have certainly experienced this problem yourself: You inform a firm of your new address, and nonetheless many shipments are wrongly addressed. The reason? Your address is stored by the firm in several places. One department has received your notification of change of address, but two other departments continue to use the old address.)

Querying Data

You need to be concerned with the organization of information in the various tables as described above only when you create queries with SQL commands. (SQL stands for *Standard Query Language* and is a type of programming language for manipulation of databases.) Often, instead of having to formulate queries in SQL code you can use one of a number of convenient tools, such as MS Query, described in the next section. The database program Access possesses a so-called query generator, with which you can easily define queries.

The Northwind Database

The imaginary firm *Northwind* provides gastronomical specialties to customers all over the world. Figure 12.1 shows only a portion of the tables in the *Northwind* database. The complete database schema is somewhat more complex and can be seen in Figure 12.3. First we give some information about the construction of the database:

In *Products* is stored information about the origin of each product. Category and supplier data are stored in two additional tables, in order to avoid redundancy. The table *Orders* contains data on each order. In three *1:n* relations reference is made to the *Customers* table, the *Shippers* table, and the *Employees* table. So that arbitrarily many articles can be included in an order, an *n:m* relation between *Orders* and *Products* is established via the intermediate table *Order Details*.

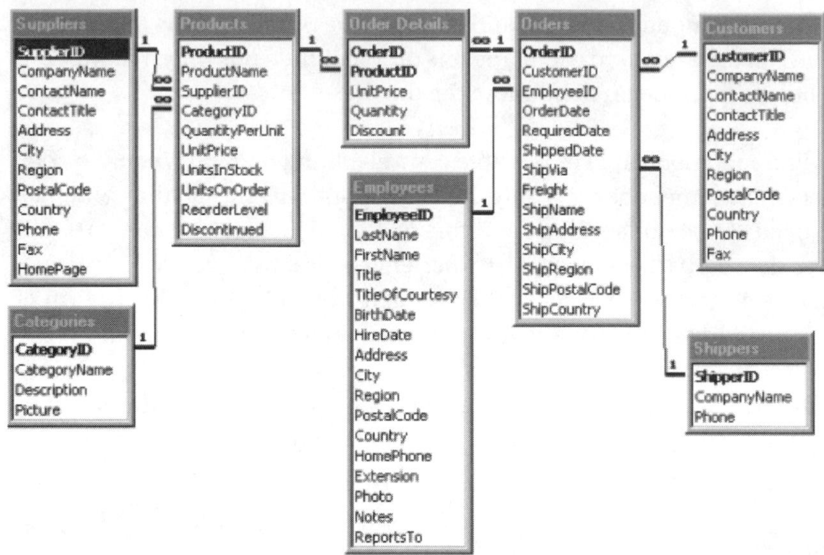

Figure 12.3. Tables and relations of the Northwind example database

The database contains about eighty products in eight categories from thirty suppliers. There are eight hundred orders from ninety customers stored. There are three shipping firms, and the employee count is nine.

The table *order details* contains, among other things, the data field *unitprice.* This field appears to contradict the rule for the construction of a relational database in that it is redundant (the unit price can be obtained from the product ID in the associated table *products*). A possible reason for the unit being stored a second time is to make it easier to deal with price changes: When the price of a product is changed, this change does not affect the record of orders already placed in *order details.*

Importing External Data

This section deals with the Excel menu command DATA|GET EXTERNAL DATA and the associated *QueryTable* object for executing database queries.

> **POINTER** *The* QueryTable *object can also be used for importing text files or HTML documents. These uses are described in Chapters 5 and 14.*

Importing Data from Databases (MS Query)

It sometimes happens that you are managing your data with a regular database program but you wish to analyze or process data with Excel. In this case the first step consists in importing the data into an Excel worksheet. To do this you execute the command DATA|GET EXTERNAL DATA|NEW DATABASE QUERY. A query wizard appears to help you with the importation.

> **REMARKS** *To be precise, we are dealing here not with one of the many traditional Excel forms or wizards, but with a freestanding program with the name MS Query (*`Msqry32.exe`*). We are dealing also with a supplementary program to the Office suite, which is usually installed in the directory* `Office2000\Office`.
>
> *Alas, the program has never been famous for user-friendliness, and in Office 2000 the program seems even more out of date: The program seems not to have heard of OLE-DB-datalink files (this is the successor of the ODBC data source). And that the help button still has no effect whatsoever is to some extent symptomatic of the entire program.*
>
> *A short description of two abbreviations: ODBC stands for* Open Database Connectivity. *Behind this is a standard (even older) for integrated access to various database systems. OLE DB stands for* Object Linking *and* Embedding Database. *By this is meant a new standard that has the same goal as ODBC (that is, unified data access), but that makes use of Microsoft component technology.*

Selecting a Data Source

The definition of a new query begins with selecting a so-called data source. (By a query is meant all parameters with the help of which MS Query creates a list ordered and filtered according to various criteria from a database.)

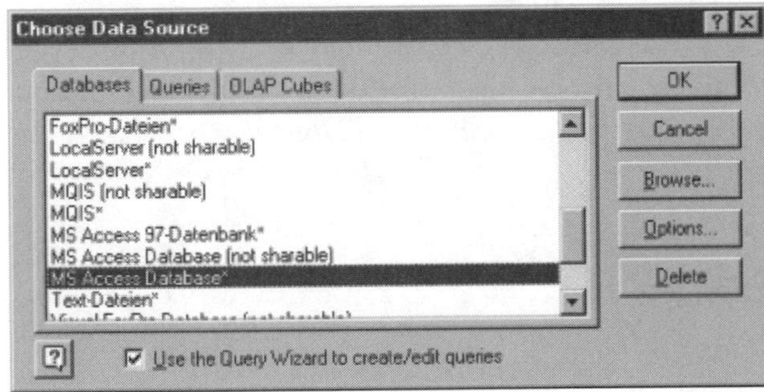

Figure 12.4. Selecting a data source

There are three possibilities for selecting a data source:

- The usual case consists in simply naming a database. This can be done in two ways:

  In simple cases—for example, in dealing with an Access file—you simply select this database type with a double click. Then a dialog appears in which you can select the name of the database file.

  On the other hand, when the database is managed by a database server, you must define a new data source. For this you select the first entry of the listbox, <New Data Source>. A double click leads to a sequence of further dialogs, in which you declare the name of the data source, the driver for the database (for example, SQL server), and the connection information (name of the server, name of the database, password if required). As a result you obtain a new ODBC data source, which is then cited in the dialog CHOOSE DATA SOURCE. The advantage of this elaborate process is that the connection data are saved as an ODBC data source and can be easily reused with additional queries. (If you wish to edit an existing data source, you simply carry it out in the control panel at the point ODBC DATA.)

- If you have already set up a query with MS Query and saved it in a `*.dqy` file, you can use this query file as the starting point for a new query.

- A third option is the so-called OLAP cubes. This variant is of interest only in combination with pivot tables and therefore will be discussed in the next chapter (and there not in great detail).

Introductory Example: Product List

After a successful selection of a database file or data source, the next step consists in selecting the table or fields in a table from which you wish to read data. In the dialog are shown tables as well as predefined queries (Access) or so-called *views* (database server). Since this is somewhat confusing at the outset, you can use the Options button to restrict the selection to tables.

For our first example of the use of MS Query we would like to import into Excel a list of all *Northwind* products (consisting of product ID, name, and price). To this end the three fields *ProductID, ProductName,* and *UnitPrice* are selected from the table *Products* (Figure 12.5).

Query Wizard - Choose Columns

What columns of data do you want to include in your query?

Available tables and columns: Employees, Order Details, Orders, Products, SupplierID, CategoryID, QuantityPerUnit

Columns in your query: ProductID, ProductName, UnitPrice

Preview of data in selected column:

Preview Now | Options... | < Back | Next > | Cancel

Figure 12.5. Selecting the table fields

The following two dialogs make it possible to filter the data (for example with *UnitPrice<10,* to select only inexpensive products) and to sort them (for example, by product name). We shall not make use of these possibilities here.

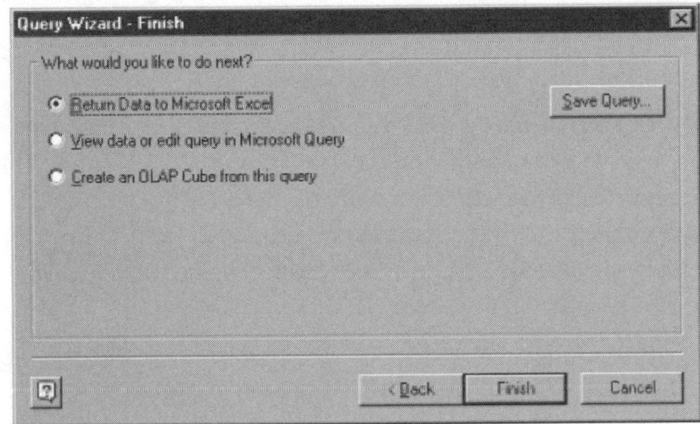

Figure 12.6. Final dialog of the MS Query Wizard

In the final dialog (Figure 12.6) you have three possibilities: You can return the selected data to Excel, you can view the data in MS Query and there process the query further, or you can create an OLAP cube from the data (see the next chapter).

The first option makes sense only if your query (as in the current example) is so trivial that further refinement is unnecessary. In this case a further dialog appears, in which you specify where and how the data are to be placed in Excel. As a rule, you need to give only the start cell and click OK. (The numerous options are described somewhat further below.)

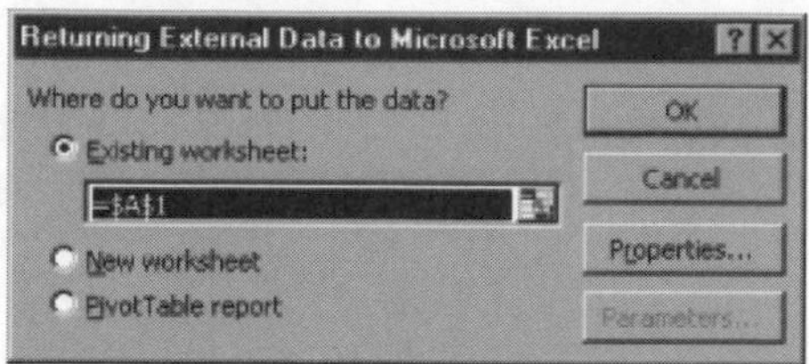

Figure 12.7. Inserting data into Excel

Book1

	A	B	C
1	ProductID	ProductName	UnitPrice
2	1	Chai	18
3	2	Chang	19
4	3	Aniseed Syrup	10
5	4	Chef Anton's Cajun Seasoning	22
6	5	Chef Anton's Gumbo Mix	21.35
7	6	Grandma's Boysenberry Spread	25
8	7	Uncle Bob's Organic Dried Pears	30
9	8	Northwoods Cranberry Sauce	40
10	9	Mishi Kobe Niku	97
11	10	Ikura	31

Sheet1 / Sheet2 / Sheet3

Figure 12.8. Data imported into a worksheet

Updating Data, Altering Queries

The data that have been imported into Excel are a copy of those in the database. If the database is altered, the imported Excel table must be updated. To this end Excel keeps track of the query parameters. To update the data, place the cell pointer in the data range and execute DATA|REFRESH DATA.

> **CAUTION** *Updating the data works only if the data source has not changed its location. For example, if the database file has been moved to another folder, Excel displays an error message when updating is attempted. The new location of the database file can be given in the login dialog that then appears.*
>
> *Particularly annoying is the condition that the file names of database files must be stored absolutely, that is, with complete drive and directory information. Therefore, if you rename a directory with your Excel application together with the associated Access database, Excel will no longer be able to locate the database file. This problem, which existed in earlier versions of Excel as well, can be solved with a few lines of program code (see below).*

Perhaps you have also discovered that the imported data do not quite meet your requirements. In this case you can summon the Query wizard again with the command DATA|GET EXTERNAL DATA|EDIT QUERY. The previous settings serve as the default setting.

Example: A Listing of All Orders

As our second example we would like to create a listing of all *Northwind* orders, where the list consists of order number, order data, name of the salesperson, and name of the customer. The construction of the query begins again with selecting the database. Then the worksheet field must be selected. Instead of spending time with the convoluted wizard, simply select the *Orders* table and skip the further dialogs. In the last step select the option VIEW DATA OR EDIT QUERY IN MICROSOFT QUERY in order to formulate the query more conveniently there.

Figure 12.9 shows the user interface of MS Query, when it is not hidden by the wizard. The advantage over the wizard is that you can actually see the data that result from the query.

First of all, these data in fact do not yet correspond to the requirements of this example: On the one hand, instead of the customer and employee name, only the employee ID numbers and customer letter codes are displayed, while on the other hand, the table contains a host of information that is of no interest.

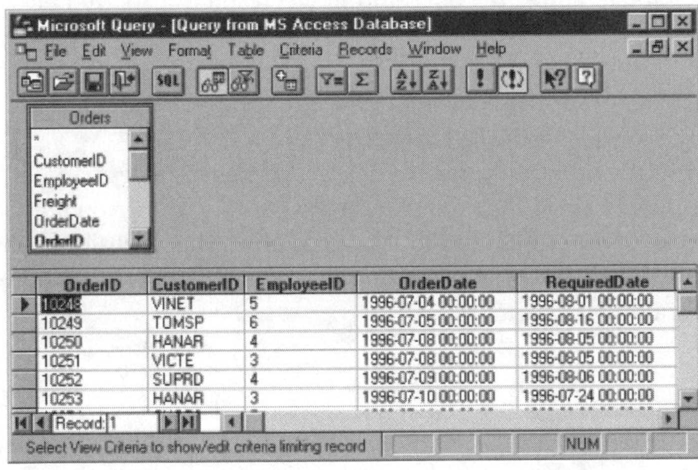

OrderID	CustomerID	EmployeeID	OrderDate	RequiredDate
10248	VINET	5	1996-07-04 00:00:00	1996-08-01 00:00:00
10249	TOMSP	6	1996-07-05 00:00:00	1996-08-16 00:00:00
10250	HANAR	4	1996-07-08 00:00:00	1996-08-05 00:00:00
10251	VICTE	3	1996-07-08 00:00:00	1996-08-05 00:00:00
10252	SUPRD	4	1996-07-09 00:00:00	1996-08-06 00:00:00
10253	HANAR	3	1996-07-10 00:00:00	1996-07-24 00:00:00

Figure 12.9. The program MS Query with the Orders table

To delete unwanted columns , simply click on the header row and press the Delete key. In this way you can get rid of all columns other than *OrderID* and *OrderDate*. (With Shift you can select several columns for deletion.)

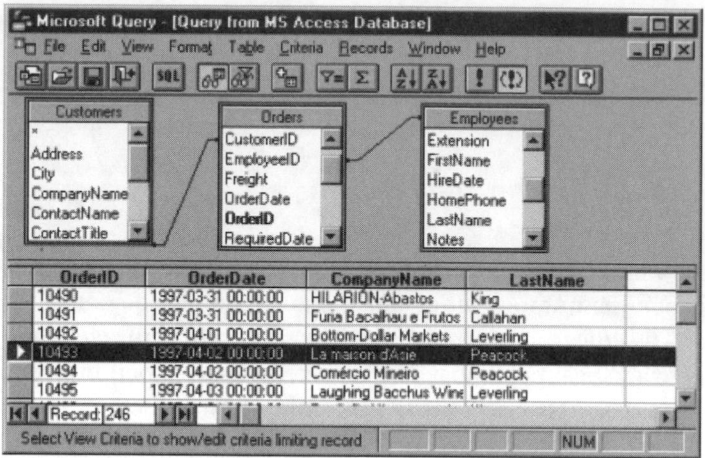

Figure 12.10. A listing of all Northwind orders

The customer and employee names are not accessible in the *Orders* table. However, with TABLE|ADD TABLES you can easily integrate the tables *Customers* and *Employees* into the query. MS Query recognizes the connections between tables on its own and represents these connections with linkage lines. From the tables *Customers* and *Employees* you can use *Drag & Drop* to move the fields *CompanyName* and *LastName* into the table. Finally, to order the table by order date, first click the *OrderDate* column and then the Sort button. The result is displayed in Figure 12.10.

If you wish to change the column headings (say, *salesperson* instead of *LastName*), you can access the appropriate dialog by double clicking on the column head. The heading holds as well for the resulting Excel table.

If you wish to restrict the table to those orders, say, executed by salesman *King*, execute the command CRITERIA|ADD CRITERIA. In the CRITERIA dialog you may specify that the last name of the employee should equal *King*. (Theoretically, it is possible that several employees have the surname *King*. To avoid such ambiguity, you could use the criterion *EmployeeID=7*.

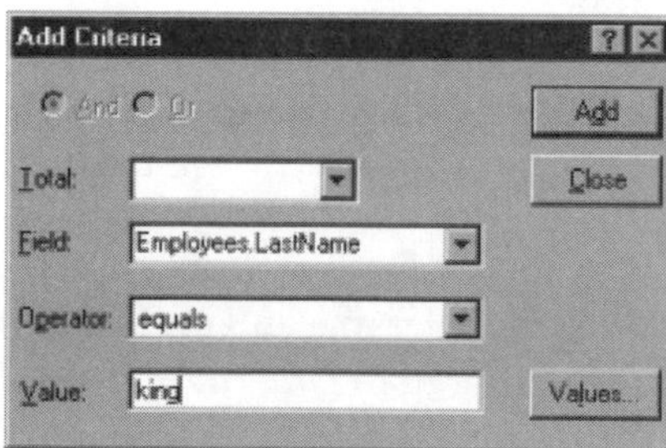

Figure 12.11. Filter criterion for the orders

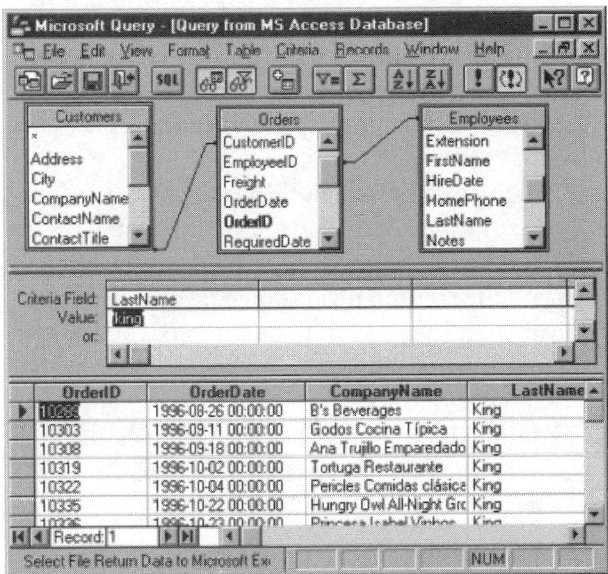

Figure 12.12. A listing of orders of the employee King

Tables and Relations

If a database query affects several tables, a relation among these tables must be established. Unfortunately, MS Query is capable of recognizing relations among tables on its own only if the tables are linked by like-named data fields. If that is not the case, you must establish the connection yourself via TABLE|JOINS. This, however, presupposes a good knowledge of the structure of the database.

> **TIP** *There exist various possibilities for defining a relation between the data fields of two tables. With a double click on the linkage lines between tables, or via the command* TABLE|JOINS, *you can select from among three different relation types and among several join operators. A change in the standard setting (join type 1, operator "=") is rarely required and presupposes a deep understanding of relational databases. In this book we shall consider only relations with the standard setting.*

Example: Sales by Employee

The goal of this example is to calculate the sales achieved by each employee. To do this, the product of *Quantity* and *Unit Price* must be obtained for each item ordered (*Order Details*). These products must then be summed for each employee.

The underlying data are to be found in three tables: *Order Details* for the actual numbers, *Orders* to allocate the different items sold to the different employees, and, finally, *EmployeesK* for the names of the salespersons. In MS Query you add two columns to the result table: *Lastname* for the employee name and *Quantity* for the quantity of each individual item sold.

A double click on the *Quantity* field opens the dialog EDIT COLUMN. There you input as data field the formula *Quantity*UnitPrice*—you are not interested merely in the quantity ordered, but in the product of this quantity with the price of the corresponding article. For this reason the column head should be changed to something like *Sales*. Finally, indicate that the result is to be summed. MS Query recognizes from context (that is, since the query contains only one additional column, with the employee name) that the sum is to be taken for each employee. After you have sorted the *Sales* column in increasing order, the result should look like Figure 12.12. *Peacock* appears to be the most successful salesman.

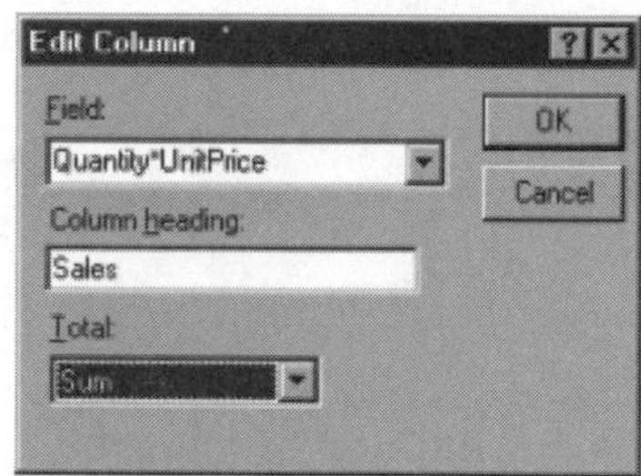

Figure 12.13. MS Query can execute calculations for each column

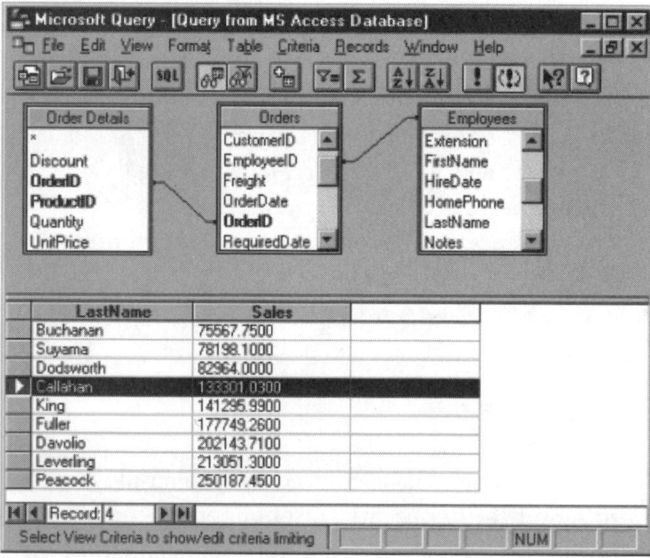

Figure 12.14. A listing of the total sales of each employee

In addition to the summation formula presented here, MS Query recognizes four additional calculational functions (minimum, maximum, average, and count). Basically, these functions come into play only when the list contains identical data records—with the exception of the data field of the current column. In this case these data records are united into a single record, where the calculational function is then applied. However, it is impossible in MS Query to group and sum data records that have only one field in common but differ in other fields. Such advanced analytical methods are available only after the entire list has been imported into Excel in the form of a pivot table.

Sort and Filter Criteria

With the sort symbol (A_Z) you can sort the database according to the current column or selected columns. The command RECORDS|SORT allows sorting according to several criteria. However, these criteria—as compared to the corresponding dialog in Excel—are quite confusedly ordered in a list. Sorting takes place first according to the first entry in the list, then the second, and so on.

In setting the filter criteria it is a good idea to activate the third window area provided in MS Query with VIEW|CRITERIA. There then appears between the table and list area a list of criteria. For the criteria there generally holds a similar control as in Excel for the so-called special filters: In the table, adjacent formulated conditions must be satisfied simultaneously (logical "and"), while conditions formed one below the other are connected by a logical "or."

The insertion of a new filter criterion is accomplished with CRITERIA|ADD CRITERIA or with a double click on the column head in the criteria table. In the dialog that appears you must specify the data field, the operator ("equals," "is greater than," etc.), and a comparison value or text. Again, a join of several data fields (for example, *quantity*unitprice*) is allowed as data field.

With the button VALUES you can choose comparison values. Note that a multiple selection is possible. In specifying several filter criteria you must always be aware that the criteria must be joined either with "and" or with "or."

An immediate change in the entries of the criteria table can be accomplished via the keyboard as well as in the dialog obtainable by a double click. The criteria can be deleted entirely with CRITERIA|REMOVE ALL CRITERIA. You can also select and remove individual columns of the criteria table with the mouse.

A Look at SQL Code

SQL ("standard query language") is a standardized language for the formulation of database commands. MS Query uses SQL internally to express and evaluate queries that you input with the mouse and keyboard.

If you would like to see how your queries look in SQL, you can look at the SQL code with View|SQL. (For database pros, this is also a method by which you can determine, more reliably and quickly than with the on-line help or documentation, how MS Query actually functions.)

The SQL code can be edited; then MS Query reconstructs the query on the monitor on the basis of this code. Changing SQL code assumes a certain degree of technical knowledge. Moreover, MS Query recognizes only a subset of SQL. Therefore, it is not possible simply to construct a query in Access and then copy the SQL code from there into MS Query.

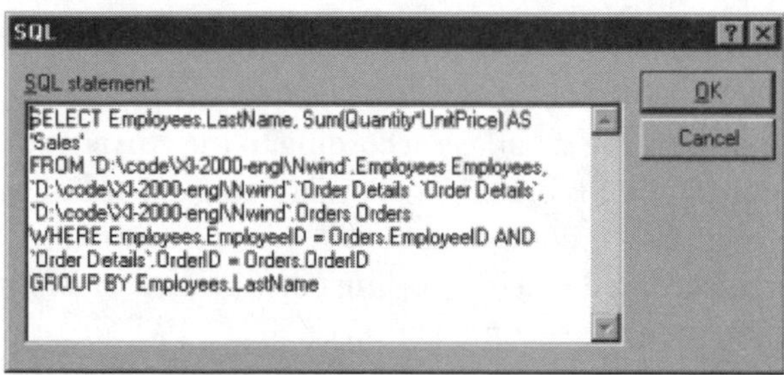

Figure 12.15. SQL code for the query of Figure 12.14

More clearly formatted, the SQL code in Figure 12.15 looks as follows:

```
SELECT Employees.LastName,
       Sum(Quantity*UnitPrice) AS 'Sales'
FROM 'D:\code\Xl-2000-engl\Nwind'.Employees Employees,
     'D:\code\Xl-2000-engl\Nwind'.'Order Details' 'Order Details',
     'D:\code\Xl-2000-engl\Nwind'.Orders Orders
WHERE Employees.EmployeeID = Orders.EmployeeID AND
      'Order Details'.OrderID = Orders.OrderID
GROUP BY Employees.LastName
ORDER BY Sum(Quantity*UnitPrice) DESC
```

POINTER *A brief introduction to SQL can be found later in this chapter.*

Queries Executed on Request

MS Query executes at once every change in a query, whether a new sort order or a new filter criterion. This is practical for experimentation with small databases, but with larger quantities of data it can lead to unbearable wait times. Therefore, there exists the possibility of deactivating automatic queries via Records|Automatic Query. Excel now no longer updates the list of data records in the lower window region automatically, but only on request via the command Records|Query Now.

Options for Inserting External Data

Immediately before data resulting from a new query are imported into Excel, the dialog RETURNING EXTERNAL DATA TO MICROSOFT EXCEL appears. With its PROPERTIES button you can select a host of options. These same options can be set after the fact with DATA|GET EXTERNAL DATA|DATA RANGE PROPERTIES.

SAVE QUERY DEFINITION means that in Excel not only the data from the database are inserted, but also the definition of the query in MS Query. This has the advantage that the data can easily be updated later or the query parameters edited.

> **TIP** *Sometimes, you would like precisely the opposite: You wish to import data once and then never alter them. Above all, you wish to be spared the constantly recurring question of whether you wish to update the data. This holds in particular when you wish to pass the Excel file to another user without the underlying database.*
>
> *In this case you should deactivate the option* SAVE QUERY DEFINITION. *The data remain in the table, but Excel no longer knows where they came from. (It is as if the data had been input from the keyboard.) Ideally, you could first store the code of the SQL query in MS Query in a small file, so that you can access it if at some later time you need to insert the data again.*

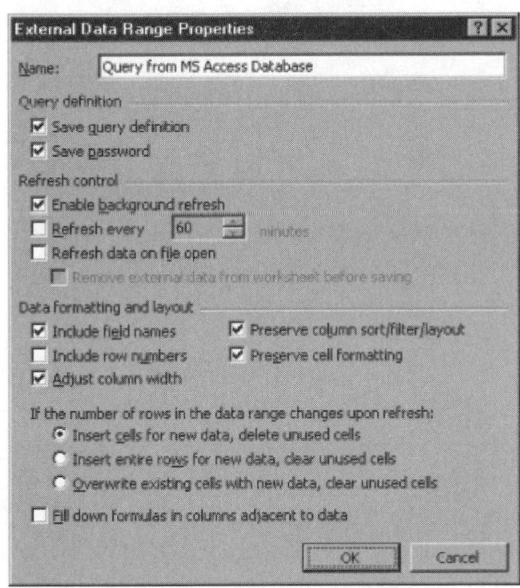

Figure 12.16. External Data Range Properties

The option SAVE PASSWORD is useful only for queries that apply to a password-secured database. If the option is activated, Excel stores the password together with the other parameters of the query. The advantage is that the password need not be typed in each time the data are updated. The disadvantage, of course, is that every user with access to the Excel file can use MS Query to access, and even alter, the database. You have thus created a security risk.

The refresh options specify whether the data are to be updated automatically when the Excel file is loaded. This costs time, of course, and is useful only for data that change often.

The data formatting options govern whether column headings and row numbers should be added, whether Excel should attempt to format the table automatically, and how Excel should behave when the data set changes during an update.

Loading and Saving Queries

When MS Query is used from within Excel, the basic information of the query is carried over into Excel and stored in the worksheet. In addition, there exists the possibility in MS Query to save the query data via FILE|SAVE. In this case only the parameters of the query are saved—such as tables, data fields, sort and filter criteria—and not the list of the data records. These must be regenerated when the query is loaded. For this reason query files with the suffix `*.dqy` are very small.

The QueryTable Object

Inside MS Query

Internally, Excel creates a *Name* object and a *QueryTable* object for every imported table. The *Name* object defines a name for the affected range of cells. You may retrieve a list of all defined *Name* objects in the immediate window with the following instruction:

```
For Each n In Names: ?n.Name & "  " & n.Value: Next
```

For the file `MS-Query.xls`, with the three examples of the foregoing section the loop returns the following result:

```
Sheet1!sample1  =Sheet1!$A$1:$C$78
Sheet2!sample2  =Sheet2!$A$1:$D$73
Sheet3!sample3  =Sheet3!$A$1:$B$10
```

The associated *QueryTable* object saves the settings of the above displayed options dialog in a host of properties. The most important properties are *Connection*, with path information about the database file; *CommandText*, with the SQL code of the query; and *Connection*, with the cell into which the data are to be inserted. (*Destination* thus refers to a *Range* object. *CommandText* replaces the property *Sql*, which is available only for reasons of compatibility.) Once again, you can see the details in the immediate window:

```
For Each ws In Worksheets: For Each q in ws.QueryTables: _
  ?q.Name, q.CommandText, q.Connection, q.Destination.Address: _
Next: Next
```

For the query from the first worksheet the results (suitably formatted) are as follows:

```
Name = "sample1"
Sql  = "SELECT Products.ProductID, Products.ProductName,
               Products.UnitPrice
        FROM `I:\Code\XL-2000\NWIND`.Products Products"
Connection = "ODBC;DBQ=I:\Code\XL-2000\NWIND.MDB;
        DefaultDir=I:\Code\XL-2000;
        Driver={Microsoft Access Driver (*.mdb)};DriverId=25;
        FIL=MS Access;MaxBufferSize=2048;MaxScanRows=8;PageTimeout=5;
        SafeTransactions=0;Threads=3;UID=admin;UserCommitSync=Yes;"
Destination.Address = "$A$1"
```

The QueryTable Object

The function of the *QueryTable* object is, then, to store all information that is necessary for the importation of the data. In this book, *QueryTable* was presented for the first time in Chapter 5 on the subject of *Textimport*. *QueryTable* is thus responsible not only for importation from databases, but for the most varied sources of data. In addition to databases and text files there are also web pages to be considered (Chapter 14).

The property ***QueryType*** gives information about the data source. If the importation took place via MS Query, as in the preceding section, then this property always has the value *xlODBCQuery (1)*. An instance of the correct setting of *Connection* and *CommandText* for this case is given in the above example. It is also made clear that it is not quite a simple matter to set this character string manually (not least because the documentation for the construction of character strings is meager; usable information is to be found only in the ODBC documentation or in the description of comparable properties of DAO objects).

If you wish to edit *QueryTable* objects via program code, the usual modus operandi is first to create a query using MS Query and then use this character string as the starting point for your program code.

A similar way of proceeding was also chosen to get around the greatest deficit of *QueryTable* objects. If you open the example file `MS-Query.xls` on your computer, under normal circumstances Excel cannot update the data, because it cannot find the database file (unless you happen to have installed the database file `Nwind.mdb` in the same folder as that on the author's computer, namely, `I:\Code\Xl-2000\`).

To help remedy this sad state of affairs, in the procedure *Workbook_Open* the *Connection* and *CommandText* properties are set to the valid path. An updating of the data is now possible, provided that `MS-Query.xls` is in the same folder as the database `Nwind.mdb`.

The two *For* loops are used to ensure that all *QueryTable* objects will run through all tables. The additional program code has, in fact, rather little to do with database programming, but rather demonstrates the use of character string functions: In *ExtractDir* the setting of the default directory is determined from the *Connection* character string. (It is a question of the path to the database file.) In what follows this path will be replaced, using *Replace*, by the path to the Excel file.

```
' MS Query.xls, ThisWorkbook
Private Sub Workbook_Open()
  Dim oldDir$, newDir$
  Dim ws As Worksheet
  Dim qt As QueryTable
  newDir = ThisWorkbook.Path
  If Right(newDir, 1) = "\" Then newDir = Left(newDir, Len(newDir) - 1)
  For Each ws In Worksheets
    For Each qt In ws.QueryTables
      If qt.QueryType = xlODBCQuery Then
        ' extract previous path from Connection string
        oldDir = ExtractDir(qt.Connection)
        ' if successful: replace previous path by new one
        If oldDir  "" Then
          qt.Connection = Replace(qt.Connection, oldDir, newDir, _
                                  Compare:=vbTextCompare)
          qt.CommandText = Replace(qt.CommandText, oldDir, newDir, _
                                  Compare:=vbTextCompare)
        End If
      End If
    Next
  Next
End Sub
```

```
' extracts "xyz" from "abc;DefaultDir=xyz;abc"
Public Function ExtractDir$(connStr$)
  Dim pos1&, pos2&
  pos1 = InStr(1, connStr, "DefaultDir", vbTextCompare)
  If pos1 = 0 Then Exit Function
  pos1 = pos1 + Len("DefaultDir=")
  pos2 = InStr(pos1, connStr, ";", vbTextCompare)
  If pos2 = 0 Then pos2 = Len(connStr)
  ExtractDir = Mid(connStr, pos1, pos2 - pos1)
  ' remove \ character at the end of the string
  If Right(ExtractDir, 1) = "\" Then
    ExtractDir = Left(ExtractDir, Len(ExtractDir) - 1)
  End If
End Function
```

CAUTION *Please note that the above program code depends on the path to the database file being saved in the attribute* DefaultDir *of the* Connection *property. This was the case with all the author's experiments with MS Query in accessing Access databases. However, the exact construction of the* Connection *character string is not documented. It is thus unclear whether this way of proceeding will function under all circumstances, that is, with other database systems or in future versions of Excel.*

TIP *A function similar to that of* QueryTable *is fulfilled for pivot tables by the object* PivotCache. *Here, too—just as in the case of* QueryTable*—the parameters for the database are stored. In contrast to* QueryTable, Pivot-Cache *can also store a copy of the data (without these data being immediately visible). In this way the situation is avoided that each time the structure of the pivot table is changed the data must be read again from the database.*

Syntax Summary

QueryTable Object

ws.QueryTables(n)	access to the *QueryTable* object of a table
ws.QueryTables.Add	create a new object
qt.BackgroundQuery	background updating (*True/False*)
qt.Connection	(array of) character string(s) with information on the data's origin
qt.Destination	cell range (*Range*), in which the data are to be displayed
qt.QueryType	type of data source (such as *xlODBCQuery*)
qt.CommandText	SQL command for the query
qt.Refresh	update data (method)

Exporting Excel Data

Exporting to a Database

The main topic of this chapter is actually the importation of data, but sooner or later one is faced with the converse, namely, exporting Excel tables. For this Excel offers a number of options:

- In executing FILE|SAVE AS you can specify "dBase III" or "dBase IV. "Then the current database (the range of cells in which the cell pointer is currently located) of the active worksheet is saved. If a range of cells is selected before the command is executed, then only this range is copied. Excel thus behaves in a manner similar to that for the execution of various DATA commands. The column labels are shortened to ten characters, with any spaces being replaced by the underscore character "_". (Take care that columns have unique labels.) The first data record of the table determines the data format.

- The command DATA|CONVERT TO MS ACCESS is provided for such conversion. The command is available only if the ACCESSLINKS ADD-IN has been activated.

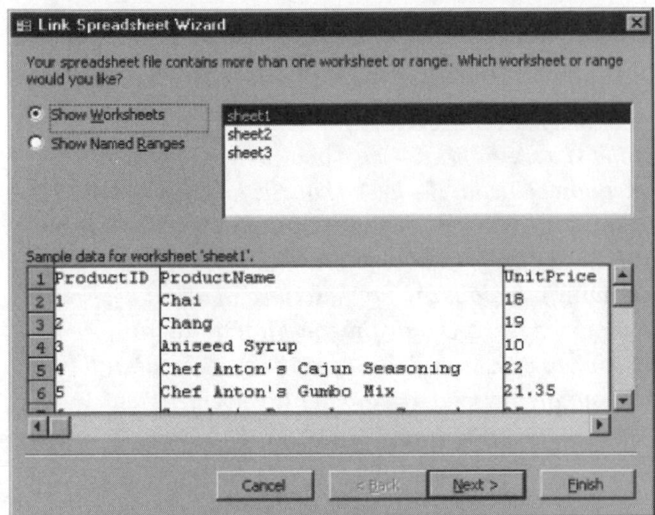

Figure 12.17. The Access import wizard during the importation of an Excel table

- Finally, you can also tackle the problem of exporting an Excel table to Access from the opposite direction: To do so, save and close the file in Excel. Then launch Access and execute FILE|GET EXTERNAL DATA|IMPORT. In the file selection form that opens choose your Excel file, which takes you to the import wizard (see Figure 12.17). (Many other database systems are capable of importing Excel tables.)

Exporting as a Text File; Form Letters in Word

> **POINTER** *Various possibilities for exporting Excel tables in the form of text files are described in Chapter 5. You can also use Excel files as the basis for form letters in MS Word. Information on this topic together with a brief example can be found in Chapter 11.*

Database Access with the ADO Library

> **REMARKS** *As the author of this book I face a dilemma at the start of this section. I have just completed a six-hundred-page book dealing exclusively with ADO (from the viewpoint of Visual Basic). Of course, I would love to discuss all of this here, though to be sure, a complete description is out of the question. Therefore, I can say only that the following description is greatly compressed, that many functions are not described at all, that from among the many options offered by ADO only the most important are mentioned, and so on. For simple tasks and those first baby steps this information should suffice. If your desires lead to a greater involvement with ADO, then you should consult the specialized literature on this subject.*

Introduction

What Is ADO?

ADO stands for *ActiveX Data Objects* and is a comparatively new library for database programming. ADO is the successor to the DAO library (which is still available; see below).

With ADO you can

- establish a connection to almost any database operating under Windows (provided that this database possesses an ODBC, or, better, OLE-DB driver)
- query data and evaluate them in your program
- add new data, edit, and delete (to the extent that you have access privileges)

If you are working with Office Developer, then you have available, in addition to the ADO library, several control elements with which you can represent simply and conveniently the results of your queries (*DataList, DataCombo, MSHFlexGrid*) or edit them (*DataGrid*).

> **POINTER** *In order for the ADO functions to be available for use in your Excel programs, you must activate them with* TOOLS|REFERENCES. *The full name of the library is* Microsoft ActiveX Data Objects 2.1 Library. *In the object browser the abbreviation is* ADODB. *Take care that you do not select one of the numerous related libraries.*
>
> *ADO 2.1 was provided with Office 2000. By the time you are reading this, there will probably be an ADO 2.5, delivered with Windows 2000. If you wish to develop programs that function with Excel 2000, then you should continue to use ADO 2.1. On the other hand, if you wish to use new functions provided in ADO 2.5 or higher, then you can use as well a newer version of ADO in Excel (if it is installed on your computer).*

ADO Versus DAO

Both the DAO and ADO libraries are included with Excel 2000. According to Microsoft, ADO is the wave of the database future. DAO is still supported for backward compatibility (that is, basically, that newly discovered errors will be corrected), but will not be further developed (thus there will be no new functions provided).

There is, then, no good reason not to leave existing DAO code as it is. DAO may be somewhat out of fashion, but in exchange it functions rather reliably, in particular in combination with Access databases. However, with new projects you should opt for ADO, for the following reasons in particular:

- The ADO object hierarchy is considerably simpler and clearer.
- The ADO object model supports events. This is of help, in principle, to keep code readable. (The greatest limitation in Excel is that it is rather complex to receive events; see Chapter 4.)
- ADO supports asynchronous operations.
- The ADO *Recordset* object, in comparison to the DAO-*Recordset*, has completely new functions, such as for the management of hierarchical data records.
- While DAO was conceived above all for Access databases, ADO enables efficient code with other database systems as well. This facilitates a later migration of an initially small Jet database to a larger client/server system.
- Office Developer makes available attractive supplementary control elements and tools for database development, but only for ADO.

> **TIP** *It is possible, in principle, to use both DAO and ADO in the same program (during the changeover phase from one to the other, say). However, one is then faced with a number of like-named objects, such as the DAO and ADO* Recordset *objects. For unique identification, in declaring variables you will now have to prefix the library name (that is,* DAO.Recordset *or* ADODB. Recordset*).*

> **TIP** *The ADO library supports many, but not all, functions of DAO. If you wish to use new Access databases or tables, or need to manage indexes or access privileges, then you must install the ADOX library in addition to ADO.*

ADO and DAO are not mutually compatible (even if many objects have the same names), and furthermore, there are no tools to transform DAO code automatically into ADO. Such a transformation is burdensome work and is to be recommended only for projects that must be fundamentally enlarged. Otherwise, the golden rule is, *never change a running system*. If your program is running just fine with DAO, then let it be! Even though DAO is no longer under active development, one may rest assured that DAO code will run for many years to come.

Introductory Example

As with all the examples of the section, the following procedure accesses the database `Nwind.mdb`. (The construction of the database is described in the previous chapter. The database file is located in the sample files for this book at `http://www.apress.com`.)

In the first two lines of the procedure *intro* two new objects are created, a *Connection* object and a *Recordset* object. The task of *conn* is to establish the connection to the database. To this end the method *Open* must be executed, in which a character string is passed that contains the parameters of the connection. The *Connection* character string can become somewhat long and complex, but in the simplest case two parameters suffice for access to an Access database:

```
Provider=microsoft.jet.oledb.4.0;Data Source=C:\path\name.mdb
```

Provider denotes the driver that is to be used for the access. For each database system (Access, SQL Server, Oracle, etc.) there is a separate driver. *Data Source* specifies the location at which the database file is located, while *intro* presupposes that `Nwind.mdb` is in the same folder as the Excel file.

If the construction of a connection is successful, then in the next step a query can be executed. For this two things are necessary: a *Recordset* object (which actually serves for evaluating the query result) and a character string with the SQL command of the query. Without a minimal knowledge of SQL, ADO programming is unthinkable. In the following example we have the following query:

```
SELECT LastName, FirstName FROM employees
ORDER BY LastName, FirstName
```

This crates a list of all employees of the *Northwind* company, ordered alphabetically. (The names of all employees are stored in the table *employees.*) For the execution of the query the method *Open* serves as well.

The following loop selects from the *Recordset* object all the data records found. Here it is important to understand that the *Recordset* object indeed enables access to all the found data records, but that at any time only one data record (one line, so to speak) is active and can be read. To select the next data record the method *MoveNext* must be executed. If it happens that there are no more records, then the property *EOF* attains the value *True.*

It now remains only to explain how the individual fields of the active record are read: Quite simply, the *rec* variable is followed by an exclamation point and then the name of the field. In the course of the loop the cells A1, A2, A3, etc., will be filled with *employees* names one after the other (Figure 12.18).

```
' ADO.xls, Module1
Sub intro()
  Dim conn As New Connection, rec As New Recordset
  Dim ws As Worksheet
  Dim sql$, i&
  Set ws = ThisWorkbook.Worksheets("intro")
  conn.Open "Provider=microsoft.jet.oledb.4.0;" + _
    "Data Source=" + ThisWorkbook.Path + "\nwind.mdb"
  sql = "SELECT LastName, FirstName " & _
        "FROM employees ORDER BY LastName, FirstName"
  rec.Open sql, conn
  While Not rec.EOF
    i = i + 1
    ws.[A1].Cells(i) = rec!LastName + ", " + rec!FirstName
    rec.MoveNext
  Wend
  rec.Close: conn.Close
End Sub
```

It is a part of good ADO programming practice that ADO objects that are no longer needed be closed with *Close*. With *intro* that would not be absolutely necessary, since in any case the variables *conn* and *rec* exist only so long as the procedure is being executed. Nonetheless, if you get used to the logical use of *Close*, then you make possible a more efficient use of the database and save yourself annoyance and possible access conflicts.

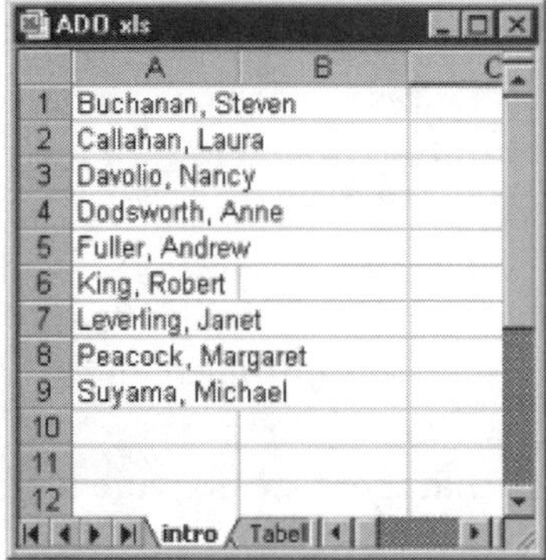

Figure 12.18. The result of our introductory example

ADO Overview

ADO Object Hierarchy

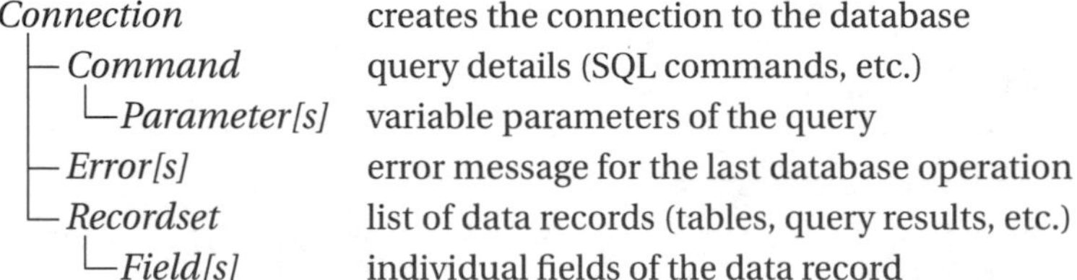

Connection	creates the connection to the database
├ *Command*	query details (SQL commands, etc.)
│ └ *Parameter[s]*	variable parameters of the query
├ *Error[s]*	error message for the last database operation
└ *Recordset*	list of data records (tables, query results, etc.)
└ *Field[s]*	individual fields of the data record

Even though the above hierarchy represents a logical connection among the objects, this hierarchy is not a requirement for the creation of new objects. Figure 12.19 better represents this very flat object hierarchy. For example, you can create a new *Recordset* object without previously explicitly creating a connection to a database.

```
Dim rec As New Recordset
rec.Open "SELECT * FROM table …", "Provider=…"
```

Naturally, you must specify at some point the data source, and internally, in any case, a *Connection* object is generated. In many cases this convenience leads to code that is difficult to maintain and to unnecessarily many connections to the database. But there are exceptions, for example in generating *Recordsets* from a file instead of from a database, where in truth no *Connection* is necessary.

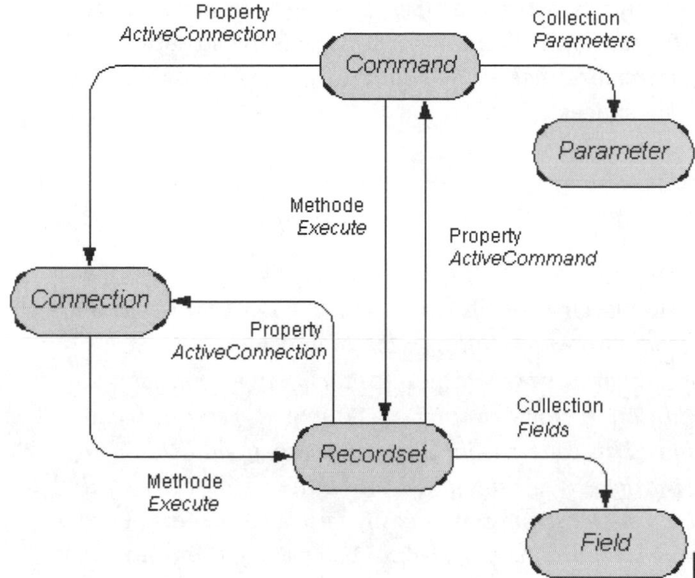

Figure 12.19. Connections between objects

> **TIP** *The indices of all ADO enumerations go from 0 to* Count*-1. However, this does not hold for enumerations of the* DataEnvironment *designer (Office Developer), whose indices, as in Excel, go from 1 to* Count.

Additional (Dynamic) Properties

The objects *Connection, Command, Field, Parameter,* and *Recordset* refer to the enumeration object *Properties,* which for the sake of clarity was not given in the hierarchy above. With *Properties* additional (dynamic) properties can be addressed. Access to individual properties is via the *Property* object. Which dynamic properties exist depends on the driver being used. In the case of simple applications it is not necessary that you be concerned with these properties.

Connections

In principle, it is simple to create a connection to a database: Simply create a new ***Connection*** object and then execute *Open*, passing a character string with the connection information. This character string has the structure *"parameter1=value1;parameter 2=value2;…"*. Both the parameter names and their settings may contain spaces.

```
Dim conn As New Connection
conn.Open "Provider=…"
```

> **TIP** *You can also execute* Open *the first time without additional parameters if you first save the connection information in the* ConnectionString *property. This property contains, after* Open, *a much longer character string, which in addition to* Provider *and* Data Source *also contains a host of other information. (This concerns the default settings of additional parameters that give the default settings for various other parameters.) Individual parts of the character string can be easily selected with* conn.Properties("xy"), *where* xy *is a parameter of the character string (for example,* "DataSource"*).*

ADO limits the establishment of the connection to the time span contained in ***ConnectionTimeout*** (the default is 15 seconds). If the connection does not succeed within this time frame, then an error occurs. In making connections to database servers that are overburdened it makes sense to raise this time limit before executing the *Open* method.

The property ***Mode*** specifies which database operations are allowed (for example, read-only access) and whether other users are allowed to access the database at the same time. The default setting in the case of Jet databases is *adModeShareDenyNone*. In contrast to the information in the ADO documentation, this means that other users may likewise open, read, and edit the database. If you wish to open the database in another mode, you must set the *Mode* property differently before executing the *Open* method. The two most important settings are *adModeShareExclusive* (excludes any further access) and *adModeRead* (read-only access).

ConnectionString *for Access-2000 Databases*

The real problem in establishing a database connection is in correctly setting the *ConnectionString* character string. The construction of the character string depends heavily on the database system. In the case of Access 2000 databases the most important parameters are the following:

Access Databases

Provider	*Microsoft.Jet.OLEDB.4.0*
Data Source	*<file name of the database file>*
User ID	*<user name>* (optional)
Password	*<password>* (optional)

In any case, if you plan on working only with Access databases, you can skip the remainder of this section. The following information is relevant only if you wish to establish a connection to another database system. The examples in this book deal exclusively with Access databases.

ConnectionString *for SQL Server 7 or MSDE (OLEDB)*

If your data are being administered by an SQL Server 7 or the MSDE (Microsoft Data Engine), then you must provide more information:

SQL Server 7 / MSDE

Provide	*SQLOLEDB* or *SQLOLEDB.1*
Data Source	*<network name of the computer on which the SQL server runs>*
Initial Catalog	*<name of the database on the SQL server>*
Integrated Security	*SSPI* (if you use Windows NT for authentication)
User ID	*<user name>* (only if no NT authentication)
Password	*<password>* (only if no NT authentication)
Prompt	*Prompt* or *Complete* (if login dialog is to be displayed)

Here is another remark on the optional *Prompt* parameter. If you use here the setting *Prompt*, then before each attempt to establish a connection a login dialog appears, in which the name and password can be provided. The setting *Complete* means that the dialog appears only when the connection fails. If you do not specify *Prompt*, then an error occurs if the connection fails.

Finally, we offer an example for establishing a connection to the example database *pubs* where the SQL server runs on the computer *mars* and you rely on NT authentication:

```
Dim conn As New Connection
conn.Open "Provider=SQLOLEDB;Data Source=mars;" & _
  "Initial Catalog=pubs;Integrated Security=SSPI"
```

With the following instruction you leave the login to the user:

```
conn.Open "Provider=SQLOLEDB;Data Source=mars;" & _
  "Initial Catalog=pubs;Prompt=Complete"
```

ConnectionString *for ODBC Data Sources*

Not every database possesses a new, ADO-compatible, OLE-DB driver. (OLE-DB is the internal basis on which ADO rests.) In such a case an ODBC driver can be used. (ODBC is the precursor technology to OLE DB: old, but reliable and usable on almost every database system.) The communication between your program and the database proceeds on three fronts: database ⇒ ODBC ⇒ OLE DB ⇒ ADO. The keywords for the *ConnectionString* character string are then once again different:

ODBC

Provider	*MSDASQL.1*
DNS	*<name of an ODBC data source>*
Driver	*<name of the ODBC driver> (e.g., SQL Server)*
Server	*<network name of the computer on which the database server runs>*
Database	*<name of the database on the SQL server>*
Trusted Connection	*yes* (if you use Windows NT for authentication)
UID	*<user name>* (only if no NT authentication)
PWD	*<password>* (only if no NT authentication)

To create again a connection to the SQL server, but this time via its ODBC driver, the following template can be followed:

```
conn.Open "Provider=MSDASQL.1;Driver=SQL Server;" & _
  "Server=mars;Database=pubs"
```

If an ODBC data source was defined (with the ODBC system administration tools), its name can be simply specified with *DNS*=.... All further information is omitted.

*Reading a Connection String from a *.udl File*

A fourth variant consists in saving the connection parameters in a so-called DataLink file with the suffix `*.udl`. Such a file can be created in Explorer: File|New|Microsoft DataLink. A dialog appears in which you can specify all the settings.

DataLink File

File Name	*<file name of the *.udl file>*
Prompt	*same as for an SQL server*

```
conn.Open "File Name=C:\path\name.udl"
```

Recordset

The *Recordset* object handles the management of data records that result from a database query. In comparison to the other ADO objects here there are many properties and methods available. The reason for this complexity lies in the great range of applications for *Recordset* objects. The following list enumerates the most important functions of this object:

- You can read all the records in sequence.
- You can edit, insert, and delete data records.
- You can move through the list of data records (that is, jump to the first, last, next, or previous record or search for a particular record).
- You can search within a list of records and alter the local sort order.
- You can save the list of records in a local file (independent of the database) and load it again later from there.

With a number of properties, the purpose of the object must be specified before the creation of a *Recordset* object. Here there is a simple rule: The less you require of the *Recordset* object, the fewer methods and properties you may use, but the more efficiently the remaining operations can be executed.

```
rec.Open sql, conn [,cursortype [,locktype]]
```

TIP *If you create a list of data records simply with* rec.Open sql, conn, *the* Recordset *object is automatically optimized with respect to optimally efficient performance. This means, however, among other restrictions, that you cannot change any data (read only) and that you can move through the record list only with* MoveNext *(forward only), that you cannot sort data locally, that you cannot use the property* Bookmark. *If you wish to execute more demanding operations, you must make this known in the optional parameters of the* Open *method (see the heading* Recordset Types*).*

SQL Abbreviations

As a rule, to open a *Recordset* object is required that you pass the database query as an SQL command. For this reason we provide, in the subsection after next, an overview of the most important SQL commands. In many cases, however, you can avoid formulating an SQL command:

- If you wish to access all the fields of a table, it suffices to specify in the first parameter of *Open* simply the name of the table. Internally, this is interpreted as *SELECT * FROM table.*

- If you have Access available, you can define queries there. When accessing Access databases you can then simply specify in *Open* the name of the query (just as with the name of a table).

- If you are working with a database server (such as Oracle), you cannot predefine any queries, but you can define so-called *views.* Even the name of a view suffices for *Open*; the internal interpretation is again *SELECT * FROM view.*

Recordset Types

The three properties *CursorLocation, CursorType,* and *LockType* determine the type of the *Recordset.* These properties must be set in advance or sent as optional parameters to *Open.* Once the object has been opened once, no further changes are possible.

The easiest property to understand is certainly ***LockType.*** This property specifies whether data can be altered and how possible conflicts are to be handled (when two or more users wish to alter the same record simultaneously).

LockType *Settings*

adLockReadOnly	data may be read, but not changed (default)
adLockPessimistic	pessimistic conflict control
adLockOptimistic	optimistic conflict control (more efficient)
adLockBatchOptimistic	several data records may be changed simultaneously

There is insufficient space here to go deeply into the fine distinctions between optimistic and pessimistic locking. In most cases *adLockOptimistic* is the better choice. If a conflict arises, an error occurs only at the first attempt actually to save the data (as a rule, during execution of the *Update* method). It is this point in the program that you must therefore protect. The setting *adLockBatchOptimistic* enables so-called batch updating, by which several data records are changed simultaneously. This is efficient, but also complicated and seldom necessary in Excel applications, for which reason we shall omit mention of the details here.

The property ***CursorType*** determines how the list of data records is to be managed internally (that is, by the database system and by ADO). The setting influences the degree of flexibility with which you can move through the record list.

CursorType Settings

adOpenForwardOnly	minimal administrative overhead (that is, very efficient), but fewer supported functions (default)
adOpenDynamic	relatively low administrative overhead, but better navigation options
adOpenKeyset	higher administrative overhead, all functions
adOpenStatic	even greater administrative overhead; comparatively slow access to the first records, fast in subsequent accesses

The setting *adOpenForwardOnly* is suitable when you simply wish to read all the data records in sequence (and possibly edit them as well). It is not possible to reactivate a record that has already been processed, and any type of local processing (search, sort, filter) is excluded.

It is impossible to describe the differences among the other three types without going deeply into the principles of database design. The main issue is at what moment how much data is to be transferred from the database into the *Recordset*, and whether subsequent changes to the data are to be visible to other users in *Recordset*. In case of doubt, *adOpenKeyset* is often a good compromise between efficiency and versatility.

Finally, the property ***CursorLocation*** determines where the management of the record list is to take place: directly in the database (*adUseServer*) or through the ADO library (*adUseClient*). This makes a great deal of difference, particularly in the case of a network system: In one case the computer with the database server is more computationally burdened, while in the other case it is the computer on which your Excel program is running.

If you are working with large quantities of data (record lists with many more than one thousand records), then *adUseServer* is often the better choice: This avoids the necessity of transferring unnecessarily many data records. However, with *adUseServer* a large number of ADO features are unavailable.

With *adUseClient* all data are immediately transferred when the *Recordset* is opened. For large record lists this can involve a large amount of time while the program is blocked. Furthermore, the data must be maintained in local RAM. The advantages are that once the data are present, there are very versatile and efficient forms of further processing.

Here, too, we make a recommendation without being able to illuminate all the background issues: If you wish to move more through the record list than you can with simply *MoveNext*, then *adUseClient* is usually the better choice. ADO is better optimized with respect to this access method.

CursorLocation Settings

adUseServer	data management directly in the database (default)
adUseClient	data management by the ADO library

The situation is made more complicated in that not every combination of these three properties is permissible. For example, with *CursorLocation=adUse-Client* only *CursorType=adOpenStatic* is possible. (If you request a *Recordset* in an impermissible combination, you receive automatically a *Recordset* with other settings. No error message occurs.) Which combinations are allowed depends again on the database driver. With Access databases different combinations are allowed from those in a database run by Oracle.

If you wish to determine which operations are possible with the *Recordset* type that has just been selected, you can use the method ***Supports***. With *Supports(adBookmark)*, for example, you can test whether *Bookmarks* are supported (*True* or *Falses*).

Data Fields

Every data record of a *Recordset* consists of one or more fields. (Data fields correspond to the column names of a table.) As already demonstrated in the introductory example, access to fields is accomplished by writing *rec!feld*. If the field name contains special or blank characters, the name must be placed in square brackets, for example, *rec![article-nr]*.

Here *name* is an abbreviation for *rec.Fields("name").Value*. Internally, the data fields are managed in a ***Fields*** enumeration. Not surprisingly, *Fields(n)* or *Fields("name")* refers to ***Field*** objects. Each of these objects provides information about the field name (*Name*), the data type (*Type*), its size (*DefinedSize* and *ActualSize*), and so on. Here *Value* contains the value of the field for the current data record.

The following example provides field information for all data fields of the *employee* table. The result is shown in Figure 12.20.

```
' ADO.xls, Module1
Sub rec_fields()
  Dim conn As New Connection
  Dim rec As New Recordset, f As Field
  Dim ws As Worksheet, i&
```

```
  Set ws = ThisWorkbook.Worksheets("fields")
  conn.Open "Provider=microsoft.jet.oledb.4.0;" + _
    "Data Source=" + ThisWorkbook.Path + "\nwind.mdb;"
  rec.Open "employees", conn
  For Each f In rec.Fields
    i = i + 1
    ws.[a1].Cells(i) = f.Name
    ws.[b1].Cells(i) = f.Type
    ws.[c1].Cells(i) = TypeName(f.Value)
  Next
  rec.Close: conn.Close
End Sub
```

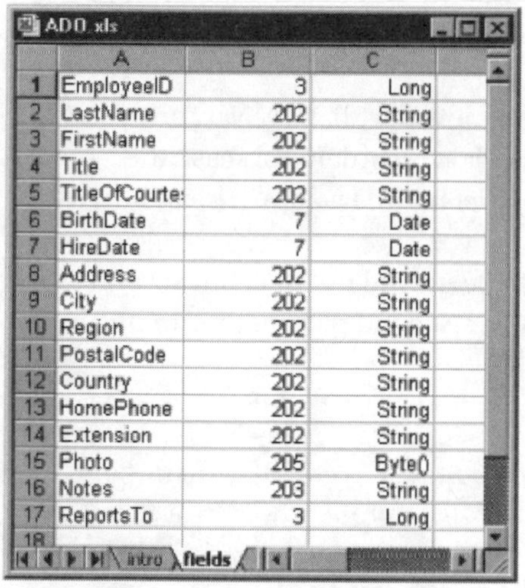

ADO.xls

	A	B	C
1	EmployeeID	3	Long
2	LastName	202	String
3	FirstName	202	String
4	Title	202	String
5	TitleOfCourte	202	String
6	BirthDate	7	Date
7	HireDate	7	Date
8	Address	202	String
9	City	202	String
10	Region	202	String
11	PostalCode	202	String
12	Country	202	String
13	HomePhone	202	String
14	Extension	202	String
15	Photo	205	Byte()
16	Notes	203	String
17	ReportsTo	3	Long

intro | fields

Figure 12.20. The data fields of the employee table

> **TIP** *Please note that most databases can place* NULL *in a field. This means that no data are available. This can lead to problems if you wish to allocate a particular type to the field of a variable, such as* x$ = rec!comment. *You must test with* IsNull(rec!comment) *whether the field contains any data at all.*

Navigation in Data Records

Navigation within the list of data records is accomplished primarily with the help of five methods:

MoveNext	activates the next record
MovePrevious	activates the previous record
MoveFirst	activates the first record
MoveLast	activates the last record
Move n	move forward *n* records (or backward in the case of negative *n*)

Note that you must not proceed on the assumption that the data records appear in any particular order, unless the record list is based on an SQL query with an *ORDER-BY* clause.

The pointer to the current record may be moved with *MoveNext* or *MovePrevious* to a position beyond the first or last record. In this case the property ***EOF*** (*end of file*) or ***BOF*** (*bottom of file*) has the value *True*, and there is no valid record being pointed to.

The method *Move* enables the pointer to be moved not one, but several, positions from the current data record. Optionally, a second parameter can be given that relates *n* to the first or last record.

> **CAUTION** *Let us underscore the following point:* EOF *and* BOF *do not indicate the last valid data record. When one of these properties is* True, *then the region of valid records has been exceeded. At this point an invalid data record is indicated, which cannot be further processed.*

Positional Information

The property ***AbsolutePosition*** determines which of the ***RecordCount*** records is currently active (the first, second, etc.). *AbsolutePosition* can also contain the value *adPosUnknown (-1)*, *adPosBOF (-2)*, or *adPosEOF (-3)*. This allocation of a value to *AbsolutePosition* represents a further possibility, namely, to select the currently active record.

Sometimes one wishes to return to the current record at a later time. To accomplish this, save the contents of the ***Bookmark*** property in a *Variant* variable. (This variable serves, then, as a bookmark.) To return, allocate the saved value again to the *Bookmark* property.

Searching and Locally Sorting Data Records

With the method ***Find*** you can find, beginning with the current record, the next data record that satisfies a particular criterion. All parameters other than the first are optional. If no suitable record is found, the *Recordset* object points to an invalid record (*EOF=True* for forward search, *BOF=True* for backward search).

```
rec.Find criterion, offset, direction
```

As search criterion you provide a character string with the column name and comparison operation, such as *"UnitPrice > 10"*. In the case of text comparison with the operator *Like*, the underscore character can serve as a wildcard for a text character, the asterisk for several characters, say *"Name Like 'M*'"*. The asterisk can be used only at the end of the search pattern, or at the beginning and the end. More complex expressions such as *Like 'a*b'* are not allowed.

offset specifies at which record the search is to begin. In the default setting the search is begun at the current record. To begin with the first record, execute the method *MoveFirst* before *Find*.

If the current record satisfies the search criterion, then it will be returned. In order to find the next satisfactory record, you must execute either *MoveNext* or *Find* with *offset:=1*. With *direction* you can specify the search direction (*adSearchForward* / *-Backward*).

Editing Existing Records

In order for data records to be edited, deleted, or inserted, the *Recordset* object must be opened with a suitable *LockType* setting.

To edit an existing data record, you need to change only one of the fields (thus *rec!fieldname = newvalue*). In contrast to the DAO library there is no longer an *Edit* method to introduce the editing process.

Changes made are saved as soon as the method ***Update*** is explicitly executed. However, saving is automatic if another data record is activated (such as with a *Move* method).

Unsaved changes can be undone with ***CancelUpdate***. In this case all fields of the current record reassume their original values. (These values can also be determined without *CancelUpdate*, by evaluating the *Field* property ***OriginalValue***, that is, by *rec!fieldname.OriginalValue*.)

Adding a Data Record

If you wish to generate a new data record, execute ***AddNew***. (This will also save any unsaved changes.) You will have created a new, empty, data record, which is now the active record. Furthermore, the record fields that are managed automatically by the database (usually ID fields, in which the next number in a running sequence is inserted) are automatically initialized. All other operations follow the same course as with editing a data record: You must set the properties and save changes with *Update.*

Deleting a Record

It is much simpler to delete a record. Simply execute the method ***Delete.***

Possible Errors

In all these three operations there is a rather large chance that an error will occur. The most probable causes are the following:

- An edited/new record cannot be saved because certain data field have impermissible values. Depending on how the table has been defined, certain fields may not be empty or may not contain the value *Null* or "".
- An altered record cannot be saved because a second user is editing the same record or perhaps has already edited it.
- A record cannot be deleted or changed because the conditions of referential integrity would be violated. (That is, the relation to a record in another table would be destroyed. In such cases the dependent records of the other table must first be deleted.)
- The record cannot be changed because you do not have sufficient privileges. (Often, databases are so strongly secured that except for the administrator, no one may directly change a table. Changes must then be carried out via the specific procedures provided.)

Note that these errors can occur at any point of your program at which the current data record can be altered. Thus very thorough error handling is required.

SQL Commands (*Command*)

The ***Command*** object has as its purpose the execution of SQL commands. You are perhaps wondering how this differs from *Recordset,* with which an SQL command can also be executed. The *Command* object must be used if the query (Access) or an SQL procedure (various database servers) is to be executed with parameters.

A command executed with *Command* can also return as result a list of data records, but that need not be the case. For example, you can execute a *DELETE* command that deletes a particular data record. In this case you do not obtain an immediate result (at most an error message if the deletion is impossible).

We cannot go into all of the many particularities of the *Command* object here, such as asynchronous queries, the use of a wide variety of types of parameters, the multiplicity of syntax variants for executing commands. Instead, the following example demonstrates a possible application, whereby in *command_parameters* we shall pose a new query with a parameter:

```
SELECT companyname FROM customers WHERE country = ?
```

This query returns a list of all customers in a particular country. Before the query can be executed, the *Command* object must be given a country name by means of the *Parameters* enumeration, such as *"germany"*, for example. To execute the command, *Open* will be used again for the *Recordset* object. But as the first parameter an SQL command will not be given, but rather the *Command* object.

This example also demonstrates the application of the method ***CopyFromRecordset***. This method is defined for the Excel *Range* object and enables it to transfer most efficiently the entire contents of a *Recordset* into a worksheet. The process begins with the cell that is specified as object by *CopyFromRecordset*. (The *While–Wend* loop used in the other examples is strictly for didactic purposes. It is supposed to show how data records are read.)

```
Sub command_parameters()
  Dim conn As New Connection
  Dim rec As New Recordset
  Dim comm As New Command
  Dim ws As Worksheet
  Dim countryname$
  Set ws = ThisWorkbook.Worksheets("command")
  conn.Open "Provider=microsoft.jet.oledb.4.0;" + _
    "Data Source=" + ThisWorkbook.Path + "\nwind.mdb;"
  Set comm.ActiveConnection = conn
  comm.CommandText = _
    "SELECT companyname FROM customers WHERE country = ?"
  countryname = InputBox("Please input the name of a country " & _
    "(for example, 'germany').")
  comm.Parameters(0) = countryname
  rec.Open comm
  ws.[a1].CopyFromRecordset rec
  rec.Close: conn.Close
End Sub
```

SQL Basics

In the previous examples a bit of SQL code has appeared here and there, but almost always of the most elementary kind. Although this section can discuss only the first five percent of the fine art of SQL, it should at least communicate the fact that SQL is a rather powerful language. Perhaps you will acquire an appetite for more.

> **POINTER** *In this book SQL commands are written with uppercase letters to distinguish them from Visual Basic keywords. SQL commands are not case sensitive. All examples here refer to the* Northwind *database.*

SQL Queries

SELECT selects the fields from the table named with *FROM*. The field names are separated by commas. If the names of fields contains special or blank characters, you must place them in square brackets. If the same field names are used in several tables, then the table name must be prefixed to the field name, for example, *table.name*. The asterisk holds for all fields in the table.

FROM specifies the tables from which the fields previously named with *SELECT* are to be taken.

INNER JOIN joins two tables through a common field (for example, an ID number). *INNER JOIN* is of central importance in relational databases when data are to be combined from several tables.

WHERE specifies the conditions that the fields must satisfy. If *WHERE* is not used, then the resulting *Recordset* contains all the data records of the table.

GROUP BY *field* combines all the resulting rows for which the given data field has the same value. For the other fields in the query so-called aggregate functions must be applied, such as *SUM(field)*, to calculate the sum.

ORDER BY specifies the fields according to which the list resulting from the previous instructions is to be ordered. With the suffixed command *ASC* or *DESC* one specifies whether the sort order is to be ascending or descending (default is ascending).

> **TIP** *If you encounter difficulties in constructing an SQL query, try to formulate it in Access or MS Query. Both of these programs allow convenient interactive posing of queries; and both programs then reveal to you the associated SQL code. If you are processing databases in Access format, you can save your queries directly in the database. In VBA code you can use such predefined queries immediately, without worrying about the underlying SQL code.*

In the following examples, SQL instructions are divided among several lines merely to improve the visual presentation. In a program the SQL instruction must be within a single character string.

SELECT Example 1

We shall create a list of all products that cost more than 50 pricing units. The list is sorted according to product name.

```
SELECT ProductName, UnitPrice
FROM Products
WHERE UnitPrice > 50
ORDER BY ProductName
```

```
Product Name                Unit Price
Carnarvon Tigers            62.50
Côte de Blaye               263.50
Manjimup Dried Apples       53.00
Mishi Kobe Niku             97.00
...
```

SELECT Example 2

Our second example is a variant of the first. The only difference is that in addition to the product name, its category is shown. To be sure, this is more easily said than done: Since the category name is defined in another table, a linkage between the two tables must be established with *INNER JOIN*. Note that the field *CategoryID* appears in both tables *Categories* and *Products*. For this reason, with *INNER JOIN* the fields must be prefixed by the table name.

```
SELECT ProductName, CategoryName, UnitPrice
FROM Categories
INNER JOIN Products ON Categories.CategoryID = Products.CategoryID
WHERE UnitPrice>50
ORDER BY ProductName
```

```
Product Name                Category Name        Unit Price
Carnarvon Tigers            Seafood              62.50
Côte de Blaye               Beverages            263.50
Manjimup Dried Apples       Produce              53.00
Mishi Kobe Niku             Meat/Poultry         97.00
...
```

SELECT Example 3

In *SELECT* queries so-called aggregate functions can be employed. The following example returns the number of products and their average price. The keyword *AS* is used to name the result field.

```
SELECT COUNT(*) AS nrOfProducts, AVG(unitprice) AS avgPrice
FROM products
```

```
nrOfProducts      avgPrice
77                28.87
```

SELECT Example 4

Our last example proves that Access can calculate. The query returns a list with the value of every order. To this end, for each row of the table *Order Details* the product of unit price, quantity, and discount is computed. The resulting list is broken into groups with common order IDs. For each group the sum of the order values of the individual items is calculated.

```
SELECT OrderID, SUM(UnitPrice * Quantity * (1-Discount)) AS Sales
FROM [Order Details]
GROUP BY OrderID
```

```
Order ID          Sales
10248             440
10249             1863.4
10250             1552.59998965263
10251             654.059999750555
...
```

Editing Data

The previous examples of queries had the task of creating an ordered list according to certain criteria, that is, to read data. You can also use SQL to edit data, and indeed, in many cases this is much more efficient than line by line processing in program code. This holds particularly for network applications: The amount of data required to send a SQL command over a network is so small that it won't affect the performance at all. On the other hand, if you first read each record over the network and then must edit and write it, much time will be lost in data transfer. In Access such commands are called action commands.

DELETE deletes the records selected with *WHERE.*

UPDATE updates individual data fields with *SET,* to the extent that they satisfy conditions named in *WHERE.* (For example, you could raise all prices by ten percent.)

INSERT INTO inserts data records into an existing table.

SELECT INTO creates a new table.

Syntax Summary

Connection Properties and Methods

ConnectionString	character string with connection data (*Data Source, Provider, ...*)
ConnectionTimeout	maximal time to establish connection (in seconds)
CursorLocation	create *Recordset*s with client or server cursor
Mode	access privileges (read only, write, sharing, etc.)
Close	terminate connection
Execute	execute database query or command
Open	establish connection

Recordset Properties

ActiveConnection	reference to *Connection* object
BOF	the invalid record before the first record is active
Bookmark	identification of the current data record
CursorLocation	client or server cursor
CursorType	cursor type (e.g., *adOpenForwardOnly, adOpenStatic*)
EditMode	edit mode (e.g., *adEditNone, adEditAdd*)
EOF	the invalid record after the last record is active
Fields	reference to the listing of the data record fields
Filter	specifies which data records are visible
LockType	locking mechanism (e.g., *adReadOnly, adLockOptimistic*)
RecordCount	number of all data records belonging to the object
Sort	contains the column name (text) for local sorting (client)
State	state of the entire *Recordset* object (e.g., *adStateOpen*)
!Name	shorthand for *Fields("name")*

Recordset Methods

CancelUpdate	undo changes in the current record (do not save)
Close	close *Recordset*
Find	find record satisfying a particular criterion
GetRows	copy contents of entire *Recordsets* into two-dimensional field
Move n	move record cursor by *n* positions
MoveFirst	activate first record
MoveLast	activate last record
MoveNext	activate next record
MovePrevious	activate previous record
Open	open *Recordset* (execute query, load from file, etc.)
Save	save *Recordset* in a file
Supports	test whether the *Recordset* supports specific functions
Update	save changes in current record
rng.CopyFromRecordset	copy *Recordset* in Excel table(*rng* is a *Range* object)

Field Properties

ActualSize	actual memory usage in bytes
Attributes	special attributes (e.g., *adFldUpdatable*)
DefinedSize	maximal size (for character string of variable length)
Name	name of the data field
NumericScale	number of decimal places (for fixed-point numbers)
OriginalValue	original value (only for batch updating)
Precision	number of digits (for fixed-point numbers)
Type	data type
Value	value

Command Properties and Methods

ActiveConnection	refers to the associated *Connection* object
CommandText	code of the command/query (normally SQL)
CommandTimeout	maximal time for query (in seconds)
CommandType	command type (e.g., *adCmdText, adCmdTable*)
Parameters	refers to *Parameter* object
State	state of asynchronous query (e.g., *adStateExecuting, -Closed*)
!Name	shorthand for *Parameters("name")*
Execute	execute command/query

Elementary SQL Commands

SELECT field1, field2	which fields
FROM table1, table2	from which tables
WHERE condition	under what conditions
GROUP BY field	how to group
ORDER BY field	how to sort
DELETE ...	command for deleting records
UPDATE ...	command for updating several records
INSERT INTO ...	command for inserting records into a table
SELECT INTO ...	command for creating a new table

Example: Evaluating a Questionnaire

Overview

The idea of the following example is fairly simple: A survey is to be conducted. Instead of the participants being given a printed form to fill out whose results later have to be tabulated by hand, the questionnaire is to be formulated in the form of an Excel worksheet. Thus various controls (listboxes, check boxes) can be used to make input as simple as possible; see the example questionnaire `survey.xls` in Figure 12.21.

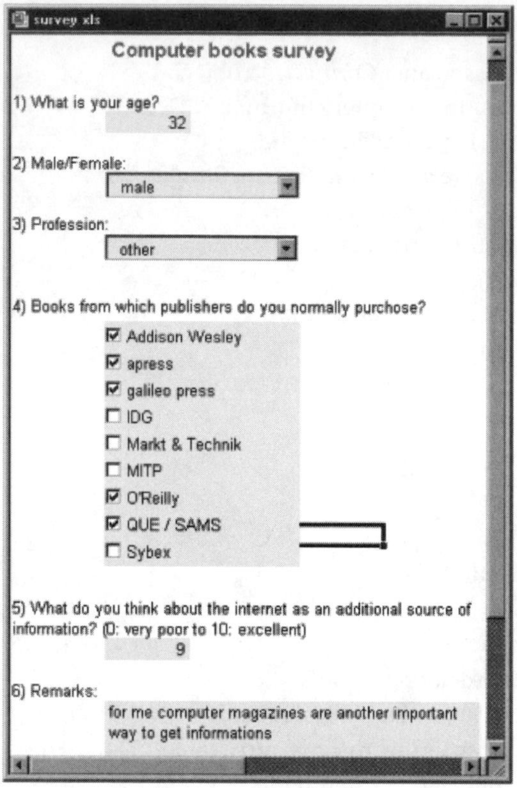

Figure 12.21. Example questionnaire

Thus instead of receiving a carton of fill-out questionnaires, you will have a folder full of Excel files. At this point the database aspect of the example kicks in. The file `analyzedata.xls` offers a function that transfers from all the Excel files in a given folder all the responses into an Access database. In a second step you can immediately evaluate all available responses; see Figure 12.22.

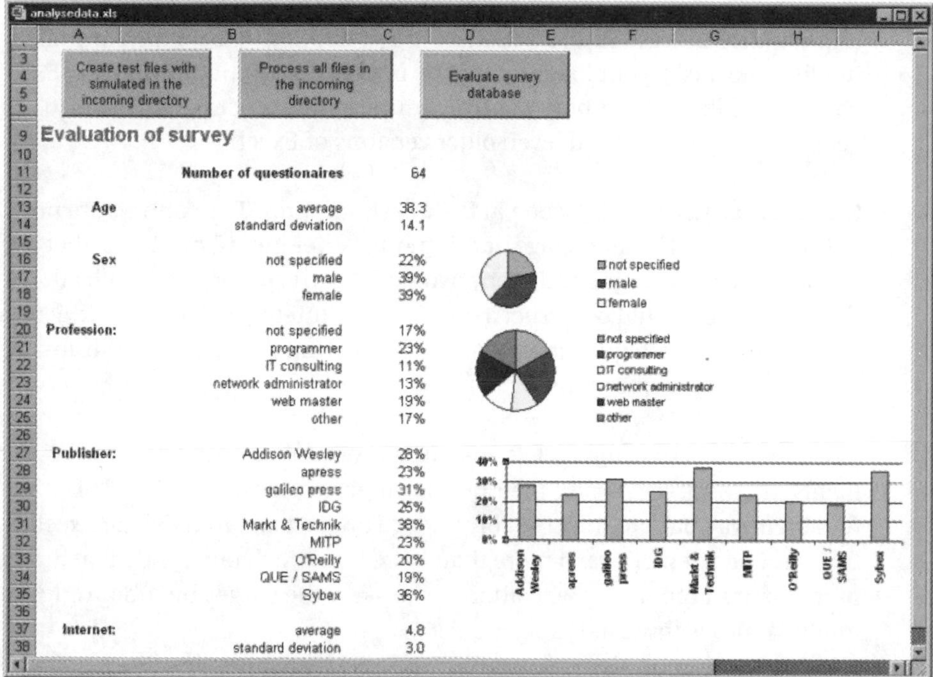

Figure 12.22. Evaluation of the questionnaires

Files and Directories

The entire project can be found in the sample files in the directory `survey`. Filled-out surveys must be placed in the directory `incoming`. After they have been read in, the files are reduced (unnecessary worksheets are deleted) and moved into the directory `archive`.

The questionnaire is located in the file `survey.xls`, a supplementary template of this questionnaire in `survey_template.xls`. This file is used to generate test files with random data. (Thus you do not have to fill out ten questionnaires in order to try out the program.)

The file `analyzedata.xls` is for evaluating the questionnaires. This file contains all the VBA code of the example. The survey data are stored in the Access database `dbsurvey.mdb`.

Alternatives, Variants, Improvements

As with most problems, here there is not a single solution, but many. To prevent my setting you, dear reader, loose with this one example without your considering some alternatives, the following list gives some suggestions as to alternatives, variants, and possible improvements.

- The example presented here uses MS Forms controls in the questionnaire. This requires at least Excel 9. If you would prefer to use the older controls (toolbar "Forms"), your Excel file will be backward compatible to Excel 5. If you would like to do without controls entirely, then you might be able to achieve compatibility with even older versions of Excel.

- Our example uses no VBA code in the questionnaire. (The controls are not linked to code.) The advantage of this modus operandi is, of course, that the macro virus warning is thereby avoided. On the other hand, with additional code you could construct a much more "intelligent" form, in which, for example, certain questions could be posed that depended on the answers to previous questions.

- The question of data flow is left open in this example. How do the participants in the survey receive their questionnaires? How do the Excel files find their way back to the host computer? How is it ensured that an Excel file is not accidentally read more than once into the database? Or that a participant in the survey who attempts to skew the survey by submitting multiple files is thwarted?

  Possible solutions depend greatly on the particular application. If you are collecting data on hospital patients, for example, you could place the questionnaire on a few computers. If you can assume that survey participants have internet access, then e-mail could become your medium of communication. Theoretically, your Excel files could be provided with a serial number, to avoid duplicates, but that would jeopardize the anonymity of the participants.

- If not the participant but a third person transmits the answers (as in a telephone survey), there is the possibility of linking the input form directly to the database (say, with Access). Excel files have the advantage that they are independent of the database and place few demands on the computer on which the data are recorded.

- Finally, we should mention the internet. This is, of course, the only completely up-to-date way of carrying out such surveys. From a technical standpoint it is really no problem, but in practice it may not be so simple.

  You need access to a web server, as well as someone to create a dynamic web page for you and manage the associated database. Particularly for smaller projects—such as a student survey—the Excel variant is simpler and less bureaucratic. Also, from the standpoint of data security (with medical or psychological data) the Excel variant is rather attractive.

REMARKS *If the anonymity of the data is a decisive criterion, then the old-fashioned paper questionnaire is (alas) still the most secure variant. Office 97 made headlines in the computer press because all documents created in it had to be given new ID numbers. These numbers make it possible (at least within a network) to identify the computer on which the document was created. Microsoft spoke of an error, provided an update, and promised that this would not happen with Office 2000, but one can no longer speak of confidence with respect to Microsoft. Perhaps Microsoft has found a better solution, but as of December 1999 it has not appeared.*

Constructing the Questionnaire

In order not to make our example overly bloated, the questionnaire has been made relatively simple. There are only six questions. The answer to three of the questions can be input directly into an Excel cell, which is the easiest solution both in setting up the questionnaire and the later evaluation of the results.

Internal Structure

The file `survey.xls` consists of three worksheets (Figure 12.23), of which normally only the first is visible. The sheet "listdata" contains the entries of the two listboxes, "results" contains a summary of the result cells.

Here are a few explanatory remarks: In the two listboxes *ListFillRange* was set in such a way that the data can be read from "listdata" (for the first listbox we have *ListFillRange="listdata:A1:A3"*). With *BoundColumn=0* we have achieved that the result of the selection is a number (0 for the first entry, etc.). *LinkedCell* refers to a result cell in "results," so that there the number of the active list entry is displayed. Finally, the setting *fmStyleDropDownList (2)* prevents the participant from inserting text into the listbox. The check boxes for input of the preferred computer book publisher are also linked to the corresponding cells in "results" via *LinkedCell*. In questions 1, 5, and 6 simple formulas have been placed in "results" (for example, *=survey!$B$5* for the age).

The main reason for the separation between the questionnaire table "survey" and the result table "results" is that you can edit the questionnaire easily (for example, by inserting a new question) without mixing up the order of result cells in "results." All of the code for evaluating the questionnaire is connected to "results" and depends on the structure of this table being constant. (Any change here would involve difficult changes in the program code.)

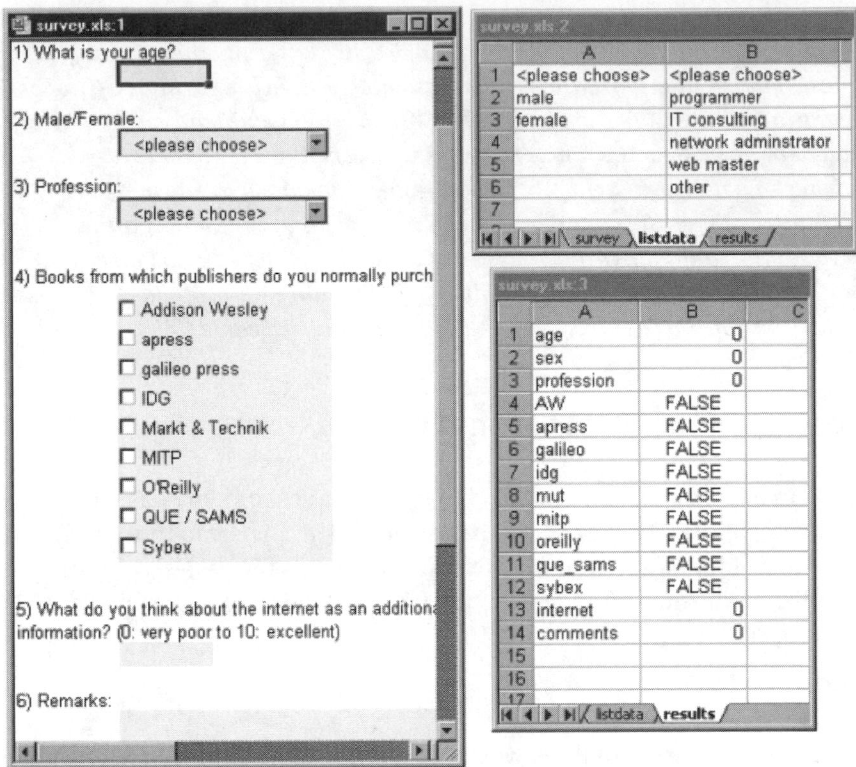

Figure 12.23. The internal structure of survey.xls

Protection, Validation Control

Both the worksheet survey and the Excel file as a whole are protected. Previously, the sheets "listdata" and "results" were invisible (FORMAT|SHEET). Thus the user can make changes only in particular cells or by means of particular controls. (The protection in this example is not backed up with a password; in practice, of course, this would be recommended.)

In question 5 the input cell B29 is protected by DATA|VALIDATION. In this cell only whole numbers between 0 and 10 can be entered. An attempt to input any other value leads to an error message.

Option Fields and Selection Fields in Questionnaires

For the selection of a profession the example file `survey.xls` uses a combo box (1 of *n*), and for the selection of a publisher, a whole sequence of check boxes (*m* of *n*). There are no option fields. For the sake of completeness, Figure 12.24 shows some further design possibilities.

First we discuss the selection of *m* of *n* options. Instead of inserting a sequence of checkboxes into the questionnaire and then labeling them and later evaluating them, you can use a normal listbox. With *ListFillRange* you associate to the listbox a range of cells with the label of the option. Then you set *fmListStyleOption (1)* and *MultiSelect=fmMultiSelectMulti (1)*. The listbox no longer looks like a listbox, but like a sequence of check boxes. The advantage is that both the design and evaluation by program code are simpler. The drawback is that it is not possible to represent the result of the selection in a single associated cell (*LinkedCell*).

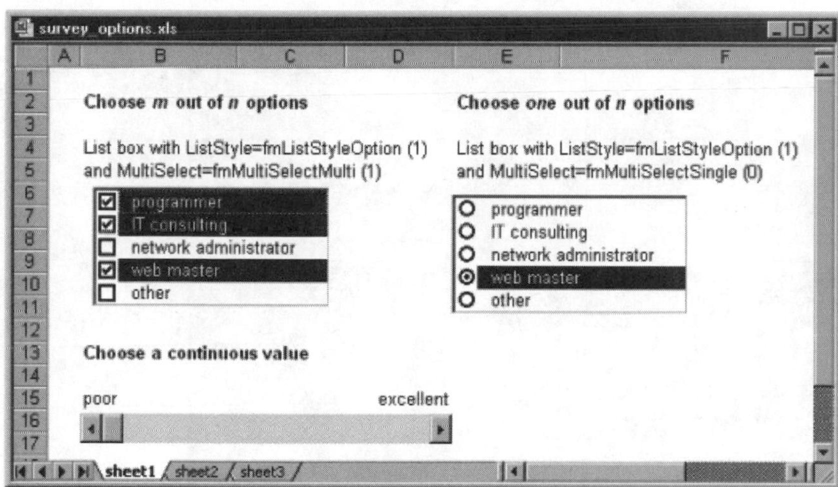

Figure 12.24. Further design possibilities for questionnaires

To select *one* of the *n* options you can use the same procedure, though now with *MultiSelect=fmMultiSelectSingle (0)*. Since Excel is incapable of managing several independent groups of option fields in one worksheet, this is the only way of managing several independent option groups in a single worksheet. It is a matter of taste as to whether this variant or a combo box as in `survey.xls` is seen to be more elegant or practical, since internally they are the same thing. The variant presented here takes more space (which may be a drawback with longer questionnaires) but is also easier to read.

Finally, Figure 12.24 shows the insertion of a scroll bar for selecting a value. In `survey.xls` the scroll bar could be used, for example, for evaluating the internet as a source of information (0 for very poor, 10 for very good). The decisive drawback of scroll bars is that you face a dilemma if the control is left in the initial position. Did the participant in the survey skip this question, or does the result correspond to the participant's opinion?

Construction of the Database

The function of the database dbsurvey.mdb is to save the results of the survey. The database consists of a single table, *dbsurveydata*, and there are no relations. The database was created with Access 2000. Figure 12.25 shows the table under construction, while Figure 12.26 shows some saved data records.

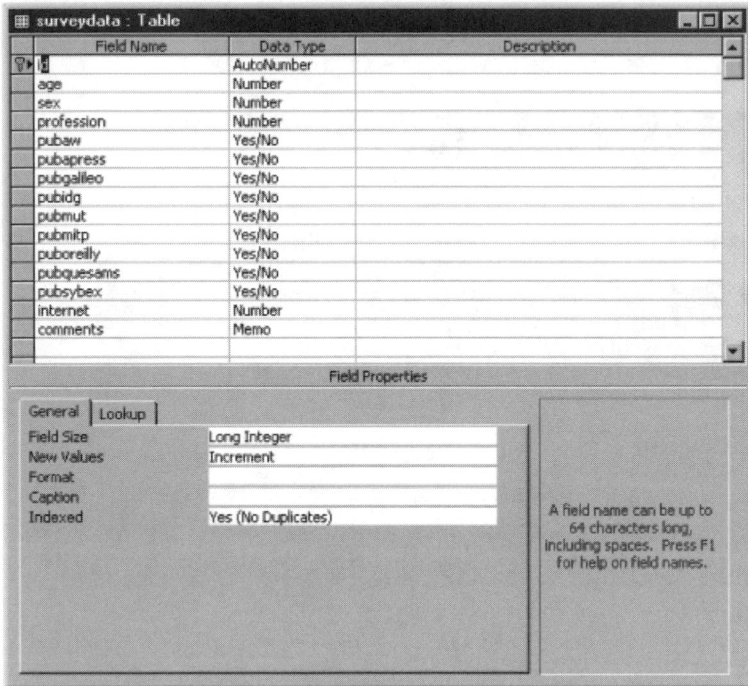

Figure 12.25. The table surveydata under construction

In addition to the database fields that arise directly from the questionnaire, the table also contains an *id* field of type *Increment*. This field has the task of identifying the data records and simplifying the internal management of the data. (It is part of the "good housekeeping" of database creation that every table be outfitted with such an *id* field and then be defined as primary index. Such *id* fields are of particular importance when several tables are linked by relations.)

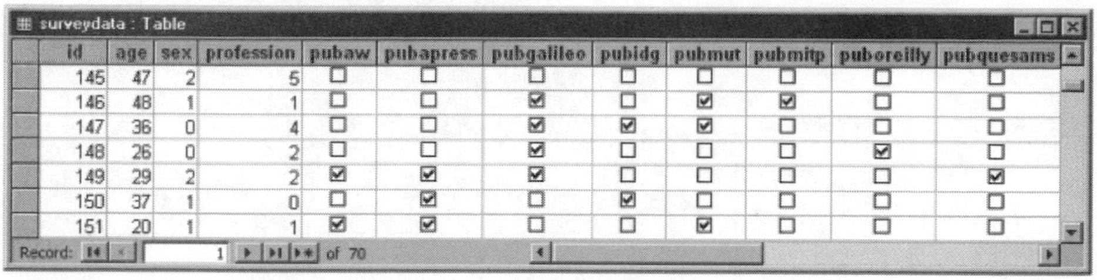

surveydata : Table

id	age	sex	profession	pubaw	pubapress	pubgalileo	pubidg	pubmut	pubmitp	puboreilly	pubquesams
145	47	2	5	☐	☐	☐	☐	☐	☐	☐	☐
146	48	1	1	☐	☐	☑	☐	☑	☑	☐	☐
147	36	0	4	☐	☐	☑	☑	☑	☐	☐	☐
148	26	0	2	☐	☐	☑	☐	☐	☐	☑	☐
149	29	2	2	☑	☑	☑	☐	☐	☐	☐	☑
150	37	1	0	☐	☑	☐	☑	☐	☐	☐	☐
151	20	1	1	☑	☑	☐	☐	☑	☐	☐	☐

Record: 1 of 70

Figure 12.26. Some data records from the table surveydata

Program Code

Reading the Questionnaires into the Database

First, *ProcessIncomingFolder* opens a connection to the database `dbsurvey.mdb` and then a *Recordset* object to the table *surveydata*. Instead of an actual SQL command in the *Open* method, only the name of the table is given, which is shorthand, allowed in ADO, for *SELECT * FROM table*.

Then a loop is run over all `*.xls` files. Each file is processed separately in the procedure *ProcessSurveyFile* (see below). During the process many Excel files are opened, edited, and then saved. To make this happen as quickly as possible, several measures are taken for speed optimization (no screen updating, for example; see Chapter 5.10). To make the waiting time bearable (about one second per file on a Pentium II 400), the status bar displays the number of files that have been processed so far.

```
' survey\analyzedata.xls, Module1
Sub ProcessIncomingFolder()
  Dim fil As File, fld As Folder
  Dim conn As New Connection
  Dim rec As New Recordset
  Dim nrOfFiles&, i&
  On Error GoTo error_processincoming
  ' optimize speed
  Application.Calculation = xlCalculationManual
  Application.ScreenUpdating = False
  Application.DisplayStatusBar = True
  ' connection to dbsurvey.mdb
  Set conn = OpenSurveyDatabase
  If conn Is Nothing Then Exit Sub
  ' short form for "SELECT * FROM surveydata"
  rec.Open "surveydata", conn, adOpenKeyset, adLockOptimistic
  Set fld = fso.GetFolder(ThisWorkbook.Path + "\incoming")
```

```
  nrOfFiles = fld.Files.Count
  For Each fil In fld.Files
    i = i + 1
    Application.StatusBar = "process file " & fil.Name & _
      " (" & i & " from " & nrOfFiles & ")"
    If LCase(Right(fil.Name, 4)) = ".xls" Then
      ProcessSurveyFile fil, rec
    End If
  Next
  rec.Close
  conn.Close
error_processincoming:
  Application.Calculation = xlCalculationAutomatic
  Application.DisplayAlerts = True
  Application.ScreenUpdating = True
  Application.StatusBar = False
  If Err  0 Then
    MsgBox Error + vbCrLf + _
      "The procedure ProcessIncomingFolder will be stopped."
  End If
End Sub
```

Transferring Data to the Database

ProcessSurveyFile is invoked for each file in the `incoming` folder. The file is opened, and protection is removed for the entire file. Then the result cells in "results" are replaced by their copies. This is necessary so that the source data can be deleted, to make the archived files as small as possible.

> **CAUTION** *The initial plan was simply to delete the sheets "survey" and "listdata." But it turned out that* wb.Worksheets("survey").Delete *leaves the file in a damaged state. The file can be saved, but at the next attempt to open it, Excel crashes. For this reason this sheet is not deleted in its entirety, but only its contents (*Cells.Clear *for the cells,* Shapes(...).Delete *for the controls).*

The insertion of a new data record into the *surveydata* table of the database is simply accomplished with *AddNew*. Then the result cells of the worksheet *results* are read and saved in various fields of the data record. Finally, the method *Update* saves the new record.

```
Sub ProcessSurveyFile(fil As Scripting.File, rec As Recordset)
  Dim newfilename$
  Dim wb As Workbook, ws As Worksheet
  Dim shp As Shape
  ' open file
  Set wb = Workbooks.Open(fil.Path)
  ' sheet "results": replace formula by their results
  ' sheets "survey" and "listdata": delete
  wb.Unprotect
  Set ws = wb.Worksheets("results")
  ws.[a1].CurrentRegion.Copy
  ws.[a1].CurrentRegion.PasteSpecial xlPasteValues
  ws.Visible = xlSheetVisible
  Application.CutCopyMode = False
  With wb.Worksheets("survey")
    .Unprotect
    .Cells.Clear
    For Each shp In .Shapes
      shp.Delete
    Next
  End With
  Application.DisplayAlerts = False  'don't show alerts
  '  wb.Worksheets("survey").Delete  'caution: would cause corrupt file
  wb.Worksheets("listdata").Delete
  Application.DisplayAlerts = True
  ' copy data from survey to database
  With rec
    .AddNew
    !age = ws.[b1]
    !sex = ws.[b2]
    !profession = ws.[b3]
    !pubaw = -CInt(ws.[b4])  'False->0, True->1
    !pubapress = -CInt(ws.[b5])
    !pubgalileo = -CInt(ws.[b6])
    !pubidg = -CInt(ws.[b7])
    !pubmut = -CInt(ws.[b8])
    !pubmitp = -CInt(ws.[b9])
    !puboreilly = -CInt(ws.[b10])
    !pubquesams = -CInt(ws.[b11])
    !pubsybex = -CInt(ws.[b12])
    !internet = ws.[b13]
    If ws.[b14]  0 And ws.[b14]  "" Then
      !Comments = [b14]
    End If
```

```
    .Update
  End With
  ' close file and move it into archive directory
  wb.Save
  ' Stop
  wb.Close
  ' new filename:
  '  directory incoming instead of archive
  '  yyyymmdd-hhmmss-oldname.xls instead of oldname.xls
  newfilename = Replace(fil.Path, _
    "incoming", "archive", compare:=vbTextCompare)
  newfilename = Replace(newfilename, _
    fil.Name, Format(Now, "yyyymmdd-hhmmss-") + fil.Name)
  fso.MoveFile fil, newfilename
End Sub
```

It is worth mentioning the use of the function *Cint* in the evaluation of the "publishers" check box (*True/False*). The function *Cint* transforms the Boolean values into 0 (*False*) and –1 (*True*). The minus sign in front of *Cint* has the effect of saving the truth values in the database as 0 and 1.

The new file name is formed from the previous name in two steps: First, the folder `incoming` is replaced by `archive`. Here a case-insensitive text comparison is carried out in *Replace* (*Compare:=vbTextCompare*). In the second step the former name (that is, *fil.Name*) is replaced by a new name, to which the current date and time are prefixed. This serves to resolve conflicts between like-named files.

The Auxiliary Function OpenSurveyDatabase

The first few lines for opening the connection to the database were taken from *ProcessIncomingFolder* and *CreateDummyFilesInIncoming*, primarily to avoid redundancy in error testing. Otherwise, these lines present few surprises.

```
' open connection to database
Function OpenSurveyDatabase() As Connection
  Dim conn As Connection
  On Error Resume Next
  Set conn = New Connection
  conn.Open "provider=microsoft.jet.oledb.4.0;" + _
    "data source=" + ThisWorkbook.Path + "\dbsurvey.mdb;"
  If Err  0 Then
    MsgBox "Could not connect to database: " & _
      Error & vbCrLf & "The procedure will be stopped."
    Exit Function
```

```
    End If
    Set OpenSurveyDatabase = conn
End Function
```

Analyzing the Survey Database

From the point of view of database programming, the most interesting procedure is certainly *AnalyzeDatabase*. In it queries are carried out in the database `dbsurvey.mdb` by means of various SQL commands, and the results then transferred into the cells of the worksheet "surveyresults." The procedure assumes that this worksheet looks like the one depicted in Figure 12.22, thus that the result cells are sensibly formatted (for example, as percentages), the charts refer to the appropriate data, and so on. This can all be accomplished interactively during program development and requires no VBA code.

All the database queries are executed with the same *Recordset* variable, which is opened with a variety of SQL commands, and after reading the result(s) is again closed. The first two commands are easily understood: *SELECT COUNT(id)* determines the number of data records, while *AVG(age)* and *STDEV(age)* calculate the mean and standard deviation of the age. Both commands return a list of records with only one record in it. For testing commands of this sort it is useful to have access to Access (see Figure 12.27).

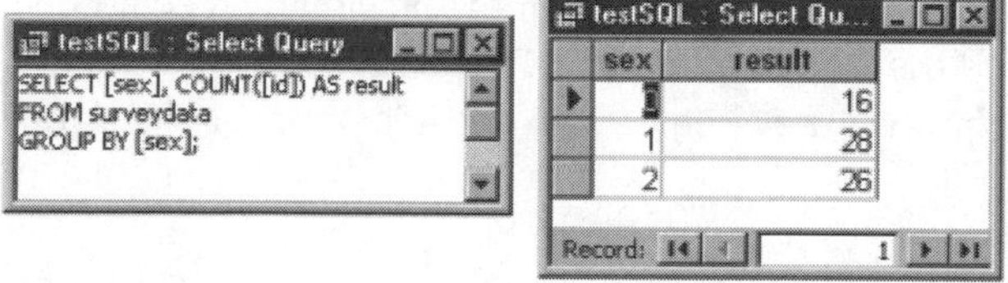

Figure 12.27. Testing an SQL query in Access

> **TIP** *Please note that* STDEV *does not conform to the SQL standard, but belongs to an extension of the SQL syntax for Access. This aggregate function, therefore, in contrast to* AVG, *is not available on all database systems.*

```
Sub AnalyzeDatabase()
  Dim conn As Connection
  Dim rec As New Recordset
  Dim ws As Worksheet
  Dim publ As Variant
  Dim p, i&
  Set ws = ThisWorkbook.Worksheets("surveyresults")
  ' connection to table surveydata of database dbsurvey.mdb
  Set conn = OpenSurveyDatabase
  If conn Is Nothing Then Exit Sub
  ' nr. of questionnaires
  rec.Open "SELECT COUNT(id) AS result FROM surveydata", conn
  ws.[c11] = rec!result
  rec.Close
  ' average age, standard deviation
  rec.Open "SELECT AVG(age) AS result1, STDEV(age) AS result2 " & _
    "FROM surveydata", conn
  ws.[c13] = rec!result1
  ws.[c14] = rec!result2
  rec.Close
```

Of greater interest is the evaluation of the column *sex* in the database (which provides this book with its "R" rating). Here three values are permissible: 0 (no input), 1 (male), and 2 (female). The query is to determine how many records belong to each group. To this end the SQL construct *GROUP BY* is employed. To facilitate understanding of the query it may help first to consider a simpler variant:

```
SELECT sex, id AS result FROM surveydata

sex          result
…            …
2            19
1            20
2            21
0            22
```

You thus obtain a list (one line for each record) where the first column contains the gender and the second, the sequential ID number. This list can then be organized using *GROUP BY sex* in such a way that entries with the same gender are collected on a single line. In this case you have to specify how the entries in the second column are to be summarized. This is done with an aggregate function (in this case *COUNT*).

```
SELECT sex, COUNT(id) AS result FROM surveydata GROUP BY sex
```

```
sex         result
0           35
1           29
2           24
```

The *Recordset* variable *rec* probably contains three records as in the table above; probably, because it is theoretically possible for one of the three permissible *sex* values to have no entries in the database. In this case the corresponding row would be lacking. For this reason the three result cells are first cleared with *ClearContents*, in order to prevent an old value from remaining behind. *ClearContents* has the advantage over a simple *Clear* in that the cell format is kept intact.

The appearance of the contents of *rec* is now clear. But the evaluation is interesting as well: A loop is run over all the data records of *rec*. Here *sex* is used as index for *[c16].Cells(1 + n)*. In this way cells C16, C17, and C18 are addressed. It is not simply a value that is moved into these cells, but a formula, by means of which the result is divided by the total number of records (cell C11).

```
' sex (0: missing, 1: male, 2: female)
ws.[c16:c18].Clear
rec.Open "SELECT sex, COUNT(id) AS result " &
         "FROM surveydata GROUP BY sex"
While Not rec.EOF
  ws.[c16].Cells(1 + rec!sex).Formula = "=" & rec!result & " / $C$11"
  rec.MoveNext
Wend
rec.Close
```

This same method is used for grouping the professions.

```
' profession (0: missing, 1-5: various prof.)
rec.Open "SELECT profession, COUNT(id) AS result " & _
         "FROM surveydata GROUP BY profession"
While Not rec.EOF
  ws.[c20].Cells(1 + rec!profession).Formula = _
     "=" & rec!result & " / $C$11"
  rec.MoveNext
Wend
rec.Close
```

To determine by what percentage of the participants the individual publishers were chosen, a host of similar queries are necessary.

```
SELECT COUNT(id) AS result FROM surveydata WHERE pubXyz = True
```

To execute this query with a minimum of programming effort a loop is run over the field names given in an *Array*. For each field name the SQL query is executed and the result placed in the corresponding cell in the worksheet.

```
 ' publishers
 publ = Array("pubaw", "pubapress", "pubgalileo", "pubidg", _
   "pubmut", "pubmitp", "puboreilly", "pubquesams", "pubsybex")
 For Each p In publ
   i = i + 1
   rec.Open "SELECT COUNT(id) AS result FROM surveydata " & _
            "WHERE " & p & " = True"
   ws.[c27].Cells(i).Formula = "=" & rec!result & " / $C$11"
   rec.Close
 Next
```

The evaluation of the internet question is done in the same way as the age question: The mean and standard deviation of all responses are computed.

```
 ' internet
 rec.Open "SELECT AVG(internet) AS result1, " & _
          "STDEV(internet) AS result2 FROM surveydata", conn
 ws.[c37] = rec!result1
 ws.[c38] = rec!result2
 rec.Close
 ' close connection
 conn.Close
End Sub
```

AnalyzeDatabase deliberately avoids the speed optimization measures carried out in the other procedures. If the execution of the SQL query takes some time (which is the case only if there are very many questionnaires in the database), then the user sees how, gradually, one result cell after the other is updated.

Naturally, the analysis commands demonstrated here cannot replace proper statistical analysis. For example, if for a medical test you wish to compute cross-correlations among several parameters, then there is no avoiding a real statistics program (such as SPSS). But even in this case it is convenient to have the data already in electronic form, so that they can be imported into the statistics program with relatively little effort. (Furthermore, Excel, too, offers some sophisticated statistics functions with the add-in "Analysis ToolPak." These functions cannot replace a professional statistics program and in their application in VBA code frequently present problems.)

Generating Test Files for the `incoming` *Directory*

If you would like to try out the program, you can, of course, fill out some questionnaires yourself and then copy them into the directory `incoming`. But you can save yourself the effort and instead call upon *CreateDummyFilesInIncoming*.

The program generates a variable number of files `nnnn.xls` in the `incoming` directory and inserts random data into the worksheet "results."

The procedure begins with the same instructions for speed optimization as in *ProcessIncomingFolder*. Then the file `survey_template.xls` is opened *nrOfFiles* times, edited, and saved under a new name in the directory `incoming`. To avoid the necessity of the file having to be later processed "by hand," all cells in the worksheet "survey" are struck through with a diagonal pattern.

```
Sub CreateDummyFilesInIncoming()
  Const nrOfFiles = 50
  Dim i&, j&
  Dim newfilename$
  Dim wb As Workbook, ws As Worksheet
  On Error GoTo error_createdummy
  Randomize
  ' optimize speed
  Application.Calculation = xlCalculationManual
  Application.ScreenUpdating = False
  Application.DisplayStatusBar = True
  Application.DisplayAlerts = False
  ' open survey_template.xls, insert random data, save
  newfilename = ThisWorkbook.Path + "\incoming\"
  For i = 1 To nrOfFiles
    Application.StatusBar = "Create file " & i & " from " & nrOfFiles
    Set wb = Workbooks.Open(ThisWorkbook.Path + "\survey_template.xls")
    ' random data
    Set ws = wb.Worksheets("results")
    ws.[b1] = Int(15 + Rnd * 50)
    ws.[b2] = Int(Rnd * 3)  '0: missing, 1: male, 2: female
    ws.[b3] = Int(Rnd * 6)  '0: missing, 1-5: various prof.
    For j = 1 To 9          'for all publishers
      If Rnd > 0.7 Then
        ws.[b4].Cells(j) = True
      Else
```

```
        ws.[b4].Cells(j) = False
      End If
    Next
    ws.[b13] = Int(Rnd * 11) 'Internet: 0-10
    ' mark survey sheet as inactive
    Set ws = wb.Worksheets("survey")
    ws.Unprotect
    ws.Cells.Interior.Pattern = xlLightUp
    ws.[a1] = "contains random data, do not edit manually"
    ws.Protect
    ' overwrite existing files (DisplayAlerts=False)
    wb.SaveAs newfilename + Format(i, "0000") + ".xls"
    wb.Close
  Next
error_createdummy:
  Application.Calculation = xlCalculationAutomatic
  Application.DisplayAlerts = True
  Application.ScreenUpdating = True
  Application.StatusBar = False
  If Err  0 Then
    MsgBox Error + vbCrLf + _
      "the procedure CreateDummyFilesInIncoming will be stopped."
  End If
End Sub
```

CHAPTER 13

Data Analysis in Excel

Excel is not a database system. Its strengths are in its extensive data analysis capabilities. The central section of this chapter is devoted to pivot tables. These are a very capable tool for grouping and organizing data with several parameters clearly. A feature of pivot tables is that with them data can be analyzed that are not even located in an Excel worksheet, but, for example, in an external database.

Chapter Overview

Grouping Data (Subtotals)

Introduction

Behind the rather cryptic command DATA|SUBTOTALS lies the possibility of distributing sorted data into groups, provide each group with a partial sum, and finally finish things off with a final sum for all the data. Instead of summation, other possibilities include calculation of means, minima, and maxima.

The precondition for being able to use this command sensibly is having a column through which several associated data records can be identified. The entire database must be sorted according to this column (and perhaps by further criteria as well).

Let us begin with an example. Figure 13.1 shows a very simple database of products (example file `Subtotal.xls`). The database is sorted primarily by the product category (a–c) and secondarily by the quality of the product (I or II). Using the SUBTOTALS form the data are grouped by category; at the same time, for each group the mean of the prices is computed. Internally, the worksheet function *=SUBTOTAL(typ, range)* is used.

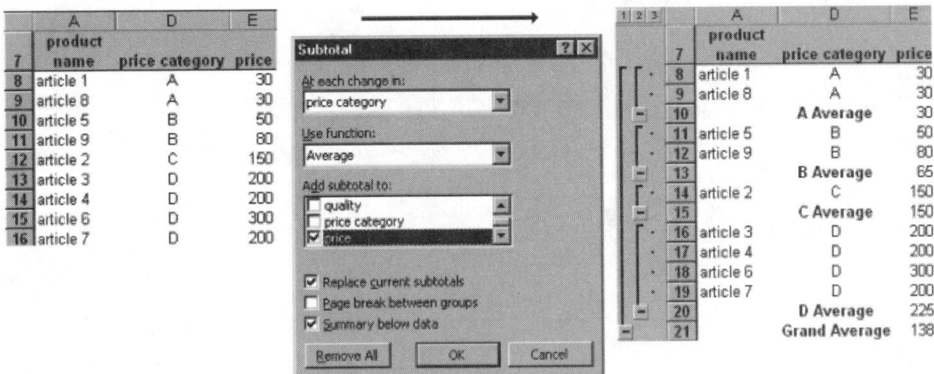

Figure 13.1. The product database was grouped by category

The command SUBTOTALS not only creates groups, it automatically divides the table up according to these groups. Both the formation of groups and the subtotals can be easily deleted by clicking on the Remove All button in the SUBTOTALS form.

Normally, each time the command is executed the most recently created grouping is dissolved. If you deactivate the option REPLACE CURRENT SUBTOTALS, then Excel adds new groups to those already existing. In many cases this can be used to create multilevel groupings. However, as a rule, this attempt fails because Excel includes the subtotals of the previous group into its calculation and thus returns nonsensical results.

In general, the command is incapable of creating groups of the type *0<=x<10* or *10<=x<20*. It can create only those groups that are identified by a unique feature. This restriction can be circumvented by creating a new column in your table with formulas that return category codes as result. For example,

```
=IF(E8<50,"A",IF(E8<100,"B",IF(E8<200,"C","D")))
```

The above formula returns the result A if E8 contains a value smaller than 50, B if E8 is smaller than 100, and so on. (If the division into categories is more complex, you can write a macro to deal with it; see Chapter 5.) In Figure 13.2 the product database of Figure 13.1 has been extended to include a price category column with the above formula, according to which it has been sorted and grouped.

Subtotal.xls

Remove subtotals

Build subtotals for price category, calculate average price

product name	product category	quality	price category	price
article 1	a	I	A	30
article 8	c	II	A	30
			A Average	30
article 5	b	I	B	50
article 9	c	II	B	80
			B Average	65
article 2	a	I	C	150
			C Average	150
article 3	a	II	D	200
article 4	b	I	D	200
article 6	c	I	D	300
article 7	c	I	D	200
			D Average	225
			Grand Average	138

sheet1

Figure 13.2. The product database has been divided into four price groups

Programming

The Method SubTotal

To generate subtotals in VBA code we have the method ***SubTotal***, which can be applied to any cell of a table. The parameter *GroupBy* specifies the number of the column (relative to the first column of the data) whose values are to be grouped. *TotalList* expects a list of all columns for which subtotals are to be computed. The function for the subtotal (which is the same for all columns) is set by *Function*.

The choices are *xlAverage, xlCount, xlMax, xlMin, xlStDev,* and *xlSum.* (For details, see the on-line help.)

> **TIP** *Please note that you must first sort the table, with the* GroupBy *column as the primary sort criterion.*

```
' Subtotals.xls, Sheet1
Private Sub btnBuildSubtotals_Click()
  With ThisWorkbook.Worksheets(1).[a7]
    .Sort Key1:=[D7], Order1:=xlAscending, Header:=xlYes, _
        MatchCase:=False, Orientation:=xlTopToBottom
    .Subtotal GroupBy:=4, Function:=xlAverage, TotalList:=Array(5), _
      Replace:=True, PageBreaks:=False, SummaryBelowData:=True
  End With
End Sub
```

To remove the grouping, apply ***RemoveSubtotal*** to the table.

```
Private Sub btnRemoveSubtotals_Click()
  ThisWorkbook.Worksheets(1).[a7].RemoveSubtotal
End Sub
```

With the method *SubTotal* the data are not only grouped and provided subtotals, but also on the left-hand table border there appear buttons for displaying and hiding the subgroups. This can be a great help, particularly with large tables, to provide a quick overview and then allow interesting subtotals to be analyzed.

The Object Outline

Internally, the division created by *SubTotal* is managed by the object ***Outline***. This object is equipped with relatively few properties and methods. The method *ShowLevels* specifies how many levels of rows or columns should be displayed. By giving the value 1, you reduce the view to the end result.

```
ThisWorkbook.Worksheets(1).Outline.ShowLevels 1
```

The largest permissible value for *ShowLevels* is 8. This value can be given even if the outline has fewer hierarchical levels. This has the effect of showing all data.

The properties *SummaryColumn* and *SummaryRow* specify whether result cells are located to the right of, respectively below, the data (default) or to the left, respectively above.

You can also structure the table without the command SUBTOTALS. In the Excel menu there is the command DATA|GROUP AND OUTLINE. In VBA code you can instead apply various methods to ranges of cells (*Range* object).

The simplest outlines are created for the specified range with *AutoOutline* and deleted with *ClearOutline*. An individual outline is possible with the methods *Group* and *Ungroup*, where here entire rows or columns must be specified as range (use the properties *EntireRow*, respectively *EntireColumn*). The property *OutlineLevel* specifies the outline level of an individual column or row, or changes it. The property *ShowDetail* of a result column or row determines whether the subsidiary detailed data are displayed.

With the *Window* property *DisplayOutline* you can show or hide outlines without altering the structure of the outline.

Syntax Summary

rng is a *Range* object, *ws* a *Worksheet* object, *wnd* a *Window* object, *outl* an *Outline* object.

SubTotal

rng.SubTotal	groups a table and creates subtotals
rng.RemoveSubTotal	removes subtotals

Outline

ws.Outline	refers to the *Outline* object
outl.ShowLevel	determines the number of visible hierarchical levels
rng.AutoOutline	analyzes the data and automatically creates subgroups
rng.Group	creates a subgroup for the range
rng.Ungroup	clears the subgroup
rng.ClearOutline	clears all grouping
rng.ShowDetail	shows or hides a subgroup
wnd.DisplayOutline	shows or hides outline column

Pivot Tables

Introduction

Pivot tables are a special type of table. In a pivot table data at least two categories are gathered into a matrix. Pivot tables are useful for representing extensive data sets compactly by creating associated groups. Pivot tables thus represent the most important tool in Excel's data analysis toolbox. With MS Query you can also use the pivot table commands for analyzing data that are managed by an external database system.

Pivot tables should, if possible, be located in a worksheet where they can be enlarged without difficulty down and to the right. The reason is that depending on the ordering of the outline fields of a pivot table the size of the pivot table can vary greatly.

In contrast to most other Excel functions, pivot tables are conceived from a statistical point of view: A change in the underlying data has no effect on the pivot table. Only when the command DATA|REFRESH DATA is executed, a command that is available only when the cell pointer is in the pivot table, can the contents of the pivot table be brought to updated status.

Introductory Example

Figure 13.3 shows a small database, in which twenty-two articles stored in a warehouse are kept track of, together with two associated, also simple, pivot tables (example file `Pivot.xls`). The database contains a list of articles in three product categories and in two quality classes. The first pivot table gives information about how many different articles there are in a particular category and quality group as well as its average price. For example, we can see from the pivot table that there are fourteen articles of quality class I, but only eight articles of quality class II. In the second pivot table the total values of the articles are given by group, though this time as a percentage of the total value of all the items in the warehouse.

Pivot tables are created with the command DATA|PIVOTTABLE AND PIVOTCHART REPORT. This command summons the PivotTable wizard. The goal of this example (that is, pivot table 1 in Figure 13.3) is to determine for each product category and quality level the number of articles and their mean value. To accomplish this the following steps were executed:

Step 1: Determines the origin of the data, which in the current example is the current worksheet.

Step 2: Determines the range of cells containing the data: B4:G26.

Step 3: Determines whether the pivot table is to be placed in the same worksheet or in a new one. As result there appears an empty matrix of a pivot table. At the same time the pivot toolbar is made visible, and the wizard disappears.

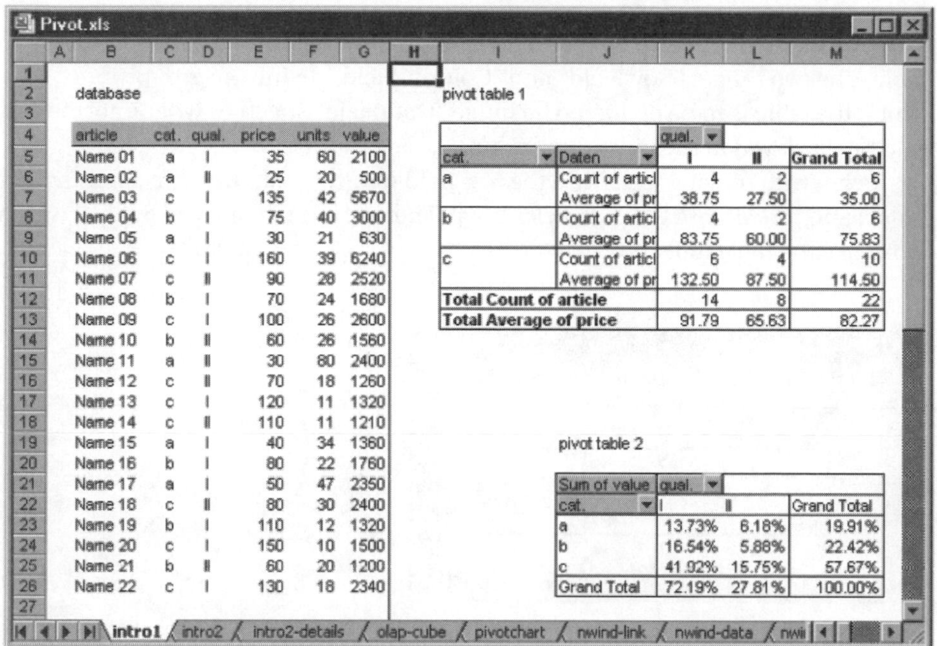

Figure 13.3. A database with two pivot tables

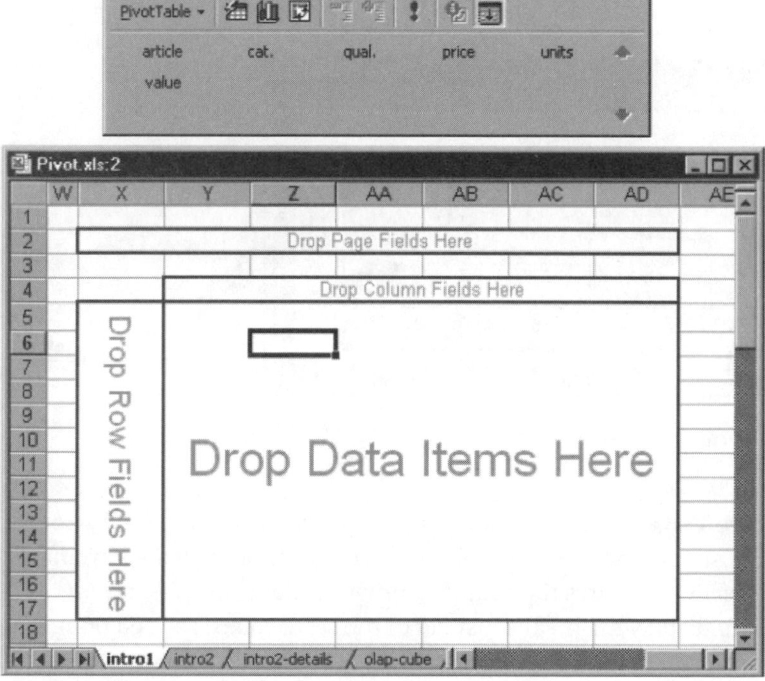

Figure 13.4. Above, the pivot table toolbar; below, the new, still empty, pivot table

Step 4: Now it is time to move, with the mouse, data fields (column headers from the initial data) from the pivot table toolbar to their proper place in the table. The two ranges "RowField" and "ColumnField" define the groups into which the table is to be divided. The range "DataField" specifies what information is to be displayed in the individual groups.

Begin with moving "cat." into the row field range, "qual." into the column field range, and "price" into the data field range. The result is the first pivot table, which looks like the table in Figure 13.5.

Sum of price	qual.		
cat.	I	II	Grand Total
a	155	55	210
b	335	120	455
c	795	350	1145
Grand Total	1285	525	1810

Figure 13.5. One step on the way to pivot table 1

In addition to the price, the number of articles is of interest, so drag the article field from the toolbar into the data range of the table (Figure 13.6).

		qual.		
cat.	Daten	I	II	Grand Total
a	Sum of price	155	55	210
	Count of article	4	2	6
b	Sum of price	335	120	455
	Count of article	4	2	6
c	Sum of price	795	350	1145
	Count of article	6	4	10
Total Sum of price		1285	525	1810
Total Count of article		14	8	22

Figure 13.6. Yet another step

Step 5: Figure 13.6 almost corresponds the requirements of the table. However, it is not the sum of the prices, but their mean that should be displayed. (Excel automatically calculates the sum for numerical data, and the number of items for text.) To display the means instead of the sums, place the cell pointer on a price field of the table (it doesn't matter which) and execute the command FIELD SETTINGS. In the form that appears select the function AVERAGE and terminate the dialog. The result is that all the price fields are accommodated to the new function.

Step 6: Because averages are being computed, a number of decimal places are displayed, too many of which make the table unreadable. Therefore, open FIELD SETTINGS once again, click on the button labeled Number, and select a new number format. In contrast to formatting with FORMAT|CELLS, the new format holds not just for the selected cell, but for all the price cells.

Example 2

The purpose of pivot table 2, shown in Figure 13.3 , is to calculate the value of the total contents of the warehouse. What percentage of the warehouse's value is tied up in a particular combination of product category and quality level? We proceed as follows:

Steps 1, 2, and 3: Data source as above. (You can specify pivot table 1 as the data source, which is based on the same data.)

Step 4: Drag "cat." into the row field range, "qual." into the column field range, and "value" to the data field range.

Step 5: Excel automatically creates sum fields for "value." This is correct in itself, but the results should be formatted as percentages. Therefore, invoke, using the pivot table toolbar, the FIELD SETTINGS dialog for the value field. The button `Options` expands the dialog box. There you can indicate that the data are to be displayed as "% of total."

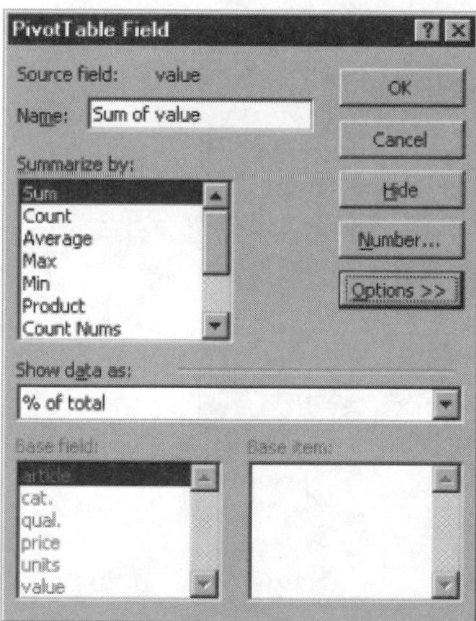

Figure 13.7. Representing a sum as a percentage of the total

Layout Options

Table Layout

Excel provides three grouping ranges for pivot tables: rows, columns, and sheets. At least one of these three group ranges must be taken up with a data field, so that a pivot table can be created in the first place. The simplest case is usually (as in the example above) that the column and row fields each contain a data field, as a result of which one has a "classic" data table in matrix form.

If several data fields are inserted into the row or column range, then Excel creates subcolumns or subrows and enlarges the table with subtotals. This makes the table more difficult to read, but it makes possible the creation of arbitrarily complex groupings into categories.

Greater clarity can be achieved by using one or more page ranges: With these are displayed list selection boxes above the actual pivot table, as we have seen in the case of the autofilter command. With these list selection boxes a single category can be selected; the pivot table is then reduced by this category. Additionally, the list selection field offers the possibility of displaying all categories simultaneously.

With the command FORMAT|AUTOFORMAT the visual presentation of the pivot table can be completely changed. Excel offers in this respect a variety of predefined format combinations.

Layout Dialog

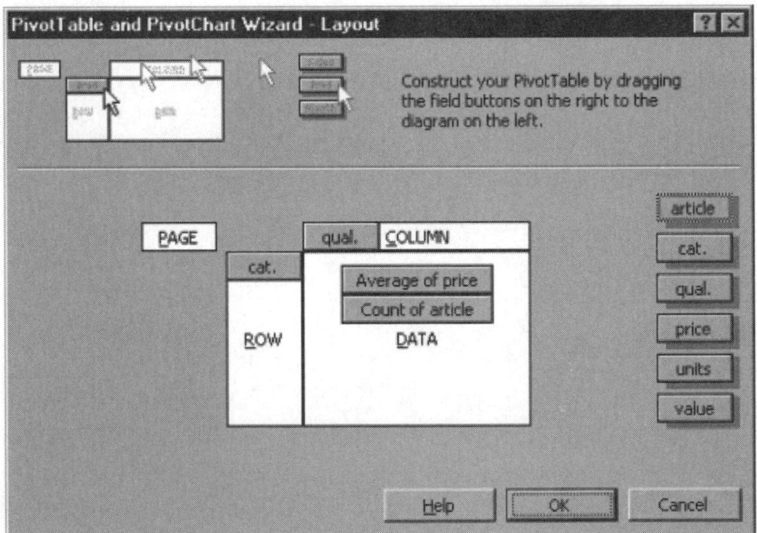

Figure 13.8. Dialog for altering the layout of a pivot table

In Excel 97 the main structure of a pivot table could be changed only in step 3 of the pivot table wizard. The new pivot table toolbar is perhaps more intuitive to use, but on the other hand, you may nonetheless experience some nostalgia for the old dialog, which was often easier to use with very large pivot tables. It still exists: Summon the pivot table wizard (this works for an existing pivot table) and click in step 3 on the button Layout. The dialog pictured in Figure 13.8 then appears.

Changing Pivot Tables After the Fact

There are almost endlessly many ways of changing existing pivot tables. (The number of variants often causes some degree of confusion. Take a half hour to do some experimentation so that you become familiar with the most important operations.)

As soon as you move the cell pointer into a pivot table the pivot table toolbar should automatically appear. (If it does not, then you must activate the toolbar with VIEW|TOOLBARS.) The most important command in the toolbar is REFRESH DATA. With this the indicated data are calculated afresh. The command must be executed when the source data have been changed, because Excel does not automatically recalculate pivot tables (in contrast to its behavior with almost all of its other worksheet functions).

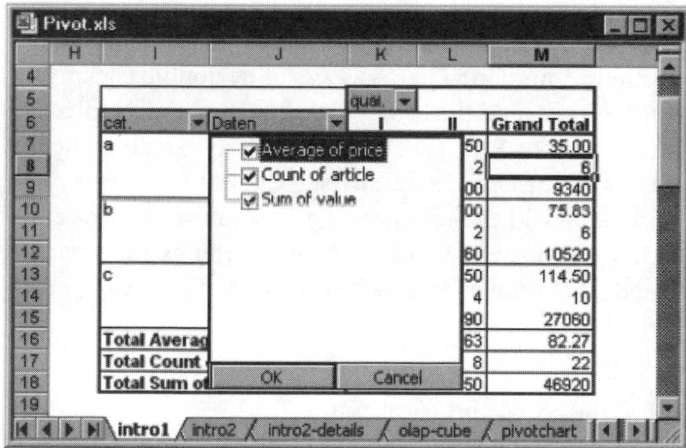

Figure 13.9. In the listbox individual fields can be deactivated

With the toolbar you can perform such tasks as extending the pivot table with additional categories and inserting additional data fields. Of course, you can also remove fields from the table to make it smaller.

TIP *When a pivot table contains several data fields, you can remove all of them from the table (field "data"). Often, you will wish to remove only a single data field and not all of them. To do this, click the arrow button and deactivate those fields that you wish to remove (Figure 13.9).*

Pivot table fields can be most easily reformatted with the pop-up menu command FIELD SETTINGS. With the gray group fields the location (row, column, page) and number of subtotals can be set. In the case of data fields the type of calculation, display format, and number format can be defined (see below, under *field settings*). Such changes affect *all* pivot table fields of the given group.

With the command DATA|SORT the order of the data fields within the pivot table can be changed. The position of the cell pointer when the command is invoked determines the sort criterion.

CAUTION *Excel cannot change a pivot table to accommodate a fundamental change in the underlying data. For example, if you change the labels in your database and then wish to update the pivot table, Excel returns an error message and removes the changed columns from the table.*

Field Settings

For formatting individual data fields Excel provides a number of rather complex options: With the pop-up menu command FIELD SETTINGS or by double clicking on a data field (either in the table itself or in the layout dialog in step 3 of the pivot table wizard) you open the dialog box PIVOTTABLE FIELD, which reveals its complexity only after you have clicked on the Options button (see Figure 13.7 above).

The listbox SUMMARIZE BY allows for the selection of one of a number of calculational functions and is self-explanatory. In the list SHOW DATA AS things are already becoming more complicated. The settings options can be divided into two groups:

Calculation proceeds automatically

Normal:	Displays the actual numerical values.
% of total:	Displays data as a percentage of the grand total of all the data in the table.
% of row/column:	Displays data in each row or column as a percentage of the total for that row or column.
Index:	Shows values in relation to row and column totals using the following formula: *(cell value * total result) / (row total * column total)*

Calculation considers the value of other data fields

Difference from:	Displays the data as the difference with respect to another item, specified by the base field and base item.
% Of:	Displays the data as a percentage of the value for the base field and base item.
% Difference From:	Displays the data as the difference from the specified value, but as a percentage difference.
Running Total In:	Unclear what this does. According to the documentation, it displays data as a running total.

For the last four named settings a second data field must be specified in relation to which the calculation is to proceed.

Grouping Results in Pivot Tables

The result lines in a pivot table can be grouped with the command DATA|GROUP AND OUTLINE|GROUP. This type of further processing of pivot tables is most useful with time-related data. Figure 13.10 presents an example.

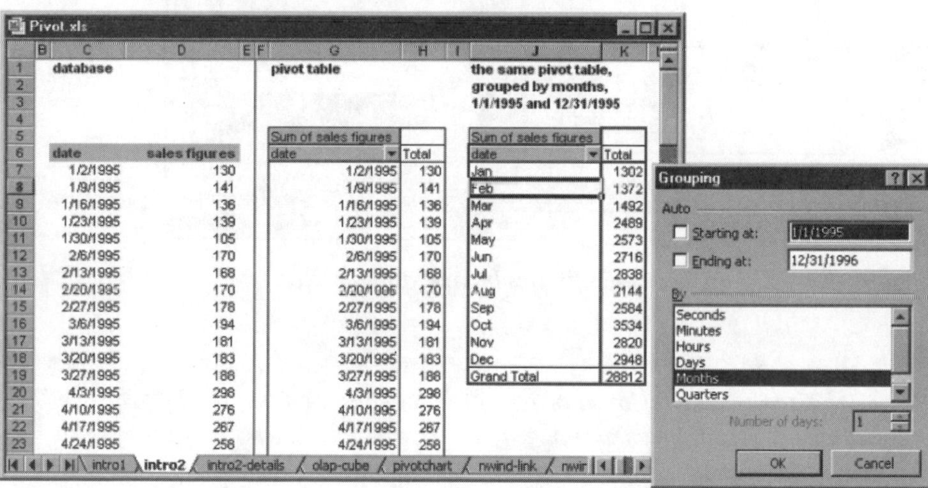

Figure 13.10. Sales figures for 1995 grouped by month

TIP *If, as in the above example, grouping is by month only, but the time period encompasses more than a year, Excel nonetheless forms only twelve groups. This means that the results for January comprise the results for all years in the time period, which is seldom a useful arrangement. The problem can be circumvented by specifying start and end dates explicitly in the* GROUPING *dialog.*

Another way of proceeding consists in grouping by year and another interval (months or quarters) simultaneously. Excel then constructs two principal groups (1995 and 1996) and within these groups, subgroups for each interval. Figure 13.11 shows an example of this, where the subsidiary grouping is for quarters instead of for months.

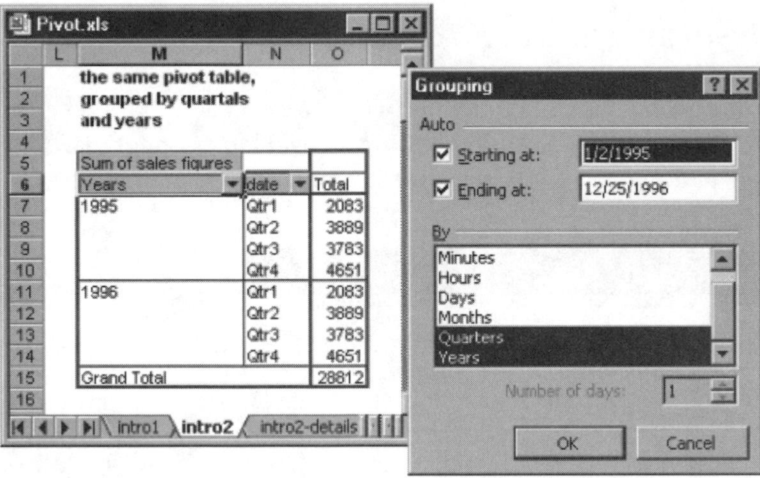

Figure 13.11. Grouping of sales figures by year and quarter

TIP *Excel is unable, for some reason that defies explanation, to group a data field if this is used as a page field of a pivot table (that is, in the region above the table). Fortunately, a solution is at hand: Drag the field into the column area, group it there, and then drag the resulting fields (year, quarter, etc.) back into the page area.*

Drilldown and Rollup

Drilldown and *rollup* are the usual terms for the opening and closing of detailed results. There are two main options for this. The first consists in executing a double click for a cell in the grouping range. The result is that the affected group is made visible or invisible (Figure 13.12).

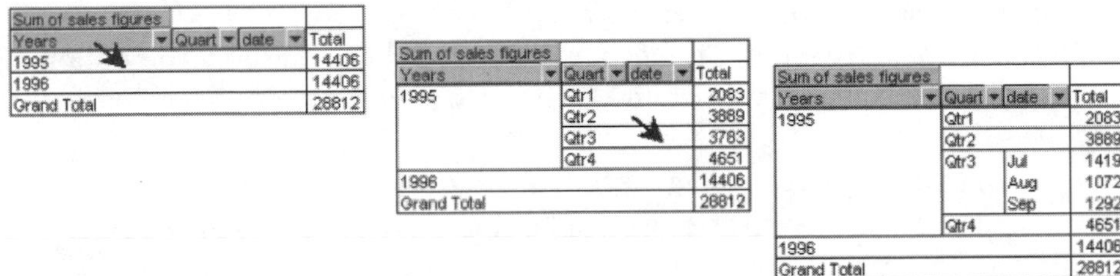

Figure 13.12. Making detailed results visible (drilldown)

On the other hand, if you execute a double click on a data field, Excel inserts one or more worksheets that contain the detailed results (Figure 13.13).

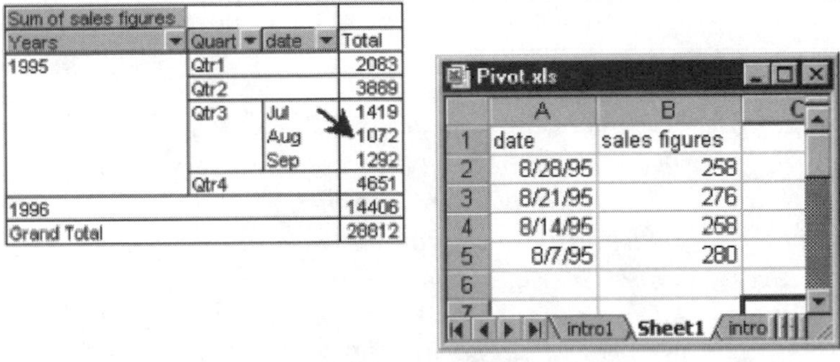

Figure 13.13. Sales figures for August 1996

Deleting Pivot Tables

There is no command for removing a pivot table from a worksheet. But that causes no difficulties: Simply select the entire range of cells and execute the command EDIT|CLEAR|ALL). With this the contents and the formatting of the cells will be deleted.

Pivot Tables for External Data

Pivot Tables can also be created for source data that do not reside in an Excel worksheet. The wizard accomplishes this in the first step with the command MULTIPLE CONSOLIDATION RANGES or EXTERNAL DATA SOURCE.

If you select the option MULTIPLE CONSOLIDATION RANGES, the pivot table wizard displays the appropriate dialog (see Chapter 11). With its assistance you can combine data from several Excel tables.

By an EXTERNAL DATA SOURCE is meant a database. When you select this option, Excel launches the auxiliary program MS Query to read in the data (see Chapter 12).

In each case the selected data are brought into Excel and stored there internally. The data are displayed as a pivot table. The raw data remain invisible.

CAUTION *The problem mentioned in the last chapter in connection with MS Query, that the names of Access databases are stored with the absolute pathname (with drive and directory), affects pivot tables as well. When both the Excel file and Access database file are moved into another directory, Excel no longer can find the source data and therefore cannot update the pivot table. A way out of this dilemma is presented later in this chapter.*

REMARKS *There are two principal ways of dealing with pivot tables with external data: The first consists in importing as much data as possible and then ordering it with the means available to pivot tables. This gives you maximal freedom in constructing the pivot table, but also requires a large amount of memory for storage. The other option is to attempt at the time of importation of the data to attempt to reduce this to a minimum. (This, then, costs more time in managing the often unwieldy MS Query.) The advantage is that the system requirements in Excel (processor demand, storage) are considerably less, and the processing speed correspondingly greater.*

OLAP Cube Files

OLAP stands for *Online Analytical Processing*. By this is meant special methods for managing and analyzing multidimensional data. This again means data that are ordered according to several parameters. The *Northwind* table in Figure 13.14 presents a good example: Only two columns contain the actual data (*quantity* and *price*). All the other columns can be used as parameters or dimensions for grouping the data: order date, product category, country of the recipient, and so on. With every pivot table, then, you are ordering multidimensional data.

Thus even though the *Northwind* database is through and through an example of multidimensional data, the notion of OLAP is usually used only when considerably more data are being analyzed (often gigabytes of data). Such databases are then called *data warehouses*. OLAP refers to the fact that the analytic functions can be executed quickly despite the huge volume of data, that is, *online*. For this a clever organization of data is necessary, and that is the particular feature of OLAP-capable database systems. (Such a system, which is particularly well optimized for the OLAP functions available from Microsoft, is, of course, Microsoft's own SQL server.)

Let us return from this brief excursion into the wonderful world of OLAP to Excel. With pivot tables you can analyze not only traditional data sources (tables, relational databases), but OLAP data sources as well. MS Query provides the key. With this program you can access OLAP data sources directly. On the other hand, you can save the results of a database query—even if with respect to a relational database—as a so-called OLAP cube.

Yet another new concept! A *cube* is a very general name for a multdimensional data set. An OLAP cube file with suffix `*.cub` makes it possible to store a static portrayal of a segment of the entire data set separate from the database. This offers a number of advantages: First, the cube file can be easily passed to another user. Second, the data are stored in a space-saving manner. Third, one can obtain very efficient access to these data. Of course, there are drawbacks: The organization of the data in the cube file is rigid (which limits the evaluation options). Moreover, changes in the source data (that is, in the database system) are not taken into account (that is, they can be accounted for only by rebuilding the cube file).

Even if you do not have access to a *data warehouse*, you can nonetheless try out the OLAP function. To do this, pose a query with MS Query that refers to a relational database (for example, as in Figure 13.14).

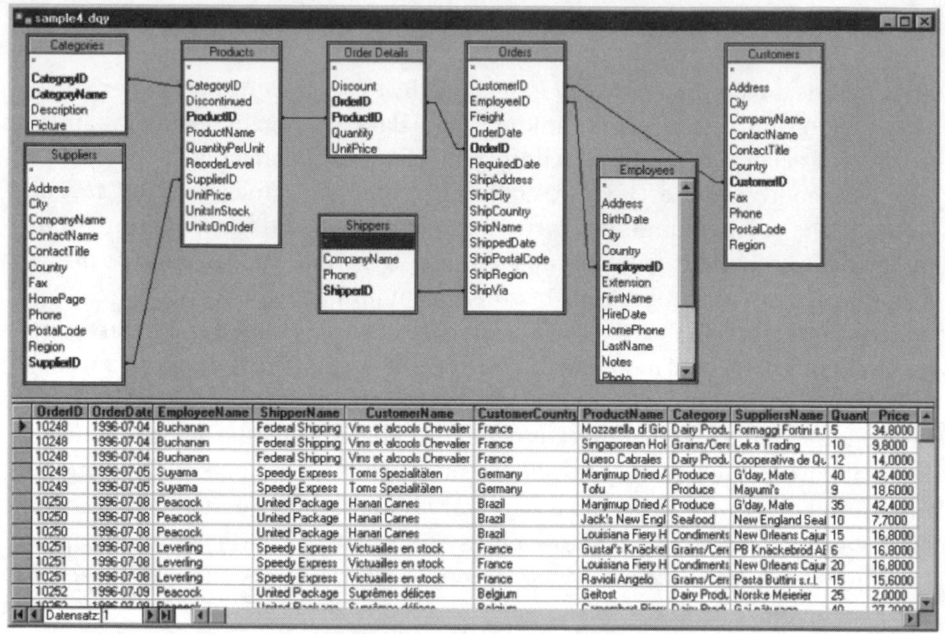

Figure 13.14. Development of a complex query with MS Query

Now either you can specify in the last step of the query wizard that you wish to create an OLAP cube from this query, or you may execute in MS Query the command FILE|CREATE OLAP CUBE. In both cases the OLAP cube wizard appears. There you select in the first step the data fields (for example, sum of *Quantity* and sum of *UnitPrice*). In the second step you specify the parameters of the data (for example, *OrderDate, LastName* of the *Employees, CategoryName*). With time data you can also provide subcategories (year, quarter, month, etc.). In the third step you save the cube into another file.

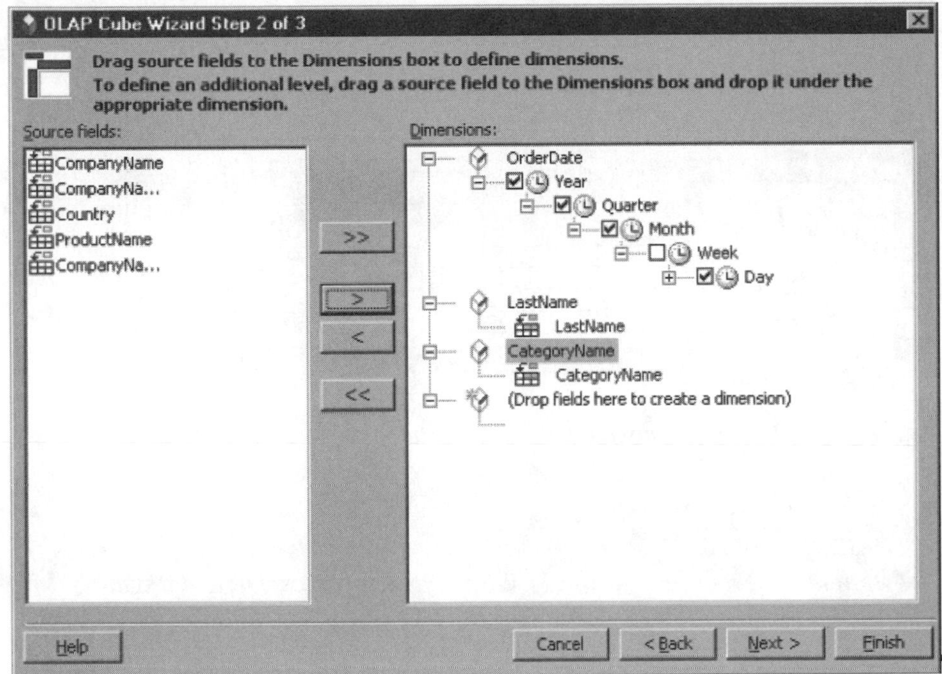

Figure 13.15. The OLAP cube wizard

Now you can create a pivot table in Excel based on this cube. In principle, this way of proceeding is the same as for the analysis of data that are available directly in Excel. But some details are different. For example, you cannot change the calculational function of the data fields (such as *Sum*), since in the cube only the sum data are stored. If you now determine that you require the mean values, you must create the cube anew. What is new as well is that time series can be more easily evaluated (without the occasionally complicated GROUP command). But even here, time categories that you have not specified in the cube wizard are not available and cannot be reproduced with DATA|GROUP.

When you exit the OLAP wizard, two files are saved in the directory `userprofile\Application Data\Microsoft\Queries`: The first is `name1.oqy`, with the SQL code of the OLAP query, and the other is `name2.cub`, with the results of the query. For the following example, `olap.cub` was stored in the same folder as the Excel file.

> **TIP** *It is impossible to create a new pivot table on the basis of a* `*.cub` *file if the associated* `*.oqy` *file is absent.*

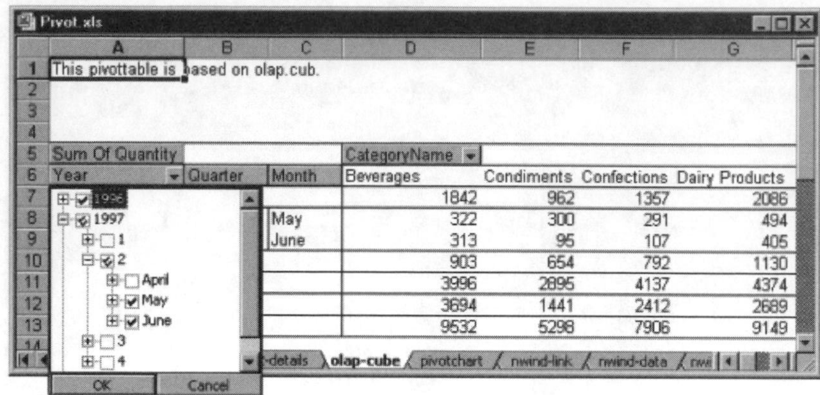

Figure 13.16. Pivot table based on an OLAP cube

POINTER *Among the Microsoft OLAP libraries can also be found* ADOMD *(that is, ADO* multidimensional*). With it you can access OLAP data sources as with the ADO library. There is insufficient space to go into this topic here.*

A good introduction to the Microsoft OLAP world (with a chapter on ADOMD *and a further chapter on Excel as OLAP analytical tool) is given in the book* MS OLAP Services, *by Gerhard Brosius.*

Pivot Table Options

If you execute the command TABLE OPTIONS in the pivot table toolbar, the dialog shown in Figure 13.17 appears. The first block of options relates to formatting the pivot table. The significance of most of the options is clear, or else can be understood from the on-line help. (Click first on the question mark and then on the option in question.) It is often overlooked that in this dialog one can also give a new name to the pivot table. This is of particular practicality when you are managing several pivot tables in an Excel file.

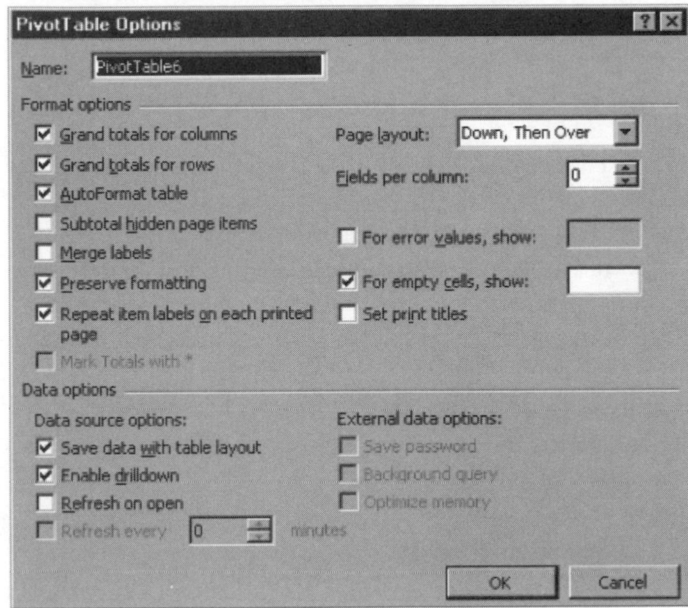

Figure 13.17. Pivot table options

The data options, on the other hand, require a bit more explanation.

SAVE DATA WITH TABLE LAYOUT means that the query data are saved together with the Excel file. The advantage is that on next loading the data are immediately available. The disadvantage is that a large data set will bloat the Excel file. (The setting is relevant only when the data come from an external data source.)

ENABLE DRILLDOWN relates to the behavior of the table following a double click. Normally, this will make visible or hide the detailed results. If this option is deactivated, Excel stops this behavior, which for pivot table novices is often confusing.

The REFRESH options govern whether and when the basis data should be automatically updated. (In the default setting, updating takes place only when the corresponding command is explicitly executed.)

BACKGROUND QUERY means that during updating of the data you can continue to work in Excel. This is above all interesting if access to an external database is relatively time-consuming.

The option OPTIMIZE MEMORY is, alas, only sketchily documented. Excel attempts in reading external data to proceed with minimal use of RAM. It is unclear how this is done and what disadvantages may accrue. (If there were no drawbacks, the option would be unnecessary.)

Pivot Charts

Pivot charts are something new in Excel 2000. These are charts that are directly connected to a pivot table. It is not possible to generate a pivot chart without an associated pivot table. Every change in the structure of the table leads to a change in the chart, and vice versa.

To generate a new pivot chart execute the command DATA|PIVOTTABLE AND PIVOTCHART REPORT as you would for a new pivot table. In the first step of the pivot table wizard you specify that you wish to create a chart (not a table). The further steps are as before, though at the end both a table and chart are created (in a single sheet).

You can also equip an existing table with a pivot chart. Either start with the chart assistant (with the cell pointer in the pivot table or execute the command PIVOTCHART in the pivot toolbar.

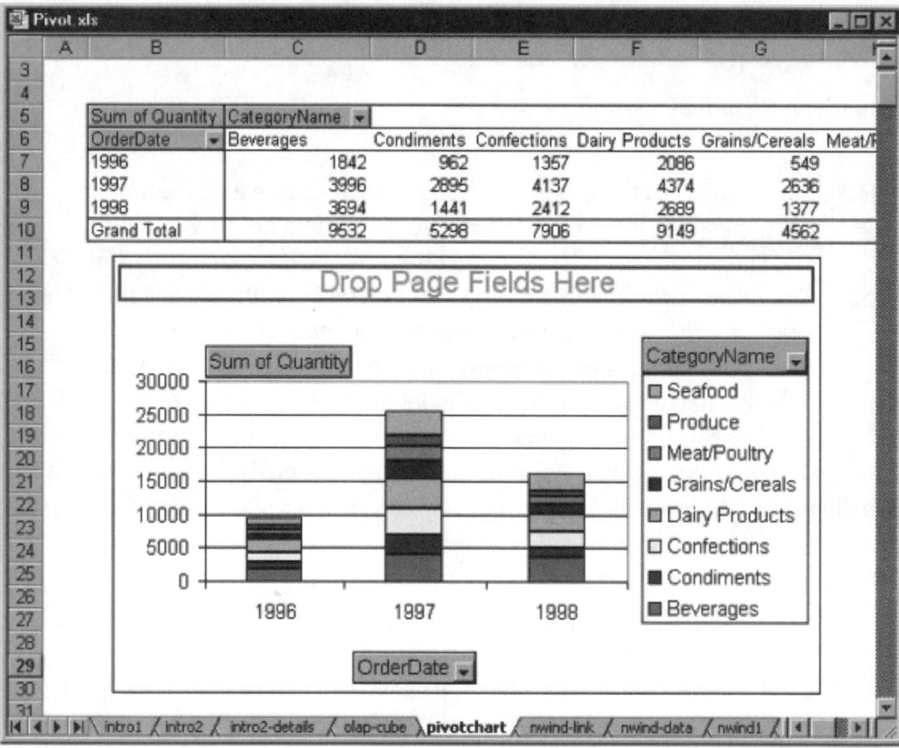

Sum of Quantity	CategoryName					
OrderDate	Beverages	Condiments	Confections	Dairy Products	Grains/Cereals	Meat/P
1996	1842	962	1357	2086	549	
1997	3996	2895	4137	4374	2636	
1998	3694	1441	2412	2689	1377	
Grand Total	9532	5298	7906	9149	4562	

Figure 13.18. A pivot table with a pivot chart

> **TIP** *Excel always generates a pivot chart in its own sheet. If you want to represent the chart next to or beneath the pivot table as an independent object, you must use a trick. Move the cell pointer outside the pivot table and launch the chart wizard. In step 2 specify the pivot table as data source. (Click on an arbitrary cell in the table.) In step 4 you now have available the option* As object in worksheet.

Programming Techniques

The starting point for most of the examples of this chapter is a rather extensive table (11 columns, 2100 rows; see Figure 13.14). These data were imported with MS Query from `nwind.mdb` into the worksheet *nwind-data*. The worksheets *nwind-1, nwind-2,* etc., access these data. All these examples can be found in the file `Pivot.xls`. The following list gives a brief description of the worksheets contained in this file:

intro1	introductory example 1 (data and two pivot tables)
intro2	introductory example2 (data and three pivot tables, time grouping)
intro2-details	detail data for intro2 (sales figures August 1996)
olap-cube	pivot table, based on `olap.cub`
pivot-chart	pivot table with chart, data basis `nwind.mdb`
nwind-link	pivot table, data basis `nwind.mdb`
nwind-data	data table (imported by MS Query from `nwind.mdb`)
nwind1, -2 …	various pivot tables based on the data in *nwind-data*
code1, -2 …	various pivot tables plus VBA code

Generating and Deleting Pivot Tables

CreatePivotTable Method

There are several ways in which you can generate a new pivot table. However, here we are going to present only two variants. The first corresponds to what can be produced with the macro recorder. We begin with the data basis of a *PivotCache* object, from which a pivot table, initially empty, is created with the method *CreatePivotTable*. The structure of the pivot table is then determined by changing the *Orientation* property of some pivot fields. The apostrophes in the pivot field names come from MS Query. This program uses this unnecessary character in the names of some imported columns. The method *CreatePivotTable* adopts this notation from the *nwind-data* worksheet. Therefore, we must stick with this notation.

> **TIP** PivotField *objects are presented more fully in the next subsection, and the* PivotCache *object in the one following.*

```
' Pivot.xls, code1
Private Sub btnCreatePivot1_Click()
  Dim pc As PivotCache, pt As PivotTable
  Dim ptName$
  ' Me refers to the worksheet associated to this module
  ptName = Me.Name + "_ptsample1"
  btnDeletePivot_Click  ' delete existing pivot table
Set pc = ThisWorkbook.PivotCaches.Add(xlDatabase, _
    "'nwind-data'!R3C1:R2158C11")
  Set pt = pc.CreatePivotTable([a8], ptName)
  With pt
    .PivotFields("Quantity").Orientation = xlDataField
    .PivotFields("'Category'").Orientation = xlColumnField
    .PivotFields("'EmployeeName'").Orientation = xlRowField
    .PivotFields("'CustomerCountry'").Orientation = xlPageField
  End With
End Sub
```

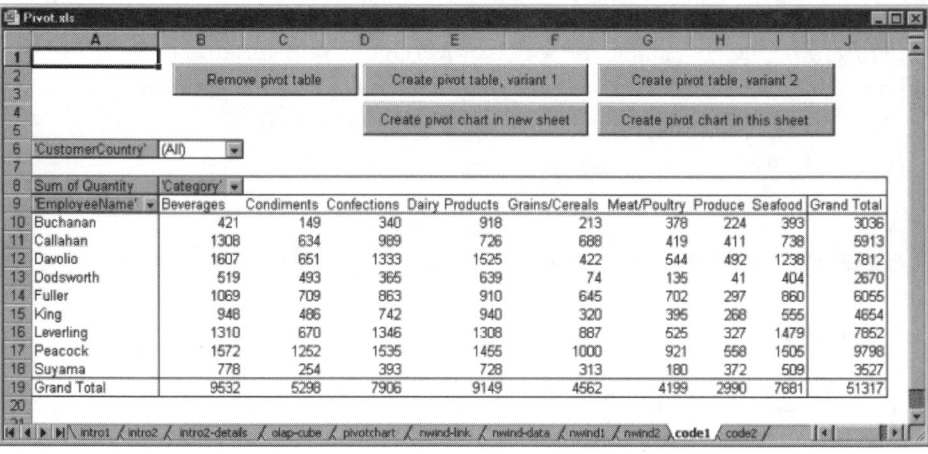

Sum of Quantity	'Category'								
'EmployeeName'	Beverages	Condiments	Confections	Dairy Products	Grains/Cereals	Meat/Poultry	Produce	Seafood	Grand Total
Buchanan	421	149	340	918	213	378	224	393	3036
Callahan	1308	634	989	726	688	419	411	738	5913
Davolio	1607	651	1333	1525	422	544	492	1238	7812
Dodsworth	519	493	365	639	74	135	41	404	2670
Fuller	1069	709	863	910	645	702	297	860	6055
King	948	486	742	940	320	395	268	555	4654
Leverling	1310	670	1346	1308	887	525	327	1479	7852
Peacock	1572	1252	1535	1455	1000	921	558	1505	9798
Suyama	778	254	393	728	313	180	372	509	3527
Grand Total	9532	5298	7906	9149	4562	4199	2990	7681	51317

Figure 13.19. The result of the procedure code1.btnCreatePivot1_Click

PivotTableWizard Method

The second variant for creating new pivot tables is the ***PivotTableWizard*** method. Here all the information for generating an empty pivot table is passed in a number of parameters. The *PivotCache* object is generated automatically. The lines for generating the table structure are as in the first example.

```
' direct generation of a pivot table
Private Sub btnCreatePivot2_Click()
  Dim pt As PivotTable
  Dim ptName$
  ' Me references the worksheet associated to this module
ptName = Me.Name + "_ptsample1"
  btnDeletePivot_Click   'delete existing pivot table
  Set pt = Me.PivotTableWizard(SourceType:=xlDatabase, _
    SourceData:="'nwind-data'!R3C1:R2158C11", _
    TableDestination:="R8C1", TableName:=ptName)
  With pt
    .PivotFields("…").Orientation = … ' as in btnCreatePivot1_Click
  End With
End Sub
```

Generating a Pivot Chart

If you want to generate a new pivot chart, you will require first a pivot table. If one is at hand, then a new chart sheet can be generated with *Charts.Add*. ***SetSourceData*** assigns the range of the pivot table as data source. Done!

```
Private Sub btnPivotChart1_Click()
  Dim ch As Chart
  If Me.PivotTables.Count = 0 Then Exit Sub
  Set ch = Charts.Add
  ch.ChartType = xlColumnStacked
  ch.SetSourceData Source:=Me.PivotTables(1).TableRange2
End Sub
```

Things become a bit more complicated if the pivot chart is to be located in the same worksheet as the pivot table. Again the chart is generated with *Charts.Add*. However, this time, the new object is inserted into the worksheet with the ***Location*** method. At this point, and for some strange reason, the object variable *ch* can no longer be accessed. All further operations must therefore be carried out with *ActiveChart*.

Now the underlying *ChartObject* is accessed via *Parent.* (This object is responsible for embedding the chart in the worksheet; see Chapter 10.) With *Left* and *Top* the location of the object is set such that the chart appears directly under the table.

```
Private Sub btnPivotChart2_Click()
  Dim ch As Chart
  Dim pt As PivotTable
  If Me.PivotTables.Count = 0 Then Exit Sub
  Set pt = Me.PivotTables(1)
  Set ch = Charts.Add
  With ch
    .ChartType = xlColumnStacked
    .SetSourceData Source:=pt.TableRange2
    .Location Where:=xlLocationAsObject, Name:="code1"
  End With
  ' from here on ActiveChart must be used
  With ActiveChart.Parent  ' refers to ChartObject
    .Left = 20
    .Top = pt.TableRange2.Top + pt.TableRange2.Height + 10
  End With
End Sub
```

Deleting a Pivot Table

In Excel there is no command for deleting a pivot table. It is thus a bit surprising that there is also no *Remove* or *Delete* method for the *PivotTables* enumeration. Nevertheless, it is a simple matter to delete a pivot table: Simply delete the entire range of cells reserved for the table, thereby automatically deleting the *PivotTable* object. (*TableRange2* refers to the cell range of the entire pivot table. The property is discussed in the following section.)

```
' delete all pivot tables in a worksheet
Private Sub btnDeletePivot_Click()
  Dim pt As PivotTable, ws As Worksheet
  Set ws = Me  'references the worksheet connected to this module
  For Each pt In ws.PivotTables
    pt.TableRange2.Clear
  Next
End Sub
```

If the table was linked to a pivot chart, this chart remains. The data therein displayed are now static, however. You can delete the chart with *Charts(...).Delete ChartObjects(...).Delete.* However, you can also link this chart with a new (or existing) pivot table by again executing the method *SetSourceData.*

Macro Recording with Pivot Tables

In the case of pivot tables the macro recorder once again leads to a rapid understanding of how particular operations can be executed in code. But as usual, code produced by the macro recorder is seldom optimal. In particular, if you record the insertion of a new pivot table (that is, the steps that you usually carry out with the pivot table wizard), the resulting code is unusually complex. This is due primarily to the fact that for some strange reason Excel breaks up long character strings into a two-dimensional *Array.* Instead of

```
.Connection= "..."
```

the macro recorder produces

```
.Connection = Array(Array("part1"), Array("partw") ...)
```

Of course, the recorder splits the character strings in arbitrary locations, which has an adverse effect on readability. Before you begin to transform the *Array* conglomerate into a readable instruction, you should have the contents of the character string displayed in the immediate window, for example via the following instruction:

```
?ActiveSheet.PivotTables(1).PivotCache.Connection
```

You can then insert the result into the program code via the clipboard. You will still have to insert quotation marks and split the string into several lines as required, but this method is usually faster than working directly on the code produced by the macro recorder.

SQL2String

If your pivot table is based on a very complex SQL instruction (for example, in the case of an OLAP query), the macro recording often fails completely due to the maximum number of line extension characters (the underscore) being exceeded. In this case you will have to write the code yourself, where again you can extract the character strings from the existing pivot tables.

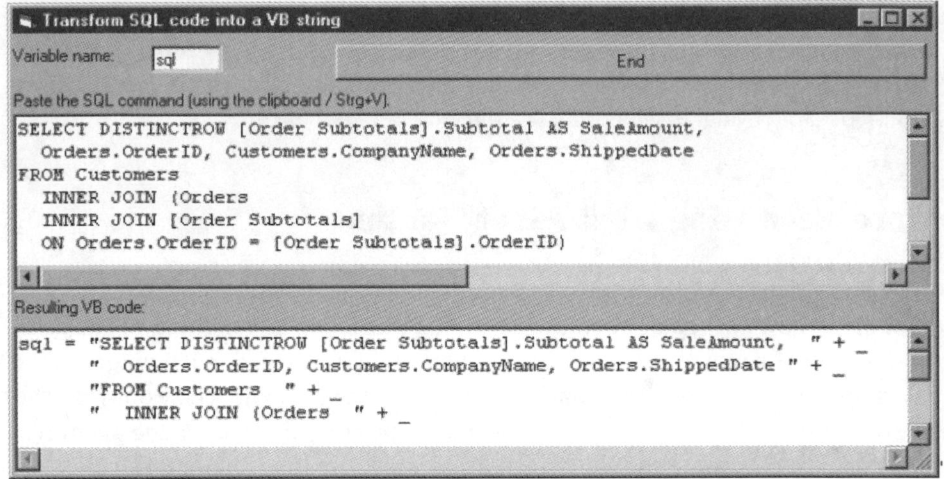

Figure 13.20. Converting long character strings into Visual Basic Syntax

If manual division of the SQL code results in more than twenty lines, you must work with a *String* variable, which you can extend via *x* = *x* + "..." as much as you like. You can be assisted in this task with the small program `sql2string.exe`, which can be found in the book's sample files (Figure 13.20). It takes the text displayed in the upper window region and creates the variable allocation corresponding to Visual Basic syntax. The text in the upper window region can be edited as in a text editor (line folding).

Construction and Reconstruction of Existing Pivot Tables

Cell Ranges

The starting point for any manipulation in a pivot table is first of all the three enumerations *PivotTables, PivotFields,* and *PivotItems*: ***PivotTables*** refers to all pivot tables in a worksheet. With the *PivotTable* object, alongside the method *PivotFields* described below, you can evaluate the properties *TableRange1, TableRange2, PageRange, ColumnRange, RowRange, DataBodyRange,* and *DataLabelRange. RowGrand* and *ColumnGrand* specify whether the result rows or columns of a pivot table are to be displayed.

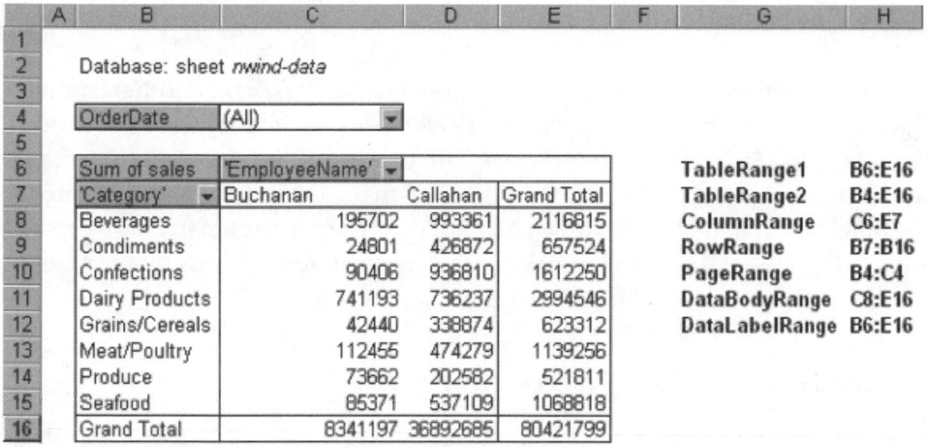

Database: sheet *nwind-data*

OrderDate	(All)		

Sum of sales	'EmployeeName'		
'Category'	Buchanan	Callahan	Grand Total
Beverages	195702	993361	2116815
Condiments	24801	426872	657524
Confections	90406	936810	1612250
Dairy Products	741193	736237	2994546
Grains/Cereals	42440	338874	623312
Meat/Poultry	112455	474279	1139256
Produce	73662	202582	521811
Seafood	85371	537109	1068818
Grand Total	8341197	36892685	80421799

TableRange1	**B6:E16**
TableRange2	**B4:E16**
ColumnRange	**C6:E7**
RowRange	**B7:B16**
PageRange	**B4:C4**
DataBodyRange	**C8:E16**
DataLabelRange	**B6:E16**

Figure 13.21. Ranges of a pivot table

Pivot Fields (PivotField)

PivotFields contains all the pivot fields defined for a table. (Each pivot field represents a column of the source data.) The ***Orientation*** property of the *PivotField* object determines whether the field is used for structuring the data, returning results, or nothing at all. If you alter the *Orientation* property of a pivot field, you create thereby, for example, a data field, a page field, or you make the field disappear.

PivotField objects govern the structure of the pivot table. With the methods *ColumnFields, DataFields, HiddenFields, PageFields, RowFields,* and *VisibleFields* you can access all *PivotField* objects of a particular *Orientation* type.

A large number of *PivotField* properties govern the layout details of a pivot table: *DataRange* and *LabelRange* specify the location of the label and result cells. *Function* determines according to which function the results are to be calculated for the data fields. *Subtotals* contains a data field that specifies what types of subtotals are to appear in the pivot table. In the case of page fields, *CurrentPage* specifies which page is currently selected.

> **POINTER** *This description is anything but complete. A host of additional properties are listed in the object browser and described in the on-line help. You might also experiment with the macro recorder by changing a single detail of an existing pivot table.*

OLAP Fields (CubeField)

If your table is based on OLAP data, then the landscape takes on another cast altogether: In this case the manipulation of pivot fields is accomplished not with the aid of *PivotFields*, but with ***CubeFields***. In the case of the *CubeField* object we are dealing with a reduced variant of *PivotField* that corresponds to the possibilities inherent in OLAP data. (With OLAP data you can carry out many fewer operations. The layout of the table is greatly limited by the query options that were chosen when the OLAP cube was created.)

Calculated Fields (Formula Fields)

It is possible to create a new pivot table from existing pivot fields: If, say, there are columns *price* and *quantity* in the source data, a new pivot field *sales* can be calculated from the product of these two. In interactive mode you execute the command FORMULAS|CALCULATED FIELD on the pivot table toolbar. In VBA code you execute *CalculatedFields.Add "sales", "=price * quantity"*. Then you can use *sales* as you would any other pivot field. ***CalculatedFields*** refers to all pivot fields that do not come directly from the source data but are calculated. For these fields the equality *IsCalculated=True* holds. The property *Formula* contains the calculational formula.

> **TIP** *Calculated fields that are placed as data fields cannot be hidden with* Orientation = xlHidden. *(The error message reports that the* Orientation *property cannot be set.) Since the macro recorder produces precisely this code, this constitutes an error in Excel 2000. Despite lengthy experiments, the author has been unable to find another way to get such a field out of the table via code. There seems to be no other solution than to delete the entire table.*

Grouping of Pivot Tables

Some of the possibilities for analysis of pivot tables can be explored with the grouping function. The necessary ***Group*** method has an existence independent of pivot tables (see Chapter 11). As object reference it expects simply a cell or range of cells. If this range happens to lie within a pivot table, then the grouping will be carried out for that table.

As a rule, only date and time fields lend themselves to grouping. The key parameter of *Group* is then *Periods*: A data field is passed to it that specifies for what units of time the grouping is to be carried out (seconds, minutes, hours, days, months, quarters, or years). As a result of the grouping new pivot fields arise, which can then be edited like all other pivot fields.

```
' group date fields (months, quarters, years)
[c3].Group Start:=True, End:=True, _
    Periods:=Array(False, False, False, False, True, True, True)
 pt.PivotFields("Years").Orientation = xlPageField
```

When grouping takes place, then usually, subtotals are to be displayed. For this we have the ***Subtotals*** property, which must be applied directly to a pivot field. A data field is also associated to *Subtotals*. It is specified in several *True* and *False* values what types of subtotals are to be created (sum, mean, etc.)

The sequence of parameters is documented in the on-line help.

```
.PivotFields("Quarters").Subtotals = Array(False, True, False, _
    False, False, False, False, False, False, False, False, False)
```

Pivot Items (PivotItem)

One level below *Pivotfields* and *CubeFields* are the ***PivotItem*** objects: These have to do with result columns or rows of the pivot table. *PivotItem* objects are associated to a *PivotField*. For example, with the *Visible* property of the *PivotItem* the visibility of individual result columns or rows can be changed. In interactive mode this corresponds to a change in the check boxes of a pivot field (see Figure 13.22).

Figure 13.22. Showing or hiding individual rows (PivotItems) of a pivot field

Example

The following procedure demonstrates the application of many of the above-described objects and properties. The results can be seen in Figure 13.23.

```
' Pivot.xls, Code2
Private Sub btnCreatePivot1_Click()
  Dim pc As PivotCache, pt As PivotTable, pf As PivotField
  Dim ptName$
  ' Me is sheet for this code
  ' remove existing pivot tables
  For Each pt In Me.PivotTables
    pt.TableRange2.Clear
  Next
  Set pc = ThisWorkbook.PivotCaches.Add(xlDatabase, _
    "'nwind-data'!R3C1:R2158C11")
  Set pt = pc.CreatePivotTable([a8], ptName)
  With pt
    .PivotFields("OrderDate").Orientation = xlRowField
    .PivotFields("'Category'").Orientation = xlColumnField
    ' new field, number format without decimal places
    .CalculatedFields.Add "sales", "= Quantity * '''Price'''"
    .PivotFields("sales").Orientation = xlDataField
    .PivotFields("Sum of sales").NumberFormat = "0"
    ' group date field (months, quarters, years)
    ' use years fields as page field, show only 1997
    ' results for each quarter
    .PivotFields("OrderDate").VisibleItems(1).LabelRange.Group _
      Start:=True, End:=True, _
      Periods:=Array(False, False, False, False, True, True, True)
    .PivotFields("Years").Orientation = xlPageField
    .PivotFields("Years").CurrentPage = "1997"
    .PivotFields("Quarters").Subtotals = Array(False, True, False, _
        False, False, False, False, False, False, False, False, False)
  End With
End Sub
```

Pivot.xls

	A	B	C	D	E	F
1						
2	Create grouped pivot table					
3						
4						
5						
6	Years	1997				
7						
8	Sum of sales		'Category'			
9	Quarters	OrderDate	Beverages	Condiments	Confections	Dairy Products
10	Qtr1	Jan	176616	41761	204718	146944
11		Feb	36080	46649	112625	60512
12		Mar	196124	13650	37392	96410
13	Qtr1 Sum					
14	Qtr2		1275036	393119	643920	1464932
15	Qtr3		981543	379907	893100	1245411
16	Qtr4		1676444	506845	1143788	2018418
17	Grand Total		20213167	6403306	14676545	22176180
18						

pivotchart / nwind-link / nwind-data / nwind1 / nwind2 / nwind3 / code1 / **code2**

Figure 13.23. Result of the procedure code2.btnCreatePivot1_Click

Internal Management (*PivotCache*)

The data basis of pivot tables is managed internally by ***PivotCache*** objects (one per pivot table). Such an object does not itself store the data, but contains a description of the parameters that are necessary for reading in external data. The property ***MemoryUsed*** specifies the requirements for intermediate data storage. For example, if the large *Northwind* table from Figure 13.14 is used as a data basis, then the memory requirement is about 200 kByte. ***RecordCount*** specifies how many data records (rows) the data source comprises.

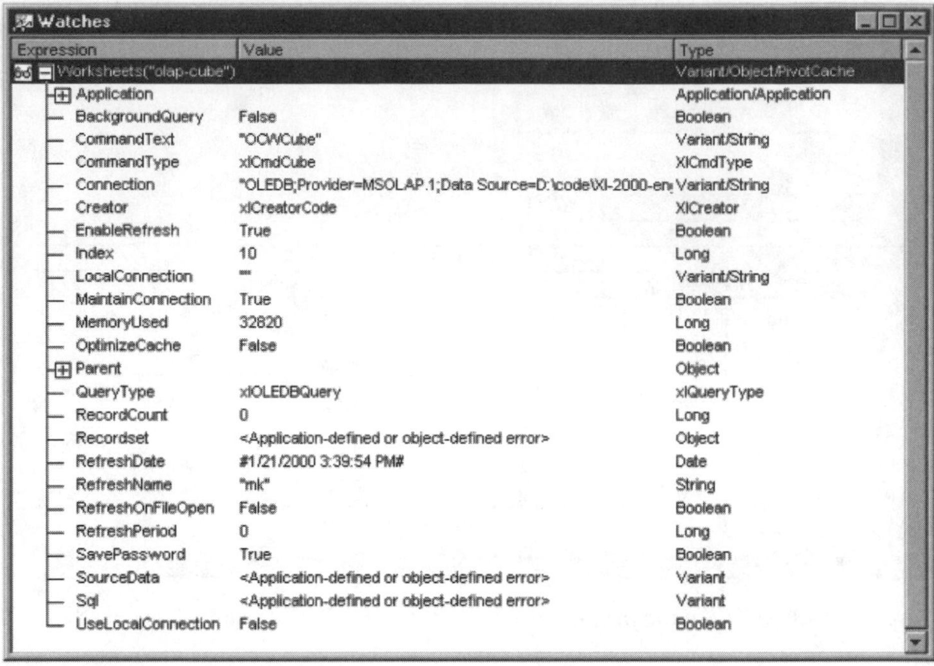

Figure 13.24. Analysis of the PivotCache object in the Watches window

According to the data source, various properties of the object are employed. An attempt to access other properties leads to an error message. For some strange reason there is no property that is always available and that specifies the type of the data source. Thus if you execute a loop over all *PivotCache* objects, you must protect the code with *On Error Resume Next* and test *Err* after accessing particular properties to obtain information about the data source type.

Excel Tables as Data Source

QueryType not initialized; access results in an error
CommandType not initialized; access results in an error
Connection not initialized; access results in an error
CommandText not initialized; access results in an error
SourceData contains as a character string (not a *Range* object) the address of the table fields; the character string is localized for some unclear reason: Thus the German version of Excel contains, for example, *"intro1!Z4S2:Z26S7"*, while the English-language version has *"intro1!R4C2:R26C7"*

External Data Source (via MS Query)

QueryType	contains *xlODBCQuery*
CommandType	contains *xlCmdSql*
Connection	contains connection information as with a *QueryTable* object (*"ODBC;..."*)
CommandText	contains the SQL command
SourceData	contains again the SQL; however, it is broken into an *Array* of character strings of 256 characters each

OLAP Cube as Data Source

QueryType	contains *xlOLEDBQuery*
CommandType	contains *xlCmdCube*
CommandText	contains *"OCWCube"*
Connection	contains in a single (usually huge) character string both the connection information and the SQL command for the OLAP cube
SourceData	not initialized; access results in an error

Updating Relations Between Pivot Tables and Data Sources

The reason for the relatively extensive treatment of *PivotCache* is that the transfer of the pivot table example files in the book's sample files produces errors unless certain measures are taken. The file names `Nwind.mdb` and `Olap.cub` are stored in the *Connection* and *CommandText* character strings with drive and path information. If you were then to open these pivot example files on your computer, Excel would complain during an attempt to update the data that it was unable to find the source data (and I would be deluged with e-mail that my examples don't work).

Unfortunately, in contrast to the case of the *QueryTable* object, it is not permitted simply to change the properties of the *PivotCache* object in order to correct the path to the database files.

The only, and alas truly costly, alternative consists in deleting the pivot tables and recreating it based on existing information. The problem with this modus operandi is that some of the layout information for the pivot table is lost.

On the other hand, the "fix-it code" reveals a great deal of internal affairs about the management of pivot tables and is therefore of interest from the point of view of general understanding.

Code execution begins in *Workbook_Open*, that is, in the first procedure that is executed when an Excel file is opened. There the first thing that happens is that *CheckMSQueryData* is called, in order to set the paths to external Access files for all tables imported with MS Query (see Chapter 12).

```
' Pivot.xls, ThisWorkbook
Private Sub Workbook_Open()
  CheckMSQueryData      ' see Workbook_Open in Chapter 12
  CheckPivotTableData
End Sub
```

In *CheckPivotTableData* a loop is run over all *PivotTable* objects in the worksheet. For each table a test is made as to whether it is based on external data. (For tables for which this is not the case the attempt to read *QueryType* leads immediately to an error. The line of code is thus adequately protected.)

If there are external data, then with *ExtractDir* (see again Chapter 12) the directory with the data is returned. If this does not agree with *ThisWorkbook.Path*, then a question appears (only for the first such table) whether the tables should really be created anew. This task is then accomplished in *RecreatePivotTable.*

```
Sub CheckPivotTableData()
  Dim ws As Worksheet
  Dim pt As PivotTable
  Dim pc As PivotCache
  Dim qtype&
  Dim oldDir$, newDir$
  Dim result&
  ' current directory (without \ at the end)
  newDir = ThisWorkbook.Path
  If Right(newDir, 1) = "\" Then
    newDir = Left(newDir, Len(newDir) - 1)
  End If
  For Each ws In ThisWorkbook.Worksheets
    For Each pt In ws.PivotTables
      Set pc = pt.PivotCache
      qtype = -1
      On Error Resume Next
      qtype = pc.QueryType  'here an error can occur
      On Error GoTo 0
      If qtype = xlODBCQuery Or qtype = xlOLEDBQuery Then
        ' extract previous path from Connection string
        oldDir = ExtractDir(pc.Connection)
        ' replace by new path
        If oldDir  "" And LCase(oldDir)  LCase(newDir) Then
```

```
        If result = 0 Then
          result = MsgBox("…?", vbYesNo, "Recreate pivot tables?")
        End If
        If result = vbYes Then
          RecreatePivotTable pt, oldDir, newDir
        End If
      End If
    End If
  Next
 Next
End Sub
```

RecreatePivotTable begins by determining the properties of the current pivot table. With the character strings for *Connection* and *CommandText* the prior path is replaced by the new path.

The new table should be recreated exactly in the place of the former table. Therefore, in determining the start cell (variable *ptRange*) it is tested whether the table is equipped with pivot page fields. This test is necessary, since in creating a new pivot table space is automatically reserved for a row with pivot page fields.

```
Sub RecreatePivotTable(pt As PivotTable, oldDir$, newDir$)
  Dim pc As PivotCache
  Dim chrt As Chart, chobj As ChartObject
  Dim ws As Worksheet
  Dim i&, cmdType&, hasChart&
  Dim con$, cmdText$, ptName$
  Dim ptRange As Range
  Dim ptLayout()
  ' retrieve current properties
  Set pc = pt.PivotCache
  con = Replace(pc.Connection, oldDir, newDir, Compare:=vbTextCompare)
  cmdType = pc.CommandType
  cmdText = Replace(pc.CommandText, oldDir, newDir, _
    Compare:=vbTextCompare)
  ptName = pt.Name
  If pt.PageFields.Count > 0 Then
    '2 rows below first page field
    Set ptRange = pt.TableRange2.Cells(3, 1)
  Else
    'first cell of table
    Set ptRange = pt.TableRange1.Cells(1)
  End If
```

The layout of the table is actually not completely recreated, but at least the principal features of its construction should be preserved. Therefore, the names and locations of all visible pivot fields are saved in the field *ptLayout*. One must take care that for OLAP pivot tables, *CubeFields* must be evaluated, while for traditional pivot tables, it should be *VisibleFields*.

```
If LCase(cmdText) = "ocwcube" Then
  ' OLAP pivot table
 ReDim ptLayout(pt.CubeFields.Count, 2)
 For i = 1 To pt.CubeFields.Count
   ptLayout(i, 1) = pt.CubeFields(i).Name
   ptLayout(i, 2) = pt.CubeFields(i).Orientation
 Next
Else
  ' standard pivot table
  ReDim ptLayout(pt.VisibleFields.Count, 2)
  For i = 1 To pt.VisibleFields.Count
    ptLayout(i, 1) = pt.VisibleFields(i).SourceName
    ptLayout(i, 2) = pt.VisibleFields(i).Orientation
  Next
End If
```

Then the entire workbook is searched for a *Chart* object that might just happen to be associated to the table. Thus a test is run whether a *Chart* object exists whose *PivotLayout.PivotTable* property refers to the *PivotTable* object under examination. For some mysterious reason a direct object comparison using *Is* fails. For this reason the properties *Worksheet.Name* and *Address* of *TableRange1* are compared with the auxiliary function *PtCompare* (method *trial by error*).

```
' connected chart in this sheet?
hasChart = False
For Each chrt In ThisWorkbook.Charts
  If PtCompare(chrt.PivotLayout.PivotTable, pt) Then
    hasChart = True
    Exit For
  End If
Next
' connected chart in another sheet?
If hasChart = False Then
  For Each ws In ThisWorkbook.Worksheets
    For Each chobj In ws.ChartObjects
      If Not (chobj.Chart.PivotLayout Is Nothing) Then
        If PtCompare(chobj.Chart.PivotLayout.PivotTable, pt) Then
          hasChart = True
```

```
          Set chrt = chobj.Chart
          Exit For
        End If
      End If
    Next
  Next
End If
```

This completes the preliminary preparations. The old pivot table is deleted and immediately recreated. Then an attempt is made to place the pivot fields in their previous locations. Here problems can arise if there are no longer existing pivot fields in *ptLayout*. This case occurs, for example, if in the original table a data field was grouped. Then the grouping fields (such as "year," "month") are also valid. In the new table these fields are missing, in the absence of grouping. Be sure to note here as well the distinction between *PivotFields* and *CubeFields* (OLAP).

```
' delete old pivot table (including cache)
pt.TableRange2.Clear
' build new pivot table
Set pc = ThisWorkbook.PivotCaches.Add(xlExternal)
pc.Connection = con
pc.CommandType = cmdType
pc.CommandText = cmdText
Set pt = pc.CreatePivotTable(ptRange, ptName)
For i = 0 To UBound(ptLayout(), 1)
  If ptLayout(i, 2)  xlHidden Then
    On Error Resume Next  'error occurs if field from
                          'date group (e.g. 'years')
    If LCase(cmdText) = "ocwcube" Then
      ' OLAP pivot table
      pt.CubeFields(ptLayout(i, 1)).Orientation = ptLayout(i, 2)
    Else
      ' standard pivot table
      pt.PivotFields(ptLayout(i, 1)).Orientation = ptLayout(i, 2)
    End If
    On Error GoTo 0
  End If
Next
```

In *Chart* objects that are present the old data continue to be displayed. The underlying data are not dynamically linked, but only a static copy of the original data. With *SetSourceData* the new table can be relinked with the *Chart* object.

```
  ' reconnect new pivot table with existing chart
  If hasChart Then
    chrt.SetSourceData pt.TableRange2
    chrt.Refresh
  End If
End Sub
' for unknown reasons the expression 'pt2 Is pt2' is sometimes False
' even though pt1 and pt2 reference the same pivot table
Function PtCompare(pt1 As PivotTable, pt2 As PivotTable) As Boolean
  Dim rng1 As Range, rng2 As Range
  Set rng1 = pt1.TableRange1
  Set rng2 = pt2.TableRange1
  If rng1.Address = rng2.Address And _
     rng1.Worksheet.Name = rng2.Worksheet.Name Then
    PtCompare = True
  Else
    PtCompare = False
  End If
End Function
```

CAUTION *Just as in Chapter 12 the following warning should be issued: The following procedures depend on the path to the database file being stored in the attribute* DefaultDir *of the* Connection *property. In the current version of Excel this is the case is the data source in directly an Access file or an OLAP cube based on an Access file. It is thus uncertain whether this process functions for other data sources or whether it will function in future versions of Excel.*

Furthermore, the procedures assume that all affected databases are located in the same directory as the Excel file. The assumption holds as well only in the present case, but certainly not for every Excel application.

Syntax Summary

wsh stands for a *WorkSheet* object, *rng* for a range of cells.

Pivot Tables

wsh.PivotTableWizard ...	creates or changes a pivot table
wsh.PivotTables(..)	access to pivot table objects
chrt.PivotLayout	access to the *PivotLayout* object
chrt.PivotLayout.PivotCache	access to the *PivotCache* object
chrt.PivotLayout.PivotFields	access to the *PivotField* object
chrt.PivotLayout.PivotTable	access to the *PivotTable* object
chrt.SetSourceData rng	associate chart to pivot table

PivotTable Properties and Methods

TableRange1	cell range of the table without page fields
TableRange2	cell range of the table including page fields
PageRange	cell range of page fields
ColumnRange	cell range of column fields
RowRange	cell range of row fields
DataBodyRange	data range
DataLabelRange	label of data range (upper left corner)
PivotFields(..)	access to all pivot fields of the pivot table
VisibleFields(..)	access to all visible fields
PageFields(..)	access to page fields
ColumnFields(..)	access to column fields
RowFields(..)	access to row fields
DataFields(..)	access to data fields
HiddenFields(..)	access to currently visible pivot fields
CubeFields(..)	access to pivot fields for OLAP data (*CubeField* object)
PivotCache	access to the *PivotCache* object
RefreshData	updates pivot table (rereads source data)

PivotField Properties

DataRange	cell range of the data fields of a pivot field
LabelRange	cell range of the label fields of a pivot field
Orientation	type of pivot field (*xlPageField, xlColumnField, xlRowField, xlDataField, xlHidden*)
Subtotals	governs which subtotals are displayed
Function	determines the calculational function (for data fields only)
CurrentPage	determines the currently visible page (for page fields only)
PivotItems(..)	access to individual pivot elements
CubeField	OLAP-specific additional properties

PivotCache Properties and Methods

CommandType	type of SQL command (SQL, OLAP-Cube)
CommandText	SQL command with external data
Connection	access to data source with external data
MemoryUsed	memory requirement (RAM) in bytes
QueryType	data type with external data (ODBC, OLE DB)
RecordCount	number of data records (rows)
SourceData	address of source data in worksheet
CreatePivotTable	create pivot table from *PivotCache*

CHAPTER 14

VBA Programming for Pros, Office Developer

For those wishing to create add-ins, call API functions, or control external programs via ActiveX automation, this chapter provides the necessary know-how. In addition, some functions of interest to Excel programmers and some tools of the Office Developer Edition will be introduced.

Please note that not all the functions introduced in this chapter require the Developer Edition. Relevant indications are provided at the beginning of each section.

Chapter Overview

Office Developer Edition

The Office Developer Edition consists of a collection of supplementary tools that are installed as an extension of the Office suite of programs. This section attempts to provide an initial overview of the functions and features of interest to Excel programmers (with no attempt at completeness!).

Extension of the Development Environment

After installation of Office Developer the VBA development environment looks no different than it did before, at least not at first glance. In fact, however, much has transpired.

VBA Projects

The most basic extension of the development environment is that now so-called VBA projects can be created. Such projects can consist of modules, class modules, formulas, and designers (see below). They will no longer be housed in an Excel file, but in an independent `*.vba` file (binary format). A VBA project has very little to do with a traditional Excel project. For example, it is impossible to integrate Excel tables or charts into a VBA project.

The code is compiled into an ActiveX-DLL. For this there is a genuine compiler that produces binary code. The DLL can be used as a component in another program. At present, the only use for VBA projects seems to be as COM add-ins. (VBA projects are not, alas, documented in their general form. The documentation refers exclusively to COM add-ins, which are actually only a special case of VBA projects.)

Designers

Designers are components that can be inserted into VBA projects. For visual editing of designer components there are available dialogs or windows that extend the VBA user interface. In addition, every designer has an associated code module. The code module gives the possibility of providing the designer components with event procedures and other code.

Both the designer window and the code module are opened via the project window. For the designer window it suffices to give a double click on the module name, while for the code module you must press the button View Code (in the project window) or the F7 key.

In principle, designers are nothing new. Even forms (dialogs) (*UserForm* objects) are created with designers (although this fact remains hidden from the developer). What is new, on the other hand, is that three supplementary designers are provided with the Developer Edition: the add-in designer, which is needed for COM add-ins, as well as two designers that assist in the development of database applications.

Designer components are inserted into the current project in the VBA development environment with Insert|DesignerName. This command is available only if a VBA project is edited in Office Developer (not, however, when a garden-variety Excel project is edited). Furthermore, the commands are available only if the designers were previously activated with Insert|Components|Designers (Figure 14.1).

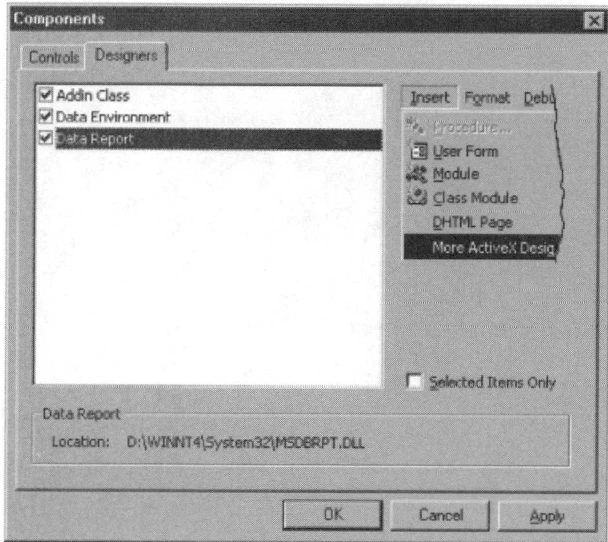

Figure 14.1. Dialog for activating designer components

COM Add-In Programming

COM add-ins are in many cases an alternative to traditional add-ins. From the developer's point of view this holds in the case of VBA projects with add-in designer components. Passing on COM add-ins as ActiveX-DLL is associated with various advantages and disadvantages. COM add-ins are described in detail later in this chapter.

Add-Ins for the Development Environment

After Office Developer has been installed, the VBA development environment contains a number of additional add-ins, which, however, cannot be used until they have been activated with the add-in manager. A simple double click loads the selected add-in. Furthermore, if you activate the option Load on Startup, the add-in will always be available in the future. Most of the add-ins will be presented in this section. Some of these are more in the line of gimmicks than genuine tools.

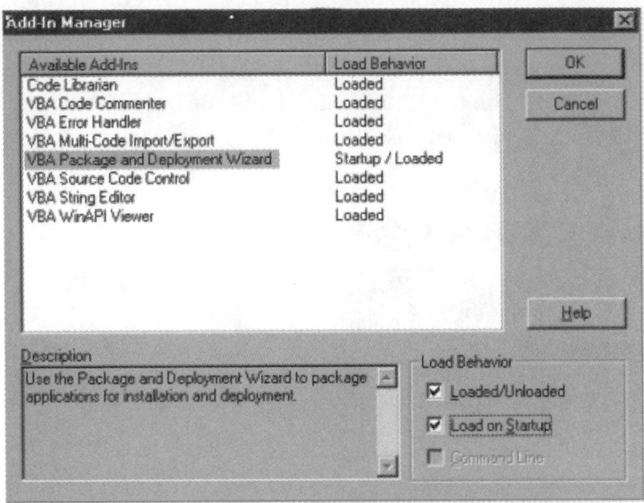

Figure 14.2. Add-ins for the development environment

Installation Assistant

If you are developing COM add-ins or if you start working in your Excel file without supplementary controls or libraries provided with Office, then if you wish to give your program to others, you must create a setup program. The installation assistant can help, which is described below in this chapter.

VBA String Editor

This mini-add-in converts a character string into VBA syntax and inserts it into the current module. This tool is of particular use with very long character strings (often SQL commands) that must be divided among several lines in VBA code (*"part1"* & _ *"part2"*, etc.). A similar task is accomplished by the program `sql2string.exe`, which is provided in the book's sample files.

VBA Error Handler

This add-in inserts error handling routines into a single procedure or into every procedure of a module or project. But do not expect too much. Only the following lines shown in boldface will be inserted:

```
Sub name()
  On Error Goto HandleErr
  … previous code
ExitHere:
  Exit Sub
  ' Error handling block added by Error Handler Add-In. DO NOT EDIT '
  ' this block of code. Automatic error handler last updated at
  ' 01-24-2000 09:34:37 'ErrorHandler:$$D=01-24-2000
  'ErrorHandler:$$T=09:34:37
HandleErr:
  Select Case Err.Number
  Case Else
    'ErrorHandler:$$N=Module1.test
    Msgbox "error " & Err.Number & ": " & _
      Err.Description, vbCritical, "procedurename"
  End Select
End Sub
```

The template for the error handler can be changed. The add-in saves you some typing, but not the mental effort to determine how your code should react to particular errors.

VBA Code Commenter

This add-in provides all the procedures in your program with comments. Since the code commenter has not been equipped with excessive artificial intelligence, this add-in comments only small things, such as the names of the parameters of the procedure. You must add the relevant information to the template. If you are being paid by line of program code, then this tool is indispensable (for each procedure it adds about twenty comment lines).

VBA Multicode Import/Export

With the MULTICODE EXPORT command you can save a number of (or all) components of the currently active project in a number of individual ASCII files. (In the case of Excel objects such as worksheets only some properties and the VBA code, and not the actual worksheet, are saved.) Such exported files can then be imported into another project with MULTICODE IMPORT.

VBA WinAPI Viewer

This program enables access to a database in which are to be found DLL declarations for most Windows system functions. These declarations are extremely useful if you wish to use these functions in your programs (see the penultimate section in this chapter).

Code Librarian

The code librarian is perhaps the most beloved tool in the Developer Edition. This program contains an enormous collection of completed programs that can be copied into your program simply by *Drag & Drop*. The code is generally well commented. Even if you employ this code unchanged in only a few instances, the examples will perhaps lead you in the proper direction. You can also use this program to compile a collection of functions or code fragments that you use frequently. Particularly attractive is that the entire code database can be searched very rapidly by keyword.

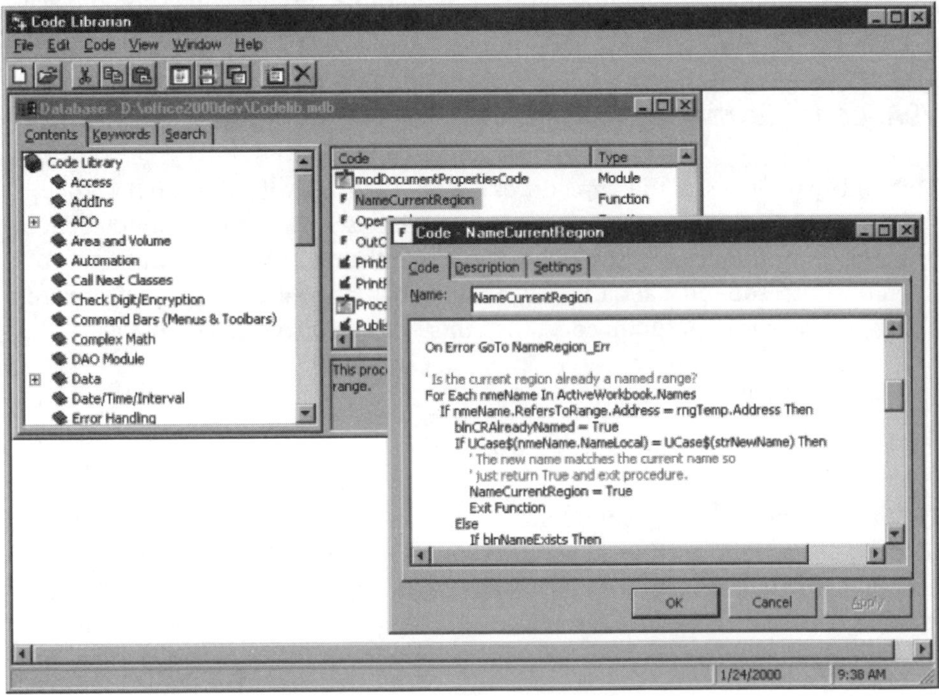

Figure 14.3. The code librarian

VBA Source Code Control

If several developers are working simultaneously on the same project, it is a good thing if at a later time it is possible to determine who made what changes, and to have these changes be undoable. A help in this is the supplementary program Visual SourceSafe, which is run in the development environment by the VBA Source Code Control add-in.

Digital Signature

With TOOLS|DIGITAL SIGNATURE Excel files and traditional add-ins can be provided with a digital signature. Unfortunately, this command is not available for COM add-ins. For COM add-ins you will need the program `signcode.exe`, which Microsoft makes available on its web site in the area Internet Client Software Development Kits. It is a mystery why this program is not simply supplied with the Developer Edition.

Some brief background information: Together with the signed files information is stored that provides details about the file's origins. If you want to be able to sign a file yourself, you must apply for a digital signature. You obtain one (after shelling out some money, of course) from national authentication organizations (in the U.S.A., for example, from VeriSign; in Europe usually from telecommunications firms).

A signature does not exclude the possibility that the code contains errors or even viruses, but it prevents subsequent changes in code that has been signed and gives positive identification as to from whom or from what company the code derives. For this reason it is unlikely that signed viruses will be sent forth into the world (unless a hacker succeeds in cracking the signature mechanism; but that, at least, has not happened yet). Therefore, even code in signed files is executed by Excel with maximal virus protection.

Database Tools and Controls

Supplementary Controls

The supplementary controls *DataList, DataCombo, DataGrid,* and *MSHFlexGrid* assist in representing the results of database queries (of course, only on the basis of ADO, not DAO); see the section after next.

Designers

The *DataEnvironment* designer simplifies the creation of a connection to a database. The *DataReport* designer is conceived for the creation of database reports, but in this respect it cannot compete with Access. Both designers are discussed later in this chapter.

Access Runtime Version and Microsoft Data Engine (MSDE)

If you are developing plain Excel projects, then neither the Access runtime version nor MSDE is of interest to you. However, there are applications that use both Access and Excel functions. In such cases you can install the Access runtime version on your client's computer without the necessity of a license. (For Excel there exists no such runtime version. If you use Excel functions, your customer must possess Excel 2000.)

The Microsoft data engine is a somewhat limited version of the Microsoft SQL server. These are the limitations: Internally, at most five queries are processed simultaneously, for which reason MSDE is suitable only for database systems that will be accessed by few persons at a time. Furthermore, the tools provided with the complete version are lacking (for example, the enterprise manager). Nonetheless, MSDE is attractive: Like the Access runtime version you can give this SQL server miniversion to your clients (however, only together with programs that you have produced with Office Developer).

Custom On-Line Help (HTMLHelp)

If you wish to provide your Excel application with its own on-line help system, you can use the HTMLHelp Workshop 1.2 (which is hidden among the documentation and examples as the installation file `HtmlHelp.exe` in the folder `ODETools\v9\HHWkshop`) to assist in the development of help files.

> **REMARKS** *The development of custom help files with the Workshop is, unfortunately, a very time-consuming and painstaking undertaking. An alternative is instead of the Workshop to use a commercial third-party tool (for example, DocToHelp, RoboHelp, Help Magician). A less expensive variant is simply to provide your client with a help text in the form of a Word document or HTML document. You can display such files within Excel via ActiveX automation (see the last section of this chapter). However, you then lose the possibility of displaying context-sensitive on-line help via* `F1`.

There is insufficient space here to go deeply into the HTMLHelp Workshop. If you are not satisfied with the on-line documentation, you may obtain further information in the Microsoft programmer's handbook or in my book on Visual Basic 6.

Once you have a completed help file, you must still establish a link between this file and the Excel application. There are relatively few places within an Excel application in which a link to a help file can be established:

- With the method *Application.Help* an arbitrary help topic can be displayed.

- To every VBA procedure in the object browser a help topic can be associated with the pop-up menu entry PROPERTIES. The help text is summoned with `F1` in the Excel form INSERT FUNCTION or via the "?" button in the object browser. This form of linking help texts is most useful if you wish to pass along a library of supplementary tables or VBA functions.

- Menu entries and icons in the toolbar can be linked to a help text. For this the properties *HelpFile* and *HelpContextID* of the affected *CommandBar* object must be set.

- MS-Forms forms and the controls contained therein can also have an associated help text via the property *HelpContextID. HelpFile* is missing, however; instead, the file name must be specified in the development environment with TOOLS|XY PROPERTIES (where xy is the name of the project).

In all of the variants described above it is unpleasant that the file name of the help file and a so-called context ID number must be specified. Since the help file is usually saved in the same folder as the workbook when an Excel application is installed, the procedure *Workbook_Open* must see to it that *HelpFile* is properly set up. The *HelpContextID* number has to do with the identification numbers of the relevant help topics. These numbers must agree with the numbers specified in HTMLHelp Workshop.

Microsoft Developer Network (MSDN)

Three MSDA CDs are provided with Office Developer. These CDs contain not only the documentation for developer-specific Office components, but comprehensive documentation for almost all Microsoft products. Included, for example, are a reference for all operating system functions, background information on (D)HTML, and articles on database programming. Altogether, the library contains more than a gigabyte of condensed text and images. (For comparison, this book in a similarly compressed form would take up about two megabytes.)

Once you have installed MSDN, you can launch the help system as a freestanding application. Moreover, the MSDN window appears automatically when you press on F1 in the VBA development environment with certain functions or libraries.

The MSDN offers excellent search options. Unfortunately, there are two serious drawbacks:

- It is rather difficult to filter relevant data from the abundance of information. (Hint: Limit the search domain.)

- The data are divided among three CD-ROMs, which requires constant changing of CDs. (Here, too, there is a way out, which consists in installing the complete MSDN library on your hard drive. The storage requirement is more than a gigabyte, and so requires a large hard drive. Alternatively, you could use a DVD drive and order the MSDN-DVD-Abo. Then every quarter you would receive a current version of the MSDN library on DVD.)

Excel Add-Ins

> **TIP** *This section deals with saving Excel files as add-in files (`*.xla`). This function is available in all Excel versions. The next section deals with a second add-in variant, the so-called COM add-ins. These can be created with the Office Developer Edition (or with the Visual Basic programming language from version 5 on), and they display a number of advantages and disadvantages in relation to the traditional add-ins as described in this section.*

Excel comes equipped with a host of so-called add-in files. These files are located in the directory `Office2000\Office\Library` and have the task of extending the functionality of Excel at a number of points. They can be activated and deactivated with the add-in manager. Since loading an add-in function requires a certain amount of memory, you should activate only those add-ins that you truly need. Add-in files can be recognized by the suffix `*.xla`.

In addition to the add-in files supplied with Excel, the command FILE|SAVE AS offers the possibility of saving your own Excel files in add-in format. (The add-in format is the last entry in the file type list.) The suggested location in which to save such a file is `userprofile\Application Data\Microsoft\AddIns`. This means that the add-in is available only for the current user. (If you wish to make an add-in generally available, you should save it in the Library directory mentioned above.)

Add-in files differ from normal `*.xls` files in the following ways:

- The (user-defined) functions contained therein are available to all other workbooks. It is not necessary (as it is otherwise) for the name of the add-in file to be prefixed or to provide a reference. The function call is effected directly with *Functionname*, not in the form *filename!functionname*. Access to these functions is, of course, possible only when the add-in file has previously been loaded. (This is the concern of the add-in manager.)

- The worksheets of the add-in are invisible and cannot be made visible.

- The property *IsAddin* of the object *ThisWorkbook* contains the value *True*.

CAUTION *In contrast to Excel 5 and 7 the program code of add-ins is unrestrictedly viewable in the development environment. There the code can be edited and saved. If you do not wish the user to see the code to your add-in, it must be password protected via* TOOLS|PROPERTIES|PROTECTION.

TIP *Add-ins can be easily converted again into normal files. Simply load the add-in file, open the properties window to "this workbook" in the development environment, and set* IsAddin *to* False. *With this the worksheets become visible, and the file can be saved in Excel with* SAVE AS *as a normal* `*.xls` *file.*

Applications of Custom Add-Ins

- You can write an add-in with a collection of new tables or VBA functions that you use frequently. As soon as the add-in is loaded, these functions are available in other VBA programs and also for use directly in worksheets. The add-in is not visible, that is, neither in menu nor toolbar nor dialog. Such libraries of functions present the fewest difficulties from the programming point of view. The add-in consists exclusively of code in module sheets. Normally, a *Workbook_Open* procedure is not necessary (unless your functions require some global variables or fields that are initialized in *Workbook_Open*).

- You can equip Excel with additional commands or wizards, thereby extending Excel's user interface. For this the add-in must extend the existing menu (usually with the worksheet menu TOOLS), so that the new commands can be invoked. The selection of these commands then leads to the display of a dialog by means of which the further use of the command is governed.

- The third variant consists in using the add-in as "packaging" for freestanding applications. This variant involves the greatest amount of programming effort. Normally, supplementary menu entries do not suffice, and therefore a custom menu or toolbar must be created and managed. In addition, as a rule, the opening and controlling of other Excel files is necessary. Further information on the problems that occur in realizing freestanding add-in programs is given below under "limitations."

> **TIP** *Among the example programs presented in this book there is one that is predestined to be transformed into an add-in. The euro conversion tool (Chapter 5). Load the* `*.xls` *file, save it as a* `*.xla` *file as an add-in, and you are done.*

Loading Add-In Files With and Without the Add-In Manager

In principle, there are two ways of starting an add-in file: Either open the file like a normal Excel file with FILE|OPEN or invoke the add-in manager (via TOOLS|ADD-INS), there click on the Browse button, and select the file. With add-ins corresponding to the first two variants, installation via the add-in manager is the better choice. You can then activate and deactivate the add-in file at will, as with other add-ins. For add-ins belonging to the third variant (custom applications) it is more practical to open the add-in file only when needed, via FILE|OPEN.

> **TIP** *Normally, only the file name of the selected file is displayed in the add-in manager, not (as with built-in add-ins) a more meaningful name for the add-in together with a brief commentary about its significance. You can alter this state of affairs as follows: Before changing your workbook into an add-in file, execute* FILE|PROPERTIES|SUMMARY *and there provide a title and short commentary.*

The form for the add-in manager has the drawback that it provides no opportunity to delete an entry from the add-in list. The only way to do this is to delete the relevant `*.xla` file or rename it and then attempt to activate the add-in. At this moment Excel realizes that the add-in no longer exists and asks whether it may be permitted to delete the entry from the add-in list.

> **TIP** *An add-in file that has been loaded via* FILE|OPEN *cannot then be deleted from Excel's memory while it is running. Add-in files are "invisible," and therefore they cannot be activated as an Excel window and then closed. To get around this deficiency you should use the add-in manager to load the add-in.*

Using Functions Defined in Add-Ins

User-defined functions that are defined in the code of an add-in can be used directly in worksheets. The functions are displayed in the form INSERT|FUNCTION in the category "User Defined. " The only condition is that the add-in file have been opened (whether via FILE|OPEN or the add-in manager). Functions or procedures that are used only within the add-in but should remain otherwise unavailable must be identified in program code with the keyword *Private.*

If you wish to use a function (or procedure) in the VBA code of a new workbook, then you must establish a reference to the add-in file (with the command TOOLS|REFERENCES). All available functions are then displayed in the object browser. See Chapter 4 on the subject of the object browser and references.

In the example below (`AddInFn.xls` and `.xla`) the generally accessible function *AITest* is defined, which multiplies its parameter by 6. The function *AITest* uses, in turn, the function *InternalFunction,* which is unavailable to the user of the add-in file.

```
' AddInFn.xls, Module1
Function AITest(x)
  AITest = 2 * InternalFunction(x)
End Function
Private Function InternalFunction(x)
  InternalFunction = x * 3
End Function
```

If you create a large function library and wish to distribute it, then you should provide each function with a brief informational text that will be displayed in the function assistant and the object browser. Such texts can be inserted into the object browser with the pop-up menu command PROPERTIES. This command opens a dialog box in which you can also set a reference to a help file.

Event Procedures in Add-Ins

In addition to the procedures *Workbook_Open* and *Workbook_BeforeClose*, which are also available in normal workbooks, for add-ins there are two additional procedures that are automatically executed: ***Workbook_AddinInstall***, when an add-in is taken into the add-in list of the add-in manager, and ***Workbook_AddinUninstall***, when the add-in is removed from this list. The two procedures are not executed every time the add-in is loaded, but only once upon installation as a permanent addition to Excel and again upon deinstallation. You can use these procedures to carry out one-time preparatory tasks (for example, to copy template files into the template directory) or corresponding cleanup tasks.

Limitations in the Programming of Custom Add-In Applications

Add-in files are completely "invisible." By this is meant that the worksheet or chart sheet of an add-in file cannot be displayed. Add-in files can be made perceptible only through a menu extension, independent menu, toolbar, or dialog.

The data in the worksheets of an add-in file are internally available and can, for example, be transferred via VBA code into a newly opened workbook and there edited. However, it is impossible to translate unchanged an application such as `DB_Share.xls` (formula and database application) for the car sharing club; see Chapter 11) into an add-in file. The application depends on its worksheets being visible on the computer monitor, where they can be changed by the user, and this is impossible with an add-in file.

There are two ways of solving this problem. The first variant consist in separating the application into two files. One file contains code, menus, and forms and is transmitted as an add-in file. The second file contains the tables in which the user is to work and is opened by the first file via *Workbook_Open*. In *Workbook_Open* you can set up event procedures for the newly opened table file (say for changing sheets). This modus operandi has two drawbacks: First, the application depends on the presence of both files, and second, the application is subject to intentional or unintentional changes in the table file.

The second solution consists in leaving all the worksheets in the add-in file. With *Workbook_Open* you generate a new workbook and copy the relevant worksheets into it. This solution requires somewhat greater effort in programming but in compensation is less subject to breakdown.

In either case there is a restriction to be reckoned with: Although you can change the (invisible) tables in the add-in while it is operational, it is impossible to save these changes. This is inconvenient in applications in which a running serial number (receipt number, data record number) must be maintained and be set to the last valid value when the program is launched. A serial number or other data that you will require at the next launch of the add-in must be saved in a different file.

In sum, add-ins are well suited for the distribution of a set of functions or to extend Excel's user interface (such as the euro conversion tool). However, add-ins seldom represent a usable solution for freestanding applications, such as can be found in Chapters 9 through 13. In this case add-ins offer no recognizable advantages over normal Excel files.

COM Add-Ins

COM add-ins are a rather curious affair. On the one hand, Microsoft has marketed this innovation as the greatest thing since DOS: finally, an integrated format by which all the Office components can be extended (instead of the alleged nine different older variants to create such extensions in Word, Excel, and Access).

On the other hand, the documentation for COM add-ins is a disaster area. There is not a single example available (as of the end of 1999, three-quarters of a year after Office 2000 was delivered) that shows how a COM add-in can be developed with Office Developer. (All the examples relate to the programming language Visual Basic 6, which is not provided with Office Developer.) There is no menu command for managing COM add-ins in Excel and in the other Office components. (The command exists, but it must be explicitly added to the menu with VIEW|TOOLBARS|CUSTOMIZE|COMMANDS.) It is no wonder, then, that all the add-ins provided with Excel are traditional in nature (that is, `*.xla` files).

This leads one to experience grave doubts as to whether the Microsoft development division is of the same opinion as the marketing division. And when you have read this section to the bitter end, it will have become clear to you that this doubt is well warranted. COM add-ins are a version-1.0 product and as such are to be avoided! Perhaps in Office 2002 (or whatever the next version number may be) COM add-ins will deliver what they promise.

> **TIP** *To develop COM add-ins you need the Office Developer Edition or the programming language Visual Basic 5 or 6. (This section discusses only the first variant.)*

Basics

What Are COM Add-Ins?

From the user's point of view a COM add-in is an extension of the Excel user interface (or other Office application). This extension can involve such objects as menu commands, forms, and wizards (assistants). The possibilities are endless.

From the programmer's point of view COM add-ins are independent projects that are developed with Office Developer (command FILE|NEW PROJECT|ADD-IN PROJECT).

From the technical point of view one is dealing with ActiveX-DLLs that communicate via the so-called *IDTExtensibility2* interface with an Office component. (IDT apparently stands for *Interrupt Dispatch Table,* but this abbreviation is not conclusively documented.)

Using COM Add-Ins

Before you can use an add-in you must install it. (This holds only for the client's computer. On your computer, where the add-in was developed, explicit installation is not required. You need only start the add-in in the development environment or compile it to a DLL file. In both cases the add-in is automatically registered.)

The second step consists in activating the COM add-in. According to how the property INITIAL LOAD BEHAVIOR was set, the add-in activates itself automatically the next time Excel is launched. This case is the most customer friendly, since in this case the new commands simply become available.

On the other hand, if no such automatic activation is provided for, then you must explicitly breathe life into the add-in with the command COM ADD-INS. You will search long and hard for this command, since it is not integrated into the normal Excel menu. (Who knows what the wise persons at Microsoft were thinking? The add-in manager is unsuitable for COM add-ins, having been conceived for traditional add-ins.) Therefore, execute in Excel VIEW|TOOLBARS|CUSTOMIZE|COMMANDS, search for the command in the category "tools," and drag it into the TOOLS menu.

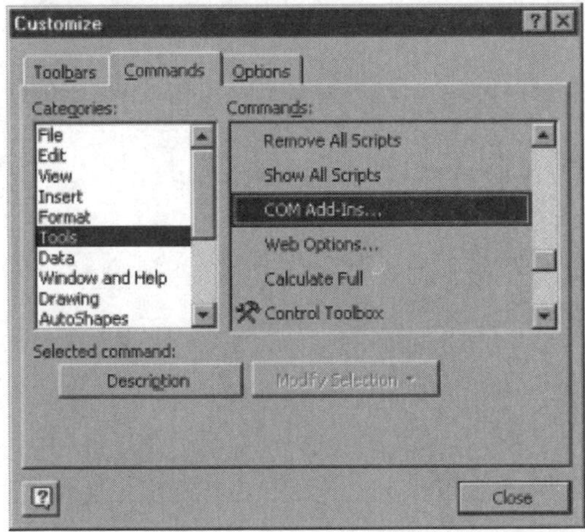

Figure 14.4. The menu command COM Add-Ins is not in the standard Excel menu

Now that the command Tools|COM Add-Ins is available to be executed, go ahead and execute it. The form displayed in Figure 14.5 appears, in which you can activate or deactivate any registered add-in. In the case of unregistered COM add-ins you can select the `*.dll` file directly with Add, though as a rule that should not be necessary.

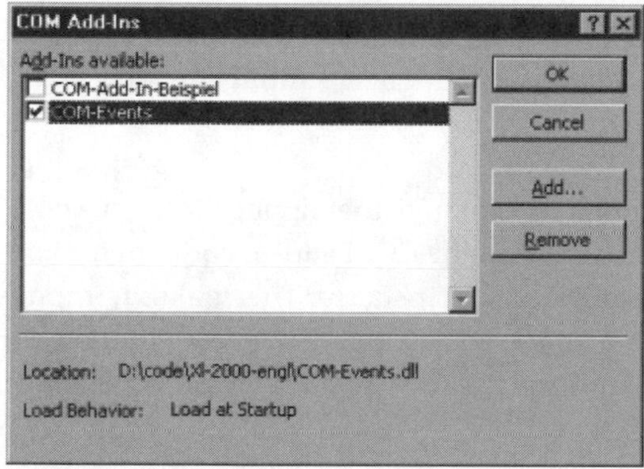

Figure 14.5. The COM Add-Ins dialog

Once activated, the add-in acquires the ability to be integrated into the user interface. How that happens depends on the add-in, but as a rule it will involve a new menu entry or toolbar.

Differences Between Traditional Add-Ins and COM Add-Ins

- To develop a COM add-in you need Office Developer Edition or the programming language Visual Basic 5 or 6.
- Program code is compiled, which in many cases produces a small increase in speed of execution. (Don't expect too much.)
- Compilation has another advantage: Your code is better protected from prying eyes.
- COM add-ins can be designed so that they can be used in various Office components (such as Outlook, Word). Depending on the application, a large portion of the code and dialogs can be used in common, with only the immediate interface components having to be programmed individually.
- COM add-ins cannot contain Excel worksheets or charts (nor invisible sheets as with traditional add-ins, nor toolbars).

A COM add-in has to this extent nothing more to do with a traditional Excel file. For this reason the menu of the VBA development environment must be used to load or save the project in a `*.vba` file. The Excel menu is unsuitable for this purpose.

In the References form no Excel file or traditional Excel add-in can be activated. This means, for example, that it is impossible to use the *EuroConvert* function of the Excel euro add-in in a COM add-in.

Instead, in developing a COM add-in the *DataEnvironment* and *DataReport* designers can be accessed. These two designers simplify the development of database applications.

- In the case of database applications (and many other applications as well), however, there is a difficulty in that within the COM add-in code there is no property to tell you where the COM DLL was installed. This makes it impossible to include a (database) file with the add-in and then access that file. (Of course, you can display a dialog and ask the user to search for the file, but that is hardly an elegant solution.)

- The distribution of an add-in is complicated, requiring a setup program (which fortunately can be created with the installation assistant). The COM add-in must be recorded in the registration database before it can be used. (This is one of the tasks of the setup program.)

  For unexplained reasons the add-in must be recorded separately for each user—at this point the setup program breaks down (for details see the next section).

- More complicated is the management of COM add-ins on the client's computer, since the required command TOOLS|COM-ADD-INS is not part of the standard menu (see above).

> **TIP** *To make the point once more: COM add-ins have as good as nothing to do with traditional Excel projects (and thus with traditional add-ins). Thus it is not surprising that it is impossible to transform a traditional project into an add-in project. (However, you can conveniently copy modules and dialogs from a traditional project into a COM add-in in via* Drag & Drop.

Applications

In the previous section three typical applications for add-ins were listed: function libraries, extensions of the user interface, and freestanding Excel applications. Traditional Excel add-ins are best suited for the first two types of application.

With COM add-ins the spectrum of possible applications is again reduced; they are suitable exclusively to extend the user interface of Excel or another Office component (assistants, additional menu commands, etc.) A definite advantage vis-à-vis traditional add-ins is to be had when the add-in is to be used not for Excel, but for other office applications, which in practice occurs relatively rarely.

> **REMARKS** *In principle, it is also possible to program COM add-ins for the VBA development environment, that is, for example, tools to simplify program development. A portion of the add-ins provided with Office Developer were presumably created in this way. However, this section deals only with COM add-ins for Excel.*

Development of a COM Add-In

The development of a new COM add-in begins with executing the command FILE|NEW PROJECT|ADD-IN PROJECT in the development environment. (This command is available if you are using the Office Developer Edition.) The project is saved in a file with the identifier `*.vba`. In contrast to normal Excel projects the open and save commands must be executed in the development environment. Excel "knows" nothing about the project, and in fact, it has nothing to do with Excel.

> **POINTER** *This section describes how a COM add-in is developed with the Office Developer Edition. If you prefer Visual Basic 6 as your development environment, you will find relevant information in the Office 2000 programmer's handbook as well as in the MSDN library ("Technical Articles"). All of the example programs on the Office Developer CD in the directory* `ODETools\V9\OPG\SampleApplications` *are conceived for Visual Basic 6.*

Add-In Designer

After the command FILE|NEW PROJECT|ADD-IN PROJECT has been executed, the new COM add-in project at first consists of only a single component (an object belonging to the class *AddInDesigner*). This class is made available by the add-in designer. (Designers were discussed at the beginning of this chapter.)

In the add-in designer window (Figure 14.6) you can set a number of properties of the add-in. The ADDIN DISPLAY NAME is the text that will be displayed in the form for activating COM add-ins (Figure 14.5). The DESCRIPTION, on the other hand, is used (for the present) only internally and is not displayed.

In APPLICATION and VERSION you specify for which Office components your add-in has been conceived. Only one component can be selected for each add-in designer. If you develop an add-in for several Office components, you must insert correspondingly many add-in designers into the project, one for each Office component.

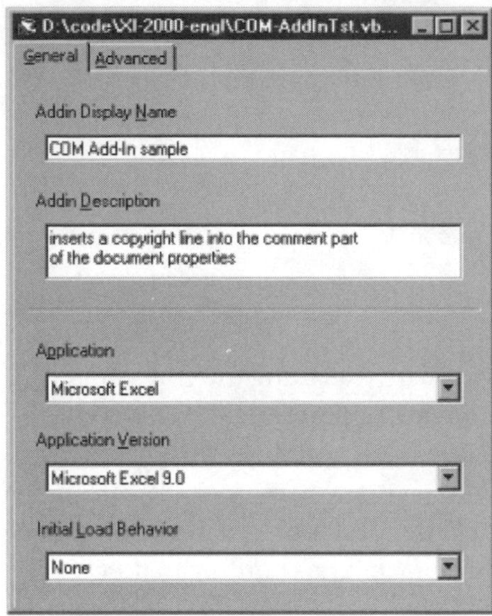

Figure 14.6. The add-in designer window

It is more difficult to explain the listbox INITIAL LOAD BEHAVIOR, for which reason we have devoted a separate subsection to it (see below). In the sheet ADVANCED of the designer window you will find additional settings, which as a rule, however, are not necessary and will not be described here.

TIP *The designer window looks like a dialog (form), but in reality it is a window. Thus it is possible to open several designer windows simultaneously or to activate other windows while a design window is open. For this reason there is no* OK *button. When the window is closed all settings are automatically saved.*

TIP *You can change the name of the add-in in the properties window only while the design window is open.*

Load Behavior of COM-Add-Ins

In the listbox INITIAL LOAD BEHAVIOR you can set how the COM add-in should behave when the application program for which it was designed (Excel, for example) is launched. (This setting is valid only for the compiled add-in DLL, not for the test of the add-in in the development environment. Information on compiling add-ins follows further below.)

The loading behavior is also related to the activation of the add-in in the COM ADD-IN dialog. Depending on how the loading behavior was set, the add-in is automatically activated (without this dialog having to be displayed). Considering the fact that the command TOOLS|COM ADD-INS is usually lacking, this is of great significance.

These are the load options:

- *startup*: The next time Excel is launched the add-in is automatically activated and loaded. When Excel is again launched the add-in will likewise be loaded, provided that the user has not specifically deactivated it via TOOLS|COM ADD-INS.

- *none*: The next time Excel is launched nothing happens; that is, the add-in remains inactive. Not until the user activates it in the COM ADD-IN dialog is the add-in loaded for the first time. Upon all further launches of Excel the add-in is loaded as long as it remains activated in TOOLS|COM ADD-INS.

- *load at next startup only*: The next time Excel is launched the add-in is automatically launched and activated. The add-in is now able to alter menu entries, add new buttons to toolbars, and so on. Upon further launches of Excel the add-in behaves as in the *load on demand* option.

- *load on demand*: The add-in is not loaded, even if it is active in the COM ADD-IN dialog. The add-in is brought to life only when an associated menu command is executed or the relevant button clicked. This is an attractive option to the extent that the add-in is loaded into memory only when it is actually needed. However, it is necessary, of course, that the menu command or button be visible. For this reason it usually makes more sense to choose the *load at next startup only* setting.

Load Behavior	Add-in is automatically activated in the COM ADD-IN dialog when the application program is first launched	Add-in is loaded only when it is actually needed
startup	•	
none		
load at next startup only	•	•
load on demand		•

If you wish for the add-in to be automatically activated (without burdening your client with the absent COM ADD-IN command), then you should choose *startup* or *load on demand.* The setting *load on demand* is the more attractive variant on technical grounds, while it is only with *startup* that the event procedures described below are executed at every launch. In these procedures you can ensure, for example, that a (possibly erroneously) deleted menu entry is restored.

During programming *none* is the most sensible setting, since the behavior is then the easiest to understand. The add-in must be explicitly activated in the COM ADD-IN dialog for it to be loaded. (Since during development Excel usually is running continuously and not continually terminated and restarted, automatic activation does not occur. And once more the following advice: The setting holds only for the compiled code. While you are testing the add-in in the development environment it behaves like the compiled version with the launch setting *none.*)

COM Add-In Events

In the module of the add-in designer there are seven events provided for the object *AddinInstance.* The events *Initialize* and *Terminate* come from the VBA development environment, while the *OnXxx* events come from the already mentioned *IDTExtensibility2* interface, which enables communication between the add-in and the Office component.

AddinInstance *Events*

Initialize	add-in initialization
OnAddInsUpdate	another add-in was activated or deactivated
OnBeginShutdown	the application program (e.g., Excel) was terminated
OnConnection	connection between add-in and application
OnDisconnection	no connection between add-in and application
OnStartupComplete	initialization of the application program is complete
Terminate	add-in termination

Some remarks on the above: ***OnConnection*** and ***OnDisconnection*** mark the beginning and end of the time during which the add-in is in contact with the application program (such as Excel).

Four parameters are passed to *OnConnection*:

```
Sub AddinInstance_OnConnection(ByVal Application As Object, _
  ByVal ConnectMode As AddInDesignerObjects.ext_ConnectMode, _
  ByVal AddInInst As Object, custom() As Variant)
```

Application refers to the application program. *ConnectMode* specifies why the add-in was loaded, either *ext_cm_Startup* (Excel program launch) or *ext_cm_AfterStartup* (later activation in the COM ADD-IN dialog). *AddInInst* refers to a *COMAddIn* object (*Office* library), which contains some properties of the add-in; *custom()* is not in use at the present time.

Of comparable significance is the parameter *RemoveMode* of the *OnDisconnection* procedure. The two possible values are *ext_dm_HostShutdown* (Excel program end) and *ext_dm_UserClosed* (deactivation in the COM ADD-IN dialog).

OnStartupComplete occurs only if the add-in is loaded during the launch of Excel (since it was already activated the last time, that is, *ConnectMode* = *ext_cm_Startup*). The difference between this and *OnConnection* is that now initialization of Excel is excluded, and the add-in can now access all Excel objects. ***OnBeginShutdown*** is the complement to *OnStartupComplete* and indicates that Excel will now be terminated. At this time all Excel objects are still accessible. If later *OnDisconnection* occurs, Excel can no longer be completely controlled.

If several add-ins are loaded (at program launch, for example), then ***OnAddInsUpdate*** occurs the corresponding number of times. This procedure is practical, then, if there is a dependency between several add-ins and this is to be tested. You can determine which COM add-ins are active via the ***ComAddIns*** enumeration. (Here we are dealing with a property of the Excel *Application* object, which refers to *ComAddIn* objects of the Office library.)

In very rare cases you will really need event procedures for all these events. Usually, *OnConnection* and *OnDisconnection* routines suffice to set or delete a menu entry or toolbar.

Finally, we present an overview of which events occur in what order:

- Launch Excel (the add-in was activated the previous time): *Initialize, OnConnection, OnAddInsUpdate, OnStartupComplete*

  Please note that with the launch behavior *load on demand* and (from the second launch) also with *load at next startup only* the events occur only when the add-in is actually loaded. In this case *OnStartupComplete* does not occur.

- Terminate Excel (add-in is still active): *OnBeginShutdown, OnDisconnection, Terminate*
- Activate add-in in the COM Add-In dialog: *Initialize, OnConnection, OnAddInsUpdate*
- Deactivate add-in in the COM Add-In dialog: *OnDisconnection, Terminate*

TIP *The example file* `COM-Events.vba` *contains, for all seven events mentioned, a simple procedure that displays with* MsgBox *the name of the event. You can use this example as a starting point for your own experiments with COM events.*

REMARKS *In the Office Developer programmer's handbook as well as in the on-line documentation there is a rather long-winded discussion of how you can implement the* IDTExtensibility2 *interface with* Implements. *However, this information is valid only if you do not use the add-in designer from Office Developer for programming. If you proceed as described in this section, you do not need* Implements.

CAUTION *The events described here occur reliably only when the add-in is compiled and the resulting DLL tested. On the other hand, if you attempt to test the add-in in the development environment, many events do not occur (for example,* OnDisconnection *and* Terminate *during deactivation of the add-in in the* COM Add-In *dialog). Of course, this makes debugging much more difficult during program development.*

Furthermore, the events occur only when the add-in is loaded into the memory of the application program. Whether and when this is the case depends on the (extensively described above) setting of the load behavior. For your first experiments you should definitely use startup *or* none.

Testing COM Add-Ins

To test a COM add-in, simply execute in the development environment Run|Run Project or press the corresponding button on the toolbar. To terminate execution of the code, use the command Run|Stop Project.

TIP *That well-known command from traditional Excel projects* RUN|RUN MACRO (F5) *is also available for COM projects, for testing individual procedures in a module (but not, however, in the code region of the add-in designer) or to test a dialog.*

The first time you use the RUN PROJECT command a PROJECT PROPERTIES form appears, in which a number of peculiar DEBUGGING settings can be made. This dialog is based on the circumstance that with a COM project one is not dealing with a freestanding program but with a component that can be used only in combination with another program (for example, Excel). The DEBUGGING settings relate to the development of other ActiveX components.

As long as you are developing COM add-ins, leave the option WAIT FOR COMPONENTS TO BE CREATED activated and click OK. This means that program execution begins only when the add-in has been activated by another program (as a rule, then, by Excel or another Office component). The dialog with the DEBUGGING settings is irritating in that WAIT FOR COMPONENTS TO BE CREATED is the only worthwhile option, and thus there is nothing really to set.

Given that the development environment has discovered no errors in your code, the new add-in is now logged into the registration database. Switch over to Excel, and there execute TOOLS|COM ADD-INS. You will discover a new entry with the name of your add-in, which you should activate. Now execution of the add-in begins, usually with one of the above-mentioned event procedures.

CAUTION *Once more a piece of advice: Testing a COM add-in in the development environment is convenient, to be sure (since you can set break points, and so on, as in Excel projects), but many events do not, alas, occur there. To give a final test to your COM add-in, you must compile it. See below.*

Compiling a COM Add-In

To convert the code of your add-in into a DLL (which stands for *Dynamic Link Library* and denotes a file with executable binary code) simply execute FILE|CREATE NAME.DLL. The DLL is automatically logged into the registration database during compilation.

> **TIP** *Internally, COM add-ins are handled like ordinary ActiveX components whose only special feature is that the* IDTExtensibility2 *event procedures enable communication with Office components. Some background information on the concepts ActiveX and DLL can be found in the last section of this chapter. Considerably more information can be found in any good book on Visual Basic, which is by far the most popular programming language for creating ActiveX components of all varieties.*

After compilation, the add-in DLL can be tested in Excel: Again execute TOOLS|COM ADD-INS in Excel and activate the add-in again. Although you seem to be executing the same operation as above, the new DLL version of the add-in is activated.

> **CAUTION** *As soon as you have compiled a COM add-in for the first time, this DLL is known on your computer (at least under your login ID). The situation becomes unclear as soon as you improve or correct the code of your add-in in the development environment. Registration continues to relate to the DLL, and this contains the old code.*
>
> *To test the new code you must either create the DLL anew in the development environment or use the command* RUN|RUN PROJECT. *In this case the registration database is changed so that now the add-in version of the development environment has priority over the DLL. However, this holds only so long as the add-in is executed in the development environment.*

> **TIP** *You can create a new DLL only when the existing DLL is not in use. Thus you must first execute* TOOLS|COM ADD-INS *in Excel (and in all other Office components in which the compiled add-in is in use) and there deactivate the add-in.*

Error Protection

If an error occurs in a COM add-in that has not been foreseen with *On Error*, then the add-in will terminate at once (that is, be removed from memory). However, Excel will not be affected by this occurrence; that is, Excel continues to run.

File Access

As already mentioned, there is the possibility to access the directory in the code of an add-in in which the COM add-in DLL was installed. But access to data(base) files that might be present there is impossible without the intervention of the user.

The VBA method *CurDir* normally refers to the data directory of the user (that is, for example, `H:\WINNT4\Profiles\Administrator\Personal`). You cannot, however, rely on this, since the current directory can be changed at will by the user or by the VBA code in an Excel file. (For Excel there is only one current directory, which is shared with all add-ins.)

Activating and Deactivating COM Add-Ins in Program Code

In principle, it is also possible via program code to activate or deactivate add-ins that have been registered. (This corresponds to a change in the check box in the COM ADD-INS dialog.) For this purpose the Excel *Application* object is equipped with the property ***ComAddIns***, which refers to a like-named enumeration of the Office library. With *ComAddIns* you can, not surprisingly, access ***ComAddIn*** objects, which contain the most important properties of the COM add-in. The ***Connect*** property specifies whether the COM add-in is currently linked with Excel. You activate or deactivate a COM add-in by setting *Connect* to *True* or *False*.

Saving Data in the Registration Database

If you wish to store information in an add-in for the long term, you are faced with a dilemma: Where should the data be stored so that they can be found at a later date? There is no installation directory or another data directory that you can access without further ado.

One possibility would be to access Excel-specific directories (whose location you can determine with properties such as *Application.**TemplatesPath***; see Chapter 5). For small data sets—a few character strings, for example—there is a more elegant alternative: You save the data not in a file, but in the Windows registration database. For this the VBA library offers the methods *SaveSetting, GetSetting, GetAllSettings*, and *DeleteSetting*.

> **TIP** *These methods are, of course, also available in all Excel programs, not only in COM add-ins. In an Excel program, however, there are much simpler options to store data, such as in the cells of a worksheet!*

SaveSetting *"progname", "directory", "key", "content"* saves the character string given in the last parameter in the following entry of the registration database:

```
HKEY_CURRENT_USER\Software\VB and VBA Program Settings\progname\directory
```

The group `VB and VBA Program Settings` is fixed. *SaveSetting* can save only character strings. The parameters *directory* and *key* must be specified (no empty character strings). If you execute the following instructions, the resulting entry in the registration database looks like that in Figure 14.7.

```
SaveSetting "xl2000test", "testdir", "testkey", "content"
```

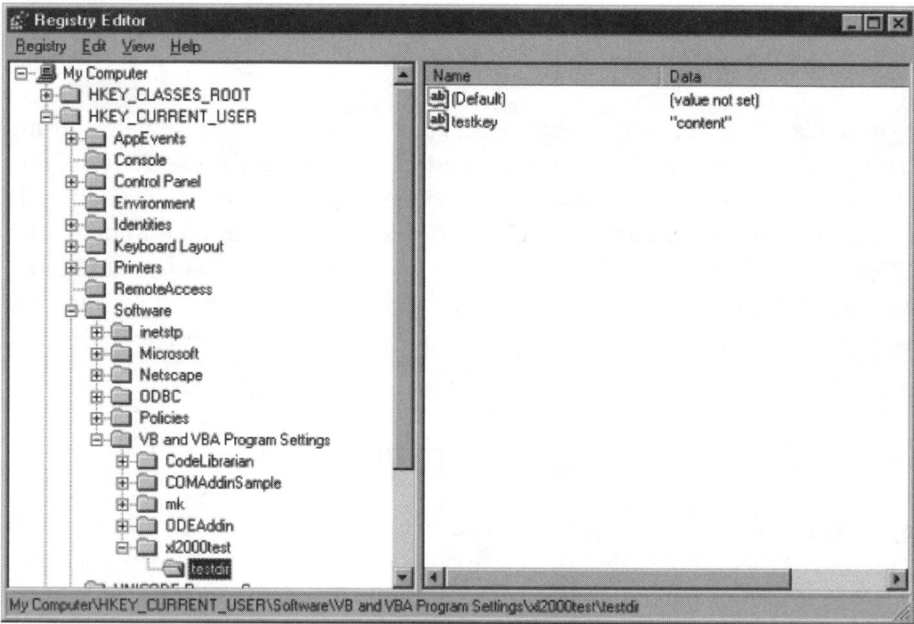

Figure 14.7. The character string "content" has been saved in the registration database

The function complementary to *SaveSetting* is ***GetSetting****("p", "v", "s", "default")*. The first three parameters are the same as those for *SaveSetting*. A default value can be specified in the fourth parameter that is then used if the registry entry being sought does not exist (in particular, the first time the program is run). The following instruction reads again the entry just saved from the registration database and returns as result the character string *content"*.

```
GetSetting("xl2000test", "testdir", "testkey")
```

GetAllSettings reads all keys and entries of a directory into a data field:

```
Dim x   'Variant
x = GetAllSettings("xl2000test", "testdir")
```

Here *x* is a two-dimensional field; *x(n,0)* contains the key, and *x(n,1)* the corresponding value of the registry directory *Window1*. The range of values for *n* is from 0 to *Ubound(x,1)*.

DeleteSettings *"p", "v" [,"s"]* deletes either all entries in a directory or only individual entries.

> **TIP** *Do not misuse the registration database for saving large amounts of data, which are better saved in a file. The registration database is not optimized for managing large data sets.*

Registry Functions

SaveSetting progname, directory, key, content	save entry
content = GetSetting(progname, directory, key[,default])	read entry
datafield = GetAllSettings(progname, directory)	read all entries of a group
DeleteSetting progname, directory[,key]	delete entry

Example: Copyright Entry for Excel and Word

The example program has been conceived for both Excel and Word (and its domain of use could easily be expanded to include other Office components as well). This add-in adds two new commands, TOOLS|INSERT COPYRIGHT TEXT and TOOLS|SET COPYRIGHT TEXT, into the menus of Excel and Word. With the command SET COPYRIGHT-TEXT a character string can be created that the program remembers (registration database). When the command INSERT COPYRIGHT TEXT is executed, then the add-in inserts the line © *2000 character string* into the comments field of the PROPERTIES dialog of the currently active document. (Instead of 2000, the current year will of course be used, and instead of "character string" the preset text.)

Thus the add-in is designed for those for whom it is a bother to invoke FILE|PROPERTIES in every document and to enter certain data in the dialog. (Of course, you can easily extend this add-in so that not only the copyright line, but other data as well are entered into the PROPERTIES dialog.

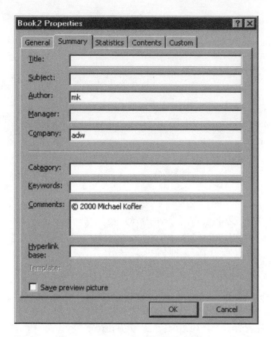

Figure 14.8. *An entry in the Properties dialog carried out by an add-in*

Overview

The project consists of four components (Figure 14.9): *addinExcel* contains the Excel-specific add-in settings and the associated code, while *addinWord* has the corresponding data for Word. There are no special features of the add-in's properties. As load behavior *load at next startup only* is set. Finally, *Module1* contains the code common to both *addin* components.

With TOOLS|REFERENCES, in addition to the libraries that are always available, the Office, Excel, and Word object libraries are activated.

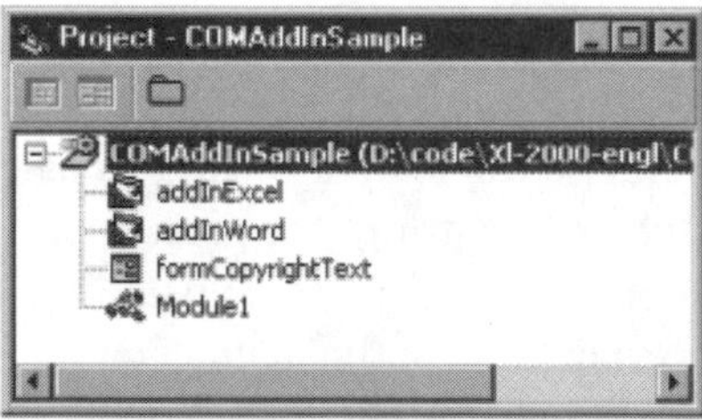

Figure 14.9. The components of the example add-in

The Code to addInExcel

In the add-in designer component *addInExcel* three general variables have been declared: In *app* a reference to the Excel *Application* object is saved. (The object is passed as parameter to the *OnConnection* event procedure.) The two *cbbName* variables refer to the pair of menu entries of the program. The variables are declared with *WithEvents* so that the associated events can be received.

```
' COM-AddInTst.vba, addinExcel
Dim app As Excel.Application
Dim WithEvents cbbNewCopyrightText  As CommandBarButton
Dim WithEvents cbbInsertCopyright  As CommandBarButton
```

In the *OnConnection* event procedure some variables are initialized. Then the procedure *InitializeCommandbar* is called to insert the two new menu commands into the menu. (The procedure is located in *Module1*. It is printed further below.)

Access to the TOOLS menu is accomplished by naming this character string directly. This means that the code functions only if this is the actual name of the menu (which would not be the case, say, for the Italian version of Excel). The alternative would be to access *Controls(6)*, but then the program is dependent on the TOOLS menu being the sixth menu. (This position is not constant. It might change in a future version of Excel. It is also possible that the user or another add-in has previously inserted another menu.)

The second feature is the variables *cbb1* and *cbb2*. They are changed in the procedure *InitializeCommandbar* and then accessed with *cbbNewCopyrightText* and *cbbInsertCopyright*. This raises the question of why not simply pass *cbbXy* to *InitializeCommandbar*. It doesn't work! There is no error that occurs, but *cbbXy* contains, after the call to *InitializeCommandbar*, still *Nothing*, and the menu events can therefore not be received. The reason for this erroneous behavior remains unclear. Perhaps it has something to do with *WithEvents*.

When *InitializeCommandbar* is called, the last parameter is *AddInInst.**ProgId***. This is a character string that specifies the add-in components, for example, *"COMAddInSample.addInExcel"*. This character string is necessary so that the COM add-in menus function even when the COM add-in is not loaded (*load on demand*).

```
' create menu entry for Excel
Private Sub AddinInstance_OnConnection(ByVal Application As Object, ByVal
ConnectMode As AddInDesignerObjects.ext_ConnectMode, ByVal AddInInst As Object,
custom() As Variant)
  Dim cbp As CommandBarPopup
  Dim cbs As CommandBars
  Dim cbb1 As CommandBarButton, cbb2 As CommandBarButton
  Set app = Application
  Set cbs = app.CommandBars
  ' localize Tools!
  Set cbp = app.CommandBars("Worksheet Menu Bar").Controls("Tools")
  ' caution: the program doesn't work if cbbNewCopyrightText
  ' and cbbInsertCopyright are used as parameters directly;
  ' therefore, we have to use local variables instead
  InitializeCommandbar cbs, cbp, cbb1, cbb2, AddInInst.ProgId
  Set cbbNewCopyrightText = cbb1
  Set cbbInsertCopyright = cbb2
End Sub
```

TIP *Please note that access to the* TOOLS *menu in program code is problematic. In international versions of Excel the menu may have a different name (such as* EXTRAS *in the German version). Another way of proceeding would be to give the number of the menu instead of the character string* "Tools". *But then the code may not function in the next version of Excel if the menus are rearranged.*

In the *OnDisconnection* event procedure the two menu entries are deleted if the add-in is explicitly deactivated in the COM ADD-IN dialog. On the other hand, if *OnDisconnection* appears at the end of the program, then the menu entries remain. (Here as well, the actual work is delegated to an auxiliary procedure. In any case, *RemoveCommandBarButtons* is located in *module1*.)

```
' delete menu entries in the add-in has been explicitly deactivated
Private Sub AddinInstance_OnDisconnection( _
    ByVal RemoveMode As AddInDesignerObjects.ext_DisconnectMode, _
    custom() As Variant)
  If RemoveMode = ext_dm_UserClosed Then
    RemoveCommandBarButtons app.CommandBars
  End If
End Sub
```

In the event procedure to Set Copyright Text the dialog shown in Figure 14.10 is displayed. The new text is saved in the registration database. This is the task of the event procedure *btnOK_Click* of the dialog (see below).

```
' event procedure for the menu entry 'Set Copyright Text
Private Sub cbbNewCopyrightText_Click( _
    ByVal Ctrl As Office.CommandBarButton, CancelDefault As Boolean)
  formCopyrightText.Show
End Sub
```

The event procedure for Set Copyright Text saves the character string saved in the registration database in the document properties. Access is via *BuiltinDocumentProperties("comments").*

```
' event procedure for the menu entry 'Set Copyright Text
Private Sub cbbInsertCopyright_Click( _
    ByVal Ctrl As Office.CommandBarButton, CancelDefault As Boolean)
  Dim wb As Workbook
  Set app = Ctrl.Application
  On Error GoTo insert_error
  Set wb = app.ActiveWorkbook
  If wb Is Nothing Then Exit Sub
  wb.BuiltinDocumentProperties("comments") = _
    "© " + Format(Now, "yyyy") + " " + _
    GetSetting("COMAddinSample", "Copyright", "copyrighttext", "")
  Exit Sub
insert_error:
  MsgBox "The Copyright Text could not be set. " & _
    "error message: " & Error
End Sub
```

The Code for AddInWord

The code for the Word add-in looks similar to that for Excel. The differences are in several details: *app* is declared as *Word.Application* (instead of *Excel.Application*). Access to the Tools menu is somewhat different from that in Excel. (The menu bar is here called *Menu Bar*, instead of *Worksheet Menu Bar*.) In *cbbInsertCopyright_Click*, *ActiveDocument* is edited instead of *ActiveWorksheet.*

```
' COM-AddInTst.vba, addinWord
Dim app As Word.Application
Dim WithEvents cbbNewCopyrightText As CommandBarButton
Dim WithEvents cbbInsertCopyright As CommandBarButton
```

```
Private Sub AddinInstance_OnConnection(…)
  … as above
  Set cbp = app.CommandBars("Menu Bar").Controls("Tools")
  … as above
End Sub
Private Sub AddinInstance_OnDisconnection(…) … as above
Private Sub cbbNewCopyrightText_Click(…)      … as above
Private Sub cbbInsertCopyright_Click(…)
  Dim doc As Document
  Set app = Ctrl.Application
  On Error GoTo insert_error
  Set doc = app.ActiveDocument
  If doc Is Nothing Then Exit Sub
  doc.BuiltinDocumentProperties("comments") = _
    "© " + Format(Now, "yyyy") + " " + _
    GetSetting("COMAddinSample", "Copyright", "copyrighttext", "")
  Exit Sub
insert_error:
  MsgBox "The copyright text could not be entered. " & _
    "Error message: " & Error
End Sub
```

The Code in Module1

InitializeCommandbar is perhaps the most interesting procedure of the example program. Here the menu commands are generated by which later the commands of the add-in will be executed. The procedure tests whether the menu commands already exist (perhaps from an earlier loading of the add-in).

For the COM add-in to be compatible with the load behavior of *load on demand* or *load at next startup only*, when new *CommandBarButton* objects are created two things must be attended to: First, the parameter *Temporary:=False* must be used, so that the menu entry is saved upon termination of Word or Excel. Second, in the *OnAction* property the name of the add-in components must be saved, and indeed in the syntax *!<addinname>*. This has the effect of loading the application program of the add-in in question when the menu command is executed, so that a reaction can follow. The add-in name can be taken from the third parameter of the *OnConnection* event procedure (see above).

The setting of the *Tag* property helps in finding the menu entry later. Finally, at the end of the initialization procedure a test is made as to whether a character string is already stored in the registration database. If that is not the case (at the first loading of the add-in), then the input dialog appears automatically.

```
' COM-AddInTst.vba, Module1
' create menu entries
Sub InitializeCommandbar(cbs As CommandBars, cbp As CommandBarPopup, _
    cbb1 As CommandBarButton, cbb2 As CommandBarButton, instancename$)
  ' test if menu entry 'Set copyright text' already exists
  Set cbb1 = cbs.FindControl(msoControlButton, Tag:="COM-Sample-1")
  If cbb1 Is Nothing Then
    Set cbb1 = cbp.Controls.Add(msoControlButton, Temporary:=False)
    With cbb1
      .BeginGroup = True
      .Caption = "Set copyright text"
      .DescriptionText = "sets the copyright text to be " & _
         "inserted into documents"
      .Tag = "COM-Sample-1"
      .OnAction = "!<" & instancename & ">"
    End With
  End If
  ' test if menu entry 'Insert copyright text' already exists
  Set cbb2 = cbs.FindControl(msoControlButton, Tag:="COM-Sample-2")
  If cbb2 Is Nothing Then
    Set cbb2 = cbp.Controls.Add(msoControlButton, Temporary:=False)
    With cbb2
      .Caption = "Insert copyright text"
      .DescriptionText = "inserts copyright text into the field " & _
        "'comment' of the document properties"
      .Tag = "COM-Sample-2"
      .OnAction = "!<" & instancename & ">"
    End With
  End If
  ' test if copyright text has already been saved in the registry
  If GetSetting("COMAddinSample", "Copyright", _
      "copyrighttext", "") = "" Then
    formCopyrightText.Show
  End If
End Sub
```

RemoveCommandBarButtons searches in the menu bar for menu commands with the *Tag* setting *"COM-Sample-n"*. Such commands are removed from the menu bar.

```
Sub RemoveCommandBarButtons(cbs As CommandBars)
  Dim cbb As CommandBarButton
  Set cbb = cbs.FindControl(msoControlButton, Tag:="COM-Sample-1")
  If Not (cbb Is Nothing) Then cbb.Delete
  Set cbb = cbs.FindControl(msoControlButton, Tag:="COM-Sample-2")
  If Not (cbb Is Nothing) Then cbb.Delete
End Sub
```

The Dialog for Setting the Copyright Text

The code for setting the copyright text demonstrates the application of the methods *GetSetting* and *SaveSetting* introduced in the previous section for reading and writing data in the registration database.

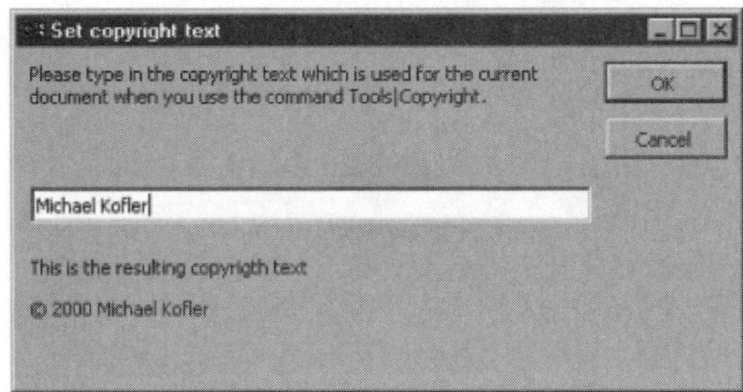

Figure 14.10. The dialog for setting the copyright text

```
' COMAddInSample.vba, formCopyrightText
Private Sub UserForm_Initialize()
  txtCopyright = GetSetting("COMAddinSample", "Copyright", _
    "copyrighttext", "")
  txtCopyright_Change
End Sub
Private Sub txtCopyright_Change()
  lblCopyright = "© " + Format(Now, "yyyy") + " " + txtCopyright
End Sub
Private Sub btnOK_Click()
  SaveSetting "COMAddinSample", "Copyright", "copyrighttext", _
    txtCopyright
  Unload Me
End Sub
Private Sub btnCancel_Click()
  Unload Me
End Sub
```

Installation Assistant

As we have already mentioned, COM add-ins must be installed and registered on the computer before they can be used. For installation it is not enough simply to copy the `addin.dll` file into some directory or other. (Moreover, a host of additional libraries are necessary in the `*.dll` file for the add-in to be able to be executed. If these libraries are not installed on the client's computer, this lack must be remedied.)

You see, then, that the distribution of a COM add-in is not a simple matter. To assist you in this task Microsoft has provided with the Office Developer Edition the so-called *Package and Deployment Wizard* (*PDW* for short), which in this section we shall call simply the installation assistant. Those who have worked with Visual Basic are familiar with this assistant, perhaps under a different name. This assistant has been the source of constant annoyance for more than half a decade. Sad to say, this holds true for the Office variant as well!

> **TIP** *Basically, the application of the installation assistant in not limited to COM add-ins. The assistant is also useful in distributing normal Excel files in which you access libraries (such as a new version of the ADO library) or supplementary controls (for example, the database controls introduced in the next section) that are not normally included with Office 2000. This section, however, is limited to COM add-ins, certainly the most important reason for Excel programmers to make friends with this assistant.*

Creating the Setup Program (Developer's Point of View)

The installation assistant is loaded in the VBA development environment via the ADD-IN menu. If the assistant does not appear, it must first be activated in the add-in manager. (There select LOAD ON STARTUP, thereby ensuring that the assistant will always be available in the future.

In the first step of the assistant select the command PACKAGE. (The other options serve for transmittal or the management of various configuration files for previously created installation files for the internet information server. Both options are normally not needed by Excel developers.)

In the next two steps you twice confirm that you wish to create a standard setup package (and not a dependency file that contains information as to which components are dependent on which other components; this option, too, is seldom of use to Excel developers).

In the step Package Folder you can specify a directory in which the installation files are to be collected. It is worthwhile to set a subdirectory `setup` as the current directory.

In the step Included Files the assistant shows which files have been installed on the client's computer. Don't be surprised about the large number of files! The files are needed by the setup program, and also by your COM DLL (which at least is very small). As a rule, you should not delete any files from the selection. If additional files belong to your project that the assistant does not automatically know about (database, help, or documentation files, for example), you can add these files to the list with Add. In Figure 14.11 the info file `COM-Events.txt` was added.

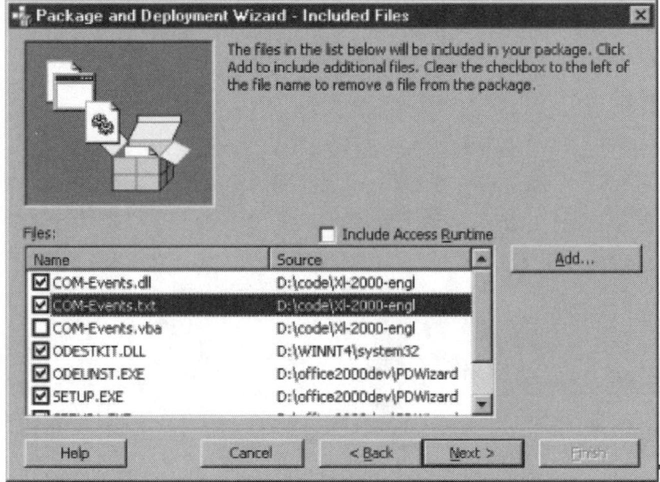

Figure 14.11. Selection of files that should be installed on the client's computer

The option Include Access Runtime is of no interest to Excel projects. It enables the installation of a limited variant of Access on the client's computer, but that makes sense only for Access projects.

In the next step you specify whether a single (large) `*.cab` file should be created or a series of smaller files. The second option is useful if you plan to distribute your program on several diskettes. (Cab files are condensed files with installation data.)

In the step Installation Options you can give your installation program a title. This text will be displayed during installation. The default is the project name.

In the step Start Menu Items you can specify where in the Windows start menu the program should be installed. Of course, this is useful only if you are using the assistant for an independently executable program (`*.exe` file). With a COM add-in, however, this is not the case. Instead, a `*.dll` file is installed, which cannot be launched independently but only as a part of Excel. Therefore, remove the last entry from the four-stage hierarchy. The `*.dll` file will, of course, be installed in any case, but in the Windows start menu a confusing reference will not appear.

So that the add-in directory in the start menu does not now remain totally empty, it is a good idea to provide a documentation file, for example, a small `Readme` file that briefly describes the use and activation of the add-in. This file is taken into the start menu with NEW ITEM (see Figure 14.12).

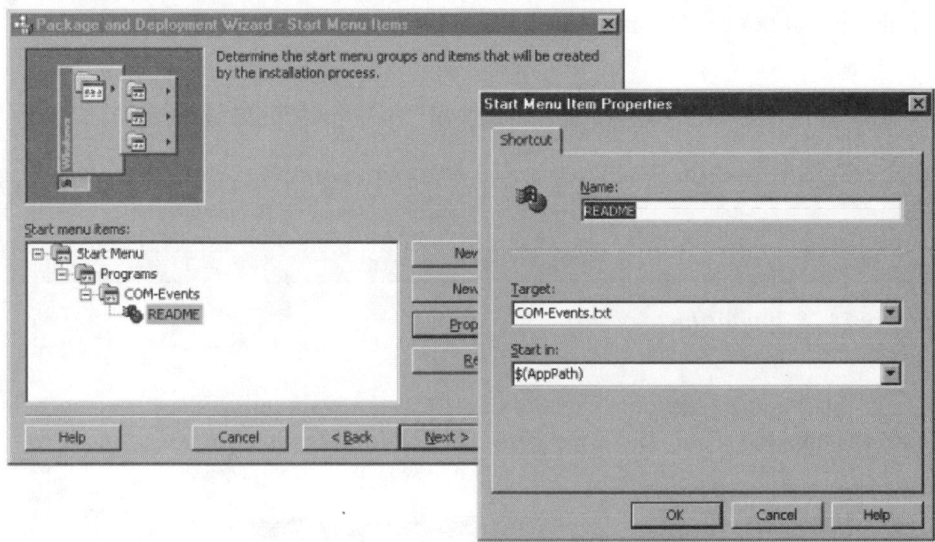

Figure 14.12. The last entry in the four-stage start menu element list should be replaced by a reference to a Readme file

The next step in the assistant makes it possible to change the installation location of several files. As a rule, you may leave these settings intact.

In the step SHARED FILES you may specify whether the installation files are of general interest and should thus remain during a deinstallation (so that they can be used by other programs). This is not generally useful for COM add-ins.

Finally, in the last step you can save all settings made in the assistant to a file. This is extremely practical, since you do not need to repeat all the settings when you wish to set the installation package a second time.

The assistant now creates the installation package, which generally consists of three files: the file `setup.exe` from the installation program, the text file `setup.lst` (with a list of all files that are installed), and `setup.exe`, with the actual installation data.

The assistant collects all additional files in uncompressed form in the directory `support`. This directory helps to create quickly (without calling upon the assistant) a new installation package by replacing individual files and then executing `name.bat`. The `support` directory is not meant to be distributed to clients! The three files listed above suffice for installation.

Installation (Client's Point of View)

Installation on the client's computer is carried out easily with `setup.exe`. When an installation program created by the Office installation assistant is executed for the first time, a suggestion to restart the computer at once appears (Figure 14.13): In order for the setup program to be executed, certain system files that appear not to be current must be replaced (for example, Windows NT 4 with Service Pack 5). It is doubtful that the client will be particularly pleased with this.

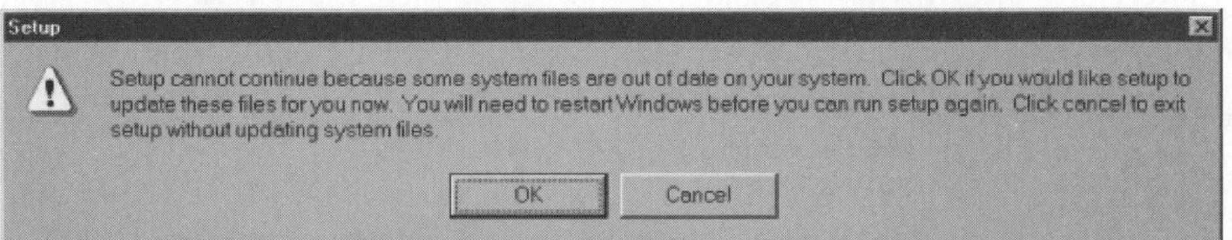

Figure 14.13. Invitation to restart

In the second attempt to execute `setup.exe` the installation should succeed. With the button CHANGE DIRECTORY you can choose an installation location.

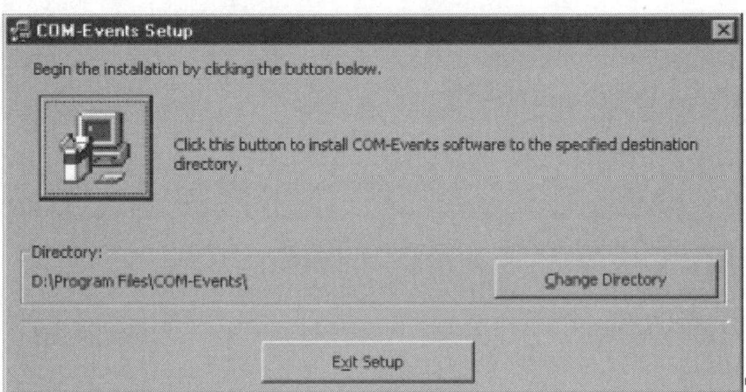

Figure 14.14. The installation program

Problems

- The COM add-in is always registered only for the login name for which it was installed. On a computer with several login IDs the COM add-in must be installed for each user.
- When the COM add-in is installed several times (once for each login ID), a different installation directory must be given for each instance.
- Under Windows NT installation requires administrator's privileges. Otherwise, the installation is interrupted by a series of completely useless error messages ("an unexpected error has occurred"). (Such problems, and other, similar, ones result in practically every user operating as administrator, which opens the door, naturally, to viruses. But we are wandering from our subject.)

TIP *That COM add-ins have to be multiply installed for multiple users is crazy, and clearly represents a design error. The only way out of this nutty situation is to execute* TOOLS|COM ADD-INS *and press the button* Add *in order to select all (previous!)* `*.dll` *files. The file will then be taken into the registration database. The drawback to this way of proceeding is that you must then explain this complex procedure to your client.*

Deinstallation

A big plus in the installation program is that deinstallation proceeds smoothly. Deinstallation is accomplished via the icon ADD/REMOVE PROGRAMS in the control panel.

Database Designers and Controls

TIP *The* DataEnvironment *and* DataReport *designers briefly described in this section, as well as supplementary database tools, are available only if you are working with the Office Developer Edition.*

> **POINTER** *This section can only hint at the many possibilities offered by designers and additional tools. For a proper description one would need a much more detailed introduction to ADO than was offered in Chapter 12, as well as many more pages of text.*
>
> *The database designers and additional controls provided with Office Developer have been available for Visual Basic programming since version 6 (that is, since mid-1998). Therefore, you will find a detailed description of these tools in any good Visual Basic book that deals with ADO. An additional source of information is, of course, the MSDN library (which also contains the complete documentation for Visual Basic).*
>
> *Information on the specific features for the use of designers and controls in Office projects can be found in the file* `wpapers\DataBinding.doc` *on the Office Developer CD-ROM. This file discusses what things do not function properly and by what means the components can nonetheless be used. This is, so to speak, the introduction to the next subsection.*

Problems and Shortcomings

The tools presented in this section perform very well by and large. However, they are not completely enjoyable to use, because Microsoft has not taken the slightest effort to adapt these tools that have been available since Visual Basic 6 (that is, since mid-1998) to the demands of the Office program development environment.

- The designers can be used only for COM add-ins. Yet they would also be useful in traditional Excel projects.

- In activating a designer or supplementary control the ADO library 2.0 is automatically activated, which was just barely current in mid-1998. (Since then, the designers have apparently not been changed.)

  However, with Office 2000 it is ADO 2.1 that is included, and it is advisable to work with it. (In ADO 2.1 many errors in ADO 2.0 have been corrected.) However, if you replace ADO 2.0 with ADO 2.1 via TOOLS|REFERENCES, then you are faced with compatibility problems. In many event procedures of the *DataEnvironment* designer and some controls, ADO-2.0 *Recordset* objects are passed, which are incompatible with ADO 2.1 *Recordsets*.

  Here is a solution: In the declarations line of the event procedure declare the *Recordset* variable with *rec As ADODB.Recordset20*. For reasons of compatibility the object *Recordset20* continues to be available in ADO 2.1. It is not shown in the object browser, since it is invisible. (In the object browser (pop-up menu) execute the command SHOW HIDDEN MEMBERS, and then you will discover a number of such objects, methods, and properties.)

- Among the most attractive features of the *DataEnvironment* designer is the SQL generator. This is a tool for formulating SQL queries (similar to query formulation in Access). Precisely this SQL generator is absent in the designer variant delivered with Office Developer.

- Among the most elementary properties of controls is that their properties are set during the creation of the dialog. This is also usually the case with database controls—but not with Office Developer! In the properties window are missing precisely those properties that are necessary for setting the data source. These properties definitely exist, but they must be set in program code. (And doing so creates massive problems that can be solved only with the help of some tricks described in `wpapers\DataBinding.doc`.)

- Likewise unavailable is the so-called properties dialog for controls. This is a complex variant of the properties window that helps in the setting of countless parameters—but not in the Office application.

- Furthermore, the info file for Office Developer 2000 indicates that in the current version the included supplementary database controls can be placed only in *UserForm* dialogs. On the other hand, embedding them in an Excel worksheet leads to difficulties. (Microsoft continues to promise to publish a corrected version of the additional controls. Perhaps they will already have been hidden somewhere out there on Microsoft's web site by the time you are reading this. In December 1999 there was still nothing available.)

- The fact that *UserForm* dialogs cannot be resized by the user causes additional problems. An extensive database table or database report that can be viewed only in a tiny window is practically useless.

To be sure, the long list of tools included with the Developer Edition looks great in the promotional literature, and most computer journals dutifully copy these reports. But a glance under the hood shows, at least in the case of database tools, more of a Potemkin village: plenty of façade, not much to back it up.

Data Environment and the DataReport Designer

Before its first use a designer must be activated with INSERT|COMPONENTS|DESIGNERS. Then it is possible to insert designer components into COM add-in projects.

DataEnvironment Designer

The *DataEnvironment* designer (which we shall abbreviate by *DE*) performs two functions: It makes possible a visual setting of the connection to an ADO-compatible database (that is, a database for which there is an OLE DB or ODBC driver). The connection information is represented in the designer window as a *Connection* object. The great advantage over manually setting the connection with the ADO *Connection* object is that the *ConnectionString* character string is conveniently composed in a dialog. For the example program of this section the database `Nwind.mdb` is again used as data source.

Once a *DE-Connection* object exists, it can be augmented with SQL commands. In a six-page dialog one may set various properties of this command, from SQL code to the properties that should be exhibited by the *Recordset* object derived from this command (the page called ADVANCED).

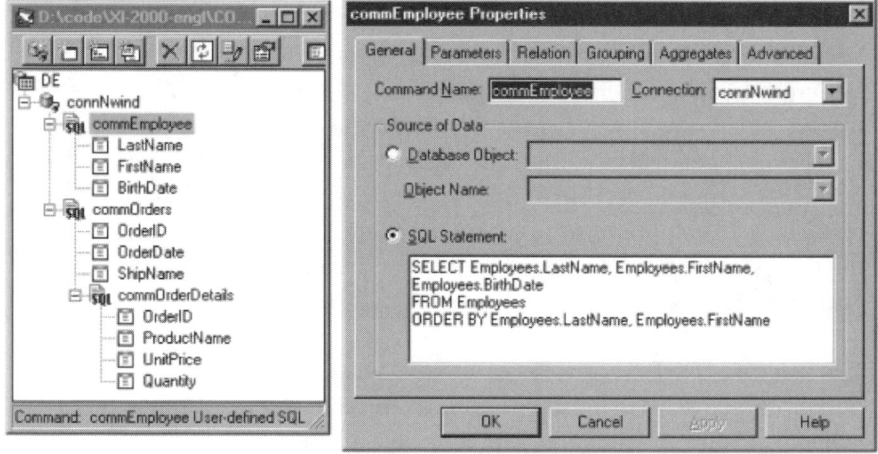

Figure 14.15. On the left, the window of the DataEnvironment designer; on the right, the dialog for setting the properties of an SQL command

A peculiarity of the designer is that two commands can be joined into a hierarchical group. To do this choose the subordinate command and in the dialog sheet RELATION set the command that is to lie above it in the hierarchy and via which data field the relationship is to be established. In the left part of Figure 14.15 *commOrders* is set to lie above *commOrderDetails.* The relationship is set via the *OrderID* field.

If now in a program you attempt to access the *commOrders* object and the derived object *Recordset,* then there exists a so-called hierarchical *Recordset.* To every master data record (that is, to every order with a certain *OrderID*-value), detailed data records (i.e. the list of ordered products) can be read. There is insufficient space here to discuss background information about hierarchical *Recordsets* in full. The key point, however, is this: Both the *MSHFlexGrid* control and *DataReport* designer have no trouble with such *Recordsets* and indicate the hierarchy on their own (see Figure 14.18).

> **TIP** *As is usual with all ADO components, the* DE *designer, too, stores the absolute path to the database file. Therefore, if you load the example file* `COM-Database.vba`, *the designer will complain that it cannot find the database. The solution to this is simple: Click with the right mouse button on the* connNwind *object, execute the command* PROPERTIES, *and set the path to the database file correctly.*

A few further thoughts on designer program code: First of all, you should give the designer objects mnemonically useful names in the properties window. The name of the designer object is taken care of by *DE.*

Then the *DE* object is available in all other components of the project. *DE.connectionName* refers to the *Connection* object defined therein. (Not surprisingly, we are dealing here with objects defined in the ADO library.) *DE.commandName* refers to the commands defined in the designer. *DE.rscommandName* (note the two additional letters *rs*) enables convenient access to the derived *Recordset* object.

The connection to the database is automatically opened once data provided via the designer are displayed in a control. Quite frequently, you will wish to (or have to) set the connection in code. That, too, is simple.

```
DE.connNwind.Open
```

Before the connection is established, the event *WillConnect* occurs in the designer. This can be used to reset the path to the database if necessary. In the lines below, the file name is read from the registration database. (How the file name got there will be revealed further below.)

```
' COM-Database.vba, DE
Private Sub connNwind_WillConnect(ConnectionString As String, _
    UserID As String, Password As String, Options As Long, _
    adStatus As ADODB.EventStatusEnum, _
    ByVal pConnection As ADODB.Connection)
  ' reset datasource
  pConnection.Properties("Data Source") = _
    GetSetting("COMDatabaseSample", "nwind", "fullname")
End Sub
```

DataReport Designer

The *DataReport* designer was actually developed as a database report generator for Visual Basic. In Excel projects you will fall back on it only for databases that are not Access or SQL server databases. In such cases Access offers many much better possibilities for creating database reports. The *DataReport* designer is a rather primitive tool in comparison to Access. Its only advantage is that it can process hierarchical *Recordsets* as a data source. (More precisely, that is the only data source type that can be adequately represented by the *DataReport* designer.

To develop a database report, open the designer window and move, via *Drag & Drop*, the data fields from the *DE* window into the *DataReport* window. We cannot go into the details of report generation here; see the on-line documentation. Note that the size of the *DataReport* cannot be changed during operation. The size it had when it was created is fixed.

A crucial point is the setting of the data source. For this one has the properties *DataSource* and *DataMember*. These, however, are not displayed in the properties window and can thus be set only in program code. For this it is best to use the *Initialize* event procedure. Of course, you must take care that the data sources set in code are compatible with the data fields that you have previously dragged into the report window.

```
' VBA-Database.vba, reportOrders
Private Sub DataReport_Initialize()
  Set Me.DataSource = DE
  Me.DataMember = "commOrders"
End Sub
```

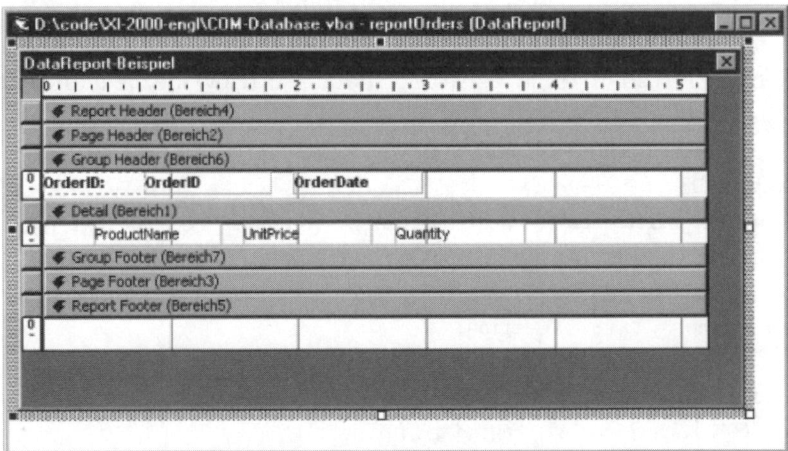

Figure 14.16. A database report under development

Database Supplementary Tools

The Office Developer Edition comes with a number of supplementary tools for representing the data of ADO database queries. Here we shall describe only the four most important of these.

As in the example program, the controls can be used in combination with the *DataEnvironment* designer. But that is not necessary. Instead, you can generate an ADO *Recordset* object in code as described in Chapter 12 and allocate this directly to the *Data* or *RowSource* property of the control.

Before you can insert the controls into a *UserForm* dialog you must incorporate them into the toolbox. To do this execute the pop-up menu command ADDITIONAL CONTROLS.

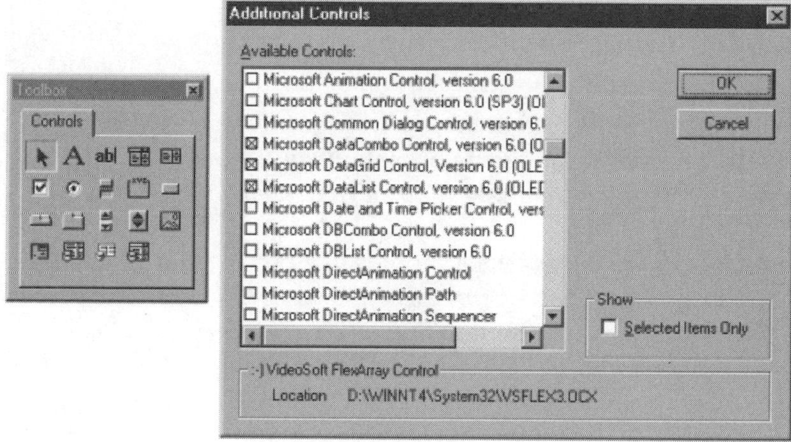

Figure 14.17. The UserForm toolbox with some database controls

Although the two designers described above can be used only for COM add-in projects, you can use the supplementary database controls also in a *UserForm* dialog of an ordinary Excel file. However, you must then use the installation assistant for distributing the Excel file, since you cannot assume that the supplementary controls are installed on your client's computer. (Since you possess Office Developer you have the right to distribute the controls together with an application, but you must make sure to do it!)

DataCombo, DataList

These two controls make it possible to display a column of a *Recordset* object. To fill the control with data you must first create the *Recordset* object. Then execute the instructions shown in the following template:

```
Dim dc As DataCombo  ' or DataList
Dim rec As Recordset
rec.Open …
Set dc = DataCombo1  ' or the name of the control in the dialog.
Set dc.RowSource = rec
dc.ListField = "column name"
```

If you wish to use a command of the *DE* designer as data source, then directly link a reference to the *DE* designer to *RowSource*. You must now specify *RowMember* as well, so that it is clear which object of the *DE* designer is meant.

```
Set dc = DataCombo1
Set dc.RowSource = DE
dc.RowMember = "commEmployee"
dc.ListField = "lastname"
```

> **TIP** *Perhaps you are thinking that the above code could be simplified a bit: Why the variable* dc*? The object* DataCombo1 *could be edited directly. Well, that is again one of the many peculiarities that hold only for Office projects.*
>
> *Although in Visual Basic* Set DataCombo1.RowSource = … *works, this does not, of course, work in Office projects. In this connection please read the Word file* `wpapers\DataBinding.doc` *on the Office Developer CD. There the necessary programming techniques are explained (without, however, giving a truly plausible reason why this is necessary).*

Apart from the data allocation the *DataList* and *DataCombo* controls look like normal listboxes and can be used as such. Furthermore, the evaluation of input takes place as with listboxes (see Chapter 7).

DataGrid

While in *DataList* and *DataCombo* only one column of a *Recordset* can be represented, the *DataGrid* control displays all columns. In addition, all data records can be placed, edited, and deleted in the control (however, only if the *AllowAddNew*, *AllowDelete*, and *AllowUpdate* properties are set to *True*). One could write a small tome about programming the *DataGrid* controls (at least a lengthy chapter), since they offer so many options.

In order for data to be displayed in the control, the property *DataSource* must be linked to a *Recordset* object. When as in the following code segment a *DE* command serves as data source, then additionally, *DataMember* must be set. With the method *Rebind* the data are retrieved and displayed in the control.

```
Dim dg As DataGrid
Set dg = DataGrid1
Set dg.DataSource = DE
dg.DataMember = "commEmployee"
dg.ReBind
```

Hierarchical FlexGrid *(MSHFlexGrid)*

The *MSHFlexGrid* has the function of displaying tabular data from a *Recordset*. However, there are many differences between it and the *DataGrid* control: On the one hand, the data cannot be altered. On the other hand, the control also works well with hierarchical *Recordsets*, that is, detailed data can be hidden and unhidden (see Figure 14.18).

For data to be displayed, *DataSource* and (only for *DE* data sources) *DataMember* must be set again. The method *CollapseAll* has the effect that at the outset no detailed data are displayed (which keeps one from becoming overwhelmed by too much detail).

```
Dim fg As MSHFlexGrid
Set fg = MSHFlexGrid1
Set fg.DataSource = DE
fg.DataMember = "commOrders"
fg.CollapseAll
```

Example Program

The purpose of the program `COM-Database.vba` is to demonstrate the application of the controls and help you with the first steps in developing your own programs. Otherwise, the program accomplishes no meaningful tasks (Figure 14.18).

The program is conceived as a COM add-in and can be invoked in Excel with the command TOOLS|DATENBASE DEMO. When it is first started, a file selection dialog appears, in which you should select the database file `nwind.mdb`. The path is then stored in the registration database and is available thereafter.

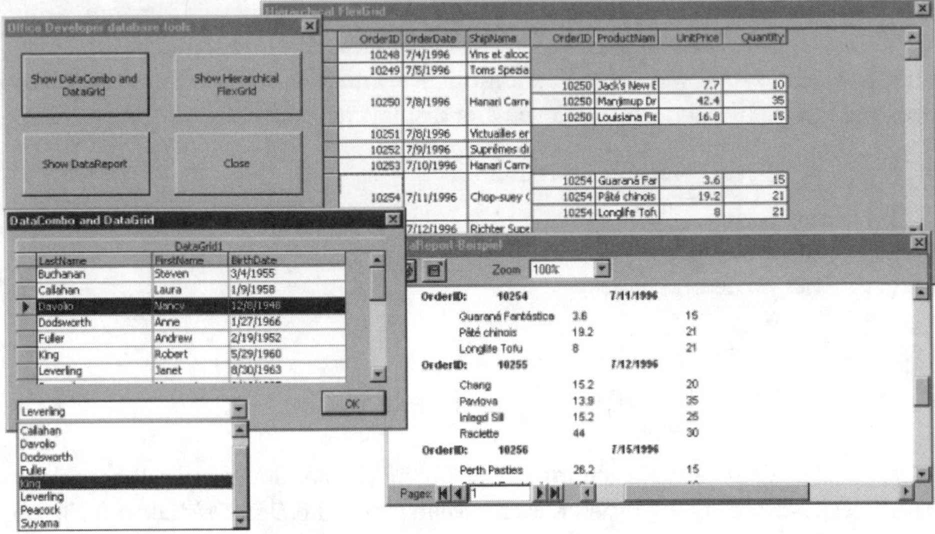

Figure 14.18. The window of the database example program

Program Code

The COM add-in project consists of an add-in designer for Excel, a *DE* designer, a *DataReport* designer, and three dialogs. Program execution begins in the *OnConnection* event procedure of the add-in designer. There a menu command is inserted in the Excel TOOLS menu (as described in the section after next). Furthermore, the auxiliary function *FindDatabase* is called, which ensures that the correct file name of the database file is stored in the registration database.

```
' COM-Database.vba, AddInExcel
Function FindDatabase$()
  Dim dbfilename
  dbfilename = GetSetting("COMDatabaseSample", "nwind", "fullname", "")
  While LCase(Dir(dbfilename))  "nwind.mdb"
    MsgBox "please select the file nwind.mdb…"
    dbfilename = app.GetOpenFilename("Database, *.mdb", , _
      "Select nwind.mdb!", "OK")
    If dbfilename = False Then Exit Function
  Wend
  SaveSetting "COMDatabaseSample", "nwind", "fullname", dbfilename
  FindDatabase = dbfilename
End Function
```

Main Dialog

With TOOLS|DATENBASE DEMO *formMain* is displayed. In its initialization procedure the connection to the database is established. The other event procedures have no special features.

```
' COM-Database.vba, formMain
Dim conn As Connection
Private Sub UserForm_Initialize()
  On Error Resume Next
  Set conn = DE.connNwind
  conn.Open
  If Err Then
    MsgBox "The connection to the database could not be" & _
      "established."
    Unload Me
  End If
End Sub
Private Sub btnShowDataGrid_Click()
  formDataGrid.Show vbModeless
End Sub
Private Sub btnShowFlexGrid_Click()  '... as above
Private Sub btnShowReport_Click()    '... as above
Private Sub btnEnd_Click()
  On Error Resume Next
  If formDataGrid.Visible Then Unload formDataGrid
  If formFlexGrid.Visible Then Unload formFlexGrid
  If reportOrders.Visible Then Unload reportOrders
  Unload Me
End Sub
Private Sub UserForm_Terminate()
  On Error Resume Next
  conn.Close
End Sub
```

DE Designer

The *DE* designer is equipped with a tiny event procedure that ensures that when the program is launched the preset path to the database is not used, but the one stored in the registration database.

```
' COM-Database.vba, DE
Private Sub connNwind_WillConnect(ConnectionString As String, …)
  ' set data source correctly
  pConnection.Properties("Data Source") = _
    GetSetting("COMDatabaseSample", "nwind", "fullname")
End Sub
```

Data Report Forms, DataReport *Designer*

In the data report forms (*DataGrid* and *MSHFlexGrid*) and in the *DataReport* designer the connection between the controls and the *DE* objects are set in the *Initialize* procedures. The code for this has appeared already in the previous section.

Excel and the Internet

TIP *The functions described in this section are available in all versions of Excel. Office Developer is not required.*

Sending Excel Files as E-Mail

With the method ***SendMail*** of the *Workbook* object the workbook is immediately passed to the "installed mail system," as the on-line documentation somewhat vaguely puts it.

If you are working with Outlook or Outlook Express as your e-mail client, everything works just beautifully. Your e-mail lands right in the program's mail "out" folder. According to the setting in Outlook the e-mail is either sent at once, or otherwise the next time the button SEND AND RECEIVE is pressed (if Outlook is configured for off-line modem operation).

Three parameters are passed to the method *SendMail*: the recipient's address, the subject (that is, the *Subject* text), and, optionally, the Boolean value *True* or *False* depending on whether a confirmation from the recipient is desired. (Please note, however, that only relatively few e-mail systems support recipient confirmation, regardless of what is set.)

```
ThisWorkbook.SendMail "joyce@dublin.eire", "Bloomsday events"
```

If you wish to send e-mail to several recipients simultaneously, you can pass an *Array* of character strings in the first parameter. It is unfortunately not possible to set an informational text. Before executing *SendMail* you do not need first to save the workbook. Excel sends the current version automatically.

Determining the Type of Installed Mail System

With the property ***MailSystem*** of the *Application* object you can determine whether an e-mail system is installed on the local computer, and if so, which e-mail system it is. This property can assume three values:

xlMAPI	The e-mail system is MAPI compatible (Messaging Application Program Interface, a Microsoft Standard).
xlPowerTalk	The e-mail system is based on PowerTalk (an e-mail system for Apple Macintosh computers). In this case, with the Macintosh version of Excel e-mail can be sent via the *Mailer* object.
xlNoMailSystem	No e-mail system is available (none, at least, compatible with MAPI or PowerTalk).

It is not explicitly documented, but it appears that *SendMail* is used only when *MailSystem* = *xlMAPI* is true. How well it functions when Outlook is not used as the e-mail system could not be tested (on my computer, at least under Windows NT, no other e-mail system is installed).

Sending E-Mail Interactively

If you wish to give the user control over the sending of e-mail and to select the receiver as well as an info text, there are two variants. The first consists in invoking a dialog for sending an e-mail message. Then an Outlook window appears in which the current workbook has already been inserted in the otherwise empty message:

```
Application.Dialogs(xlDialogSendMail).Show
```

The second variant consists in setting the property ***EnvelopeVisible*** for the current workbook to *True*. Then beneath the menus and toolbars four lines appear that enable the input of a recipient address and direct dispatch of the e-mail. You can use the following instruction to turn *EnvelopeVisible* on and off:

```
ThisWorkbook.EnvelopeVisible = Not ThisWorkbook.EnvelopeVisible
```

If you execute the instruction in the event procedure of a button, take care that you have set *TakeFocusOnClick* for the button to *False*. Otherwise, you will get an error message.

Again, it remains unclear whether both methods work without Outlook.

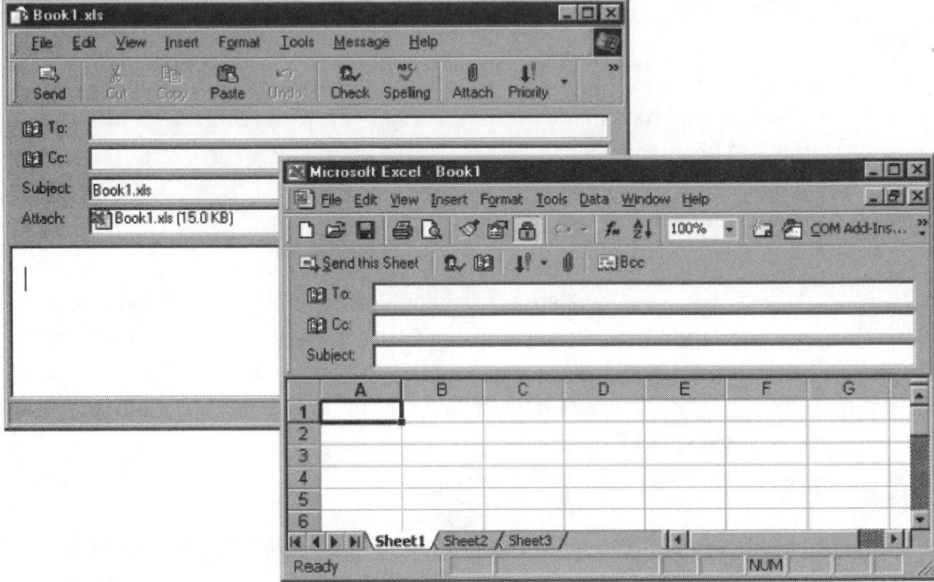

Figure 14.19. Left: the xlDialogSendMail dialog; right: Excel with EnvelopeVisible=True

HTML Import

POINTER *The importation of text (Chapter 5), databases (Chapter 12), and HTML documents are all accomplished in Excel with the same* QueryTable *object. Here we shall describe only the HTML features. The data source type is derived from the property* QueryType *of the* QueryTable *object* (xlODBCQuery, xlTextImport, *or* xlWebQuery). *According to* QueryType *it is then other properties of the* QueryTable *object that describe the parameters of the import.*

With Data|Get External Data|New Web Query you can select any HTML file (either on the internet or in a local network). Pressing Browse Web starts Internet Explorer. The web address set there is automatically taken into the Excel dialog (Figure 14.20).

In the following importation Excel attempts, depending on the settings of the options, to import the entire document, a particular table from the document, or simply all tables in the document. (Considered as tables are all parts of the HTML file that are enclosed between *<TABLE>* and *</TABLE>*. Because of the many possible formats for tables in HTML documents, *<TABLE>* constructions are often used for text passages that do not look at all like a table.)

In principle, web importation functions surprisingly well. The problem is that the internet changes rapidly, and many web sites are completely restructured at least once a year. An application that, say, regularly reads stock quotations from the internet must therefore regularly be adapted to the current layout of the quotation web page.

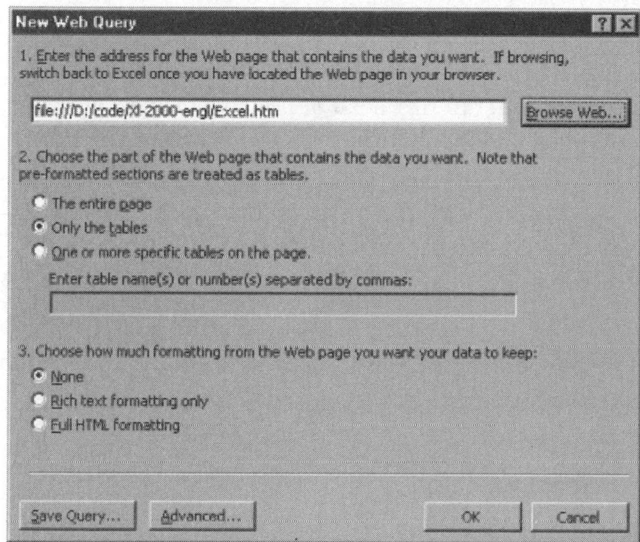

Figure 14.20. Importation from an HTML file

A few words on setting the *QueryTable* properties: *QueryType* contains *xlWebQuery (4)*. *Name* must agree with the name of the range of cells into which the data were imported. *Destination* specifies the first cell of the import range. The *Connection* character string has the structure *"URL;http://www.name.com/seite.htm"*. Various details of the importation are set in the *WebXxx* properties. As usual, the quickest way to find plausible settings for these properties is via the macro recorder.

HTML Export, Web Components

In interactive mode, HTML exportation is accomplished via the command FILE|SAVE AS WEB PAGE. What can be exported is a range of cells (the current selection), a worksheet, the whole workbook, or a chart.

Independent of the exported data there are two export variants: The resulting HTML code can be static or interactive. Static means that traditional HTML code is produced that can be viewed with almost any HTML browser. On the other hand, if the option ADD INTERACTIVITY is chosen, then the HTML page contains a reference to a so-called web component (see below).

Setting the many export options is a bit confusing, since it is distributed among three dialogs:

- The dialog SAVE AS appears when FILE|SAVE AS WEB PAGE is executed. It is sufficient for simple saves.
- The dialog PUBLISH AS WEB PAGE is invoked by the **Publish** button in the SAVE AS dialog. It contains, among other things, a list of previously exported objects in the current workbook and thereby simplifies repeating an export.
- The dialog WEB OPTIONS is invoked with the menu command TOOLS|WEB OPTIONS in the SAVE AS dialog. There a host of options can be set that determine how the HTML document is to be constructed.

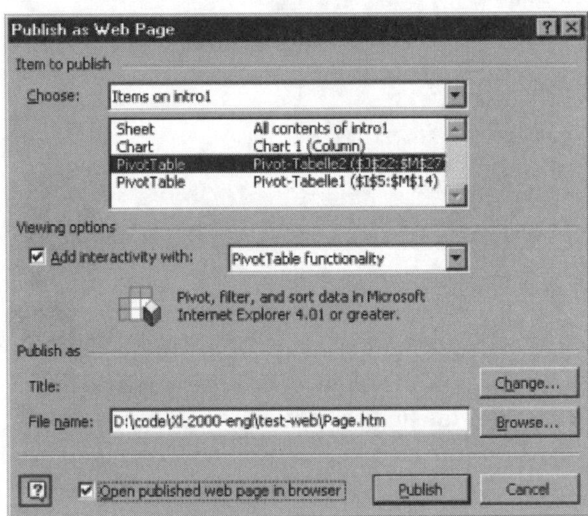

Figure 14.21. One of the three exportation dialogs

Web Components

Web components refers to ActiveX controls that make available some of Excel's functions. For users this has the advantage that they can change data (for example, input new numerical values, sort differently, reorganize pivot tables, change the chart type). To this end there are three primary web components: *Spreadsheet* for normal worksheets, *PivotTableList* for pivot tables, and *Chart* for charts. (There are, in addition, some web components for navigation and for creating a database link, but we shall not discuss them further here.)

Web components offer an impressive array of functions (connected with a very attractive design), but they have two serious drawbacks:

- The resulting web pages can be displayed only with Internet Explorer versions 4.01 and higher. Of course, Windows is necessary as well.

- Web components can be used only if the user has a license for Office 2000. In an intranet (an office network, say) with an Office network license it is permitted to transfer the web components from the local server and install them only when needed. Otherwise, Office 2000 must already be installed for the web components to be used.

Thus web components may be technologically fascinating, but for the internet they are perhaps unsuitable on account of their numerous restrictions. (Internet pages should be constructed in such a way that they can be read by as many internet users as possible. This is definitely not the case here.)

The central area of application for web components may thus be in intranets (although there it is actually simpler to make an Excel file as such available on the network).

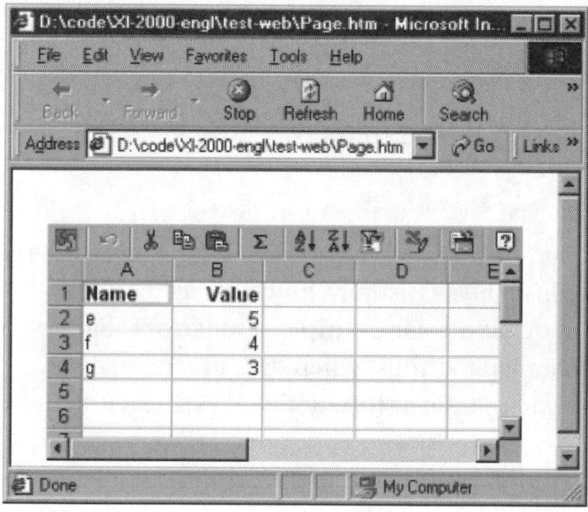

Figure 14.22. A small range of cells that was exported with interactivity (that is, as a web component)

> **POINTER** *The functions of web components can be controlled via VBScript of Visual Basic code in DHTML pages. Web components are thus programmable, where in principle there is an object model such as Excel, although this is, of course, greatly restricted in its scope. A description of these functions would overreach the bounds of this book and does not really have anything to do with Excel. More information can be found in the programmer's handbook to the Office Developer Edition, in the MSDN library (look under* OWC *or* Office Web Components*), and in good books on Frontpage 2000.*

HTML Export via VBA Code with PublishObject

If you wish to save an Excel object via VBA code in an HTML document, you will need to make the acquaintance of ***PublishObject***. Access to such objects is by way of *Workbook.PublishObjects*. To export an Excel object for the first time, you must create a new *PublishObject* with *Add*.

```
Dim publ As PublishObject
Dim fname$
fname = "c:\test.htm"
Set publ = ThisWorkbook.PublishObjects.Add( _
  SourceType:=xlSourceRange, Sheet:="Sheet1", Source:="$B$3:$C$5", _
  Filename:=fname, HtmlType:=xlHtmlStatic, DivID:="ID1")
publ.Publish
```

To the *Add* method must be added a number of parameters, for which there are like-named properties of the *PublishObject* (usually, however, read only): *SourceType* specifies the data type in question (for example, a range of cells or a chart). *Sheet* and *Source* specify in character strings which data are to be saved. *HtmlType* determines whether to create a static or interactive HTML document with web components.

The parameter *DivID* is strange indeed: With it an identification character string can be specified by means of which later the *PublishObject* can be accessed. *DivID* takes over the function that with all other objects is played by *Name*. (If the specified character string is already in use, the associated object will be overwritten with the new data. If you do not specify the parameter, Excel generates a character string automatically.)

Finally, you must execute the method ***Publish*** for the *PublishObject*. Only then is the HTML file generated.

Export Options

For fine control of the HTML export you can set the countless properties of the object ***DefaultWebOptions*** (global for Excel) or ***WebOptions*** (only for the current workbook). Neither option deals with an enumeration object, despite the *-s* ending. The most important properties of both objects are collected in Chapter 5, in the subsection "setting options with program code."

Dynamic Link Libraries (DLLs)

Dynamic link libraries are libraries of functions. With DLLs you have access to almost all Windows system functions and can even—if necessary—replace time-critical VBA procedures with your own C routines in the form of a DLL. The following sections are restricted to a discussion of how the so-called API functions in VBA can be invoked. (API stands for *Application Programming Interface* and denotes the entirety of DLLs with Windows system functions.)

> **TIP** *The use of DLL functions requires a great amount of background knowledge about the inner workings of Windows and about Windows programming that cannot be supplied in this section.*
>
> *The Office Developer Edition is not in itself necessary for the invocation of API functions in Excel. However, with the Developer Edition there are two things included that are very valuable in the development of such code:*
>
> - *First, in the VBA development environment you can invoke the so-called WinAPI viewer as an add-in. This a sort of database that contains the associated declarations for many DLL functions in VBA syntax, thereby saving much effort.*
> - *Second, the MSDN library contains a complete and extensive description of all API functions and represents an excellent source of fundamental information.*

Basics

A *Library* is a collection of functions. The words *Dynamic Link* attached thereto indicate that the library is loaded only when it is actually needed. Loading proceeds automatically when a function from the DLL is used.

DLLs are usually saved as `*.dll` files. DLLs are located either in the Windows system folder (with DLLs common to all programs) or directly in the folder of a program (if the DLL is conceived for that program alone).

Many of the system functions in Windows are contained in DLLs. The three most important libraries are the GDI library (graphics functions), the User library (window, menus, mouse), and the Kernel library (memory management).

In addition to these system functions (whose DLL files come with Microsoft Windows) there exist application-specific DLLS. These DLLs have been created for a specific program. In the Office directory, for example, there are many such DLLs. However, there DLLs are of little interest to application programmers to the extent that they are seldom publicly documented. Thus you do not know what functions are contained there and how they are used. (Moreover, you can access almost all Office functions much more conveniently with VBA-compatible object libraries.)

If you work with the programming language C or C++, you can program your own DLLs. This has the advantage that time-critical VBA procedures can be replaced with very efficient C code. Perhaps you are thinking that you can write the entire program in C. That would entail an enormous effort. With DLLs you can unite the advantages of VBA and C in a single program: Fast program development of 95 percent with VBA with time-critical special functions programmed in C.

Problems and Limitations

You will use DLLs mostly when a function provided for in Windows is not accessible with a VBA command or method. A significant problem is that first, you must know which DLLs even exist, and second, how these DLLs are used (what parameters, what return values, etc.). Windows system functions are well documented, to be sure, but the documentation is oriented to C syntax and is included only with the Office Developer Edition.

Even when the documentation problem is solved, there are further difficulties under Excel: For many system functions an identification number internal to Windows must be passed, such as the identification number of the active window or of a graphics object. In VBA, however, there is no possibility to determine the identification numbers of Excel objects. Thus it is impossible to call many elementary DLL functions (such as determining the definition of the graphics system).

Declaring DLL Functions

In principle it is easy to invoke DLL functions in VBA programs: You simply declare the function and then call it as you would any other VBA procedure. However, you will at once determine that the declaration of DLL functions is not always so easy.

A function declaration is necessary so that Visual Basic knows in what DLL file the function is located, what parameters must be passed to the function, and what the format of the return value of the function is (if indeed there is a return value).

The declaration is accomplished with the command ***Declare***. Immediately after *Declare* either the keyword *Function* (if the DLL function has a return value) or *Sub* (no return value) is placed. There follow the name of the function, the keyword ***Lib***, and the name of the DLL library in quotation marks. Thereafter, the declaration follows the same rules as those for a VBA procedure: There follows the parameter list and, if needed, the data type of the return value.

```
Declare Sub subname Lib "biblioname" (parameterlist)
Declare Function functname Lib "biblioname" (parameterlist) As
    datatype
```

You specify the data type of the return value either with a type identifier &, %, !, #, $, or @ after the function name or with *As datatype* after the parameter list. The following two declarations have the same effect:

```
Declare Function fname& Lib "biblname" (parameterlist)
Declare Function fname Lib "biblname" (parameterlist) As Long
```

The library name normally contains the file name of the DLL, for example, `Shell32.dll`. An exception is the system libraries "GDI32," "User32," and "Kernel32," whose names are given without the identifier `*.dll`.

If you wish to save a function under VBA under another name, you must use the keyword *Alias* in the declaration. In the example below the DLL function *GetWindowsDirectoryA* is declared in such a way that it can be used in VBA under the abbreviated name *GetWindowsDirectory*. (The additional letter "A" indicates that the function expects character strings in ANSI format. This is a requirement for the deployment of any DLL function in VBA.)

```
Declare Sub GetWindowsDirectory Lib "kernel32" _
  Alias "GetWindowsDirectoryA" (parameterlist)
```

As soon as a DLL function is actually used, Windows searches the DLL file in the Windows directory, in the Windows system directory, and in the Excel directory. If your DLL is located in none of these directories, you must specify the exact library name, say, *"C:\Test\Mine.dll"*. Note that DLLs that are located in the same directory as that in which the Excel file will be located only if the exact path is specified.

The Parameter List of the DLL Declaration

You must supply the data types of the parameters of the DLL function and the type of parameter passing in the parameter list. Many difficulties arise from the differing data types between VBA and the programming language C, for which the DLL functions are usually conceived.

Visual Basic	*C*
ByVal x As Byte	BYTE x
x As Byte	LPBYTE x
ByVal x As Integer	short x
x As Integer	short far *x
ByVal x As Long	LONG x
x As Long	LPLONG x
ByVal x As Single	float x
x As Single	float far *x
ByVal x As Double	double x
x As Double	double far *x

It is true, in general, that most DLL functions expect values, while VBA usually passes a pointer. For this reason numerical parameters must be declared *ByVal* almost without exception.

With character strings the main problem is that the DLL functions expect and return character strings in which the last character contains the code 0 to signify the end of the string. In passing character strings to DLL functions the keyword *ByVal* suffices for the parameter: VBA automatically appends a 0 character to the character string.

Somewhat more difficult is dealing with DLL functions that return character strings. First of all, the variable in question must be supplied with a sufficiently long character string before the function call; otherwise, the DLL function writes to memory in an uncontrolled manner and can even cause a crash. And second, you must evaluate the result variable after the call and change the character string therein, which is terminated with a 0, into a "genuine" VBA character string. Both of these details are demonstrated in the following example.

If a DLL function expects a compound data type, you must reproduce this data type with a *Type* instruction. Many DLL functions are capable of processing variable data types. Such parameters should be declared with the data type *As Any*. VBA then does no automatic data type checking and when called passes along the given parameters as addresses to the DLL function. If the parameters are to be passed by value, then use the keyword *ByVal*.

The passing of an address (*pointer*) causes few problems, since VBA normally passes all parameters by reference, using 32-bit-far addressing (the standard address format for Windows). If you wish to pass a null pointer to a DLL function, you must set the data type of this parameter in the declaration with *As Any*. In calling the function, specify *ByVal 0&*.

Calling DLL Functions

Calling a DLL function follows (given that the function has previously been declared) in the same way as for normal procedures.

```
Dim tmp$
tmp = Space(256)    ' filled with 256 characters
GetWindowsDirectory tmp, 255
```

Example: Determine Windows Directory

The following example can be found in `DLL.xls`. It determines the location of the Windows directory. This directory can be located on an arbitrary hard drive and can have an arbitrary name. Therefore, in the kernel library there is the function *GetWindowsDirectory* that determines the path of this directory.

Before this function can be used it must be defined with *Declare*. The actual function call takes place in *WinDir*. There the variable *tmp* is first filled with 256 blank characters and then passed to *GetWindowsDirectory*. The DLL function returns a 0-terminated character string; that is, the actual length of the character string must be determined up to this 0 character. To accomplish this the function *NullString* is called, which removes all characters beyond the 0 character.

```
' DLL.xls, Module1
Declare Sub GetWindowsDirectory Lib "kernel32"
  Alias "GetWindowsDirectoryA" (ByVal lpBuffer$, ByVal nSize&)
Function WinDir() As String
  Dim tmp$
  tmp = Space(256)    ' fill with 256 blank characters
  GetWindowsDirectory tmp, 255
  WinDir = NullString(tmp)
End Function
Function NullString(x)
  NullString = Left(x, InStr(x, Chr(0)) - 1)
End Function
' DLL.xls, Tabelle1
Private Sub btnShowWindowsDir_Click()
  MsgBox "The path of the Windows directory is " & WinDir()
End Sub
```

> **TIP** *The above example is of a strictly pedagogical nature. The Windows directory can be found much more easily, namely, with the method* Environ("windir") *of the VBA library or with the method* GetSpecialFolder (WindowsFolder), *which is defined for the object* FileSystemObject *of the Microsoft Scripting library (see also Chapter 5).*

Syntax Summary

DLL Functions

Declare Sub subname _ Lib "dllname" (parameterlist)	declare DLL function without return value
Declare Function funcname _ Lib "dllname" (paralist) As datatype	DLL function with return value
Declare Sub/Function vbname _ Lib "dllname" Alias "dllfnname"	DLL function, where the function name in the DLL and the name in VBA code differ

ActiveX Automation

ActiveX automation is a control mechanism by means of which one application (Excel, say) can control another application (Word, say). Usually, the controlling program is called the client, the controlled program the server.

VBA in combination with the object library of the server program serves as the control language. If this is to function smoothly, the object library of the server must be activated (TOOLS|REFERENCES in the development environment). Then all objects, methods, and properties of the server can be used as if they were built-in keywords; that is, the object catalog, on-line help, and so on, are available for the controlling components.

In principle *every* library under Excel is controlled via ActiveX automation, thus also the VBA, Scripting, and ADO libraries, described extensively in this book. ActiveX automation is actually nothing new, but your daily bread and butter (except that you perhaps did not know till now that every day you are employing ActiveX automation as an internal control mechanism).

You may be asking at this point, Why devote here an entire section to ActiveX automation if everything has already been explained? In fact, there is no systematic reason, but rather a practical one: All that to this point has been written about the use of ActiveX libraries dealt with standard applications. In the foreground was the use of the libraries, not the technical background. In this section we shall consider some of the more exotic forms of ActiveX automation:

- Starting Internet Explorer and displaying an HTML document
- Printing a database report with Access
- Programming a new object library with Visual Basic and using this library in Excel.
- Controlling Excel with an external program

The Limits of ActiveX Automation

The potential of ActiveX automation is immense, but alas, there are problems:

- The mechanisms for control of external programs are seldom as developed as the use of pure function libraries such as ADO. A desire to experiment is still a requirement for the creation of a functioning program. And if it finally runs with version *n*, it is completely uncertain whether it will continue to run with version *n*+1.
- ActiveX automation presupposes that the external program in question is installed. This may be the case on your computer, but not necessarily on your client's computer.
- A great advantage of the combination of ActiveX automation and VBA is that you do not need to learn a new programming language for each program. But this argument may be somewhat deceptive: To be sure, you do not need to learn a new programming language, but you do have to work with an entirely new object model. This book, in which only the objects of Excel are explored to any great extent (and even they have not been described completely), demonstrates that this is no trivial task.

The Limits of Excel

With Excel you can *use* the mechanism of ActiveX automation. If you are working with the Office Developer Edition, you can even create COM add-ins, which are nothing other than a special case of an ActiveX-capable library. But it is only with the programming language Visual Basic (which is sold as a separate product by Microsoft, at present in version 6) that you acquire the full potential of ActiveX programming.

- With Visual Basic you can create new object libraries. (From Visual Basic's point of view these libraries are called ActiveX servers or, according to the original documentation, code components.) In each case what is meant is programs or DLLs that are controlled via ActiveX automation. Thus if you are lacking a particular function in Excel, you can program the necessary objects, methods, and properties in Visual Basic.

In contrast to COM add-ins such libraries are not restricted to applications in the Microsoft Office family. Moreover, in programming, all the possibilities of Visual Basic are available, which in some cases go a bit beyond those of Excel.

- Visual Basic also makes possible the programming of new ActiveX controls, which can be used like the MS Forms controls in Excel dialogs and worksheets.

Excel as Client (Controlling External Programs)

Creating a Connection to the Partner Program

Before you can use the control mechanism of ActiveX automation you must create a connection to the OLE program. For this there are the following two possibilities:

- You simply create a start object of the ActiveX program. However, this variant functions only if the object library supports this (which is usually the case only for libraries that are not designed as freestanding programs). An example is the ADO library, for which the following two lines suffice to create a connection:

```
Dim conn As New Connection
conn.Open …
```

  This form of ActiveX automation is the simplest and most convenient variant. (The use of ADO objects is described extensively in Chapter 12.)

- You create an object with *CreateObject*. As parameter you must specify the object class that identifies the program. The following lines create the connection to Word.

```
Dim word As Object
Set word = CreateObject("Word.Document.8")
```

- The character string "`Word.Document.8`" identifies the object that you wish to create. Many application programs recognize a number of objects (in Word, for example, "Word.Document" or "Word.Picture.6"; a portion of the available character strings are displayed in the system information program HELP|ABOUT MICROSOFT EXCEL|SYSTEM INFO). A very long list of all registered objects can be obtained with the registration editor (program `Regedit.exe` in the Windows directory) under the rubric HKEY_CLASSES_ROOT.

- You generate an object with *GetObject*. As parameter you must specify the file name. The associated program is loaded automatically. However, this variant does not function with all OLE programs. The following lines create a connection to the database Access.

```
Dim access As Object
Set access = GetObject("filename.mdb")
```

  To execute these lines Access must be installed. The program will be launched automatically. Not all the objects of the Access library are available for programming.

- You may fall back on the *Object* property of an OLE object in Excel. This method functions only when the program supports OLE.

```
Dim oleobj as OLEObject, word As Object
Set oleobj = Sheets(1).OLEObjects(1)
Set word = oleobj.Object.Application
```

Regardless of which method you use to establish the connection to the OLE server, insofar as the OLE server supports an object library, you should activate this library with TOOLS|REFERENCES. For this you have available the on-line help (via F1); in the program code upper- and lowercase are automatically corrected, and then you can use the object catalog.

As soon as you have activated the object library, you can more precisely declare the object variables, for example, *Dim word As Word.Application*. This has the advantage that the development environment recognizes all allowed methods and properties and thus is of use in both code input and syntax checking.

> **TIP** *Object libraries that have never been used will usually not appear in the* REFERENCES *dialog. Click on* Browse *and search for the object library in question. The libraries of the Office components are located in* `Office2000/Office` *and have the identifier* `*.olb`.

> **REMARKS** *It is absolutely necessary to activate the object library via* TOOLS|REFERENCES *only for the first four variants above. If the connection to the ActiveX server is accomplished via* CreateObject *or* GetObject, *then the program runs in principle even without a reference to the object library. Now the object variable must be declared with the generally applicable* Dim x As Object.
>
> *For this reason, however, Excel can test only at run time whether the method or property that you have specified exists. Furthermore, the code that is generated in this case is less efficient than it would have been if an object library had been used (because the definition of the method cannot take place at compile time, but only at run time).*

Example: Printing an Access Report

The following example assumes that you have access to Access. (The ADO library is not sufficient!) Although the code looks completely unspectacular, this short procedure actually accomplishes something: Access is launched, and the *Northwind* database, our old friend from Chapter 12, is loaded.

Here some relatively complicated error protection is necessary: It could happen that Access will refuse to be launched (perhaps because it has not been installed). It could also happen that Access is running from the last time the procedure was called, but in the meantime the database file `nwind.mdb` has been closed. In this case the database is reopened with *OpenCurrentDatabase.*

One further detail is worth special mention: With *GetObject* it is explicitly specified in the second parameter that Access 2000 (internal version number 9) should be launched. If you do not do this and an older version of Access happens to be installed on your computer, then it could happen that this older version will be launched. But `nwind.mdb` assumes Access 2000.

The variable *acc* is defined as static. This has the advantage that Access does not have to be launched anew when the procedure is called. Beginning with the second time, Access appears almost without hesitation (assuming that you have sufficient RAM). However, you must execute *Set acc=Nothing* explicitly, so that Access will be terminated. (If you execute FILE|EXIT in Access, then Access will become invisible, but it will continue to run. Under Windows NT you can convince yourself of this with the task manager. Thus it is not always a good idea to declare *acc* as *Static.*)

```
' ActiveX-Access.xls, Table1
Private Sub btnAccessReport_Click()
  Dim ok, fil$, prjName$
```

```
  On Error GoTo report_error
  Static acc As Access.Application
report_anothertry:
  fil$ = ThisWorkbook.Path + "\nwind.mdb"
' start Access, load database
  If acc Is Nothing Then
    Set acc = GetObject(fil, "access.project.9")
  End If
  On Error Resume Next  ' error if no CurrentProject
  prjName = acc.CurrentProject.Name
  On Error GoTo report_error
  If LCase(prjName)  "nwind.mdb" Then
    acc.OpenCurrentDatabase fil, False
  End If
```

With the Access property *DoCmd* you can now print out the report defined in `Nwind.mdb`. (The definition of the report has already taken place in Access.) *OpenReport* here is a method of the *DoCmd* object.

Altogether, this object construction works a bit weirdly: There indeed exists a *Report* object together with a *Reports* enumeration, but only reports that have already been opened can be accessed. Here *DoCmd* represents an artificial object that is used simply to call all commands that do not fit into the Access object model. Only in comparison with other object libraries does one recognize the elegance of the objects and methods in Excel.

Via the parameter *acViewPreview* with *OpenReport* you are able to display the report on the computer monitor, but not to print it. (The constant *acViewPreview* is defined in the Access object library.) *ActivateMicrosoftApp* makes Access the active window; otherwise, Access would be visible only as an icon in the task bar.

```
  acc.DoCmd.OpenReport "Products by Category", acViewPreview
  acc.DoCmd.Maximize
  acc.Visible = True
  Application.ActivateMicrosoftApp xlMicrosoftAccess
  Exit Sub
report_error:
  ok = MsgBox("An error has occurred: " & Error & vbCrLf & _
    vbCrLf & "Another try?", vbYesNo)
  Set acc = Nothing
  If ok = vbYes Then
    On Error GoTo report_error
    GoTo report_anothertry
  End If
End Sub
```

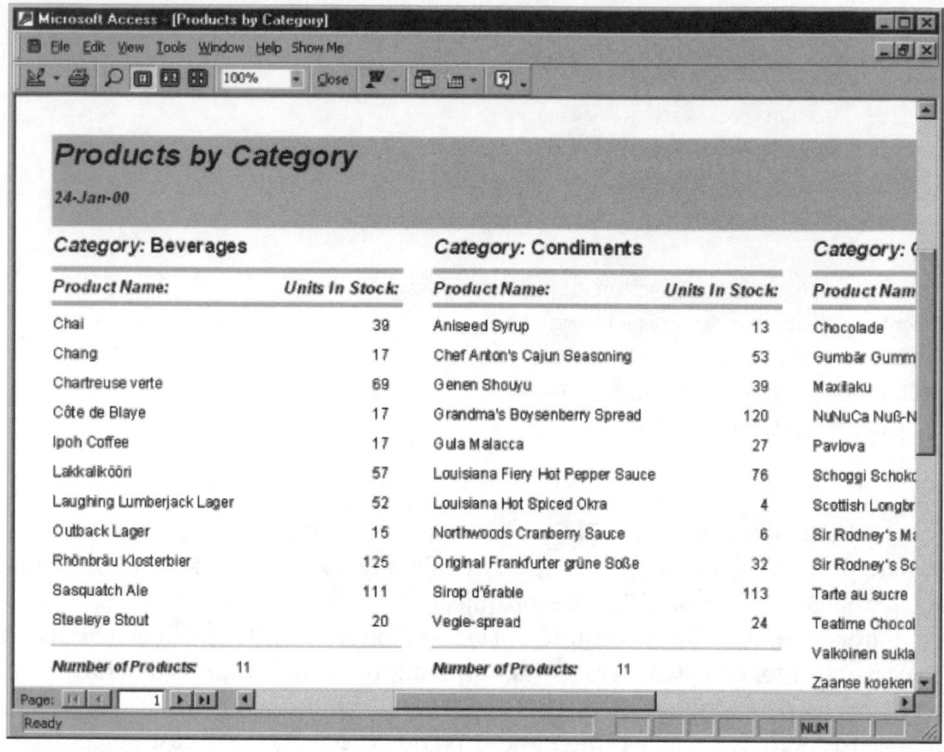

Figure 14.23. The first page of the report printed by Access

Example: Displaying HTML Files (Internet Explorer)

In our second ActiveX example Internet Explorer will be launched. Within it an HTML file will be displayed. This way of proceeding can serve, for example, as an alternative to displaying one's own help text. (The advantage is that you save the tiresome task of working with the HTMLHelp Workshop.)

For our example the library Microsoft Internet Controls, file `Windows\System32\Shdocvw.dll`, was activated. Explorer was first launched with *CreateObject*. Then with the method *Navigate* the file `Excel.htm` from the same directory is loaded. In *CommandButton2_Click* Explorer is terminated with the method *Quit*.

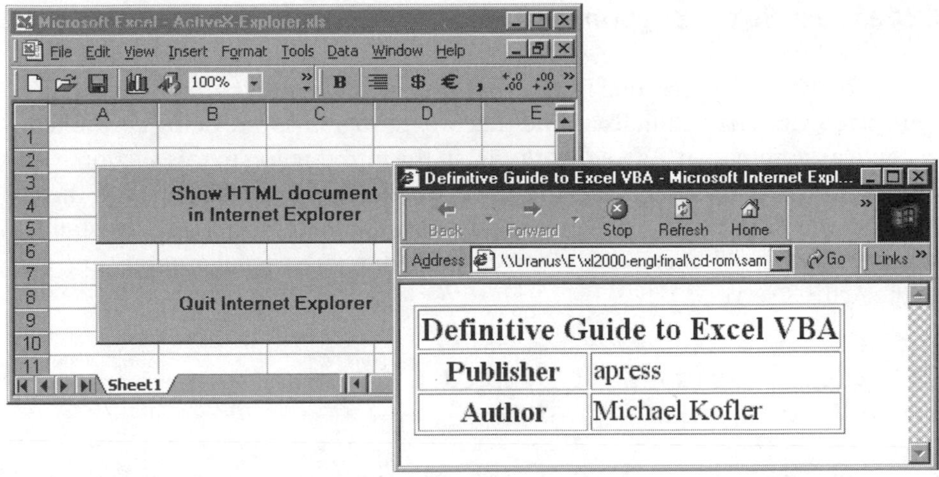

Figure 14.24. Display of an HTML file in Internet Explorer

```
' ActiveX-Explorer.xls, "Table1"
Dim obj As InternetExplorer
' display Internet Explorer with file
Private Sub CommandButton1_Click()
  On Error Resume Next
  Set obj = CreateObject("InternetExplorer.Application")
  If Dir(ThisWorkbook.Path + "\excel.htm")  "" Then
    obj.Navigate ThisWorkbook.Path + "\excel.htm"
  Else
    obj.GoHome
  End If
  obj.StatusBar = False  'deactivate statusbar
  obj.MenuBar = False    'deactivate menu
  obj.Toolbar = 1        'activate toolbar
  obj.Visible = True     'display Internet Explorer
End Sub
' terminate Explorer
Private Sub CommandButton2_Click()
  On Error Resume Next
  If Not obj Is Nothing Then
    obj.Quit
    Set obj = Nothing
  End If
End Sub
```

Excel as Server (Control by an External Program)

Up to now we have proceeded from the assumption that program development took place with VBA within Excel and that other programs were being controlled via ActiveX automation. As we mentioned in the introduction to this section, quite another scenario is possible: Program development can take place in the VBA dialect of another application program (Access, Project) or in the freestanding program Visual Basic. Excel is then controlled by an external program and acts as the ActiveX server.

Example: Displaying an Excel Chart in a Visual Basic Program

I have taken this example from my book on Visual Basic 6 (see the References). The example program is a freestanding program (that is, it is not an Excel file, but an independent `*.exe` file). If you do have not Visual Basic 6 installed on your computer, you must execute the setup program in the example directory `VB6\Chart\Setup` to install all the necessary Visual Basic libraries.

After the program is launched Excel is automatically launched as well (if it is not already running). Excel is then used to draw a chart based on the file `ExcelChart.xls`. This chart is displayed in the Visual Basic program in an OLE field.

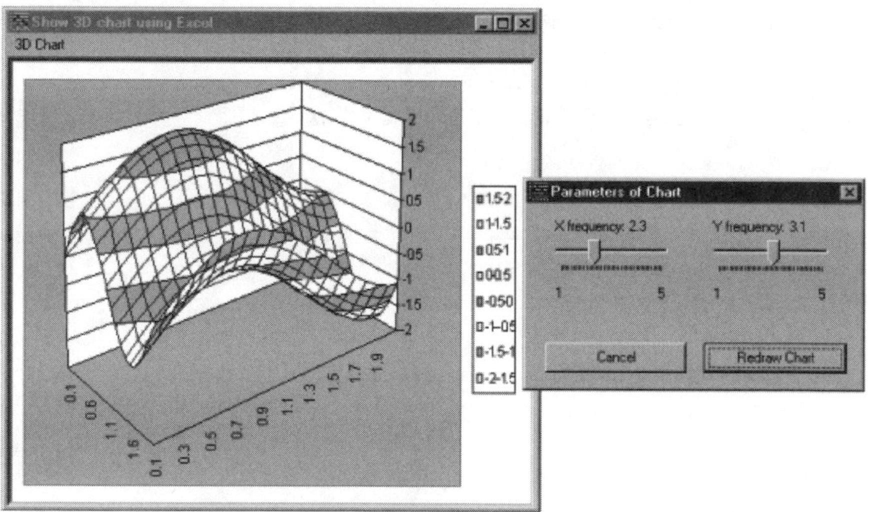

Figure 14.25. A Visual Basic program that relies on Excel's chart functions

With the menu command CHART|CHANGE PARAMETER two parameters of the graphic can be set. The Visual Basic program then recalculates the *z*-coordinates for all the points of the graphic and inserts these data via the clipboard into the Excel table. Then the chart is redrawn on the basis of these data. With two CHART commands the appearance of the chart can be changed. In program code the corresponding Excel dialogs are easily inserted. The chart can be printed with CHART|PRINT.

This Visual Basic program shows how ActiveX automation can be used to display and print a 3-D chart equipped with every refinement, without having to program all these functions anew. Why do otherwise, when Excel does it all so effortlessly?

Installation

The program `ExcelChart.exe` is located in the directory `VB6\Chart` as a freestanding `*.exe` file. However, you can execute it only if you have installed Visual Basic. If that is not the case, you must first run the program `Setup\Setup.exe`. This program installs all necessary Visual Basic libraries on your computer.

> **TIP** *You can easily undo this installation: With a double click on the* ADD/REMOVE PROGRAMS *icon in the control panel you find yourself in the Windows dialog for deinstallation of programs.*

Creating a Connection

The connection to Excel is created in the procedure *MDIForm_Load*. In this the method *CreateEmbed* of the OLE field is used. An OLE field of Visual Basic corresponds approximately to the Excel object *OleObject*. The method *CreateEmbed* is comparable to *CreateObject*.

A loop follows in which all currently open windows in Excel are processed, until the currently loaded file is found. As an identifier the character string "ActiveX_Chart_keyword" is used, which was specified as the title in the file `ExcelChart.xls` (FILE|PROPERTIES|SUMMARY). The loop gets around a weak point of *CreateEmbed*: The method creates an object, but it does not return a reference to an object. If Excel is already running and several files are open, this process makes certain that the wrong workbook is not processed. As soon as the window has been found, the *Workbook* object of the workbook is returned via the *Parent* property and stored in the global variable *wb*.

```
'VB6\Chart\formOLE.frm
Dim wb As Workbook
' initialization: loads Excel file, reference to
' the file in which to save variables wb,
' insert data, display via OLE Field
Private Sub Form_Load()
  Dim xl As Object, win As Window
  On Error Resume Next
  ChDrive App.Path
  ChDir App.Path
  Me.OLE1.Visible = False  ' currently invisible
  formWait.Show           ' please wait …
  MousePointer = vbHourglass
  With Me
    .OLE1.CreateEmbed App.Path + "\ActiveX_Chart.xls"
    Set xl = .OLE1.object.Application
    ' process all Excel windows,
    ' search for newly generated window
    For Each win In xl.Windows
      If win.Parent.Title = "ActiveX_Chart_keyword" Then
        ' we have found it!
        Set wb = win.Parent
        Exit For
      End If
    Next
  End With
  ' If an error has occurred, Excel is
  ' perhaps no longer available
  If Err  0 Then
    MsgBox "An error has occurred. " _
      & "The program will be terminated. To" _
      & "execute this example program Excel 2000 must be installed" _
    Unload Me
  End If
  PlotChart
  Me.OLE1.Visible = True
  MousePointer = 0
  formWait.Hide
End Sub
```

Drawing a Chart

Drawing the chart takes place in a separate procedure. The idea is simple: In two loops for each point in a 21-by-21 element region the *Z*-coordinate of the surface is computed. These *Z* values are arranged in a single enormous character string, where the individual values are separated by *vbTab* and the rows by *vbCr* (carriage return). This character string is then transferred to the clipboard.

With the Excel method *Paste* the data are taken from the clipboard and inserted into table 1 beginning with cell B2. The chart in `ExcelChart.xls` expects its data in the range A1:V22, where the first row and column are reserved for the axis labels and are already supplied with values. In principle, it would also be possible to write the data directly into the individual cells of the worksheet in a loop, but that would take much longer.

After the transfer of the data the table (and not the chart) is displayed in the OLE field. To overcome this shortcoming the chart sheet is activated and the worksheet made invisible. In principle, each of these measures should suffice individually, but experience has shown that only both commands accomplish the task. It is precisely these niggling details that make life with ActiveX automation so difficult and lead to a great loss of time in the debugging process.

```
Sub PlotChart()
  Dim xfreq, yfreq
  Dim x#, y#, z#, data$
  xfreq = formPara.SliderX
  yfreq = formPara.SliderY
  ' calculate new data
  For y = 0 To 2.00001 Step 0.1
    For x = 0 To 2.00001 Step 0.1
      z = Sin(x * xfreq / 10) + Sin(y * yfreq / 10)
      data = data & DecimalPoint(Str(z)) & vbTab
    Next x
    data = data & vbCr
  Next y
  Clipboard.Clear
  Clipboard.SetText data
  wb.Sheets("table").Paste wb.Sheets("table").Cells(2, 2)
  ' so that the chart and not the table is displayed
  wb.Sheets("chart").Activate
  ' Activate alone does not help, for whatever
  wb.Sheets("table").Visible = False
End Sub
```

```
' replace comma by decimal point
Private Function DecimalPoint$(x$)
  DecimalPoint = Replace(x, ",", ".")
End Function
```

> **TIP** *In transferring data via the clipboard a period must be given as the decimal point, even if one is using an international version of Excel in which this function is taken over by the comma. Since the Visual Basic function* Str *provides a comma in some local settings, this is replaced by a period in* DecimalPoint.

Printing the Chart

```
Private Sub menuPrint_Click()
  On Error Resume Next
  wb.Sheets("Chart1").PrintOut  ' print chart
  If Err  0 Then
    MsgBox "In the attempt to print the chart " & _
           "an error occurred"
  End If
End Sub
```

The remaining code of the program has little to do with Excel and is therefore not of interest to us. If you have Visual Basic, you can look at the remaining procedures yourself. If you do not have access to Visual Basic, you can examine the four `*.frm` files in the directory `Vb6\Chart` in any text editor. These files contain the definition of the program's forms and the program code in ASCII format.

New Objects for Excel (ClipBoard Example)

In the two previous sections we have seen how to use already existing object libraries of another program, where Excel was treated once as client, and then as server. Visual Basic offers another, far-reaching, possibility: You can program a new ActiveX server with Visual Basic and then use it from within Excel. In this way you can define new objects, methods, and properties.

This section gives a simple example of this: In Excel there is no way to access properly the contents of the clipboard. You can copy a range of cells to the clipboard or copy the clipboard contents to another range. However, you cannot read or write a character string to or from the clipboard. For many applications this would be desirable. In particular, large data sets could be much more efficiently inserted into a range of cells via the clipboard than in the traditional way (that is, processing each cell individually).

> **TIP** *Since this book is about Excel and not Visual Basic, we shall not go into the details of server programming. In this section we consider only in principle how this could be done and to demonstrate the application of a new OLE server under Excel.*

Installation

The new *ClipBoard* object is made available by an ActiveX server in the form of a DLL. This program must be registered in the Windows registration database before it can be used for ActiveX automation. For this you must execute the program `Vb6\ClipBoard\Setup\Setup.exe`. This program installs any Visual Basic libraries that might be needed.

Using the ClipBoard Object in Excel

To use the server it is necessary that a reference to the library "ClipBoard Object" be established via TOOLS|REFERENCES. In the example file `Vb6\ClipBoard\ActiveX_Clip.xls` this is, of course, already the case.

If these preparations have been carried out, the *ClipBoard* object, with four methods, is now available for use: *Clear* deletes the contents of the clipboard; *GetFormat* tests whether the clipboard contains data in a particular format (for example, text data); *SetText* inserts text into the clipboard; *GetText* reads the text contained in the clipboard.

The Excel Program Code

The procedure *test1* demonstrates the use of the new object: With *CreateObject* the connection to the OLE server is set. The reference to the new object is stored in the object variable *clip*, which is of the new *ClipBoard* object type. Then the methods listed above can be applied to *clip*. In *test1* a short character string is written to the clipboard with *SetText*. The following lines are traditional VBA code: The current contents of the clipboard are copied into cell A1, to show that *SetText* has functioned correctly.

```
' Vb6\ClipBoard\ActiveX_Clip.xls, "Module1"
Sub test1()
  Dim clip As ClipBoard
  Set clip = CreateObject("ClipBiblio.Clipboard")
  clip.Clear
  clip.SetText "abc"
  With Sheets("Sheet1")
    .Activate
    .[a1].CurrentRegion.Clear
    .[a1].Select
    .Paste
  End With
End Sub
```

Next we look at *test2,* which is not much more exciting. There with *GetFormat* a test is made as to whether the clipboard contains data in text format. For this an ID number must be passed to *GetFormat.* For VBA applications there are two ID numbers that are relevant: 1 for normal text and 2 for bitmaps. (Moreover, the clipboard can simultaneously contain data in several formats, say ASCII text and text with Word formatting codes. For this reason the format *GetFormat* must be tested and is not directly returned.) If the clipboard contains text, this is read with *GetText* and displayed via *MsgBox.* If a text is too long, *MsgBox* will truncate it.

```
Sub test2()
  Dim clip As ClipBoard
  Set clip = CreateObject("ClipBiblio.Clipboard")
  If clip.GetFormat(1) Then
    MsgBox "The clipboard contains data in text format: " & _
      Chr(13) & Chr(13) & clip.GetText
  End If
End Sub
```

The Program Code of the ActiveX Server

The Visual Basic program `ClipBoard.vbp` consists of nothing more than the class module `Class.cls`. There the methods of the new class *ClipBoard* are defined. The code is very short, since under Visual Basic there is already a predefined *ClipBoard* object, whose methods have only to be applied.

```
' Vb6\Clipboard\Code\Class.cls with Instancing=5 (MultiUser)
' Method Clear: clears the clipboard
Sub Clear()
  On Error Resume Next
  ClipBoard.Clear
End Sub
' Method GetText: reads text from the clipboard
Function GetText$(Optional format)
  On Error Resume Next
  If IsMissing(format) Then
    GetText = ClipBoard.GetText(1)
  Else
    GetText = ClipBoard.GetText(format)
  End If
End Function
' Method SetText: places text in the clipboard
Sub SetText(txt$, Optional format)
  On Error Resume Next
  If IsMissing(format) Then
    ClipBoard.SetText txt
  Else
    ClipBoard.SetText txt, format
  End If
End Sub
' Method GetFormat: tests whether the clipboard
' has data in the given format
Function GetFormat(format)
  On Error Resume Next
  GetFormat = ClipBoard.GetFormat(format)
End Function
```

In order that these lines of code result in a usable ActiveX server, a number of settings in PROJECT|PROPERTIES in the Visual Basic development environment are necessary. As project name, "clipBiblio" is set; as project type, ACTIVEX DLL.

Object Linking and Embedding (OLE)

OLE denotes the embedding of a document *x* in another document *y* and the mechanisms by which *x* can be processed without leaving the program for *y*. (More concretely: You embed a Corel Draw graphic in Excel and can edit the graphic without leaving Excel.)

> **TIP** *The abbreviation OLE was used by Microsoft for a while also as a synonym for COM, that is, for* Component Object Model *(Microsoft's technology for communication between objects). Later, the notion OLE was replaced by ActiveX, so that OLE today (almost) always is used only in its original sense.*

For programmers OLE is interesting insofar as an object embedded in an Excel worksheet can be addressed via the Excel object model. This works particularly well when the embedded object on its part can be processed via ActiveX automation, but that is not a necessary presupposition.

Fundamentals

If you wish to embed an object in Excel in interactive mode, you execute INSERT|OBJECT. The object is now visible within Excel, although its source is another program. If you wish to process an OLE object, you activate it with a double click. Instead of the Excel menu bar the menu bar of the other program is shown.

More precisely, OLE should really stand for "object linking *or* embedding," since in question are two completely separate mechanisms. What we have just described was object embedding: A freestanding object was embedded in Excel. The data of this object are saved in the Excel file.

In contrast to this we have object linking: In this case a part of a file of the partner program is copied and inserted via the clipboard (in Excel EDIT|PASTE SPECIAL, option PASTE LINK) into a second program. If the data in the original program are changed, the data are updated in Excel as well. The data are, however, a part of the original program and are saved by it. A change in the data can be made only in the original program (and not within the object framework in Excel).

Editing Existing OLE Objects

With the method *OLEObjects* you can access OLE objects embedded in a worksheet. This method refers to *OLEObject* objects. The property ***OLEType*** of this object specifies whether the object is freestanding and embedded (*xlOLEEmbed*) or linked (*xlOLELink*). This distinction is important in programming, since according to the OLE type different properties and methods of *OLEObject* can, or must, be used.

Embedded and Linked Objects

Embedded and linked objects can be made active with ***Select*** (corresponds to a simple mouse click). ***Activate*** enables editing of the object and corresponds to a double click on the object. According to the OLE type the editing can take place immediately in Excel (with a different menu), or else the OLE program in question appears in its own window. Note that *Activate* cannot be used in the immediate window.

With various properties of *OLEObject* you can set the position and size of the object within the worksheet as well as visual formatting details (frame, shadow, etc.). *Delete* removes the object (where in the case of an embedded object all the data are lost, while with a linked object it is only the reference to the data in the original program).

A command can be passed to the object via the ***Verb*** method. Many OLE programs support only two commands, whose ID numbers are stored in the constants *xlOpen* and *xlPrimary. Verb xlOpen* results in the OLE object being able to be edited in a separate window (even if this OLE program would support direct editing within Excel). *Verb xlPrimary* executes the default command of the OLE program. In many cases the editing of the object is thereby begun within Excel (such as with the method *Activate*). However, depending on the OLE program the default command can have a different effect. Additionally, many OLE programs support further commands. The ID numbers of these commands must be taken from the documentation of these programs.

For Linked Objects Only

Linked objects can be updated with the method ***Update***. Any changes in the data in the source program are then displayed in Excel. The property *AutoUpdate* specifies whether the object will be automatically updated when changes are made. This property can be read, but not changed. Even if the property is set to *True*, updating takes place only at regular time intervals and not at every change, since the computational requirements would be too great.

Editing OLE Objects with ActiveX Automation

If the OLE program also supports ActiveX automation (which is the case, for example, with all Office components), then with the *Object* property of the *OLEObject* object you reach the interface for ActiveX automation. Presumably, you have become dizzy by now with all these objects. Therefore, here is a brief explanation of what is meant by each object: *OLEObject* is a normal VBA object like *Range* or *Font. Object* is a property of *OLEObject* and refers to a new object that represents the starting point for ActiveX automation.

The following example inserts the two words "new text" into a Word OLE object. The program assumes that in the first worksheet an OLE Word object is embedded as the first object (menu command INSERT|OBJECT). Access is made to the OLE object via *Sheets* and *OLEObjects.* Via *Object.Application* you arrive at the Word *Application* object (which plays the same role as the Excel *Application* object, thus representing the basis of the object library). With the property *Selection* the like-named object can be edited. The method *Typetext* finally inserts some text characters, and with *vbCrLf,* a line break.

Note that the OLE object must be activated with *Activate* before execution of the automation command. A command for deactivation is lacking, and thus finally a cell of the Excel worksheet is activated, which results in the deactivation of Word.

```
' OLE-WinWord.xls, "Table1"
Private Sub CommandButton1_Click()
  Dim winword As Word.Application
  On Error GoTo btn1_error
  Application.ScreenUpdating = False
  Sheets(1).OLEObjects(1).Activate
  Set winword = Sheets(1).OLEObjects(1).Object.Application
  With winword
    .Selection.Typetext "new text" + vbCrLf
  End With
  Sheets(1).[A1].Activate
btn1_error:
  Application.ScreenUpdating = True
End Sub
```

So that the program can be executed, the Microsoft Word 9.0 Object Library must be activated via TOOLS|REFERENCES. Now the expansion of properties and methods of the Word library functions as with the Excel library. The Word object library is available in the object browser; on-line help can be summoned with `F1`; and so on.

> **TIP** *If the Microsoft Word 9.0 Object Library is not displayed in the* REFERENCES *dialog, click the button* BROWSE *and select the file* `Office2000/Office/MSO9.olb`.

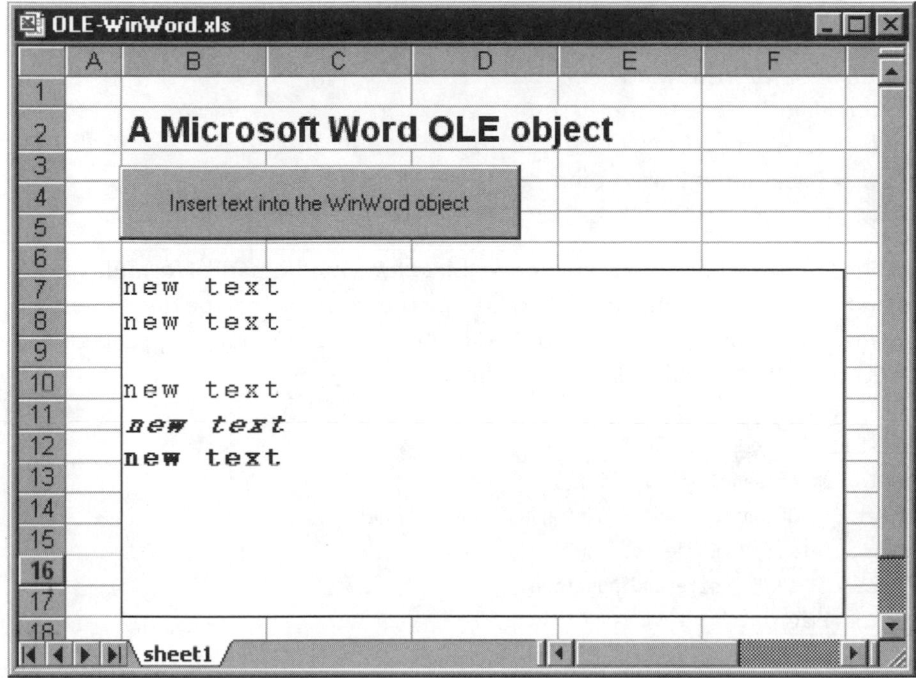

Figure 14.26. ActiveX-Automation for an OLE-Object

Inserting New OLE Objects

If you do not wish to edit existing objects—as described in the previous pages—but would like to insert new objects into tables, charts, or dialogs, then you have a number of options: Embedding a new, empty, OLE object; embedding a file; linking a file; and linking an object from the clipboard.

Embedding a New, Empty, OLE Object

To insert a new OLE object you apply *Add* to the *OLEObjects,* where you must specify the name of the OLE program in the first parameter. The syntax of this name varies from program to program, and it changes with almost every version.

Two examples of character strings that are valid at the moment are *"Word.Document.8"*, for a Word object, and *"Equation.3"*, for an Office formula object. (These character strings are valid for both Office 97 and Office 2000, probably because these two Office versions are similar. In general, you should count on these character strings changing in the next Office version.)

> **TIP** *A list of OLE types available on your computer and their names can be obtained in the system information program, which you can launch with* HELP|ABOUT MICROSOFT EXCEL|SYSTEMINFO. *The program displays a list of the installed OLE programs in the directory* OLE Registration|Registration.

The following lines insert an empty object for a mathematical formula into the first worksheet of your workbook. Editing the formula must be done manually. The formula editor cannot be controlled by ActiveX automation. The procedure works only if the formula editor is installed.

```
' OLE-Equation.xls, "Table1"
Private Sub CommandButton1_Click()
  Sheets(1).OLEObjects.Add(Equation.3).Name = "new"
  With Sheets(1).OLEObjects("new")
    .Left = 10   ' size and position
    .Top = 10
    .Width = 50
    .Height = 50
    .Activate   'edit OLE object
  End With
  Sheets(1).[a1].Activate
End Sub
```

Embedding an OLE Object Based on a File

To embed a new object whose contents are prescribed by a file of the OLE program, you again use *Add*. However, now you specify the two named parameters *Filename* and *Link*. In the example instruction below the new object is activated at once. You could also proceed as in the example above and first change the position of the object.

```
Sheets(1).OLEObjects.Add( _
  Filename:="C:\Test\dok2.doc", Link:=False).Activate
```

Linking an OLE Object Based on a File

From a programming point of view the only difference here is that now you specify *Link:=True*. This has the result that the actual data continue to be saved by the OLE program (and not within Excel). Moreover, it is possible to edit the data only in the OLE program (and not within Excel).

Inserting and Linking an OLE Object from the Clipboard

The insertion of OLE data from the clipboard proceeds, interestingly, not via *OLEObjects* and *Add*, but via the methods *Pictures* and *Paste*. The object so inserted counts as a "normal" OLE object, which can be edited after insertion via *OLEObjects*. A necessity for the correct execution of the following lines is that you first select data in a suitable OLE program and copy it to the clipboard (for example, a paragraph from a Word document).

```
Sheets(1).Pictures.Paste(Link:=True).Select
```

Launching and Controlling Programs Without ActiveX

Launching a Program

If you wish from within a VBA program to launch another Windows or DOS program that cannot be controlled via ActiveX automation, then you must make use of the command ***Shell***. As parameters you must specify the file name and a mode value. The mode determines in what form the program will appear on the monitor:

1 as a normal window with focus

2 as an Icon with focus (the program appears in the task bar, but its window is not opened)

3 as full-screen window with focus

4 as a normal window without focus

7 as an icon without focus

Surprisingly, the default mode is number 2, which is the least used. The most useful modes are 1 (if the user is to work with the program) and 7 (if the program is to run undisturbed in the background).

The file name must usually be given in full form (with the suffix `*.exe` and the complete path). Even without these specifications Excel will find programs that are located in the Windows directory.

If *Shell* is used as a function, it returns the ID number of the program. It is under this ID number that Windows runs the program internally. The number can be used to reactivate the program at a later time with *AppActivate*. The following instruction starts the Notepad program.

```
ID = Shell("notepad", 2)
```

Note, please, that VBA continues its work on the procedure after a short hesitation. Excel and the newly started program now run quasi-simultaneously and independently of one another. There is no way to determine within VBA whether a program is running yet or continues to run. (You would have to employ various DLL system functions that determine information about all running processes. This requires some rather difficult programming that would go outside the subject matter of this book. Details can be found in the KB article Q129796 in the MSDN library.)

Activating a Running Program

The command ***AppActivate*** activates an already loaded program. The command is passed as parameter the ID number of an earlier *Shell* command or the name of the window of the program to be activated. VBA is relatively forgiving in the way it interprets these parameters: Case plays no role. The program is activated as soon as it can be uniquely identified.

AppActivate activates the program, but does not change its state. If the program is currently showing itself as an icon, then it remains an icon. Attempts to shift the program into another state with *SendKeys* (say, with Alt+spacebar, Ctrl+W) fails because Excel assumes that the key combination is meant for it (because after *AppActivate* it takes a while until the program is truly activated). If *AppActivate* cannot find the specified program, then error 5 occurs (invalid procedure call).

Launching and Activating Microsoft Application Programs

If your goal is not to launch an arbitrary program, but one of the Microsoft application programs (in particular, Word, Access, and so on), you can use the method ***ActivateMicrosoftApp***. This method has the advantage over *Shell* that you do not need to know the precise file name of the program.

ActivateMicrosoftApp is passed a constant that identifies the program (see the on-line help). Sadly, in the list of programs that can be activated you will not find the most elementary Windows programs (such as Explorer).

If the program is already running, it will be activated as with *AppActivate*. This method returns *True* if the program launch or activation was successful, and otherwise, *False*.

```
Application.ActivateMicrosoftApp xlMicrosoftWord
```

Controlling the Active Program

The simplest way of controlling a program launched or activated with *Shell*, *AppActivate*, or *ActivateMicrosoftApp* is provided by the command ***SendKeys***: It simulates keyboard input for the currently active program. The syntax for the character string that is passed as parameter to *SendKeys* can be retrieved from the on-line help.

Although the possibilities offered by *SendKeys* seem attractive at first glance, in practice it is as good as impossible to control a program effectively with it. Control of Excel usually fails because the keys simulated by *SendKeys* can be processed only when no VBA macro is running. The control of external programs fails because you cannot always foresee how the program will behave. Moreover, you must take care not to send the keys too quickly; otherwise, keys will be "swallowed" or incorrectly interpreted. The speed of the program to be controlled depends, in turn, on the speed of the computer. In short, *SendKeys* is suitable for a few cute gags, but not for controlling a program.

In addition to this truly inflexible control option VBA recognizes two more intelligent ways to proceed: ActiveX and DDE. ActiveX has already been discussed extensively. DDE stands for "dynamic data exchange" and denotes an already rather old control mechanism that by Windows 95 meant hardly a thing and in this book will not be discussed further.

Syntax Summary

sh stands for a worksheet or chart sheet, *oleob* for an OLE object.

Program Launch and Control

id= Shell("datname")	launch external program
AppActivate "windowtitle"	activate running program
AppActivate id	
Application.ActivateMicrosoftApp xlXxx	start or activate MS program
SendKeys ".."	simulates keyboard input

OLE, ActiveX Automation

sh.OLEObjects(..)	access OLE objects
sh.OLEObjects.Add ...	create new OLE object
sh.Pictures.Paste link:=True	insert OLE object from the clipboard
oleob.Select	select object (normal mouse click)
oleob.Activate	activate object (double click)
oleob.Verb xlOpen/xlPrimary	execute OLE command
oleob.Update	update linked OLE object
oleob.Delete	delete OLE object
oleob.Object	reference for ActiveX automation
obj = GetObject("", "ole-name")	reference for ActiveX automation

Part IV

Reference

CHAPTER 15

Object Reference

The biggest problem in working with VBA is the enormous number of keywords. This reference chapter makes no attempt to list or describe the more than one thousand keywords. (One thousand keywords at two paragraphs each equals about five hundred pages!) That is the task of the on-line help, which despite its manifest insufficiencies is much preferable to a printed text.

This chapter gives, rather, an overview of about two hundred objects that constantly arise in VBA programming. The most important objects of the Excel, ADO, MS Forms, Office, Binder, Scripting, VBA, and VBE libraries are described in alphabetical order. I have attempted to make clear above all the connections among the various objects and to name the properties and methods that form these connections.

Chapter Overview

Object Hierarchy

This section contains several hierarchical lists, in which the logical relationship among VBA objects is represented. These lists are restricted to various segments of the object hierarchy. Do not expect completeness! Alas, this book is too small to contain a complete hierarchical listing of all objects, because the object list contains countless ramifications, which in part lead to a common object, then branch off again, and so on, and so on. A complete object hierarchy would be much too long to satisfy any reasonable requirement of clarity.

In connection with the object hierarchy the concepts of *above* and *below* must be clarified. An object that is higher in the hierarchy is placed higher in the following lists and, in the next section, to the left of the basic object. The highest object in the hierarchy is thus the *Application* object, through whose methods and properties all other objects can be reached. Here is an example: Above the *Workbook* object lie first *Workbooks* and then *Application*, while *Sheets* and each individual *Worksheet* lie below.

In the following lists only objects are named, not properties and methods that lead from one object to another. It is sometimes irritating that there are often like-named objects and methods and like-named objects and properties.

Within the lists the symbol ⇒ frequently appears. This symbol indicates that at this juncture a further ramification occurs that is represented separately further below.

Excel

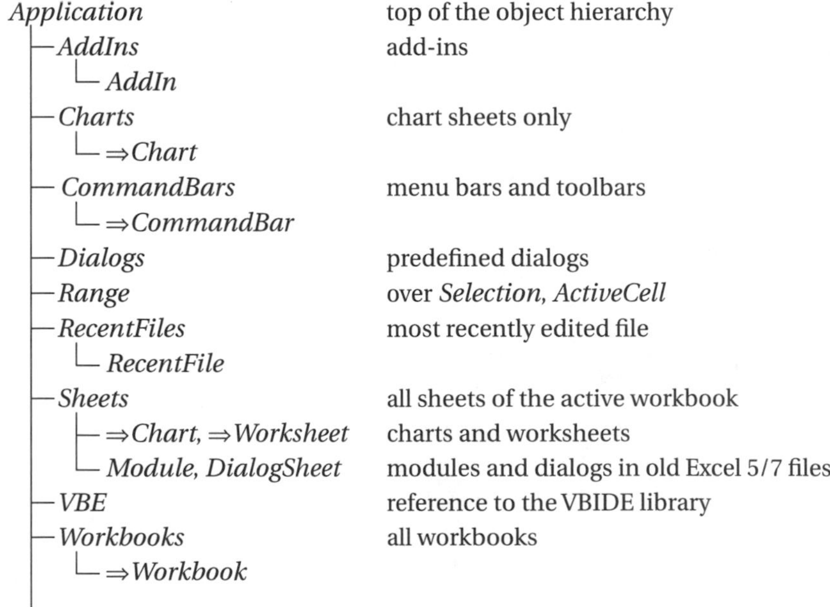

Application	top of the object hierarchy
├─ *AddIns*	add-ins
│ └─ *AddIn*	
├─ *Charts*	chart sheets only
│ └─ ⇒*Chart*	
├─ *CommandBars*	menu bars and toolbars
│ └─ ⇒*CommandBar*	
├─ *Dialogs*	predefined dialogs
├─ *Range*	over *Selection, ActiveCell*
├─ *RecentFiles*	most recently edited file
│ └─ *RecentFile*	
├─ *Sheets*	all sheets of the active workbook
│ ├─ ⇒*Chart*, ⇒*Worksheet*	charts and worksheets
│ └─ *Module, DialogSheet*	modules and dialogs in old Excel 5/7 files
├─ *VBE*	reference to the VBIDE library
├─ *Workbooks*	all workbooks
│ └─ ⇒*Workbook*	

├─*Windows*	all windows (including hidden windows)
│ └─⇒*Window*	
├─*WorksheetFunctions*	access to worksheet functions
└─*Worksheets*	worksheets only
└─⇒*Worksheet*	

Workbook

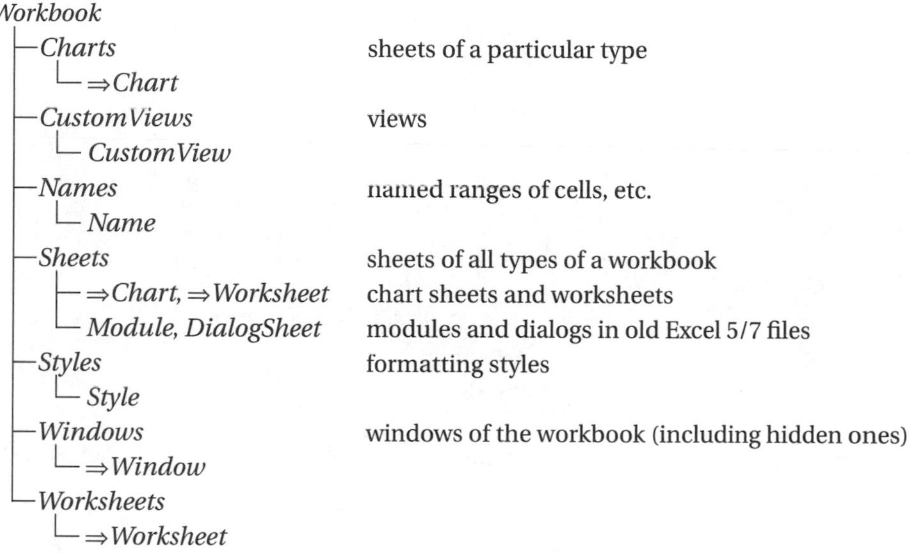

Workbook	
├─*Charts*	sheets of a particular type
│ └─⇒*Chart*	
├─*CustomViews*	views
│ └─*CustomView*	
├─*Names*	named ranges of cells, etc.
│ └─*Name*	
├─*Sheets*	sheets of all types of a workbook
│ ├─⇒*Chart*, ⇒*Worksheet*	chart sheets and worksheets
│ └─*Module, DialogSheet*	modules and dialogs in old Excel 5/7 files
├─*Styles*	formatting styles
│ └─*Style*	
├─*Windows*	windows of the workbook (including hidden ones)
│ └─⇒*Window*	
└─*Worksheets*	
└─⇒*Worksheet*	

Window

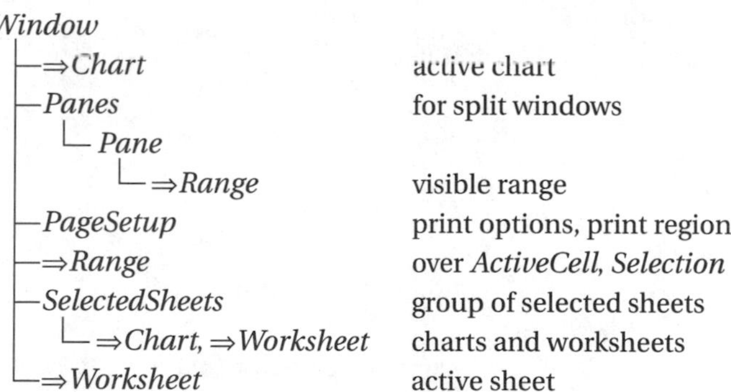

Window	
├─⇒*Chart*	active chart
├─*Panes*	for split windows
│ └─*Pane*	
│ └─⇒*Range*	visible range
├─*PageSetup*	print options, print region
├─⇒*Range*	over *ActiveCell, Selection*
├─*SelectedSheets*	group of selected sheets
│ └─⇒*Chart*, ⇒*Worksheet*	charts and worksheets
└─⇒*Worksheet*	active sheet

Worksheet

```
Worksheet
  ├─ChartObjects                   embedded charts
  ├─Comments                       comments
  │   └─Comment
  ├─H/VBreaks                      horizontal and vertical page breaks
  │   └─H/VBreak
  ├─HyperLinks                     cross references/internet links
  │   └─Hyperlinks
  ├─OLEObjects                     embedded OLE objects
  ├─Outline                        table structure
  ├─PageSetup                      page layout/printer
  ├─PivotTables                    pivot tables
  │   └─⇒PivotTable
  ├─QueryTables                    external data
  │   └─QueryTable
  ├─⇒Range                         over Selection, Range, Columns, UsedRange,
  │                                Cells, etc.
  ├─Scenarios                      scenarios
  │   └─Scenario
  └─⇒Shapes                        drawing and control elements, object groups
```

Range

```
Range
  ├─⇒Areas                         partial range of multiple selection
  │   └─Range
  ├─Borders                        border
  │   └─Border
  ├─Characters                     individual text characters
  │   └─Font
  ├─Comment                        comments
  ├─Font                           font
  ├─FormatConditions               conditional formatting
  │   └─FormatCondition
  ├─Interior                       background color and pattern
  ├─⇒PivotTable                    pivot tables
  ├─PivotField                     pivot fields
  ├─PivotItem                      pivot items
  │
```

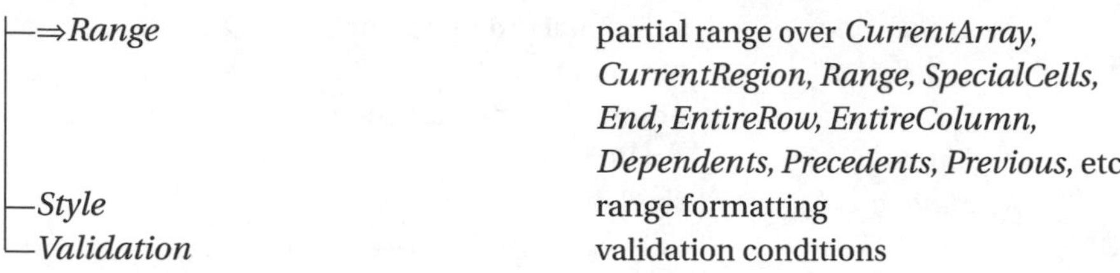

├─⇒*Range*	partial range over *CurrentArray, CurrentRegion, Range, SpecialCells, End, EntireRow, EntireColumn, Dependents, Precedents, Previous,* etc.
├─*Style*	range formatting
└─*Validation*	validation conditions

PivotTable

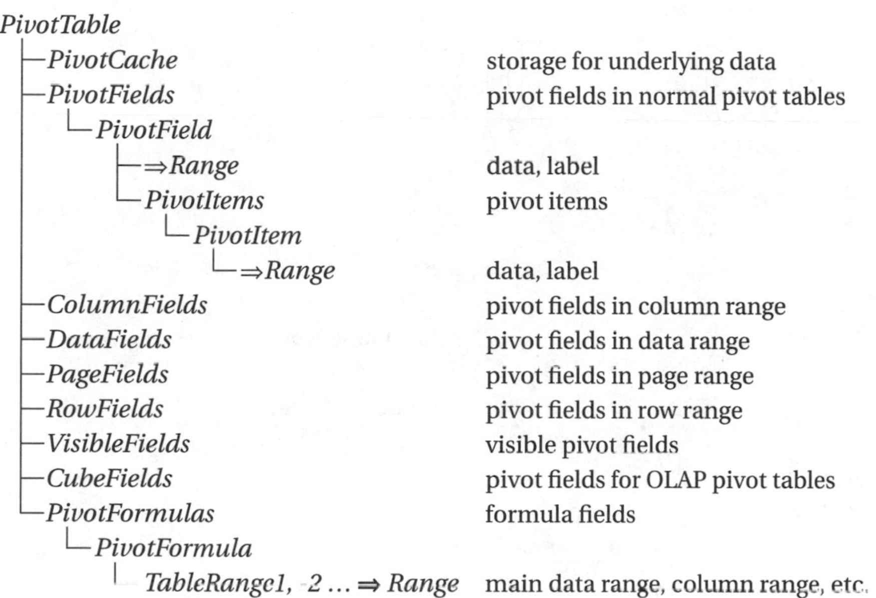

PivotTable	
├─*PivotCache*	storage for underlying data
├─*PivotFields*	pivot fields in normal pivot tables
│ └─*PivotField*	
│ ├─⇒*Range*	data, label
│ └─*PivotItems*	pivot items
│ └─*PivotItem*	
│ └─⇒*Range*	data, label
├─*ColumnFields*	pivot fields in column range
├─*DataFields*	pivot fields in data range
├─*PageFields*	pivot fields in page range
├─*RowFields*	pivot fields in row range
├─*VisibleFields*	visible pivot fields
├─*CubeFields*	pivot fields for OLAP pivot tables
└─*PivotFormulas*	formula fields
└─*PivotFormula*	
TableRange1, 2 … ⇒ *Range*	main data range, column range, etc.

Shape Objects

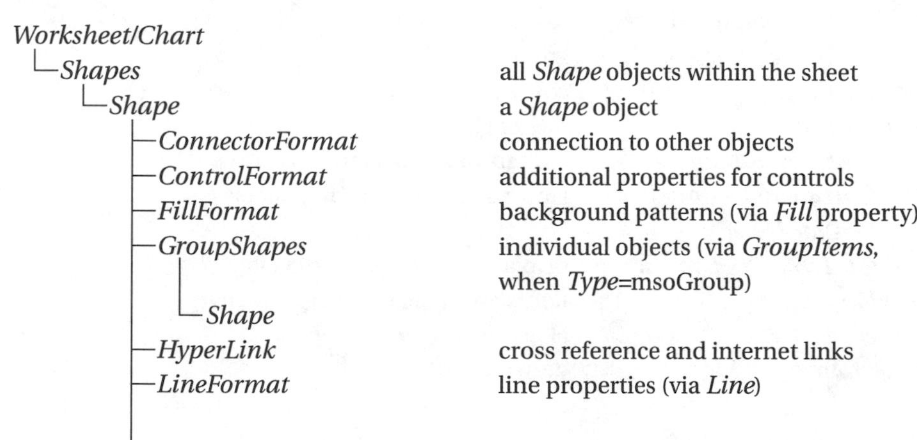

Worksheet/Chart	
└─*Shapes*	all *Shape* objects within the sheet
└─*Shape*	a *Shape* object
├─*ConnectorFormat*	connection to other objects
├─*ControlFormat*	additional properties for controls
├─*FillFormat*	background patterns (via *Fill* property)
├─*GroupShapes*	individual objects (via *GroupItems*, when *Type*=msoGroup)
│ └─*Shape*	
├─*HyperLink*	cross reference and internet links
├─*LineFormat*	line properties (via *Line*)

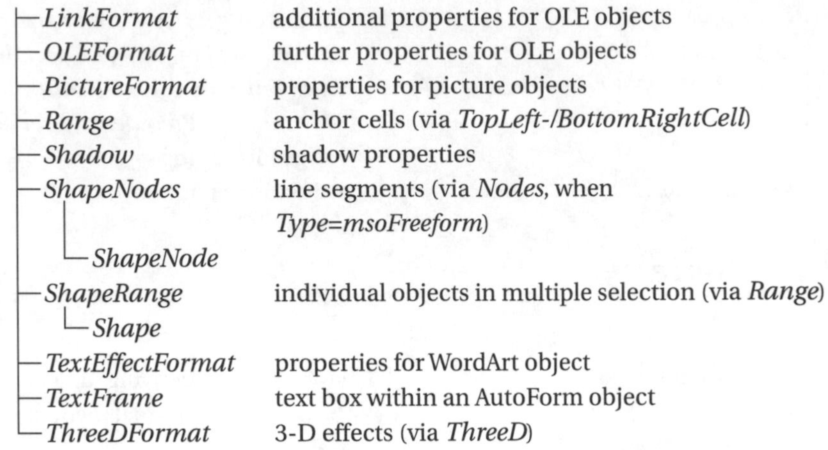

Object	Description
├ *LinkFormat*	additional properties for OLE objects
├ *OLEFormat*	further properties for OLE objects
├ *PictureFormat*	properties for picture objects
├ *Range*	anchor cells (via *TopLeft-/BottomRightCell*)
├ *Shadow*	shadow properties
├ *ShapeNodes*	line segments (via *Nodes*, when *Type=msoFreeform*)
│ └ *ShapeNode*	
├ *ShapeRange*	individual objects in multiple selection (via *Range*)
│ └ *Shape*	
├ *TextEffectFormat*	properties for WordArt object
├ *TextFrame*	text box within an AutoForm object
└ *ThreeDFormat*	3-D effects (via *ThreeD*)

Chart Objects

Object	Description
Workbook	**Part 1: access**
└ *Charts*	
└ *Chart*	main chart in chart sheet
└ *ChartObjects*	
└ ⇒*Chart*	additional embedded charts
Worksheet	
└ *ChartObjects*	
└ *ChartObject*	
└ ⇒*Chart*	embedded chart in a worksheet

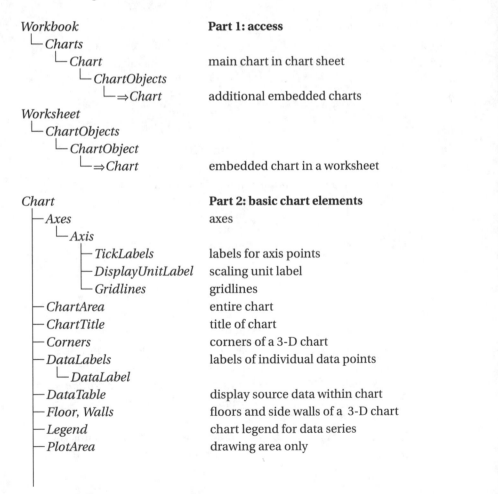

Object	Description
Chart	**Part 2: basic chart elements**
├ *Axes*	axes
│ └ *Axis*	
│ ├ *TickLabels*	labels for axis points
│ ├ *DisplayUnitLabel*	scaling unit label
│ └ *Gridlines*	gridlines
├ *ChartArea*	entire chart
├ *ChartTitle*	title of chart
├ *Corners*	corners of a 3-D chart
├ *DataLabels*	labels of individual data points
│ └ *DataLabel*	
├ *DataTable*	display source data within chart
├ *Floor, Walls*	floors and side walls of a 3-D chart
├ *Legend*	chart legend for data series
├ *PlotArea*	drawing area only
│	

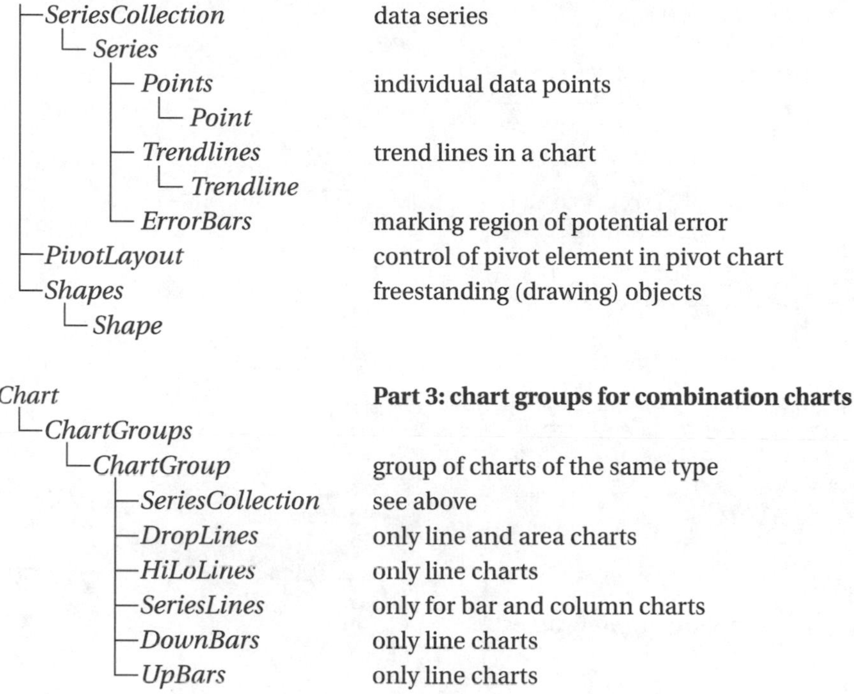

├─*SeriesCollection*	data series
│ └─ *Series*	
│ ├─ *Points*	individual data points
│ │ └─ *Point*	
│ ├─ *Trendlines*	trend lines in a chart
│ │ └─ *Trendline*	
│ └─ *ErrorBars*	marking region of potential error
├─*PivotLayout*	control of pivot element in pivot chart
└─*Shapes*	freestanding (drawing) objects
└─ *Shape*	

Chart	**Part 3: chart groups for combination charts**
└─*ChartGroups*	
└─*ChartGroup*	group of charts of the same type
├─*SeriesCollection*	see above
├─*DropLines*	only line and area charts
├─*HiLoLines*	only line charts
├─*SeriesLines*	only for bar and column charts
├─*DownBars*	only line charts
└─*UpBars*	only line charts

Database Programming (ADO Library)

ADO Object Hierarchy

Connection	creates connection to database
├─*Command*	query details (SQL command, etc.)
│ └─*Parameter[s]*	variable parameters of the query
├─*Error[s]*	error message for most recent database operation
└─*Recordset*	data record list (tables, query results, etc.)
└─*Field[s]*	individual fields of a data record

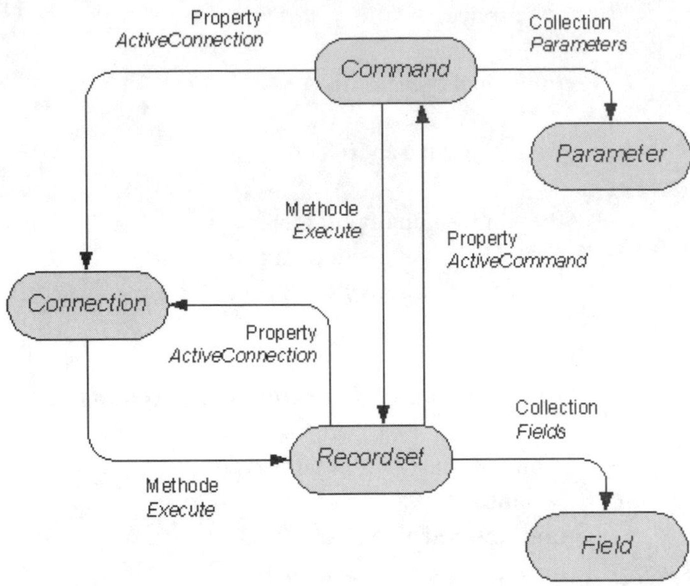

Figure 15.1. Connections among objects

Control of the Development Environment (VBIDE Library)

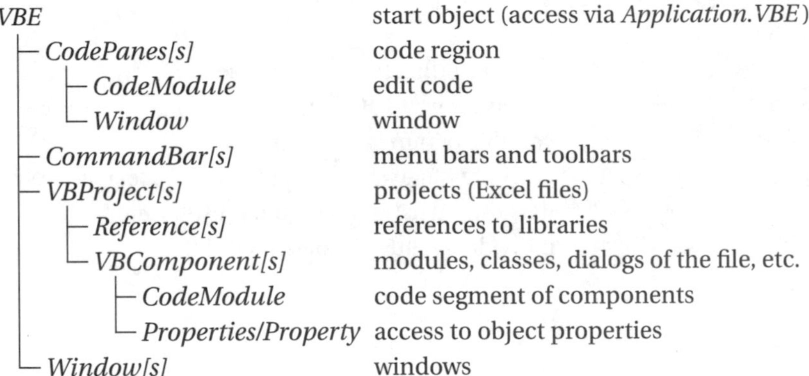

VBE	start object (access via *Application.VBE*)
├ *CodePanes[s]*	code region
│ ├ *CodeModule*	edit code
│ └ *Window*	window
├ *CommandBar[s]*	menu bars and toolbars
├ *VBProject[s]*	projects (Excel files)
│ ├ *Reference[s]*	references to libraries
│ └ *VBComponent[s]*	modules, classes, dialogs of the file, etc.
│ ├ *CodeModule*	code segment of components
│ └ *Properties/Property*	access to object properties
└ *Window[s]*	windows

User-Defined Dialogs and Controls (MS Forms Library)

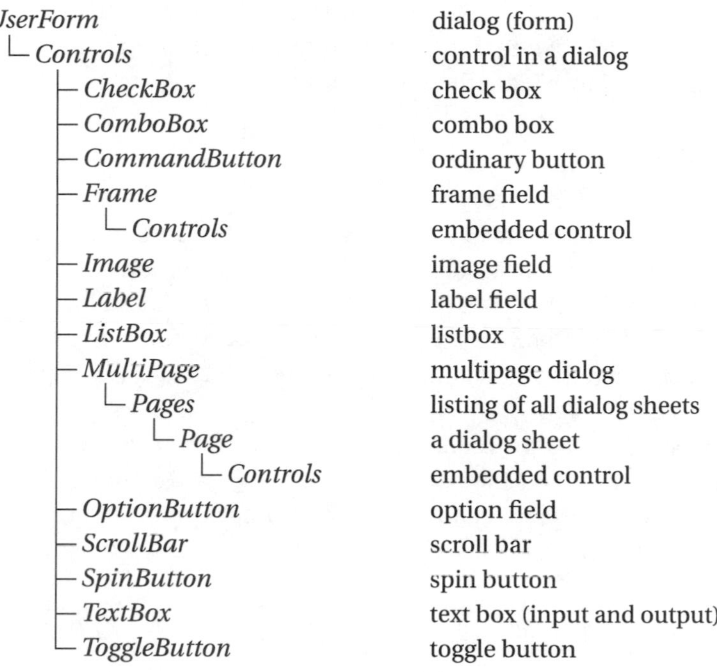

UserForm	dialog (form)
└ *Controls*	control in a dialog
├ *CheckBox*	check box
├ *ComboBox*	combo box
├ *CommandButton*	ordinary button
├ *Frame*	frame field
└ *Controls*	embedded control
├ *Image*	image field
├ *Label*	label field
├ *ListBox*	listbox
├ *MultiPage*	multipage dialog
└ *Pages*	listing of all dialog sheets
└ *Page*	a dialog sheet
└ *Controls*	embedded control
├ *OptionButton*	option field
├ *ScrollBar*	scroll bar
├ *SpinButton*	spin button
├ *TextBox*	text box (input and output)
└ *ToggleButton*	toggle button

File Access with File System Objects (Scripting Library)

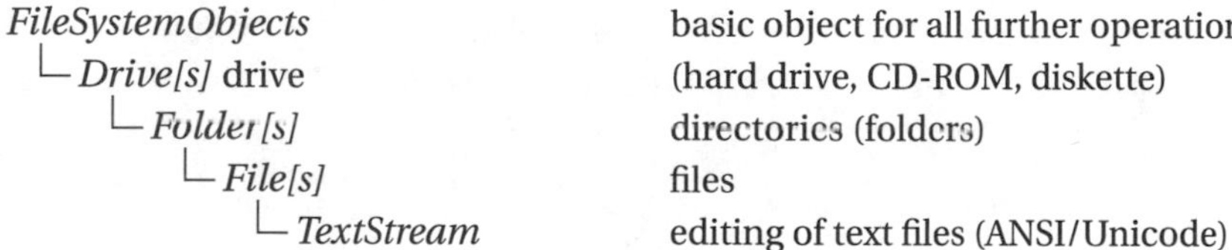

FileSystemObjects	basic object for all further operations
└ *Drive[s]* drive	(hard drive, CD-ROM, diskette)
└ *Folder[s]*	directories (folders)
└ *File[s]*	files
└ *TextStream*	editing of text files (ANSI/Unicode)

Menu Bars and Toolbars (Office Library)

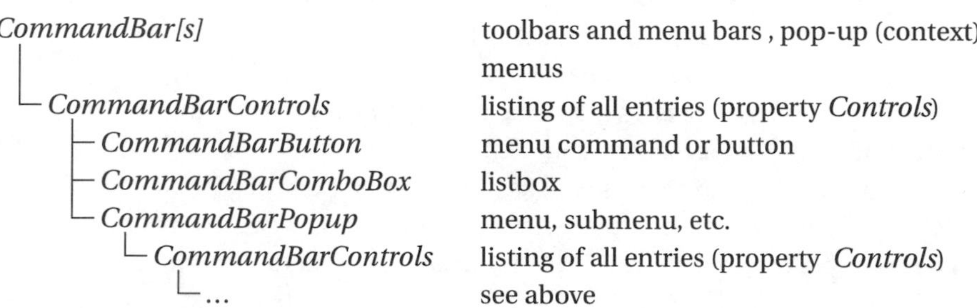

CommandBar[s]	toolbars and menu bars , pop-up (context) menus
└ *CommandBarControls*	listing of all entries (property *Controls*)
├ *CommandBarButton*	menu command or button
├ *CommandBarComboBox*	listbox
└ *CommandBarPopup*	menu, submenu, etc.
└ *CommandBarControls*	listing of all entries (property *Controls*)
└ ...	see above

Alphabetical Reference

In the reference that follows are described all basic objects of Excel as well as the most important objects of the Office, MS Forms, and ADO libraries. Further, an attempt has been made to emphasize the most important and characteristic properties and methods and to explain their functions.

Enumeration Objects

For enumeration objects the like-named method is given to the left, and the parameters of this method to the right. More precisely, to the right we are actually dealing with the *Item* method, which is almost never written out (that is, instead of *Axes.Item(xlValue)* one typically writes the short form *Axes(xlValue)*). In most cases an object of an enumeration is identified by specifying an index number or name (*Sheets(1)* or *Sheets("Table 1")*).

With most methods that lead to enumeration objects, data fields are also allowed as arguments. For example, the method *Sheets(Array(1,2,3))* returns a ***Sheets*** object that contains sheets 1, 2, and 3. Now, for example, you can select all three sheets at once with *Select*.

Identical or Similar Properties of Multiple Objects

Properties that are associated with practically all objects in the same or similar form will not be described anew each time. In particular, we have *Count* (specifies the number of elements of an enumeration object), *Index* (specifies the index number of an object within an enumeration), *Parent* (refers to the object lying above), *Application* (refers to the object ***Application***), and *Creator* (contains an ID number of the program from which the object comes, as a rule the ID number of Excel).

Default Properties, Default Objects, Shorthand Notation

With many properties and methods the object ***Application*** is considered the default object. An object must be named only if the property or method refers to a different object (for example, to a particular ***Workbook*** object).

With all objects that possess a *Value* property this property is the default property, and need not be explicitly named.

In accessing ranges of cells as well as objects in worksheets the shorthand form *[A1]* is permitted. The complete notation would be *Range("A1")*. The shorthand with square brackets corresponds internally to a call to the *Evaluate* or *Item* method.

Formalities

In order that we may distinguish from among the many like-named methods and properties without further reference, in this section all objects are written in boldface.

In the left portion of the syntax box are listed methods and properties that lead to the object in question (symbol ↗). In the right-hand portion of the syntax box are listed the methods, properties, or indices that lead from the object under consideration to other objects (symbol ↘).

In the upper right corner of the syntax box appears the library from which the object comes. (In order for objects from the ADO, Binder, Office, and MS Forms libraries to be able to be used, the library in question must be activated with TOOLS|REFERENCES.)

ADO	An object of the ActiveX Data Objects library (access to external databases).
Excel	A normal Excel object. These objects are available in every VBA program under Excel.
Office	An object of the Office library (document properties, menu bars, toolbars, etc.).
OfficeBinder	An object of the OfficeBinder library (folders).
MSForms	Controls and other objects of the MS Forms library (structure of forms).
Scripting	An object from the Microsoft Scripting-Runtime library (concerns above all File Scripting Objects).
StdOLE	An object from thc OLE Automation library (concerns only *StdPicture* and *StdFont*).
VBA	An object that has been made available from the programming language VBA (concerns only *Collection* and *ErrObject*).
VBE	An object from the VBA Extension library (VBIDE in the object browser).

Order in the Object Hierarchy

For each object in the gray syntax boxes, to the left are placed the most important higher-ranking objects that lead to the object described. To the right are named the most important properties or methods of the described object that lead to lower-ranking objects. In this way an immediate ordering of the object in the object hierarchy is achieved.

For example, take a look at the ***Axis*** object (a couple of pages further): The method *Axes* of the higher-ranked ***Chart*** object leads to the ***Axis*** object. The two properties *MajorGridlines* and *MinorGridlines* refer to the lower-ranked object ***Gridlines***.

The cross references in the left and right sides of the syntax box are in many cases incomplete. For example, dozens of higher-ranking methods and properties lead to the ***Range*** object. Conversely, above the properties and methods of the ***Workbook*** object there are countless further objects that can be reached. Thus a complete cross reference is essentially impossible due to restrictions of space and the desideratum of comprehensibility.

AddIn	Excel
***Application**.AddIns(..)* ↗	

The object ***AddIn*** contains certain data for the add-ins registered in Excel. The property *Installed* specifies whether the add-in is currently activated or deactivated. A change in the value of this property also changes the state of the add-in. *Path, Name,* and *FullName* specify the file name of the add-in file, *Title* the title displayed in the ADD-IN dialog, and *Comments* a brief related explanation.

AddIns	Excel
Application.*AddIns* ↗	*(index* or *name)* ↘ ***AddIn***

The object refers to the list of all add-ins registered in Excel. Whether these add-ins are actually activated can be determined via the *Installed* property of the ***add-in*** object. With the method *Add* you can install new add-ins. For this you have merely to specify the file name of the add-in.

Adjustments	Excel
***Shape**.Adjustments* ↗	
***ShapeRange**.Adjustments* ↗	

Many ***Shape*** objects (to which belong, among others, all AutoShapes, see the Drawing toolbar) possess yellow adjustment points with which in interactive mode the appearance of the object can be changed (such as the width of an arrow or the shape of its point). These changes are stored in several floating-point numbers, which can be addressed with *Adjustments(n)*. Whether and how many adjustment parameters are available can be determined with *Adjustments.Count*. It is more difficult to determine the meaning of the *n*th parameter for the object, since it is not documented. Take the advice of the on-line help and use the macro recorder.

Application Excel

***Excel**.Application* ↗

.Workbooks ↘ ***Workbook***
.ActiveWorkbook ↘ ***Workbook***
.Windows ↘ ***Window***
.ActiveWindow ↘ ***Window***
.ActiveSheet ↘ ***Worksheet, Chart***
.Commandbars ↘ ***Commandbar***
.AddIns ↘ ***AddIn***

The object ***Application*** lies above all Excel objects. With its various properties and methods you can reach, sometimes directly, sometimes indirectly, all other objects described in this chapter. In the syntax box above are listed only some particularly frequently needed properties and methods.

Application refers to many properties that control global Excel options (for example, *DisplayFormulaBar, Calculation, ScreenUpdating, WindowState, DisplayFullScreen, DisplayStatusBar, DisplayAlerts*). *Path* specifies the path to `Excel.exe`. *Version* contains the number of the current Excel version.

With ***Application*** you can access certain worksheet functions, so these can be used in VBA code as well (such as *Count, Index, Sum, VLookup, Lookup*).

Application is the default object for many methods and properties, so it does not always have to be specifically named (such as *ActiveSheet, ActiveWindow*).

If you are controlling Excel from an external program via ActiveX automation, you must prefix *Excel* to the *Application* property in order to specify that the command is to be applied to Excel. *Excel* can also be used in VBA code within Excel, but it has no effect there.

Areas Excel

***Range**.Areas* ↗

(index) ↘ ***Range***

If a cell range is made up of several partial ranges, then the object ***Areas*** refers to the rectangular partial areas of this range. Whether a composite range is at hand can be determined by the *Count* property of ***Areas***.

AutoCorrect Excel

***Application**.AutoCorrect* ↗

The ***AutoCorrect*** object controls that autocorrect feature in Excel (optional) during input of text. The property *ReplaceText* specifies whether the automatic correction is active. *ReplacementList* contains a data field with the text to be replaced and the associated corrections. With the methods *AddReplacement* and *DeleteReplacement* entries to this list can be added or deleted. *CapitalizeNamesOfDays* specifies whether the first letter of a weekday should be automatically written in uppercase; *TwoInitialCapitals* determines whether such a typographical error (e.g., GOliath) should be automatically corrected.

	AutoFilter	Excel
Worksheet.*AutoFilter* ↗		*.Filters* ↘ ***Filter***

The ***AutoFilter*** object is listed in the object browser, but it is not, alas, documented. (The same can be said for the related objects ***Filters*** and ***Filter***). Thus the following remarks should be taken with due caution.

With the *AutoFilter* method of the ***Range*** object you can construct filters for databases and lists in worksheets. Within a worksheet only one autofilter can be active at a given time. However, this can contain several filters (one for each column of the database). The ***AutoFilter*** object enables access to the corresponding ***Filter*** objects (*AutoFilter.Filters.Count* and *AutoFilter.Filters(n)*). The property *Range* specifies the range of cells of the entire database that should be processed by the autofilter.

	Axes	Excel
Chart.*Axes* ↗		*(type, group)* ↘ ***Axis***

The enumeration object ***Axes*** refers to the coordinate axes of a chart (see ***Axis***). Identification comes from the input of the type (*xlCategory* for the *X*-axis, *xlValue* for the *Y*-axis, and *xlSeries* for the third axis in the case of a 3-D chart). For 2-D charts with two *Y*-axes the axis group must be specified via the second parameter (*xlPrimary* or *xlSecondary*).

There are two methods for adding or deleting axes. Axes are generated and deleted by changing the *AxisGroup* properties of the objects ***Chart*** and ***Series***, respectively.

	Axis	Excel
Chart.*Axes(..)* ↗		*.AxisTitle* ↘ ***AxisTitle***
		.MajorGridlines ↘ ***Gridlines***
		.MinorGridlines ↘ ***Gridlines***
		.TickLabels ↘ ***TickLabels***

The ***Axis*** object is used in charts for describing the features of the coordinate axes. Charts are usually equipped with *X*- and *Y*-axes, while 3-D charts have a *Z*-axis as well. In the case of combination charts it is possible to have two independent *X*- and *Y*-axes (ordered by *AxisGroup*). Access to all axes is accomplished via the method *Axes*.

The most important properties are *MinimumScale* and *MaximumScale* (range of values), *MajorUnit* and *MinorUnit* (distance between major and minor tick marks and gridlines), *MajorTickMark* and *MinorTickMark* (for turning on and off the subsidiary tick marks), and *ScaleType* (for choosing between linear and logarithmic scaling).

Visual details for labeling can be set by the subsidiary objects ***AxisTitle*** and ***TickLabels***.

	AxisTitle	Excel
Axis.*AxisTitle* ↗		*.Interior* ↘ ***Interior***
		.Border ↘ ***Border***
		.Font ↘ ***Font***

The object ***AxisTitle*** describes the appearance of the title of a coordinate axis of a chart. The text of the axis label is controlled by the *Caption* or *Text* property, and the font by the like-named lower-ranking object. The location of the title can be changed via *Left* and *Top*. In order that unlabeled axes can be labeled, first the *HasTitle* property of the ***Axis*** object must be set to *True*.

	Binder	OfficeBinder
CreateObject("Office.Binder") ↗		*.ActiveSection* ↘ ***Section***
GetObject(..., "Office.Binder") ↗		
		.Sections ↘ ***Section***
		.BuiltinDocumentProperties ↘ ***DocumentProperty***
		.CustomDocumentProperties ↘ ***DocumentProperty***

The ***Binder*** object enables VBA control of binders. Integration into the Excel object model is via ActiveX automation. An object of type ***Binder*** must therefore be created with *CreateObject* or *GetObject*. Finally, the individual sections of the binder can be accessed via the properties *ActiveSection* and *Sections*.

For managing the binders there are available, among others, the methods *Open, Close, Save, SaveAs,* and *PrintOut*. The visibility of the binder bar at the left border can be controlled with the property *LeftPane*. *Path* and *Name* specify the path and name of the binder file (identifier `*.odb`). Additional binder properties can be read and altered via the *XxxDocumentProperties* properties.

	Border	Excel
Range.*Borders(..)* ↗		
`chartobject`.*Border* ↗		

The object ***Border*** controls the border and line style of individual cells, ranges of cells, and countless chart objects (such as ***Series***, ***ChartObject***, ***ChartTitle***, ***Oval***, ***Legend***). The three most important properties are *Color*, *LineStyle* (such as dotted, for example), and *Weight* (width of the lines). To facilitate the setting of the ***Border*** properties for a range of cells one has the *Range* method *BorderAround*.

	Borders	***Excel***
FormatCondition.*Borders* ↗		*(index)* ↘ ***Border***
Range.*Borders* ↗		
Style.*Borders* ↗		

This enumeration object refers to the six ***Border*** objects that determine the appearance of the border lines of a range of cells as well as a pair of diagonal lines. As index the *XlBordersIndex* constant is specified.

CalculatedFields	Excel
PivotTable.*CalculatedFields* ↗	*(name* or *index)* ↘ ***PivotField***

This enumeration object refers to those pivot fields of a pivot table that do not come directly from the source data but are calculated. (If in the source data there are columns with *price* and *quantity*, then from the product of these numbers a new pivot field *sales* can be calculated. In interactive mode you execute the command FORMULAS|CALCULATED FIELD in the pivot table toolbar.) For calculated pivot fields one has *IsCalculated=True*. The property *Formula* contains the calculational formula.

CalculatedItems	Excel
PivotField.*CalculatedItems* ↗	*(name* or *index)* ↘ ***PivotItem***

This enumeration object refers to pivot elements (not fields) that result from a formula. (In interactive mode to create such formulas you use the command FORMULAS|CALCULATED ITEM from the pivot table toolbar. You can thus, for example, insert a partial result row into a pivot table that summarizes data from several rows.) For calculated pivot items one has, as with pivot fields, *IsCalculated=True*. The property *Formula* contains the calculational formula.

CalloutFormat	Excel
Shape*.CalloutFormat* ↗	
ShapeRange*.CalloutFormat* ↗	

According to the on-line help, the ***CalloutFormat*** object controls various properties of ***Shape*** objects of the type "legend with line." However, after several attempts I have been unable to generate an AutoForm object that would allow access to ***CalloutFormat*** without an error message.

Characters	Excel
Range*.Characters(..)* ↗	*.Font* ↘ ***Font***
object*.Characters(..)* ↗	

With the *Characters* method you can access individual characters of a text in a cell or in an object (such as ***ChartTitle***, ***TextBox***) and change its type style. The properties *Text* and *Caption* contain the selected text. The number of the first character and the number of characters must be passed to the *Characters* method.

Chart	***Excel***
Workbook*.Charts(..)* ↗	*.ChartArea* ↘ ***ChartArea***
ChartObject*.Chart* ↗	*.Axes* ↘ ***Axis***
Workbook*.ActiveChart* ↗	*.SeriesCollection* ↘ ***Series***

The ***Chart*** object can refer either to an embedded chart in a worksheet or to the principal chart in a chart sheet. (There is no independent type of object for chart sheets.) In each case ***Chart*** represents the basic object for the content and visual appearance of a chart. For charts that are embedded in worksheets there is, in addition, the ***ChartObject***, standing between the worksheet and the chart, which determines the position and size of the chart.

From the ***Chart*** object more than thirty properties and methods refer to subordinate objects, by means of which most details of content and form in the chart can be controlled. The three most important properties and methods are named in the syntax box above. A complete overview is given in the previous section by the object hierarchy list, under the topic of chart objects.

Ordered directly beneath the ***Chart*** object are the properties *Type* and *SubType*, through which the chart type is set. The method *ChartWizard* creates a new chart. *AutoFormat* forms the chart via an autoformat. *Elevation, Rotation*, and *Perspective* determine the viewing direction of a 3-D chart.

ChartArea	Excel
Chart.*ChartArea* ↗	.*Interior* ↘ ***Interior***
	.*Border* ↘ ***Border***

The object ***ChartArea*** describes the visual appearance of the entire chart (including axes, legend, title, etc.). In contrast to ***ChartArea***, we have the object ***PlotArea***, which concerns only the background portion of the chart.

The appearance of the chart area is handled principally by the subobjects ***Interior*** (color and pattern) and ***Border*** (border). This object acquires additional significance via the methods *Copy, ClearFormats, ClearContents*, and *Clear*. These methods concern not the chart area, but the entire chart.

ChartColorFormat	Excel
ChartFillFormat.*Fore-/BackColor* ↗	

This object enables the setting of color transitions in various chart objects. There is no recognizable difference between this and ***ColorFormat***. See also ***ChartFillFormat*** and ***ColorFormat***.

ChartFillFormat	Excel
ChartObject.*Fill* ↗	.*Fore-/BackColor* ↘ ***ChartColorFormat***

With this object background effects can be set, as with ***FillFormat*** (which see). However, ***ChartFillFormat*** is specifically for chart objects, while ***FillFormat*** is only for ***Shape*** and ***ShapeRange***.

ChartGroup	Excel
***Chart**.ChartGroups(..)* ↗	*.SeriesCollection* ↘ ***Series***
***Chart**.XxxGroups(..)* ↗	

Chart groups bring together within a chart several data series with a common chart type. Chart groups are required only for combination charts (combination charts are charts in which two chart types are united, for example, a line chart and a scatter chart or two line charts with different *Y*-axes). The most important properties are *Type* and *SubType*, through which the chart type of the group is determined.

ChartGroups	Excel
***Chart**.ChartGroups* ↗	*(name* or *index)* ↘ ***ChartGroup***

This enumeration object refers to ***ChartGroup*** objects, which are necessary for constructing combination charts (see above). In addition to *ChartGroups* there exist countless other methods that refer to specific subcollections of ***ChartGroup*** objects, for example, *AreaGroups*, *PieGroups*, and *LineGroups*. There is no separate method for constructing combination charts, which arise simply from the separate settings of the *Type* or *SubType* property of individual data series.

ChartObject	Excel
***Worksheet**.ChartObjects(..)* ↗	*.Chart* ↘ ***Chart***
	.Interior ↘ ***Interior***

The chart object lies between an embedded ***Chart*** object and the worksheet. Above all, it determines the size and position of the chart. Chart objects are allowed, in principle, in chart sheets and dialog sheets as well, though they seldom appear in those contexts. Chart objects can be reproduced with the method *Duplicate* and with *Copy* can be copied to the clipboard.

ChartObjects	Excel
***Worksheet**.ChartObjects* ↗	*(index* or *name)* ↘ ***Chart***

This enumeration object refers to the embedded ***ChartObject*** objects of a worksheet, dialog sheet, or chart sheet. See ***ChartObject***.

Charts	Excel
***Workbook**.Charts* ↗	*(index* or *name)* ↘ ***Chart***

This enumeration object refers to chart sheets. Note that there is no separate object type for chart sheets, for which reason ***Charts*** actually refers to the main chart of a chart sheet. The page/chart is activated by the method *Select* and sent to the printer or represented in page view with *PrintOut*. To access embedded charts in a worksheet you must use the object ***ChartObjects***.

ChartTitle	Excel
Chart.*ChartTitle* ↗	.*Interior* ↘ ***Interior***
	.*Font* ↘ ***Font***

This object describes text, font, position, and appearance of the title of a chart. Whether a chart has a title at all is determined by the ***Chart*** property *HasTitle*. Finally, the appearance of the title can be set with the properties/methods *Caption*, *Interior*, *Border*, and *Font*.

CheckBox	MS Forms
UserForm.*Controls(..)* ↗	

This object represents the check box (yes/no choice) in MS Forms dialogs. The most important property is *Value*, which contains, according to the setting, *True*, *False*, or *Null* (undetermined).

CodeModule	VBE
CodePane.*CodeModule* ↗	
VBComponent.*CodeModule* ↗	

The ***CodeModule*** object enables changes in program code. For this purpose methods such as *InsertLines*, *DeleteLines*, *AddFromFile* are available.

CodePane[s]	VBE
VBE.*CodePanes* ↗	.*CodeModule* ↘ ***CodeModule***
	.*Window* ↘ ***Window***

The enumeration object ***CodePanes*** and the derived ***CodePane*** objects describe regions of code in the VBA development environment. (Tip: If you wish to edit VBA code you must rely on the ***CodeModule*** object.)

Collection	VBA
	(*index* or *name*) ↘ ***object***

This object enables the definition of separate listings (enumeration objects). New objects can be added with *Add*, while existing objects can be deleted with *Remove*. The number of saved objects can be determined with *Count*.

ColorFormat Excel

***FillFormat**.Fore-/BackColor* ↗
***LineFormat**.Fore-/BackColor* ↗
***ShadowFormat**.ForeColor* ↗
***ThreeDFormat**.ExtrusionColor* ↗

With some objects that were introduced in Excel 97 the color is not set directly as an RGB value, but via the detour of a ***ColorFormat*** object. The default property of ***ColorFormat*** is *RGB*, and according to the *Type* setting the color can be set as well with the property *SchemeColor*. *SchemeColor* expects index numbers for the valid color palette (whose setting, however, can be neither read nor changed).

ComAddIn[s] Office

***Application**.ComAddIns(..)* ↗

Application**.ComAddins* refers to the like-named enumeration of all COM add-ins registered with Excel. ***ComAddIns refers to the individual ***ComAddIn*** objects, whose property *Description* contains the name of the COM add-in (that is, the text that is displayed in the dialog Tools|COM Add-Ins). The property *Connect* determines whether the add-in is currently active. A change in *Connect* has the same effect as a change in the corresponding checkbox in the COM Add-Ins dialog.

ComboBox MS-Forms

***UserForm**.Controls(..)* ↗

This control offers a combination of a collapsible listbox with a text field. *List(n)* enables access to the list. With *RowSource* the list can be taken from a range of cells in the table. (When the control is used in a worksheet, instead of the above, *ListFillRange* must be used. *LinkedCell* then specifies into which cell the result of the selection should be transferred.) *Text* contains the selected or input text, while *Value* contains, according to the setting of *BoundColumn*, the text of the number of the selected list elements.

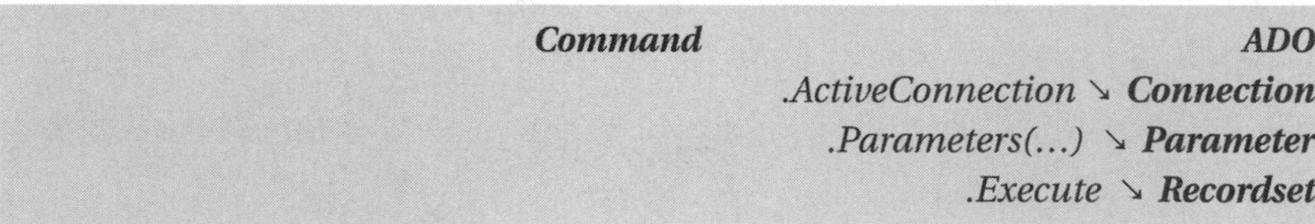
Command ***ADO***

.ActiveConnection ↘ ***Connection***
.Parameters(...) ↘ ***Parameter***
.Execute ↘ ***Recordset***

This object makes it possible to execute SQL commands with parameters and so-called *stored procedures* (SQL procedures that are managed by the database server). The SQL code of the query or name of the *stored procedure* is given in *CommandText*. Then the values of the parameters are set. Finally, the command can be executed with the method *Execute*. If the command deals with a query, then *Execute* returns a ***Recordset*** object.

CommandBar Office
Application.*CommandBars(..)* ↗ .*Controls* ↘ ***CommandBarControls***

This object describes a menu bar or toolbar. More precisely, there are three types (property *Type*): normal toolbars (*msoBarTypeNormal*), regular menu bars (*msoBarTypeMenuBar*), and pop-up menus (*msoBarTypePopup*).

CommandBarButton Office
CommandBar.*Controls(..)* ↗

This object represents a normal entry in a menu or toolbar. Depending on the setting of *Style* the object is represented as an icon and/or text.

CommandBarComboBox Office
CommandBar.*Controls(..)* ↗

A menu element can be used either as a text input field or as a listbox (in a toolbar). The type of use is determined by *Style* (*msoControlDropdown, msoControlEdit,* or *msoControlComboBox*). When a listbox is used the list is processed with the methods *AddItem, RemoveItem,* and *Clear.* In each case the input text or selected entry can be taken from *Text.*

CommandBarControl Office
CommandBar.*Controls(..)* ↗ (*index* or *name)* ↘ ***CommandBarControl***

CommandBarControl is an object lying above ***CommandBarButton***, ***CommandBarComboBox***, or ***CommandBarPopup***. Which object type is currently valid can be determined with *Type.* (Please note that there are some *CommandBar* types that appear in built-in menus, but currently cannot be used in programming and therefore are represented by their own objects.)

Important properties are *Caption* (the label text), *TooltipText* (the yellow infotext if this differs from *Caption*), *BeginGroup* (display a separation line above or to the left), and *OnAction* (the event procedure to be called).

CommandBarControls Office
CommandBar.*Controls* ↗ (*index* or *name)* ↘ ***CommandBarControl***

This enumeration object leads to the individual entries of a toolbar or menu bar or of a menu or submenu. Formally, with subordinate objects we are dealing with ***CommandBarControl*** objects. In fact, you usually receive a ***CommandBarButton***, ***CommandBarComboBox***, or ***CommandBarPopup*** object (see ***CommandControl***). With *Add* new menu items can be added.

CommandBarPopup	Office
***CommandBar**.Controls(..)* ↗	*.Controls* ↘ ***CommandBarControls***

This object is the key to individual menus in a menu bar or toolbar, to submenus in menus, and so on. *Controls* refers to the subordinate entries that come into play with a ***CommandBarButton***, ***CommandBarComboBox***, or ***CommandBar-Popup*** object.

The possibility of placing this object at any level of the hierarchy makes access to the object complicated. Furthermore, this object is not suited for pop-up menus, which must be defined as ***CommandBar*** objects with *Position=msoBar-Popup*.

CommandBars	Office
***Application**.CommandBars* ↗	*(index* or *name)* ↘ ***CommandBar***

This object enumerates all predefined and user-defined toolbars and menu bars.

CommandButton	MS-Forms
***UserForm**.Controls(..)* ↗	*.Picture* ↘ ***StdPicture***

The most important button property is *Caption*, for the label text. Optionally, a picture can be displayed in the button (properties *Picture* and *PicturePosition*). A click triggers, not surprisingly, a *Click* event.

If you use a control in a worksheet, you should set *TakeFocusOnClick* to *False*. You thereby avoid the input focus remaining in the button when it is clicked (which in VBA code can lead to problems).

Comment	Excel
***Range**.Comment* ↗	*.Next/.Previous* ↘ ***Comment***
***Range**.AddComment(..)* ↗	*.Shape* ↘ ***Shape***

This object stores the content and other information as notes (also called comments since Excel 97). With the method *Text* the comment can be read and edited. The methods *Previous* and *Next* refer to additional comments in the worksheet. New comments can be created with the method *AddComment* of the ***Range*** object. ***Range.**ClearComments* deletes all comments in a given range of cells.

Comments	Excel
***Worksheet**.Comments* ↗	*(index* or *name)* ↘ ***Comment***

This enumeration object enables access to all comments within a worksheet without the necessity of examining all the cells.

Connection ADO

Recordset.*ActiveConnection* ↗ .*Execute* ↘ ***Recordset***

Before data can be read from a database, access thereto must be established via the ***Connection*** object. For this a character string is passed with the method *Open* that contains all necessary parameters (the desired database driver, the name of the database, the network name of the database server, login name and password, etc.).

ConnectorFormat Excel

Shape/ShapeRange.*ConnectorFormat* ↗ .*Begin-/EndConnectedShape* ↘ ***Shape***

ConnectorFormat describes the connection between two *Shape* objects. For example, two AutoForm rectangles can be connected with an AutoForm connection line. In this case the connection is described by the ***ConnectorFormat*** object of the ***Shape*** object

The most important properties are *BeginConnectedShape* and *EndConnectedShape*, which refer to the two objects that are connected to each other. To create or delete the connection the methods *BeginConnect/EndConnect* and *BeginDisconnect/EndDisconnect* are available (for the source and goal objects).

Control MS-Forms

This object makes available common properties, methods, and events for all MS Forms controls. It is seldom used directly (at most in the declaration of variables or parameters).

ControlFormat Excel

Shape.*ControlFormat* ↗

If a ***Shape*** object is used to embed a control (usually from the MS Forms library) into a worksheet, the ***ControlFormat*** object has some objects available for the control. The object enables the communication between worksheet and control. Among others, these properties include *LinkedCell, ListFillRange,* and *PrintObject.* See also Chapter 7.

Controls ***MS-Forms***

Frame.*Controls* ↗ (*index* or *name*) ↘ ***control***

Page.*Controls* ↗

UserForm.*Controls* ↗

This enumeration object refers to all controls of a frame field, dialog page, or an entire dialog. The only property is *Count.* With the methods *Add* and *Remove* new controls can be added or deleted via program code.

Corners	Excel
Chart.*Corners* ↗	

This object describes the corner points of the rectangular box that surrounds a 3-D chart. The only useful method is *Select.* This object is of no significance for programming. In manual editing of charts the corners can be selected and the entire chart then turned with the mouse.

CubeField	Excel
CubeFields*(...)* ↗	*.TreeViewControl* ↘ ***TreeViewControl***
PivotField.*CubeField* ↗	

This object describes certain features of pivot fields that hold specifically for OLAP data sources (for example, *CubeFieldType=xlHierarchy* or *xlMeasure*). A host of additional properties have the same meaning as they do with ***PivotField***, which refers to pivot fields of traditional data sources.

CubeFields	Excel
PivotTable.*CubeFields* ↗	*(index* or *name)* ↘ ***CubeField***

This enumeration object refers to all OLAP pivot fields and corresponds essentially to *PivotFields* for pivot fields of traditional data sources.

CustomView	Excel
Workbook.*CustomViews(..)* ↗	

Since Excel 97, for one Excel file several settings for the printer and for the display of columns and rows (hide and unhide) can be saved. In interactive mode these settings can be saved or activated with VIEW|CUSTOM VIEWS.

With the ***CustomView*** object one can determine whether printer settings (*PrintSettings*) or column and row settings (*RowColSettings*) are saved for a particular view. What these settings look like can be determined only when the view in question is activated by *Show.*

CustomViews	Excel
Workbook.*CustomViews* ↗	*(index* or *name)* ↘ ***CustomView***

This object enumerates all saved views belonging to a workbook. With the *Add* method the current settings for the printer or for row and column views are saved as a new view. See also ***CustomView***.

DataLabel	***Excel***
Series.*DataLabels(..)* ↗	*.Interior* ↘ ***Interior***
Point.*DataLabel* ↗	*.Border* ↘ ***Border***
Trendline.*DataLabel* ↗	*.Font* ↘ ***Font***

With this object the label of individual data points in a data series of a chart can be set. Before the object ***DataLabel*** can be changed the property *HasDataLabels* of the object ***Series*** must be set to *True*.

The type of label (value, percentage, or separate text) is set with the *Type* property. Individual texts are specified with *Caption* or *Text*. Visual formatting is accomplished via *Orientation*, *Interior*, *Border*, and *Font*.

In many cases it is easier to use the method *ApplyDataLabels* than to label each individual data point. With it all points of a ***Series*** object or all data series of a ***Chart*** object can be labeled uniformly with values, percentages, etc.

DataLabels	Excel
Series.*DataLabels* ↗	*(index)* ↘ ***DataLabel***

This enumeration object refers to ***DataLabel*** objects of a data series. As *index* the number of the data point must be given. See ***DataLabel***.

DataObject	MS-Forms

This object is passed with OLE Drop events (*BeforeDragOver*, *BeforeDropOrPaste*) to the corresponding event procedure. It makes possible the evaluation of drag-and-drop operations, for example, the placement of a file from Explorer in an MS Forms dialog. The object can be used to read data from or write it to the clipboard (methods *GetFromClipboard* and *PutInClipboard*).

DataTable	Excel
Chart.*DataTable* ↗	*.Border* ↘ ***Border***
	.Font ↘ ***Font***

Since Excel 97 source data can be displayed as numerical values within a chart object (usually below the chart itself) (CHART OPTIONS|DATA SOURCE). In program code the data table can be activated or deleted with ***Chart***.*HasDataTable=True/False*. The appearance of the data table can be controlled with the properties of ***DataTable***, for example, with *HasBorderOutline*, *ShowLegendKey*.

Debug	VBA

With the object ***Debug*** we are dealing with a general VBA object. ***Debug*** refers to the immediate window in the programming environment. There is only one method for ***Debug***: *Print* directs output to the immediate window.

DefaultWebOptions	Excel
Application.*DefaultWebOptions* ↗	

The properties of this object control the parameters of HTML export by Excel (FILE|SAVE AS|TOOLS|WEBOPTIONS). In spite of the *-s* on the end this is not an enumeration object. If the web properties are to be set not globally for Excel but individually for one file, then the ***WebOptions*** object can be used (access via ***Workbook***.*WebOptions*).

Dialog	Excel
Application.*Dialogs(..)* ↗	

This object serves for the internal management of predefined Excel dialogs. These dialogs can be displayed with the *Show* method. Custom dialogs are managed with the ***DialogSheet*** object.

Dialogs	Excel
Application.*Dialogs* ↗	*(index)* ↘ ***Dialog***

This enumeration object contains a list of all predefined Excel dialogs. Selection proceeds by specifying the index in an *xlDialogNamexxx* constant.

Dictionary	Scripting
	(index or *name)* ↘ ***object***

This object corresponds essentially to the VBA object ***Collection***. However, it is somewhat more versatile. It enables the definition of individual listings (enumeration objects). New objects can be added with *Add*, while existing objects can be deleted with *Remove*. The number of saved objects is determined with *Count*.

DisplayUnitLabel	Excel
Axis.*DisplayUnitLabel* ↗	*.Font* ↘ ***Font***

This object describes text, style, position, and appearance of the label of the scaling unit of a coordinate axis of a chart. Whether this axis is scaled at all is determined by the ***Axis*** property *HasTitle*. If one of the predefined factors is used (for example, ***Axis***.*DisplayUnit = xlMillions*), then ***Axis***.*DisplayUnitLabel.Text* automatically contains a suitable label character string (for example, *"Millions"*). On the other hand, if some other arbitrary factor is used as scaling factor (property *DisplayUnitCustom*), then *DisplayUnitLabel.Text* is to be set accordingly.

DocumentProperties ***Office***
Workbook. *BuiltinDocumentProperties* ↗ *(name* or *index)* ↘ ***DocumentProperty***
Workbook. *CustomDocumentProperties* ↗
Binder*:XxxDocumentProperties* ↗

This enumeration object contains a list of all properties of the specified Excel file or binder. These properties serve to identify and search for documents, and they were new in the Office 95 package. Among the twenty-eight properties for Excel workbooks are *"Title", "Subject", "Author", "Last Author", "Revision Number"*. Additionally, with the *Add* method custom properties may be defined. In interactive mode the document properties can be set or newly defined via FILE|PROPERTIES.

DocumentProperty Office
Workbook.*BuiltinDocumentProperties(..)* ↗
Binder.*CustomDocumentProperties(..)* ↗

The ***DocumentProperty*** object describes a property of an Excel file or binder. Here *Name* specifies the property name, *Type* the type, and *Value* the current setting. With the properties *LinkSource* and *LinkToContent* the value of a custom (user-defined) property can be linked directly with the contents of a worksheet. For this *LinkToContent* must be set to *True* and *LinkSource* allocated to a named range of cells.

Drive Scripting
Drives*(...)* ↗ *RootFolder* ↘ ***Folder***

This object describes a hard drive, a floppy drive, a CD-ROM drive, etc. *DriveType* specifies the type of drive, *TotalSize* the total capacity, *FreeSpace* the amount of available space. *RootFolder* refers to the root directory (through which the files and all other directories can be addressed).

Drives Scripting
FileScriptingObject.*Drives* ↗ *(name* or *index)* ↘ ***Drive***

This enumeration object refers to all drives on the computer.

DropLines Excel
ChartGroup*.DropLines* ↗ *.Border* ↘ ***Border***

With line charts and area charts vertical drop lines can be applied to the individual data points. For this the ***ChartGroup*** property *HasDropLines* must be set to *True*. The drop lines stretch from the *X*-axis to the data point. With the object ***DropLines*** (or its subobject ***Border***) the appearance of the drop line can be set.

ErrObject VBA

This object contains information about the most recent error and can be evaluated, for example, in an error-handling routine. The two most important properties are *Number*, with the error number, and *Description*, with a brief description. This object is seldom used, because the same information is available from the previously available functions *Err* and *Error.*

Errors/Error Excel

***Connection**.Errors* ↗

This enumeration object refers to the error that occurred during the previous ADO database operation. (During the execution of a single command several errors can occur that are reported by different database libraries or the database system itself.) The usually cryptic error text is to be found in *Description.* Furthermore, *Number* and *NativeNumber* contain the internal provider error number as well as the ADO error number.

ErrorBars Excel

Series**.ErrorBars* ↗ *.Border* ↘ ***Border

Error bars are small vertical or horizontal lines associated with each data point of a two-dimensional chart that indicate the range of possible error of the data point. Error bars are normally generated with the like-named method of the ***Series*** object. With the ***Border*** subobject the visual display of the error bars can be set. Setting the ***Series*** property *HasErrorBars* to *False* removes the error bars.

Field ADO

***Recordset**!name* ↗
***Fields**("name")* ↗

This object enables access to a single field of the currently active data record of a *Recordset* object. The property *Value* receives the contents of the field. *Name, Type, Attributes,* etc., provide additional information about the type of the field. ***Recordset**!name* is the usual shorthand for ***Recordsets.**Fields("name").Value.*

Fields ADO

Recordset.**Fields* ↗ *(index* or *name)* ↘ ***Field

This enumeration object refers to all data fields of a *Recordset* object.

	File	Scripting
Files(...) ↗		*.Drive* ↘ ***Drive***
		.OpenAsStream ↘ ***TextStream***

This object describes a file on the hard drive (or on another drive). Important properties are *Name* (the file name), *Path* (combination of drive, directory, and file name), *Size* (file size), *Attributes* (for example, write protected). Files can be copied with *Copy*, moved with *Move*, and deleted with, you guessed it, *Delete*. Additionally, text files can be opened as a ***TextStream*** object.

	Files	Scripting
Folder*.Files* ↗		*.Drives* ↘ ***Drive***

This enumeration object refers to all files within a directory.

	FileSystemObject	Scripting
		.Drives ↘ ***Drive***
		.GetSpecialFolder ↘ ***Folder***

This object forms the foundation of the *File Scripting Objects* (FSO for short), which enable object-oriented access to directories and files. Lower-ranked objects are ***Drive[s]***, ***Folder[s]***, and ***File[s]***.

	FillFormat	Excel
Shape/ShapeRange*.Fill* ↗		*.Fore-/BackColor* ↘ ***ColorFormat***

With this object it is possible to set background effects for various drawing objects (***Shape***). For color transitions two colors may be specified with *ForeColor* and *BackColor*; the color transition is then controlled via the properties *GradientDegree* and *GradientStyle*. Additionally, a texture (background bitmap) can be associated to the object with the properties *TextureName* and *TextureType*. For chart objects one has available the related object ***ChartFillFormat***.

	Filter	Excel
AutoFilter*.Filters* ↗		*(index* or *name)* ↘ ***Filter***

The three properties *Operator*, *Criteria1*, *Criteria2* of the ***Filter*** object describe the filter criterion for a column of an ***AutoFilter*** object. *On* tells whether the filter is active.

	Filters	Excel
AutoFilter*.Filters* ↗		*(index* or *name)* ↘ ***Filter***

This enumeration object refers to all filters of an autofilter (one for each column of the database).

Floor	Excel
Chart.*Floor* ↗	*.Interior* ↘ ***Interior***
	.Border ↘ ***Border***

Floor describes the floor of three-dimensional charts. The visual appearance is determined via the two subobjects ***Interior*** and ***Border***. The method *ClearFormats* restores the standard formatting of the floor. See also ***Walls*** for the side walls of a 3-D chart.

Folder	Scripting
Folders(...) ↗	*.Files* ↘ ***Files***
FileSystemObject.*GetSpecialFolder* ↗	*.SubFolders* ↘ ***Folders***

This object describes a directory on the hard drive (or another drive). Important properties are *Name* and *Path* (combination of drive and directory names), *Size* (size of all files contained therein), *Attributes* (for example, write protected).

Folders	Scripting
Folder.*SubFolders* ↗	*.Drives* ↘ ***Drive***

This enumeration object refers to all subdirectories of a directory.

Font	***Excel***
Range.*Font* ↗	
Characters.*Font* ↗	
ChartObject.*Font* ↗	

The ***Font*** object serves to set the font of a range of cells, of individual characters, and various chart objects and controls. The most important properties are *Name* (for the font name), *Size, Bold, Italic, Underline, Subscript, Superscript, Color,* and *Background.*

FormatCondition	***Excel***
Range.*FormatConditions(..)* ↗	*.Borders(..)* ↘ ***Border***
	.Font ↘ ***Font***
	.Interior ↘ ***Interior***

The formatting of a cell or range of cells can be made dependent on at most three conditions (FORMAT|CONDITIONAL FORMATTING). In this way, for example, all values that exceed a given value can be set in boldface.

The properties *Formula1* and *Formula2* as well as *Operator* describe the conditions *Borders, Font,* and *Interior* of the resulting formatting. With *Delete* the conditional formatting can be cleared.

FormatConditions	Excel
Range*.FormatConditions* ↗	*(index* or *name)* ↘ ***FormatCondition***

This enumeration object refers to the (at most three) conditional formats of a cell or range of cells. With *Add* a new format can be added, while *Delete* clears the conditional format.

Frame	MS-Forms
UserForm*.Controls(..)* ↗	*.Controls(..)* ↘ ***control***

The frame field provides visual separation in MS Forms dialogs. Controls contained within the frame are moved together with their container field and with *Zoom* can be enlarged or shrunk independently of the rest of the dialog. *Controls* provides access to the controls.

FreeFormBuilder	Excel
Shapes*.BuildFreeForm(..)* ↗	

Free forms are composed of an arbitrary number of lines or curves and are normally drawn in interactive mode. If you wish to generate free-form objects in code, then you must use the method *BuildFreeForm*. This method returns a ***FreeFormBuilder*** object, which can be extended with the method *AddNodes*. Finally, the method *ConvertToShape* changes the object into a ***Shape*** object.

Gridlines	Excel
Axis*.MajorGridlines* ↗	*.Border* ↘ ***Border***
Axis*.MinorGridlines* ↗	

This object describes the gridlines in the background of a chart. Gridlines are associated to a coordinate axis, that is, horizontal lines to the *Y*-axis and vertical lines to the *X*-axis. Whether and which gridlines are displayed is determined by the two ***Axis*** properties *HasMajorGridlines* and *HasMinorGridlines*. The distance between the principal lines is determined by the ***Axis*** property *MajorUnit*. Auxiliary lines are drawn between these, at a displacement of *MinorUnit*. The visual appearance of gridlines (color and line type) is set via the subobject ***Border***.

The object ***Gridlines*** has nothing to do with the gridlines in worksheets. Whether such a grid is displayed is determined by the ***Window*** properties *DisplayGridlines* and *GridlineColor*.

	GroupShapes	Excel
Shape/ShapeRange.*GroupItems* ↗		*(index* or *name)* ↘ ***Shapes***

When several objects are collected into a group through the pop-up menu command GROUPING, Excel generates a new ***Shape*** object, to which the previously independent objects are subordinated in the hierarchy. Access to the individual objects is via the ***GroupShapes*** enumeration, whose two most important properties are *Count* and *Item*. See also ***Shape***.

	HiLoLines	Excel
ChartGroup.*HiLoLines* ↗		*.Border* ↘ ***Border***

This object describes the appearance of HiLo lines in a line chart. These are vertical lines that connect the smallest and largest data values from several data series. Whether these lines are displayed is determined by the ***ChartGroup*** property *HasHiLoLines*. The appearance of the lines is set by the subobject ***Border***.

	HPageBreak	Excel
Worksheet.*HPageBreaks(..)* ↗		*.Location* ↘ ***Range***

This object indicates a horizontal page break in a worksheet

	HPageBreaks	Excel
Worksheet.*HPageBreaks* ↗		*(index* or *name)* ↘ ***HPageBreak***

This enumeration object enables access to all manual page breaks in a worksheet.

	HyperLink	Excel
object.*property* ↗		*.Range* ↘ ***Range***
Shape.*HyperLink* ↗		*.Shape* ↘ ***Shape***

This object describes a cross reference to a document. This can refer to a particular location in the active file, another local file, or a document on the internet. The address or file name is specified in *Address*, while the exact position in the document (a cell address, for example) is in *SubAddress*.

	HyperLinks	Excel
Chart/Worksheet.*Hyperlinks* ↗		*(index* or *name)* ↘ ***HyperLink***
Range.*Hyperlinks* ↗		

This enumeration object enables access to all cross references and internet links of a sheet or range of cells.

Image	MS-Forms
***UserForm**.Controls(..)* ↗	*.Picture* ↘ ***StdPicture***

The property ***Image*** serves to display bitmaps in dialogs. The property *Picture* refers to a ***StdPicture*** object of the StdOLE library. The image can be loaded from a file by means of the function *LoadPicture*. Various properties of ***Image*** offer formatting options (clipping, adjusting the image to the size of the control, and so on).

Interior	Excel
***Range**.Interior* ↗	
***ChartObject**.Interior* ↗	

This object describes the color and pattern of the interior (that is, the background) of numerous objects. Almost all chart objects, format templates, and such like refer to the ***Interior*** object. The most important properties are *Color*, *Pattern*, and *PatternColor*. Colors are set by allocating an *RGB* value. Alternatively, the properties *Colors* and *PatternColorIndex* can be used, to which are allocated a color index between 1 and 56 or the constant *xlNone* or *xlAutomatic*.

Label	MS-Forms
***UserForm**.Controls(..)* ↗	*.Font* ↘ ***NewFont***

The label field serves to label other controls is MS Forms dialogs. The text is set with *Caption*.

LeaderLines	Excel
***Series**.LeaderLines* ↗	*.Border* ↘ ***Border***

This object enables, in certain chart types, the formatting of lines that are drawn between chart elements and label text (Dialog FORMAT DATA POINT|DATA LABELS|SHOW LEADER LINES). The lines are displayed only if the property *HasLeaderLines* of ***Series*** is set to *True*.

Legend	Excel
***Chart**.Legend* ↗	*LegendEntries* ↘ ***LegendEntry***
	Border ↘ ***Border***

The ***Legend*** object describes the legend of a chart. (The legend is a rectangular box in which the lines, colors, or pattern of the chart is explained and labeled.

With this object's properties position, size, and format are determined (*Left, Top, Width, Height, Interior, Border, Font, Shadow*). Whether a chart has a legend at all is determined by the ***Chart*** property *HasLegend*. The actual details of the legend, that is, the pattern and labeling, are set by the subobject ***LegendEntry***.

LegendEntries Excel

Legend**.LegendEntries* ↗ *(index)* ↘ ***LegendEntry

This enumeration object refers to the entries in the legend of a chart. There is no way of increasing the number of entries with *Add*; every data series and trend line is associated to a fixed legend entry.

LegendEntry Excel

Legend**.LegendEntries(..)* ↗ *.Font* ↘ ***Font
.LegendKey ↘ ***LegendKey***

This object describes a single entry within the legend of a chart. This object has relatively few of its own properties and methods: *Font* for the label text, *LegendKey* for the visual appearance of the data series (see further below), and *Delete* to delete the entire entry. (However, the entry cannot be recreated or reinserted. You must delete the entire legend with *False* and with ...=*True* create it anew, this time with all legend entries.)

The label text of the legend entry is determined by the *Name* property of the ***Series*** object. The ordering of the legend entries within the legend is handled automatically by Excel (depending on the amount of space available).

LegendKey Excel

LegendEntry**.LegendKey* ↗ *.Border* ↘ ***Border

This object determines the visual display of a data series within the legend (see ***Legend*** object). A change in formatting changes the formatting of the associated data series in the chart (and conversely). The most important properties of this object are *MarkerStyle, MarkerBackgroundStyle,* and *MarkerForegroundColor* as well as *Border.*

LineFormat Excel

Shape/ShapeRange**.Line* ↗ *.Fore-/Backcolor* ↘ ***ColorFormat

This object describes the appearance of lines and arrows that are displayed by AutoForm objects (see ***Shape***). Among the most important properties are *ForeColor* and *BackColor, DashStyle,* and *Weight.* Arrow properties are set by *BeginArrowheadLength, BeginArrowheadStyle, BeginArrowheadWidth,* and *EndArrowheadLength, EndArrowheadStyle, EndArrowheadWidth.*

LinkFormat Excel

***Shape**.LinkFormat* ↗

This object contains essentially the property *AutoUpdate*, which for linked OLE objects specifies whether the object is to be updated automatically after a change in the source data. The method *Update* carries out this updating manually.

ListBox MS-Forms

***UserForm**.Controls(..)* ↗

ListBox enables a convenient selection of one or more entries from a list. Access to list elements is via *List*. With *RowSource* the list can be taken from a range of cells in a worksheet. (If a control is used in a worksheet, then instead of the above, *ListFillRange* must be used. *LinkedCell* specifies into which cell the result of the selection is to be transferred.) *Text* contains the selected or input text, while *Value* holds, depending on the setting of *BoundColumn*, likewise the text or else the number of the selected list element.

Mailer Excel

***Workbook**.Mailer* ↗

This object controls the transfer of a workbook over a network. It is of interest only if you work with an Apple Macintosh computer with the network extension PowerTalk. For a direct mail sending, set the properties of ***Mailer*** and start the distribution with *SendMailer*.

MultiPage MS-Forms

UserForm**.Controls(..)* ↗ *.Pages(..)* ↘ ***Page

This object serves for the management of multipage dialogs. Each dialog sheet is represented by its own ***Page*** object (access via *Pages(n)*). *Value* specifies the page of the dialog that is currently visible.

Name Excel

***Workbook**.Names(..)* ↗

This object normally describes a named range of cells. This range can be used in worksheet formulas as well as in VBA code by specifying its name (for example, *[profit]* instead of *[F17]*). For reasons of compatibility with Excel 4, ***Name*** objects can also refer to traditional macros, which is reflected in numerous extraneous properties.

The most important properties are *Name* (with the name of the ***Name*** object) and *RefersTo* (with a formula that contains the cell reference, for example, *"=Table1!$A$1"*).

Names	Excel
Workbook.*Names* ↗	*(index* or *name)* ↘ ***Name***

This enumeration object refers to all defined names in a workbook. As a rule, names are used for denoting cell ranges (command INSERT|NAME|DEFINE). In program code ranges can be named simply by changing the *Name* property of the range.

NewFont	MS-Forms
ControlElement.*Font* ↗	

This object serves the internal representation of fonts (*Font* property of many controls). The same function is also fulfilled by the object ***StdFont*** of the StdOLE library.

ODBCError	Excel
Application.*ODBCErrors(n)* ↗	

This object contains in the property *ErrorString* an error message for the most recent ODBC error. Such errors can occur during access to a database server. You may, perhaps, suppose that this object belongs rather in the ADO library for database programming. However, ODBC errors can also occur directly in Excel, such as when access is made to external data in a pivot table or ***QueryTable*** object.

ODBCErrors	Excel
Application.*ODBCErrors* ↗	*(index)* ↘ ***ODBCError***

This object lists all errors that have occurred in the most recent ODBC access. (Data access via ODBC is processed by a whole conglomerate of function libraries. At each level—the lowest represents the database server itself—errors can occur. For this reason, it is possible that an ODBC access returns several error messages.) Whether errors have occurred can be determined via the *Count* property.

OLEDBError[s]	Excel
Application.*OLEDBErrors(n)* ↗	

These two objects correspond to ***ODBCError[s]***, but hold for errors that were caused by OLE DB libraries (for example, during access to an OLAP cube via a pivot table).

OLEFormat	Excel
Shape.*OLEFormat* ↗	.*Object* ↘ ***oleprogram***

This object is a smaller variant of ***OLEObject***; that is, it contains only a subset of the properties of *OLEObject*. This object serves especially for processing OLE objects that are embedded in an Excel worksheet as ***Shape*** objects.

OLEObject	Excel
Worksheet.*OLEObjects(..)* ↗	.*Object* ↘ ***oleprogram***

OLE objects are objects of other Windows programs that are embedded within Excel and are displayed there (for example, Corel Draw drawings). OLE objects can be contained in custom dialogs, charts, and worksheets.

OLEObject describes certain external properties of the object that can be changed by Excel (without calling the OLE program), such as position, size, border, and shadow. The property *OLEType* specifies how the object is attached to Excel: as an embedded, freestanding object or as a linked object from another file. *Object* refers to the OLE program and enables object automation applications.

The method *Activate* invokes the subordinate OLE program. *Update* brings the data to its latest version (this normally occurs automatically at regular intervals). With *Verb* predefined commands (very few) can be passed to the OLE program.

OLEObjects	Excel
Worksheet.*OLEObjects* ↗	*(index* or *name)* ↘ ***OLEObject***

This enumeration object refers to all object groups in a custom dialog, chart, or worksheet. See ***OLEObject***.

OptionButton	MS-Forms
UserForm.*Controls* ↗	

The option button enables a convenient selection of one option from among several. Each option is represented by its own option button. Related option buttons must be identified by a unique *GroupName* (required only if several option groups appear in the same dialog). For evaluation, the *Value* property of all option buttons must be tested.

Outline	Excel
Worksheet.*Outline* ↗	

The object ***Outline*** serves the internal representation of a hierarchical grouping of a table. (Such groupings are formed via DATA|SUBTOTALS or DATA|GROUP AND

OUTLINE.) The method *ShowLevels* specifies how many row or column levels are to be displayed. The properties *SummaryColumn* and *SummaryRow* specify whether result cells are to be located to the right (respectively beneath) the data (default setting) or to the left (respectively above).

The construction of an outline and changes thereto take place via the methods and properties of the ***Range*** object (*AutoOutline, ClearOutline, Group, Ungroup*). *OutlineLevel* specifies or changes the outline level of an individual row or column.

Page MS-Forms

MultiPage**.Pages(..)* ↗ *.Controls(..)* ↘ ***control

This object represents a page of a multipage dialog (***MultiPage***). The controls contained therein are addressed via *Controls*. The page is labeled with *Caption*.

Pages MS-Forms

MultiPage**.Pages* ↗ *(index* or *name)* ↘ ***Page

This object lists all pages of a multipage dialog.

PageSetup Excel

***Chart**.PageSetup* ↗
***Worksheet**.PageSetup* ↗

This object describes all printer-specific data for the page setup. It is available for all sheet types as well as for the ***Window*** object. The printer setting must be carried out for each sheet individually; the data are not valid for the entire workbook.

Headers and footers are set with the six properties *Left-*, *Center-*, and *Right-Header* and *-Footer*. *Left-*, *Right-*, *Top-*, and *BottomMargin* determine the dimensions of the side margins. *Orientation* determines whether printing is to be in landscape or portrait format. *Zoom* defines a general scaling factor for printing (10 to 400 percent).

For worksheets *PrintArea* specifies the cell range to be printed. *PrintTitleColumns* and *PrintTitleLine* determine the rows/columns that are to printed on *every* page. In the case of charts *ChartSize* determines how the available page area is to be used.

The actual printing is initiated by the method *PrintOut*, which is available to various objects (***Range***, all three page types, ***Workbook***). In worksheets horizontal and vertical page breaks can be inserted with *H/VPageBreaks*.

Pane Excel

Window**.Panes(..)* ↗ *.VisibleRange* ↘ ***Range
***Window**.ActivePane* ↗

The object ***Pane*** describes one of at most four panes, which arise through the division (and freezing) of a window. The method *Activate* selects the currently active pane. The two properties *ScrollColumn* and *ScrollRow* specify the number of the first visible row/column in the pane, or else change it. *VisibleRange* refers to the visible range of cells in the pane.

Panes Excel

Window**.Panes* ↗ *(index)* ↘ ***Pane

The enumeration object ***Panes*** refers to all the panes of a window (see ***Pane***). If the window is not divided, then the property *Count* contains the value 1. Undivided windows can be divided at the current cursor position by changing the ***Window*** properties *Split* and *FreezePanes.*

Parameter ADO

***Command**!name* ↗
Parameters(...) ↗

This object describes a parameter of a database command. *Name* and *Type* specify the parameter name and its data type. *Direction* determines whether the parameter is an input or output parameter. *Value* contains the value of the parameter.

Parameter Excel

QueryTable**.Parameters(..)* ↗ *.SourceRange* ↘ ***Range

If an SQL query with parameters is used in a ***QueryTable*** object (? in the SQL text), then these parameters can be set with the *SetParam* method of the ***Parameter*** object. Another way of proceeding is to read the parameter via *SourceRange* from a table field. Finally, to update the data the *Refresh* method of ***QueryTable*** must always be executed.

Parameters ADO

Command**.Parameters* ↗ *(index* or *name)* ↘ ***Parameter

This enumeration object refers to all parameters of an SQL command that is addressed via an ADO ***Command*** object.

Parameters	Excel
QueryTable.*Parameters* ↗	*(index* or *name)* ↘ ***Parameter***

This enumeration object lists all parameters of an SQL query of a ***QueryTable*** object. (A parameter results from each "?" character in the SQL command.)

Phonetic[s]	Excel
Range.*Phonetics* ↗	

The ***Phonetics*** enumeration object refers to ***Phonetic*** objects. These objects contain phonetic information about cells that contain contents in Asian languages.

PictureFormat	Excel
Shape/ShapeRange.*PictureFormat* ↗	

This object describes features of pictures that are represented in ***Shape*** objects (*Type=mso[Linked]Picture* or *msoXxxOLEObject*). Among the most important properties are *Brightness* and *Contrast.* With *CropLeft, -Bottom, -Top,* and *-Right* the visible segment of the picture can be set.

> **NOTE** *Bitmap files should be inserted with* **Shapes**.AddPicture. *Instead of this, the macro recorder chooses the no longer supported* Pictures *enumeration.*

PivotCache	Excel
Workbook.*PivotCaches(..)* ↗ ***PivotTable***.*PivotCache* ↗	

With the ***PivotCache*** object the underlying data for a pivot table as well as (as with ***QueryTable***) the linkage information are saved. This object plays an especially important role when the basis data are not from an Excel table, but from an external database. (If an Excel file becomes unexpectedly large, printing *MemoryUsed* for all ***PivotCache*** objects often provides a conclusive solution.)

PivotCaches	Excel
Workbook.*PivotCaches* ↗	*(index* or *name)* ↘ ***PivotCache***

This enumeration object refers to the ***PivotCache*** objects in an Excel workbook.

PivotField	Excel
PivotTable.*PivotFields* ↗	.*PivotItems* ↘ ***PivotItem***

Pivot fields are the structural fields of pivot tables. These are the fields that you move from the pivot table toolbar into the regions "row field," "page field," "column field," and "data field." The properties of pivot fields control the actual content of the pivot table. With the methods *Pivot-*, *Hidden-*, *Visible-*, *Parent-*, and *ChildItems* individual pivot elements of a pivot field can be accessed.

PivotFields	Excel
PivotTable.*PivotFields* ↗	(*index* or *name*) ↘ ***PivotField***

This enumeration object refers to the ***PivotField*** object of a pivot table. This enumeration encompasses only the pivot fields that are directly created from the underlying data. Not considered here are, for example, calculated fields (see ***CalculatedFields***) and data fields (***PivotTable.***_DataFields_ and ***PivotTable.***_VisibleFields_) whose composite name differs from the original name (such as *"Sum - quantity"* instead of *"quantity"*).

PivotFormula	Excel
PivotTable.*PivotFormulas(..)* ↗	

The ***PivotFormula*** object describes a formula field in a pivot table. (In interactive mode formula fields are created with the FORMULAS submenu.)

PivotFormulas	Excel
PivotTable.*PivotFormulas* ↗	(*index*) ↘ ***PivotFormula***

This enumeration object lists all formula fields of a pivot table. (Most pivot tables do not have such fields.)

PivotItem	Excel
PivotField.*PivotItems(..)* ↗	.*ChildItems* ↘ ***PivotItems***

Pivot items contain the groups into which a pivot field is divided. (For a list of articles in which price categories I, II, and III appear, for the pivot field "price" there exist the pivot elements "I," "II," and "III.") Pivot items have hardly any of their own properties that change the structure and content of the pivot table. Only *ShowDetail* changes the display of subordinate details.

PivotItems	Excel
PivotField.*PivotItems(..)* ↗	(*index* or *name*) ↘ ***PivotItem***

This enumeration object refers to the ***PivotItem*** objects of a pivot field. See ***PivotItem***.

	PivotLayout	Excel
Chart.*PivotLayout* ↗		.*PivotFields* ↘ ***PivotField***
		.*PivotTable* ↘ ***PivotTable***

The object ***PivotLayout*** newly introduced in Excel 2000 creates the linkage between a pivot chart (***Chart***) and the associated pivot table. Furthermore, all properties of ***PivotTable*** that determine the layout of a pivot table can be accessed directly via ***PivotLayout***. ***Chart***.*PivotLayout.PivotFields* is a shorthand notation for ***Chart***.*PivotLayout.PivotTable.PivotFields*. If a chart is not linked to a pivot table (that is, if it is a run-of-the-mill chart), then ***Chart***.*PivotLayout* contains the value *Nothing*.

Please note that the object comparison ***Chart***.*PivotLayout.PivotTable Is* ***PivotTable*** can return *False* under some circumstances, even in dealing with the same pivot table. If you must carry out such a comparison, then compare the properties .*Worksheet.Name* and .*Address* of *PivotTable.TableRange1*.

	PivotTable	Excel
Worksheet.*PivotTables* ↗		.*PivotFields* ↘ ***PivotField***

Pivot tables are the most important tool that Excel has to offer for the analysis of tabular data (lists). In pivot tables the table entries are grouped according to various criteria and represented as a grid. ***PivotTable*** serves the management of pivot tables. The property *SourceData* refers to the source data of the table. Numerous properties such as *DataBodyRange*, *RowRange*, and *ColumnRange* refer to the ranges in which the results of the pivot table are displayed.

With the method *AddFields* a pivot table can be enlarged. *RefreshTable* updates the table. *ShowPages* creates for a selected page field one or more detailed pivot tables (in new worksheets).

The methods *PivotFields*, *HiddenFields*, *DataFields*, *PageFields*, *ColumnFields*, and *RowFields* refer to the selected ***PivotField*** object.

	PivotTables	Excel
Worksheet.*PivotTables* ↗		(*index* or *name*) ↘ ***PivotTable***

This enumeration object refers to all pivot tables of a worksheet. There is no *Add* method; new pivot tables are generated with the method *PivotTableWizard*. See ***PivotTable***.

	PlotArea	Excel
Chart.*PlotArea* ↗		.*Interior* ↘ ***Interior***
		.*Border* ↘ ***Border***

This object describes the background of the plot area of a chart. The plot area is the region of the chart in which the actual graphic is displayed. This object stands in contrast to ***ChartArea***, through which the entire area of the chart (including the title, legend, etc.) is described. The layout of the plot area is accomplished essentially by the subobjects ***Interior*** (color and pattern) and ***Border*** (border). See also ***Floor*** and ***Walls*** for the border surfaces of three-dimensional charts.

	Point	Excel
Series.*Points(..)* ↗		*.Border* ↘ ***Border***
		.DataLabel ↘ ***DataLabel***

The ***Point*** object describes a single data point of a chart. Data points are collected within a chart into data series, that is, into groups of associated data. With the ***Point*** object the data point itself, the line segment from the previous data point to this data point, and the label of the data point can be visually formatted. For this one has the properties *DataLabel, MarkerStyle, MarkerBackgroundColor*, and *MarkerForegroundColor* as well as *Border*.

	Points	Excel
Series.*Points* ↗		*(index)* ↘ ***Point***

This enumeration object refers to the data points of a data series. As *index* the number of the data point must be specified (that is, 5 for the fifth data point, for example). See ***Point***.

	Properties/Property	ADO
Connection.*Properties* ↗		
Recordset.*Properties* ↗		

This enumeration object lists dynamic properties of various ADO objects (***Connection, Command, Field, Parameter, Recordset***). Which properties an object has depends above all on the database driver (*Provider* setting in ***Connection.***_ConnectionString_). The most important *Property* properties are *Name, Type, Attributes*, and *Value*.

	Properties/Property	VBE
VBComponent.*Properties* ↗		

This enumeration object lists all properties (*Name*) and their settings (*Value*) of a VBA component.

PublishObject	Excel
***Chart/Range**.CreatePublisher* ↗	
***PublishObjects**(..)* ↗	

This object manages the settings of an HTML exportation operation for Excel data (for example, for certain table cells, an entire worksheet, or a chart). The exportation can be repeated at any time with the method *Publish*. Important export properties are *FileName* (the file name or HTML address), *HTMLType* (type of HTML file, for example, *xlHtmlStatic*), as well as *Sheet* and *Source* for describing the data source.

PublishObjects	Excel
***Workbook**.PublishObjects* ↗	*(index* or *name)* ↘ ***PublishObject***

This enumeration object refers to all components of the file that can be exported in HTML format.

QueryTable	Excel
***Range**.QueryTable* ↗	
***Worksheet**.QueryTables(..)* ↗	

This object saves all relevant data for carrying out data importation from a text file, a database, an OLAP cube, or a web site. The property *QueryType* specifies the type of data source. If all further properties are correctly set with respect to the query source, then the importation can be carried out or repeated with *Refresh* (for updating the data).

If the importation is carried out with MS Query (command DATA|GET EXTERNAL DATA|NEW QUERY), then one has *QueryType=xlODBCQuery*. In this case the property *Connection* contains the access information to the database file or database server. *CommandText* contains the query code.

For text importation one has *QueryType=xlTextImport*. The property *Connection* in this case contains the character string *"Text;"* followed by the complete name of the file to be imported. The various parameters of the importation are determined by a host of *TextFileXxx* properties.

QueryTables	Excel
***Worksheet**.QueryTable* ↗	*(index* or *name)* ↘ ***QueryTable***

This enumeration object refers to all external data sources in an Excel file.

Range	Excel
Worksheet.*Range(..)* ↗	*.Cells* ↘ ***Range***
Worksheet.*Cells(..)* ↗	*.Areas* ↘ ***Range***
Application.*ActiveCell* ↗	*.Font* ↘ ***Font***
Application.*Selection* ↗	*.Border* ↘ ***Border***

The object ***Range*** can comprise a single cell, an entire range of cells (under certain conditions composed of several partial ranges), or entire rows or columns of a table. There are countless properties and methods that refer to ranges from a wide variety of objects. Conversely, beginning with a ***Range*** object almost any number of other (partial) ranges can be addressed (for example, via properties and methods such as *CurrentRegion, SpecialCells, End, Dependents, EntireColumn, EntireRow, Precedents*).

Ranges composed of several subranges must in general be processed by evaluation of *Areas*. In this case the *Range* object returns the first subrange.

The character string for describing a range of cells can be determined with *Address*. (When the cells A1:B4 are selected, then *Selection.Address* returns the character string "$A$1:$B$4".) The desired address format (absolute, relative, A1 or Z1S1, or external) can be selected via several parameters.

The contents of cells can be read or edited with the properties *Val* and *Formula*. In the case of ranges with several cells, upon reading, only the contents of the first cell are returned, while writing changes all the cells. The *Text* property of a cell can only be read; it cannot be altered.

The most important properties and methods for formatting cells are *Font, Border, Interior* (for the background color), *Orientation* (of text: horizontal, vertical), *HorizontalAlignment* (left, centered, right, justified), *VerticalAlignment* (above, middle, below), *NumberFormat, Style, ColumnWidth, RowHeight.*

For moving the cell pointer or changing the selected range one has the two methods *Select* and *Offset.*

RecentFile	Excel
Application.*RecentFiles(..)* ↗	

This object specifies the file name (properties *Name* and *Path*) of a recently used Excel file. With the method *Open* this file can again be opened.

RecentFiles	Excel
Application.*RecentFiles* ↗	*(index)* ↘ ***RecentFile***

This enumeration object lists the most recently opened Excel files.

	Recordset	ADO
Command*.Open* ↗		*.ActiveConnection* ↘ ***Connection***
		!name ↘ ***Field***

This object enables the processing of lists of data records that result from an SQL query. The object thus has central importance in ADO database applications, since it makes possible both reading and editing of data.

The data record list is created with the method *Open.* The three properties *CursorLocation, CursorType,* and *LockType* determine which functions the *Recordset* object supports and how efficiently internal management proceeds.

With an open *Recordset* object *!name* can be used to access the data fields of the currently active data record. To activate another data record one has the methods *MoveNext, MovePrevious,* etc. The properties *EOF* and *BOF* indicate whether navigation led beyond the end, respectively beginning, of the data record list.

	RefEdit	RefEdit
UserForm*.Controls(..)* ↗		

The ***RefEdit*** control (formula field) is not part of the MS Forms library, but rather is made available in the freestanding RefEdit library. It is a variant of the text field and enables convenient input of cell references. *Value* contains the input text or cell reference as a character string.

	Reference[s]	VBE
VBProject*.References(..)* ↗		

References lists all object references (libraries) that are used in a VBA project. With the properties of the subordinate ***Reference*** object one can determine, among other things, their name, file name, and a short description.

	RoutingSlip	Excel
Workbook*.RoutingSlip* ↗		

This object controls the transfer of a workbook via e-mail. The most important properties are *Recipients* (list of persons/computers to whom the workbook is to be sent), *Message* and *Subject* (content input), and *Delivery.* The transfer of the workbook is launched by the ***Workbook*** method *Route.*

Scenario Excel

Worksheet**.Scenarios(..)* ↗ *.ChangingCell* ↘ ***Range

Scenarios are an aid in comparing various changes to source data in a worksheet model. The ***Scenario*** object describes which cells of a table are to be changed. The object recognizes two characteristic properties: *ChangingCell* refers to a (usually composite) range of cells with variable values; *Values* contains a data field that specifies numerical values that are to be placed in the cells. The method *ChangeScenario* offers a possibility of changing both properties simultaneously.

Scenarios Excel

Worksheet**.Scenarios* ↗ *(index* or *name)* ↘ ***Scenario

This enumeration object refers to the scenarios defined in a worksheet. *Add* creates a new scenario. The method *CreateSummary* creates, on the basis of all scenarios, a summary report (in a new worksheet) in which all changed cells and the results of those changes are given.

ScrollBar MS-Forms

***UserForm**.Controls* ↗

With a scroll bar a numerical value (*Value*) can be placed within a specified range (*Min* to *Max*).

Section Binder

***Binder**.ActiveSection* ↗
***Binder**.Sections(..)* ↗

The ***Section*** object describes a section of a binder. The *Type* property specifies what object type is at issue. This property returns a character string that describes the OLE object type (in the syntax of *GetObject* or *CreateObject*). The *Object* property enables direct access to the underlying program (Excel for worksheet, Word for a text document, for example). For managing the section one has available the methods *Activate, Copy, Delete, Move, PrintOut, SaveAs.*

Sections Binder

***Binder**.Sections(..)*

This enumeration object lists all sections of a binder. With the *Add* method new sections can be added.

	Series	Excel
Chart*.SeriesCollection(..)* ↗		*.Trendlines* ↘ ***Trendline***
ChartGroup*.SeriesCollection(..)* ↗		*.Points* ↘ ***Point***
		.ErrorBars ↘ ***ErrorBars***
		.DataLabels ↘ ***DataLabel***

Data series contain groups of associated data points of a chart. A data series can, for example, contain all values for a line in a line chart. If several lines are to be represented, then several data series will be required.

With the object ***Series*** various formatting features for the graphical display of the entire data series can be changed. For this there are generally available the same properties and methods as for the formatting of individual ***Point*** objects; see above.

Type determines the chart type for the individual data series. (By choosing differing chart types for several data series one ends up with combination charts made up of groups of charts.) With *AxisGroup* the data series is associated to one of two possible coordinate axes. *PlotOrder* moves individual data series in a 3-D chart forward or backward. *Smooth* determines whether the curve of a line chart should be smoothed. Additional effects can be achieved with the subobjects ***ErrorBars*** and ***Trendline***.

	SeriesCollection	Excel
Chart*.SeriesCollection* ↗		*(index* or *name)* ↘ ***Series***
ChartGroup*.SeriesCollection* ↗		

This enumeration object refers to the data series of a chart or chart group in a combination chart (see ***Series***).

With the methods *Paste* and *Add* the number of data series can be increased. *Extend* increases the number of data points in the data series.

	SeriesLines	Excel
ChartGroup*.SeriesLines* ↗		*.Border* ↘ ***Border***

Series lines link the bars or columns of a stacked bar or column chart. ("Stacked" means here that several data series are represented not each in its own column, but in segments of a column one above the other.) Series lines thus clarify the development of the individual values. The appearance of series lines is controlled by the ***Border*** subobject.

	ShadowFormat	Excel
Shape/ShapeRange*.ShadowFormat* ↗		*.ForeColor* ↘ ***ColorFormat***

This object describes the shadow effects of ***Shape*** objects. The most important properties are *ForeColor* (the color of the shadow), *OffsetX*, and *OffsetY*.

Shape	Excel
Comment.*Shape* ↗	*ConnectorFormat.* ↘ ***ConnectorFormat***
ConnectorFormat.*Begin/EndConnectedShape* ↗	*ControlFormat* ↘ ***ControlFormat***
FreeFormBuilder.*ConvertToShape(..)* ↗	*GroupItems* ↘ ***GroupShapes***
Hyperlink.*Shape* ↗	*Nodes* ↘ ***ShapeNodes***
Shapes.*AddShape(..)* ↗	*TopLeftCell, BottomRightCell* ↘ ***Range***
Worksheet.*Shapes(..)* ↗	...

The ***Shape*** object serves primarily to represent AutoForms (lines, rectangles, arrows, stars—see the drawing toolbar). It thereby replaces the various drawing objects from Excel 5/7. However, this object is also used to manage a completely different collection of objects (for example, MS Forms controls).

There are many related objects: ***ShapeRange*** enables the common editing of several ***Shape*** objects. Freeforms constitute a particular class of ***Shape*** objects. In this case the property *ShapeNodes* refers to a like-named enumeration of ***ShapeNode*** objects. The ***GroupShape*** object manages several items that have been collected into a group.

ShapeRange	Excel
Shapes.*Range(Array(..,..,..))* ↗	*(index* or *name)* ↘ ***Shape***
Charts/OLEObjects.*ShapeRange* ↗	

This object enables simultaneous processing of an entire collection of ***Shape*** objects. For this one has most of the properties and methods of the ***Shape*** object. Furthermore, an object group can be constructed with *Group* or *ReGroup*. (This returns a new *Shape* object that unifies the collection. The individual objects can now be addressed via ***Shape.****GroupItems*. This property again leads to a ***GroupShape*** object.)

ShapeNode	Excel
Shape/ShapeRange.*Nodes(..)* ↗	

This object describes a segment (that is, a line segment or curve) of a freeform. The coordinate points are read via *Points*. This property returns a two-dimensional *Array*. (A one-dimensional field would actually have sufficed.) Access to both coordinates can be accomplished as in the following lines:

```
' first coordinate point of the first Shape object
' assumes Type=msoFreeform
pt = Shapes(1).Nodes(1).Points
x = pt(1,1)
y = pt(1,2)
```

Other important properties are *SegmentType* (line or curve) and *EditingType* (for example, corner point or point of symmetry). All three properties can be read only. To make changes the *SetXxx* methods of the ***ShapeNodes*** object must be used.

	ShapeNodes	Excel
Shape/ShapeRange.*Nodes* ↗		(*index* or *name*) ↘ ***ShapeNode***

If a ***Shape*** object contains a freeform (say, a line segment drawn free-hand, ***Shape.***_Type=msoFreeform_), then its property *Nodes* refers to the enumeration object ***ShapeNodes***, by which the individual corner points of the line segment can be addressed. Moreover, with the methods *Insert* and *Delete* additional line segments can be added and then edited with *SetEditingType*, *SetPosition*, and *SetSegmentType*. See also ***FreeformBuilder***.

	Shapes	Excel
Chart.*Shapes* ↗		(*index* or *name*) ↘ ***Shape***
WorkSheet.*Shapes* ↗		*.Range* ↘ ***ShapeRange***

This enumeration object lists all ***Shape*** objects of a worksheet or chart. In contrast to accessing individual ***Shape*** objects, with *Range* several objects can be accessed simultaneously. To create new ***Shape*** objects one has countless *Add* methods available, such as *AddShape, AddLine, AddCurve, AddOLEObject*. Finally, *SelectAll* selects all ***Shape*** objects.

	Sheets	***Excel***
Application.*Sheets* ↗		(*index* or *name*) ↘ ***Chart***
Workbook.*Sheets* ↗		(*index* or *name*) ↘ ***Worksheet***
Window.*SelectedSheets* ↗		

This enumeration object refers to all sheets of a workbook or the currently active workbook (if the object ***Application*** or no object at all is specified) or to the commonly selected group of sheets in a window.

Please note that there is no ***Sheet*** object. ***Sheets*** refers, according to the type of sheet, to a ***Chart*** or ***Worksheet*** object. In Excel 5/7 files *Sheets* can also refer to objects of type *DialogSheet* and *Module*.

With the ***Sheets*** object all properties and methods of the relevant ***XxxSheets*** objects are accessible. In particular, with *Add* and *Delete* sheets can be created and deleted. *Select* activates a selected sheet. The property *Visible* specifies whether a sheet is to be displayed in the sheet register. With the method *FillAcrossSheets* a range of cells in a worksheet can be copied to all sheets encompassed by ***Sheets***.

SoundNote	Excel
***Range**.SoundNote* ↗	

With the ***SoundNote*** object sounds or sequences of notes can be associated with a table cell. The linking of sound information is accomplished with the methods *Play* and *Import.* With the method *Play* the notes are output to the computer's speaker.

SpinButton	MS-Forms
***UserForm**.Controls* ↗	

With a spin button a numerical value (*Value*) can be placed within a given range (*Min* to *Max*).

StdFont	StdOLE
***object**.Font* ↗	

This object serves the internal representation of fonts (*Font* property of many objects). This same function is also filled by the object ***NewFont*** of the MS Forms library.

StdPicture	StdOLE
***Image**.Picture* ↗	

This object serves the internal representation of pictures (bitmaps, *Picture* property of various MS Forms controls). The StdOLE library makes available the two functions *LoadPicture* and *SavePicture*, by means of which bitmap files can be loaded and saved.

Style	***Excel***
***Workbook**.Styles(..)* ↗	*.Interior* ↘ ***Interior***
***Range**.Style* ↗	*.Borders* ↘ ***Borders***
	.Font ↘ ***Font***

Styles are predefined formats that can be used for rapid formatting of cells or ranges of cells. Styles belong to the data of a workbook and are saved with it. To equip a range of cells with a style one must simply assign the corresponding style to the ***Range*** property *Style.*

Styles contain information about font, color, and pattern (property *Interior*), cell borders (method *Borders* for the four lines left, right, above, below), number format (*NumberFormat*), orientation (*Orientation, VerticalAlignment, Horizontal-Alignment, WrapText*), and cell protection (*Locked*). The six properties *Include-Alignment, -Pattern,* etc. specify which of the six formatting aspects are to be modified by the style. That is, you can define formats that change only the font and number format and leave the rest of the information in the range untouched.

Styles	Excel
***Workbook**.Styles* ↗	*(index* or *name)* ↘ ***Style***

This enumeration object refers to the styles defined in a workbook. With the methods *Add* and *Merge* additional styles can be added to the list.

TextBox	MS-Forms
***UserForm**.Controls* ↗	*.Font* ↘ ***NewFont***

A text field enables the input of text (including multiline) in certain dialogs. The most important property is, not surprisingly, *Text*.

TextEffectFormat	Excel
***Shape/ShapeRange**.TextEffect* ↗	

This object describes the features of a WordArt object (***Shape*** object with *Type=msoTextEffect*).

TextFrame	Excel
***Shape/ShapeRange**.TextEffect* ↗	*.Characters* ↘ ***Characters***

This object describes the extent of the text in an AutoForm object (***Shape*** object with *Type=msoAutoShape*). Access to the text itself is via the ***Characters*** object, which enables separate formatting of each individual letter. The text alignment is set with *HorizontalAlignment* and *VerticalAlignment*, the border of the AutoForm object with *MarginLeft*, *-Top*, *-Right*, and *-Bottom*.

TextStream	Scripting
***File**.OpenAsStream* ↗	

This object enables the reading and writing of a text file. The most important methods are *Read* and *ReadLine* for reading individual characters or entire lines, as well as *Write* and *WriteLine* for writing a character string or an entire line.

ThreeDFormat	Excel
***Shape/ShapeRange**.ThreeD* ↗	*.ExtrusionColor* ↘ ***ColorFormat***

This object describes the three-dimensional appearance of ***Shape*** objects. With the appropriate setting, inherently flat ***Shape*** objects can be extended into the third dimension.

> **TIP** *To understand the properties fully you should experiment with the 3-D toolbar (3-D icon on the drawing toolbar).*

TickLabels	Excel
***Axis**.TickLabels* ↗	*.Font* ↘ ***Font***

This object describes how the tick marks on a coordinate axis of a chart are to be labeled. Characteristic properties and methods are *Orientation, Font, NumberFormat, NumberFormatLinked* (*True* if the number format should be taken from the table).

This object has influence neither on the location and content of the label nor on the number of label points. These details are handled by ***Axis*** properties, in particular, by *TickLabelSpacing* and *-Position* as well as by *TickMarkSpacing* (for *X*-axes) or *MajorUnit* (for *Y*-axes).

ToggleButton	MS-Forms
***UserForm**.Controls* ↗	*.Picture* ↘ ***StdPicture***

The toggle button is a variant of an ordinary button. The special feature is that the toggle button does not spring back automatically after being pressed, but only after being clicked on again.

TreeviewControl	Excel
***CubeField**.TreeViewControl* ↗	

This object refers to the hierarchical listbox that is used in OLAP pivot fields for selecting an indicated hierarchical level and detail. With the property *Drilled* one can control the visibility of the pivot data corresponding to the ***CubeField***. For this to occur the property is passed a two-dimensional *Array* (see the example in the on-line help or use the macro recorder).

Trendline	Excel
***Series**.Trendlines(..)* ↗	*.Border* ↘ ***Border***
	.DataLabel ↘ ***DataLabel***

This object describes trend lines, approximation curves, and smoothed curves in charts. Trend lines are associated to individual data series and can be displayed only in certain two-dimensional chart types. *Type* determines the type of trend line (for example *xlPolynomial, xlLogarithmic*). For approximation curves *Period* determines the number of data points whose average value is calculated to draw the curve. In the case of polynomial approximation curves the property *Order* determines the order of the polynomial (2 to 6). *Forward* and *Backward* determine how many periods into the future or past beyond the available data range the curve should be drawn (for estimating a trend).

The visual display of a curve is handled with the subobjects ***DataLabel*** and ***Border***. *DisplayEquation* and *DisplayRSquared* determine whether the formula for the curve and a coefficient for the size of the desired approximation to the data should be displayed in a text field.

	Trendlines	Excel
Series.*Trendlines* ↗		*(index* or *name)* ↘ ***Trendline***

This enumeration object refers to the trend line, approximation curve, or smoothing curve of a data series. See ***Trendline***.

	UpBars	Excel
ChartGroup.*UpBars* ↗		*.Interior* ↘ ***Interior***
		.Border ↘ ***Border***

This object describes the appearance of positive deviation bars between two data series in a line chart. Details can be found under ***DownBars*** (for negative deviation bars).

	UserForm	***MS-Forms***
Dialogname ↗		*.ActiveControl* ↘ ***controlelement***
		.Controls ↘ ***Controls***
		.controlelementname ↘ ***controlelement***

The *UserForm* object is the basis object for all MF Forms dialogs (forms). It makes a host of properties available for the structuring of dialogs. *StartupPosition* has influence over the location at which the dialog appears. *Picture* can contain a bitmap that is displayed as the dialog background. With *Zoom* the entire dialog contents can be made larger or smaller.

With the enumeration *Controls* all controls contained within the dialog can be addressed. (In program code, however, usually the name of the control is used directly.) *ActiveControl* refers to the currently active control (with keyboard focus).

	Validation	Excel
Range.*Validation* ↗		

This object describes what input is allowed in a range of cells (interactive setting via DATA|VALIDATION). The type of number allowed (for example, integer, date) is set with *Type*. The number range can be restricted to the limit values in *Formula1* and *Formula2*. For this a comparison operator must be specified with *Operator* (such as *xlBetween*, *xlGreater*). *Formula1* and *Formula2* contain either values or cell addresses. (In the second case the boundary values are read from the cells.) *InputMessage* provides a short infotext for input, and *ErrorMessage* contains the error message that will be displayed if the rules are not adhered to.

	VBComponent[s]	VBE
***VBProject**.VBComponents(..)* ↗		*.CodeModule* ↘ ***CodeModule***
		.Properties(..) ↘ ***Property***

VBComponents contains a listing of all components of a VBA project (that is, modules and dialogs, *Type* property). The code segment of a component is addressed via *CodeModule*, the properties via *Properties.* If the component has a designer (here the dialog editor, for example, is meant), then it can be determined with *HasOpenDesigner* whether it is active.

	VBE	VBE
***Application**.VBE* ↗		*.CodePanes(..)* ↘ ***CodePane***
		.CommandBars(..) ↘ ***CommandBars***
		.VBProjects(..) ↘ ***VBProject***
		.Window(..) ↘ ***Window***

VBE is the start object for the like-named library for programming of the VBA development environment. (In the object browser this library is denoted by VBIDE.) The principal task of ***VBE*** is enabling access to the subordinate objects (see syntax box). Furthermore, the currently active components of the development environment can be addressed via *ActiveCodePane, ActiveVBProject, ActiveWindow,* and *SelectedVBComponent.*

	VBProject[s]	**VBE**
***VBE**.ActiveVBProject* ↗		*.References(..)* ↘ ***Reference***
***VBE**.VBProjects* ↗		*.VBComponents(..)* ↘ ***VBComponent***

VBProjects contains references to all currently loaded projects (Excel files and add-ins). The individual components (meaning modules and dialogs) and references to external object libraries can be addressed via the properties *VBComponents* and *References.*

	VPageBreak	Excel
***Worksheet**.VPageBreaks(..)* ↗		*.Location* ↘ ***Range***

This object denotes a vertical page break in a worksheet.

	VPageBreaks	Excel
***Worksheet**.VPageBreaks* ↗		*(index* or *name)* ↘ ***VPageBreak***

This enumeration object enables access to all manual page breaks in a worksheet.

	Walls	Excel
Chart.*Walls* ↗		*.Interior* ↘ ***Interior***
		.Border ↘ ***Border***

This object describes the two side walls of a 3-D chart. With the subobjects ***Interior*** and ***Border*** the color and border of these walls can be set, although only for both walls taken together. See also ***Floor*** for the floor of a three-dimensional chart.

	WebOptions	Excel
Workbook.*WebOptions* ↗		

The properties of this object control the parameters of the HTML exportation of an Excel file. (For the global export settings of Excel you will have to set the properties of *DefaultWebOptions.*)

	Window	Excel
Workbook.*Windows(..)* ↗		*.Panes* ↘ ***Pane***
Application.*ActiveWindow* ↗		*.SelectedSheets* ↘ ***Sheets***

This object refers to a window within Excel. Windows are made active with *Activate.* The methods *ActivateNext* and *ActivatePrevious* change to the next or previous window. With *NewWindow* and *Close* new windows are generated and closed. With *Split* and *FreezePanes* windows can be divided into several panes.

The property *Visible* determines whether a window is visible. With *WindowState* the size of the window (icon, normal, maximized) is set. *Caption* contains the window title. The properties *ScrollColumn* and *ScrollRow* determine the number of the first visible column or row. *DisplayGridlines* specifies whether gridlines are displayed within the window.

The ***Window*** properties and methods *ActivePane, ActiveSheet, ActiveChart, ActiveCell, Panes, Selection,* and *SelectedSheets* refer to various subordinate objects.

	Windows	Excel
Workbook.*Windows* ↗		*(index* or *name)* ↘ ***Window***

This enumeration object refers to the windows of a workbook. Access is accomplished via the input of the (internal) window number or the window title (*Caption-* property of the ***Window*** object).

Window[s]	VBE
***VBE**.Windows* ↗	

The enumeration object ***Windows*** and the derived object ***Window*** enable access to the windows of the VBA development environment. In the case of a conflict of names with Excel ***Window[s]*** objects you must prefix *VBE*, for example, *Dim w As VBE.Window*.

Workbook	Excel
***Application**.Workbooks(..)* ↗	*.Charts* ↘ ***Chart***
***Application**.ActiveWorkbook* ↗	*.DialogSheets* ↘ ***DialogSheet***
	.Modules ↘ ***Module***
	.Worksheets ↘ ***Worksheet***
	.Windows ↘ ***Window***

The object ***Workbook*** describes an Excel file. With the methods introduced above access can be made to the sheets of the workbook, where a distinction is made among the four types of sheet. The method *Sheets* enables access to all sheets of the workbook (independent of their type). *Windows* refers to the windows belonging to the workbook.

The workbook can be saved with the methods *Save* and *SaveAs*. *Close* closes the workbook, and with the provision of an optional parameter the workbook can be saved.

Workbooks	Excel
***Application**.Workbooks* ↗	(*index* or *name*) ↘ ***Workbook***

Workbooks contains the list of all loaded workbooks (including those that are invisible because their windows are hidden). Reference to individual workbooks can be effected either by the input of the index number or the file names (without path). With *Add* a new, empty, workbook can be declared. *Open* loads an existing workbook.

Worksheet	**Excel**
***Workbook**.Worksheets* ↗	*.Range* ↘ ***Range***
***Application**.ActiveSheet* ↗	*.Cells* ↘ ***Range***
	.XxxObjects ↘ ***XxxObject***

Worksheets belong together with dialog, chart, and module sheets to the sheets of a workbook. Countless methods and properties refer on the one hand to ranges of cells (*Range, Rows, Columns, Cells*) and on the other to embedded controls, drawing objects, charts, pivot tables, and so on.

The exchange of data via the clipboard is accomplished with the methods *Copy, Paste,* and *PasteSpecial. Calculate* leads to a manual recalculation of a table (required only if the ***Application*** property *Calculation* is set to *xlManual*). With the properties *ConsolidationFunction, -Options,* and *-Sources* the details of a consolidation process are set, which can then be executed with ***Range****.Consolidate.*

WorksheetFunctions	Excel
Application*.WorksheetFunctions* ↗	

With this object Excel worksheet functions can be used in VBA program code.

Worksheets	Excel
Workbook*.Worksheets* ↗	*(index* or *name)* ↘ ***Worksheet***

This enumeration object refers to the worksheets of a workbook. With the methods *Add* and *Copy* new methods can be generated. *Select* makes a worksheet into the active sheet.

APPENDIX A

Where to Find the Sample Files

The sample files for this book can be found at `http://www.apress.com`. The files are split into three parts:

> xl-2000-part1.zip: all basic samples
>
> xl-2000-part2.zip: sql2string (chapter 13, page 671) and VB6 code (chapter 14, page 750)
>
> xl-2000-part3.zip: setup-comevents and setup-comtest (chapter 14, page 701)

You will need WinZip (`http://www.winzip.com`) or a similar tool to extract the archives.

Alphabetical Description of the Example Files

The following list specifies the chapter in which the example file is described.

`query-definitions\`	SQL Code for MS-Query	12
`setup-COMEvents\`	setup program for `COM-Events.dll`	14
`setup-COMTest\`	setup program for `COM-AddInTst.dll`	14
`sql2string\`	change character string to Visual Basic syntax	13
`survey\`	evaluation of questionnaires	12
`vb6\Chart\`	controlling Excel via ActiveX automation	14
`vb6\ClipBoard\`	a new object library for Excel	14
`*.dll`	COM add-ins	14
`*.cub`	OLAP cube files	13
`*.mdb`	database files	12
`*.pdo, *.vbo`	files of the installation wizard	14

`*.txt`	README_files and example files for Chapter 5, "User-Defined Worksheet Functions"	5
`*.vba`	code for COM add-ins	14
`*.xla`	traditional Excel add-ins	14
`ActiveX-Access.xls`	ActiveX control by Access	14
`ActiveX-Explorer.xls`	ActiveX control of Internet Explorer	14
`AddInFn.xla`	example of a traditional add-in	14
`ADO.xls`	ADO database programming	12
`Car_Template.xlt`	template for `DB_Share.xls`	11
`Cells.xls`	using ranges of cells	5
`Chart.xls`	chart programming	10
`COM-*.*`	COM add-in programming	14
`CommandBar*.xls`	some menus and control bars	8
`Consolidate.xls`	consolidate worksheets	11
`DateTime.xls`	calculations with date and time	5
`DB_Functions.xls`	application of database worksheet functions	11
`DB_Share.xls`	balance sheet of a car-sharing club	11
`DisplayUnitLabel.xls`	chart programming	10
`DLL.xls`	use of DLL functions in VBA	14
`Euro.xls`	macros for euro conversion	5
`Excel.htm`	file for `ActiveX-Explorer.xls`	14
`Files.xls`	using files, FSO	5
`Function.xls`	definition of new worksheet functions with VBA	5
`Holidays.xls`	function for calculating holidays	5
`Implements.xls`	object-oriented programming example	4
`Intro*.xls`	introductory example	1
`Miscellaneous.xls`	tips and tricks	5
`Mma.xls`	text exportation in Mathematica format	5
`MS-Query.xls`	examples for MS Query	12
`Names.xls`	programming named ranges	5
`Nwind.mdb`	*Northwind* database	12
`Olap.cub`	OLAP cube example	13
`OLE_*.xls`	OLE and ActiveX automation	14
`Pivot.xls`	application of pivot tables	13
`Shapes.xls`	drawing objects	10
`Share.xlt`	car-sharing form	9
`Sheets.xls`	windows, workbooks, and sheets	5
`Speedy.xlt`	intelligent form	9
`Staff.xls`	employee database	11
`Staff.doc`	form letter in Word for `Staff.xls`	11
`Subtotal.xls`	grouping data, subtotals	13
`Trend.xls`	trend functions in charts	10

`Userform.xls`	examples of custom dialogs (forms)	7
`VBA-Concepts.xls`	basic concepts of VBA programming	5
`Vocabulary.xls`	vocabulary trainer	1

References

Gerhard Brosius: *Microsoft OLAP Services.* Addison Wesley 1999.

Michael Kofler: *Visual Basic Database Programming,* Addison Wesley 2000.

Microsoft: *Office 2000 / Visual Basic Programmers Manual,* 1999 (supplied with Office 2000 Developer).

Microsoft: *Microsoft Developer Network* (MSDN-Library).

Tim Peterson et al.: *Microsoft OLAP Unleashed,* SAMS 1999.

John Walkenbach: *Microsoft Excel 2000 Power Programming with VBA.* IDG Books Worldwide 1999.

Eric Wells: *Developing Microsoft Excel 95 Solutions with Visual Basic for Applications.* Microsoft Press 1996.

Sakhr Youness: *Professional Data Warehousing with SQL Server 7.0 and OLAP Services.* Wrox 2000.

Index

Note: *Italicized* page numbers denote figures or tables.

D

G

H

Q

R

S

T

X

Y

Z

The Story Behind Apress

APRESS IS AN INNOVATIVE PUBLISHING COMPANY devoted to meeting the needs of existing and potential programming professionals. Simply put, the "A" in Apress stands for the "author's press™." Our unique author-centric approach to publishing grew from conversations between Dan Appleman and Gary Cornell, authors of best-selling, highly regarded computer books. They wanted to create a publishing company that emphasized quality above all—a company whose books would be considered the best in their market.

To accomplish this goal, they knew it was necessary to attract the very best authors—established authors whose work is already highly regarded, and new authors who have real-world practical experience that professional software developers want in the books they buy. Dan and Gary's vision of an author-centric press has already attracted many leading software professionals—just look at the list of Apress titles on the following pages.

Would You Like to Write for Apress?

APRESS IS RAPIDLY EXPANDING its publishing program. If you can write and refuse to compromise on the quality of your work, if you believe in doing more then rehashing existing documentation, and if you are looking for opportunities and rewards that go far beyond those offered by traditional publishing houses, we want to hear from you!

Consider these innovations that we offer every one of our authors:

- Top royalties with *no* hidden switch statements. For example, authors typically only receive half of their normal royalty rate on foreign sales. In contrast, Apress' royalty rate remains the same for both foreign and domestic sales.

- A mechanism for authors to obtain equity in Apress. Unlike the software industry, where stock options are essential to motivate and retain software professionals, the publishing industry has stuck to an outdated compensation model based on royalties alone. In the spirit of most software companies, Apress reserves a significant portion of its equity for authors.

- Serious treatment of the technical review process. Each Apress book has a technical reviewing team whose remuneration depends in part on the success of the book since they, too, receive a royalty.

Moreover, through a partnership with Springer-Verlag, one of the world's major publishing houses, Apress has significant venture capital behind it. Thus, Apress has the resources both to produce the highest quality books *and* to market them aggressively.

If you fit the model of the Apress author who can write a book that gives the "professional what he or she needs to know™," then please contact any one of our editorial directors, Gary Cornell (`gary_cornell@apress.com`), Dan Appleman (`dan_appleman@apress.com`), or Karen Watterson (`karen_watterson@apress.com`), for more information on how to become an Apress author.